601 ITALIAN VERBS

Dr. Emanuele Occhipinti
with
Dr. Lori Langer de Ramírez
Dr. Amelia Moser
Dr. David Rose
Anthony Vittorino M.A.

601 Italian Verbs

Contacting the Editors
Every effort has been made to provide accurate information in this publication, but changes are inevitable. The publisher cannot be responsible for any resulting loss, inconvenience, or injury. We would appreciate it if readers would call our attention to any errors or outdated information by contacting Berlitz Publishing, 193 Morris Avenue, Springfield, NJ 07081, USA.
email: comments@berlitzbooks.com

First Printing: June 2010
Printed in Canada

Publishing Director: Sheryl Olinsky Borg
Project Manager/Editor: Nela Navarro
Editorial: Dr. David Rose, Susanna Pastorino
Production Manager: Elizabeth Gaynor
Cover Design: Claudia Petrilli, Leighanne Tillman
Interior Design/Art: Claudia Petrilli and Datagrafix, Inc.

Table of Contents

About the Authors

Dr. Emanuele Occhipinti

Dr. Emanuele Occhipinti is Assistant Professor and Director of the Italian program at Drew University. He holds a *Laurea* in Modern Foreign Languages and Literatures from the University of Florence and received his Ph.D. in Italian Literature from Rutgers University. He is also the editor of *New Approaches to Teaching Italian Language and Culture: Case Studies from an International Perspective*.

Dr. Lori Langer de Ramírez

Dr. Lori Langer de Ramírez holds a Master's Degree in Applied Linguistics and a Doctorate in Curriculum and Teaching from Teachers College, Columbia University. She is currently the Chairperson of the ESL and World Language Department for Herricks Public Schools in New Hyde Park, N.Y. Dr. Langer de Ramírez is the author of several Spanish-language books and texts and has contributed to many textbooks and written numerous articles about second language pedagogy and methodology. Her interactive web site, www.miscositas.com, offers teachers over 40 virtual picturebooks and other curricular materials for teaching foreign languages.

Dr. Amelia Moser

Dr. Amelia Moser is Visiting Assistant Professor of Italian at Bard College. Dr. Moser received her Ph.D. in Romance Languages from Harvard University. She has taught Italian language and literature at Harvard University, Yale University, Iona College and Columbia University. She is also Managing Editor of *Italian Poetry Review*, a pluri-lingual journal of creativity and criticism sponsored by Columbia University, The Italian Academy for Advanced Studies in America, and Fordham University.

Dr. David Rose

Dr. David Rose is currently the Director of World Languages for the Oceanside School District, in Oceanside, N.Y. Dr. Rose has an M.A. in Romance Languages and Literature and a Ph.D. in Foreign Language Instruction with a specialization in Italian from Stony Brook University. Dr. Rose has taught Italian at the middle school, high school and college levels, and has served as coordinator and chaperone for college-level study abroad programs in Italy. He has served as consultant for the New York State Regents Exam in Italian and is a member of Phi Beta Kappa.

Anthony Vittorino M.A.

Tony Vittorino is a teacher of Italian and Spanish at Herricks High School in New Hyde Park, N.Y. Mr. Vittorino holds Masters degrees in Italian and European History from New York University and St. John's University, respectively.

About the Authors/Reviewers

Mr. Vittorino has worked as a translator of historical texts and legal documents and as an adjunct instructor at St. John's University, New York. He travels to Italy frequently, most recently to Rome this past summer through an NEH grant to study Italian art in Rome and Florence. He is also an avid educational blogger and has presented at technology workshops organized by the American Council for the Teaching of Foreign Languages.

Berlitz Publishing is grateful for the valuable comments and suggestions made by the team of teacher and student reviewers during the stages of development. Their contributions, expertise, experience and passion for the Italian language are clearly reflected in this important project.

Grazie mille!

Teachers

Angelo Musto, Oceanside High School, Oceanside, New York

Nicola Nino, Columbia University, New York, New York

Renata Paolercio, Bronx Science High School, Bronx, New York

Serena Grattarola, Smith College, Northampton, Massachusetts

Susanna Pastorino, Montclair State University, Montclair, New Jersey

Students

Erika Esposito, Herricks High School, New Hyde Park, New York

Hope Ross, Drew University, Madison, New Jersey

Frank Sedita, Drew University, Madison, New Jersey

Raphael Smith, Rutgers University, Newark, New Jersey

Dear Student,

As with everything in life, if you want to become good at something, you have to practice. Learning Italian is the same: it is crucial to your growth that you practice the language in many different contexts. For example:

- *watching Italian language television and listening to Italian language songs*
- *listening to Italian language radio broadcasts and podcasts*
- *reading Italian language books, stories, and newspaper magazine articles*
- *and, most importantly: engaging native speakers of Italian in conversation*

These are all critical ways to immerse yourself with the structures and vocabulary of Italian. Along with this authentic practice is the need for precision – and this is where 601 Italian Verbs *can help you to improve your fluency. When you are through producing a story, an essay, a blog entry or an email in Italian, consult* 601 Italian Verbs *to ensure that your message is being communicated correctly. A good understanding of the verb tenses, their conjugations and their structures will enable you to express yourself freely and correctly. And take some time to work through the activities at the end of* 601 Italian Verbs. *They are aimed at assessing your understanding of the use of verbs in real-life contexts, such as conversations and short stories.*

It is our hope that 601 Italian Verbs *will become an invaluable source of information for you during your years on the road to Italian fluency.*

It is also our hope that your road will be paved with the joy of learning and the wonder of communicating in a new language. In bocca al lupo!

- Dr. Emanuele Occhipinti and Dr. Lori Langer de Ramírez

Dear Teacher,

It is so exhilarating to watch our students grow and thrive in their study of the Italian language. We watch in awe as they master subject-verb agreement and we smile with delight when they finally grasp the subjunctive mood! But there are also trying times on the road to Italian proficiency. Understanding the many different tenses and conjugations in the target language can prove challenging to many students. This is where 601 Italian Verbs *can serve as an important source of support and encouragement for our students.*

601 Italian Verbs *is an essential book for your students and you to use as a reference at home, in the classroom or at the library. We all recall times when a student wants to say or write something in Italian, but just doesn't have the verb paradigm mastered quite yet. While communication can certainly take place without this precision of language, it is less likely to be successful and can often frustrate students. By having* 601 Italian Verbs *handy when students are working in the language, teachers can help scaffold the language that students have already acquired. Students can check their work using the book, as well as use it for reference as they create essays, blog entries, original creative writing pieces and other writing or oral productions in the Italian classroom.*

601 Italian Verbs *can help students to feel secure in the language while also providing valuable information and practice that can lead to more advanced proficiency in Italian. We all know that a secure student is a student who is open to learning more. It is our hope that this book serves as an important resource for students as they continue on their road to Italian proficiency. Buon lavoro!*

- Dr. Emanuele Occhipinti and Dr. Lori Langer de Ramírez

How to Use This Book

Welcome to *601 Italian Verbs*! This is *the* verb reference book for today's student. This book was created to help you learn the Italian verb system, not for the sake of studying Italian verbs, but so that you can communicate and enjoy speaking Italian! *601 Italian Verbs* will help make studying easier and also provide you with opportunities to improve, practice and even have fun *in italiano*.

Learn to make the most of this book by becoming familiar with the contents. Go back to the Table of Contents (TOC) on page 3. The TOC will help you navigate and locate the following sections in this book:

About the Authors/Reviewers

You will notice that *601 Italian Verbs* is written by a team of experienced teachers committed to helping you learn Italian. The book was reviewed by another team of equally experienced teachers and engaged students from various schools and universities.

Letter to the Student/Letter to the Teacher

Dr. Emanuele Occhipinti, one of the book's main authors, shares tips to help you practice Italian in different contexts. Dr. Occhipinti also tells you how *601 Italian Verbs* will help you improve your overall fluency in Italian, whether you are writing an essay, a blog, an email, a text message, or prepping for an exam.

Verb Guide

The Verb Guide is a brief, clear, student-friendly overview of all the important parts of the Italian verb system. The Verb Guide also provides you with practical tips on how to place accents correctly to enhance your writing skills.
It also provides useful Memory Tips to help you understand how important verbs, such as *essere*, are used.

Alphabetical Listing of 601 Verbs

601 Italian Verbs provides an alphabetical listing of 601 of the most commonly-used Italian verbs in academic, professional and social contexts. Each verb page provides an English translation of the Italian verb. The verb conjugations have endings that are highlighted for easy reference, which in turn makes learning the conjugations of the different tenses much easier! We have identified 75 of the most useful and common Italian verbs. These "75 Must Know Verbs" are featured with a blue background for easy reference.
In addition, the authors have written Memory Tips to help you remember key verbs. These verbs are also marked for easy reference.

Italian Verb Activities/Answer Key

The activity pages provide you with a variety of accessible and practical exercises that help you practice both the conjugation and usage of verbs.
There is an Answer Key on page 686 so that you can check your own answers.

Must Know Verbs

You will find a list of Must Know Verbs. These verbs are 75 of the most useful and common Italian verbs. Remember, these verbs are marked for easy reference in the body of the book.

Tech Verb List

Here, you will find a list of verbs commonly used when talking about technology. Now you can send email, download a podcast, open documents, and use search engines in Italian!

Italian Text Messaging

Time to have fun in Italian! Use this text-messaging guide to text *in italiano.* You can also use this text-messaging guide when writing emails or when communicating on social networking sites.

Test Prep Guide

The Test Prep Guide offers a quick, bulleted list of helpful strategies for test prep for Italian and for your other classes. These tips will help you before, during and after the exam. *In bocca al lupo!*

Index of over 1900 Italian Verbs Conjugated like Model Verbs

At the beginning of the index you will find a list of model verbs. We have included these verbs since most other Italian verbs are conjugated like one of these model forms. We suggest that you study these model verbs; once you know these conjugations you will be able to conjugate almost any verb!

The index provides an additional 1900 verbs used in Italian. Each verb includes an English translation. The English translation is followed by a number, for example: *remare*, to row (90). The number 90 refers to the page where you will find the conjugation of the verb *amare*. The verb *remare* is conjugated like the model verb *amare*.

iPod Instructions

Use your iPod to communicate instantly in Italian! The free download that accompanies *601 Italian Verbs* gives you access to hundreds of words, phrases and useful expressions. See page 734 for more information.

iPhone and iPod touch Instructions

The free download that accompanies *601 Italian Verbs* enables you to use your iPhone and iPod touch to conjugate essential Italian verbs in the palm of your hand! See page 735 for more information.

Verb Guide Table of Contents

Introduction

The purpose of this book is to help you understand and successfully navigate the Italian verb system. There are three broad concepts that you need to understand to help you do this, and they are the following:

- What is meant by "conjugating" a verb
- What is meant by "tense" and how the Italian verb tenses work
- What is meant by "mood" and how the indicative, subjunctive and imperative moods are used in Italian

In this introduction, you will learn about these three concepts, and you will see that what appears to be a dauntingly complicated system is really quite simple once you understand the key, which is the use of patterns. Armed with your knowledge of patterns in the Italian verb system, you will be able to use this book to help you communicate well in Italian.

List of tenses

English/English explanation	**Italian/Italian example using "parlare"**
present indicative (what you do/are doing)	presente indicativo (*parlo*)
imperfect indicative (what you used to do/ were doing)	imperfetto indicativo (*parlavo*)
present perfect (what you have done)	passato prossimo (*ho parlato/ sono andato*)
future (what you will do)	futuro (*parlerò*)
conditional (what you would do)	condizionale presente (*parlerei*)
past absolute (what you did)	passato remoto (*parlai*)
past perfect (what you had done)	trapassato prossimo (*avevo parlato*)
preterite perfect tense	trapassato remoto (*ebbi parlato*)
future perfect (what you will have done)	futuro anteriore (*avrò parlato)*
conditional perfect (what you would have done)	condizionale passato (*avrei parlato*)
present subjunctive*	presente congiuntivo (*parli*)
imperfect subjunctive*	imperfetto congiuntivo (*parlassi*)
present perfect subjunctive*	passato congiuntivo (*abbia parlato*)
past perfect subjunctive*	trapassato congiuntivo (*avessi parlato*)

*Translation of these tenses will vary with the context. See examples in sections on the uses of the subjunctive mood.

What is conjugation?

Let's start by thinking about what you know about verbs in general. You know that they are sometimes called "action words" and that no sentence is complete without a verb. In English, verbs almost always have a subject or word that does the action of the verb. Without the subject, the sentence seems incomplete. What you will find about Italian verbs that makes them special is that each verb form gives you more information than its English counterpart. While an English verb form communicates only the action, an Italian verb form also tells who does the action and when it takes place.

The infinitive

In Italian, the basic form of a verb that you will see when you look in the dictionary is called an infinitive. This form has no subject because it is unconjugated, but it carries the basic meaning of the verb, the action. In Italian, all infinitives end in "-are," "-ere" or "-ire," and each one of these endings indicates how you will conjugate or change the verb to make it agree with a subject. While there are times when you will leave the verb in the infinitive form, most of the time you will need to change the infinitive ending to agree with a subject and to show a tense. Once you learn the basic pattern that all Italian verbs follow for conjugation, you will see that changing a subject or a tense is very simple. Most irregular verbs, however, do not follow a pattern, and you will need to memorize them.

When can you leave a verb in the infinitive, or unconjugated, form?

- An infinitive may act like an English gerund. A gerund is a verb form that is used as a noun. In the English sentence "*Running* is good for your health," the subject of the sentence is the gerund "running." In Italian, however, you use an infinitive to express the same idea: "*Correre fa bene alla salute.*"
- An infinitive is frequently used as a complement to a conjugated verb. A complement is a second verb form that completes the meaning of the first verb, as in these examples:

Voglio *praticare* l'italiano.	I want *to practice* Italian.
Devo *andare* a scuola.	I have *to go* to school.
Mi piace *studiare* l'italiano.	I like *to study* Italian.

- An infinitive is often used after a preposition in Italian, where a gerund might be used in English:

prima di *mangiare*	before *eating*
invece di *arrivare*	instead of *arriving*
senza *entrare*	without *entering*

How do I conjugate a verb so that I can use it in a sentence?

In order to master the conjugation pattern that all Italian verbs follow, you just need to learn the basic format. Here is a simple chart to help you visualize the pattern:

Singular forms	Plural forms
1st person = the one speaking/acting	1st person = the ones speaking/acting
2nd person = the one spoken to	2nd person = the ones spoken to
3rd person = the one spoken about	3rd person = the ones spoken about

In any tense, Italian verbs always have six forms, and they always follow this pattern. Which form you need to use depends on who or what the subject of the verb is, no matter what tense you are using. You can always use this pattern to help you understand and use verbs in Italian. It will never change, no matter what the verb or the tense.

Subject pronouns

The first thing you need to learn is the pattern for personal (or subject) pronouns in Italian, which are the same for all verb conjugations.

1st person singular = io (I)	1st person plural = noi (we)
2nd person singular = tu (you, informal)	2nd person plural = voi (you plural)
3rd person singular = lui, lei, Lei (he, she, you formal)	3rd person plural = loro (they)

Notice that while in English there is only one way to say "you," in Italian there are two variations. That is because in Italian there is a social distinction between the two ways to address others, depending on how well you know someone. The second person subject pronoun and verb form are used to indicate familiarity, while the third person form indicates a social distance and is therefore more formal.

In Italy, you use the "tu" form of the verb when you are addressing someone with whom you are on a first-name basis, like a friend or family member, especially someone younger. The "Lei" form is used with strangers, people you know but with whom you have a more formal relationship or with older people who deserve your respect, like your teacher.

The last big difference about personal pronouns used with verbs in Italian is that you can often omit them, unlike in English. This is because the endings in different verb conjugations will generally tell you who the subject is. Examples will be given later to show you how all these concepts work.

What is meant by "tense" in Italian?

In any language, the verb's tense indicates the time frame for the action of the verb. In fact, in Italian the word for "tense" (tempo) is also the word for "time." So, if you want to talk about what is going on now, you will choose the present tense. If you want to talk about what happened yesterday or last year, you will choose the past tense. If you want to talk about your life in twenty years, you will choose the future tense, and so on. This is the same in Italian as it is in English. What is different about Italian is that the verb endings you will learn for each tense convey more information than those in English. They will tell you not only what time period is being referred to, but also who or what the subject of the verb is.

The Present Indicative Tense (il presente indicativo)

Let's start with the present tense, which can be used to talk about current action or routine action. Verbs whose infinitives end in "-are" are called first conjugation verbs and are the most common type of verb in Italian. All "-are" verbs are conjugated the same way, unless they are irregular. A regular verb is simply one that follows the rules for conjugation, and an irregular verb does not follow those rules. Once you learn the pattern for each conjugation, you can apply it to any regular verb in that category. If a verb is irregular, you will use the same basic pattern, but you will have to memorize the irregular forms.

In order to conjugate a regular verb, you start with the infinitive stem, which is the infinitive minus the "-are," "-ere" or "-ire." So, for the verb "parlare" (to speak, to talk), you remove the "-are" and get the infinitive stem "parl-." Then you simply add the present tense endings for "-are" verbs, which are given below:

-o	-iamo
-i	-ate
-a	-ano

These endings correspond to the chart of personal pronouns given previously and automatically tell you who the subject is. For example, if a verb form is "stem + -o", you know right away that the subject is "io" (I) and that you are using the present tense. If it ends in "-i," the subject can only be "tu" (the informal, singular "you"). Let's look at an example to see how this works. A common regular "-are" verb in Italian is "parlare." Here is the chart for the present tense conjugation of this verb:

io parlo = I speak	noi parliamo = we speak
tu parli = you speak	voi parlate = you (pl.) speak
lui, lei, Lei parla = he speaks, she speaks, you speak	loro parlano = they speak

The translation of the present tense in Italian is pretty flexible. For example, "io parlo" may mean "I speak," "I do speak" or "I am speaking," depending on the context. As we saw before, since each verb form in Italian is directly related to a specific subject, it is perfectly normal to drop the personal pronoun and use only the verb. Consider the following brief interchange:

Parli italiano? = Do you speak Italian?
Sì, parlo un po' d'italiano. = Yes, I speak a little Italian.

Anyone who heard this conversation would know right away who was speaking, simply by the endings used. Only "io" can be the subject of "parlo," and only "tu" can be the subject of "parli," so the subject pronouns are not necessary, except for emphasis. This is true for the first and second person plural forms as well. The third person form is a bit different, since there is more than one possible subject for this form. Therefore, unless you have already made it clear whom you are talking about, it is more likely that a subject will be used with these forms (either a noun or a pronoun). For example, if you hear someone say "*Parla italiano molto bene,*" you have no clue who speaks Italian well unless the speaker has already mentioned him or her. If the speaker has previously said "*Mio fratello Peter vive in Italia,*" (My brother Peter lives in Italy), then you can assume that the subject of "*Parla italiano molto bene*" is "he," even though it is not directly stated.

Second conjugation verbs are those whose infinitives end in "-ere," and their present tense endings are slightly different than those of "-are" verbs. Here is the chart for these verbs:

-o	-iamo
-i	-ete
-e	-ono

Here is the present tense conjugation the for verb "leggere" (to read):

In regular verbs, in the third person plural of the present tense, the third last syllable is normally stressed: **par**lano, **leg**gono, **par**tono.

io leggo = I read	noi leggiamo = we read
tu leggi = you read	voi leggete = you (pl.) read
lui, lei, Lei legge = he reads, she reads, you read	loro leggono = they read

What you will notice right away is that two of these endings use the vowel "e" where "-are" verbs use the vowel "a." First person, or the "io" and "noi" forms, are the same for all regular verbs in the present tense, since they all end in "o" and "iamo."

Third conjugation verbs are those whose infinitives end in "-ire," and the chart for their present-tense endings is below:

-o	-iamo
-i	-ite
-e	-ono

All of these endings but the "voi" ending are the same as those used for "-ere" verbs, so that means you only have to learn one different ending. That ending will always let you know whether the verb is a second or third conjugation verb.

Here is the present tense conjugation of the verb "partire" (to leave):

io parto = I leave	noi partiamo = we leave
tu parti = you leave	voi partite = you (pl.) leave
lui, lei, Lei parte = he leaves, she leaves, you leave	loro partono = they leave

Notice that the three conjugations follow the same pattern in the "io," "tu" and "noi" forms.
Verbs in "-ere" and "-ire" follow the same pattern in the "Lei," "lui/lei" and "loro" forms.

Verbs in *-isc*:

Most "-ire" verbs like "preferire," "costruire," "capire," "pulire" etc., add "-isc" between the stem and the endings in all persons but the first and second plural. Look at the present tense conjugation of the verb "capire" (to understand):

io cap**isc**o = I understand	noi capiamo = we understand
tu cap**isc**i = you understand	voi capite = you (pl.) understand
lui, lei, Lei cap**isc**e = he understands, she understands, you understand	loro cap**isc**ono = they understand

Spelling changes in the present tense

Certain verbs in Italian undergo spelling changes for phonetic reasons in the second person singular "tu" and in the first person plural "noi" (see chart on next page). There are three types of changes possible: verbs that end in "-iare," verbs that end in "-care" and verbs that end in "-gare."

An example of the first of these changes is the verb "studiare" (to study). Like other verbs in "-iare," it has only one "i" in the "tu" and "noi" forms. The chart of the present tense conjugation of "studiare" is below:

studio* = I study	studiamo = we study
studi* = you study	studiate = you (pl.) study
studia* = he studies, she studies, you study	studiano* = they study

*Note that verbs like "inviare" (to send) and "sciare" (to ski) have a stressed "i" in the first person singular (*invio*, *scio*), so they retain a double "i" in the "tu" form: "tu invii," "tu scii."

Verbs ending in "-care" and "-gare" add an "h" between the stem and the ending "i" in the second person singular and first person plural in order to maintain the hard sound of the letters "c" and "g" ("c" and "g" have an hard sound in front of "a," "o" and "u," but a soft sound before "e" and "i;" to produce a hard "c" or "g" in front of "e" or "i," we need an "h"). Look at the examples of the verbs "cercare" (to look for) and "pagare" (to pay):

cerco = I look for	cerchiamo = we look for
cerchi = you look for	cercate = you (pl.) look for
cerca = he looks for, she looks for, you look for	cercano = they look for

pago = I pay	paghiamo = we pay
paghi = you pay	pagate = you (pl.) pay
paga = he pays, she pays, you pay	pagano = they pay

Reflexive verbs in the present tense

Verbs whose subjects and objects are the same are called reflexive verbs, and in order to conjugate these verbs, you must add a reflexive pronoun that agrees with the subject pronoun. An example of this in English is seen in the constructions "I hurt myself" and "He saw himself in the mirror."

Below is a chart with all the reflexive pronouns:

mi (myself)	ci (ourselves)
ti (yourself)	vi (yourselves)
si (himself, herself, yourself)*	si (themselves)*

*Note that there is only one reflexive pronoun for third person verb forms, whether the verb is singular or plural.

You can see that the reflexive pronouns correspond to the subject pronouns. If the subject of a reflexive verb is "io," then the reflexive pronoun for that verb form must be "mi." An example of a common reflexive verb is "vestirsi" (to get dressed):

(io) mi vesto = I dress myself	(noi) ci vestiamo = we dress ourselves
(tu) ti vesti = you dress yourself	(voi) vi vestite = you (pl.) dress yourselves
(lui, lei, Lei) si veste = he, she dresses himself/herself, you dress yourself	(loro) si vestono = they dress themselves

Note that the appropriate reflexive pronoun is placed before the conjugated verb form. In the infinitive form of a reflexive verb, the pronoun is often attached to the end, as in the sentence: "*Voglio vestirmi*" (I want to dress myself).

In English, the reflexive construction is relatively uncommon, but in Italian it is extremely common. While in English we are more likely to use a possessive adjective (as in the expression, "I am washing my hands."), in Italian that same construction will be reflexive, without the possessive adjective ("*Mi lavo le mani.*"). The use of the reflexive pronoun makes the possessive adjective redundant and unnecessary in Italian.

You can recognize a reflexive verb, because the infinitive of the verb will have the reflexive pronoun "si" attached to the end, without the final "e" of the infinitive. These verbs end in "-arsi," "-ersi" and "-irsi." In order to conjugate them, drop the reflexive endings and add the endings you already know for the present. The verb "chiamare" means to call, but when it is reflexive, it means to call oneself, as in the expression "*Come ti chiami?*" or "What is your name?" (Literally, this expression means "What do you call yourself?") When you want to say, "My name is ..." you use this verb and say "*Mi chiamo* ...."

There are several reasons why a verb may be reflexive:

- To create a truly reflexive construction, in which the subject and the object are the same:

  Lei si trucca. She puts on makeup.

- To distinguish between two verbs with different meanings:

  Laura lava la macchina. Laura washes the car.
  Laura si lava le mani. Laura washes her hands.

- To express reciprocal action when the subject is plural:

  I due amici si telefonano. The two friends call each other.

Irregular forms in the present tense

There are some verbs that are completely irregular in the present tense, and you simply have to memorize their conjugations. Fortunately, most are very common verbs which you will use so frequently that it doesn't take long to remember them. An example of this type of verb is the verb "andare," which means "to go."

io vado = I go	noi andiamo = we go
tu vai = you go	voi andate = you (pl.) go
lui, lei, Lei va = he goes, she goes, you go	loro vanno = they go

Note that most irregular verbs belong to the second and third conjugations.

Verbs like "sapere" (to know), "dare" (to give) and "stare" (to stay) follow a similar pattern, and like "andare," have a double "n" in the third person plural. Here is the conjugation of "sapere":

so = I know	sappiamo = we know
sai = you know	sapete = you (pl.) know
sa = he knows, she knows, you know	sanno = they know

The verb "uscire" (to go out) forms the conjugation of the three singular persons and the third plural person by using the stem "esc-." Look at its conjugation:

esco = I go out	usciamo = we go out
esci = you go out	uscite = you (pl.) go out
esce = he goes out, she goes out, you go out	escono = they go out

Some verbs, like "rimanere" (to stay, to remain), "salire" (to go up) and "venire" (to come) add a "g" to the stem in the first person singular and third person plural. Here is the conjugation of "venire":

vengo* = I come	veniamo = we come
vieni = you come	venite = you (pl.) come
viene = he comes, she comes, you come	vengono* = they come

Some verbs — "bere" (to drink), "dire" (to say) and "tradurre" (to translate) — form the conjugation using the Latin stem: "bev-," "dic-" and "traduc-" and then adding the appropriate ending for the present tense. Look at the conjugation of the verb "bere":

bevo = I drink	beviamo = we drink
bevi = you drink	bevete = you (pl.) drink
beve = he drinks, she drinks, you drink	bevono = they drink

The verb "fare" (to do/make) forms the present using the Latin stem "fac-" in the first person singular and plural. In the other persons, it follows the pattern of a verb like "andare" or "sapere." Look at the conjugations of "fare":

faccio = I do/make	facciamo = we do/make
fai = you do/make	fate = you (pl.) do/make
fa = he does/makes, she does/makes, you do/make	fanno = they do/make

Note that this verb adds an extra "-c-" to the Latin stem "fac-": "faccio," "facciamo."

The verbs "dovere" (to have to, must), "potere" (to be able, can, may) and "volere" (to want) are irregular and are often followed by the infinitive:

dovere	**potere**	**volere**
devo	posso	voglio
devi	puoi	vuoi
deve	può	vuole
dobbiamo	possiamo	vogliamo
dovete	potete	volete
devono	possono	vogliono

Note the accent mark in the "lui," "lei," "Lei" form of "potere": può. Also, note the pattern of "potere" and "volere" in the "io," "noi" and "loro" forms.

The irregular verbs *essere* and *avere*

There are two very important verbs used for descriptions and as helping verbs in compound tenses: "avere" and "essere." Here are the charts for the present tense of these two verbs:

"essere"

sono = I am	siamo = we are
sei = you are	siete = you (pl.) are
è = he is, she is, you are	sono = they are

"avere"

ho = I have	abbiamo = we have
hai = you have	avete = you (pl.) have
ha = he has, she has, you have	hanno = they have

Note the accent mark in the third person of the verb "essere": "è." Also note that the "h" in Italian is always silent.

Uses of *essere* and *avere*

"Essere" is used to name the general categories that identify people and things, such as profession, race, religion, political affiliation, relationships, etc., as in these examples:

Mio padre è insegnante.	My dad is a teacher.
Molte persone in Italia sono cattoliche.	Lots of people in Italy are Catholic.

The verb "essere" also describes relationships:

Lui è mio fratello.	He is my brother.

It is also used to describe possession and origin:

Di chi è il libro? È di Massimo.	Whose book is it? It's Massimo's.
Di dov'è Laura? È italiana.	Where is Laura from? She's Italian.

If you want to describe instrinsic qualitites of people or things, you use "essere," as in the following sentences:

Mio fratello è alto e bello.	My brother is tall and handsome.
La lezione è difficile, però è interessante.	The class is hard, but it's interesting.

"Avere" is used to describe physical features:

Luca ha i capelli biondi e gli occhi verdi.	Luca has blond hair and green eyes.

It is used to indicate possession:

Io ho una casa in Italia.	I have a house in Italy.

"Avere" is also used in some idiomatic expressions. These are very important to remember, since in English the verb "to be" is used instead.

avere fretta = to be in a hurry	avere ... anni = to be ... years old
avere voglia di = to be up for, to want	avere fame/sete = to be hungry/thirsty
avere bisogno di = to need	avere freddo/caldo = to be cold/hot
avere paura di = to be afraid	avere ragione/torto = to be right/wrong
avere sonno = to be sleepy	

Look at some examples:

Laura ha 30 anni.	Laura is 30 years old.
Maria ha fame.	Maria is hungry.
Noi abbiamo sonno perché siamo stanchi.	We are sleepy because we are tired.
Luca ha voglia di un gelato.	Luca is up for an ice cream.

Notice the preposition "di" after "avere paura di," "avere bisogno di" and "avere voglia di."

The Imperative Mood (l'imperativo)

The imperative is used to give commands but also instructions like directions or recipes. The "tu," (except in the first conjugation) "noi" and "voi" forms are the same as the present indicative. You will learn the formal form ("Lei") at the end of the book.

Look at the following chart with the imperative of the three conjugations:

	parlare (to speak)	**leggere (to read)**	**partire (to leave)**
(tu)	parla!*	leggi!	parti!
(noi)	parliamo!	leggiamo!	partiamo!
(voi)	parlate!	leggete!	partite!

*Note that in first conjugation verbs only, the ending for the "tu" form is "-a" and not "-i" like in the present tense.

Third conjugation verbs in "-isc" like "pulire" (to clean) add "-isc" just in the "tu" form only, as they do in the present tense:

(tu) pulisci! (noi) puliamo! (voi) pulite!

To form the negative imperative, just put "non" in front of the "noi" and "voi" forms. For the "tu" form, the construction is "non" + infinitive:

Non puliamo! Let's not clean!

Non partite! Don't leave!

But:

Luca, non partire! Luca, don't leave!

The verbs "andare" (to go), "dare" (to give), "fare" (to do, to make) and "stare" (to stay) also have a contracted form in the second person singular:

vai/va' dai/da' fai/fa' stai/sta'

The verb "dire" (to say) only has a contracted form:

di'

The reflexive pronouns are attached to imperative endings:

Vestiti! Dress yourself!

Vestiamoci! Let's dress!

Vestitevi! Dress yourselves!

Object pronouns follow the same pattern:

Leggilo! Read it!

The contracted forms of "andare," "dare," "dire," "fare" and "stare" lose the apostrophe and attach to all pronouns except *gli*, doubling the first consonant in the process:

Dammi il libro!	Give me the book!
Dille "ciao"!	Tell her "ciao."

But:

Dagli il libro!	Give the book to him!

The contracted form of *"andare"* has the same construction with *ci:*

Vacci!	Go there!

Note that "essere" and "avere" have irregular "tu" and "voi" forms:

	essere	**avere**
(tu)	sii	abbi
(voi)	siate	abbiate

Expressing Past Actions: The Present Perfect Tense (il passato prossimo)

In Italian, the most commonly used past tenses are the present perfect tense (which we'll call by its better-known Italian name, the *passato prossimo*) and the imperfect. Each has different uses, so you will need to learn them both. The *passato prossimo* describes completed actions in the past and can be translated by both the past absolute (I ate) and the present perfect (I have eaten) in English, while the imperfect tense expresses repeated actions, ongoing actions or conditions in the past. (A chart and examples explaining the different uses of these two tenses follows the section on the formation of both tenses.)

The present perfect tense (il passato prossimo)

To form the present perfect tense, you need to use the present tense of the irregular helping verbs that you already know – "avere" or "essere" – plus the past participle. As a general rule, all transitive verbs (verbs that take a direct object) use the helping verb "avere." Intransitive verbs (verbs that don't have a direct object) take either "avere" or "essere," but there is no rule, so you will have to learn from practice. Reflexive verbs and verbs of motion and change of state use "essere."

The easiest way to recognize a transitive verb from an intransitive one is whether or not you can answer the questions "Who?" or "What?" If you can, the verb is transitive. For example: *Luigi has seen Maria.* (Whom did he see? Maria.) *I have eaten pasta.* (What did I eat? Pasta.).

Forming the regular past participle:

- For "-are" verbs, drop the infinitive ending and add "-ato."

  The past participle for the verb "parlare" is "parlato."
- For "-ere" verbs, drop the infinitive ending and add "-uto."

  The past participle for the verb "ricevere" is "ricevuto."
- For "-ire" verbs, drop the infinitive ending and add "-ito."

  The past participle for the verb "partire" is "partito."

Here is the present perfect tense of the verb "parlare":

ho parlato = I have spoken/I spoke	abbiamo parlato = we have spoken/ we spoke
hai parlato = you have spoken/you spoke	avete parlato = you (pl.) have spoken/ you all spoke
ha parlato = he, she has spoken/you have spoken/he, she, you spoke	hanno parlato = they have spoken/ they spoke

Here is the present perfect tense of the verb "andare":

sono andato/a = I have gone/I went	siamo andati/e = we have gone/we went
sei andato/a = you have gone/you went	siete andati/e = you (pl.) have gone/ you all went
è andato/a = he, she has gone/you have gone/he, she, you went	sono andati/e = they have gone/they went

Remember that the *passato prossimo* corresponds to the English present perfect but also the past absolute or simple past.

Agreement of the past participle

When the present perfect is formed with the helping verb "avere," the past participle doesn't change in any person unless a direct object pronoun ("lo," "la," "La," "li" or "le") precedes the verb, in which case the past participle agrees in gender and number with the pronoun.

Examples:

*Hai mangiato la pasta? Sì, **l**'ho **mangiata**.*	Have you eaten the pasta? Yes, I have eaten it.
*Hai visto Luisa e Maria? No, non **le** ho **viste**.*	Have you seen Luisa and Maria? No, I haven't seen them.

Note that "lo," "la" and "La" elide in front of "h," but "li" and "le" do not.

When the present perfect is formed with the helping verb "essere," it must always agree in gender and number with the subject of the verb:

Laura è **andata** a Roma.
Luca è **andato** a Roma.
Noi siamo **andati/e** a Roma. ("-i" or "-e" depending whether the subject is masculine or feminine plural.)

Some verbs can either take "avere"or "essere" in the passato prossimo

-Verbs indicating weather conditions like "piovere" and "nevicare" can take both.
-Some verbs require "essere" when there is no direct object afterwards, but with a direct object they require "avere":

La lezione è cominciata alle 8:00.	Class started at 8:00.

But:

Ho cominciato la lezione di yoga.	I started the yoga class.
Sono scesi dal treno.	They got off the train.

But:

Hanno sceso le scale.	They went down the stairs.
Le lezioni sono finite alle 12:00.	Classes ended at 12:00.

But:

Ho finito i compiti.	I have finished the homework.

Irregular Past Participles:

There are some irregular past participles, just like in English, and you must memorize them. Here are the most common irregular past participles used with the helping verb "avere":

Infinitive	**Irregular past participle**
aprire (to open)	*aperto* (opened)
avere (to have)	*avuto* (had)
bere (to drink)	*bevuto* (drunk)
chiedere (to ask)	*chiesto* (asked)
chiudere (to close)	*chiuso* (closed)
dare (to give)	*dato* (given)
decidere (to decide)	*deciso* (decided)
dire (to say)	*detto* (said)
fare (to do/make)	*fatto* (done/made)
leggere (to read)	*letto* (read)
mettere (to put)	*messo* (put)
prendere (to take)	*preso* (taken)
promettere (to promise)	*promesso* (promised)
ridere (to laugh)	*riso* (laughed)
scegliere (to choose)	*scelto* (chosen)
scrivere (to write)	*scritto* (written)
vedere (to see)	*visto* (seen)
vincere (to win)	*vinto* (won)

Here are some of the most common past participles used with the helping verb "essere":

Infinitive	**Irregular past participle**
essere (to be)	*stato* (been)
morire (to die)	*morto* (died)
nascere (to be born)	*nato* (born)
rimanere (to remain)	*rimasto* (remained)
succedere (to happen)	*successo* (happened)
venire (to come)	*venuto* (come)

Uses of past participles

- The past participle follows the verbs "avere" (in which case it is invariable and does NOT agree with the subject of the verb) and "essere" (in which case it is variable and agrees in gender and number with the subject of the verb) in the perfect tenses. An example of this is the sentence "*Ho aperto la porta.*" (I have opened the door.) or the sentence "*Lei è partita.*" (She left.) These sentences describe an action.
- The past participle may be used as an adjective, either with or without "essere," in which case the ending will change to agree in gender and number with the word being modified. Here is an example of this use: "*La porta è aperta.*" (The door is open.) This sentence describes the result of an action.
- The past participle may follow the verb "essere" to form the passive voice, and in this case it is also considered an adjective and must agree with the subject of the verb "essere." An example of this is the sentence "*La porta è stata aperta dall'insegnante.*" (The door was opened by the teacher.) This form of the passive voice is mainly used when the speaker wishes to indicate by whom the action was done. When this is not important, you will most often use the common form of the passive voice, formed by adding the impersonal "si" to the verb in the third person singular or plural (depending on the subject), as in the following examples:

In Italia si mangia spesso la pasta.	In Italy, pasta is eaten often.
In Svizzera si parlano tre lingue.	In Switzerland, three languages are spoken.

The Imperfect Indicative Tense (l'imperfetto indicativo)

In order to talk about routine past actions in Italian (the way things used to be) or progressive actions (what someone was doing when something else happened), you need to use the imperfect tense. While the past absolute and the present perfect (a tense presented later) allow you to describe actions and reactions in the past, the imperfect tense lets you describe past conditions, feelings and circumstances, as well as routine or progressive actions. This is the most regular of all Italian tenses. The imperfect has only one set of endings for "-are," "-ere" and "-ire" verbs, and unlike the preterite, there are very few irregular verbs to memorize. To form this tense, you drop "-re" from the infinitive stem and add the imperfect endings.

Below is the chart for the endings for this tense:

-vo	-vamo
-vi	-vate
-va	-vano

Remember to add the consonant "v" throughout the conjugation.

Here is the chart for the imperfect of the verb "parlare" (to speak, to talk):

parlavo = I used to speak/I was speaking	parlavamo = we used to speak/we were speaking
parlavi = you used to speak/you were speaking	parlavate = you (pl.) used to speak/you (pl.) were speaking
parlava = he, she, you used to speak/he, she was speaking, you were speaking	parlavano = they used to speak/they were speaking

Here is the chart for the imperfect of the verb "leggere" (to read):

leggevo = I used to read/I was reading	leggevamo = we used to read/we were reading
leggevi = you used to read/you were reading	leggevate = you (pl.) used to read/you (pl.) were reading
leggeva = he, she, you used to read/he, she was reading, you were reading	leggevano = they used to read/they were reading

Here is the chart for the imperfect of the verb "partire" (to leave):

partivo = I used to leave/I was leaving	partivamo = we used to leave/we were leaving
partivi = you used to leave/you were leaving	partivate = you (pl.) used to leave/you (pl.) were leaving
partiva = he, she, you used to leave/ he, she was leaving, you were leaving	partivano = they used to leave/they were leaving

Irregular forms in the imperfect tense

Only a few verbs have any irregular forms; "essere" has irregular forms in all the persons. Here is its chart:

essere (to be)

ero = I was/I used to be	eravamo = we were/we used to be
eri = you were/you used to be	eravate = you (pl.) were/you (pl.) used to be
era = he, she was, you were/you used to be	erano = they were/they used to be

Some verbs use a Latin stem but with the imperfect regular endings. Here are the charts of the three most common ones:

fare (to do/make)

facevo = I was doing, making/I used to do, make	facevamo = we were doing, making/ we used to do, make
facevi = you were doing, making/you used to do, make	facevate = you (pl.) were doing, making/you (pl.) used to do, make
faceva = he, she was doing, making/ you were doing, making/you used to do, make	facevano = they were doing, making/ they used to do, make

bere (to drink)

bevevo = I was drinking/I used to drink	bevevamo = we were drinking/we used to drink
bevevi = you were drinking/you used to drink	bevevate = you (pl.) were drinking/you (pl.) used to drink
beveva = he, she was drinking, you were drinking/he, she, you used to drink	bevevano = they were drinking/they used to drink

dire (to say)

dicevo = I was saying/I used to say	dicevamo = we were saying/we used to say
dicevi = you were saying/you used to say	dicevate = you (pl.) were saying/you (pl.) used to say
diceva = he, she was saying, you were saying/he, she, you used to say	dicevano = they were saying/they used to say

Uses of the present perfect and the imperfect

Here is a chart to help you remember the different uses of these two tenses:

Present perfect	**Imperfect**
-describes completed, specific past actions or events	-describes routine or repeated past actions
	-describes reactions to past actions or events
	-describes ongoing or progressive past actions
	-describes conditions or circumstances in the past
	-describes background actions, as opposed to main actions

Here are some examples to help you see the difference in the two tenses:

Leri c'è stato un incidente.	Yesterday there was an accident. (an event happened)
Lo ero spaventato.	I was scared. (my reaction to the event)
C' erano molte persone ferite.	There were many injured people. (the resulting condition)
La settimana scorsa sono andato al cinema.	Last week, I went to the movies. (a single event)
Quando ero piccolo andavo sempre al parco.	When I was a child, I always used to go the park. (condition or circumstance/ repeated past action)
Mentre cenavo è squillato il telefono.	While I was eating dinner, the phone rang. (action in progress when main action occurred)

Because they are conditions, time of day and age are always imperfect, but what happened at a certain time or age could be *passato prossimo*.

Quando è arrivato mio padre erano le cinque.	It was five o'clock when my father arrived.
Quando mi sono rotto il braccio avevo cinque anni.	I was five when I broke my arm.

You can think of the imperfect tense as a long, unbroken line, with no beginning or end. The *passato prossimo* could be represented by specific points on that line or by a limited segment of that line, a moment framed in time. If you know when an action started, when it ended or how long it lasted, use the *passato prossimo*.

There are some verbs, like "conoscere" (to know, to meet) and "sapere" (to know), whose definitions in English change in these two tenses, but this makes sense if you understand the overall concept of *passato prossimo* versus *imperfect*. Here are a couple of examples:

Leri ho conosciuto Marco.	Yesterday I met Marco. (a specific action)
Quando ero piccolo non conoscevo Luisa.	When I was little, I did not know Luisa. (an ongoing condition)
Non sapevo la risposta giusta.	I did not know the right answer. (a condition)
L'ho saputo dopo.	I found it out later. (a specific action)

The Past Absolute (il passato remoto)

To talk about completed actions in the past you will use the past absolute. This tense is used mainly to describe actions in the distant past and to talk about historical events. It is used in literary texts and in formal writing. In Central and Southern Italy, it is sometimes used in everyday Italian, too. Usually, to talk about the past, the *passato prossimo* is used instead.

Verbs in "-are" add the following endings:

-ai	-ammo
-asti	-aste
-ò	-arono

The chart for the past absolute of the verb "parlare" (to speak, to talk) is given below:

parlai = I spoke	parlammo = we spoke
parlasti = you spoke	parlaste = you (pl.) spoke
parlò = he, she, you spoke	parlarono = they spoke

Verbs in "-ere" add the following endings:

-ei or -etti	-emmo
-esti	-este
-é or -ette	-erono or -ettero

Note the alternate endings for the "io," "lui"/"lei"/"Lei" and "loro" forms. However, in verbs with a stem ending in "-t" like "potere," there is no second alternate form.

The chart for the verb "credere" (to believe) in the past absolute is given below:

credei/credetti = I believed	credemmo = we believed
credesti = you believed	credeste = you (pl.) believed
credé/credette = he, she, you believed	crederono/credettero = they believed

Verbs in "-ire" add the following endings:

ii	immo
isti	iste
ì	irono

Note the accent mark in the third person singular in the three conjugations.

Here is the chart for the verb "finire" (to finish) in the past absolute:

finii = I finished	finimmo = we finished
finisti = you finished	finiste = you (pl.) finished
finì = he, she, you finished	finirono = they finished

Irregular verbs in the past absolute

Most verbs with an irregular past absolute are "-ere" verbs and they follow a 1-3-3 pattern meaning that they are regular in all persons but in the "io," "lui"/"lei"/"Lei" and "loro" forms, when they have the following endings: "-i," "-e," "-ero." You can predict the conjugation if you know the first person singular and the infinitive.

As an example, the verb "scrivere" (to write) belongs to this group. The first person is "scrissi" so the conjugation will be:

scrissi = I wrote	scrivemmo = we wrote
scrivesti = you wrote	scriveste = you (pl.) wrote
scrisse = he, she, you wrote	scrissero = they wrote

Note that verbs that have two alternate stems like "scrivere/scrissi" have no accents.

Here are the most common irregular verbs that follow the 1-3-3 pattern. The infinitive and first person singular are provided:

Infinitive	**First person singular**
avere (to have)	*ebbi*
conoscere (to know, to meet)	*conobbi*
leggere (to read)	*lessi*
mettere (to put)	*misi*
nascere (to be born)	*nacqui*
piacere (to like)	*piacqui*
rimanere (to stay, to remain)	*rimasi*
rispondere (to answer)	*risposi*
scegliere (to choose)	*scelsi*
vedere (to see)	*vidi*
venire (to come)	*venni*
vivere (to live)	*vissi*
volere (to want)	*volli*

There is a small group of verbs that use the Latin stem to form the "tu," "noi" and "voi" persons. Some of these are "bere" (to drink), which uses "bev-," "dire" (to say), which uses "dic-" and "fare" (to do/make), which uses "fac-." Here is the chart of the verb "fare" (to do/make):

feci = I did/made	facemmo* = we did/made
facesti* = you did/made	faceste* = you (pl.) did/made
fece = he, she, you did/made	fecero = they did/made

Finally, the verb "essere" (to be) is irregular in all persons and must therefore be memorized. Here is the conjugation:

fui = I was	fummo = we were
fosti = you were	foste = you (pl.) were
fu = he was, she was, you were	furono = they were

The Future Tense and Conditional Mood (il futuro presente e il condizionale presente)

The future tense is used to say what will happen, and the conditional mood (attitude of the speaker) is used to say what would happen under certain conditions. Here you will learn the future tense and the present conditional mood. The future and the conditional are the only ones that in Italian are not formed by using the infinitive stem. Instead, for all regular verbs, the future and the conditional are based on the entire infinitive form. In addition, for each – the future tense and the conditional mood – there is only one set of endings, which are used with all verbs, both regular and irregular. And, finally, the future and the conditional share the same set of irregular stems. So, once you learn the future tense, the present conditional mood is really easy.

Here is the chart for future tense endings, which are added directly to the infinitive of regular verbs:

-ò	-emo
-ai	-ete
-à	-anno

Note that only the "io" and "lui"/"lei"/"Lei" forms carry an accent mark.

These same endings are used for all verbs, both regular and irregular, regardless of the conjugation. All regular "-are," "-ere" and "-ire" verbs work the same way in this tense and add only the future endings. Verbs in "-are" change the stem "-ar" into "-er" before adding them.

For the verb "parlare" (to speak, to talk), the future tense looks like this:

parl**er**ò = I will speak	parl**er**emo = we will speak
parl**er**ai = you will speak	parl**er**ete = you (pl.) will speak
parl**er**à = he, she, you will speak	parl**er**anno = they will speak

For the verb "leggere" (to read), the future tense looks like this:

leggerò = I will read	leggeremo = we will read
leggerai = you will read	leggerete = you (pl.) will read
leggerà = he, she, you will read	leggeranno = they will read

For the verb "partire" (to leave), the future tense looks like this:

partirò = I will leave	partiremo = we will leave
partirai = you will leave	partirete = you (pl.) will leave
partirà = he, she, you will leave	partiranno = they will leave

Uses of the future tense:

- To express predictions in the present, as in the sentence: *Lei dice che arriverà alle cinque.* (She says that she will arrive at 5:00 p.m.)
- After expressions of time such as "quando," "se," "appena," "non appena" and "finché" when it is implied that the event will occur in the future: *Se pioverà, prenderò l'ombrello.* (If it rains, I will take the umbrella.)
- To express conjecture or probability in the present, as in this question and answer: *Che ore saranno? Saranno le otto.* (I wonder what time it is. It must be 8:00 p.m.)

In the first two cases, you can use the present tense instead of the future.

English uses the present tense in these cases.

Here is the chart for conditional mood endings, which are also added directly to the infinitive of regular verbs:

-ei	-emmo
-esti	-este
-ebbe	-ebbero

Note that the stem is the same as the one in the future tense, so verbs in "-are" change the stem "-ar" into "-er" before adding the conditional endings.

Here is the chart for the verb "parlare" in the conditional mood:

parlerei = I would speak	parleremmo = we would speak
parleresti = you would speak	parlereste = you (pl.) would speak
parlerebbe = he, she, you would speak	parlerebbero = they would speak

For the verb "leggere," the conditional mood looks like this:

leggerei = I would read	leggeremmo = we would read
leggeresti = you would read	leggereste = you (pl.) would read
leggerebbe = he, she, you would read	leggerebbero = they would read

For the verb "partire," the conditional mood looks like this:

partirei = I would leave	partiremmo = we would leave
partiresti = you would leave	partireste = you (pl.) would leave
partirebbe = he, she, you would leave	partirebbero = they would leave

Don't confuse the future "noi" form with the conditional one: "parleremo" vs. "parleremmo." In the conditional there is a double "m," and in Italian, doubles are pronounced with more emphasis.

Uses of the conditional mood:

- To make a request, expressing desire seems less rude or direct: *Potresti parlarmi del tuo amico?* (Could you tell me about your friend?)
- In past tense "if" clauses that express contrary-to-fact conditions, such as this sentence: *Se potessi, ti aiuterei.* (If I could, I would help you.)

Spelling changes in the future tense and conditional mood

Verbs ending in "-care" and "-gare" add an "h" after a "-c"or "-g" and then change the vowel "-a" into an "-e," like all "-are" verbs:

"Cercare" (to look for) becomes "cer**ch**erò" in the future, "cer**ch**erei" in the conditional.
"Pagare" (to pay) becomes "pa**gh**erò" in the future, "pa**gh**erei" in the conditional.

Verbs ending in "-ciare" and "-giare" drop the "-i" and change the "-a" into "-e":

"Cominciare" (to start) becomes "comin**c**erò" in the future, "comin**c**erei" in the conditional.
"Mangiare" (to eat) becomes "man**g**erò" in the future, "man**g**erei" in the conditional.

Irregular stems for the future and conditional

Both the future and the conditional use the same irregular stems, which are listed below:

Infinitive	**Irregular stem**
avere	*avr-*
andare	*andr-*
dovere	*dovr-*
essere	*sar-*
fare	*far-*
dare	*dar-*
potere	*potr-*
sapere	*sapr-*
vedere	*vedr-*
volere	*vorr-*
venire	*verr-*
bere	*berr-*
tenere	*terr-*

Since the irregular stems are the same for both the future and the conditional, you simply need to learn these once, and then the two sets of endings.

Here are the charts for the verb "avere" (to have) in the future and the conditional. Note that the same irregular stem is used for both; only the endings change.

The future of "avere":

avrò = I will have	avremo = we will have
avrai = you will have	avrete = you (pl.) will have
avrà = he, she, you will have	avranno = they will have

The conditional of "avere":

avrei = I would have	avremmo = we would have
avresti = you would have	avreste = you (pl.) would have
avrebbe = he, she, you would have	avrebbero = they would have

Simple Versus Compound Tenses

Simple tenses are those that are formed by a single word, and compound tenses, as the name implies, have two parts, like a compound word. The simple tenses you have learned are the present, the past absolute, the imperfect, the future and the conditional. You have also learned one of the compound tenses, the *passato prossimo*. There are five compound tenses, known as the "perfect tenses."

The perfect tenses, of which the *passato prossimo* is the most common, use the helping verbs "avere" (to have) or "essere" (to be) and the past participle of the verb or the "-ed" form. The rules for subject-past participle agreement with "essere" or agreement with a preceding direct object with "avere" are the same as they are in the *passato prossimo* in all these tenses. Once you know how to form the past participle, in order to form the four perfect tenses, you merely need to change the tense of the helping verb.

The past perfect tense (il trapassato prossimo)

The past perfect tense is used to describe an action that took place further back in the past than another past action either mentioned or implied in the same sentence: *Carlo ha domandato se avevo già visto il film.* (Carlo asked if I had already seen the film.) To form the past perfect tense, also known as the pluperfect, the helping verbs "essere" and "avere" are conjugated in the imperfect tense. Here is the chart for the verb "mangiare" (to eat) in this tense:

avevo mangiato = I had eaten	avevamo mangiato = we had eaten
avevi mangiato = you had eaten	avevate mangiato = you (pl.) had eaten
aveva mangiato = he, she, you had eaten	avevano mangiato = they had eaten

And here is the chart for the verb "uscire" (to go out) in the past perfect tense:

ero uscito/a = I had gone out	eravamo usciti/e = we had gone out
eri uscito/a = you had gone out	eravate usciti/e = you (pl.) had gone out
era uscito/a = he, she, you had gone out	erano usciti/e = they had gone out

The preterite perfect tense (il trapassato remoto)

There is another compound tense, known as the preterite perfect or anterior preterite, but it is not commonly used in Italian. This tense is translated exactly like the past perfect, or pluperfect, so it is not necessary in everyday speech. However, if you read a lot in Italian, you will probably see it. It is formed by adding the preterite tense of the helper verbs "avere" and "essere" to the past participle. It is used only in subordinate clauses with time expressions like "quando," "dopo che" and "appena" if there is a passato remoto (past absolute) in the main clause:

Tornai a casa appena ebbi finito le lezioni. I came back home, as soon as I had finished classes.

Here is the chart for the verb "fare" (to do/make) in this tense:

ebbi fatto = I had done/made	avemmo fatto = we had done/made
avesti fatto = you had done/made	aveste fatto = you (pl.) had done/made
ebbe fatto = he, she, you had done/made	ebbero fatto = they had done/made

Here is the chart for the verb "arrivare" (to arrive) in this tense:

fui arrivato/a = I had arrived	fummo arrivati/e = we had arrived
fosti arrivato/a = you had arrived	foste arrivati/e = you (pl.) had arrived
fu arrivato/a = he, she, you had arrived	furono arrivati/e = they had arrived

The future perfect tense and conditional perfect mood (il futuro anteriore e il condizionale passato)

The future perfect tense is used to describe an action that will have been completed either before a future point in time or before another future event occurs: *Noi avremo finito i compiti entro le cinque.* (We will have finished our homework by five o'clock.) To form the future perfect tense, "avere" or "essere" are conjugated in the future tense. Here is the chart for the verb "dormire" (to sleep) in this tense:

avrò dormito = I will have slept	avremo dormito = we will have slept
avrai dormito = you will have slept	avrete dormito = you (pl.) will have slept
avrà dormito = he, she, you will have slept	avranno dormito = they will have slept

And here is the chart for the verb "partire" (to leave) in the future perfect tense:

sarò partito/a = I will have left	saremo partiti/e = we will have left
sarai partito/a = you will have left	sarete partiti/e = you (pl.) will have left
sarà partito/a = he, she, you will have left	saranno partiti/e = they will have left

When the future tense is used in the main clause of a sentence containing the conjunctions "dopo che," "appena," "quando," etc. the future perfect is used after the conjunction: *Lei ci dirà quando sarà partito l'aereo*. (She will tell us when the plane has left.)

The future perfect is also used to express a probability in the past: *Dov'è Stefania? Non lo so, sarà uscita.* (Where is Stefania? I don't know. She probably went out.)

The conditional perfect mood is used to describe a past event that did not take place: *L'estate scorsa sarei andato in Italia ma non avevo abbastanza soldi.* (Last summer, I would have gone to Italy, but I didn't have enough money.)

It is also used in an indirect statement after verbs like "to know," "to say" or "to tell" (this construction is also known as "future in the past."):

Luca ha detto che Barbara sarebbe venuta a cena. (Luca said that Barbara would come to dinner.) Note that in this construction, English uses the conditional present.

To form the conditional perfect, "avere" and "essere" are conjugated in the conditional tense and used with the past participle. Here is the chart for the verb "restituire" (to return, to give back) in this tense:

avrei restituito = I would have given back	avremmo restituito = we would have given back
avresti restituito = you would have given back	avreste restituito = you (pl.) would have given back
avrebbe restituito = he, she, you would have given back	avrebbero restituito = they would have given back

Here is the chart for the verb "partire" (to leave) in this tense:

sarei partito/a = I would have left	saremmo partiti/e = we would have left
saresti partito/a = you would have left	sareste partiti/e = you (pl.) would have left
sarebbe partito/a = he, she, you would have left	sarebbero partiti/e = they would have left

The Progressive Forms

The present progressive

The progressive forms of the simple tenses are composed of the verb "stare" (to stay) and the present participle of the verb, what we know as the "-ing" form of the verb. "I am eating now" is an example of the present progressive tense in English. There are two progressive tenses in Italian, which are formed by changing the tense of the verb "stare." The present participle never changes, no matter what the subject or the tense of "stare."

Forming the present participle

- For "-are" verbs, simply drop the infinitive ending and add "-ando." The present participle of the verb parlare is "parlando."
- For "-ere" and "-ire" verbs, drop the infinitive ending and add "-endo." For the verb "vedere," the present participle is "vedendo," and for "partire," the present participle is "partendo."
- Some verbs use the Latin stem to form the present participle. So, the present participle of the verb "bere" is "bevendo," of "dire" is "dicendo," and of "fare" is "facendo."
- Reflexive and object pronouns may be attached to the end of a present participle. For example, you can say both *Sto leggendolo* and *Lo sto legendo* (I am reading it).

Using the present participle

- While the translation of the present participle makes it seem like an English gerund, this is not the case. A gerund in English is a verb form that is used as a noun, as in the sentence "Skating is fun." In Italian, a present participle is NEVER used as a noun. (Remember that the Italian infinitive is the equivalent of the English gerund.)
- The present participle may follow the verb "stare" in progressive constructions. An example is seen in the sentence "*Lei sta parlando.*" (She is talking.)
- The present participle may be used as an adverb to modify the action of a verb. An example of this is in the sentence "*Loro arrivarono gridando.*" (They arrived shouting.)
- The present participle is used to express the phrase "by doing something," as in this example: "*Sbagliando, s'impara.*" (By making mistakes, one learns.)

Forming the present progressive

To form the present progressive, the verb "stare" must be conjugated in the present tense. Here is the chart for the verb "parlare" (to speak, to talk):

sto parlando = I am talking	stiamo parlando = we are talking
stai parlando = you are talking	state parlando = you (pl.) are talking
sta parlando = he, she is talking/you are talking	stanno parlando = they are talking

In English, you can use the present progressive to indicate future intention, as in the sentence "This weekend I am going to the beach." In Italian, this form is NEVER used to express intention. It is used chiefly to emphasize actions in progress.

The past progressive

To form the past progressive, you will conjugate the verb "stare" in the imperfect tense. Here is the chart for the past progressive of the verb "partire":

stavo partendo = I was leaving	stavamo partendo = we were leaving
stavi partendo = you were leaving	stavate partendo = you (pl.) were leaving
stava partendo = he, she was leaving/you were leaving	stavano partendo = they were leaving

What is the Subjunctive Mood?

All the verb tenses you have seen so far, are in the "indicative, imperative and conditional moods," which must be distinguished from the "subjunctive mood." While "tense" refers to time, "mood" refers to the attitude of the speaker towards the action being described. Because the subjunctive mood is very rarely used in English, it is not a concept English speakers immediately recognize. However, it is extremely common in Italian, and you must use it in many situations. You will find that there are different tenses in the subjunctive mood, just as in the indicative mood. The subjunctive has four tenses: present, past, imperfect and past perfect.

Basically, in Italian you use the indicative mood when you are objectively describing your experience in the world around you, and you use the subjunctive mood when you are reacting subjectively to your experience. Here is a simple chart to help you understand the difference between the indicative and subjunctive mood:

Verbs in the indicative mood	**Verbs in the subjunctive mood**
-state objective truth or facts	-give subjective reactions
-imply certainty	-imply doubt
-inform, confirm or verify	-suggest, question or deny

Formation of the present subjunctive (il congiuntivo presente)

The present subjunctive — with the exception of irregular forms — is formed by dropping the infinitive endings and adding the subjunctive ones. For "-ere" and "-ire" verbs these are the same. Also, "-ire" verbs that add "-isc" in all forms but "noi" and "voi" in the present indicative do the same in the subjunctive.

Here is a chart of the subjunctive endings for the present:

	-are	**-ere** and **-ire**
io	-i	-a
tu	-i	-a
lui, lei, Lei	-i	-a
noi	-iamo	-iamo
voi	-iate	-iate
loro	-ino	-ano

*Note that the first three persons are the same, so it is important to specify the subject pronoun to distinguish them. The "loro" form is the same as the present indicative and the "noi" and "voi" forms are the same in all three conjugations.

Here is an example of this pattern for the "-are" verb "parlare" (to speak, to talk):

parli	parliamo
parli	parliate
parli	parlino

Here is the present subjunctive of the verb "scrivere" (to write):

scriva	scriviamo
scriva	scriviate
scriva	scrivano

Here is the present subjunctive of the verb "partire" (to leave):

parta	partiamo
parta	partiate
parta	partano

A common "-ire" verb in "-isc" in the present subjunctive is "capire" (to understand):

capisca	capiamo
capisca	capiate
capisca	capiscano

Translations have not been given for these forms because the present subjunctive has several possible translations in English. Here are some examples:

- The present subjunctive may refer to present or future actions, depending on the context:

  Spero che *adesso non piova.* — I hope that *it is not raining now.*
  Spero che *più tardi non piova.* — I hope that *it will not rain* later.

- Although in Italian the present subjunctive is almost always in a dependent clause following the relative pronoun "che" (that), in English the same construction may be expressed with an infinitive clause:

  Voglio che *mi aiutino.* — I want *them to help me.*

Spelling changes in the present subjunctive

Just as in the present indicative, there are some verbs whose stem has a spelling change before the present subjunctive endings are added. Verbs whose stem ends in "-care" and "-gare" change the "-c" and "-g" to "-ch" and "-gh;" verbs whose stem ends in "-ciare," "-giare," "-sciare" or "-gliare," drop the "-i." Verbs in "-iare" drop the "-i" as well, but they retain it in the first three persons singular and in the third person plural when it is stressed in the "io" form of the present indicative. i.e.: the stem for verb "inviare" (to send) will be "invii-." See the charts below for some examples:

pagare (to pay)

paghi	paghiamo
paghi	paghiate
paghi	paghino

mangiare (to eat)

mangi	mangiamo
mangi	mangiate
mangi	mangino

studiare (to study)

studi	studiamo
studi	studiate
studi	studino

Verbs with irregular present subjunctive forms

There are some verbs whose present subjunctive forms are irregular. Some of these verbs are given below:

avere (to have)

abbia	abbiamo
abbia	abbiate
abbia	abbiano

essere (to be)

sia	siamo
sia	siate
sia	siano

andare (to go)

vada	andiamo
vada	andiate
vada	vadano

fare (to do/make)

faccia	facciamo
faccia	facciate
faccia	facciano

dare (to give)

dia	diamo
dia	diate
dia	diano

venire (to come)

venga	veniamo
venga	veniate
venga	vengano

uscire (to go out)

esca	usciamo
esca	usciate
esca	escano

volere (to want)

voglia	vogliamo
voglia	vogliate
voglia	vogliano

Uses of the present subjunctive

In general, the subjunctive mood is used in sentences with a dependent clause when there is an element in the main clause that requires the subjunctive in the dependent clause. Here is what many of these sentences will look like:

Main clause* + "che" + second subject + dependent clause

*must contain a subjunctive cue

There are four general categories of what we can call "subjunctive cues," or expressions that require the use of the subjunctive mood. These categories are doubt/negation, emotion, opinion, and command/request.

Here are some lists of common subjunctive cues in all four categories:

Doubt/negation

dubitare	to doubt	*non essere sicuro**	not to be sure
negare	to deny	*non è vero**	it is not true
non credere	not to believe	*sospettare*	to suspect

*If these expressions drop the "no," they become expressions of certainty and do NOT require the use of the subjunctive mood.

Non sono sicuro che piova.	I'm not sure that it's going to rain.
Sono sicuro che pioverà.	I am sure that it's going to rain.

Emotion*

essere contento	to be glad	*preoccuparsi*	to worry
dispiacere	to be sorry, to regret	*dare fastidio*	to bother
essere sorpreso	to be surprised	*piacere*	to like, to please
temere/avere paura	to fear, to be afraid	*non piacere*	to dislike
essere contento, triste, etc.	to be happy, sad, etc.	*sperare*	to hope

*These expressions of emotion require the subjunctive mood whether they are affirmative or negative. Either way, they express your feelings, which are subjective.

Sono contento che tu venga alla festa.	I am glad that you will come to my party.
Sono sorpreso che lei non sia ancora qui.	I am surprised that she is not here yet.

Opinion

There are too many expressions of opinion to list here, but here are a few to help you understand the concept. These are most often impersonal expressions that may contain adjectives.

È importante	It's important	*È meglio*	It's better
È necessario/bisogna	It's necessary	*È incredibile*	It's incredible
È interessante	It's interesting	*È possibile*	It's possible
È bene/male	It's good/bad	*pensare*	to think
Sembra	It seems	*credere*	to believe
		immaginare	to imagine

È possibile che lei arrivi domani. — It's possible that she will arrive tomorrow.

Penso che loro abbiano ragione. — I think they are right.

Command/request

volere	to want	*ordinare*	to order, to command
insistere	to insist	*pregare*	to beg
desiderare	to desire	*esigere*	to demand
chiedere	to ask, to request	*raccomandare*	to recommend

Remember that the pattern of these sentences is a main clause with a subjunctive cue followed by a dependent clause that uses the subjunctive. Let's look at another sentence that follows this pattern, contrasted with a similarly constructed sentence that uses the indicative.

Dubito che oggi ci sia un esame. — I doubt that there is a test today.

The verb "dubitare" (to doubt) requires the use of the subjunctive of the verb "esserci" in the dependent clause. In contrast to this sentence, if there were no doubt, you would use the indicative of the verb "esserci" in the dependent clause:

So che oggi c'è un esame. — I know that there is a test today.

Since we so often react to the world around us, the subjunctive mood is used extensively in Italian. If we merely reported information, we would not need to use the subjunctive mood, but since we frequently express our opinions, feelings and wishes, the subjunctive mood is essential for more sophisticated communication in Italian.

The following is an example of a statement in which we merely report information:

Mio fratello Giacomo è malato.	My brother Giacomo is sick.

The following is an example of a subjective response to that information:

Mi dispiace che tuo fratello Giacomo sia malato.	I am sorry that your brother Giacomo is sick.

In this sentence, the verb in the dependent clause is in the subjunctive, because the main clause expresses an emotion.

When you give your opinion about something, it is always subjective. For that reason, the subjunctive is used after impersonal expressions of opinion. Here are some examples:

È bene che voi siate qui.	It's good that you are here.
È importante che tutti si preparino.	It's important that everyone get ready.

However, if the impersonal clause expresses truth or certainty, the indicative is used, as in these examples:

È vero che oggi abbiamo un esame.	It's true that we have a test today.
Sono sicuro che non pioverà.	I'm sure that it isn't going to rain.

Another common use of the present subjunctive is in the formation of indirect commands, when we are expressing our wish that someone else do something. Here is an example of that structure:

Raccomando che tutti imparino il congiuntivo.	I recommend that everyone learn the subjunctive.

The verb "raccomandare" (to recommend) in the first clause requires the use of the subjunctive in the second clause.

As you can see, the subjunctive is used when the subjects of the main clause and of the subordinate clause are different. But if you have the same subject you need to use the infinitive. Here are some examples:

Voglio che gli studenti imparino il congiuntivo (**different subjects:** *io/gli studenti*)	I want students to learn the subjunctive.

Gli studenti vogliono imparare il congiuntivo. (Same subject: *studenti*)	Students want to learn the subjunctive.
Mio padre spera che io impari l'italiano. (Different subject: *mio padre/io*)	My father hopes I learn Italian.
Spero di imparare l'italiano. (Same subject: *io*)	I hope to learn Italian.

Notice that "pensare" (to think), "credere" (to believe) and "sognare" (to dream) add "di" before the infinitive.

Other uses of the subjunctive

Certain expressions ALWAYS require the use of the subjunctive mood. We have grouped these conjunctions according to their theme.

Concession

sebbene	although
benché	although
malgrado	although
Sebbene piova spesso, fa molto caldo.	Although it rains a lot, it's very hot.

Condition

a meno che non	unless
a condizione che	provided that
a patto che	provided that
Sarò felice di aiutarla a patto che me lo dica prima.	Provided that she tells me beforehand, I will be happy to help her.

Intention

affinché	in order that
*perché**	in order that
in modo che	so that

*When "perché" means "because," it takes the indicative.

Massimo pulisce la sua stanza in modo che i suoi genitori non si arrabbino.	Massimo cleans his room so that his parents won't get mad.

Negation

*senza che**	without
Lui non fa niente senza che i suoi genitori lo sappiano.	He does nothing without his parents knowing.

Time

finché *prima che **	until before
Voglio andare via prima che sia troppo tardi.	I want to leave before it is too late.

**These expressions take the infinitive when the subjects of the main and dependent clauses are the same.*

The subjunctive in relative clauses

The subjunctive is used in relative clauses when in the main clause we have verbs like "desiderare" (to desire), "volere" (to want), "cercare" (to look for) and "avere bisogno di" (to need). Here are some examples:

Cerco un meccanico che mi possa riparare la macchina.	I am looking for a mechanic who can fix my car.
Abbiamo bisogno di una persona che sappia parlare l'italiano.	We need a person who can speak Italian.

If you are describing something that is definite, you don't need to use the subjunctive:

Ho un meccanico che mi può riparare la macchina.	I have a mechanic who can fix my car.

The subjunctive after superlatives

The subjunctive is also used after the superlative, which often expresses subjectivity:

È la donna più bella che io conosca.	She is the most beautiful woman I know.
Quelle sono le scarpe più care che abbia.	Those are the most expensive shoes I have.

It is also used after the following expressions, when they are used subjectively: "l'ultimo" (the last), "il primo" (the first) and "il solo" (the only):

È il solo che scriva poesia.	He is the only one who writes poetry.

The subjunctive after indefinite expressions

The subjunctive is used after certain indefinite expressions ending in "-unque" (-ever). Here are the most common:

chiunque	whoever
dovunque	wherever
qualunque	whatever
comunque	however
Dovunque tu vada in Italia, ti troverai bene.	Wherever you go in Italy, you'll be happy.

Other subjunctive tenses

There are only three other tenses of the subjunctive mood that are commonly used. These are the imperfect subjunctive, the past subjunctive and the past perfect subjunctive.

The past subjunctive (il congiuntivo passato)

To form the past of the subjunctive, you need to change the helping verbs "avere" and "essere" to the appropriate subjunctive present tense plus the past participle. The past subjunctive of "parlare" (to speak, to talk) looks like this:

abbia parlato	abbiamo parlato
abbia parlato	abbiate parlato
abbia parlato	abbiano parlato

The present subjunctive of "andare" (to go) looks like this:

sia andato/a	siamo andati/e
sia andato/a	siate andati/e
sia andato/a	siano andati/e

The imperfect subjunctive (il congiuntivo imperfetto)

To form the imperfect subjunctive, of regular verbs just drop "-re" from the infinitive and add the following endings:

-ssi	-ssimo
-ssi	-ste
-sse	-ssero

Here is the verb "parlare" (to speak, to talk) in the imperfect subjunctive:

parlassi	parlassimo
parlassi	parlaste
parlasse	parlassero

Here is the verb "leggere" (to read):

leggessi	leggessimo
leggessi	leggeste
leggesse	leggessero

All "-ire" verbs form the subjunctive in the same way. Notice that verbs with "-isc" lose it in all persons in the imperfect subjunctive.

Here is the verb "partire" (to leave):

partissi	partissimo
partissi	partiste
partisse	partissero

Few verbs are irregular in this tense. The most common are: "essere," "dire," "dare," "fare" and "stare." Here is the conjugation of "essere" (to be):

fossi	fossimo
fossi	foste
fosse	fossero

Notice that all forms have a double "s" except the "voi" form, which has "st."

The past perfect subjunctive (il congiuntivo trapassato)

The past perfect, or pluperfect, subjunctive is formed from the imperfect subjunctive of the helping verbs "avere" and "essere" and the past participle. The pluperfect subjunctive of "parlare" looks like this:

avessi parlato	avessimo parlato
avessi parlato	aveste parlato
avesse parlato	avessero parlato

The pluperfect subjunctive of "partire" looks like this:

fossi partito/a	fossimo partiti/e
fossi partito/a	foste partiti/e
fosse partito/a	fossero partiti/e

Sequence of tenses

The subjunctive tense you choose will depend on the tense of the verb in the main clause. If the main verb is in the present, future, present perfect or command form, you may choose either the present subjunctive or the past subjunctive, depending on whether or not the action of the dependent clause has happened. Here is a chart to help you remember which tense to choose:

Main clause	**Subjunctive tenses**
Present	present subjunctive (to express present or future action) past subjunctive (to express a completed past action) imperfect (action typical of imperfect uses: habit, description, etc.)

Examples:

Spero che tu arrivi in tempo. I hope that you will arrive on time.

(The dependent clause refers to an action that has not happened yet.)

Dubito che siano partiti ieri.	I doubt that they left yesterday.

(The dependent clauses refer to actions in the past.)

When expressing past actions, there is also a sequence of tenses that you must observe. If the main verb is in any past tense, or in the conditional, you may choose either the imperfect subjunctive or the past perfect subjunctive, depending on whether or not the action of the dependent clause has happened.

Main clause	**Subjunctive tenses**
Present perfect Past absolute	imperfect or conditional past (to express a future action)
Imperfect	imperfect (to express a simultaneous action)
Conditional	past perfect (to express a past action)

Examples:

Speravo che arrivassero in tempo.	I was hoping that they would arrive on time.

(Although both clauses are in the past, the action of the dependent clause has not yet occurred.)

Dubitavamo che fossero già arrivati.	We doubted that they had already arrived.

(The action of the dependent clause is prior to the action of the main clause.)

The Imperative Mood (formal)

An important use of the present subjunctive is to form commands, also known as the "imperative mood" in English. You are already familiar with the informal imperative (see p. 23). Here are the "Lei" and "Loro" forms (note that the "Loro" form is very rarely used) of "parlare" (to speak, to talk), "leggere" (to read) and "partire" (to leave):

(Lei)	parli	legga	parta
(Loro)	parlino	leggano	partano

Indicative command forms

To form the negative formal imperative, just put "non" in front of the "Lei" and "Loro" forms:

Non parta!	Don't leave!

Reflexive and object pronouns always precede the formal imperative:

Si vesta!	Dress yourself!
Mi dica!	Tell me!

Note that while the pronouns are attached to the verb in the informal imperative, because they always precede the "Lei" and "Loro" forms, they come before the verb in the formal imperative.

Special Cases

Although each of the 601 verbs in the reference section of conjugated verbs is shown in all tenses and forms, there are some verbs that are not generally used in all tenses and/or forms. These verbs include "piacere" (to like), "costare" (to cost) and "capitare" (to happen), which are normally used in the third person singular or plural, and verbs used to describe weather conditions like "piovere" (to rain), "nevicare" (to snow) and "grandinare" (to hail), which are generally used only in the third person singular.

Conclusion

Now that you understand how to conjugate a verb in Italian, how to form and use the different tenses, and when to use the subjunctive mood, you are ready to start using this knowledge to help you communicate in Italian. The rest of this book will give you a handy reference to hundreds of common verbs, as well as practice exercises to help you learn and remember how these verbs work in Italian. Don't be discouraged if it is challenging at first. Learning how to navigate through the Italian verb system will take time and effort, but it will be worth it when you can read, write and speak Italian, and understand what others say. Always remember to practice what you have learned, because *vale più la pratica della grammatica* (experience is more important than theory) in any language!

Emanuele Occhipinti
Drew University

to abandon — abbandonare

gerundio **abbandonando** participio passato **abbandonato**

SINGULAR	PLURAL	SINGULAR	PLURAL
indicativo presente		**passato prossimo**	
abbandon**o**	abbandon**iamo**	**ho** abbandonato	**abbiamo** abbandonato
abbandon**i**	abbandon**ate**	**hai** abbandonato	**avete** abbandonato
abbandon**a**	abbandon**ano**	**ha** abbandonato	**hanno** abbandonato
imperfetto		**trapassato prossimo**	
abbandona**vo**	abbandona**vamo**	**avevo** abbandonato	**avevamo** abbandonato
abbandona**vi**	abbandona**vate**	**avevi** abbandonato	**avevate** abbandonato
abbandona**va**	abbandona**vano**	**aveva** abbandonato	**avevano** abbandonato
passato remoto		**trapassato remoto**	
abbandon**ai**	abbandon**ammo**	**ebbi** abbandonato	**avemmo** abbandonato
abbandon**asti**	abbandon**aste**	**avesti** abbandonato	**aveste** abbandonato
abbandon**ò**	abbandon**arono**	**ebbe** abbandonato	**ebbero** abbandonato
futuro semplice		**futuro anteriore**	
abbandoner**ò**	abbandoner**emo**	**avrò** abbandonato	**avremo** abbandonato
abbandoner**ai**	abbandoner**ete**	**avrai** abbandonato	**avrete** abbandonato
abbandoner**à**	abbandoner**anno**	**avrà** abbandonato	**avranno** abbandonato
condizionale presente		**condizionale passato**	
abbandoner**ei**	abbandoner**emmo**	**avrei** abbandonato	**avremmo** abbandonato
abbandoner**esti**	abbandoner**este**	**avresti** abbandonato	**avreste** abbandonato
abbandoner**ebbe**	abbandoner**ebbero**	**avrebbe** abbandonato	**avrebbero** abbandonato
congiuntivo presente		**congiuntivo passato**	
abbandon**i**	abbandon**iamo**	**abbia** abbandonato	**abbiamo** abbandonato
abbandon**i**	abbandon**iate**	**abbia** abbandonato	**abbiate** abbandonato
abbandon**i**	abbandon**ino**	**abbia** abbandonato	**abbiano** abbandonato
congiuntivo imperfetto		**congiuntivo trapassato**	
abbandon**assi**	abbandon**assimo**	**avessi** abbandonato	**avessimo** abbandonato
abbandon**assi**	abbandon**aste**	**avessi** abbandonato	**aveste** abbandonato
abbandon**asse**	abbandon**assero**	**avesse** abbandonato	**avessero** abbandonato

imperativo

	abbandoniamo
abbandona; non abbandonare	abbandonate
abbandoni	abbandonino

abbassare — to lower, to dim, to reduce

gerundio **abbassando** — participio passato **abbassato**

A

SINGULAR	PLURAL	SINGULAR	PLURAL
indicativo presente		passato prossimo	
abbass**o**	abbass**iamo**	**ho** abbassato	**abbiamo** abbassato
abbass**i**	abbass**ate**	**hai** abbassato	**avete** abbassato
abbass**a**	abbass**ano**	**ha** abbassato	**hanno** abbassato
imperfetto		trapassato prossimo	
abbassa**vo**	abbassa**vamo**	**avevo** abbassato	**avevamo** abbassato
abbassa**vi**	abbassa**vate**	**avevi** abbassato	**avevate** abbassato
abbassa**va**	abbassa**vano**	**aveva** abbassato	**avevano** abbassato
passato remoto		trapassato remoto	
abbass**ai**	abbass**ammo**	**ebbi** abbassato	**avemmo** abbassato
abbass**asti**	abbass**aste**	**avesti** abbassato	**aveste** abbassato
abbass**ò**	abbass**arono**	**ebbe** abbassato	**ebbero** abbassato
futuro semplice		futuro anteriore	
abbasser**ò**	abbasser**emo**	**avrò** abbassato	**avremo** abbassato
abbasser**ai**	abbasser**ete**	**avrai** abbassato	**avrete** abbassato
abbasser**à**	abbasser**anno**	**avrà** abbassato	**avranno** abbassato
condizionale presente		condizionale passato	
abbasser**ei**	abbasser**emmo**	**avrei** abbassato	**avremmo** abbassato
abbasser**esti**	abbasser**este**	**avresti** abbassato	**avreste** abbassato
abbasser**ebbe**	abbasser**ebbero**	**avrebbe** abbassato	**avrebbero** abbassato
congiuntivo presente		congiuntivo passato	
abbass**i**	abbass**iamo**	**abbia** abbassato	**abbiamo** abbassato
abbass**i**	abbass**iate**	**abbia** abbassato	**abbiate** abbassato
abbass**i**	abbass**ino**	**abbia** abbassato	**abbiano** abbassato
congiuntivo imperfetto		congiuntivo trapassato	
abbass**assi**	abbass**assimo**	**avessi** abbassato	**avessimo** abbassato
abbass**assi**	abbass**aste**	**avessi** abbassato	**aveste** abbassato
abbass**asse**	abbass**assero**	**avesse** abbassato	**avessero** abbassato
imperativo			
	abbassiamo		
abbassa; non abbassare	abbassate		
abbassi	abbassino		

to subscribe abbonarsi

gerundio **abbonandosi** participio passato **abbonatosi**

SINGULAR	PLURAL	SINGULAR	PLURAL
indicativo presente		passato prossimo	
mi abbon**o**	**ci** abbon**iamo**	**mi sono** abbonato(a)	**ci siamo** abbonati(e)
ti abbon**i**	**vi** abbon**ate**	**ti sei** abbonato(a)	**vi siete** abbonati(e)
si abbon**a**	**si** abbon**ano**	**si è** abbonato(a)	**si sono** abbonati(e)
imperfetto		trapassato prossimo	
mi abbona**vo**	**ci** abbona**vamo**	**mi ero** abbonato(a)	**ci eravamo** abbonati(e)
ti abbona**vi**	**vi** abbona**vate**	**ti eri** abbonato(a)	**vi eravate** abbonati(e)
si abbona**va**	**si** abbona**vano**	**si era** abbonato(a)	**si erano** abbonati(e)
passato remoto		trapassato remoto	
mi abbon**ai**	**ci** abbon**ammo**	**mi fui** abbonato(a)	**ci fummo** abbonati(e)
ti abbon**asti**	**vi** abbon**aste**	**ti fosti** abbonato(a)	**vi foste** abbonati(e)
si abbon**ò**	**si** abbon**arono**	**si fu** abbonato(a)	**si furono** abbonati(e)
futuro semplice		futuro anteriore	
mi abboner**ò**	**ci** abboner**emo**	**mi sarò** abbonato(a)	**ci saremo** abbonati(e)
ti abboner**ai**	**vi** abboner**ete**	**ti sarai** abbonato(a)	**vi sarete** abbonati(e)
si abboner**à**	**si** abboner**anno**	**si sarà** abbonato(a)	**si saranno** abbonati(e)
condizionale presente		condizionale passato	
mi abboner**ei**	**ci** abboner**emmo**	**mi sarei** abbonato(a)	**ci saremmo** abbonati(e)
ti abboner**esti**	**vi** abboner**este**	**ti saresti** abbonato(a)	**vi sareste** abbonati(e)
si abboner**ebbe**	**si** abboner**ebbero**	**si sarebbe** abbonato(a)	**si sarebbero** abbonati(e)
congiuntivo presente		congiuntivo passato	
mi abbon**i**	**ci** abbon**iamo**	**mi sia** abbonato(a)	**ci siamo** abbonati(e)
ti abbon**i**	**vi** abbon**iate**	**ti sia** abbonato(a)	**vi siate** abbonati(e)
si abbon**i**	**si** abbon**ino**	**si sia** abbonato(a)	**si siano** abbonati(e)
congiuntivo imperfetto		congiuntivo trapassato	
mi abbon**assi**	**ci** abbon**assimo**	**mi fossi** abbonato(a)	**ci fossimo** abbonati(e)
ti abbon**assi**	**vi** abbon**aste**	**ti fossi** abbonato(a)	**vi foste** abbonati(e)
si abbon**asse**	**si** abbon**assero**	**si fosse** abbonato(a)	**si fossero** abbonati(e)

imperativo

	abboniamoci
abbonati; non abbonarti/ non ti abbonare	abbonatevi
si abboni	si abbonino

A

abbordare — to approach

gerundio **abbordando** participio passato **abbordato**

indicativo presente

SINGULAR	PLURAL
abbord**o**	abbord**iamo**
abbord**i**	abbord**ate**
abbord**a**	abbord**ano**

imperfetto

SINGULAR	PLURAL
abborda**vo**	abborda**vamo**
abborda**vi**	abborda**vate**
abborda**va**	abborda**vano**

passato remoto

SINGULAR	PLURAL
abbord**ai**	abbord**ammo**
abbord**asti**	abbord**aste**
abbord**ò**	abbord**arono**

futuro semplice

SINGULAR	PLURAL
abborder**ò**	abborder**emo**
abborder**ai**	abborder**ete**
abborder**à**	abborder**anno**

condizionale presente

SINGULAR	PLURAL
abborder**ei**	abborder**emmo**
abborder**esti**	abborder**este**
abborder**ebbe**	abborder**ebbero**

congiuntivo presente

SINGULAR	PLURAL
abbord**i**	abbord**iamo**
abbord**i**	abbord**iate**
abbord**i**	abbord**ino**

congiuntivo imperfetto

SINGULAR	PLURAL
abbord**assi**	abbord**assimo**
abbord**assi**	abbord**aste**
abbord**asse**	abbord**assero**

imperativo

SINGULAR	PLURAL
	abbordiamo
abborda; non abbordare	abbordate
abbordi	abbordino

passato prossimo

SINGULAR	PLURAL
ho abbordato	**abbiamo** abbordato
hai abbordato	**avete** abbordato
ha abbordato	**hanno** abbordato

trapassato prossimo

SINGULAR	PLURAL
avevo abbordato	**avevamo** abbordato
avevi abbordato	**avevate** abbordato
aveva abbordato	**avevano** abbordato

trapassato remoto

SINGULAR	PLURAL
ebbi abbordato	**avemmo** abbordato
avesti abbordato	**aveste** abbordato
ebbe abbordato	**ebbero** abbordato

futuro anteriore

SINGULAR	PLURAL
avrò abbordato	**avremo** abbordato
avrai abbordato	**avrete** abbordato
avrà abbordato	**avranno** abbordato

condizionale passato

SINGULAR	PLURAL
avrei abbordato	**avremmo** abbordato
avresti abbordato	**avreste** abbordato
avrebbe abbordato	**avrebbero** abbordato

congiuntivo passato

SINGULAR	PLURAL
abbia abbordato	**abbiamo** abbordato
abbia abbordato	**abbiate** abbordato
abbia abbordato	**abbiano** abbordato

congiuntivo trapassato

SINGULAR	PLURAL
avessi abbordato	**avessimo** abbordato
avessi abbordato	**aveste** abbordato
avesse abbordato	**avessero** abbordato

to embrace, to hug **abbracciare**

gerundio **abbracciando** participio passato **abbracciato**

SINGULAR	PLURAL	SINGULAR	PLURAL
indicativo presente		passato prossimo	
abbracci**o**	abbracci**amo**	**ho** abbracciato	**abbiamo** abbracciato
abbracci	abbracci**ate**	**hai** abbracciato	**avete** abbracciato
abbracci**a**	abbracci**ano**	**ha** abbracciato	**hanno** abbracciato
imperfetto		trapassato prossimo	
abbraccia**vo**	abbraccia**vamo**	**avevo** abbracciato	**avevamo** abbracciato
abbraccia**vi**	abbraccia**vate**	**avevi** abbracciato	**avevate** abbracciato
abbraccia**va**	abbraccia**vano**	**aveva** abbracciato	**avevano** abbracciato
passato remoto		trapassato remoto	
abbracci**ai**	abbracci**ammo**	**ebbi** abbracciato	**avemmo** abbracciato
abbracci**asti**	abbracci**aste**	**avesti** abbracciato	**aveste** abbracciato
abbracci**ò**	abbracci**arono**	**ebbe** abbracciato	**ebbero** abbracciato
futuro semplice		futuro anteriore	
abbraccer**ò**	abbraccer**emo**	**avrò** abbracciato	**avremo** abbracciato
abbraccer**ai**	abbraccer**ete**	**avrai** abbracciato	**avrete** abbracciato
abbraccer**à**	abbraccer**anno**	**avrà** abbracciato	**avranno** abbracciato
condizionale presente		condizionale passato	
abbraccer**ei**	abbraccer**emmo**	**avrei** abbracciato	**avremmo** abbracciato
abbraccer**esti**	abbraccer**este**	**avresti** abbracciato	**avreste** abbracciato
abbraccer**ebbe**	abbraccer**ebbero**	**avrebbe** abbracciato	**avrebbero** abbracciato
congiuntivo presente		congiuntivo passato	
abbracc**i**	abbracc**iamo**	**abbia** abbracciato	**abbiamo** abbracciato
abbracc**i**	abbracc**iate**	**abbia** abbracciato	**abbiate** abbracciato
abbracc**i**	abbracc**ino**	**abbia** abbracciato	**abbiano** abbracciato
congiuntivo imperfetto		congiuntivo trapassato	
abbracci**assi**	abbracci**assimo**	**avessi** abbracciato	**avessimo** abbracciato
abbracci**assi**	abbracci**aste**	**avessi** abbracciato	**aveste** abbracciato
abbracci**asse**	abbracci**assero**	**avesse** abbracciato	**avessero** abbracciato
imperativo			
	abbracciamo		
abbraccia; non abbracciare	abbracciate		
abbracci	abbraccino		

abbronzarsi — to tan

gerundio **abbronzandosi** participio passato **abbronzatosi**

SINGULAR	PLURAL
indicativo presente	
mi abbronz**o**	**ci** abbronz**iamo**
ti abbronz**i**	**vi** abbronz**ate**
si abbronz**a**	**si** abbronz**ano**
imperfetto	
mi abbronza**vo**	**ci** abbronza**vamo**
ti abbronza**vi**	**vi** abbronza**vate**
si abbronza**va**	**si** abbronza**vano**
passato remoto	
mi abbronz**ai**	**ci** abbronz**ammo**
ti abbronz**asti**	**vi** abbronz**aste**
si abbronz**ò**	**si** abbronz**arono**
futuro semplice	
mi abbronzer**ò**	**ci** abbronzer**emo**
ti abbronzer**ai**	**vi** abbronzer**ete**
si abbronzer**à**	**si** abbronzer**anno**
condizionale presente	
mi abbronzer**ei**	**ci** abbronzer**emmo**
ti abbronzer**esti**	**vi** abbronzer**este**
si abbronzer**ebbe**	**si** abbronzer**ebbero**
congiuntivo presente	
mi abbronz**i**	**ci** abbronz**iamo**
ti abbronz**i**	**vi** abbronz**iate**
si abbronz**i**	**si** abbronz**ino**
congiuntivo imperfetto	
mi abbronz**assi**	**ci** abbronz**assimo**
ti abbronz**assi**	**vi** abbronz**aste**
si abbronz**asse**	**si** abbronz**assero**
imperativo	
	abbronziamoci
abbronzati; non abbronzarti/ non ti abbronzare	abbronzatevi
si abbronzi	si abbronzino

SINGULAR	PLURAL
passato prossimo	
mi sono abbronzato(a)	**ci siamo** abbronzati(e)
ti sei abbronzato(a)	**vi siete** abbronzati(e)
si è abbronzato(a)	**si sono** abbronzati(e)
trapassato prossimo	
mi ero abbronzato(a)	**ci eravamo** abbronzati(e)
ti eri abbronzato(a)	**vi eravate** abbronzati(e)
si era abbronzato(a)	**si erano** abbronzati(e)
trapassato remoto	
mi fui abbronzato(a)	**ci fummo** abbronzati(e)
ti fosti abbronzato(a)	**vi foste** abbronzati(e)
si fu abbronzato(a)	**si furono** abbronzati(e)
futuro anteriore	
mi sarò abbronzato(a)	**ci saremo** abbronzati(e)
ti sarai abbronzato(a)	**vi sarete** abbronzati(e)
si sarà abbronzato(a)	**si saranno** abbronzati(e)
condizionale passato	
mi sarei abbronzato(a)	**ci saremmo** abbronzati(e)
ti saresti abbronzato(a)	**vi sareste** abbronzati(e)
si sarebbe abbronzato(a)	**si sarebbero** abbronzati(e)
congiuntivo passato	
mi sia abbronzato(a)	**ci siamo** abbronzati(e)
ti sia abbronzato(a)	**vi siate** abbronzati(e)
si sia abbronzato(a)	**si siano** abbronzati(e)
congiuntivo trapassato	
mi fossi abbronzato(a)	**ci fossimo** abbronzati(e)
ti fossi abbronzato(a)	**vi foste** abbronzati(e)
si fosse abbronzato(a)	**si fossero** abbronzati(e)

gerundio **abitando** participio passato **abitato**

SINGULAR	PLURAL	SINGULAR	PLURAL
indicativo presente		*passato prossimo*	
abit**o**	abit**iamo**	**ho** abitato	**abbiamo** abitato
abit**i**	abit**ate**	**hai** abitato	**avete** abitato
abit**a**	abit**ano**	**ha** abitato	**hanno** abitato
imperfetto		*trapassato prossimo*	
abita**vo**	abita**vamo**	**avevo** abitato	**avevamo** abitato
abita**vi**	abita**vate**	**avevi** abitato	**avevate** abitato
abita**va**	abita**vano**	**aveva** abitato	**avevano** abitato
passato remoto		*trapassato remoto*	
abit**ai**	abit**ammo**	**ebbi** abitato	**avemmo** abitato
abit**asti**	abit**aste**	**avesti** abitato	**aveste** abitato
abit**ò**	abit**arono**	**ebbe** abitato	**ebbero** abitato
futuro semplice		*futuro anteriore*	
abiter**ò**	abiter**emo**	**avrò** abitato	**avremo** abitato
abiter**ai**	abiter**ete**	**avrai** abitato	**avrete** abitato
abiter**à**	abiter**anno**	**avrà** abitato	**avranno** abitato
condizionale presente		*condizionale passato*	
abiter**ei**	abiter**emmo**	**avrei** abitato	**avremmo** abitato
abiter**esti**	abiter**este**	**avresti** abitato	**avreste** abitato
abiter**ebbe**	abiter**ebbero**	**avrebbe** abitato	**avrebbero** abitato
congiuntivo presente		*congiuntivo passato*	
abit**i**	abit**iamo**	**abbia** abitato	**abbiamo** abitato
abit**i**	abit**iate**	**abbia** abitato	**abbiate** abitato
abit**i**	abit**ino**	**abbia** abitato	**abbiano** abitato
congiuntivo imperfetto		*congiuntivo trapassato*	
abit**assi**	abit**assimo**	**avessi** abitato	**avessimo** abitato
abit**assi**	abit**aste**	**avessi** abitato	**aveste** abitato
abit**asse**	abit**assero**	**avesse** abitato	**avessero** abitato

imperativo

	abitiamo
abita; non abitare	abitate
abiti	abitino

MEMORY TIP

The animals live in a **habitat**.

abituarsi — to get used to

gerundio **abituandosi** participio passato **abituatosi**

A

SINGULAR	PLURAL
indicativo presente	
mi abitu**o**	**ci** abitu**iamo**
ti abitu**i**	**vi** abitu**ate**
si abitu**a**	**si** abitu**ano**
imperfetto	
mi abitua**vo**	**ci** abitua**vamo**
ti abitua**vi**	**vi** abitua**vate**
si abitua**va**	**si** abitua**vano**
passato remoto	
mi abitu**ai**	**ci** abitu**ammo**
ti abitu**asti**	**vi** abitu**aste**
si abitu**ò**	**si** abitu**arono**
futuro semplice	
mi abituer**ò**	**ci** abituer**emo**
ti abituer**ai**	**vi** abituer**ete**
si abituer**à**	**si** abituer**anno**
condizionale presente	
mi abituer**ei**	**ci** abituer**emmo**
ti abituer**esti**	**vi** abituer**este**
si abituer**ebbe**	**si** abituer**ebbero**
congiuntivo presente	
mi abitu**i**	**ci** abitu**iamo**
ti abitu**i**	**vi** abitu**iate**
si abitu**i**	**si** abitu**ino**
congiuntivo imperfetto	
mi abitu**assi**	**ci** abitu**assimo**
ti abitu**assi**	**vi** abitu**aste**
si abitu**asse**	**si** abitu**assero**
imperativo	
	abituiamoci
abituati; non abituarti; non ti abituare	abituatevi
si abitui	si abituino

SINGULAR	PLURAL
passato prossimo	
mi sono abituato(a)	**ci siamo** abituati(e)
ti sei abituato(a)	**vi siete** abituati(e)
si è abituato(a)	**si sono** abituati(e)
trapassato prossimo	
mi ero abituato(a)	**ci eravamo** abituati(e)
ti eri abituato(a)	**vi eravate** abituati(e)
si era abituato(a)	**si erano** abituati(e)
trapassato remoto	
mi fui abituato(a)	**ci fummo** abituati(e)
ti fosti abituato(a)	**vi foste** abituati(e)
si fu abituato(a)	**si furono** abituati(e)
futuro anteriore	
mi sarò abituato(a)	**ci saremo** abituati(e)
ti sarai abituato(a)	**vi sarete** abituati(e)
si sarà abituato(a)	**si saranno** abituati(e)
condizionale passato	
mi sarei abituato(a)	**ci saremmo** abituati(e)
ti saresti abituato(a)	**vi sareste** abituati(e)
si sarebbe abituato(a)	**si sarebbero** abituati(e)
congiuntivo passato	
mi sia abituato(a)	**ci siamo** abituati(e)
ti sia abituato(a)	**vi siate** abituati(e)
si sia abituato(a)	**si siano** abituati(e)
congiuntivo trapassato	
mi fossi abituato(a)	**ci fossimo** abituati(e)
ti fossi abituato(a)	**vi foste** abituati(e)
si fosse abituato(a)	**si fossero** abituati(e)

We were so used to it that it became habit.

gerundio **abusando** participio passato **abusato**

SINGULAR	PLURAL
indicativo presente	
abus**o**	abus**iamo**
abus**i**	abus**ate**
abus**a**	abus**ano**
imperfetto	
abusa**vo**	abusa**vamo**
abusa**vi**	abusa**vate**
abusa**va**	abusa**vano**
passato remoto	
abus**ai**	abus**ammo**
abus**asti**	abus**aste**
abus**ò**	abus**arono**
futuro semplice	
abuser**ò**	abuser**emo**
abuser**ai**	abuser**ete**
abuser**à**	abuser**anno**
condizionale presente	
abuser**ei**	abuser**emmo**
abuser**esti**	abuser**este**
abuser**ebbe**	abuser**ebbero**
congiuntivo presente	
abus**i**	abus**iamo**
abus**i**	abus**iate**
abus**i**	abus**ino**
congiuntivo imperfetto	
abus**assi**	abus**assimo**
abus**assi**	abus**aste**
abus**asse**	abus**assero**
imperativo	
	abusiamo
abusa; non abusare	abusate
abusi	abusino

SINGULAR	PLURAL
passato prossimo	
ho abusato	**abbiamo** abusato
hai abusato	**avete** abusato
ha abusato	**hanno** abusato
trapassato prossimo	
avevo abusato	**avevamo** abusato
avevi abusato	**avevate** abusato
aveva abusato	**avevano** abusato
trapassato remoto	
ebbi abusato	**avemmo** abusato
avesti abusato	**aveste** abusato
ebbe abusato	**ebbero** abusato
futuro anteriore	
avrò abusato	**avremo** abusato
avrai abusato	**avrete** abusato
avrà abusato	**avranno** abusato
condizionale passato	
avrei abusato	**avremmo** abusato
avresti abusato	**avreste** abusato
avrebbe abusato	**avrebbero** abusato
congiuntivo passato	
abbia abusato	**abbiamo** abusato
abbia abusato	**abbiate** abusato
abbia abusato	**abbiano** abusato
congiuntivo trapassato	
avessi abusato	**avessimo** abusato
avessi abusato	**aveste** abusato
avesse abusato	**avessero** abusato

accadere — to happen, to occur

gerundio **accadendo** participio passato **accaduto**

A

SINGULAR	PLURAL	SINGULAR	PLURAL
indicativo presente		passato prossimo	
accad**e**	accad**ono**	**è** accaduto(a)	**sono** accaduti(e)
imperfetto		trapassato prossimo	
accade**va**	accade**vano**	**era** accaduto(a)	**erano** accaduti(e)
passato remoto		trapassato remoto	
accadd**e**	accadd**ero**	**fu** accaduto(a)	**furono** accaduti(e)
futuro semplice		futuro anteriore	
accadr**à**	accadr**anno**	**sarà** accaduto(a)	**saranno** accaduti(e)
condizionale presente		condizionale passato	
accadr**ebbe**	accadr**ebbero**	**sarebbe** accaduto(a)	**sarebbero** accaduti(e)
congiuntivo presente		congiuntivo passato	
accad**a**	accad**ano**	**sia** accaduto(a)	**siano** accaduti(e)
congiuntivo imperfetto		congiuntivo trapassato	
accad**esse**	accad**essero**	**fosse** accaduto(a)	**fossero** accaduti(e)

to caress, to pet **accarezzare**

gerundio **accarezzando** participio passato **accarezzato**

SINGULAR	PLURAL	SINGULAR	PLURAL
indicativo presente		passato prossimo	
accarezz**o**	acarezz**iamo**	**ho** accarezzato	**abbiamo** accarezzato
accarezz**i**	accarezz**ate**	**hai** accarezzato	**avete** accarezzato
accarezz**a**	accarezz**ano**	**ha** accarezzato	**hanno** accarezzato
imperfetto		trapassato prossimo	
accarezza**vo**	accarezza**vamo**	**avevo** accarezzato	**avevamo** accarezzato
accarezza**vi**	accarezza**vate**	**avevi** accarezzato	**avevate** accarezzato
accarezza**va**	accarezza**vano**	**aveva** accarezzato	**avevano** accarezzato
passato remoto		trapassato remoto	
accarezz**ai**	accarezz**ammo**	**ebbi** accarezzato	**avemmo** accarezzato
accarezz**asti**	accarezz**aste**	**avesti** accarezzato	**aveste** accarezzato
accarezz**ò**	accarezz**arono**	**ebbe** accarezzato	**ebbero** accarezzato
futuro semplice		futuro anteriore	
accarezzer**ò**	accarezzer**emo**	**avrò** accarezzato	**avremo** accarezzato
accarezzer**ai**	accarezzer**ete**	**avrai** accarezzato	**avrete** accarezzato
accarezzer**à**	accarezzer**anno**	**avrà** accarezzato	**avranno** accarezzato
condizionale presente		condizionale passato	
accarezzer**ei**	accarezzer**emmo**	**avrei** accarezzato	**avremmo** accarezzato
accarezzer**esti**	accarezzer**este**	**avresti** accarezzato	**avreste** accarezzato
accarezzer**ebbe**	accarezzer**ebbero**	**avrebbe** accarezzato	**avrebbero** accarezzato
congiuntivo presente		congiuntivo passato	
accarezz**i**	accarezz**iamo**	**abbia** accarezzato	**abbiamo** accarezzato
accarezz**i**	accarezz**iate**	**abbia** accarezzato	**abbiate** accarezzato
accarezz**i**	accarezz**ino**	**abbia** accarezzato	**abbiano** accarezzato
congiuntivo imperfetto		congiuntivo trapassato	
accarezz**assi**	accarezz**assimo**	**avessi** accarezzato	**avessimo** accarezzato
accarezz**assi**	accarezz**aste**	**avessi** accarezzato	**aveste** accarezzato
accarezz**asse**	accarezz**assero**	**avesse** accarezzato	**avessero** accarezzato
imperativo			
	accarezziamo		
accarezza; non accarezzare	accarezzate		
accarezzi	accarezzino		

accendere — to light, to turn on, to switch on

gerundio **accendendo** participio passato **acceso**

SINGULAR	PLURAL	SINGULAR	PLURAL
indicativo presente		passato prossimo	
accend**o**	accend**iamo**	**ho** acceso	**abbiamo a**cceso
accend**i**	accend**ete**	**hai** acceso	**avete** acceso
accend**e**	accend**ono**	**ha** acceso	**hanno** acceso
imperfetto		trapassato prossimo	
accende**vo**	accende**vamo**	**avevo** acceso	**avevamo** acceso
accende**vi**	accende**vate**	**avevi** acceso	**avevate** acceso
accende**va**	accende**vano**	**aveva** acceso	**avevano** acceso
passato remoto		trapassato remoto	
acces**i**	accend**emmo**	**ebbi** acceso	**avemmo** acceso
accend**esti**	accend**este**	**avesti** acceso	**aveste** acceso
acces**e**	acces**ero**	**ebbe** acceso	**ebbero** acceso
futuro semplice		futuro anteriore	
accender**ò**	accender**emo**	**avrò** acceso	**avremo** acceso
accender**ai**	accender**ete**	**avrai** acceso	**avrete** acceso
accender**à**	accender**anno**	**avrà** acceso	**avranno** acceso
condizionale presente		condizionale passato	
accender**ei**	accender**emmo**	**avrei** acceso	**avremmo** acceso
accender**esti**	accender**este**	**avresti** acceso	**avreste** acceso
accender**ebbe**	accender**ebbero**	**avrebbe** acceso	**avrebbero** acceso
congiuntivo presente		congiuntivo passato	
accend**a**	accend**iamo**	**abbia** acceso	**abbiamo** acceso
accend**a**	accend**iate**	**abbia** acceso	**abbiate** acceso
accend**a**	accend**ano**	**abbia** acceso	**abbiano** acceso
congiuntivo imperfetto		congiuntivo trapassato	
accend**essi**	accend**essimo**	**avessi** acceso	**avessimo** acceso
accend**essi**	accend**este**	**avessi** acceso	**aveste** acceso
accend**esse**	accend**essero**	**avesse** acceso	**avessero** acceso
imperativo			
	accendiamo		
accendi; non accendere	accendete		
accenda	accendano		

to accept — accettare

gerundio **accettando** — participio passato **accettato**

SINGULAR	PLURAL	SINGULAR	PLURAL
indicativo presente		passato prossimo	
accett**o**	accett**iamo**	**ho** accettato	**abbiamo** accettato
accett**i**	accett**ate**	**hai** accettato	**avete** accettato
accett**a**	accett**ano**	**ha** accettato	**hanno** accettato
imperfetto		trapassato prossimo	
accetta**vo**	accetta**vamo**	**avevo** accettato	**avevamo** accettato
accetta**vi**	accetta**vate**	**avevi** accettato	**avevate** accettato
accetta**va**	accetta**vano**	**aveva** accettato	**avevano** accettato
passato remoto		trapassato remoto	
accett**ai**	accett**ammo**	**ebbi** accettato	**avemmo** accettato
accett**asti**	accett**aste**	**avesti** accettato	**aveste** accettato
accett**ò**	accett**arono**	**ebbe** accettato	**ebbero** accettato
futuro semplice		futuro anteriore	
accetter**ò**	accetter**emo**	**avrò** accettato	**avremo** accettato
accetter**ai**	accetter**ete**	**avrai** accettato	**avrete** accettato
accetter**à**	accetter**anno**	**avrà** accettato	**avranno** accettato
condizionale presente		condizionale passato	
accetter**ei**	accetter**emmo**	**avrei** accettato	**avremmo** accettato
accetter**esti**	accetter**este**	**avresti** accettato	**avreste** accettato
accetter**ebbe**	accetter**ebbero**	**avrebbe** accettato	**avrebbero** accettato
congiuntivo presente		congiuntivo passato	
accett**i**	accett**iamo**	**abbia** accettato	**abbiamo** accettato
accett**i**	accett**iate**	**abbia** accettato	**abbiate** accettato
accett**i**	accett**ino**	**abbia** accettato	**abbiano** accettato
congiuntivo imperfetto		congiuntivo trapassato	
accett**assi**	accett**assimo**	**avessi** accettato	**avessimo** accettato
accett**assi**	accett**aste**	**avessi** accettato	**aveste** accettato
accett**asse**	accett**assero**	**avesse** accettato	**avessero** accettato

imperativo

	accettiamo
accetta; non accettare	accettate
accetti	accettino

accogliere to welcome, to greet, to receive

gerundio **accogliendo** participio passato **accolto**

A

SINGULAR	PLURAL	SINGULAR	PLURAL
indicativo presente		passato prossimo	
accolgo	accogl**iamo**	**ho** accolto	**abbiamo** accolto
accogl**i**	accogl**iete**	**hai** accolto	**avete** accolto
accogl**ie**	**accolgono**	**ha** accolto	**hanno** accolto
imperfetto		trapassato prossimo	
accoglie**vo**	accoglie**vamo**	**avevo** accolto	**avevamo** accolto
accoglie**vi**	accoglie**vate**	**avevi** accolto	**avevate** accolto
accoglie**va**	accoglie**vano**	**aveva** accolto	**avevano** accolto
passato remoto		trapassato remoto	
accolsi	accogl**iemmo**	**ebbi** accolto	**avemmo** accolto
accogl**iesti**	accogl**ieste**	**avesti** accolto	**aveste** accolto
accolse	**accolsero**	**ebbe** accolto	**ebbero** accolto
futuro semplice		futuro anteriore	
accoglier**ò**	accoglier**emo**	**avrò** accolto	**avremo** accolto
accoglier**ai**	accoglier**ete**	**avrai** accolto	**avrete** accolto
accoglier**à**	accoglier**anno**	**avrà** accolto	**avranno** accolto
condizionale presente		condizionale passato	
accoglier**ei**	accoglier**emmo**	**avrei** accolto	**avremmo** accolto
accoglier**esti**	accoglier**este**	**avresti** accolto	**avreste** accolto
accoglier**ebbe**	accoglier**ebbero**	**avrebbe** accolto	**avrebbero** accolto
congiuntivo presente		congiuntivo passato	
accolg**a**	accogl**iamo**	**abbia** accolto	**abbiamo** accolto
accolg**a**	accogl**iate**	**abbia** accolto	**abbiate** accolto
accolg**a**	accolg**ano**	**abbia** accolto	**abbiano** accolto
congiuntivo imperfetto		congiuntivo trapassato	
accogl**iessi**	accogl**iessimo**	**avessi** accolto	**avessimo** accolto
accogl**iessi**	accogl**ieste**	**avessi** accolto	**aveste** accolto
accogl**iesse**	accogl**iessero**	**avesse** accolto	**avessero** accolto
imperativo			
	accogliamo		
accogli; non accogliere	accogliete		
accolga	accolgano		

to accompany **accompagnare**

gerundio **accompagnando** participio passato **accompagnato**

indicativo presente

SINGULAR	PLURAL
accompagn**o**	accompagn**iamo**
accompagn**i**	accompagn**ate**
accompagn**a**	accompagn**ano**

imperfetto

SINGULAR	PLURAL
accompagna**vo**	accompagna**vamo**
accompagna**vi**	accompagna**vate**
accompagna**va**	accompagna**vano**

passato remoto

SINGULAR	PLURAL
accompagn**ai**	accompagn**ammo**
accompagn**asti**	accompagn**aste**
accompagn**ò**	accompagn**arono**

futuro semplice

SINGULAR	PLURAL
accompagner**ò**	accompagner**emo**
accompagner**ai**	accompagner**ete**
accompagner**à**	accompagner**anno**

condizionale presente

SINGULAR	PLURAL
abbasser**ei**	abbasser**emmo**
abbasser**esti**	abbasser**este**
abbasser**ebbe**	abbasser**ebbero**

congiuntivo presente

SINGULAR	PLURAL
accompagn**i**	accompagn**iamo**
accompagn**i**	accompagn**iate**
accompagn**i**	accompagn**ino**

congiuntivo imperfetto

SINGULAR	PLURAL
accompagn**assi**	accompagn**assimo**
accompagn**assi**	accompagn**aste**
accompagn**asse**	accompagn**assero**

imperativo

SINGULAR	PLURAL
	accompagniamo
accompagna; non accompagnare	accompagnate
accompagni	accompagnino

passato prossimo

SINGULAR	PLURAL
ho accompagnato	**abbiamo** accompagnato
hai accompagnato	**avete** accompagnato
ha accompagnato	**hanno** accompagnato

trapassato prossimo

SINGULAR	PLURAL
avevo accompagnato	**avevamo** accompagnato
avevi accompagnato	**avevate** accompagnato
aveva accompagnato	**avevano** accompagnato

trapassato remoto

SINGULAR	PLURAL
ebbi accompagnato	**avemmo** accompagnato
avesti accompagnato	**aveste** accompagnato
ebbe accompagnato	**ebbero** accompagnato

futuro anteriore

SINGULAR	PLURAL
avrò accompagnato	**avremo** accompagnato
avrai accompagnato	**avrete** accompagnato
avrà accompagnato	**avranno** accompagnato

condizionale passato

SINGULAR	PLURAL
avrei accompagnato	**avremmo** accompagnato
avresti accompagnato	**avreste** accompagnato
avrebbe accompagnato	**avrebbero** accompagnato

congiuntivo passato

SINGULAR	PLURAL
abbia accompagnato	**abbiamo** accompagnato
abbia accompagnato	**abbiate** accompagnato
abbia accompagnato	**abbiano** accompagnato

congiuntivo trapassato

SINGULAR	PLURAL
avessi accompagnato	**avessimo** accompagnato
avessi accompagnato	**aveste** accompagnato
avesse accompagnato	**avessero** accompagnato

MEMORY TIP

I would like to accompany you to the reception.

accorgersi — to realize, to notice

gerundio **accorgendosi** participio passato **accortosi**

A

SINGULAR	PLURAL
indicativo presente	
mi accorg**o**	**ci** accorg**iamo**
ti accorg**i**	**vi** accorg**ete**
si accorg**e**	**si** accorg**ono**
imperfetto	
mi accorge**vo**	**ci** accorge**vamo**
ti accorge**vi**	**vi** accorge**vate**
si accorge**va**	**si** accorge**vano**
passato remoto	
mi accors**i**	**ci** accorg**emmo**
ti accorg**esti**	**vi** accorg**este**
si accors**e**	**si** accors**ero**
futuro semplice	
mi accorger**ò**	**ci** accorger**emo**
ti accorger**ai**	**vi** accorger**ete**
si accorger**à**	**si** accorger**anno**
condizionale presente	
mi accorger**ei**	**ci** accorger**emmo**
ti accorger**esti**	**vi** accorger**este**
si accorger**ebbe**	**si** accorger**ebbero**
congiuntivo presente	
mi accorg**a**	**ci** accorg**iamo**
ti accorg**a**	**vi** accorg**iate**
si accorg**a**	**si** accorg**ano**
congiuntivo imperfetto	
mi accorg**essi**	**ci** accorg**essimo**
ti accorg**essi**	**vi** accorg**este**
si accorg**esse**	**si** accorg**essero**
imperativo	
	accorgiamoci
accorgiti; non accorgerti/ non ti accorgere	accorgetevi
si accorga	si accorgano

SINGULAR	PLURAL
passato prossimo	
mi sono accorto(a)	**ci siamo** accorti(e)
ti sei accorto(a)	**vi siete** accorti(e)
si è accorto(a)	**si sono** accorti(e)
trapassato prossimo	
mi ero accorto(a)	**ci eravamo** accorti(e)
ti eri accorto(a)	**vi eravate** accorti(e)
si era accorto(a)	**si erano** accorti(e)
trapassato remoto	
mi fui accorto(a)	**ci fummo** accorti(e)
ti fosti accorto(a)	**vi foste** accorti(e)
si fu accorto(a)	**si furono** accorti(e)
futuro anteriore	
mi sarò accorto(a)	**ci saremo** accorti(e)
ti sarai accorto(a)	**vi sarete** accorti(e)
si sarà accorto(a)	**si saranno** accorti(e)
condizionale passato	
mi sarei accorto(a)	**ci saremmo** accorti(e)
ti saresti accorto(a)	**vi sareste** accorti(e)
si sarebbe accorto(a)	**si sarebbero** accorti(e)
congiuntivo passato	
mi sia accorto(a)	**ci siamo** accorti(e)
ti sia accorto(a)	**vi siate** accorti(e)
si sia accorto(a)	**si siano** accorti(e)
congiuntivo trapassato	
mi fossi accorto(a)	**ci fossimo** accorti(e)
ti fossi accorto(a)	**vi foste** accorti(e)
si fosse accorto(a)	**si fossero** accorti(e)

gerundio **addormentandosi** participio passato **addormentatosi**

SINGULAR	PLURAL
indicativo presente	
mi addorment**o**	**ci** addorment**iamo**
ti addorment**i**	**vi** addorment**ate**
si addorment**a**	**si** addorment**ano**
imperfetto	
mi addormenta**vo**	**ci** addormenta**vamo**
ti addormenta**vi**	**vi** addormenta**vate**
si addormenta**va**	**si** addormenta**vano**
passato remoto	
mi addorment**ai**	**ci** addorment**ammo**
ti addorment**asti**	**vi** addorment**aste**
si addorment**ò**	**si** addorment**arono**
futuro semplice	
mi addormenter**ò**	**ci** addormenter**emo**
ti addormenter**ai**	**vi** addormenter**ete**
si addormenter**à**	**si** addormenter**anno**
condizionale presente	
mi addormenter**ei**	**ci** addormenter**emmo**
ti addormenter**esti**	**vi** addormenter**este**
si addormenter**ebbe**	**si** addormenter**ebbero**
congiuntivo presente	
mi addorment**i**	**ci** addorment**iamo**
ti addorment**i**	**vi** addorment**iate**
si addorment**i**	**si** addorment**ino**
congiuntivo imperfetto	
mi addorment**assi**	**ci** addorment**assimo**
ti addorment**assi**	**vi** addorment**aste**
si addorment**asse**	**si** addorment**assero**
imperativo	
	addormentiamoci
addormentati; non addormentarti/ non ti addormentare	addormentatevi
si addormenti	si addormentino

SINGULAR	PLURAL
passato prossimo	
mi sono addormentato(a)	**ci siamo** addormentati(e)
ti sei addormentato(a)	**vi siete** addormentati(e)
si è addormentato(a)	**si sono** addormentati(e)
trapassato prossimo	
mi ero addormentato(a)	**ci eravamo** addormentati(e)
ti eri addormentato(a)	**vi eravate** addormentati(e)
si era addormentato(a)	**si erano** addormentati(e)
trapassato remoto	
mi fui addormentato(a)	**ci fummo** addormentati(e)
ti fosti addormentato(a)	**vi foste** addormentati(e)
si fu addormentato(a)	**si furono** addormentati(e)
futuro anteriore	
mi sarò addormentato(a)	**ci saremo** addormentati(e)
ti sarai addormentato(a)	**vi sarete** addormentati(e)
si sarà addormentato(a)	**si saranno** addormentati(e)
condizionale passato	
mi sarei addormentato(a)	**ci saremmo** addormentati(e)
ti saresti addormentato(a)	**vi sareste** addormentati(e)
si sarebbe addormentato(a)	**si sarebbero** addormentati(e)
congiuntivo passato	
mi sia addormentato(a)	**ci siamo** addormentati(e)
ti sia addormentato(a)	**vi siate** addormentati(e)
si sia addormentato(a)	**si siano** addormentati(e)
congiuntivo trapassato	
mi fossi addormentato(a)	**ci fossimo** addormentati(e)
ti fossi addormentato(a)	**vi foste** addormentati(e)
si fosse addormentato(a)	**si fossero** addormentati(e)

aderire — to adhere, to comply

gerundio **aderendo** participio passato **aderito**

SINGULAR	PLURAL
indicativo presente	
aderisc**o**	ader**iamo**
aderisc**i**	ader**ite**
aderisc**e**	aderisc**ono**
imperfetto	
aderi**vo**	aderi**vamo**
aderi**vi**	aderi**vate**
aderi**va**	aderi**vano**
passato remoto	
ader**ii**	ader**immo**
ader**isti**	ader**iste**
ader**ì**	ader**irono**
futuro semplice	
aderir**ò**	aderir**emo**
aderir**ai**	aderir**ete**
aderir**à**	aderir**anno**
condizionale presente	
aderir**ei**	aderir**emmo**
aderir**esti**	aderir**este**
aderir**ebbe**	aderir**ebbero**
congiuntivo presente	
ader**isca**	ader**iamo**
ader**isca**	ader**iate**
ader**isca**	ader**iscano**
congiuntivo imperfetto	
ader**issi**	ader**issimo**
ader**issi**	ader**iste**
ader**isse**	ader**issero**
imperativo	
	aderiamo
aderisci; non aderire	aderite
aderisca	aderiscano

SINGULAR	PLURAL
passato prossimo	
ho aderito	**abbiamo** aderito
hai aderito	**avete** aderito
ha aderito	**hanno** aderito
trapassato prossimo	
avevo aderito	**avevamo** aderito
avevi aderito	**avevate** aderito
aveva aderito	**avevano** aderito
trapassato remoto	
ebbi aderito	**avemmo** aderito
avesti aderito	**aveste** aderito
ebbe aderito	**ebbero** aderito
futuro anteriore	
avrò aderito	**avremo** aderito
avrai aderito	**avrete** aderito
avrà aderito	**avranno** aderito
condizionale passato	
avrei aderito	**avremmo** aderito
avresti aderito	**avreste** aderito
avrebbe aderito	**avrebbero** aderito
congiuntivo passato	
abbia aderito	**abbiamo** aderito
abbia aderito	**abbiate** aderito
abbia aderito	**abbiano** aderito
congiuntivo trapassato	
avessi aderito	**avessimo** aderito
avessi aderito	**aveste** aderito
avesse aderito	**avessero** aderito

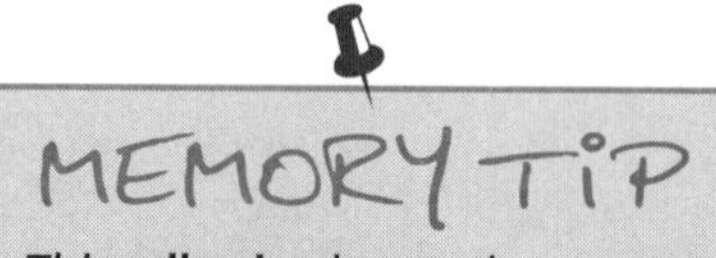

This adhesive keeps the poster stuck to the wall.

to adore **adorare**

gerundio **adorando** participio passato **adorato**

SINGULAR	PLURAL
indicativo presente	
ador**o**	ador**iamo**
ador**i**	ador**ate**
ador**a**	ador**ano**
imperfetto	
adora**vo**	adora**vamo**
adora**vi**	adora**vate**
adora**va**	adora**vano**
passato remoto	
ador**ai**	ador**ammo**
ador**asti**	ador**aste**
ador**ò**	ador**arono**
futuro semplice	
adorer**ò**	adorer**emo**
adorer**ai**	adorer**ete**
adorer**à**	adorer**anno**
condizionale presente	
adorer**ei**	adorer**emmo**
adorer**esti**	adorer**este**
adorer**ebbe**	adorer**ebbero**
congiuntivo presente	
ador**i**	ador**iamo**
ador**i**	ador**iate**
ador**i**	ador**ino**
congiuntivo imperfetto	
ador**assi**	ador**assimo**
ador**assi**	ador**aste**
ador**asse**	ador**assero**
imperativo	
	adoriamo
adora; non adorare	adorate
adori	adorino

SINGULAR	PLURAL
passato prossimo	
ho adorato	**abbiamo** adorato
hai adorato	**avete** adorato
ha adorato	**hanno** adorato
trapassato prossimo	
avevo adorato	**avevamo** adorato
avevi adorato	**avevate** adorato
aveva adorato	**avevano** adorato
trapassato remoto	
ebbi adorato	**avemmo** adorato
avesti adorato	**aveste** adorato
ebbe adorato	**ebbero** adorato
futuro anteriore	
avrò adorato	**avremo** adorato
avrai adorato	**avrete** adorato
avrà adorato	**avranno** adorato
condizionale passato	
avrei adorato	**avremmo** adorato
avresti adorato	**avreste** adorato
avrebbe adorato	**avrebbero** adorato
congiuntivo passato	
abbia adorato	**abbiamo** adorato
abbia adorato	**abbiate** adorato
abbia adorato	**abbiano** adorato
congiuntivo trapassato	
avessi adorato	**avessimo** adorato
avessi adorato	**aveste** adorato
avesse adorato	**avessero** adorato

affermare — to affirm, to declare

gerundio **affermando** — participio passato **affermato**

A

SINGULAR	PLURAL
indicativo presente	
afferm**o**	afferm**iamo**
afferm**i**	afferm**ate**
afferm**a**	afferm**ano**
imperfetto	
afferma**vo**	afferma**vamo**
afferma**vi**	afferma**vate**
afferma**va**	afferma**vano**
passato remoto	
afferm**ai**	afferm**ammo**
afferm**asti**	afferm**aste**
afferm**ò**	afferm**arono**
futuro semplice	
affermer**ò**	affermer**emo**
affermer**ai**	affermer**ete**
affermer**à**	affermer**anno**
condizionale presente	
affermer**ei**	affermer**emmo**
affermer**esti**	affermer**este**
affermer**ebbe**	affermer**ebbero**
congiuntivo presente	
afferm**i**	afferm**iamo**
afferm**i**	afferm**iate**
afferm**i**	afferm**ino**
congiuntivo imperfetto	
afferm**assi**	afferm**assimo**
afferm**assi**	afferm**aste**
afferm**asse**	afferm**assero**
imperativo	
	affermiamo
afferma; non affermare	affermate
affermi	affermino

SINGULAR	PLURAL
passato prossimo	
ho affermato	**abbiamo** affermato
hai affermato	**avete** affermato
ha affermato	**hanno** affermato
trapassato prossimo	
avevo affermato	**avevamo** affermato
avevi affermato	**avevate** affermato
aveva affermato	**avevano** affermato
trapassato remoto	
ebbi affermato	**avemmo** affermato
avesti affermato	**aveste** affermato
ebbe affermato	**ebbero** affermato
futuro anteriore	
avrò affermato	**avremo** affermato
avrai affermato	**avrete** affermato
avrà affermato	**avranno** affermato
condizionale passato	
avrei affermato	**avremmo** affermato
avresti affermato	**avreste** affermato
avrebbe affermato	**avrebbero** affermato
congiuntivo passato	
abbia affermato	**abbiamo** affermato
abbia affermato	**abbiate** affermato
abbia affermato	**abbiano** affermato
congiuntivo trapassato	
avessi affermato	**avessimo** affermato
avessi affermato	**aveste** affermato
avesse affermato	**avessero** affermato

The defendant **affirmed** his innocence.

to grab, to grasp — afferrare

gerundio **afferrando** participio passato **afferrato**

indicativo presente

SINGULAR	PLURAL
afferr**o**	afferr**iamo**
afferr**i**	afferr**ate**
afferr**a**	afferr**ano**

imperfetto

SINGULAR	PLURAL
afferra**vo**	afferra**vamo**
afferra**vi**	afferra**vate**
afferra**va**	afferra**vano**

passato remoto

SINGULAR	PLURAL
afferr**ai**	afferr**ammo**
afferr**asti**	afferr**aste**
afferr**ò**	afferr**arono**

futuro semplice

SINGULAR	PLURAL
afferrer**ò**	afferrer**emo**
afferrer**ai**	afferrer**ete**
afferrer**à**	afferrer**anno**

condizionale presente

SINGULAR	PLURAL
afferrer**ei**	afferrer**emmo**
afferrer**esti**	afferrer**este**
afferrer**ebbe**	afferrer**ebbero**

congiuntivo presente

SINGULAR	PLURAL
afferr**i**	afferr**iamo**
afferr**i**	afferr**iate**
afferr**i**	afferr**ino**

congiuntivo imperfetto

SINGULAR	PLURAL
afferr**assi**	afferr**assimo**
afferr**assi**	afferr**aste**
afferr**asse**	afferr**assero**

imperativo

SINGULAR	PLURAL
	afferriamo
afferra; non afferrare	afferrate
afferri	afferrino

passato prossimo

SINGULAR	PLURAL
ho afferrato	**abbiamo** afferrato
hai afferrato	**avete** afferrato
ha afferrato	**hanno** afferrato

trapassato prossimo

SINGULAR	PLURAL
avevo afferrato	**avevamo** afferrato
avevi afferrato	**avevate** afferrato
aveva afferrato	**avevano** afferrato

trapassato remoto

SINGULAR	PLURAL
ebbi afferrato	**avemmo** afferrato
avesti afferrato	**aveste** afferrato
ebbe afferrato	**ebbero** afferrato

futuro anteriore

SINGULAR	PLURAL
avrò afferrato	**avremo** afferrato
avrai afferrato	**avrete** afferrato
avrà afferrato	**avranno** afferrato

condizionale passato

SINGULAR	PLURAL
avrei afferrato	**avremmo** afferrato
avresti afferrato	**avreste** afferrato
avrebbe afferrato	**avrebbero** afferrato

congiuntivo passato

SINGULAR	PLURAL
abbia afferrato	**abbiamo** afferrato
abbia afferrato	**abbiate** afferrato
abbia afferrato	**abbiano** afferrato

congiuntivo trapassato

SINGULAR	PLURAL
avessi afferrato	**avessimo** afferrato
avessi afferrato	**aveste** afferrato
avesse afferrato	**avessero** afferrato

Ferrari grabbed first place again.

affliggere — to afflict, to plague, to distress

gerundio **affliggendo** — participio passato **afflitto**

SINGULAR	PLURAL	SINGULAR	PLURAL
indicativo presente		*passato prossimo*	
affligg**o**	affligg**iamo**	**ho** afflitto	**abbiamo** afflitto
affligg**i**	affligg**ete**	**hai** afflitto	**avete** afflitto
affligg**e**	affligg**ono**	**ha** afflitto	**hanno** afflitto
imperfetto		*trapassato prossimo*	
affligge**vo**	affligge**vamo**	**avevo** afflitto	**avevamo** afflitto
affligge**vi**	affligge**vate**	**avevi** afflitto	**avevate** afflitto
affligge**va**	affligge**vano**	**aveva** afflitto	**avevano** afflitto
passato remoto		*trapassato remoto*	
afflissi**i**	affligg**emmo**	**ebbi** afflitto	**avemmo** afflitto
affligg**esti**	affligg**este**	**avesti** afflitto	**aveste** afflitto
affliss**e**	affliss**ero**	**ebbe** afflitto	**ebbero** afflitto
futuro semplice		*futuro anteriore*	
affligger**ò**	affligger**emo**	**avrò** afflitto	**avremo** afflitto
affligger**ai**	affligger**ete**	**avrai** afflitto	**avrete** afflitto
affligger**à**	affligger**anno**	**avrà** afflitto	**avranno** afflitto
condizionale presente		*condizionale passato*	
affligger**ei**	affligger**emmo**	**avrei** afflitto	**avremmo** afflitto
affligger**esti**	affligger**este**	**avresti** afflitto	**avreste** afflitto
affligger**ebbe**	affligger**ebbero**	**avrebbe** afflitto	**avrebbero** afflitto
congiuntivo presente		*congiuntivo passato*	
affligg**a**	affligg**iamo**	**abbia** afflitto	**abbiamo** afflitto
affligg**a**	affligg**iate**	**abbia** afflitto	**abbiate** afflitto
affligg**a**	affligg**ano**	**abbia** afflitto	**abbiano** afflitto
congiuntivo imperfetto		*congiuntivo trapassato*	
affligg**essi**	affligg**essimo**	**avessi** afflitto	**avessimo** afflitto
affligg**essi**	affligg**este**	**avessi** afflitto	**aveste** afflitto
affligg**esse**	affligg**essero**	**avesse** afflitto	**avessero** afflitto

imperativo

	affliggiamo
affliggi; non affliggere	affliggete
affligga	affliggano

to hurry, to hasten — affrettarsi

gerundio **affrettandosi** participio passato **affrettatosi**

A

SINGULAR	PLURAL	SINGULAR	PLURAL
indicativo presente		passato prossimo	
mi affrett**o**	**ci** affrett**iamo**	**mi sono** affrettato(a)	**ci siamo** affrettati(e)
ti affrett**i**	**vi** affrett**ate**	**ti sei** affrettato(a)	**vi siete** affrettati(e)
si affrett**a**	**si** affrett**ano**	**si è** affrettato(a)	**si sono** affrettati(e)
imperfetto		trapassato prossimo	
mi affretta**vo**	**ci** affretta**vamo**	**mi ero** affrettato(a)	**ci eravamo** affrettati(e)
ti affretta**vi**	**vi** affretta**vate**	**ti eri** affrettato(a)	**vi eravate** affrettati(e)
si affretta**va**	**si** affretta**vano**	**si era** affrettato(a)	**si erano** affrettati(e)
passato remoto		trapassato remoto	
mi affrett**ai**	**ci** affrett**ammo**	**mi fui** affrettato(a)	**ci fummo** affrettati(e)
ti affrett**asti**	**vi** affrett**aste**	**ti fosti** affrettato(a)	**vi foste** affrettati(e)
si affrett**ò**	**si** affrett**arono**	**si fu** affrettato(a)	**si furono** affrettati(e)
futuro semplice		futuro anteriore	
mi affretter**ò**	**ci** affretter**emo**	**mi sarò** affrettato(a)	**ci saremo** affrettati(e)
ti affretter**ai**	**vi** affretter**ete**	**ti sarai** affrettato(a)	**vi sarete** affrettati(e)
si affretter**à**	**si** affretter**anno**	**si sarà** affrettato(a)	**si saranno** affrettati(e)
condizionale presente		condizionale passato	
mi affretter**ei**	**ci** affretter**emmo**	**mi sarei** affrettato(a)	**ci saremmo** affrettati(e)
ti affretter**esti**	**vi** affretter**este**	**ti saresti** affrettato(a)	**vi sareste** affrettati(e)
si affretter**ebbe**	**si** affretter**ebbero**	**si sarebbe** affrettato(a)	**si sarebbero** affrettati(e)
congiuntivo presente		congiuntivo passato	
mi affrett**i**	**ci** affrett**iamo**	**mi sia** affrettato(a)	**ci siamo** affrettati(e)
ti affrett**i**	**vi** affrett**iate**	**ti sia** affrettato(a)	**vi siate** affrettati(e)
si affrett**i**	**si** affrett**ino**	**si sia** affrettato(a)	**si siano** affrettati(e)
congiuntivo imperfetto		congiuntivo trapassato	
mi affrett**assi**	**ci** affrett**assimo**	**mi fossi** affrettato(a)	**ci fossimo** affrettati(e)
ti affrett**assi**	**vi** affrett**aste**	**ti fossi** affrettato(a)	**vi foste** affrettati(e)
si affrett**asse**	**si** affrett**assero**	**si fosse** affrettato(a)	**si fossero** affrettati(e)

imperativo

	affrettiamoci
affrettati; non affrettarti/ non ti affrettare	affrettatevi
si affretti	si affrettino

MEMORY TIP

They started to **fret** because they were in a rush.

aggiungere — to add, to append

gerundio **aggiungendo** — participio passato **aggiunto**

A

SINGULAR	PLURAL	SINGULAR	PLURAL
indicativo presente		*passato prossimo*	
aggiung**o**	aggiung**iamo**	**ho** aggiunto	**abbiamo** aggiunto
aggiung**i**	aggiung**ete**	**hai** aggiunto	**avete** aggiunto
aggiung**e**	aggiung**ono**	**ha** aggiunto	**hanno** aggiunto
imperfetto		*trapassato prossimo*	
aggiunge**vo**	aggiunge**vamo**	**avevo** aggiunto	**avevamo** aggiunto
aggiunge**vi**	aggiunge**vate**	**avevi** aggiunto	**avevate** aggiunto
aggiunge**va**	aggiunge**vano**	**aveva** aggiunto	**avevano** aggiunto
passato remoto		*trapassato remoto*	
aggiun**si**	aggiung**emmo**	**ebbi** aggiunto	**avemmo** aggiunto
aggiung**esti**	aggiung**este**	**avesti** aggiunto	**aveste** aggiunto
aggiun**se**	aggiun**sero**	**ebbe** aggiunto	**ebbero** aggiunto
futuro semplice		*futuro anteriore*	
aggiunger**ò**	aggiunger**emo**	**avrò** aggiunto	**avremo** aggiunto
aggiunger**ai**	aggiunger**ete**	**avrai** aggiunto	**avrete** aggiunto
aggiunger**à**	aggiunger**anno**	**avrà** aggiunto	**avranno** aggiunto
condizionale presente		*condizionale passato*	
aggiunger**ei**	aggiunger**emmo**	**avrei** aggiunto	**avremmo** aggiunto
aggiunger**esti**	aggiunger**este**	**avresti** aggiunto	**avreste** aggiunto
aggiunger**ebbe**	aggiunger**ebbero**	**avrebbe** aggiunto	**avrebbero** aggiunto
congiuntivo presente		*congiuntivo passato*	
aggiung**a**	aggiung**iamo**	**abbia** aggiunto	**abbiamo** aggiunto
aggiung**a**	aggiung**iate**	**abbia** aggiunto	**abbiate** aggiunto
aggiung**a**	aggiung**ano**	**abbia** aggiunto	**abbiano** aggiunto
congiuntivo imperfetto		*congiuntivo trapassato*	
aggiung**essi**	aggiung**essimo**	**avessi** aggiunto	**avessimo** aggiunto
aggiung**essi**	aggiung**este**	**avessi** aggiunto	**aveste** aggiunto
aggiung**esse**	aggiung**essero**	**avesse** aggiunto	**avessero** aggiunto
imperativo			
	aggiungiamo		
aggiungi; non aggiungere	aggiungete		
aggiunga	aggiungano		

gerundio **aiutando** participio passato **aiutato**

SINGULAR	PLURAL
indicativo presente	
aiut**o**	aiut**iamo**
aiut**i**	aiut**ate**
aiut**a**	aiut**ano**
imperfetto	
aiuta**vo**	aiuta**vamo**
aiuta**vi**	aiuta**vate**
aiuta**va**	aiuta**vano**
passato remoto	
aiut**ai**	aiut**ammo**
aiut**asti**	aiut**aste**
aiut**ò**	aiut**arono**
futuro semplice	
aiuter**ò**	aiuter**emo**
aiuter**ai**	aiuter**ete**
aiuter**à**	aiuter**anno**
condizionale presente	
aiuter**ei**	aiuter**emmo**
aiuter**esti**	aiuter**este**
aiuter**ebbe**	aiuter**ebbero**
congiuntivo presente	
aiut**i**	aiut**iamo**
aiut**i**	aiut**iate**
aiut**i**	aiut**ino**
congiuntivo imperfetto	
aiut**assi**	aiut**assimo**
aiut**assi**	aiut**aste**
aiut**asse**	aiut**assero**
imperativo	
	aiutiamo
aiuta; non aiutare	aiutate
aiuti	aiutino

SINGULAR	PLURAL
passato prossimo	
ho aiutato	**abbiamo** aiutato
hai aiutato	**avete** aiutato
ha aiutato	**hanno** aiutato
trapassato prossimo	
avevo aiutato	**avevamo** aiutato
avevi aiutato	**avevate** aiutato
aveva aiutato	**avevano** aiutato
trapassato remoto	
ebbi aiutato	**avemmo** aiutato
avesti aiutato	**aveste** aiutato
ebbe aiutato	**ebbero** aiutato
futuro anteriore	
avrò aiutato	**avremo** aiutato
avrai aiutato	**avrete** aiutato
avrà aiutato	**avranno** aiutato
condizionale passato	
avrei aiutato	**avremmo** aiutato
avresti aiutato	**avreste** aiutato
avrebbe aiutato	**avrebbero** aiutato
congiuntivo passato	
abbia aiutato	**abbiamo** aiutato
abbia aiutato	**abbiate** aiutato
abbia aiutato	**abbiano** aiutato
congiuntivo trapassato	
avessi aiutato	**avessimo** aiutato
avessi aiutato	**aveste** aiutato
avesse aiutato	**avessero** aiutato

allarmare — to alarm

gerundio **allarmando** participio passato **allarmato**

SINGULAR	PLURAL
indicativo presente	
allarm**o**	allarm**iamo**
allarm**i**	allarm**ate**
allarm**a**	allarm**ano**
imperfetto	
allarma**vo**	allarma**vamo**
allarma**vi**	allarma**vate**
allarma**va**	allarma**vano**
passato remoto	
allarm**ai**	allarm**ammo**
allarm**asti**	allarm**aste**
allarm**ò**	allarm**arono**
futuro semplice	
allarmer**ò**	allarmer**emo**
allarmer**ai**	allarmer**ete**
allarmer**à**	allarmer**anno**
condizionale presente	
allarmer**ei**	allarmer**emmo**
allarmer**esti**	allarmer**este**
allarmer**ebbe**	allarmer**ebbero**
congiuntivo presente	
allarm**i**	allarm**iamo**
allarm**i**	allarm**iate**
allarm**i**	allarm**ino**
congiuntivo imperfetto	
allarm**assi**	allarm**assimo**
allarm**assi**	allarm**aste**
allarm**asse**	allarm**assero**
imperativo	
	allarmiamo
allarma; non allarmare	allarmate
allarmi	allarmino

SINGULAR	PLURAL
passato prossimo	
ho allarmato	**abbiamo** allarmato
hai allarmato	**avete** allarmato
ha allarmato	**hanno** allarmato
trapassato prossimo	
avevo allarmato	**avevamo** allarmato
avevi allarmato	**avevate** allarmato
aveva allarmato	**avevano** allarmato
trapassato remoto	
ebbi allarmato	**avemmo** allarmato
avesti allarmato	**aveste** allarmato
ebbe allarmato	**ebbero** allarmato
futuro anteriore	
avrò allarmato	**avremo** allarmato
avrai allarmato	**avrete** allarmato
avrà allarmato	**avranno** allarmato
condizionale passato	
avrei allarmato	**avremmo** allarmato
avresti allarmato	**avreste** allarmato
avrebbe allarmato	**avrebbero** allarmato
congiuntivo passato	
abbia allarmato	**abbiamo** allarmato
abbia allarmato	**abbiate** allarmato
abbia allarmato	**abbiano** allarmato
congiuntivo trapassato	
avessi allarmato	**avessimo** allarmato
avessi allarmato	**aveste** allarmato
avesse allarmato	**avessero** allarmato

to allude, to refer — alluderere

gerundio **alludendo** participio passato **alluso**

SINGULAR	PLURAL
indicativo presente	
allud**o**	allud**iamo**
allud**i**	allud**ete**
allud**e**	allud**ono**
imperfetto	
allude**vo**	allude**vamo**
allude**vi**	allude**vate**
allude**va**	allude**vano**
passato remoto	
allusi	allud**emmo**
allud**esti**	allud**este**
alluse	**allusero**
futuro semplice	
alluder**ò**	alluder**emo**
alluder**ai**	alluder**ete**
alluder**à**	alluder**anno**
condizionale presente	
alluder**ei**	alluder**emmo**
alluder**esti**	alluder**este**
alluder**ebbe**	alluder**ebbero**
congiuntivo presente	
allud**a**	allud**iamo**
allud**a**	allud**iate**
allud**a**	allud**ano**
congiuntivo imperfetto	
allud**essi**	allud**essimo**
allud**essi**	allud**este**
allud**esse**	allud**essero**
imperativo	
	alludiamo
alludi; non alludere	alludete
alluda	alludano

SINGULAR	PLURAL
passato prossimo	
ho alluso	**abbiamo** alluso
hai alluso	**avete** alluso
ha alluso	**hanno** alluso
trapassato prossimo	
avevo alluso	**avevamo** alluso
avevi alluso	**avevate** alluso
aveva alluso	**avevano** alluso
trapassato remoto	
ebbi alluso	**avemmo** alluso
avesti alluso	**aveste** alluso
ebbe alluso	**ebbero** alluso
futuro anteriore	
avrò alluso	**avremo** alluso
avrai alluso	**avrete** alluso
avrà alluso	**avranno** alluso
condizionale passato	
avrei alluso	**avremmo** alluso
avresti alluso	**avreste** alluso
avrebbe alluso	**avrebbero** alluso
congiuntivo passato	
abbia alluso	**abbiamo** alluso
abbia alluso	**abbiate** alluso
abbia alluso	**abbiano** alluso
congiuntivo trapassato	
avessi alluso	**avessimo** alluso
avessi alluso	**aveste** alluso
avesse alluso	**avessero** alluso

alzare — to lift up, to raise

gerundio **alzando** participio passato **alzato**

SINGULAR	PLURAL	SINGULAR	PLURAL
indicativo presente		passato prossimo	
alz**o**	alz**iamo**	**ho** alzato	**abbiamo** alzato
alz**i**	alz**ate**	**hai** alzato	**avete** alzato
alz**a**	alz**ano**	**ha** alzato	**hanno** alzato
imperfetto		trapassato prossimo	
alza**vo**	alza**vamo**	**avevo** alzato	**avevamo** alzato
alza**vi**	alza**vate**	**avevi** alzato	**avevate** alzato
alza**va**	alza**vano**	**aveva** alzato	**avevano** alzato
passato remoto		trapassato remoto	
alz**ai**	alz**ammo**	**ebbi** alzato	**avemmo** alzato
alz**asti**	alz**aste**	**avesti** alzato	**aveste** alzato
alz**ò**	alz**arono**	**ebbe** alzato	**ebbero** alzato
futuro semplice		futuro anteriore	
alzer**ò**	alzer**emo**	**avrò** alzato	**avremo** alzato
alzer**ai**	alzer**ete**	**avrai** alzato	**avrete** alzato
alzer**à**	alzer**anno**	**avrà** alzato	**avranno** alzato
condizionale presente		condizionale passato	
alzer**ei**	alzer**emmo**	**avrei** alzato	**avremmo** alzato
alzer**esti**	alzer**este**	**avresti** alzato	**avreste** alzato
alzer**ebbe**	alzer**ebbero**	**avrebbe** alzato	**avrebbero** alzato
congiuntivo presente		congiuntivo passato	
alz**i**	alz**iamo**	**abbia** alzato	**abbiamo** alzato
alz**i**	alz**iate**	**abbia** alzato	**abbiate** alzato
alz**i**	alz**ino**	**abbia** alzato	**abbiano** alzato
congiuntivo imperfetto		congiuntivo trapassato	
alz**assi**	alz**assimo**	**avessi** alzato	**avessimo** alzato
alz**assi**	alz**aste**	**avessi** alzato	**aveste** alzato
alz**asse**	alz**assero**	**avesse** alzato	**avessero** alzato
imperativo			
	alziamo		
alza; non alzare	alzate		
alzi	alzino		

gerundio **alzandosi** participio passato **alzatosi**

SINGULAR	PLURAL	SINGULAR	PLURAL
indicativo presente		passato prossimo	
mi alz**o**	**ci** alz**iamo**	**mi sono** alzato(a)	**ci siamo** alzati(e)
ti alz**i**	**vi** alz**ate**	**ti sei** alzato(a)	**vi siete** alzati(e)
si alz**a**	**si** alz**ano**	**si è** alzato(a)	**si sono** alzati(e)
imperfetto		trapassato prossimo	
mi alza**vo**	**ci** alza**vamo**	**mi ero** alzato(a)	**ci eravamo** alzati(e)
ti alza**vi**	**vi** alza**vate**	**ti eri** alzato(a)	**vi eravate** alzati(e)
si alza**va**	**si** alza**vano**	**si era** alzato(a)	**si erano** alzati(e)
passato remoto		trapassato remoto	
mi alz**ai**	**ci** alz**ammo**	**mi fui** alzato(a)	**ci fummo** alzati(e)
ti alz**asti**	**vi** alz**aste**	**ti fosti** alzato(a)	**vi foste** alzati(e)
si alz**ò**	**si** alz**arono**	**si fu** alzato(a)	**si furono** alzati(e)
futuro semplice		futuro anteriore	
mi alzer**ò**	**ci** alzer**emo**	**mi sarò** alzato(a)	**ci saremo** alzati(e)
ti alzer**ai**	**vi** alzer**ete**	**ti sarai** alzato(a)	**vi sarete** alzati(e)
si alzer**à**	**si** alzer**anno**	**si sarà** alzato(a)	**si saranno** alzati(e)
condizionale presente		condizionale passato	
mi alzer**ei**	**ci** alzer**emmo**	**mi sarei** alzato(a)	**ci saremmo** alzati(e)
ti alzer**esti**	**vi** alzer**este**	**ti saresti** alzato(a)	**vi sareste** alzati(e)
si alzer**ebbe**	**si** alzer**ebbero**	**si sarebbe** alzato(a)	**si sarebbero** alzati(e)
congiuntivo presente		congiuntivo passato	
mi alz**i**	**ci** alz**iamo**	**mi sia** alzato(a)	**ci siamo** alzati(e)
ti alz**i**	**vi** alz**iate**	**ti sia** alzato(a)	**vi siate** alzati(e)
si alz**i**	**si** alz**ino**	**si sia** alzato(a)	**si siano** alzati(e)
congiuntivo imperfetto		congiuntivo trapassato	
mi alz**assi**	**ci** alz**assimo**	**mi fossi** alzato(a)	**ci fossimo** alzati(e)
ti alz**assi**	**vi** alz**aste**	**ti fossi** alzato(a)	**vi foste** alzati(e)
si alz**asse**	**si** alz**assero**	**si fosse** alzato(a)	**si fossero** alzati(e)

imperativo

	alziamoci
alzati; non alzarti/ non ti alzare	alzatevi
si alzi	si alzino

amare — to love

gerundio **amando** participio passato **amato**

A

SINGULAR	PLURAL	SINGULAR	PLURAL
indicativo presente		passato prossimo	
am**o**	am**iamo**	**ho** amato	**abbiamo** amato
am**i**	am**ate**	**hai** amato	**avete** amato
am**a**	am**ano**	**ha** amato	**hanno** amato
imperfetto		trapassato prossimo	
ama**vo**	ama**vamo**	**avevo** amato	**avevamo** amato
ama**vi**	ama**vate**	**avevi** amato	**avevate** amato
ama**va**	ama**vano**	**aveva** amato	**avevano** amato
passato remoto		trapassato remoto	
am**ai**	am**ammo**	**ebbi** amato	**avemmo** amato
am**asti**	am**aste**	**avesti** amato	**aveste** amato
am**ò**	am**arono**	**ebbe** amato	**ebbero** amato
futuro semplice		futuro anteriore	
amer**ò**	amer**emo**	**avrò** amato	**avremo** amato
amer**ai**	amer**ete**	**avrai** amato	**avrete** amato
amer**à**	amer**anno**	**avrà** amato	**avranno** amato
condizionale presente		condizionale passato	
amer**ei**	amer**emmo**	**avrei** amato	**avremmo** amato
amer**esti**	amer**este**	**avresti** amato	**avreste** amato
amer**ebbe**	amer**ebbero**	**avrebbe** amato	**avrebbero** amato
congiuntivo presente		congiuntivo passato	
am**i**	am**iamo**	**abbia** amato	**abbiamo** amato
am**i**	am**iate**	**abbia** amato	**abbiate** amato
am**i**	am**ino**	**abbia** amato	**abbiano** amato
congiuntivo imperfetto		congiuntivo trapassato	
am**assi**	am**assimo**	**avessi** amato	**avessimo** amato
am**assi**	am**aste**	**avessi** amato	**aveste** amato
am**asse**	am**assero**	**avesse** amato	**avessero** amato

imperativo

	amiamo
ama; non amare	amate
ami	amino

gerundio **ammettendo** participio passato **ammesso**

A

SINGULAR	PLURAL
indicativo presente	
ammett**o**	ammett**iamo**
ammett**i**	ammett**ete**
ammett**e**	ammett**ono**
imperfetto	
ammette**vo**	ammette**vamo**
ammette**vi**	ammette**vate**
ammette**va**	ammette**vano**
passato remoto	
ammisi	ammett**emmo**
ammett**esti**	ammett**este**
ammise	**ammisero**
futuro semplice	
ammetter**ò**	ammetter**emo**
ammetter**ai**	ammetter**ete**
ammetter**à**	ammetter**anno**
condizionale presente	
ammetter**ei**	ammetter**emmo**
ammetter**esti**	ammetter**este**
ammetter**ebbe**	ammetter**ebbero**
congiuntivo presente	
ammett**a**	ammett**iamo**
ammett**a**	ammett**iate**
ammett**a**	ammett**ano**
congiuntivo imperfetto	
ammett**essi**	ammett**essimo**
ammett**essi**	ammett**este**
ammett**esse**	ammett**essero**
imperativo	
	ammettiamo
ammetti; non ammettere	ammettete
ammetta	ammettano

SINGULAR	PLURAL
passato prossimo	
ho ammesso	**abbiamo** ammesso
hai ammesso	**avete** ammesso
ha ammesso	**hanno** ammesso
trapassato prossimo	
avevo ammesso	**avevamo** ammesso
avevi ammesso	**avevate** ammesso
aveva ammesso	**avevano** ammesso
trapassato remoto	
ebbi ammesso	**avemmo** ammesso
avesti ammesso	**aveste** ammesso
ebbe ammesso	**ebbero** ammesso
futuro anteriore	
avrò ammesso	**avremo** ammesso
avrai ammesso	**avrete** ammesso
avrà ammesso	**avranno** ammesso
condizionale passato	
avrei ammesso	**avremmo** ammesso
avresti ammesso	**avreste** ammesso
avrebbe ammesso	**avrebbero** ammesso
congiuntivo passato	
abbia ammesso	**abbiamo** ammesso
abbia ammesso	**abbiate** ammesso
abbia ammesso	**abbiano** ammesso
congiuntivo trapassato	
avessi ammesso	**avessimo** ammesso
avessi ammesso	**aveste** ammesso
avesse ammesso	**avessero** ammesso

MEMORY TIP

The suspect will not **admit** to any wrongdoing.

ammirare — to admire

gerundio **ammirando** participio passato **ammirato**

SINGULAR	PLURAL	SINGULAR	PLURAL
indicativo presente		*passato prossimo*	
ammir**o**	ammir**iamo**	**ho** ammirato	**abbiamo** ammirato
ammir**i**	ammir**ate**	**hai** ammirato	**avete** ammirato
ammir**a**	ammir**ano**	**ha** ammirato	**hanno** ammirato
imperfetto		*trapassato prossimo*	
ammira**vo**	ammira**vamo**	**avevo** ammirato	**avevamo** ammirato
ammira**vi**	ammira**vate**	**avevi** ammirato	**avevate** ammirato
ammira**va**	ammira**vano**	**aveva** ammirato	**avevano** ammirato
passato remoto		*trapassato remoto*	
ammir**ai**	ammir**ammo**	**ebbi** ammirato	**avemmo** ammirato
ammir**asti**	ammir**aste**	**avesti** ammirato	**aveste** ammirato
ammir**ò**	ammir**arono**	**ebbe** ammirato	**ebbero** ammirato
futuro semplice		*futuro anteriore*	
ammirer**ò**	ammirer**emo**	**avrò** ammirato	**avremo** ammirato
ammirer**ai**	ammirer**ete**	**avrai** ammirato	**avrete** ammirato
ammirer**à**	ammirer**anno**	**avrà** ammirato	**avranno** ammirato
condizionale presente		*condizionale passato*	
ammirer**ei**	ammirer**emmo**	**avrei** ammirato	**avremmo** ammirato
ammirer**esti**	ammirer**este**	**avresti** ammirato	**avreste** ammirato
ammirer**ebbe**	ammirer**ebbero**	**avrebbe** ammirato	**avrebbero** ammirato
congiuntivo presente		*congiuntivo passato*	
ammir**a**	ammir**iamo**	**abbia** ammirato	**abbiamo** ammirato
ammir**a**	ammir**iate**	**abbia** ammirato	**abbiate** ammirato
ammir**a**	ammir**ino**	**abbia** ammirato	**abbiano** ammirato
congiuntivo imperfetto		*congiuntivo trapassato*	
ammir**assi**	ammir**assimo**	**avessi** ammirato	**avessimo** ammirato
ammir**assi**	ammir**aste**	**avessi** ammirato	**aveste** ammirato
ammir**asse**	ammir**assero**	**avesse** ammirato	**avessero** ammirato
imperativo			
	ammiriamo		
ammira; non ammirare	ammirate		
ammiri	ammirino		

gerundio **andando** participio passato **andato**

SINGULAR	PLURAL	SINGULAR	PLURAL
indicativo presente		passato prossimo	
vado	and**iamo**	**sono** andato(a)	**siamo** andati(e)
vai	and**ate**	**sei** andato(a)	**siete** andati(e)
va	**vanno**	**è** andato(a)	**sono** andati(e)
imperfetto		trapassato prossimo	
anda**vo**	anda**vamo**	**ero** andato(a)	**eravamo** andati(e)
anda**vi**	anda**vate**	**eri** andato(a)	**eravate** andati(e)
anda**va**	anda**vano**	**era** andato(a)	**erano** andati(e)
passato remoto		trapassato remoto	
and**ai**	and**ammo**	**fui** andato(a)	**fummo** andati(e)
and**asti**	and**aste**	**fosti** andato(a)	**foste** andati(e)
and**ò**	and**arono**	**fu** andato(a)	**furono** andati(e)
futuro semplice		futuro anteriore	
andr**ò**	andr**emo**	**sarò** andato(a)	**saremo** andati(e)
andr**ai**	andr**ete**	**sarai** andato(a)	**sarete** andati(e)
andr**à**	andr**anno**	**sarà** andato(a)	**saranno** andati(e)
condizionale presente		condizionale passato	
andr**ei**	andr**emmo**	**sarei** andato(a)	**saremmo** andati(e)
andr**esti**	andr**este**	**saresti** andato(a)	**sareste** andati(e)
andr**ebbe**	andr**ebbero**	**sarebbe** andato(a)	**sarebbero** andati(e)
congiuntivo presente		congiuntivo passato	
vad**a**	and**iamo**	**sia** andato(a)	**siamo** andati(e)
vad**a**	and**iate**	**sia** andato(a)	**siate** andati(e)
vad**a**	vad**ano**	**sia** andato(a)	**siano** andati(e)
congiuntivo imperfetto		congiuntivo trapassato	
and**assi**	and**assimo**	**fossi** andato(a)	**fossimo** andati(e)
and**assi**	and**aste**	**fossi** andato(a)	**foste** andati(e)
and**asse**	and**assero**	**fosse** andato(a)	**fossero** andati(e)
imperativo			
	andiamo		
vai; non andare	andate		
vada	vadano		

andarsene — to go away

gerundio **andandosene** participio passato **andatosene**

A

SINGULAR	PLURAL	SINGULAR	PLURAL
indicativo presente		*passato prossimo*	
me ne vad**o**	**ce ne** and**iamo**	**me ne sono** andato(a)	**ce ne siamo** andati(e)
te ne va**i**	**ve ne** and**ate**	**te ne sei** andato(a)	**ve ne siete** andati(e)
se ne va	**se ne** va**nno**	**se ne è** andato(a)	**se ne sono** andati(e)
imperfetto		*trapassato prossimo*	
me ne anda**vo**	**ce ne** anda**vamo**	**me ne ero** andato(a)	**ce ne eravamo** andati(e)
te ne anda**vi**	**ve ne** anda**vate**	**te ne eri** andato(a)	**ve ne eravate** andati(e)
se ne anda**va**	**se ne** anda**vano**	**se ne era** andato(a)	**se ne erano** andati(e)
passato remoto		*trapassato remoto*	
me ne and**ai**	**ce ne** and**ammo**	**me ne fui** andato(a)	**ce ne fummo** andati(e)
te ne and**asti**	**ve ne** and**aste**	**te ne fosti** andato(a)	**ve ne foste** andati(e)
se ne and**ò**	**se ne** and**arono**	**se ne fu** andato(a)	**se ne furono** andati(e)
futuro semplice		*futuro anteriore*	
me ne andr**ò**	**ce ne** andr**emo**	**me ne sarò** andato(a)	**ce ne saremo** andati(e)
te ne andr**ai**	**ve ne** andr**ete**	**te ne sarai** andato(a)	**ve ne sarete** andati(e)
se ne andr**à**	**se ne** andr**anno**	**se ne sarà** andato(a)	**se ne saranno** andati(e)
condizionale presente		*condizionale passato*	
me ne andr**ei**	**ce ne** andr**emmo**	**me ne sarei** andato(a)	**ce ne saremmo** andati(e)
te ne andr**esti**	**ve ne** andr**este**	**te ne saresti** andato(a)	**ve ne sareste** andati(e)
se ne andr**ebbe**	**se ne** andr**ebbero**	**se ne sarebbe** andato(a)	**se ne sarebbero** andati(e)
congiuntivo presente		*congiuntivo passato*	
me ne vad**a**	**ce ne** and**iamo**	**me ne sia** andato(a)	**ce ne siamo** andati(e)
te ne vad**a**	**ve ne** and**iate**	**te ne sia** andato(a)	**ve ne siate** andati(e)
se ne vad**a**	**se ne** vad**ano**	**se ne sia** andato(a)	**se ne siano** andati(e)
congiuntivo imperfetto		*congiuntivo trapassato*	
me ne and**assi**	**ce ne** and**assimo**	**me ne fossi** andato(a)	**ce ne fossimo** andati(e)
te ne and**assi**	**ve ne** and**aste**	**te ne fossi** andato(a)	**ve ne foste** andati(e)
se ne and**asse**	**se ne** and**assero**	**se ne fosse** andato(a)	**se ne fossero** andati(e)

imperativo

SINGULAR	PLURAL
	andiamocene
vattene; non andartene/ non te ne andare	andatevene
se ne vada	se ne vadano

to bore — annoiare

gerundio **annoiando** — participio passato **annoiato**

SINGULAR	PLURAL
indicativo presente	
annoi**o**	annoi**amo**
annoi	annoi**ate**
annoi**a**	annoi**ano**
imperfetto	
annoia**vo**	annoia**vamo**
annoia**vi**	annoia**vate**
annoia**va**	annoia**vano**
passato remoto	
annoi**ai**	annoi**ammo**
annoi**asti**	annoi**aste**
annoi**ò**	annoi**arono**
futuro semplice	
annoier**ò**	annoier**emo**
annoier**ai**	annoier**ete**
annoier**à**	annoier**anno**
condizionale presente	
annoier**ei**	annoier**emmo**
annoier**esti**	annoier**este**
annoier**ebbe**	annoier**ebbero**
congiuntivo presente	
annoi**i**	annoi**amo**
annoi**i**	annoi**ate**
annoi**i**	annoi**no**
congiuntivo imperfetto	
annoi**assi**	annoi**assimo**
annoi**assi**	annoi**aste**
annoi**asse**	annoi**assero**
imperativo	
	annoiamo
annoia; non annoiare	annoiate
annoi	annoino

SINGULAR	PLURAL
passato prossimo	
ho annoiato	**abbiamo** annoiato
hai annoiato	**avete** annoiato
ha annoiato	**hanno** annoiato
trapassato prossimo	
avevo annoiato	**avevamo** annoiato
avevi annoiato	**avevate** annoiato
aveva annoiato	**avevano** annoiato
trapassato remoto	
ebbi annoiato	**avemmo** annoiato
avesti annoiato	**aveste** annoiato
ebbe annoiato	**ebbero** annoiato
futuro anteriore	
avrò annoiato	**avremo** annoiato
avrai annoiato	**avrete** annoiato
avrà annoiato	**avranno** annoiato
condizionale passato	
avrei annoiato	**avremmo** annoiato
avresti annoiato	**avreste** annoiato
avrebbe annoiato	**avrebbero** annoiato
congiuntivo passato	
abbia annoiato	**abbiamo** annoiato
abbia annoiato	**abbiate** annoiato
abbia annoiato	**abbiano** annoiato
congiuntivo trapassato	
avessi annoiato	**avessimo** annoiato
avessi annoiato	**aveste** annoiato
avesse annoiato	**avessero** annoiato

annoiarsi — to get bored

gerundio **annoiandosi** — participio passato **annoiatosi**

SINGULAR	PLURAL
indicativo presente	
mi annoi**o**	**ci** annoi**amo**
ti annoi	**vi** annoi**ate**
si annoi**a**	**si** annoi**ano**
imperfetto	
mi annoia**vo**	**ci** annoia**vamo**
ti annoia**vi**	**vi** annoia**vate**
si annoia**va**	**si** annoia**vano**
passato remoto	
mi annoi**ai**	**ci** annoi**ammo**
ti annoi**asti**	**vi** annoi**aste**
si annoi**ò**	**si** annoi**arono**
futuro semplice	
mi annoier**ò**	**ci** annoier**emo**
ti annoier**ai**	**vi** annoier**ete**
si annoier**à**	**si** annoier**anno**
condizionale presente	
mi annoier**ei**	**ci** annoier**emmo**
ti annoier**esti**	**vi** annoier**este**
si annoier**ebbe**	**si** annoier**ebbero**
congiuntivo presente	
mi annoi	**ci** annoi**amo**
ti annoi	**vi** annoi**ate**
si annoi	**si** anno**ino**
congiuntivo imperfetto	
mi annoi**assi**	**ci** annoi**assimo**
ti annoi**assi**	**vi** annoi**aste**
si annoi**asse**	**si** annoi**assero**
imperativo	
	annoiamoci
annoiati; non annoiarti/ non ti annoiare	annoiatevi
si annoi	si annoino

SINGULAR	PLURAL
passato prossimo	
mi sono annoiato(a)	**ci siamo** annoiati(e)
ti sei annoiato(a)	**vi siete** annoiati(e)
si è annoiato(a)	**si sono** annoiati(e)
trapassato prossimo	
mi ero annoiato(a)	**ci eravamo** annoiati(e)
ti eri annoiato(a)	**vi eravate** annoiati(e)
si era annoiato(a)	**si erano** annoiati(e)
trapassato remoto	
mi fui annoiato(a)	**ci fummo** annoiati(e)
ti fosti annoiato(a)	**vi foste** annoiati(e)
si fu annoiato(a)	**si furono** annoiati(e)
futuro anteriore	
mi sarò annoiato(a)	**ci saremo** annoiati(e)
ti sarai annoiato(a)	**vi sarete** annoiati(e)
si sarà annoiato(a)	**si saranno** annoiati(e)
condizionale passato	
mi sarei annoiato(a)	**ci saremmo** annoiati(e)
ti saresti annoiato(a)	**vi sareste** annoiati(e)
si sarebbe annoiato(a)	**si sarebbero** annoiati(e)
congiuntivo passato	
mi sia annoiato(a)	**ci siamo** annoiati(e)
ti sia annoiato(a)	**vi siate** annoiati(e)
si sia annoiato(a)	**si siano** annoiati(e)
congiuntivo trapassato	
mi fossi annoiato(a)	**ci fossimo** annoiati(e)
ti fossi annoiato(a)	**vi foste** annoiati(e)
si fosse annoiato(a)	**si fossero** annoiati(e)

to anticipate — anticipare

gerundio **anticipando** participio passato **anticipato**

SINGULAR	PLURAL
indicativo presente	
anticip**o**	anticip**iamo**
anticip**i**	anticip**ate**
anticip**a**	anticip**ano**
imperfetto	
anticipa**vo**	anticipa**vamo**
anticipa**vi**	anticipa**vate**
anticipa**va**	anticipa**vano**
passato remoto	
anticip**ai**	anticip**ammo**
anticip**asti**	anticip**aste**
anticip**ò**	anticip**arono**
futuro semplice	
anticiper**ò**	anticiper**emo**
anticiper**ai**	anticiper**ete**
anticiper**à**	anticiper**anno**
condizionale presente	
anticiper**ei**	anticiper**emmo**
anticiper**esti**	anticiper**este**
anticiper**ebbe**	anticiper**ebbero**
congiuntivo presente	
anticip**i**	anticip**iamo**
anticip**i**	anticip**iate**
anticip**i**	anticip**ino**
congiuntivo imperfetto	
anticip**assi**	anticip**assimo**
anticip**assi**	anticip**aste**
anticip**asse**	anticip**assero**
imperativo	
	anticipiamo
anticipa; non anticipare	anticipate
anticipi	anticipino

SINGULAR	PLURAL
passato prossimo	
ho anticipato	**abbiamo** anticipato
hai anticipato	**avete** anticipato
ha anticipato	**hanno** anticipato
trapassato prossimo	
avevo anticipato	**avevamo** anticipato
avevi anticipato	**avevate** anticipato
aveva anticipato	**avevano** anticipato
trapassato remoto	
ebbi anticipato	**avemmo** anticipato
avesti anticipato	**aveste** anticipato
ebbe anticipato	**ebbero** anticipato
futuro anteriore	
avrò anticipato	**avremo** anticipato
avrai anticipato	**avrete** anticipato
avrà anticipato	**avranno** anticipato
condizionale passato	
avrei anticipato	**avremmo** anticipato
avresti anticipato	**avreste** anticipato
avrebbe anticipato	**avrebbero** anticipato
congiuntivo passato	
abbia anticipato	**abbiamo** anticipato
abbia anticipato	**abbiate** anticipato
abbia anticipato	**abbiano** anticipato
congiuntivo trapassato	
avessi anticipato	**avessimo** anticipato
avessi anticipato	**aveste** anticipato
avesse anticipato	**avessero** anticipato

apparecchiare — to set (the table)

gerundio **apparecchiando** participio passato **apparecchiato**

A

SINGULAR	PLURAL	SINGULAR	PLURAL
indicativo presente		passato prossimo	
apparecchi**o**	apparecchi**amo**	**ho** apparecchiato	**abbiamo** apparecchiato
apparecchi	apparecchi**ate**	**hai** apparecchiato	**avete** apparecchiato
apparecchi**a**	apparecchi**ano**	**ha** apparecchiato	**hanno** apparecchiato
imperfetto		trapassato prossimo	
apparecchia**vo**	apparecchia**vamo**	**avevo** apparecchiato	**avevamo** apparecchiato
apparecchia**vi**	apparecchia**vate**	**avevi** apparecchiato	**avevate** apparecchiato
apparecchia**va**	apparecchia**vano**	**aveva** apparecchiato	**avevano** apparecchiato
passato remoto		trapassato remoto	
apparecchi**ai**	apparecchi**ammo**	**ebbi** apparecchiato	**avemmo** apparecchiato
apparecchi**asti**	apparecchi**aste**	**avesti** apparecchiato	**aveste** apparecchiato
apparecchi**ò**	apparecchi**arono**	**ebbe** apparecchiato	**ebbero** apparecchiato
futuro semplice		futuro anteriore	
apparecchier**ò**	apparecchier**emo**	**avrò** apparecchiato	**avremo** apparecchiato
apparecchier**ai**	apparecchier**ete**	**avrai** apparecchiato	**avrete** apparecchiato
apparecchier**à**	apparecchier**anno**	**avrà** apparecchiato	**avranno** apparecchiato
condizionale presente		condizionale passato	
apparecchier**ei**	apparecchier**emmo**	**avrei** apparecchiato	**avremmo** apparecchiato
apparecchier**esti**	apparecchier**este**	**avresti** apparecchiato	**avreste** apparecchiato
apparecchier**ebbe**	apparecchier**ebbero**	**avrebbe** apparecchiato	**avrebbero** apparecchiato
congiuntivo presente		congiuntivo passato	
apparecchi**i**	apparecchi**amo**	**abbia** apparecchiato	**abbiamo** apparecchiato
apparecchi**i**	apparecchi**ate**	**abbia** apparecchiato	**abbiate** apparecchiato
apparecchi**i**	apparecchi**no**	**abbia** apparecchiato	**abbiano** apparecchiato
congiuntivo imperfetto		congiuntivo trapassato	
apparecchi**assi**	apparecchi**assimo**	**avessi** apparecchiato	**avessimo** apparecchiato
apparecchi**assi**	apparecchi**aste**	**avessi** apparecchiato	**aveste** apparecchiato
apparecchi**asse**	apparecchi**assero**	**avesse** apparecchiato	**avessero** apparecchiato
imperativo			
	apparecchiamo		
apparecchia; non apparecchiare	apparecchiate		
apparecchi	apparecchino		

to appear, to look, to seem **apparire**

gerundio **apparendo** participio passato **apparso**

A

SINGULAR	PLURAL	SINGULAR	PLURAL
indicativo presente		passato prossimo	
appai**o**, appar**isco**	appar**iamo**	**sono** apparso(a)	**siamo** apparsi(e)
appar**i**, appar**isci**	appar**ite**	**sei** apparso(a)	**siete** apparsi(e)
appar**e**, appar**isce**	appai**ono**, appar**iscono**	**è** apparso(a)	**sono** apparsi(e)
imperfetto		trapassato prossimo	
appari**vo**	appari**vamo**	**ero** apparso(a)	**eravamo** apparsi(e)
appari**vi**	appari**vate**	**eri** apparso(a)	**eravate** apparsi(e)
appari**va**	appari**vano**	**era** apparso(a)	**erano** apparsi(e)
passato remoto		trapassato remoto	
apparv**i**, appar**ii**	appar**immo**	**fui** apparso(a)	**fummo** apparsi(e)
appar**isti**	appar**iste**	**fosti** apparso(a)	**foste** apparsi(e)
apparv**e**, appar**ì**	apparv**ero**, appar**irono**	**fu** apparso(a)	**furono** apparsi(e)
futuro semplice		futuro anteriore	
apparir**ò**	apparir**emo**	**sarò** apparso(a)	**saremo** apparsi(e)
apparir**ai**	apparir**ete**	**sarai** apparso(a)	**sarete** apparsi(e)
apparir**à**	apparir**anno**	**sarà** apparso(a)	**saranno** apparsi(e)
condizionale presente		condizionale passato	
apparir**ei**	apparir**emmo**	**sarei** apparso(a)	**saremmo** apparsi(e)
apparir**esti**	apparir**este**	**saresti** apparso(a)	**sareste** apparsi(e)
apparir**ebbe**	apparir**ebbero**	**sarebbe** apparso(a)	**sarebbero** apparsi(e)
congiuntivo presente		congiuntivo passato	
appai**a**, appar**isca**	appar**iamo**	**sia** apparso(a)	**siamo** apparsi(e)
appai**a**, appar**isca**	appar**iate**	**sia** apparso(a)	**siate** apparsi(e)
appai**a**, appar**isca**	appai**ano**, appar**iscano**	**sia** apparso(a)	**siano** apparsi(e)
congiuntivo imperfetto		congiuntivo trapassato	
appar**issi**	appar**issimo**	**fossi** apparso(a)	**fossimo** apparsi(e)
appar**issi**	appar**iste**	**fossi** apparso(a)	**foste** apparsi(e)
appar**isse**	appar**issero**	**fosse** apparso(a)	**fossero** apparsi(e)

imperativo

	appariamo
appari, apparisci; non apparire	apparite
appaia, apparisca	appaiano, appariscano

MEMORY TIP

The rain clouds **appeared** unexpectedly.

appartenere — to belong

gerundio **appartenendo** participio passato **appartenuto**

indicativo presente

SINGULAR	PLURAL
appartengo	apparteniamo
appartieni	appartenete
appartiene	appartengono

imperfetto

SINGULAR	PLURAL
appartenevo	appartenevamo
appartenevi	appartenevate
apparteneva	appartenevano

passato remoto

SINGULAR	PLURAL
appartenni	appartenemmo
appartenesti	apparteneste
appartenne	appartennero

futuro semplice

SINGULAR	PLURAL
apparterrò	apparterremo
apparterrai	apparterrete
apparterrà	apparterranno

condizionale presente

SINGULAR	PLURAL
apparterrei	apparterremmo
apparterresti	apparterreste
apparterrebbe	apparterrebbero

congiuntivo presente

SINGULAR	PLURAL
appartenga	apparteniamo
appartenga	apparteniate
appartenga	appartengano

congiuntivo imperfetto

SINGULAR	PLURAL
appartenessi	appartenessimo
appartenessi	apparteneste
appartenesse	appartenessero

imperativo

SINGULAR	PLURAL
	apparteniamo
appartieni; non appartenere	appartenete
appartenga	appartengano

passato prossimo

SINGULAR	PLURAL
sono appartenuto(a)	**siamo** appartenuti(e)
sei appartenuto(a)	**siete** appartenuti(e)
è appartenuto(a)	**sono** appartenuti(e)

trapassato prossimo

SINGULAR	PLURAL
ero appartenuto(a)	**eravamo** appartenuti(e)
eri appartenuto(a)	**eravate** appartenuti(e)
era appartenuto(a)	**erano** appartenuti(e)

trapassato remoto

SINGULAR	PLURAL
fui appartenuto(a)	**fummo** appartenuti(e)
fosti appartenuto(a)	**foste** appartenuti(e)
fu appartenuto(a)	**furono** appartenuti(e)

futuro anteriore

SINGULAR	PLURAL
sarò appartenuto(a)	**saremo** appartenuti(e)
sarai appartenuto(a)	**sarete** appartenuti(e)
sarà appartenuto(a)	**saranno** appartenuti(e)

condizionale passato

SINGULAR	PLURAL
sarei appartenuto(a)	**saremmo** appartenuti(e)
saresti appartenuto(a)	**sareste** appartenuti(e)
sarebbe appartenuto(a)	**sarebbero** appartenuti(e)

congiuntivo passato

SINGULAR	PLURAL
sia appartenuto(a)	**siamo** appartenuti(e)
sia appartenuto(a)	**siate** appartenuti(e)
sia appartenuto(a)	**siano** appartenuti(e)

congiuntivo trapassato

SINGULAR	PLURAL
fossi appartenuto(a)	**fossimo** appartenuti(e)
fossi appartenuto(a)	**foste** appartenuti(e)
fosse appartenuto(a)	**fossero** appartenuti(e)

gerundio **apprendendo** participio passato **appreso**

SINGULAR	PLURAL
indicativo presente	
apprend**o**	apprend**iamo**
apprend**i**	apprend**ete**
apprend**e**	apprend**ono**
imperfetto	
apprende**vo**	apprende**vamo**
apprende**vi**	apprende**vate**
apprende**va**	apprende**vano**
passato remoto	
appres**i**	apprend**emmo**
apprend**esti**	apprend**este**
appres**e**	appres**ero**
futuro semplice	
apprender**ò**	apprender**emo**
apprender**ai**	apprender**ete**
apprender**à**	apprender**anno**
condizionale presente	
apprender**ei**	apprender**emmo**
apprender**esti**	apprender**este**
apprender**ebbe**	apprender**ebbero**
congiuntivo presente	
apprend**a**	apprend**iamo**
apprend**a**	apprend**iate**
apprend**a**	apprend**ano**
congiuntivo imperfetto	
apprend**essi**	apprend**essimo**
apprend**essi**	apprend**este**
apprend**esse**	apprend**essero**
imperativo	
	apprendiamo
apprendi; non apprendere	apprendete
apprenda	apprendano

SINGULAR	PLURAL
passato prossimo	
ho appreso	**abbiamo** appreso
hai appreso	**avete** appreso
ha appreso	**hanno** appreso
trapassato prossimo	
avevo appreso	**avevamo** appreso
avevi appreso	**avevate** appreso
aveva appreso	**avevano** appreso
trapassato remoto	
ebbi appreso	**avemmo** appreso
avesti appreso	**aveste** appreso
ebbe appreso	**ebbero** appreso
futuro anteriore	
avrò appreso	**avremo** appreso
avrai appreso	**avrete** appreso
avrà appreso	**avranno** appreso
condizionale passato	
avrei appreso	**avremmo** appreso
avresti appreso	**avreste** appreso
avrebbe appreso	**avrebbero** appreso
congiuntivo passato	
abbia appreso	**abbiamo** appreso
abbia appreso	**abbiate** appreso
abbia appreso	**abbiano** appreso
congiuntivo trapassato	
avessi appreso	**avessimo** appreso
avessi appreso	**aveste** appreso
avesse appreso	**avessero** appreso

approvare — to accept, to approve

gerundio **approvando** participio passato **approvato**

	SINGULAR	PLURAL
indicativo presente	approv**o**	approv**iamo**
	approv**i**	approv**ate**
	approv**a**	approv**ano**
imperfetto	approva**vo**	approva**vamo**
	approva**vi**	approva**vate**
	approva**va**	approva**vano**
passato remoto	approv**ai**	approv**ammo**
	approv**asti**	approv**aste**
	approv**ò**	approv**arono**
futuro semplice	approver**ò**	approver**emo**
	approver**ai**	approver**ete**
	approver**à**	approver**anno**
condizionale presente	approver**ei**	approver**emmo**
	approver**esti**	approver**este**
	approver**ebbe**	approver**ebbero**
congiuntivo presente	approv**i**	approv**iamo**
	approv**i**	approv**iate**
	approv**i**	approv**ino**
congiuntivo imperfetto	approv**assi**	approv**assimo**
	approv**assi**	approv**aste**
	approv**asse**	approv**assero**
imperativo		approviamo
	approva; non approvare	approvate
	approvi	approvino

	SINGULAR	PLURAL
passato prossimo	**ho** approvato	**abbiamo** approvato
	hai approvato	**avete** approvato
	ha approvato	**hanno** approvato
trapassato prossimo	**avevo** approvato	**avevamo** approvato
	avevi approvato	**avevate** approvato
	aveva approvato	**avevano** approvato
trapassato remoto	**ebbi** approvato	**avemmo** approvato
	avesti approvato	**aveste** approvato
	ebbe approvato	**ebbero** approvato
futuro anteriore	**avrò** approvato	**avremo** approvato
	avrai approvato	**avrete** approvato
	avrà approvato	**avranno** approvato
condizionale passato	**avrei** approvato	**avremmo** approvato
	avresti approvato	**avreste** approvato
	avrebbe approvato	**avrebbero** approvato
congiuntivo passato	**abbia** approvato	**abbiamo** approvato
	abbia approvato	**abbiate** approvato
	abbia approvato	**abbiano** approvato
congiuntivo trapassato	**avessi** approvato	**avessimo** approvato
	avessi approvato	**aveste** approvato
	avesse approvato	**avessero** approvato

gerundio **appuntando** participio passato **appuntato**

SINGULAR	PLURAL	SINGULAR	PLURAL
indicativo presente		passato prossimo	
appunt**o**	appunt**iamo**	**ho** appuntato	**abbiamo** appuntato
appunt**i**	appunt**ate**	**hai** appuntato	**avete** appuntato
appunt**a**	appunt**ano**	**ha** appuntato	**hanno** appuntato
imperfetto		trapassato prossimo	
appunta**vo**	appunta**vamo**	**avevo** appuntato	**avevamo** appuntato
appunta**vi**	appunta**vate**	**avevi** appuntato	**avevate** appuntato
appunta**va**	appunta**vano**	**aveva** appuntato	**avevano** appuntato
passato remoto		trapassato remoto	
appunt**ai**	appunt**ammo**	**ebbi** appuntato	**avemmo** appuntato
appunt**asti**	appunt**aste**	**avesti** appuntato	**aveste** appuntato
appunt**ò**	appunt**arono**	**ebbe** appuntato	**ebbero** appuntato
futuro semplice		futuro anteriore	
appunter**ò**	appunter**emo**	**avrò** appuntato	**avremo** appuntato
appunter**ai**	appunter**ete**	**avrai** appuntato	**avrete** appuntato
appunter**à**	appunter**anno**	**avrà** appuntato	**avranno** appuntato
condizionale presente		condizionale passato	
appunter**ei**	appunter**emmo**	**avrei** appuntato	**avremmo** appuntato
appunter**esti**	appunter**este**	**avresti** appuntato	**avreste** appuntato
appunter**ebbe**	appunter**ebbero**	**avrebbe** appuntato	**avrebbero** appuntato
congiuntivo presente		congiuntivo passato	
appunt**i**	appunt**iamo**	**abbia** appuntato	**abbiamo** appuntato
appunt**i**	appunt**iate**	**abbia** appuntato	**abbiate** appuntato
appunt**i**	appunt**ino**	**abbia** appuntato	**abbiano** appuntato
congiuntivo imperfetto		congiuntivo trapassato	
appunt**assi**	appunt**assimo**	**avessi** appuntato	**avessimo** appuntato
appunt**assi**	appunt**aste**	**avessi** appuntato	**aveste** appuntato
appunt**asse**	appunt**assero**	**avesse** appuntato	**avessero** appuntato
imperativo			
	appuntiamo		
appunta; non appuntare	appuntate		
appunti	appuntino		

aprire — to open

gerundio **aprendo** participio passato **aperto**

SINGULAR	PLURAL	SINGULAR	PLURAL
indicativo presente		passato prossimo	
apr**o**	apr**iamo**	**ho** aperto	**abbiamo** aperto
apr**i**	apr**ite**	**hai** aperto	**avete** aperto
apr**e**	apr**ono**	**ha** aperto	**hanno** aperto
imperfetto		trapassato prossimo	
apri**vo**	apri**vamo**	**avevo** aperto	**avevamo** aperto
apri**vi**	apri**vate**	**avevi** aperto	**avevate** aperto
apri**va**	apri**vano**	**aveva** aperto	**avevano** aperto
passato remoto		trapassato remoto	
apri**i**	apr**immo**	**ebbi** aperto	**avemmo** aperto
apr**isti**	apr**iste**	**avesti** aperto	**aveste** aperto
apr**ì**	apr**irono**	**ebbe** aperto	**ebbero** aperto
futuro semplice		futuro anteriore	
aprir**ò**	aprir**emo**	**avrò** aperto	**avremo** aperto
aprir**ai**	aprir**ete**	**avrai** aperto	**avrete** aperto
aprir**à**	aprir**anno**	**avrà** aperto	**avranno** aperto
condizionale presente		condizionale passato	
aprir**ei**	aprir**emmo**	**avrei** aperto	**avremmo** aperto
aprir**esti**	aprir**este**	**avresti** aperto	**avreste** aperto
aprir**ebbe**	aprir**ebbero**	**avrebbe** aperto	**avrebbero** aperto
congiuntivo presente		congiuntivo passato	
apr**a**	apr**iamo**	**abbia** aperto	**abbiamo** aperto
apr**a**	apr**iate**	**abbia** aperto	**abbiate** aperto
apr**a**	apr**ano**	**abbia** aperto	**abbiano** aperto
congiuntivo imperfetto		congiuntivo trapassato	
apr**issi**	apr**issimo**	**avessi** aperto	**avessimo** aperto
apr**issi**	apr**iste**	**avessi** aperto	**aveste** aperto
apr**isse**	apr**issero**	**avesse** aperto	**avessero** aperto
imperativo			
	apriamo		
apri; non aprire	aprite		
apra	aprano		

gerundio **ardendo** participio passato **arso**

SINGULAR	PLURAL	SINGULAR	PLURAL
indicativo presente		passato prossimo	
ard**o**	ard**iamo**	**ho** arso	**abbiamo** arso
ard**i**	ard**ete**	**hai** arso	**avete** arso
ard**e**	ard**ono**	**ha** arso	**hanno** arso
imperfetto		trapassato prossimo	
arde**vo**	arde**vamo**	**avevo** arso	**avevamo** arso
arde**vi**	arde**vate**	**avevi** arso	**avevate** arso
arde**va**	arde**vano**	**aveva** arso	**avevano** arso
passato remoto		trapassato remoto	
ars**i**	ard**emmo**	**ebbi** arso	**avemmo** arso
ard**esti**	ard**este**	**avesti** arso	**aveste** arso
ars**e**	ars**ero**	**ebbe** arso	**ebbero** arso
futuro semplice		futuro anteriore	
arder**ò**	arder**emo**	**avrò** arso	**avremo** arso
arder**ai**	arder**ete**	**avrai** arso	**avrete** arso
arder**à**	arder**anno**	**avrà** arso	**avranno** arso
condizionale presente		condizionale passato	
arder**ei**	arder**emmo**	**avrei** arso	**avremmo** arso
arder**esti**	arder**este**	**avresti** arso	**avreste** arso
arder**ebbe**	arder**ebbero**	**avrebbe** arso	**avrebbero** arso
congiuntivo presente		congiuntivo passato	
ard**a**	ard**iamo**	**abbia** arso	**abbiamo** arso
ard**a**	ard**iate**	**abbia** arso	**abbiate** arso
ard**a**	ard**ano**	**abbia** arso	**abbiano** arso
congiuntivo imperfetto		congiuntivo trapassato	
ard**essi**	ard**essimo**	**avessi** arso	**avessimo** arso
ard**essi**	ard**este**	**avessi** arso	**aveste** arso
ard**esse**	ard**essero**	**avesse** arso	**avessero** arso
imperativo			
	ardiamo		
ardi; non ardere	ardete		
arda	ardano		

arrabbiarsi — to get angry

gerundio **arrabbiandosi** participio passato **arrabbiatosi**

SINGULAR	PLURAL
indicativo presente	
mi arrabbi**o**	**ci** arrabbi**amo**
ti arrabbi	**vi** arrabbiat**e**
si arrabbi**a**	**si** arrabbi**ano**
imperfetto	
mi arrabbia**vo**	**ci** arrabbia**vamo**
ti arrabbia**vi**	**vi** arrabbia**vate**
si arrabbia**va**	**si** arrabbia**vano**
passato remoto	
mi arrabbi**ai**	**ci** arrabbi**ammo**
ti arrabbi**asti**	**vi** arrabbi**aste**
si arrabbi**ò**	**si** arrabbi**arono**
futuro semplice	
mi arrabbier**ò**	**ci** arrabbier**emo**
ti arrabbier**ai**	**vi** arrabbier**ete**
si arrabbier**à**	**si** arrabbier**anno**
condizionale presente	
mi arrabbier**ei**	**ci** arrabbier**emmo**
ti arrabbier**esti**	**vi** arrabbier**este**
si arrabbier**ebbe**	**si** arrabbier**ebbero**
congiuntivo presente	
mi arrabbi	**ci** arrabbi**amo**
ti arrabbi	**vi** arrabbi**ate**
si arrabbi	**si** arrabbi**no**
congiuntivo imperfetto	
mi arrabbi**assi**	**ci** arrabbi**assimo**
ti arrabbi**assi**	**vi** arrabbi**aste**
si arrabbi**asse**	**si** arrabbi**assero**
imperativo	
	arrabbiamoci
arrabbiati; non arrabbiarti/ non ti arrabbiare	arrabbiatevi
si arrabbi	si arrabbino

SINGULAR	PLURAL
passato prossimo	
mi sono arrabbiato(a)	**ci siamo** arrabbiati(e)
ti sei arrabbiato(a)	**vi siete** arrabbiati(e)
si è arrabbiato(a)	**si sono** arrabbiati(e)
trapassato prossimo	
mi ero arrabbiato(a)	**ci eravamo** arrabbiati(e)
ti eri arrabbiato(a)	**vi eravate** arrabbiati(e)
si era arrabbiato(a)	**si erano** arrabbiati(e)
trapassato remoto	
mi fui arrabbiato(a)	**ci fummo** arrabbiati(e)
ti fosti arrabbiato(a)	**vi foste** arrabbiati(e)
si fu arrabbiato(a)	**si furono** arrabbiati(e)
futuro anteriore	
mi sarò arrabbiato(a)	**ci saremo** arrabbiati(e)
ti sarai arrabbiato(a)	**vi sarete** arrabbiati(e)
si sarà arrabbiato(a)	**si saranno** arrabbiati(e)
condizionale passato	
mi sarei arrabbiato(a)	**ci saremmo** arrabbiati(e)
ti saresti arrabbiato(a)	**vi sareste** arrabbiati(e)
si sarebbe arrabbiato(a)	**si sarebbero** arrabbiati(e)
congiuntivo passato	
mi sia arrabbiato(a)	**ci siamo** arrabbiati(e)
ti sia arrabbiato(a)	**vi siate** arrabbiati(e)
si sia arrabbiato(a)	**si siano** arrabbiati(e)
congiuntivo trapassato	
mi fossi arrabbiato(a)	**ci fossimo** arrabbiati(e)
ti fossi arrabbiato(a)	**vi foste** arrabbiati(e)
si fosse arrabbiato(a)	**si fossero** arrabbiati(e)

gerundio **arrestando** participio passato **arrestato**

SINGULAR	PLURAL	SINGULAR	PLURAL
indicativo presente		passato prossimo	
arrest**o**	arrest**iamo**	**ho** arrestato	**abbiamo** arrestato
arrest**i**	arrest**ate**	**hai** arrestato	**avete** arrestato
arrest**a**	arrest**ano**	**ha** arrestato	**hanno** arrestato
imperfetto		trapassato prossimo	
arresta**vo**	arresta**vamo**	**avevo** arrestato	**avevamo** arrestato
arresta**vi**	arresta**vate**	**avevi** arrestato	**avevate** arrestato
arresta**va**	arresta**vano**	**aveva** arrestato	**avevano** arrestato
passato remoto		trapassato remoto	
arrest**ai**	arrest**ammo**	**ebbi** arrestato	**avemmo** arrestato
arrest**asti**	arrest**aste**	**avesti** arrestato	**aveste** arrestato
arrest**ò**	arrest**arono**	**ebbe** arrestato	**ebbero** arrestato
futuro semplice		futuro anteriore	
arrester**ò**	arrester**emo**	**avrò** arrestato	**avremo** arrestato
arrester**ai**	arrester**ete**	**avrai** arrestato	**avrete** arrestato
arrester**à**	arrester**anno**	**avrà** arrestato	**avranno** arrestato
condizionale presente		condizionale passato	
arrester**ei**	arrester**emmo**	**avrei** arrestato	**avremmo** arrestato
arrester**esti**	arrester**este**	**avresti** arrestato	**avreste** arrestato
arrester**ebbe**	arrester**ebbero**	**avrebbe** arrestato	**avrebbero** arrestato
congiuntivo presente		congiuntivo passato	
arrest**i**	arrest**iamo**	**abbia** arrestato	**abbiamo** arrestato
arrest**i**	arrest**iate**	**abbia** arrestato	**abbiate** arrestato
arrest**i**	arrest**ino**	**abbia** arrestato	**abbiano** arrestato
congiuntivo imperfetto		congiuntivo trapassato	
arrest**assi**	arrest**assimo**	**avessi** arrestato	**avessimo** arrestato
arrest**assi**	arrest**aste**	**avessi** arrestato	**aveste** arrestato
arrest**asse**	arrest**assero**	**avesse** arrestato	**avessero** arrestato
imperativo			
	arrestiamo		
arresta; non arrestare	arrestate		
arresti	arrestino		

A

arrivare — to arrive

gerundio **arrivando** — participio passato **arrivato**

A

SINGULAR	PLURAL	SINGULAR	PLURAL
indicativo presente		passato prossimo	
arriv**o**	arriv**iamo**	**sono** arrivato(a)	**siamo** arrivati(e)
arriv**i**	arriv**ate**	**sei** arrivato(a)	**siete** arrivati(e)
arriv**a**	arriv**ano**	**è** arrivato(a)	**sono** arrivati(e)
imperfetto		trapassato prossimo	
arriva**vo**	arriva**vamo**	**ero** arrivato(a)	**eravamo** arrivati(e)
arriva**vi**	arriva**vate**	**eri** arrivato(a)	**eravate** arrivati(e)
arriva**va**	arriva**vano**	**era** arrivato(a)	**erano** arrivati(e)
passato remoto		trapassato remoto	
arriv**ai**	arriv**ammo**	**fui** arrivato(a)	**fummo** arrivati(e)
arriv**asti**	arriv**aste**	**fosti** arrivato(a)	**foste** arrivati(e)
arriv**ò**	arriv**arono**	**fu** arrivato(a)	**furono** arrivati(e)
futuro semplice		futuro anteriore	
arriver**ò**	arriver**emo**	**sarò** arrivato(a)	**saremo** arrivati(e)
arriver**ai**	arriver**ete**	**sarai** arrivato(a)	**sarete** arrivati(e)
arriver**à**	arriver**anno**	**sarà** arrivato(a)	**saranno** arrivati(e)
condizionale presente		condizionale passato	
arriver**ei**	arriver**emmo**	**sarei** arrivato(a)	**saremmo** arrivati(e)
arriver**esti**	arriver**este**	**saresti** arrivato(a)	**sareste** arrivati(e)
arriver**ebbe**	arriver**ebbero**	**sarebbe** arrivato(a)	**sarebbero** arrivati(e)
congiuntivo presente		congiuntivo passato	
arriv**i**	arriv**iamo**	**sia** arrivato(a)	**siamo** arrivati(e)
arriv**i**	arriv**iate**	**sia** arrivato(a)	**siate** arrivati(e)
arriv**i**	arriv**ino**	**sia** arrivato(a)	**siano** arrivati(e)
congiuntivo imperfetto		congiuntivo trapassato	
arriv**assi**	arriv**assimo**	**fossi** arrivato(a)	**fossimo** arrivati(e)
arriv**assi**	arriv**aste**	**fossi** arrivato(a)	**foste** arrivati(e)
arriv**asse**	arriv**assero**	**fosse** arrivato(a)	**fossero** arrivati(e)
imperativo			
	arriviamo		
arriva; non arrivare	arrivate		
arrivi	arrivino		

gerundio **asciugando** participio passato **asciugato**

SINGULAR	PLURAL
indicativo presente	
asciug**o**	asciugh**iamo**
asciugh**i**	asciug**ate**
asciug**a**	asciug**ano**
imperfetto	
asciuga**vo**	asciuga**vamo**
asciuga**vi**	asciuga**vate**
asciuga**va**	asciuga**vano**
passato remoto	
asciug**ai**	asciug**ammo**
asciug**asti**	asciug**aste**
asciug**ò**	asciug**arono**
futuro semplice	
asciugher**ò**	asciugher**emo**
asciugher**ai**	asciugher**ete**
asciugher**à**	asciugher**anno**
condizionale presente	
asciugher**ei**	asciugher**emmo**
asciugher**esti**	asciugher**este**
asciugher**ebbe**	asciugher**ebbero**
congiuntivo presente	
asciugh**i**	asciugh**iamo**
asciugh**i**	asciugh**iate**
asciugh**i**	asciugh**ino**
congiuntivo imperfetto	
asciug**assi**	asciug**assimo**
asciug**assi**	asciug**aste**
asciug**asse**	asciug**assero**
imperativo	
	asciughiamo
asciuga; non asciugare	asciugate
asciughi	asciughino

SINGULAR	PLURAL
passato prossimo	
ho asciugato	**abbiamo** asciugato
hai asciugato	**avete** asciugato
ha asciugato	**hanno** asciugato
trapassato prossimo	
avevo asciugato	**avevamo** asciugato
avevi asciugato	**avevate** asciugato
aveva asciugato	**avevano** asciugato
trapassato remoto	
ebbi asciugato	**avemmo** asciugato
avesti asciugato	**aveste** asciugato
ebbe asciugato	**ebbero** asciugato
futuro anteriore	
avrò asciugato	**avremo** asciugato
avrai asciugato	**avrete** asciugato
avrà asciugato	**avranno** asciugato
condizionale passato	
avrei asciugato	**avremmo** asciugato
avresti asciugato	**avreste** asciugato
avrebbe asciugato	**avrebbero** asciugato
congiuntivo passato	
abbia asciugato	**abbiamo** asciugato
abbia asciugato	**abbiate** asciugato
abbia asciugato	**abbiano** asciugato
congiuntivo trapassato	
avessi asciugato	**avessimo** asciugato
avessi asciugato	**aveste** asciugato
avesse asciugato	**avessero** asciugato

ascoltare — to listen (to)

gerundio **ascoltando** participio passato **ascoltato**

A

SINGULAR	PLURAL	SINGULAR	PLURAL
indicativo presente		passato prossimo	
ascolt**o**	ascolt**iamo**	**ho** ascoltato	**abbiamo** ascoltato
ascolt**i**	ascolt**ate**	**hai** ascoltato	**avete** ascoltato
ascolt**a**	ascolt**ano**	**ha** ascoltato	**hanno** ascoltato
imperfetto		trapassato prossimo	
ascolta**vo**	ascolta**vamo**	**avevo** ascoltato	**avevamo** ascoltato
ascolta**vi**	ascolta**vate**	**avevi** ascoltato	**avevate** ascoltato
ascolta**va**	ascolta**vano**	**aveva** ascoltato	**avevano** ascoltato
passato remoto		trapassato remoto	
ascolt**ai**	ascolt**ammo**	**ebbi** ascoltato	**avemmo** ascoltato
ascolt**asti**	ascolt**aste**	**avesti** ascoltato	**aveste** ascoltato
ascolt**ò**	ascolt**arono**	**ebbe** ascoltato	**ebbero** ascoltato
futuro semplice		futuro anteriore	
ascolter**ò**	ascolter**emo**	**avrò** ascoltato	**avremo** ascoltato
ascolter**ai**	ascolter**ete**	**avrai** ascoltato	**avrete** ascoltato
ascolter**à**	ascolter**anno**	**avrà** ascoltato	**avranno** ascoltato
condizionale presente		condizionale passato	
ascolter**ei**	ascolter**emmo**	**avrei** ascoltato	**avremmo** ascoltato
ascolter**esti**	ascolter**este**	**avresti** ascoltato	**avreste** ascoltato
ascolter**ebbe**	ascolter**ebbero**	**avrebbe** ascoltato	**avrebbero** ascoltato
congiuntivo presente		congiuntivo passato	
ascolt**i**	ascolt**iamo**	**abbia** ascoltato	**abbiamo** ascoltato
ascolt**i**	ascolt**iate**	**abbia** ascoltato	**abbiate** ascoltato
ascolt**i**	ascolt**ino**	**abbia** ascoltato	**abbiano** ascoltato
congiuntivo imperfetto		congiuntivo trapassato	
ascolt**assi**	ascolt**assimo**	**avessi** ascoltato	**avessimo** ascoltato
ascolt**assi**	ascolt**aste**	**avessi** ascoltato	**aveste** ascoltato
ascolt**asse**	ascolt**assero**	**avesse** ascoltato	**avessero** ascoltato
imperativo			
	ascoltiamo		
ascolta; non ascoltare	ascoltate		
ascolti	ascoltino		

to wait (for) — aspettare

gerundio **aspettando** — participio passato **aspettato**

SINGULAR	PLURAL
indicativo presente	
aspett**o**	aspett**iamo**
aspett**i**	aspett**ate**
aspett**a**	aspett**ano**
imperfetto	
aspetta**vo**	aspetta**vamo**
aspetta**vi**	aspetta**vate**
aspetta**va**	aspetta**vano**
passato remoto	
aspett**ai**	aspett**ammo**
aspett**asti**	aspett**aste**
aspett**ò**	aspett**arono**
futuro semplice	
aspetter**ò**	aspetter**emo**
aspetter**ai**	aspetter**ete**
aspetter**à**	aspetter**anno**
condizionale presente	
aspetter**ei**	aspetter**emmo**
aspetter**esti**	aspetter**este**
aspetter**ebbe**	aspetter**ebbero**
congiuntivo presente	
aspett**i**	aspett**iamo**
aspett**i**	aspett**iate**
aspett**i**	aspett**ino**
congiuntivo imperfetto	
aspett**assi**	aspett**assimo**
aspett**assi**	aspett**aste**
aspett**asse**	aspett**assero**
imperativo	
	aspettiamo
aspetta; non aspettare	aspettate
aspetti	aspettino

SINGULAR	PLURAL
passato prossimo	
ho aspettato	**abbiamo** aspettato
hai aspettato	**avete** aspettato
ha aspettato	**hanno** aspettato
trapassato prossimo	
avevo aspettato	**avevamo** aspettato
avevi aspettato	**avevate** aspettato
aveva aspettato	**avevano** aspettato
trapassato remoto	
ebbi aspettato	**avemmo** aspettato
avesti aspettato	**aveste** aspettato
ebbe aspettato	**ebbero** aspettato
futuro anteriore	
avrò aspettato	**avremo** aspettato
avrai aspettato	**avrete** aspettato
avrà aspettato	**avranno** aspettato
condizionale passato	
avrei aspettato	**avremmo** aspettato
avresti aspettato	**avreste** aspettato
avrebbe aspettato	**avrebbero** aspettato
congiuntivo passato	
abbia aspettato	**abbiamo** aspettato
abbia aspettato	**abbiate** aspettato
abbia aspettato	**abbiano** aspettato
congiuntivo trapassato	
avessi aspettato	**avessimo** aspettato
avessi aspettato	**aveste** aspettato
avesse aspettato	**avessero** aspettato

assaggiare — to taste

gerundio **assaggiando** — participio passato **assaggiato**

SINGULAR	PLURAL	SINGULAR	PLURAL
indicativo presente		passato prossimo	
assaggi**o**	assaggi**amo**	**ho** assaggiato	**abbiamo** assaggiato
assaggi	assaggi**ate**	**hai** assaggiato	**avete** assaggiato
assaggi**a**	assaggi**ano**	**ha** assaggiato	**hanno** assaggiato
imperfetto		trapassato prossimo	
assaggia**vo**	assaggia**vamo**	**avevo** assaggiato	**avevamo** assaggiato
assaggia**vi**	assaggia**vate**	**avevi** assaggiato	**avevate** assaggiato
assaggia**va**	assaggia**vano**	**aveva** assaggiato	**avevano** assaggiato
passato remoto		trapassato remoto	
assaggi**ai**	assaggi**ammo**	**ebbi** assaggiato	**avemmo** assaggiato
assaggi**asti**	assaggi**aste**	**avesti** assaggiato	**aveste** assaggiato
assaggi**ò**	assaggi**arono**	**ebbe** assaggiato	**ebbero** assaggiato
futuro semplice		futuro anteriore	
assagger**ò**	assagger**emo**	**avrò** assaggiato	**avremo** assaggiato
assagger**ai**	assagger**ete**	**avrai** assaggiato	**avrete** assaggiato
assagger**à**	assagger**anno**	**avrà** assaggiato	**avranno** assaggiato
condizionale presente		condizionale passato	
assagger**ei**	assagger**emmo**	**avrei** assaggiato	**avremmo** assaggiato
assagger**esti**	assagger**este**	**avresti** assaggiato	**avreste** assaggiato
assagger**ebbe**	assagger**ebbero**	**avrebbe** assaggiato	**avrebbero** assaggiato
congiuntivo presente		congiuntivo passato	
assagg**i**	assagg**iamo**	**abbia** assaggiato	**abbiamo** assaggiato
assagg**i**	assagg**iate**	**abbia** assaggiato	**abbiate** assaggiato
assagg**i**	assagg**ino**	**abbia** assaggiato	**abbiano** assaggiato
congiuntivo imperfetto		congiuntivo trapassato	
assaggi**assi**	assaggi**assimo**	**avessi** assaggiato	**avessimo** assaggiato
assaggi**assi**	assaggi**aste**	**avessi** assaggiato	**aveste** assaggiato
assaggi**asse**	assaggi**assero**	**avesse** assaggiato	**avessero** assaggiato
imperativo			
	assaggiamo		
assaggia; non assaggiare	assaggiate		
assaggi	assaggino		

to assault — assalire

gerundio **assalendo** participio passato **assalito**

SINGULAR	PLURAL
indicativo presente	
assalg**o**	assal**iamo**
assal**i**	assal**ite**
assal**e**	assalg**ono**
imperfetto	
assali**vo**	assali**vamo**
assali**vi**	assali**vate**
assali**va**	assali**vano**
passato remoto	
assal**ii**	assal**immo**
assal**isti**	assal**iste**
assal**ì**	assal**irono**
futuro semplice	
assalir**ò**	assalir**emo**
assalir**ai**	assalir**ete**
assalir**à**	assalir**anno**
condizionale presente	
assalir**ei**	assalir**emmo**
assalir**esti**	assalir**este**
assalir**ebbe**	assalir**ebbero**
congiuntivo presente	
assalg**a**	assal**iamo**
assalg**a**	assal**iate**
assalg**a**	assalg**ano**
congiuntivo imperfetto	
assal**issi**	assal**issimo**
assal**issi**	assal**iste**
assal**isse**	assal**issero**
imperativo	
	assaliamo
assali; non assalire	assalite
assalga	assalgano

SINGULAR	PLURAL
passato prossimo	
ho assalito	**abbiamo** assalito
hai assalito	**avete** assalito
ha assalito	**hanno** assalito
trapassato prossimo	
avevo assalito	**avevamo** assalito
avevi assalito	**avevate** assalito
aveva assalito	**avevano** assalito
trapassato remoto	
ebbi assalito	**avemmo** assalito
avesti assalito	**aveste** assalito
ebbe assalito	**ebbero** assalito
futuro anteriore	
avrò assalito	**avremo** assalito
avrai assalito	**avrete** assalito
avrà assalito	**avranno** assalito
condizionale passato	
avrei assalito	**avremmo** assalito
avresti assalito	**avreste** assalito
avrebbe assalito	**avrebbero** assalito
congiuntivo passato	
abbia assalito	**abbiamo** assalito
abbia assalito	**abbiate** assalito
abbia assalito	**abbiano** assalito
congiuntivo trapassato	
avessi assalito	**avessimo** assalito
avessi assalito	**aveste** assalito
avesse assalito	**avessero** assalito

assistere — to assist, to attend

gerundio **assistendo** participio passato **assistito**

SINGULAR	PLURAL	SINGULAR	PLURAL
indicativo presente		passato prossimo	
assist**o**	assist**iamo**	**ho** assistito	**abbiamo** assistito
assist**i**	assist**ete**	**hai** assistito	**avete** assistito
assist**e**	assist**ono**	**ha** assistito	**hanno** assistito
imperfetto		trapassato prossimo	
assiste**vo**	assiste**vamo**	**avevo** assistito	**avevamo** assistito
assiste**vi**	assiste**vate**	**avevi** assistito	**avevate** assistito
assiste**va**	assiste**vano**	**aveva** assistito	**avevano** assistito
passato remoto		trapassato remoto	
assist**ei**, assist**etti**	assist**emmo**	**ebbi** assistito	**avemmo** assistito
assist**esti**	assist**este**	**avesti** assistito	**aveste** assistito
assist**é**, assist**ette**	assist**erono**, assist**ettero**	**ebbe** assistito	**ebbero** assistito
futuro semplice		futuro anteriore	
assister**ò**	assister**emo**	**avrò** assistito	**avremo** assistito
assister**ai**	assister**ete**	**avrai** assistito	**avrete** assistito
assister**à**	assister**anno**	**avrà** assistito	**avranno** assistito
condizionale presente		condizionale passato	
assister**ei**	assister**emmo**	**avrei** assistito	**avremmo** assistito
assister**esti**	assister**este**	**avresti** assistito	**avreste** assistito
assister**ebbe**	assister**ebbero**	**avrebbe** assistito	**avrebbero** assistito
congiuntivo presente		congiuntivo passato	
assist**a**	assist**iamo**	**abbia** assistito	**abbiamo** assistito
assist**a**	assist**iate**	**abbia** assistito	**abbiate** assistito
assist**a**	assist**ano**	**abbia** assistito	**abbiano** assistito
congiuntivo imperfetto		congiuntivo trapassato	
assist**essi**	assist**essimo**	**avessi** assistito	**avessimo** assistito
assist**essi**	assist**este**	**avessi** assistito	**aveste** assistito
assist**esse**	assist**essero**	**avesse** assistito	**avessero** assistito
imperativo			
	assistiamo		
assisti; non assistere	assistete		
assista	assistano		

MEMORY TIP

I **assist** my grandmother who is bedridden.

gerundio **associando** participio passato **associato**

SINGULAR	PLURAL	SINGULAR	PLURAL
indicativo presente		passato prossimo	
associ**o**	associ**amo**	**ho** associato	**abbiamo** associato
associ	associ**ate**	**hai** associato	**avete** associato
associ**a**	associ**ano**	**ha** associato	**hanno** associato
imperfetto		trapassato prossimo	
associa**vo**	associa**vamo**	**avevo** associato	**avevamo** associato
associa**vi**	associa**vate**	**avevi** associato	**avevate** associato
associa**va**	associa**vano**	**aveva** associato	**avevano** associato
passato remoto		trapassato remoto	
associ**ai**	associ**ammo**	**ebbi** associato	**avemmo** associato
associ**asti**	associ**aste**	**avesti** associato	**aveste** associato
associ**ò**	associ**arono**	**ebbe** associato	**ebbero** associato
futuro semplice		futuro anteriore	
associer**ò**	associer**emo**	**avrò** associato	**avremo** associato
associer**ai**	associer**ete**	**avrai** associato	**avrete** associato
associer**à**	associer**anno**	**avrà** associato	**avranno** associato
condizionale presente		condizionale passato	
associer**ei**	associer**emmo**	**avrei** associato	**avremmo** associato
associer**esti**	associer**este**	**avresti** associato	**avreste** associato
associer**ebbe**	associer**ebbero**	**avrebbe** associato	**avrebbero** associato
congiuntivo presente		congiuntivo passato	
associ**i**	associ**amo**	**abbia** associato	**abbiamo** associato
associ**i**	associ**ate**	**abbia** associato	**abbiate** associato
associ**i**	associ**ino**	**abbia** associato	**abbiano** associato
congiuntivo imperfetto		congiuntivo trapassato	
associ**assi**	associ**assimo**	**avessi** associato	**avessimo** associato
associ**assi**	associ**aste**	**avessi** associato	**aveste** associato
associ**asse**	associ**assero**	**avesse** associato	**avessero** associato
imperativo			
	associamo		
associa; non associare	associate		
associ	associno		

assumere — to hire, to undertake, to assume

gerundio **assumendo** participio passato **assunto**

A

SINGULAR	PLURAL	SINGULAR	PLURAL
indicativo presente		passato prossimo	
assum**o**	assum**iamo**	**ho** assunto	**abbiamo** assunto
assum**i**	assum**ete**	**hai** assunto	**avete** assunto
assum**e**	assum**ono**	**ha** assunto	**hanno** assunto
imperfetto		trapassato prossimo	
assume**vo**	assume**vamo**	**avevo** assunto	**avevamo** assunto
assume**vi**	assume**vate**	**avevi** assunto	**avevate** assunto
assume**va**	assume**vano**	**aveva** assunto	**avevano** assunto
passato remoto		trapassato remoto	
assuns**i**	assum**emmo**	**ebbi** assunto	**avemmo** assunto
assum**esti**	assum**este**	**avesti** assunto	**aveste** assunto
assuns**e**	assuns**ero**	**ebbe** assunto	**ebbero** assunto
futuro semplice		futuro anteriore	
assumer**ò**	assumer**emo**	**avrò** assunto	**avremo** assunto
assumer**ai**	assumer**ete**	**avrai** assunto	**avrete** assunto
assumer**à**	assumer**anno**	**avrà** assunto	**avranno** assunto
condizionale presente		condizionale passato	
assumer**ei**	assumer**emmo**	**avrei** assunto	**avremmo** assunto
assumer**esti**	assumer**este**	**avresti** assunto	**avreste** assunto
assumer**ebbe**	assumer**ebbero**	**avrebbe** assunto	**avrebbero** assunto
congiuntivo presente		congiuntivo passato	
assum**a**	assum**iamo**	**abbia** assunto	**abbiamo** assunto
assum**a**	assum**iate**	**abbia** assunto	**abbiate** assunto
assum**a**	assum**ano**	**abbia** assunto	**abbiano** assunto
congiuntivo imperfetto		congiuntivo trapassato	
assum**essi**	assum**essimo**	**avessi** assunto	**avessimo** assunto
assum**essi**	assum**este**	**avessi** assunto	**aveste** assunto
assum**esse**	assum**essero**	**avesse** assunto	**avessero** assunto
imperativo			
	assumiamo		
assumi; non assumere	assumete		
assuma	assumano		

to abstain, to refrain **astenersi**

gerundio **astenendosi** participio passato **astenutosi**

SINGULAR	PLURAL
indicativo presente	
mi asteng**o**	**ci** asten**iamo**
ti astien**i**	**vi** asten**ete**
si astien**e**	**si** asteng**ono**
imperfetto	
mi astene**vo**	**ci** astene**vamo**
ti astene**vi**	**vi** astene**vate**
si astene**va**	**si** astene**vano**
passato remoto	
mi asten**ni**	**ci** asten**emmo**
ti asten**esti**	**vi** asten**este**
si asten**ne**	**si** asten**nero**
futuro semplice	
mi aster**rò**	**ci** aster**remo**
ti asterr**ai**	**vi** aster**rete**
si asterr**à**	**si** aster**ranno**
condizionale presente	
mi asterr**ei**	**ci** asterr**emmo**
ti asterr**esti**	**vi** asterr**este**
si asterr**ebbe**	**si** asterr**ebbero**
congiuntivo presente	
mi asteng**a**	**ci** asten**iamo**
ti asteng**a**	**vi** asten**iate**
si asteng**a**	**si** asteng**ano**
congiuntivo imperfetto	
mi asten**essi**	**ci** asten**essimo**
ti asten**essi**	**vi** asten**este**
si asten**esse**	**si** asten**essero**
imperativo	
	asteniamoci
astieniti; non astenerti/ non ti astenere	astenetevi
si astenga	si astengano

SINGULAR	PLURAL
passato prossimo	
mi sono astenuto(a)	**ci siamo** astenuti(e)
ti sei astenuto(a)	**vi siete** astenuti(e)
si è astenuto(a)	**si sono** astenuti(e)
trapassato prossimo	
mi ero astenuto(a)	**ci eravamo** astenuti(e)
ti eri astenuto(a)	**vi eravate** astenuti(e)
si era astenuto(a)	**si erano** astenuti(e)
trapassato remoto	
mi fui astenuto(a)	**ci fummo** astenuti(e)
ti fosti astenuto(a)	**vi foste** astenuti(e)
si fu astenuto(a)	**si furono** astenuti(e)
futuro anteriore	
mi sarò astenuto(a)	**ci saremo** astenuti(e)
ti sarai astenuto(a)	**vi sarete** astenuti(e)
si sarà astenuto(a)	**si saranno** astenuti(e)
condizionale passato	
mi sarei astenuto(a)	**ci saremmo** astenuti(e)
ti saresti astenuto(a)	**vi sareste** astenuti(e)
si sarebbe astenuto(a)	**si sarebbero** astenuti(e)
congiuntivo passato	
mi sia astenuto(a)	**ci siamo** astenuti(e)
ti sia astenuto(a)	**vi siate** asienuti(e)
si sia astenuto(a)	**si siano** astenuti(e)
congiuntivo trapassato	
mi fossi astenuto(a)	**ci fossimo** astenuti(e)
ti fossi astenuto(a)	**vi foste** astenuti(e)
si fosse astenuto(a)	**si fossero** astenuti(e)

attaccare — to attack, to attach, to begin

gerundio **attaccando** participio passato **attaccato**

A

SINGULAR	PLURAL	SINGULAR	PLURAL
indicativo presente		passato prossimo	
attacc**o**	attacch**iamo**	**ho** attaccato	**abbiamo** attaccato
attacch**i**	attacc**ate**	**hai** attaccato	**avete** attaccato
attacc**a**	attacc**ano**	**ha** attaccato	**hanno** attaccato
imperfetto		trapassato prossimo	
attacca**vo**	attacca**vamo**	**avevo** attaccato	**avevamo** attaccato
attacca**vi**	attacca**vate**	**avevi** attaccato	**avevate** attaccato
attacca**va**	attacca**vano**	**aveva** attaccato	**avevano** attaccato
passato remoto		trapassato remoto	
attacc**ai**	attacc**ammo**	**ebbi** attaccato	**avemmo** attaccato
attacc**asti**	attacc**aste**	**avesti** attaccato	**aveste** attaccato
attacc**ò**	attacc**arono**	**ebbe** attaccato	**ebbero** attaccato
futuro semplice		futuro anteriore	
attaccher**ò**	attaccher**emo**	**avrò** attaccato	**avremo** attaccato
attaccher**ai**	attaccher**ete**	**avrai** attaccato	**avrete** attaccato
attaccher**à**	attaccher**anno**	**avrà** attaccato	**avranno** attaccato
condizionale presente		condizionale passato	
attaccher**ei**	attaccher**emmo**	**avrei** attaccato	**avremmo** attaccato
attaccher**esti**	attaccher**este**	**avresti** attaccato	**avreste** attaccato
attaccher**ebbe**	attaccher**ebbero**	**avrebbe** attaccato	**avrebbero** attaccato
congiuntivo presente		congiuntivo passato	
attacch**i**	attacch**iamo**	**abbia** attaccato	**abbiamo** attaccato
attacch**i**	attacch**iate**	**abbia** attaccato	**abbiate** attaccato
attacch**i**	attacch**ino**	**abbia** attaccato	**abbiano** attaccato
congiuntivo imperfetto		congiuntivo trapassato	
attacc**assi**	attacc**assimo**	**avessi** attaccato	**avessimo** attaccato
attacc**assi**	attacc**aste**	**avessi** attaccato	**aveste** attaccato
attacc**asse**	attacc**assero**	**avesse** attaccato	**avessero** attaccato
imperativo			
	attacchiamo		
attacca; non attaccare	attaccate		
attacchi	attacchino		

gerundio **attendendo** participio passato **atteso**

SINGULAR	PLURAL	SINGULAR	PLURAL
indicativo presente		passato prossimo	
attend**o**	attend**iamo**	**ho** atteso	**abbiamo** atteso
attend**i**	attend**ete**	**hai** atteso	**avete** atteso
attend**e**	attend**ono**	**ha** atteso	**hanno** atteso
imperfetto		trapassato prossimo	
attende**vo**	attende**vamo**	**avevo** atteso	**avevamo** atteso
attende**vi**	attende**vate**	**avevi** atteso	**avevate** atteso
attende**va**	attende**vano**	**aveva** atteso	**avevano** atteso
passato remoto		trapassato remoto	
attes**i**	attend**emmo**	**ebbi** atteso	**avemmo** atteso
attend**esti**	attend**este**	**avesti** atteso	**aveste** atteso
attes**e**	attes**ero**	**ebbe** atteso	**ebbero** atteso
futuro semplice		futuro anteriore	
attender**ò**	attender**emo**	**avrò** atteso	**avremo** atteso
attender**ai**	attender**ete**	**avrai** atteso	**avrete** atteso
attender**à**	attender**anno**	**avrà** atteso	**avranno** atteso
condizionale presente		condizionale passato	
attender**ei**	attender**emmo**	**avrei** atteso	**avremmo** atteso
attender**esti**	attender**este**	**avresti** atteso	**avreste** atteso
attender**ebbe**	attender**ebbero**	**avrebbe** atteso	**avrebbero** atteso
congiuntivo presente		congiuntivo passato	
attend**a**	attend**iamo**	**abbia** atteso	**abbiamo** atteso
attend**a**	attend**iate**	**abbia** atteso	**abbiate** atteso
attend**a**	attend**ano**	**abbia** atteso	**abbiano** atteso
congiuntivo imperfetto		congiuntivo trapassato	
attend**essi**	attend**essimo**	**avessi** atteso	**avessimo** atteso
attend**essi**	attend**este**	**avessi** atteso	**aveste** atteso
attend**esse**	attend**essero**	**avesse** atteso	**avessero** atteso

imperativo

SINGULAR	PLURAL
	attendiamo
attendi; non attendere	attendete
attenda	attendano

attrarre — to attract

gerundio **attraendo** participio passato **attratto**

A

SINGULAR	PLURAL	SINGULAR	PLURAL
indicativo presente		passato prossimo	
attragg**o**	attra**iamo**	**ho** attratto	**abbiamo** attratto
attra**i**	attra**ete**	**hai** attratto	**avete** attratto
attra**e**	attragg**ono**	**ha** attratto	**hanno** attratto
imperfetto		trapassato prossimo	
attrae**vo**	attrae**vamo**	**avevo** attratto	**avevamo** attratto
attrae**vi**	attrae**vate**	**avevi** attratto	**avevate** attratto
attrae**va**	attrae**vano**	**aveva** attratto	**avevano** attratto
passato remoto		trapassato remoto	
attra**ssi**	attra**emmo**	**ebbi** attratto	**avemmo** attratto
attra**esti**	attra**este**	**avesti** attratto	**aveste** attratto
attra**sse**	attra**ssero**	**ebbe** attratto	**ebbero** attratto
futuro semplice		futuro anteriore	
attrarr**ò**	attrarr**emo**	**avrò** attratto	**avremo** attratto
attrarr**ai**	attrarr**ete**	**avrai** attratto	**avrete** attratto
attrarr**à**	attrarr**anno**	**avrà** attratto	**avranno** attratto
condizionale presente		condizionale passato	
attrarr**ei**	attrarr**emmo**	**avrei** attratto	**avremmo** attratto
attrarr**esti**	attrarr**este**	**avresti** attratto	**avreste** attratto
attrarr**ebbe**	attrarr**ebbero**	**avrebbe** attratto	**avrebbero** attratto
congiuntivo presente		congiuntivo passato	
attragg**a**	attra**iamo**	**abbia** attratto	**abbiamo** attratto
attragg**a**	attra**iate**	**abbia** attratto	**abbiate** attratto
attragg**a**	attragg**ano**	**abbia** attratto	**abbiano** attratto
congiuntivo imperfetto		congiuntivo trapassato	
attra**essi**	attra**essimo**	**avessi** attratto	**avessimo** attratto
attra**essi**	attra**este**	**avessi** attratto	**aveste** attratto
attra**esse**	attra**essero**	**avesse** attratto	**avessero** attratto

imperativo

SINGULAR	PLURAL
	attraiamo
attrai; non attrarre	attraete
attragga	attraggano

SINGULAR	PLURAL
indicativo presente	
attribu**isco**	attribu**iamo**
attribu**isci**	attribu**ite**
attribu**isce**	attribu**iscono**
imperfetto	
attribui**vo**	attribui**vamo**
attribui**vi**	attribui**vate**
attribui**va**	attribui**vano**
passato remoto	
attribu**ii**	attribu**immo**
attribu**isti**	attribu**iste**
attribu**ì**	attribu**irono**
futuro semplice	
attribuir**ò**	attribuir**emo**
attribuir**ai**	attribuir**ete**
attribuir**à**	attribuir**anno**
condizionale presente	
attribuir**ei**	attribuir**emmo**
attribuir**esti**	attribuir**este**
attribuir**ebbe**	attribuir**ebbero**
congiuntivo presente	
attribu**isca**	attribu**iamo**
attribu**isca**	attribu**iate**
attribu**isca**	attribu**iscano**
congiuntivo imperfetto	
attribu**issi**	attribu**issimo**
attribu**issi**	attribu**iste**
attribu**isse**	attribu**issero**
imperativo	
	attribuiamo
attribuisci; non attribuire	attribuite
attribuisca	attribuiscano

SINGULAR	PLURAL
passato prossimo	
ho attribuito	**abbiamo** attribuito
hai attribuito	**avete** attribuito
ha attribuito	**hanno** attribuito
trapassato prossimo	
avevo attribuito	**avevamo** attribuito
avevi attribuito	**avevate** attribuito
aveva attribuito	**avevano** attribuito
trapassato remoto	
ebbi attribuito	**avemmo** attribuito
avesti attribuito	**aveste** attribuito
ebbe attribuito	**ebbero** attribuito
futuro anteriore	
avrò attribuito	**avremo** attribuito
avrai attribuito	**avrete** attribuito
avrà attribuito	**avranno** attribuito
condizionale passato	
avrei attribuito	**avremmo** attribuito
avresti attribuito	**avreste** attribuito
avrebbe attribuito	**avrebbero** attribuito
congiuntivo passato	
abbia attribuito	**abbiamo** attribuito
abbia attribuito	**abbiate** attribuito
abbia attribuito	**abbiano** attribuito
congiuntivo trapassato	
avessi attribuito	**avessimo** attribuito
avessi attribuito	**aveste** attribuito
avesse attribuito	**avessero** attribuito

avere — to get, to have

gerundio **avendo** participio passato **avuto**

A

SINGULAR	PLURAL	SINGULAR	PLURAL
indicativo presente		passato prossimo	
ho	**abbiamo**	**ho** avuto	**abbiamo** avuto
hai	**avete**	**hai** avuto	**avete** avuto
ha	**hanno**	**ha** avuto	**hanno** avuto
imperfetto		trapassato prossimo	
ave**vo**	ave**vamo**	**avevo** avuto	**avevamo** avuto
ave**vi**	ave**vate**	**avevi** avuto	**avevate** avuto
ave**va**	ave**vano**	**aveva** avuto	**avevano** avuto
passato remoto		trapassato remoto	
ebbi	**avemmo**	**ebbi** avuto	**avemmo** avuto
avesti	**aveste**	**avesti** avuto	**aveste** avuto
ebbe	**ebbero**	**ebbe** avuto	**ebbero** avuto
futuro semplice		futuro anteriore	
avrò	**avremo**	**avrò** avuto	**avremo** avuto
avrai	**avrete**	**avrai** avuto	**avrete** avuto
avrà	**avranno**	**avrà** avuto	**avranno** avuto
condizionale presente		condizionale passato	
avrei	**avremmo**	**avrei** avuto	**avremmo** avuto
avresti	**avreste**	**avresti** avuto	**avreste** avuto
avrebbe	**avrebbero**	**avrebbe** avuto	**avrebbero** avuto
congiuntivo presente		congiuntivo passato	
abbia	**abbiamo**	**abbia** avuto	**abbiamo** avuto
abbia	**abbiate**	**abbia** avuto	**abbiate** avuto
abbia	**abbiano**	**abbia** avuto	**abbiano** avuto
congiuntivo imperfetto		congiuntivo trapassato	
avessi	**avessimo**	**avessi** avuto	**avessimo** avuto
avessi	**aveste**	**avessi** avuto	**aveste** avuto
avesse	**avessero**	**avesse** avuto	**avessero** avuto

imperativo

	abbiamo
abbi; non avere	abbiate
abbia	abbiano

gerundio **avvedendosi** participio passato **avvedutosi**

SINGULAR	PLURAL
indicativo presente	
mi avved**o**	**ci** avved**iamo**
ti avved**i**	**vi** avved**ete**
si avved**e**	**si** avved**ono**
imperfetto	
mi avvede**vo**	**ci** avvede**vamo**
ti avvede**vi**	**vi** avvede**vate**
si avvede**va**	**si** avvede**vano**
passato remoto	
mi avv**idi**	**ci** avved**emmo**
ti avved**esti**	**vi** avved**este**
si avv**ide**	**si** avv**idero**
futuro semplice	
mi avvedr**ò**	**ci** avvedr**emo**
ti avvedr**ai**	**vi** avvedr**ete**
si avvedr**à**	**si** avvedr**anno**
condizionale presente	
mi avvedr**ei**	**ci** avvedr**emmo**
ti avvedr**esti**	**vi** avvedr**este**
si avvedr**ebbe**	**si** avvedr**ebbero**
congiuntivo presente	
mi avved**a**	**ci** avved**iamo**
ti avved**a**	**vi** avved**iate**
si avved**a**	**si** avved**ano**
congiuntivo imperfetto	
mi avved**essi**	**ci** avved**essimo**
ti avved**essi**	**vi** avved**este**
si avved**esse**	**si** avved**essero**
imperativo	
	avvediamoci
avvediti; non avvederti/ non ti avvedere	avvedetevi
si avveda	si avvedano

SINGULAR	PLURAL
passato prossimo	
mi sono avveduto(a)	**ci siamo** avveduti(e)
ti sei avveduto(a)	**vi siete** avveduti(e)
si è avveduto(a)	**si sono** avveduti(e)
trapassato prossimo	
mi ero avveduto(a)	**ci eravamo** avveduti(e)
ti eri avveduto(a)	**vi eravate** avveduti(e)
si era avveduto(a)	**si erano** avveduti(e)
trapassato remoto	
mi fui avveduto(a)	**ci fummo** avveduti(e)
ti fosti avveduto(a)	**vi foste** avveduti(e)
si fu avveduto(a)	**si furono** avveduti(e)
futuro anteriore	
mi sarò avveduto(a)	**ci saremo** avveduti(e)
ti sarai avveduto(a)	**vi sarete** avveduti(e)
si sarà avveduto(a)	**si saranno** avveduti(e)
condizionale passato	
mi sarei avveduto(a)	**ci saremmo** avveduti(e)
ti saresti avveduto(a)	**vi sareste** avveduti(e)
si sarebbe avveduto(a)	**si sarebbero** avveduti(e)
congiuntivo passato	
mi sia avveduto(a)	**ci siamo** avveduti(e)
ti sia avveduto(a)	**vi siate** avveduti(e)
si sia avveduto(a)	**si siano** avveduti(e)
congiuntivo trapassato	
mi fossi avveduto(a)	**ci fossimo** avveduti(e)
ti fossi avveduto(a)	**vi foste** avveduti(e)
si fosse avveduto(a)	**si fossero** avveduti(e)

avvenire — to happen, to occur

gerundio **avvenendo** participio passato **avvenuto**

A

SINGULAR	PLURAL	SINGULAR	PLURAL
indicativo presente		passato prossimo	
avvien**e**	avveng**ono**	**è** avvenuto(a)	**sono** avvenuti(e)
imperfetto		trapassato prossimo	
avveni**va**	avveni**vano**	**era** avvenuto(a)	**erano** avvenuti(e)
passato remoto		trapassato remoto	
avvenn**e**	avvenn**ero**	**fu** avvenuto(a)	**furono** avvenuti(e)
futuro semplice		futuro anteriore	
avverr**à**	avverr**anno**	**sarà** avvenuto(a)	**saranno** avvenuti(e)
condizionale presente		condizionale passato	
avverr**ebbe**	avverr**ebbero**	**sarebbe** avvenuto(a)	**sarebbero** avvenuti(e)
congiuntivo presente		congiuntivo passato	
avveng**a**	avveng**ano**	**sia** avvenuto(a)	**siano** avvenuti(e)
congiuntivo imperfetto		congiuntivo trapassato	
avven**isse**	avven**issero**	**fosse** avvenuto(a)	**fossero** avvenuti(e)

to warn, to inform — avvertire

gerundio **avvertendo** participio passato **avvertito**

SINGULAR	PLURAL	SINGULAR	PLURAL
indicativo presente		passato prossimo	
avvert**o**	avvert**iamo**	**ho** avvertito	**abbiamo** avvertito
avvert**i**	avvert**ite**	**hai** avvertito	**avete** avvertito
avvert**e**	avvert**ono**	**ha** avvertito	**hanno** avvertito
imperfetto		trapassato prossimo	
avverti**vo**	avverti**vamo**	**avevo** avvertito	**avevamo** avvertito
avverti**vi**	avverti**vate**	**avevi** avvertito	**avevate** avvertito
avverti**va**	avverti**vano**	**aveva** avvertito	**avevano** avvertito
passato remoto		trapassato remoto	
avvert**ii**	avvert**immo**	**ebbi** avverino	**avemmo** avvertito
avvert**isti**	avvert**iste**	**avesti** avvertito	**aveste** avvertito
avvert**ì**	avvert**irono**	**ebbe** avvertito	**ebbero** avvertito
futuro semplice		futuro anteriore	
avvertir**ò**	avvertir**emo**	**avrò** avvertito	**avremo** avvertito
avvertir**ai**	avvertir**ete**	**avrai** avvertito	**avrete** avvertito
avvertir**à**	avvertir**anno**	**avrà** avvertito	**avranno** avvertito
condizionale presente		condizionale passato	
avvertir**ei**	avvertir**emmo**	**avrei** avvertito	**avremmo** avvertito
avvertir**esti**	avvertir**este**	**avresti** avvertito	**avreste** avvertito
avvertir**ebbe**	avvertir**ebbero**	**avrebbe** avvertito	**avrebbero** avvertito
congiuntivo presente		congiuntivo passato	
avvert**a**	avvert**iamo**	**abbia** avvertito	**abbiamo** avvertito
avvert**a**	avvert**iate**	**abbia** avvertito	**abbiate** avvertito
avvert**a**	avvert**ano**	**abbia** avvertito	**abbiano** avvertito
congiuntivo imperfetto		congiuntivo trapassato	
avvert**issi**	avvert**issimo**	**avessi** avvertito	**avessimo** avvertito
avvert**issi**	avvert**iste**	**avessi** avvertito	**aveste** avvertito
avvert**isse**	avvert**issero**	**avesse** avvertito	**avessero** avvertito
imperativo			
	avvertiamo		
avverti; non avvertire	avvertite		
avverta	avvertano		

A

avviare — to begin, to start

gerundio **avviando** participio passato **avviato**

A

SINGULAR	PLURAL
indicativo presente	
avvi**o**	avvi**amo**
avv**ii**	avvi**ate**
avvi**a**	avvi**ano**
imperfetto	
avvia**vo**	avvia**vamo**
avvia**vi**	avvia**vate**
avvia**va**	avvia**vano**
passato remoto	
avvi**ai**	avvi**ammo**
avvi**asti**	avvi**aste**
avvi**ò**	avvi**arono**
futuro semplice	
avvier**ò**	avvier**emo**
avvier**ai**	avvier**ete**
avvier**à**	avvier**anno**
condizionale presente	
avvier**ei**	avvier**emmo**
avvier**esti**	avvier**este**
avvier**ebbe**	avvier**ebbero**
congiuntivo presente	
avv**ii**	avvi**amo**
avv**ii**	avvi**ate**
avv**ii**	avv**iino**
congiuntivo imperfetto	
avvi**assi**	avvi**assimo**
avvi**assi**	avvi**aste**
avvi**asse**	avvi**assero**
imperativo	
	avviamo
avvia; non avviare	avviate
avvii	avviino

SINGULAR	PLURAL
passato prossimo	
ho avviato	**abbiamo** avviato
hai avviato	**avete** avviato
ha avviato	**hanno** avviato
trapassato prossimo	
avevo avviato	**avevamo** avviato
avevi avviato	**avevate** avviato
aveva avviato	**avevano** avviato
trapassato remoto	
ebbi avviato	**avemmo** avviato
avesti avviato	**aveste** avviato
ebbe avviato	**ebbero** avviato
futuro anteriore	
avrò avviato	**avremo** avviato
avrai avviato	**avrete** avviato
avrà avviato	**avranno** avviato
condizionale passato	
avrei avviato	**avremmo** avviato
avresti avviato	**avreste** avviato
avrebbe avviato	**avrebbero** avviato
congiuntivo passato	
abbia avviato	**abbiamo** avviato
abbia avviato	**abbiate** avviato
abbia avviato	**abbiano** avviato
congiuntivo trapassato	
avessi avviato	**avessimo** avviato
avessi avviato	**aveste** avviato
avesse avviato	**avessero** avviato

gerundio **avvisando** participio passato **avvisato**

SINGULAR	PLURAL	SINGULAR	PLURAL
indicativo presente		passato prossimo	
avvis**o**	avvis**iamo**	**ho** avvisato	**abbiamo** avvisato
avvis**i**	avvis**ate**	**hai** avvisato	**avete** avvisato
avvis**a**	avvis**ano**	**ha** avvisato	**hanno** avvisato
imperfetto		trapassato prossimo	
avvisa**vo**	avvisa**vamo**	**avevo** avvisato	**avevamo** avvisato
avvisa**vi**	avvisa**vate**	**avevi** avvisato	**avevate** avvisato
avvisa**va**	avvisa**vano**	**aveva** avvisato	**avevano** avvisato
passato remoto		trapassato remoto	
avvis**ai**	avvis**ammo**	**ebbi** avvisato	**avemmo** avvisato
avvis**asti**	avvis**aste**	**avesti** avvisato	**aveste** avvisato
avvis**ò**	avvis**arono**	**ebbe** avvisato	**ebbero** avvisato
futuro semplice		futuro anteriore	
avviser**ò**	avviser**emo**	**avrò** avvisato	**avremo** avvisato
avviser**ai**	avviser**ete**	**avrai** avvisato	**avrete** avvisato
avviser**à**	avviser**anno**	**avrà** avvisato	**avranno** avvisato
condizionale presente		condizionale passato	
avviser**ei**	avviser**emmo**	**avrei** avvisato	**avremmo** avvisato
avviser**esti**	avviser**este**	**avresti** avvisato	**avreste** avvisato
avviser**ebbe**	avviser**ebbero**	**avrebbe** avvisato	**avrebbero** avvisato
congiuntivo presente		congiuntivo passato	
avvis**i**	avvis**iamo**	**abbia** avvisato	**abbiamo** avvisato
avvis**i**	avvis**iate**	**abbia** avvisato	**abbiate** avvisato
avvis**i**	avvis**ino**	**abbia** avvisato	**abbiano** avvisato
congiuntivo imperfetto		congiuntivo trapassato	
avvis**assi**	avvis**assimo**	**avessi** avvisato	**avessimo** avvisato
avvis**assi**	avvis**aste**	**avessi** avvisato	**aveste** avvisato
avvis**asse**	avvis**assero**	**avesse** avvisato	**avessero** avvisato

imperativo

	avvisiamo
avvisa; non avvisare	avvisate
avvisi	avvisino

A

baciare — to kiss

gerundio **baciando** — participio passato **baciato**

B

SINGULAR	PLURAL
indicativo presente	
bacio	baciamo
baci	baciate
bacia	baciano
imperfetto	
baciavo	baciavamo
baciavi	baciavate
baciava	baciavano
passato remoto	
baciai	baciammo
baciasti	baciaste
baciò	baciarono
futuro semplice	
bacerò	baceremo
bacerai	bacerete
bacerà	baceranno
condizionale presente	
bacerei	baceremmo
baceresti	bacereste
bacerebbe	bacerebbero
congiuntivo presente	
baci	baciamo
baci	baciate
baci	bacino
congiuntivo imperfetto	
baciassi	baciassimo
baciassi	baciaste
baciasse	baciassero
imperativo	
	baciamo
bacia; non baciare	baciate
baci	bacino

SINGULAR	PLURAL
passato prossimo	
ho baciato	abbiamo baciato
hai baciato	avete baciato
ha baciato	hanno baciato
trapassato prossimo	
avevo baciato	avevamo baciato
avevi baciato	avevate baciato
aveva baciato	avevano baciato
trapassato remoto	
ebbi baciato	avemmo baciato
avesti baciato	aveste baciato
ebbe baciato	ebbero baciato
futuro anteriore	
avrò baciato	avremo baciato
avrai baciato	avrete baciato
avrà baciato	avranno baciato
condizionale passato	
avrei baciato	avremmo baciato
avresti baciato	avreste baciato
avrebbe baciato	avrebbero baciato
congiuntivo passato	
abbia baciato	abbiamo baciato
abbia baciato	abbiate baciato
abbia baciato	abbiano baciato
congiuntivo trapassato	
avessi baciato	avessimo baciato
avessi baciato	aveste baciato
avesse baciato	avessero baciato

to dance **ballare**

gerundio **ballando** participio passato **ballato**

SINGULAR	PLURAL	SINGULAR	PLURAL
indicativo presente		passato prossimo	
ball**o**	ball**iamo**	**ho** ballato	**abbiamo** ballato
ball**i**	ball**ate**	**hai** ballato	**avete** ballato
ball**a**	ball**ano**	**ha** ballato	**hanno** ballato
imperfetto		trapassato prossimo	
balla**vo**	balla**vamo**	**avevo** ballato	**avevamo** ballato
balla**vi**	balla**vate**	**avevi** ballato	**avevate** ballato
balla**va**	balla**vano**	**aveva** ballato	**avevano** ballato
passato remoto		trapassato remoto	
ball**ai**	ball**ammo**	**ebbi** ballato	**avemmo** ballato
ball**asti**	ball**aste**	**avesti** ballato	**aveste** ballato
ball**ò**	ball**arono**	**ebbe** ballato	**ebbero** ballato
futuro semplice		futuro anteriore	
baller**ò**	baller**emo**	**avrò** ballato	**avremo** ballato
baller**ai**	baller**ete**	**avrai** ballato	**avrete** ballato
baller**à**	baller**anno**	**avrà** ballato	**avranno** ballato
condizionale presente		condizionale passato	
ball**erei**	ball**eremmo**	**avrei** ballato	**avremmo** ballato
ball**eresti**	ball**ereste**	**avresti** ballato	**avreste** ballato
ball**erebbe**	ball**erebbero**	**avrebbe** ballato	**avrebbero** ballato
congiuntivo presente		congiuntivo passato	
ball**i**	ball**iamo**	**abbia** ballato	**abbiamo** ballato
ball**i**	ball**iate**	**abbia** ballato	**abbiate** ballato
ball**i**	ball**ino**	**abbia** ballato	**abbiano** ballato
congiuntivo imperfetto		congiuntivo trapassato	
ball**assi**	ball**assimo**	**avessi** ballato	**avessimo** ballato
ball**assi**	ball**aste**	**avessi** ballato	**aveste** ballato
ball**asse**	ball**assero**	**avesse** ballato	**avessero** ballato

imperativo

	balliamo
balla; non ballare	ballate
balli	ballino

B

MEMORY TIP

Cinderella danced at the ball.

bastare — to be enough, to suffice

gerundio **bastando** participio passato **bastato**

B

SINGULAR	PLURAL	SINGULAR	PLURAL
indicativo presente		passato prossimo	
bast**a**	bast**ano**	**è** bastato(a)	**sono** bastati(e)
imperfetto		trapassato prossimo	
basta**va**	basta**vano**	**era** bastato(a)	**erano** bastati(e)
passato remoto		trapassato remoto	
bast**ò**	bast**arono**	**fu** bastato(a)	**furono** bastati(e)
futuro semplice		futuro anteriore	
baster**à**	baster**anno**	**sarà** bastato(a)	**saranno** bastati(e)
condizionale presente		condizionale passato	
bast**erebbe**	bast**erebbero**	**sarebbe** bastato(a)	**sarebbero** bastati(e)
congiuntivo presente		congiuntivo passato	
bast**i**	bast**ino**	**sia** bastato(a)	**siano** bastati(e)
congiuntivo imperfetto		congiuntivo trapassato	
bast**asse**	bast**assero**	**fosse** bastato(a)	**fossero** bastati(e)

to bless **benedire**

gerundio **benedicendo** participio passato **benedetto**

SINGULAR	PLURAL	SINGULAR	PLURAL
indicativo presente		passato prossimo	
benedi**co**	benedi**ciamo**	**ho** benedetto	**abbiamo** benedetto
benedi**ci**	bene**dite**	**hai** benedetto	**avete** benedetto
benedi**ce**	benedi**cono**	**ha** benedetto	**hanno** benedetto
imperfetto		trapassato prossimo	
benedice**vo**, benedi**vo**	benedice**vamo**, benedi**vamo**	**avevo** benedetto	**avevamo** benedetto
benedice**vi**, benedi**vi**	benedice**vate**, benedi**vate**	**avevi** benedetto	**avevate** benedetto
benedice**va**, benedi**va**	benedice**vano**, benedi**vano**	**aveva** benedetto	**avevano** benedetto
passato remoto		trapassato remoto	
benedi**ssi**	benedic**emmo**	**ebbi** benedetto	**avemmo** benedetto
benedic**esti**	benedic**este**	**avesti** benedetto	**aveste** benedetto
benedi**sse**	benediss**ero**	**ebbe** benedetto	**ebbero** benedetto
futuro semplice		futuro anteriore	
benedir**ò**	benedir**emo**	**avrò** benedetto	**avremo** benedetto
benedir**ai**	benedir**ete**	**avrai** benedetto	**avrete** benedetto
benedir**à**	benedir**anno**	**avrà** benedetto	**avranno** benedetto
condizionale presente		condizionale passato	
benedir**ei**	benedir**emmo**	**avrei** benedetto	**avremmo** benedetto
benedir**esti**	benedir**este**	**avresti** benedetto	**avreste** benedetto
benedir**ebbe**	benedir**ebbero**	**avrebbe** benedetto	**avrebbero** benedetto
congiuntivo presente		congiuntivo passato	
benedic**a**	benedic**iamo**	**abbia** benedetto	**abbiamo** benedetto
benedic**a**	benedic**iate**	**abbia** benedetto	**abbiate** benedetto
benedic**a**	benedic**ano**	**abbia** benedetto	**abbiano** benedetto
congiuntivo imperfetto		congiuntivo trapassato	
benedic**essi**	benedic**essimo**	**avessi** benedetto	**avessimo** benedetto
benedic**essi**	benedic**este**	**avessi** benedetto	**aveste** benedetto
benedic**esse**	benedic**essero**	**avesse** benedetto	**avessero** benedetto
imperativo			
	benediciamo		
benedici; non benedire	benedite		
benedica	benedicano		

B

bere — to drink

gerundio **bevendo** — participio passato **bevuto**

SINGULAR	PLURAL	SINGULAR	PLURAL
indicativo presente		passato prossimo	
bev**o**	bev**iamo**	**ho** bevuto	**abbiamo** bevuto
bev**i**	bev**ete**	**hai** bevuto	**avete** bevuto
bev**e**	bev**ono**	**ha** bevuto	**hanno** bevuto
imperfetto		trapassato prossimo	
beve**vo**	beve**vamo**	**avevo** bevuto	**avevamo** bevuto
beve**vi**	beve**vate**	**avevi** bevuto	**avevate** bevuto
beve**va**	beve**vano**	**aveva** bevuto	**avevano** bevuto
passato remoto		trapassato remoto	
bev**vi**	bev**emmo**	**ebbi** bevuto	**avemmo** bevuto
bev**esti**	bev**este**	**avesti** bevuto	**aveste** bevuto
bev**ve**	bev**vero**	**ebbe** bevuto	**ebbero** bevuto
futuro semplice		futuro anteriore	
berr**ò**	berr**emo**	**avrò** bevuto	**avremo** bevuto
berr**ai**	berr**ete**	**avrai** bevuto	**avrete** bevuto
berr**à**	berr**anno**	**avrà** bevuto	**avranno** bevuto
condizionale presente		condizionale passato	
berr**ei**	berr**emmo**	**avrei** bevuto	**avremmo** bevuto
berr**esti**	berr**este**	**avresti** bevuto	**avreste** bevuto
berr**ebbe**	berr**ebbero**	**avrebbe** bevuto	**avrebbero** bevuto
congiuntivo presente		congiuntivo passato	
bev**a**	bev**iamo**	**abbia** bevuto	**abbiamo** bevuto
bev**a**	bev**iate**	**abbia** bevuto	**abbiate** bevuto
bev**a**	bev**ano**	**abbia** bevuto	**abbiano** bevuto
congiuntivo imperfetto		congiuntivo trapassato	
bev**essi**	bev**essimo**	**avessi** bevuto	**avessimo** bevuto
bev**essi**	bev**este**	**avessi** bevuto	**aveste** bevuto
bev**esse**	bev**essero**	**avesse** bevuto	**avessero** bevuto
imperativo			
	beviamo		
bevi; non bere	bevete		
beva	bevano		

to need **bisognare**

gerundio **bisognando**

participio passato **bisognato**

SINGULAR PLURAL

indicativo presente
bisogn**a**

imperfetto
bisogna**va**

passato remoto
bisogn**ò**

futuro semplice
bisogner**à**

condizionale presente
bisognere**bbe**

congiuntivo presente
bisogn**i**

congiuntivo imperfetto
bisogna**sse**

SINGULAR PLURAL

passato prossimo
è bisognato(a)

trapassato prossimo
era bisognato(a)

trapassato remoto
fu bisognato(a)

futuro anteriore
sarà bisognato(a)

condizionale passato
sarebbe bisognato(a)

congiuntivo passato
sia bisognato(a)

congiuntivo trapassato
fosse bisognato(a)

bloccare — to block, to prevent

gerundio **bloccando** — participio passato **bloccato**

SINGULAR	PLURAL	SINGULAR	PLURAL
indicativo presente		passato prossimo	
blocc**o**	blocc**hiamo**	**ho** bloccato	**abbiamo** bloccato
blocc**hi**	blocc**ate**	**hai** bloccato	**avete** bloccato
blocc**a**	blocc**ano**	**ha** bloccato	**hanno** bloccato
imperfetto		trapassato prossimo	
blocca**vo**	blocca**vamo**	**avevo** bloccato	**avevamo** bloccato
blocca**vi**	blocca**vate**	**avevi** bloccato	**avevate** bloccato
blocca**va**	blocca**vano**	**aveva** bloccato	**avevano** bloccato
passato remoto		trapassato remoto	
blocc**ai**	blocc**ammo**	**ebbi** bloccato	**avemmo** bloccato
blocc**asti**	blocc**aste**	**avesti** bloccato	**aveste** bloccato
blocc**ò**	blocc**arono**	**ebbe** bloccato	**ebbero** bloccato
futuro semplice		futuro anteriore	
blocche**rò**	blocche**remo**	**avrò** bloccato	**avremo** bloccato
blocche**rai**	blocche**rete**	**avrai** bloccato	**avrete** bloccato
blocche**rà**	blocche**ranno**	**avrà** bloccato	**avranno** bloccato
condizionale presente		condizionale passato	
blocche**rei**	blocche**remmo**	**avrei** bloccato	**avremmo** bloccato
blocche**resti**	blocche**reste**	**avresti** bloccato	**avreste** bloccato
blocche**rebbe**	blocche**rebbero**	**avrebbe** bloccato	**avrebbero** bloccato
congiuntivo presente		congiuntivo passato	
blocch**i**	blocch**iamo**	**abbia** bloccato	**abbiamo** bloccato
blocch**i**	blocch**iate**	**abbia** bloccato	**abbiate** bloccato
blocch**i**	blocch**ino**	**abbia** bloccato	**abbiano** bloccato
congiuntivo imperfetto		congiuntivo trapassato	
blocc**assi**	blocc**assimo**	**avessi** bloccato	**avessimo** bloccato
blocc**assi**	blocc**aste**	**avessi** bloccato	**aveste** bloccato
blocc**asse**	blocc**assero**	**avesse** bloccato	**avessero** bloccato
imperativo			
	blocchiamo		
blocca; non bloccare	bloccate		
blocchi	blocchino		

to fail, to reject, to vote down **bocciare**

gerundio **bocciando** participio passato **bocciato**

SINGULAR	PLURAL
indicativo presente	
bocc**io**	bocc**iamo**
bocc**i**	bocc**iate**
bocc**ia**	bocc**iano**
imperfetto	
boccia**vo**	boccia**vamo**
boccia**vi**	boccia**vate**
boccia**va**	boccia**vano**
passato remoto	
bocci**ai**	bocci**ammo**
bocci**asti**	bocci**aste**
bocci**ò**	bocci**arono**
futuro semplice	
bocce**rò**	bocce**remo**
bocce**rai**	bocce**rete**
bocce**rà**	bocce**ranno**
condizionale presente	
bocc**erei**	bocc**eremmo**
bocc**eresti**	bocc**ereste**
bocc**erebbe**	bocc**erebbero**
congiuntivo presente	
bocc**i**	bocc**iamo**
bocc**i**	bocc**iate**
bocc**i**	bocc**ino**
congiuntivo imperfetto	
bocci**assi**	bocci**assimo**
bocci**assi**	bocci**aste**
bocci**asse**	bocci**assero**
imperativo	
	bocciamo
boccia; non bocciare	bocciate
bocci	boccino

SINGULAR	PLURAL
passato prossimo	
ho bocciato	**abbiamo** bocciato
hai bocciato	**avete** bocciato
ha bocciato	**hanno** bocciato
trapassato prossimo	
avevo bocciato	**avevamo** bocciato
avevi bocciato	**avevate** bocciato
aveva bocciato	**avevano** bocciato
trapassato remoto	
ebbi bocciato	**avemmo** bocciato
avesti bocciato	**aveste** bocciato
ebbe bocciato	**ebbero** bocciato
futuro anteriore	
avrò bocciato	**avremo** bocciato
avrai bocciato	**avrete** bocciato
avrà bocciato	**avranno** bocciato
condizionale passato	
avrei bocciato	**avremmo** bocciato
avresti bocciato	**avreste** bocciato
avrebbe bocciato	**avrebbero** bocciato
congiuntivo passato	
abbia bocciato	**abbiamo** bocciato
abbia bocciato	**abbiate** bocciato
abbia bocciato	**abbiano** bocciato
congiuntivo trapassato	
avessi bocciato	**avessimo** bocciato
avessi bocciato	**aveste** bocciato
avesse bocciato	**avessero** bocciato

bollire — to boil

gerundio **bollendo** participio passato **bollito**

SINGULAR	PLURAL	SINGULAR	PLURAL
indicativo presente		passato prossimo	
boll**o**	boll**iamo**	**ho** bollito	**abbiamo** bollito
boll**i**	boll**ite**	**hai** bollito	**avete** bollito
boll**e**	boll**ono**	**ha** bollito	**hanno** bollito
imperfetto		trapassato prossimo	
bolli**vo**	bolli**vamo**	**avevo** bollito	**avevamo** bollito
bolli**vi**	bolli**vate**	**avevi** bollito	**avevate** bollito
bolli**va**	bolli**vano**	**aveva** bollito	**avevano** bollito
passato remoto		trapassato remoto	
boll**ii**	boll**immo**	**ebbi** bollito	**avemmo** bollito
boll**isti**	boll**iste**	**avesti** bollito	**aveste** bollito
boll**ì**	boll**irono**	**ebbe** bollito	**ebbero** bollito
futuro semplice		futuro anteriore	
bollir**ò**	bollir**emo**	**avrò** bollito	**avremo** bollito
bollir**ai**	bollir**ete**	**avrai** bollito	**avrete** bollito
bollir**à**	bollir**anno**	**avrà** bollito	**avranno** bollito
condizionale presente		condizionale passato	
boll**irei**	boll**iremmo**	**avrei** bollito	**avremmo** bollito
boll**iresti**	boll**ireste**	**avresti** bollito	**avreste** bollito
boll**irebbe**	boll**irebbero**	**avrebbe** bollito	**avrebbero** bollito
congiuntivo presente		congiuntivo passato	
boll**a**	boll**iamo**	**abbia** bollito	**abbiamo** bollito
boll**a**	boll**iate**	**abbia** bollito	**abbiate** bollito
boll**a**	boll**ano**	**abbia** bollito	**abbiano** bollito
congiuntivo imperfetto		congiuntivo trapassato	
boll**issi**	boll**issimo**	**avessi** bollito	**avessimo** bollito
boll**issi**	boll**iste**	**avessi** bollito	**aveste** bollito
boll**isse**	boll**issero**	**avesse** bollito	**avessero** bollito
imperativo			
	bolliamo		
bollisci; non bollire	bollite		
bolla	bollano		

gerundio **bruciando** participio passato **bruciato**

SINGULAR	PLURAL	SINGULAR	PLURAL
indicativo presente		passato prossimo	
bruc**io**	bruci**amo**	**ho** bruciato	**abbiamo** bruciato
bruc**i**	bruci**ate**	**hai** bruciato	**avete** bruciato
bruc**ia**	bruci**ano**	**ha** bruciato	**hanno** bruciato
imperfetto		trapassato prossimo	
brucia**vo**	brucia**vamo**	**avevo** bruciato	**avevamo** bruciato
brucia**vi**	brucia**vate**	**avevi** bruciato	**avevate** bruciato
brucia**va**	brucia**vano**	**aveva** bruciato	**avevano** bruciato
passato remoto		trapassato remoto	
bruci**ai**	bruci**ammo**	**ebbi** bruciato	**avemmo** bruciato
bruci**asti**	bruci**aste**	**avesti** bruciato	**aveste** bruciato
bruci**ò**	bruci**arono**	**ebbe** bruciato	**ebbero** bruciato
futuro semplice		futuro anteriore	
brucer**ò**	brucer**emo**	**avrò** bruciato	**avremo** bruciato
brucer**ai**	brucer**ete**	**avrai** bruciato	**avrete** bruciato
brucer**à**	brucer**anno**	**avrà** bruciato	**avranno** bruciato
condizionale presente		condizionale passato	
brucer**ei**	brucer**emmo**	**avrei** bruciato	**avremmo** bruciato
brucer**esti**	brucer**este**	**avresti** bruciato	**avreste** bruciato
brucer**ebbe**	brucer**ebbero**	**avrebbe** bruciato	**avrebbero** bruciato
congiuntivo presente		congiuntivo passato	
bruc**i**	bruci**amo**	**abbia** bruciato	**abbiamo** bruciato
bruc**i**	bruci**ate**	**abbia** bruciato	**abbiate** bruciato
bruc**i**	bruc**ino**	**abbia** bruciato	**abbiano** bruciato
congiuntivo imperfetto		congiuntivo trapassato	
bruci**assi**	bruci**assimo**	**avessi** bruciato	**avessimo** bruciato
bruci**assi**	bruci**aste**	**avessi** bruciato	**aveste** bruciato
bruci**asse**	bruci**assero**	**avesse** bruciato	**avessero** bruciato
imperativo			
	bruciamo		
brucia; non bruciare	bruciate		
bruci	brucino		

bruciarsi — to burn oneself

gerundio **bruciandosi** participio passato **bruciatosi**

SINGULAR	PLURAL
indicativo presente	
mi bruci**o**	**ci** bruc**iamo**
ti bruci	**vi** bruc**iate**
si bruci**a**	**si** bruc**iano**
imperfetto	
mi brucia**vo**	**ci** brucia**vamo**
ti brucia**vi**	**vi** brucia**vate**
si brucia**va**	**si** brucia**vano**
passato remoto	
mi bruci**ai**	**ci** bruci**ammo**
ti bruci**asti**	**vi** bruci**aste**
si bruci**ò**	**si** bruci**arono**
futuro semplice	
mi bruce**rò**	**ci** bruce**remo**
ti bruce**rai**	**vi** bruce**rete**
si bruce**rà**	**si** bruce**ranno**
condizionale presente	
mi bruc**erei**	**ci** bruc**eremmo**
ti bruc**eresti**	**vi** bruc**ereste**
si bruc**erebbe**	**si** bruc**erebbero**
congiuntivo presente	
mi bruci	**ci** bruc**iamo**
ti bruci	**vi** bruc**iate**
si bruci	**si** bruc**ino**
congiuntivo imperfetto	
mi bruci**assi**	**ci** bruci**assimo**
ti bruci**assi**	**vi** bruci**aste**
si bruci**asse**	**si** bruci**assero**
imperativo	
	bruciamoci
bruciati; non bruciarti/ non ti bruciare	bruciatevi
si bruci	si brucino

SINGULAR	PLURAL
passato prossimo	
mi sono bruciato(a)	**ci siamo** bruciati(e)
ti sei bruciato(a)	**vi siete** bruciati(e)
si è bruciato(a)	**si sono** bruciati(e)
trapassato prossimo	
mi ero bruciato(a)	**ci eravamo** bruciati(e)
ti eri bruciato(a)	**vi eravate** bruciati(e)
si era bruciato(a)	**si erano** bruciati(e)
trapassato remoto	
mi fui bruciato(a)	**ci fummo** bruciati(e)
ti fosti bruciato(a)	**vi foste** bruciati(e)
si fu bruciato(a)	**si furono** bruciati(e)
futuro anteriore	
mi sarò bruciato(a)	**ci saremo** bruciati(e)
ti sarai bruciato(a)	**vi sarete** bruciati(e)
si sarà bruciato(a)	**si saranno** bruciati(e)
condizionale passato	
mi sarei bruciato(a)	**ci saremmo** bruciati(e)
ti saresti bruciato(a)	**vi sareste** bruciati(e)
si sarebbe bruciato(a)	**si sarebbero** bruciati(e)
congiuntivo passato	
mi sia bruciato(a)	**ci siamo** bruciati(e)
ti sia bruciato(a)	**vi siate** bruciati(e)
si sia bruciato(a)	**si siano** bruciati(e)
congiuntivo trapassato	
mi fossi bruciato(a)	**ci fossimo** bruciati(e)
ti fossi bruciato(a)	**vi foste** bruciati(e)
si fosse bruciato(a)	**si fossero** bruciati(e)

to make fun of, to laugh at, to tease **burlarsi**

gerundio **burlandosi** participio passato **burlatosi**

SINGULAR	PLURAL	SINGULAR	PLURAL
indicativo presente		passato prossimo	
mi burl**o**	**ci** burl**iamo**	**mi sono** burlato(a)	**ci siamo** burlati(e)
ti burl**i**	**vi** burl**ate**	**ti sei** burlato(a)	**vi siete** burlati(e)
si burl**a**	**si** burl**ano**	**si è** burlato(a)	**si sono** burlati(e)
imperfetto		trapassato prossimo	
mi burla**vo**	**ci** burla**vamo**	**mi ero** burlato(a)	**ci eravamo** burlati(e)
ti burla**vi**	**vi** burla**vate**	**ti eri** burlato(a)	**vi eravate** burlati(e)
si burla**va**	**si** burla**vano**	**si era** burlato(a)	**si erano** burlati(e)
passato remoto		trapassato remoto	
mi burl**ai**	**ci** burl**ammo**	**mi fui** burlato(a)	**ci fummo** burlati(e)
ti burl**asti**	**vi** burl**aste**	**ti fosti** burlato(a)	**vi foste** burlati(e)
si burl**ò**	**si** burlar**ono**	**si fu** burlato(a)	**si furono** burlati(e)
futuro semplice		futuro anteriore	
mi burler**ò**	**ci** burler**emo**	**mi sarò** burlato(a)	**ci saremo** burlati(e)
ti burler**ai**	**vi** burler**ete**	**ti sarai** burlato(a)	**vi sarete** burlati(e)
si burler**à**	**si** burler**anno**	**si sarà** burlato(a)	**si saranno** burlati(e)
condizionale presente		condizionale passato	
mi burler**ei**	**ci** burler**emmo**	**mi sarei** burlato(a)	**ci saremmo** burlati(e)
ti burler**esti**	**vi** burler**este**	**ti saresti** burlato(a)	**vi sareste** burlati(e)
si burler**ebbe**	**si** burler**ebbero**	**si sarebbe** burlato(a)	**si sarebbero** burlati(e)
congiuntivo presente		congiuntivo passato	
mi burl**i**	**ci** burl**iamo**	**mi sia** burlato(a)	**ci siamo** burlati(e)
ti burl**i**	**vi** burl**iate**	**ti sia** burlato(a)	**vi siate** burlati(e)
si burl**i**	**si** burl**ino**	**si sia** burlato(a)	**si siano** burlati(e)
congiuntivo imperfetto		congiuntivo trapassato	
mi burl**assi**	**ci** burl**assimo**	**mi fossi** burlato(a)	**ci fossimo** burlati(e)
ti burl**assi**	**vi** burl**aste**	**ti fossi** burlato(a)	**vi foste** burlati(e)
si burl**asse**	**si** burl**assero**	**si fosse** burlato(a)	**si fossero** burlati(e)

imperativo

	burliamoci
burlati; non burlarti/ non ti burlare	burlatevi
si burli	si burlino

B

bussare — to knock

gerundio **bussando** participio passato **bussato**

indicativo presente

SINGULAR	PLURAL
buss**o**	buss**iamo**
buss**i**	buss**ate**
buss**a**	buss**ano**

imperfetto

SINGULAR	PLURAL
bussa**vo**	bussa**vamo**
bussa**vi**	bussa**vate**
bussa**va**	bussa**vano**

passato remoto

SINGULAR	PLURAL
buss**ai**	buss**ammo**
buss**asti**	buss**aste**
buss**ò**	buss**arono**

futuro semplice

SINGULAR	PLURAL
busser**ò**	busser**emo**
busser**ai**	busser**ete**
busser**à**	busser**anno**

condizionale presente

SINGULAR	PLURAL
busser**ei**	busser**emmo**
busser**esti**	busser**este**
busser**ebbe**	busser**ebbero**

congiuntivo presente

SINGULAR	PLURAL
buss**i**	buss**iamo**
buss**i**	buss**iate**
buss**i**	buss**ino**

congiuntivo imperfetto

SINGULAR	PLURAL
buss**assi**	buss**assimo**
buss**assi**	buss**aste**
buss**asse**	buss**assero**

imperativo

SINGULAR	PLURAL
	bussiamo
bussa; non bussare	bussate
bussi	bussino

passato prossimo

SINGULAR	PLURAL
ho bussato	**abbiamo** bussato
hai bussato	**avete** bussato
ha bussato	**hanno** bussato

trapassato prossimo

SINGULAR	PLURAL
avevo bussato	**avevamo** bussato
avevi bussato	**avevate** bussato
aveva bussato	**avevano** bussato

trapassato remoto

SINGULAR	PLURAL
ebbi bussato	**avemmo** bussato
avesti bussato	**aveste** bussato
ebbe bussato	**ebbero** bussato

futuro anteriore

SINGULAR	PLURAL
avrò bussato	**avremo** bussato
avrai bussato	**avrete** bussato
avrà bussato	**avranno** bussato

condizionale passato

SINGULAR	PLURAL
avrei bussato	**avremmo** bussato
avresti bussato	**avreste** bussato
avrebbe bussato	**avrebbero** bussato

congiuntivo passato

SINGULAR	PLURAL
abbia bussato	**abbiamo** bussato
abbia bussato	**abbiate** bussato
abbia bussato	**abbiano** bussato

congiuntivo trapassato

SINGULAR	PLURAL
avessi bussato	**avessimo** bussato
avessi bussato	**aveste** bussato
avesse bussato	**avessero** bussato

gerundio **buttando** participio passato **buttato**

SINGULAR	PLURAL	SINGULAR	PLURAL
indicativo presente		passato prossimo	
butt**o**	butt**iamo**	**ho** buttato	**abbiamo** buttato
butt**i**	butt**ate**	**hai** buttato	**avete** buttato
butt**a**	butt**ano**	**ha** buttato	**hanno** buttato
imperfetto		trapassato prossimo	
butta**vo**	butta**vamo**	**avevo** buttato	**avevamo** buttato
butta**vi**	butta**vate**	**avevi** buttato	**avevate** buttato
butta**va**	butta**vano**	**aveva** buttato	**avevano** buttato
passato remoto		trapassato remoto	
butt**ai**	butt**ammo**	**ebbi** buttato	**avemmo** buttato
butt**asti**	butt**aste**	**avesti** buttato	**aveste** buttato
butt**ò**	butt**arono**	**ebbe** buttato	**ebbero** buttato
futuro semplice		futuro anteriore	
butter**ò**	butter**emo**	**avrò** buttato	**avremo** buttato
butter**ai**	butter**ete**	**avrai** buttato	**avrete** buttato
butter**à**	butter**anno**	**avrà** buttato	**avranno** buttato
condizionale presente		condizionale passato	
butter**ei**	butter**emmo**	**avrei** buttato	**avremmo** buttato
butter**esti**	butter**este**	**avresti** buttato	**avreste** buttato
butter**ebbe**	butter**ebbero**	**avrebbe** buttato	**avrebbero** buttato
congiuntivo presente		congiuntivo passato	
butt**i**	butt**iamo**	**abbia** buttato	**abbiamo** buttato
butt**i**	butt**iate**	**abbia** buttato	**abbiate** buttato
butt**i**	butt**ino**	**abbia** buttato	**abbiano** buttato
congiuntivo imperfetto		congiuntivo trapassato	
butt**assi**	butt**assimo**	**avessi** buttato	**avessimo** buttato
butt**assi**	butt**aste**	**avessi** buttato	**aveste** buttato
butt**asse**	butt**assero**	**avesse** buttato	**avessero** buttato
imperativo			
	buttiamo		
butta; non buttare	buttate		
butti	buttino		

buttarsi — to throw oneself

gerundio **buttandosi** participio passato **buttatosi**

SINGULAR	PLURAL
indicativo presente	
mi butt**o**	**ci** butt**iamo**
ti butt**i**	**vi** butt**ate**
si butt**a**	**si** butt**ano**
imperfetto	
mi butta**vo**	**ci** butta**vamo**
ti butta**vi**	**vi** butta**vate**
si butta**va**	**si** butta**vano**
passato remoto	
mi butt**ai**	**ci** butt**ammo**
ti butt**asti**	**vi** butt**aste**
si butt**ò**	**si** butt**arono**
futuro semplice	
mi butter**ò**	**ci** butter**emo**
ti butter**ai**	**vi** butter**ete**
si butter**à**	**si** butter**anno**
condizionale presente	
mi butter**ei**	**ci** butter**emmo**
ti butter**esti**	**vi** butter**este**
si butter**ebbe**	**si** butter**ebbero**
congiuntivo presente	
mi butt**i**	**ci** butt**iamo**
ti butt**i**	**vi** butt**iate**
si butt**i**	**si** butt**ino**
congiuntivo imperfetto	
mi butt**assi**	**ci** butt**assimo**
ti butt**assi**	**vi** butt**aste**
si butt**asse**	**si** butt**assero**
imperativo	
	buttiamoci
buttati; non buttarti/ non ti buttare	buttatevi
si butti	si buttino

SINGULAR	PLURAL
passato prossimo	
mi sono buttato(a)	**ci siamo** buttati(e)
ti sei buttato(a)	**vi siete** buttati(e)
si è buttato(a)	**si sono** buttati(e)
trapassato prossimo	
mi ero buttato(a)	**ci eravamo** buttati(e)
ti eri buttato(a)	**vi eravate** buttati(e)
si era buttato(a)	**si erano** buttati(e)
trapassato remoto	
mi fui buttato(a)	**ci fummo** buttati(e)
ti fosti buttato(a)	**vi foste** buttati(e)
si fu buttato(a)	**si furono** buttati(e)
futuro anteriore	
mi sarò buttato(a)	**ci saremo** buttati(e)
ti sarai buttato(a)	**vi sarete** buttati(e)
si sarà buttato(a)	**si saranno** buttati(e)
condizionale passato	
mi sarei buttato(a)	**ci saremmo** buttati(e)
ti saresti buttato(a)	**vi sareste** buttati(e)
si sarebbe buttato(a)	**si sarebbero** buttati(e)
congiuntivo passato	
mi sia buttato(a)	**ci siamo** buttati(e)
ti sia buttato(a)	**vi siate** buttati(e)
si sia buttato(a)	**si siano** buttati(e)
congiuntivo trapassato	
mi fossi buttato(a)	**ci fossimo** buttati(e)
ti fossi buttato(a)	**vi foste** buttati(e)
si fosse buttato(a)	**si fossero** buttati(e)

gerundio **cadendo** participio passato **caduto**

SINGULAR	PLURAL	SINGULAR	PLURAL
indicativo presente		passato prossimo	
cad**o**	cad**iamo**	**sono** caduto(a)	**siamo** caduti(e)
cad**i**	cad**ete**	**sei** caduto(a)	**siete** caduti(e)
cad**e**	cad**ono**	**è** caduto(a)	**sono** caduti(e)
imperfetto		trapassato prossimo	
cade**vo**	cade**vamo**	**ero** caduto(a)	**eravamo** caduti(e)
cade**vi**	cade**vate**	**eri** caduto(a)	**eravate** caduti(e)
cade**va**	cade**vano**	**era** caduto(a)	**erano** caduti(e)
passato remoto		trapassato remoto	
cadd**i**	cad**emmo**	**fui** caduto(a)	**fummo** caduti(e)
cad**esti**	cad**este**	**fosti** caduto(a)	**foste** caduti(e)
cadd**e**	cadd**ero**	**fu** caduto(a)	**furono** caduti(e)
futuro semplice		futuro anteriore	
cadr**ò**	cadr**emo**	**sarò** caduto(a)	**saremo** caduti(e)
cadr**ai**	cadr**ete**	**sarai** caduto(a)	**sarete** caduti(e)
cadr**à**	cadr**anno**	**sarà** caduto(a)	**saranno** caduti(e)
condizionale presente		condizionale passato	
cadr**ei**	cadr**emmo**	**sarei** caduto(a)	**saremmo** caduti(e)
cadr**esti**	cadr**este**	**saresti** caduto(a)	**sareste** caduti(e)
cadr**ebbe**	cadr**ebbero**	**sarebbe** caduto(a)	**sarebbero** caduti(e)
congiuntivo presente		congiuntivo passato	
cad**a**	cad**iamo**	**sia** caduto(a)	**siamo** caduti(e)
cad**a**	cad**iate**	**sia** caduto(a)	**siate** caduti(e)
cad**a**	cad**ano**	**sia** caduto(a)	**siano** caduti(e)
congiuntivo imperfetto		congiuntivo trapassato	
cad**essi**	cad**essimo**	**fossi** caduto(a)	**fossimo** caduti(e)
cad**essi**	cad**este**	**fossi** caduto(a)	**foste** caduti(e)
cad**esse**	cad**essero**	**fosse** caduto(a)	**fossero** caduti(e)
imperativo			
	cadiamo		
cadi; non cadere	cadete		
cada	cadano		

calcolare to calculate, to compute, to estimate

gerundio **calcolando** participio passato **calcolato**

C

SINGULAR	PLURAL	SINGULAR	PLURAL
indicativo presente		passato prossimo	
calcol**o**	calcol**iamo**	**ho** calcolato	**abbiamo** calcolato
calcol**i**	calcol**ate**	**hai** calcolato	**avete** calcolato
calcol**a**	calcol**ano**	**ha** calcolato	**hanno** calcolato
imperfetto		trapassato prossimo	
calcola**vo**	calcola**vamo**	**avevo** calcolato	**avevamo** calcolato
calcola**vi**	calcola**vate**	**avevi** calcolato	**avevate** calcolato
calcola**va**	calcola**vano**	**aveva** calcolato	**avevano** calcolato
passato remoto		trapassato remoto	
calcol**ai**	calcol**ammo**	**ebbi** calcolato	**avemmo** calcolato
calcol**asti**	calcol**aste**	**avesti** calcolato	**aveste** calcolato
calcol**ò**	calcol**arono**	**ebbe** calcolato	**ebbero** calcolato
futuro semplice		futuro anteriore	
calcoler**ò**	calcoler**emo**	**avrò** calcolato	**avremo** calcolato
calcoler**ai**	calcoler**ete**	**avrai** calcolato	**avrete** calcolato
calcoler**à**	calcoler**anno**	**avrà** calcolato	**avranno** calcolato
condizionale presente		condizionale passato	
calcoler**ei**	calcoler**emmo**	**avrei** calcolato	**avremmo** calcolato
calcoler**esti**	calcoler**este**	**avresti** calcolato	**avreste** calcolato
calcoler**ebbe**	calcoler**ebbero**	**avrebbe** calcolato	**avrebbero** calcolato
congiuntivo presente		congiuntivo passato	
calcol**i**	calcol**iamo**	**abbia** calcolato	**abbiamo** calcolato
calcol**i**	calcol**iate**	**abbia** calcolato	**abbiate** calcolato
calcol**i**	calcol**ino**	**abbia** calcolato	**abbiano** calcolato
congiuntivo imperfetto		congiuntivo trapassato	
calcol**assi**	calcol**assimo**	**avessi** calcolato	**avessimo** calcolato
calcol**assi**	calcol**aste**	**avessi** calcolato	**aveste** calcolato
calcol**asse**	calcol**assero**	**avesse** calcolato	**avessero** calcolato

imperativo

	calcoliamo
calcola; non calcolare	calcolate
calcoli	calcolino

gerundio **calmandosi** participio passato **calmatosi**

SINGULAR	PLURAL	SINGULAR	PLURAL
indicativo presente		passato prossimo	
mi calm**o**	**ci** calm**iamo**	**mi sono** calmato(a)	**ci siamo** calmati(e)
ti calm**i**	**vi** calm**ate**	**ti sei** calmato(a)	**vi siete** calmati(e)
si calm**a**	**si** calm**ano**	**si è** calmato(a)	**si sono** calmati(e)
imperfetto		trapassato prossimo	
mi calma**vo**	**ci** calma**vamo**	**mi ero** calmato(a)	**ci eravamo** calmati(e)
ti calma**vi**	**vi** calma**vate**	**ti eri** calmato(a)	**vi eravate** calmati(e)
si calma**va**	**si** calma**vano**	**si era** calmato(a)	**si erano** calmati(e)
passato remoto		trapassato remoto	
mi calm**ai**	**ci** calm**ammo**	**mi fui** calmato(a)	**ci fummo** calmati(e)
ti calm**asti**	**vi** calm**aste**	**ti fosti** calmato(a)	**vi foste** calmati(e)
si calm**ò**	**si** calm**arono**	**si fu** calmato(a)	**si furono** calmati(e)
futuro semplice		futuro anteriore	
mi calmer**ò**	**ci** calmer**emo**	**mi sarò** calmato(a)	**ci saremo** calmati(e)
ti calmer**ai**	**vi** calmer**ete**	**ti sarai** calmato(a)	**vi sarete** calmati(e)
si calmer**à**	**si** calmer**anno**	**si sarà** calmato(a)	**si saranno** calmati(e)
condizionale presente		condizionale passato	
mi calmer**ei**	**ci** calmer**emmo**	**mi sarei** calmato(a)	**ci saremmo** calmati(e)
ti calmer**esti**	**vi** calmer**este**	**ti saresti** calmato(a)	**vi sareste** calmati(e)
si calmer**ebbe**	**si** calmer**ebbero**	**si sarebbe** calmato(a)	**si sarebbero** calmati(e)
congiuntivo presente		congiuntivo passato	
mi calm**i**	**ci** calm**iamo**	**mi sia** calmato(a)	**ci siamo** calmati(e)
ti calm**i**	**vi** calm**iate**	**ti sia** calmato(a)	**vi siate** calmati(e)
si calm**i**	**si** calm**ino**	**si sia** calmato(a)	**si siano** calmati(e)
congiuntivo imperfetto		congiuntivo trapassato	
mi calm**assi**	**ci** calm**assimo**	**mi fossi** calmato(a)	**ci fossimo** calmati(e)
ti calm**assi**	**vi** calm**aste**	**ti fossi** calmato(a)	**vi foste** calmati(e)
si calm**asse**	**si** calm**assero**	**si fosse** calmato(a)	**si fossero** calmati(e)
imperativo			
	calmiamoci		
calmati; non calmarti/non ti calmare	calmatevi		
si calmi	si calmino		

C

cambiare — to change

gerundio **cambiando** — participio passato **cambiato**

C

SINGULAR	PLURAL	SINGULAR	PLURAL
indicativo presente		passato prossimo	
cambi**o**	camb**iamo**	**ho** cambiato	**abbiamo** cambiato
camb**i**	cambi**ate**	**hai** cambiato	**avete** cambiato
cambi**a**	camb**iano**	**ha** cambiato	**hanno** cambiato
imperfetto		trapassato prossimo	
cambia**vo**	cambia**vamo**	**avevo** cambiato	**avevamo** cambiato
cambia**vi**	cambia**vate**	**avevi** cambiato	**avevate** cambiato
cambia**va**	cambia**vano**	**aveva** cambiato	**avevano** cambiato
passato remoto		trapassato remoto	
cambi**ai**	cambi**ammo**	**ebbi** cambiato	**avemmo** cambiato
cambi**asti**	cambi**aste**	**avesti** cambiato	**aveste** cambiato
cambi**ò**	cambi**arono**	**ebbe** cambiato	**ebbero** cambiato
futuro semplice		futuro anteriore	
cambier**ò**	cambier**emo**	**avrò** cambiato	**avremo** cambiato
cambier**ai**	cambier**ete**	**avrai** cambiato	**avrete** cambiato
cambier**à**	cambier**anno**	**avrà** cambiato	**avranno** cambiato
condizionale presente		condizionale passato	
cambier**ei**	cambier**emmo**	**avrei** cambiato	**avremmo** cambiato
cambier**esti**	cambier**este**	**avresti** cambiato	**avreste** cambiato
cambier**ebbe**	cambier**ebbero**	**avrebbe** cambiato	**avrebbero** cambiato
congiuntivo presente		congiuntivo passato	
camb**i**	camb**iamo**	**abbia** cambiato	**abbiamo** cambiato
camb**i**	camb**iate**	**abbia** cambiato	**abbiate** cambiato
camb**i**	camb**ino**	**abbia** cambiato	**abbiano** cambiato
congiuntivo imperfetto		congiuntivo trapassato	
cambi**assi**	cambi**assimo**	**avessi** cambiato	**avessimo** cambiato
cambi**assi**	cambi**aste**	**avessi** cambiato	**aveste** cambiato
cambi**asse**	cambi**assero**	**avesse** cambiato	**avessero** cambiato

imperativo

	cambiamo
cambia; non cambiare	cambiate
cambi	cambino

to walk **camminare**

gerundio **camminando** participio passato **camminato**

SINGULAR	PLURAL	SINGULAR	PLURAL
indicativo presente		passato prossimo	
cammin**o**	cammin**iamo**	**ho** camminato	**abbiamo** camminato
cammin**i**	cammin**ate**	**hai** camminato	**avete** camminato
cammin**a**	cammin**ano**	**ha** camminato	**hanno** camminato
imperfetto		trapassato prossimo	
cammina**vo**	cammina**vamo**	**avevo** camminato	**avevamo** camminato
cammina**vi**	cammina**vate**	**avevi** camminato	**avevate** camminato
cammina**va**	cammina**vano**	**aveva** camminato	**avevano** camminato
passato remoto		trapassato remoto	
cammin**ai**	cammin**ammo**	**ebbi** camminato	**avemmo** camminato
cammin**asti**	cammin**aste**	**avesti** camminato	**aveste** camminato
cammin**ò**	cammin**arono**	**ebbe** camminato	**ebbero** camminato
futuro semplice		futuro anteriore	
camminer**ò**	camminer**emo**	**avrò** camminato	**avremo** camminato
camminer**ai**	camminer**ete**	**avrai** camminato	**avrete** camminato
camminer**à**	camminer**anno**	**avrà** camminato	**avranno** camminato
condizionale presente		condizionale passato	
camminer**ei**	camminer**emmo**	**avrei** camminato	**avremmo** camminato
camminer**esti**	camminer**este**	**avresti** camminato	**avreste** camminato
camminer**ebbe**	camminer**ebbero**	**avrebbe** camminato	**avrebbero** camminato
congiuntivo presente		congiuntivo passato	
cammin**i**	cammin**iamo**	**abbia** camminato	**abbiamo** camminato
cammin**i**	cammin**iate**	**abbia** camminato	**abbiate** camminato
cammin**i**	cammin**ino**	**abbia** camminato	**abbiano** camminato
congiuntivo imperfetto		congiuntivo trapassato	
cammin**assi**	cammin**assimo**	**avessi** camminato	**avessimo** camminato
cammin**assi**	cammin**aste**	**avessi** camminato	**aveste** camminato
cammin**asse**	cammin**assero**	**avesse** camminato	**avessero** camminato
imperativo			
	camminiamo		
cammina; non camminare	camminate		
cammini	camminino		

C

cancellare — to erase, to cancel, to cross out

gerundio **cancellando** — participio passato **cancellato**

C

SINGULAR	PLURAL	SINGULAR	PLURAL
indicativo presente		passato prossimo	
cancell**o**	cancell**iamo**	**ho** cancellato	**abbiamo** cancellato
cancell**i**	cancell**ate**	**hai** cancellato	**avete** cancellato
cancell**a**	cancell**ano**	**ha** cancellato	**hanno** cancellato
imperfetto		trapassato prossimo	
cancella**vo**	cancella**vamo**	**avevo** cancellato	**avevamo** cancellato
cancella**vi**	cancella**vate**	**avevi** cancellato	**avevate** cancellato
cancella**va**	cancella**vano**	**aveva** cancellato	**avevano** cancellato
passato remoto		trapassato remoto	
cancell**ai**	cancell**ammo**	**ebbi** cancellato	**avemmo** cancellato
cancell**asti**	cancell**aste**	**avesti** cancellato	**aveste** cancellato
cancell**ò**	cancell**arono**	**ebbe** cancellato	**ebbero** cancellato
futuro semplice		futuro anteriore	
canceller**ò**	canceller**emo**	**avrò** cancellato	**avremo** cancellato
canceller**ai**	canceller**ete**	**avrai** cancellato	**avrete** cancellato
canceller**à**	canceller**anno**	**avrà** cancellato	**avranno** cancellato
condizionale presente		condizionale passato	
canceller**ei**	canceller**emmo**	**avrei** cancellato	**avremmo** cancellato
canceller**esti**	canceller**este**	**avresti** cancellato	**avreste** cancellato
canceller**ebbe**	canceller**ebbero**	**avrebbe** cancellato	**avrebbero** cancellato
congiuntivo presente		congiuntivo passato	
cancell**i**	cancell**iamo**	**abbia** cancellato	**abbiamo** cancellato
cancell**i**	cancell**iate**	**abbia** cancellato	**abbiate** cancellato
cancell**i**	cancell**ino**	**abbia** cancellato	**abbiano** cancellato
congiuntivo imperfetto		congiuntivo trapassato	
cancell**assi**	cancell**assimo**	**avessi** cancellato	**avessimo** cancellato
cancell**assi**	cancell**aste**	**avessi** cancellato	**aveste** cancellato
cancell**asse**	cancell**assero**	**avesse** cancellato	**avessero** cancellato
imperativo			
	cancelliamo		
cancella; non cancellare	cancellate		
cancelli	cancellino		

to sing **cantare**

gerundio **cantando** participio passato **cantato**

SINGULAR	PLURAL	SINGULAR	PLURAL
indicativo presente		passato prossimo	
cant**o**	cant**iamo**	**ho** cantato	**abbiamo** cantato
cant**i**	cant**ate**	**hai** cantato	**avete** cantato
cant**a**	cant**ano**	**ha** cantato	**hanno** cantato
imperfetto		trapassato prossimo	
canta**vo**	canta**vamo**	**avevo** cantato	**avevamo** cantato
canta**vi**	canta**vate**	**avevi** cantato	**avevate** cantato
canta**va**	canta**vano**	**aveva** cantato	**avevano** cantato
passato remoto		trapassato remoto	
cant**ai**	cant**ammo**	**ebbi** cantato	**avemmo** cantato
cant**asti**	cant**aste**	**avesti** cantato	**aveste** cantato
cant**ò**	cant**arono**	**ebbe** cantato	**ebbero** cantato
futuro semplice		futuro anteriore	
canter**ò**	canter**emo**	**avrò** cantato	**avremo** cantato
canter**ai**	canter**ete**	**avrai** cantato	**avrete** cantato
canter**à**	canter**anno**	**avrà** cantato	**avranno** cantato
condizionale presente		condizionale passato	
canter**ei**	canter**emmo**	**avrei** cantato	**avremmo** cantato
canter**esti**	canter**este**	**avresti** cantato	**avreste** cantato
canter**ebbe**	canter**ebbero**	**avrebbe** cantato	**avrebbero** cantato
congiuntivo presente		congiuntivo passato	
cant**i**	cant**iamo**	**abbia** cantato	**abbiamo** cantato
cant**i**	cant**iate**	**abbia** cantato	**abbiate** cantato
cant**i**	cant**ino**	**abbia** cantato	**abbiano** cantato
congiuntivo imperfetto		congiuntivo trapassato	
cant**assi**	cant**assimo**	**avessi** cantato	**avessimo** cantato
cant**assi**	cant**aste**	**avessi** cantato	**aveste** cantato
cant**asse**	cant**assero**	**avesse** cantato	**avessero** cantato
imperativo			
	cantiamo		
canta; non cantare	cantate		
canti	cantino		

C

capire

to understand

gerundio **capendo** participio passato **capito**

SINGULAR	PLURAL	SINGULAR	PLURAL
indicativo presente		passato prossimo	
capisc**o**	cap**iamo**	**ho** capito	**abbiamo** capito
capisc**i**	cap**ite**	**hai** capito	**avete** capito
capisc**e**	capisc**ono**	**ha** capito	**hanno** capito
imperfetto		trapassato prossimo	
capi**vo**	capi**vamo**	**avevo** capito	**avevamo** capito
capi**vi**	capi**vate**	**avevi** capito	**avevate** capito
capi**va**	capi**vano**	**aveva** capito	**avevano** capito
passato remoto		trapassato remoto	
cap**ii**	cap**immo**	**ebbi** capito	**avemmo** capito
cap**isti**	cap**iste**	**avesti** capito	**aveste** capito
cap**ì**	cap**irono**	**ebbe** capito	**ebbero** capito
futuro semplice		futuro anteriore	
capir**ò**	capir**emo**	**avrò** capito	**avremo** capito
capir**ai**	capir**ete**	**avrai** capito	**avrete** capito
capir**à**	capir**anno**	**avrà** capito	**avranno** capito
condizionale presente		condizionale passato	
capir**ei**	capir**emmo**	**avrei** capito	**avremmo** capito
capir**esti**	capir**este**	**avresti** capito	**avreste** capito
capir**ebbe**	capir**ebbero**	**avrebbe** capito	**avrebbero** capito
congiuntivo presente		congiuntivo passato	
capisc**a**	cap**iamo**	**abbia** capito	**abbiamo** capito
capisc**a**	cap**iate**	**abbia** capito	**abbiate** capito
capisc**a**	capisc**ano**	**abbia** capito	**abbiano** capito
congiuntivo imperfetto		congiuntivo trapassato	
cap**issi**	cap**issimo**	**avessi** capito	**avessimo** capito
cap**issi**	cap**iste**	**avessi** capito	**aveste** capito
cap**isse**	cap**issero**	**avesse** capito	**avessero** capito
imperativo			
	capiamo		
capisci; non capire	capite		
capisca	capiscano		

to fall, to fall down **cascare**

gerundio **cascando** participio passato **cascato**

SINGULAR	PLURAL	SINGULAR	PLURAL
indicativo presente		passato prossimo	
casc**o**	casch**iamo**	**sono** cascato(a)	**siamo** cascati(e)
casch**i**	casc**ate**	**sei** cascato(a)	**siete** cascati(e)
casc**a**	casc**ano**	**è** cascato(a)	**sono** cascati(e)
imperfetto		trapassato prossimo	
casca**vo**	casca**vamo**	**ero** cascato(a)	**eravamo** cascati(e)
casca**vi**	casca**vate**	**eri** cascato(a)	**eravate** cascati(e)
casca**va**	casca**vano**	**era** cascato(a)	**erano** cascati(e)
passato remoto		trapassato remoto	
casc**ai**	casc**ammo**	**fui** cascato(a)	**fummo** cascati(e)
casc**asti**	casc**aste**	**fosti** cascato(a)	**foste** cascati(e)
casc**ò**	casc**arono**	**fu** cascato(a)	**furono** cascati(e)
futuro semplice		futuro anteriore	
casche**rò**	casche**remo**	**sarò** cascato(a)	**saremo** cascati(e)
casche**rai**	casche**rete**	**sarai** cascato(a)	**sarete** cascati(e)
casche**rà**	casche**ranno**	**sarà** cascato(a)	**saranno** cascati(e)
condizionale presente		condizionale passato	
casche**rei**	casche**remmo**	**sarei** cascato(a)	**saremmo** cascati(e)
casche**resti**	casche**reste**	**saresti** cascato(a)	**sareste** cascati(e)
casche**rebbe**	casche**rebbero**	**sarebbe** cascato(a)	**sarebbero** cascati(e)
congiuntivo presente		congiuntivo passato	
casch**i**	casch**iamo**	**sia** cascato(a)	**siamo** cascati(e)
casch**i**	casch**iate**	**sia** cascato(a)	**siate** cascati(e)
casch**i**	casch**ino**	**sia** cascato(a)	**siano** cascati(e)
congiuntivo imperfetto		congiuntivo trapassato	
casc**assi**	casc**assimo**	**fossi** cascato(a)	**fossimo** cascati(e)
casc**assi**	casc**aste**	**fossi** cascato(a)	**foste** cascati(e)
casc**asse**	casc**assero**	**fosse** cascato(a)	**fossero** cascati(e)
imperativo			
	caschiamo		
casca; non cascare	cascate		
caschi	caschino		

C

causare — to cause, to bring about

gerundio **causando** participio passato **causato**

SINGULAR	PLURAL	SINGULAR	PLURAL
indicativo presente		passato prossimo	
caus**o**	caus**iamo**	**ho** causato	**abbiamo** causato
caus**i**	caus**ate**	**hai** causato	**avete** causato
caus**a**	caus**ano**	**ha** causato	**hanno** causato
imperfetto		trapassato prossimo	
causa**vo**	causa**vamo**	**avevo** causato	**avevamo** causato
causa**vi**	causa**vate**	**avevi** causato	**avevate** causato
causa**va**	causa**vano**	**aveva** causato	**avevano** causato
passato remoto		trapassato remoto	
caus**ai**	caus**ammo**	**ebbi** causato	**avemmo** causato
caus**asti**	caus**aste**	**avesti** causato	**aveste** causato
caus**ò**	caus**arono**	**ebbe** causato	**ebbero** causato
futuro semplice		futuro anteriore	
causer**ò**	causer**emo**	**avrò** causato	**avremo** causato
causer**ai**	causer**ete**	**avrai** causato	**avrete** causato
causer**à**	causer**anno**	**avrà** causato	**avranno** causato
condizionale presente		condizionale passato	
causer**ei**	causer**emmo**	**avrei** causato	**avremmo** causato
causer**esti**	causer**este**	**avresti** causato	**avreste** causato
causer**ebbe**	causer**ebbero**	**avrebbe** causato	**avrebbero** causato
congiuntivo presente		congiuntivo passato	
caus**i**	caus**iamo**	**abbia** causato	**abbiamo** causato
caus**i**	caus**iate**	**abbia** causato	**abbiate** causato
caus**i**	caus**ino**	**abbia** causato	**abbiano** causato
congiuntivo imperfetto		congiuntivo trapassato	
caus**assi**	caus**assimo**	**avessi** causato	**avessimo** causato
caus**assi**	caus**aste**	**avessi** causato	**aveste** causato
caus**asse**	caus**assero**	**avesse** causato	**avessero** causato
imperativo			
	causiamo		
causa; non causare	causate		
causi	causino		

to yield, to surrender, to grant **cedere**

gerundio **cedendo** participio passato **ceduto**

SINGULAR	PLURAL	SINGULAR	PLURAL
indicativo presente		passato prossimo	
ced**o**	ced**iamo**	**ho** ceduto	**abbiamo** ceduto
ced**i**	ced**ete**	**hai** ceduto	**avete** ceduto
ced**e**	ced**ono**	**ha** ceduto	**hanno** ceduto
imperfetto		trapassato prossimo	
cede**vo**	cede**vamo**	**avevo** ceduto	**avevamo** ceduto
cede**vi**	cede**vate**	**avevi** ceduto	**avevate** ceduto
cede**va**	cede**vano**	**aveva** ceduto	**avevano** ceduto
passato remoto		trapassato remoto	
ced**ei**, ced**etti**	ced**emmo**	**ebbi** ceduto	**avemmo** ceduto
ced**esti**	ced**este**	**avesti** ceduto	**aveste** ceduto
ced**é**, ced**ette**	ced**erono**, ced**ettero**	**ebbe** ceduto	**ebbero** ceduto
futuro semplice		futuro anteriore	
ceder**ò**	ceder**emo**	**avrò** ceduto	**avremo** ceduto
ceder**ai**	ceder**ete**	**avrai** ceduto	**avrete** ceduto
ceder**à**	ceder**anno**	**avrà** ceduto	**avranno** ceduto
condizionale presente		condizionale passato	
ceder**ei**	ceder**emmo**	**avrei** ceduto	**avremmo** ceduto
ceder**esti**	ceder**este**	**avresti** ceduto	**avreste** ceduto
ceder**ebbe**	ceder**ebbero**	**avrebbe** ceduto	**avrebbero** ceduto
congiuntivo presente		congiuntivo passato	
ced**a**	ced**iamo**	**abbia** ceduto	**abbiamo** ceduto
ced**a**	ced**iate**	**abbia** ceduto	**abbiate** ceduto
ced**a**	ced**ano**	**abbia** ceduto	**abbiano** ceduto
congiuntivo imperfetto		congiuntivo trapassato	
ced**essi**	ced**essimo**	**avessi** ceduto	**avessimo** ceduto
ced**essi**	ced**este**	**avessi** ceduto	**aveste** ceduto
ced**esse**	ced**essero**	**avesse** ceduto	**avessero** ceduto
imperativo			
	cediamo		
cedi; non cedere	cedete		
ceda	cedano		

C

celebrare — to celebrate, to praise

gerundio **celebrando** — participio passato **celebrato**

SINGULAR	PLURAL	SINGULAR	PLURAL
indicativo presente		passato prossimo	
celebr**o**	celebr**iamo**	**ho** celebrato	**abbiamo** celebrato
celebr**i**	celebr**ate**	**hai** celebrato	**avete** celebrato
celebr**a**	celebr**ano**	**ha** celebrato	**hanno** celebrato
imperfetto		trapassato prossimo	
celebra**vo**	celebra**vamo**	**avevo** celebrato	**avevamo** celebrato
celebra**vi**	celebra**vate**	**avevi** celebrato	**avevate** celebrato
celebra**va**	celebra**vano**	**aveva** celebrato	**avevano** celebrato
passato remoto		trapassato remoto	
celebr**ai**	celebr**ammo**	**ebbi** celebrato	**avemmo** celebrato
celebr**asti**	celebr**aste**	**avesti** celebrato	**aveste** celebrato
celebr**ò**	celebr**arono**	**ebbe** celebrato	**ebbero** celebrato
futuro semplice		futuro anteriore	
celebrer**ò**	celebrer**emo**	**avrò** celebrato	**avremo** celebrato
celebrer**ai**	celebrer**ete**	**avrai** celebrato	**avrete** celebrato
celebrer**à**	celebrer**anno**	**avrà** celebrato	**avranno** celebrato
condizionale presente		condizionale passato	
celebrer**ei**	celebrer**emmo**	**avrei** celebrato	**avremmo** celebrato
celebrer**esti**	celebrer**este**	**avresti** celebrato	**avreste** celebrato
celebrer**ebbe**	celebrer**ebbero**	**avrebbe** celebrato	**avrebbero** celebrato
congiuntivo presente		congiuntivo passato	
celebr**i**	celebr**iamo**	**abbia** celebrato	**abbiamo** celebrato
celebr**i**	celebr**iate**	**abbia** celebrato	**abbiate** celebrato
celebr**i**	celebr**ino**	**abbia** celebrato	**abbiano** celebrato
congiuntivo imperfetto		congiuntivo trapassato	
celebr**assi**	celebr**assimo**	**avessi** celebrato	**avessimo** celebrato
celebr**assi**	celebr**aste**	**avessi** celebrato	**aveste** celebrato
celebr**asse**	celebr**assero**	**avesse** celebrato	**avessero** celebrato
imperativo			
	celebriamo		
celebra; non celebrare	celebrate		
celebri	celebrino		

to have dinner **cenare**

gerundio **cenando**

participio passato **cenato**

indicativo presente

SINGULAR	PLURAL
cen**o**	cen**iamo**
cen**i**	cen**ate**
cen**a**	cen**ano**

imperfetto

SINGULAR	PLURAL
cena**vo**	cena**vamo**
cena**vi**	cena**vate**
cena**va**	cena**vano**

passato remoto

SINGULAR	PLURAL
cen**ai**	cen**ammo**
cen**asti**	cen**aste**
cen**ò**	cen**arono**

futuro semplice

SINGULAR	PLURAL
cener**ò**	cener**emo**
cener**ai**	cener**ete**
cener**à**	cener**anno**

condizionale presente

SINGULAR	PLURAL
cener**ei**	cener**emmo**
cener**esti**	cener**este**
cener**ebbe**	cener**ebbero**

congiuntivo presente

SINGULAR	PLURAL
cen**i**	cen**iamo**
cen**i**	cen**iate**
cen**i**	cen**ino**

congiuntivo imperfetto

SINGULAR	PLURAL
cen**assi**	cen**assimo**
cen**assi**	cen**aste**
cen**asse**	cen**asseio**

imperativo

SINGULAR	PLURAL
	ceniamo
cena; non cenare	cenate
ceni	cenino

passato prossimo

SINGULAR	PLURAL
ho cenato	**abbiamo** cenato
hai cenato	**avete** cenato
ha cenato	**hanno** cenato

trapassato prossimo

SINGULAR	PLURAL
avevo cenato	**avevamo** cenato
avevi cenato	**avevate** cenato
aveva cenato	**avevano** cenato

trapassato remoto

SINGULAR	PLURAL
ebbi cenato	**avemmo** cenato
avesti cenato	**aveste** cenato
ebbe cenato	**ebbero** cenato

futuro anteriore

SINGULAR	PLURAL
avrò cenato	**avremo** cenato
avrai cenato	**avrete** cenato
avrà cenato	**avranno** cenato

condizionale passato

SINGULAR	PLURAL
avrei cenato	**avremmo** cenato
avresti cenato	**avreste** cenato
avrebbe cenato	**avrebbero** cenato

congiuntivo passato

SINGULAR	PLURAL
abbia cenato	**abbiamo** cenato
abbia cenato	**abbiate** cenato
abbia cenato	**abbiano** cenato

congiuntivo trapassato

SINGULAR	PLURAL
avessi cenato	**avessimo** cenato
avessi cenato	**aveste** cenato
avesse cenato	**avessero** cenato

cercare — to search, to look for

gerundio **cercando** — participio passato **cercato**

SINGULAR	PLURAL	SINGULAR	PLURAL
indicativo presente		passato prossimo	
cerc**o**	cerch**iamo**	**ho** cercato	**abbiamo** cercato
cerch**i**	cerc**ate**	**hai** cercato	**avete** cercato
cerc**a**	cerc**ano**	**ha** cercato	**hanno** cercato
imperfetto		trapassato prossimo	
cerca**vo**	cerca**vamo**	**avevo** cercato	**avevamo** cercato
cerca**vi**	cerca**vate**	**avevi** cercato	**avevate** cercato
cerca**va**	cerca**vano**	**aveva** cercato	**avevano** cercato
passato remoto		trapassato remoto	
cerc**ai**	cerc**ammo**	**ebbi** cercato	**avemmo** cercato
cerc**asti**	cerc**aste**	**avesti** cercato	**aveste** cercato
cerc**ò**	cerc**arono**	**ebbe** cercato	**ebbero** cercato
futuro semplice		futuro anteriore	
cercher**ò**	cercher**emo**	**avrò** cercato	**avremo** cercato
cercher**ai**	cercher**ete**	**avrai** cercato	**avrete** cercato
cercher**à**	cercher**anno**	**avrà** cercato	**avranno** cercato
condizionale presente		condizionale passato	
cercher**ei**	cercher**emmo**	**avrei** cercato	**avremmo** cercato
cercher**esti**	cercher**este**	**avresti** cercato	**avreste** cercato
cercher**ebbe**	cercher**ebbero**	**avrebbe** cercato	**avrebbero** cercato
congiuntivo presente		congiuntivo passato	
cerch**i**	cerch**iamo**	**abbia** cercato	**abbiamo** cercato
cerch**i**	cerch**iate**	**abbia** cercato	**abbiate** cercato
cerch**i**	cerch**ino**	**abbia** cercato	**abbiano** cercato
congiuntivo imperfetto		congiuntivo trapassato	
cerc**assi**	cerc**assimo**	**avessi** cercato	**avessimo** cercato
cerc**assi**	cerc**aste**	**avessi** cercato	**aveste** cercato
cerc**asse**	cerc**assero**	**avesse** cercato	**avessero** cercato
imperativo			
	cerchiamo		
cerca; non cercare	cercate		
cerchi	cerchino		

gerundio **chiamando** participio passato **chiamato**

SINGULAR	PLURAL	SINGULAR	PLURAL
indicativo presente		passato prossimo	
chiam**o**	chiam**iamo**	**ho** chiamato	**abbiamo** chiamato
chiam**i**	chiam**ate**	**hai** chiamato	**avete** chiamato
chiam**a**	chiam**ano**	**ha** chiamato	**hanno** chiamato
imperfetto		trapassato prossimo	
chiama**vo**	chiama**vamo**	**avevo** chiamato	**avevamo** chiamato
chiama**vi**	chiama**vate**	**avevi** chiamato	**avevate** chiamato
chiama**va**	chiama**vano**	**aveva** chiamato	**avevano** chiamato
passato remoto		trapassato remoto	
chiam**ai**	chiam**ammo**	**ebbi** chiamato	**avemmo** chiamato
chiam**asti**	chiam**aste**	**avesti** chiamato	**aveste** chiamato
chiam**ò**	chiam**arono**	**ebbe** chiamato	**ebbero** chiamato
futuro semplice		futuro anteriore	
chiamer**ò**	chiamer**emo**	**avrò** chiamato	**avremo** chiamato
chiamer**ai**	chiamer**ete**	**avrai** chiamato	**avrete** chiamato
chiamer**à**	chiamer**anno**	**avrà** chiamato	**avranno** chiamato
condizionale presente		condizionale passato	
chiamer**ei**	chiamer**emmo**	**avrei** chiamato	**avremmo** chiamato
chiamer**esti**	chiamer**este**	**avresti** chiamato	**avreste** chiamato
chiamer**ebbe**	chiamer**ebbero**	**avrebbe** chiamato	**avrebbero** chiamato
congiuntivo presente		congiuntivo passato	
chiam**i**	chiam**iamo**	**abbia** chiamato	**abbiamo** chiamato
chiam**i**	chiam**iate**	**abbia** chiamato	**abbiate** chiamato
chiam**i**	chiam**ino**	**abbia** chiamato	**abbiano** chiamato
congiuntivo imperfetto		congiuntivo trapassato	
chiam**assi**	chiam**assimo**	**avessi** chiamato	**avessimo** chiamato
chiam**assi**	chiam**aste**	**avessi** chiamato	**aveste** chiamato
chiam**asse**	chiam**assero**	**avesse** chiamato	**avessero** chiamato
imperativo			
	chiamiamo		
chiama; non chiamare	chiamate		
chiami	chiamino		

C

chiamarsi — to be called

gerundio **chiamandosi** participio passato **chiamatosi**

SINGULAR	PLURAL	SINGULAR	PLURAL
indicativo presente		passato prossimo	
mi chiam**o**	**ci** chiam**iamo**	**mi sono** chiamato(a)	**ci siamo** chiamati(e)
ti chiam**i**	**vi** chiam**ate**	**ti sei** chiamato(a)	**vi siete** chiamati(e)
si chiam**a**	**si** chiam**ano**	**si è** chiamato(a)	**si sono** chiamati(e)
imperfetto		trapassato prossimo	
mi chiama**vo**	**ci** chiama**vamo**	**mi ero** chiamato(a)	**ci eravamo** chiamati(e)
ti chiama**vi**	**vi** chiama**vate**	**ti eri** chiamato(a)	**vi eravate** chiamati(e)
si chiama**va**	**si** chiama**vano**	**si era** chiamato(a)	**si erano** chiamati(e)
passato remoto		trapassato remoto	
mi chiam**ai**	**ci** chiam**ammo**	**mi fui** chiamato(a)	**ci fummo** chiamati(e)
ti chiam**asti**	**vi** chiam**aste**	**ti fosti** chiamato(a)	**vi foste** chiamati(e)
si chiam**ò**	**si** chiam**arono**	**si fu** chiamato(a)	**si furono** chiamati(e)
futuro semplice		futuro anteriore	
mi chiamer**ò**	**ci** chiamer**emo**	**mi sarò** chiamato(a)	**ci saremo** chiamati(e)
ti chiamer**ai**	**vi** chiamer**ete**	**ti sarai** chiamato(a)	**vi sarete** chiamati(e)
si chiamer**à**	**si** chiamer**anno**	**si sarà** chiamato(a)	**si saranno** chiamati(e)
condizionale presente		condizionale passato	
mi chiamer**ei**	**ci** chiamer**emmo**	**mi sarei** chiamato(a)	**ci saremmo** chiamati(e)
ti chiamer**esti**	**vi** chiamer**este**	**ti saresti** chiamato(a)	**vi sareste** chiamati(e)
si chiamer**ebbe**	**si** chiamer**ebbero**	**si sarebbe** chiamato(a)	**si sarebbero** chiamati(e)
congiuntivo presente		congiuntivo passato	
mi chiam**i**	**ci** chiam**iamo**	**mi sia** chiamato	**ci siamo** chiamati(e)
ti chiam**i**	**vi** chiam**iate**	**ti sia** chiamato	**vi siate** chiamati(e)
si chiam**i**	**si** chiam**ino**	**si sia** chiamato	**si siano** chiamati(e)
congiuntivo imperfetto		congiuntivo trapassato	
mi chiam**assi**	**ci** chiam**assimo**	**mi fossi** chiamato(a)	**ci fossimo** chiamati(e)
ti chiam**assi**	**vi** chiam**aste**	**ti fossi** chiamato(a)	**vi foste** chiamati(e)
si chiam**asse**	**si** chiam**assero**	**si fosse** chiamato(a)	**si fossero** chiamati(e)

imperativo

	chiamiamoci
chiamati; non ti chiamare	chiamatevi
si chiami	si chiamino

gerundio **chiedendo** participio passato **chiesto**

SINGULAR	PLURAL	SINGULAR	PLURAL
indicativo presente		passato prossimo	
chied**o**	chied**iamo**	**ho** chiesto	**abbiamo** chiesto
chied**i**	chied**ete**	**hai** chiesto	**avete** chiesto
chied**e**	chied**ono**	**ha** chiesto	**hanno** chiesto
imperfetto		trapassato prossimo	
chiede**vo**	chiede**vamo**	**avevo** chiesto	**avevamo** chiesto
chiede**vi**	chiede**vate**	**avevi** chiesto	**avevate** chiesto
chiede**va**	chiede**vano**	**aveva** chiesto	**avevano** chiesto
passato remoto		trapassato remoto	
chie**si**	chied**emmo**	**ebbi** chiesto	**avemmo** chiesto
chied**esti**	chied**este**	**avesti** chiesto	**aveste** chiesto
chie**se**	chie**sero**	**ebbe** chiesto	**ebbero** chiesto
futuro semplice		futuro anteriore	
chieder**ò**	chieder**emo**	**avrò** chiesto	**avremo** chiesto
chieder**ai**	chieder**ete**	**avrai** chiesto	**avrete** chiesto
chieder**à**	chieder**anno**	**avrà** chiesto	**avranno** chiesto
condizionale presente		condizionale passato	
chieder**ei**	chieder**emmo**	**avrei** chiesto	**avremmo** chiesto
chieder**esti**	chieder**este**	**avresti** chiesto	**avreste** chiesto
chieder**ebbe**	chieder**ebbero**	**avrebbe** chiesto	**avrebbero** chiesto
congiuntivo presente		congiuntivo passato	
chied**a**	chied**iamo**	**abbia** chiesto	**abbiamo** chiesto
chied**a**	chied**iate**	**abbia** chiesto	**abbiate** chiesto
chied**a**	chied**ano**	**abbia** chiesto	**abbiano** chiesto
congiuntivo imperfetto		congiuntivo trapassato	
chied**essi**	chied**essimo**	**avessi** chiesto	**avessimo** chiesto
chied**essi**	chied**este**	**avessi** chiesto	**aveste** chiesto
chied**esse**	chied**essero**	**avesse** chiesto	**avessero** chiesto
imperativo			
	chiediamo		
chiedi; non chiedere	chiedete		
chieda	chiedano		

chiudere — to close

gerundio **chiudendo** — participio passato **chiuso**

SINGULAR	PLURAL	SINGULAR	PLURAL
indicativo presente		passato prossimo	
chiud**o**	chiud**iamo**	**ho** chiuso	**abbiamo** chiuso
chiud**i**	chiud**ete**	**hai** chiuso	**avete** chiuso
chiud**e**	chiud**ono**	**ha** chiuso	**hanno** chiuso
imperfetto		trapassato prossimo	
chiude**vo**	chiude**vamo**	**avevo** chiuso	**avevamo** chiuso
chiude**vi**	chiude**vate**	**avevi** chiuso	**avevate** chiuso
chiude**va**	chiude**vano**	**aveva** chiuso	**avevano** chiuso
passato remoto		trapassato remoto	
chiu**si**	chiud**emmo**	**ebbi** chiuso	**avemmo** chiuso
chiud**esti**	chiud**este**	**avesti** chiuso	**aveste** chiuso
chiu**se**	chiu**sero**	**ebbe** chiuso	**ebbero** chiuso
futuro semplice		futuro anteriore	
chiuder**ò**	chiuder**emo**	**avrò** chiuso	**avremo** chiuso
chiuder**ai**	chiuder**ete**	**avrai** chiuso	**avrete** chiuso
chiuder**à**	chiuder**anno**	**avrà** chiuso	**avranno** chiuso
condizionale presente		condizionale passato	
chiuder**ei**	chiuder**emmo**	**avrei** chiuso	**avremmo** chiuso
chiuder**esti**	chiuder**este**	**avresti** chiuso	**avreste** chiuso
chiuder**ebbe**	chiuder**ebbero**	**avrebbe** chiuso	**avrebbero** chiuso
congiuntivo presente		congiuntivo passato	
chiud**a**	chiud**iamo**	**abbia** chiuso	**abbiamo** chiuso
chiud**a**	chiud**iate**	**abbia** chiuso	**abbiate** chiuso
chiud**a**	chiud**ano**	**abbia** chiuso	**abbiano** chiuso
congiuntivo imperfetto		congiuntivo trapassato	
chiud**essi**	chiud**essimo**	**avessi** chiuso	**avessimo** chiuso
chiud**essi**	chiud**este**	**avessi** chiuso	**aveste** chiuso
chiud**esse**	chiud**essero**	**avesse** chiuso	**avessero** chiuso

imperativo

	chiudiamo
chiudi; non chiudere	chiudete
chiuda	chiudano

to catch, to seize, to pick, to gather **cogliere**

gerundio **cogliendo** participio passato **colto**

SINGULAR	PLURAL
indicativo presente	
colg**o**	cogl**iamo**
cogl**i**	cogl**iete**
cogli**e**	colg**ono**
imperfetto	
coglie**vo**	coglie**vamo**
coglie**vi**	coglie**vate**
coglie**va**	coglie**vano**
passato remoto	
cols**i**	cogl**iemmo**
cogl**iesti**	cogl**ieste**
cols**e**	cols**ero**
futuro semplice	
coglier**ò**	coglier**emo**
coglier**ai**	coglier**ete**
coglier**à**	coglier**anno**
condizionale presente	
coglier**ei**	coglier**emmo**
coglier**esti**	coglier**este**
coglier**ebbe**	coglier**ebbero**
congiuntivo presente	
colg**a**	cogl**iamo**
colg**a**	cogl**iate**
colg**a**	colg**ano**
congiuntivo imperfetto	
cogl**iessi**	cogl**iessimo**
cogl**iessi**	cogl**ieste**
cogl**iesse**	cogl**iessero**
imperativo	
	cogliamo
cogli; non cogliere	cogliete
colga	colgano

SINGULAR	PLURAL
passato prossimo	
ho colto	**abbiamo** colto
hai colto	**avete** colto
ha colto	**hanno** colto
trapassato prossimo	
avevo colto	**avevamo** colto
avevi colto	**avevate** colto
aveva colto	**avevano** colto
trapassato remoto	
ebbi colto	**avemmo** colto
avesti colto	**aveste** colto
ebbe colto	**ebbero** colto
futuro anteriore	
avrò colto	**avremo** colto
avrai colto	**avrete** colto
avrà colto	**avranno** colto
condizionale passato	
avrei colto	**avremmo** colto
avresti colto	**avreste** colto
avrebbe colto	**avrebbero** colto
congiuntivo passato	
abbia colto	**abbiamo** colto
abbia colto	**abbiate** colto
abbia colto	**abbiano** colto
congiuntivo trapassato	
avessi colto	**avessimo** colto
avessi colto	**aveste** colto
avesse colto	**avessero** colto

colpire — to hit, to strike

gerundio **colpendo** participio passato **colpito**

C

SINGULAR	PLURAL	SINGULAR	PLURAL
indicativo presente		passato prossimo	
colpisc**o**	colp**iamo**	**ho** colpito	**abbiamo** colpito
colpisc**i**	colp**ite**	**hai** colpito	**avete** colpito
colpisc**e**	colpisc**ono**	**ha** colpito	**hanno** colpito
imperfetto		trapassato prossimo	
colpi**vo**	colpi**vamo**	**avevo** colpito	**avevamo** colpito
colpi**vi**	colpi**vate**	**avevi** colpito	**avevate** colpito
colpi**va**	colpi**vano**	**aveva** colpito	**avevano** colpito
passato remoto		trapassato remoto	
colp**ii**	colp**immo**	**ebbi** colpito	**avemmo** colpito
colp**isti**	colp**iste**	**avesti** colpito	**aveste** colpito
colp**ì**	colp**irono**	**ebbe** colpito	**ebbero** colpito
futuro semplice		futuro anteriore	
colpir**ò**	colpir**emo**	**avrò** colpito	**avremo** colpito
colpir**ai**	colpir**ete**	**avrai** colpito	**avrete** colpito
colpir**à**	colpir**anno**	**avrà** colpito	**avranno** colpito
condizionale presente		condizionale passato	
colpir**ei**	colpir**emmo**	**avrei** colpito	**avremmo** colpito
colpir**esti**	colpir**este**	**avresti** colpito	**avreste** colpito
colpir**ebbe**	colpir**ebbero**	**avrebbe** colpito	**avrebbero** colpito
congiuntivo presente		congiuntivo passato	
colpisc**a**	colp**iamo**	**abbia** colpito	**abbiamo** colpito
colpisc**a**	colp**iate**	**abbia** colpito	**abbiate** colpito
colpisc**a**	colpisc**ano**	**abbia** colpito	**abbiano** colpito
congiuntivo imperfetto		congiuntivo trapassato	
colp**issi**	colp**issimo**	**avessi** colpito	**avessimo** colpito
colp**issi**	colp**iste**	**avessi** colpito	**aveste** colpito
colp**isse**	colp**issero**	**avesse** colpito	**avessero** colpito
imperativo			
	colpiamo		
colpisci; non colpire	colpite		
colpisca	colpiscano		

gerundio **cominciando** participio passato **cominciato**

SINGULAR	PLURAL	SINGULAR	PLURAL
indicativo presente		passato prossimo	
cominci**o**	cominc**iamo**	**ho** cominciato	**abbiamo** cominciato
cominc**i**	cominc**iate**	**hai** cominciato	**avete** cominciato
cominci**a**	cominc**iano**	**ha** cominciato	**hanno** cominciato
imperfetto		trapassato prossimo	
comincia**vo**	comincia**vamo**	**avevo** cominciato	**avevamo** cominciato
comincia**vi**	comincia**vate**	**avevi** cominciato	**avevate** cominciato
comincia**va**	comincia**vano**	**aveva** cominciato	**avevano** cominciato
passato remoto		trapassato remoto	
cominci**ai**	cominci**ammo**	**ebbi** cominciato	**avemmo** cominciato
cominci**asti**	cominci**aste**	**avesti** cominciato	**aveste** cominciato
cominci**ò**	cominci**arono**	**ebbe** cominciato	**ebbero** cominciato
futuro semplice		futuro anteriore	
comincer**ò**	comincer**emo**	**avrò** cominciato	**avremo** cominciato
comincer**ai**	comincer**ete**	**avrai** cominciato	**avrete** cominciato
comincer**à**	comincer**anno**	**avrà** cominciato	**avranno** cominciato
condizionale presente		condizionale passato	
comincer**ei**	comincer**emmo**	**avrei** cominciato	**avremmo** cominciato
comincer**esti**	comincer**este**	**avresti** cominciato	**avreste** cominciato
comincer**ebbe**	comincer**ebbero**	**avrebbe** cominciato	**avrebbero** cominciato
congiuntivo presente		congiuntivo passato	
cominc**i**	cominc**iamo**	**abbia** cominciato	**abbiamo** cominciato
cominc**i**	cominc**iate**	**abbia** cominciato	**abbiate** cominciato
cominc**i**	cominc**ino**	**abbia** cominciato	**abbiano** cominciato
congiuntivo imperfetto		congiuntivo trapassato	
cominci**assi**	cominci**assimo**	**avessi** cominciato	**avessimo** cominciato
cominci**assi**	cominci**aste**	**avessi** cominciato	**aveste** cominciato
cominci**asse**	cominci**assero**	**avesse** cominciato	**avessero** cominciato

imperativo

	cominciamo
comincia; non cominciare	cominciate
cominci	comincino

C

commettere — to commit

gerundio **commettendo** participio passato **commesso**

SINGULAR	PLURAL	SINGULAR	PLURAL
indicativo presente		passato prossimo	
commett**o**	commett**iamo**	**ho** commesso	**abbiamo** commesso
commett**i**	commett**ete**	**hai** commesso	**avete** commesso
commett**e**	commett**ono**	**ha** commesso	**hanno** commesso
imperfetto		trapassato prossimo	
commette**vo**	commette**vamo**	**avevo** commesso	**avevamo** commesso
commette**vi**	commette**vate**	**avevi** commesso	**avevate** commesso
commette**va**	commette**vano**	**aveva** commesso	**avevano** commesso
passato remoto		trapassato remoto	
commis**i**	commett**emmo**	**ebbi** commesso	**avemmo** commesso
commett**esti**	commett**este**	**avesti** commesso	**aveste** commesso
commis**e**	commis**ero**	**ebbe** commesso	**ebbero** commesso
futuro semplice		futuro anteriore	
commetter**ò**	commetter**emo**	**avrò** commesso	**avremo** commesso
commetter**ai**	commetter**ete**	**avrai** commesso	**avrete** commesso
commetter**à**	commetter**anno**	**avrà** commesso	**avranno** commesso
condizionale presente		condizionale passato	
commetter**ei**	commetter**emmo**	**avrei** commesso	**avremmo** commesso
commetter**esti**	commetter**este**	**avresti** commesso	**avreste** commesso
commetter**ebbe**	commetter**ebbero**	**avrebbe** commesso	**avrebbero** commesso
congiuntivo presente		congiuntivo passato	
commett**a**	commett**iamo**	**abbia** commesso	**abbiamo** commesso
commett**a**	commett**iate**	**abbia** commesso	**abbiate** commesso
commett**a**	commett**ano**	**abbia** commesso	**abbiano** commesso
congiuntivo imperfetto		congiuntivo trapassato	
commett**essi**	commett**essimo**	**avessi** commesso	**avessimo** commesso
commett**essi**	commett**este**	**avessi** commesso	**aveste** commesso
commett**esse**	commett**essero**	**avesse** commesso	**avessero** commesso
imperativo			
	commettiamo		
commetti; non commettere	commettete		
commetta	commettano		

You **committed** a serious error in your analysis.

to move, to touch, to affect — commuovere

gerundio **commuovendo** participio passato **commosso**

SINGULAR	PLURAL
indicativo presente	
commuov**o**	commuov**iamo**
commuov**i**	commuov**ete**
commuov**e**	commuov**ono**
imperfetto	
commuove**vo**	commuove**vamo**
commuove**vi**	commuove**vate**
commuove**va**	commuove**vano**
passato remoto	
commoss**i**	commuov**emmo**
commuov**esti**	commuov**este**
commoss**e**	commoss**ero**
futuro semplice	
commuover**ò**	commuover**emo**
commuover**ai**	commuover**ete**
commuover**à**	commuover**anno**
condizionale presente	
commuover**ei**	commuover**emmo**
commuover**esti**	commuover**este**
commuover**ebbe**	commuover**ebbero**
congiuntivo presente	
commuov**a**	commuov**iamo**
commuov**a**	commuov**iate**
commuov**a**	commuov**ano**
congiuntivo imperfetto	
commuov**essi**	commuov**essimo**
commuov**essi**	commuov**este**
commuov**esse**	commuov**essero**
imperativo	
	commuoviamo
commuovi; non commuovere	commuovete
commuova	commuovano

SINGULAR	PLURAL
passato prossimo	
ho commosso	**abbiamo** commosso
hai commosso	**avete** commosso
ha commosso	**hanno** commosso
trapassato prossimo	
avevo commosso	**avevamo** commosso
avevi commosso	**avevate** commosso
aveva commosso	**avevano** commosso
trapassato remoto	
ebbi commosso	**avemmo** commosso
avesti commosso	**aveste** commosso
ebbe commosso	**ebbero** commosso
futuro anteriore	
avrò commosso	**avremo** commosso
avrai commosso	**avrete** commosso
avrà commosso	**avranno** commosso
condizionale passato	
avrei commosso	**avremmo** commosso
avresti commosso	**avreste** commosso
avrebbe commosso	**avrebbero** commosso
congiuntivo passato	
abbia commosso	**abbiamo** commosso
abbia commosso	**abbiate** commosso
abbia commosso	**abbiano** commosso
congiuntivo trapassato	
avessi commosso	**avessimo** commosso
avessi commosso	**aveste** commosso
avesse commosso	**avessero** commosso

comparire — to appear, to turn up

gerundio **comparendo** — participio passato **comparso**

C

SINGULAR	PLURAL	SINGULAR	PLURAL
indicativo presente		**passato prossimo**	
compaio	compariamo	sono comparso(a)	siamo comparsi(e)
compari	comparite	sei comparso(a)	siete comparsi(e)
compare	compaiono	è comparso(a)	sono comparsi(e)
imperfetto		**trapassato prossimo**	
comparivo	comparivamo	ero comparso(a)	eravamo comparsi(e)
comparivi	comparivate	eri comparso(a)	eravate comparsi(e)
compariva	comparivano	era comparso(a)	erano comparsi(e)
passato remoto		**trapassato remoto**	
comparvi, comparii	comparimmo	fui comparso(a)	fummo comparsi(e)
comparisti	compariste	fosti comparso(a)	foste comparsi(e)
comparve, comparì	comparvero, comparirono	fu comparso(a)	furono comparsi(e)
futuro semplice		**futuro anteriore**	
comparirò	compariremo	sarò comparso(a)	saremo comparsi(e)
comparirai	comparirete	sarai comparso(a)	sarete comparsi(e)
comparirà	compariranno	sarà comparso(a)	saranno comparsi(e)
condizionale presente		**condizionale passato**	
comparirei	compariremmo	sarei comparso(a)	saremmo comparsi(e)
compariresti	comparireste	saresti comparso(a)	sareste comparsi(e)
comparirebbe	comparirebbero	sarebbe comparso(a)	sarebbero comparsi(e)
congiuntivo presente		**congiuntivo passato**	
compaia	compariamo	sia comparso(a)	siamo comparsi(e)
compaia	compariate	sia comparso(a)	siate comparsi(e)
compaia	compaiano	sia comparso(a)	siano comparsi(e)
congiuntivo imperfetto		**congiuntivo trapassato**	
comparissi	comparissimo	fossi comparso(a)	fossimo comparsi(e)
comparissi	compariste	fossi comparso(a)	foste comparsi(e)
comparisse	comparissero	fosse comparso(a)	fossero comparsi(e)
imperativo			
	compariamo		
compari; non comparire	comparite		
compaia	compaiano		

to please, to humor, to gratify compiacere

gerundio **compiacendo** participio passato **compiaciuto**

SINGULAR	PLURAL
indicativo presente	
compiacci**o**	compiacc**iamo**
compiac**i**	compiac**ete**
compiac**e**	compiacc**iono**
imperfetto	
compiace**vo**	compiace**vamo**
compiace**vi**	compiace**vate**
compiace**va**	compiace**vano**
passato remoto	
compiacqu**i**	compiac**emmo**
compiac**esti**	compiac**este**
compiacqu**e**	compiacqu**ero**
futuro semplice	
compiacer**ò**	compiacer**emo**
compiacer**ai**	compiacer**ete**
compiacer**à**	compiacer**anno**
condizionale presente	
compiacer**ei**	compiacer**emmo**
compiacer**esti**	compiacer**este**
compiacer**ebbe**	compiacer**ebbero**
congiuntivo presente	
compiacci**a**	compiacc**iamo**
compiacci**a**	compiacc**iate**
compiacci**a**	compiacc**iano**
congiuntivo imperfetto	
compiac**essi**	compiac**essimo**
compiac**essi**	compiac**este**
compiac**esse**	compiac**essero**
imperativo	
	compiacciamo
compiaci; non compiacere	compiacete
compiaccia	compiacciano

SINGULAR	PLURAL
passato prossimo	
ho compiaciuto	**abbiamo** compiaciuto
hai compiaciuto	**avete** compiaciuto
ha compiaciuto	**hanno** compiaciuto
trapassato prossimo	
avevo compiaciuto	**avevamo** compiaciuto
avevi compiaciuto	**avevate** compiaciuto
aveva compiaciuto	**avevano** compiaciuto
trapassato remoto	
ebbi compiaciuto	**avemmo** compiaciuto
avesti compiaciuto	**aveste** compiaciuto
ebbe compiaciuto	**ebbero** compiaciuto
futuro anteriore	
avrò compiaciuto	**avremo** compiaciuto
avrai compiaciuto	**avrete** compiaciuto
avrà compiaciuto	**avranno** compiaciuto
condizionale passato	
avrei compiaciuto	**avremmo** compiaciuto
avresti compiaciuto	**avreste** compiaciuto
avrebbe compiaciuto	**avrebbero** compiaciuto
congiuntivo passato	
abbia compiaciuto	**abbiamo** compiaciuto
abbia compiaciuto	**abbiate** compiaciuto
abbia compiaciuto	**abbiano** compiaciuto
congiuntivo trapassato	
avessi compiaciuto	**avessimo** compiaciuto
avessi compiaciuto	**aveste** compiaciuto
avesse compiaciuto	**avessero** compiaciuto

comporre — to compose

gerundio **componendo** — participio passato **composto**

SINGULAR	PLURAL
indicativo presente	
compong**o**	compon**iamo**
compon**i**	compon**ete**
compon**e**	compong**ono**
imperfetto	
compone**vo**	compone**vamo**
compone**vi**	compone**vate**
compone**va**	compone**vano**
passato remoto	
compos**i**	compon**emmo**
compon**esti**	compon**este**
compos**e**	compos**ero**
futuro semplice	
comporr**ò**	comporr**emo**
comporr**ai**	comporr**ete**
comporr**à**	comporr**anno**
condizionale presente	
comporr**ei**	comporr**emmo**
comporr**esti**	comporr**este**
comporr**ebbe**	comporr**ebbero**
congiuntivo presente	
compong**a**	compon**iamo**
compong**a**	compon**iate**
compong**a**	compong**ano**
congiuntivo imperfetto	
compon**essi**	compon**essimo**
compon**essi**	compon**este**
compon**esse**	compon**essero**
imperativo	
	componiamo
componi; non comporre	componete
componga	compongano

SINGULAR	PLURAL
passato prossimo	
ho composto	**abbiamo** composto
hai composto	**avete** composto
ha composto	**hanno** composto
trapassato prossimo	
avevo composto	**avevamo** composto
avevi composto	**avevate** composto
aveva composto	**avevano** composto
trapassato remoto	
ebbi composto	**avemmo** composto
avesti composto	**aveste** composto
ebbe composto	**ebbero** composto
futuro anteriore	
avrò composto	**avremo** composto
avrai composto	**avrete** composto
avrà composto	**avranno** composto
condizionale passato	
avrei composto	**avremmo** composto
avresti composto	**avreste** composto
avrebbe composto	**avrebbero** composto
congiuntivo passato	
abbia composto	**abbiamo** composto
abbia composto	**abbiate** composto
abbia composto	**abbiano** composto
congiuntivo trapassato	
avessi composto	**avessimo** composto
avessi composto	**aveste** composto
avesse composto	**avessero** composto

to behave — comportarsi

gerundio **comportandosi** participio passato **comportatosi**

SINGULAR	PLURAL
indicativo presente	
mi comport**o**	**ci** comport**iamo**
ti comport**i**	**vi** comport**ate**
si comport**a**	**si** comport**ano**
imperfetto	
mi comporta**vo**	**ci** comporta**vamo**
ti comporta**vi**	**vi** comporta**vate**
si comporta**va**	**si** comporta**vano**
passato remoto	
mi comport**ai**	**ci** comport**ammo**
ti comport**asti**	**vi** comport**aste**
si comport**ò**	**si** comport**arono**
futuro semplice	
mi comporter**ò**	**ci** comporter**emo**
ti comporter**ai**	**vi** comporter**ete**
si comporter**à**	**si** comporter**anno**
condizionale presente	
mi comporter**ei**	**ci** comporter**emmo**
ti comporter**esti**	**vi** comporter**este**
si comporter**ebbe**	**si** comporter**ebbero**
congiuntivo presente	
mi comport**i**	**ci** comport**iamo**
ti comport**i**	**vi** comport**iate**
si comport**i**	**si** comport**ino**
congiuntivo imperfetto	
mi comport**assi**	**ci** comport**assimo**
ti comport**assi**	**vi** comport**aste**
si comport**asse**	**si** comport**assero**
imperativo	
	comportiamoci
comportati; non comportarti/non ti comportare	comportatevi
si comporti	si comportino

SINGULAR	PLURAL
passato prossimo	
mi sono comportato(a)	**ci siamo** comportati(e)
ti sei comportato(a)	**vi siete** comportati(e)
si è comportato(a)	**si sono** comportati(e)
trapassato prossimo	
mi ero comportato(a)	**ci eravamo** comportati(e)
ti eri comportato(a)	**vi eravate** comportati(e)
si era comportato(a)	**si erano** comportati(e)
trapassato remoto	
mi fui comportato(a)	**ci fummo** comportati(e)
ti fosti comportato(a)	**vi foste** comportati(e)
si fu comportato(a)	**si furono** comportati(e)
futuro anteriore	
mi sarò comportato(a)	**ci saremo** comportati(e)
ti sarai comportato(a)	**vi sarete** comportati(e)
si sarà comportato(a)	**si saranno** comportati(e)
condizionale passato	
mi sarei comportato(a)	**ci saremmo** comportati(e)
ti saresti comportato(a)	**vi sareste** comportati(e)
si sarebbe comportato(a)	**si sarebbero** comportati(e)
congiuntivo passato	
mi sia comportato(a)	**ci siamo** comportati(e)
ti sia comportato(a)	**vi siate** comportati(e)
si sia comportato(a)	**si siano** comportati(e)
congiuntivo trapassato	
mi fossi comportato(a)	**ci fossimo** comportati(e)
ti fossi comportato(a)	**vi foste** comportati(e)
si fosse comportato(a)	**si fossero** comportati(e)

comprare — to buy

gerundio **comprando** participio passato **comprato**

SINGULAR	PLURAL	SINGULAR	PLURAL
indicativo presente		passato prossimo	
compr**o**	compr**iamo**	**ho** comprato	**abbiamo** comprato
compr**i**	compr**ate**	**hai** comprato	**avete** comprato
compr**a**	compr**ano**	**ha** comprato	**hanno** comprato
imperfetto		trapassato prossimo	
compra**vo**	compra**vamo**	**avevo** comprato	**avevamo** comprato
compra**vi**	compra**vate**	**avevi** comprato	**avevate** comprato
compra**va**	compra**vano**	**aveva** comprato	**avevano** comprato
passato remoto		trapassato remoto	
compra**i**	compr**ammo**	**ebbi** comprato	**avemmo** comprato
compr**asti**	compr**aste**	**avesti** comprato	**aveste** comprato
compr**ò**	compr**arono**	**ebbe** comprato	**ebbero** comprato
futuro semplice		futuro anteriore	
comprer**ò**	comprer**emo**	**avrò** comprato	**avremo** comprato
comprer**ai**	comprer**ete**	**avrai** comprato	**avrete** comprato
comprer**à**	comprer**anno**	**avrà** comprato	**avranno** comprato
condizionale presente		condizionale passato	
comprer**ei**	comprer**emmo**	**avrei** comprato	**avremmo** comprato
comprer**esti**	comprer**este**	**avresti** comprato	**avreste** comprato
comprer**ebbe**	comprer**ebbero**	**avrebbe** comprato	**avrebbero** comprato
congiuntivo presente		congiuntivo passato	
compr**i**	compr**iamo**	**abbia** comprato	**abbiamo** comprato
compr**i**	compr**iate**	**abbia** comprato	**abbiate** comprato
compr**i**	compr**ino**	**abbia** comprato	**abbiano** comprato
congiuntivo imperfetto		congiuntivo trapassato	
compr**assi**	compr**assimo**	**avessi** comprato	**avessimo** comprato
compr**assi**	compr**aste**	**avessi** comprato	**aveste** comprato
compr**asse**	compr**assero**	**avesse** comprato	**avessero** comprato
imperativo			
	compriamo		
compra; non comprare	comprate		
compri	comprino		

to include, to understand — comprendere

gerundio **comprendendo** — participio passato **compreso**

SINGULAR	PLURAL	SINGULAR	PLURAL
indicativo presente		passato prossimo	
comprend**o**	comprend**iamo**	**ho** compreso	**abbiamo** compreso
comprend**i**	comprend**ete**	**hai** compreso	**avete** compreso
comprend**e**	comprend**ono**	**ha** compreso	**hanno** compreso
imperfetto		trapassato prossimo	
comprende**vo**	comprende**vamo**	**avevo** compreso	**avevamo** compreso
comprende**vi**	comprende**vate**	**avevi** compreso	**avevate** compreso
comprende**va**	comprende**vano**	**aveva** compreso	**avevano** compreso
passato remoto		trapassato remoto	
compres**i**	comprend**emmo**	**ebbi** compreso	**avemmo** compreso
comprend**esti**	comprend**este**	**avesti** compreso	**aveste** compreso
compres**e**	compres**ero**	**ebbe** compreso	**ebbero** compreso
futuro semplice		futuro anteriore	
comprender**ò**	comprender**emo**	**avrò** compreso	**avremo** compreso
comprender**ai**	comprender**ete**	**avrai** compreso	**avrete** compreso
comprender**à**	comprender**anno**	**avrà** compreso	**avranno** compreso
condizionale presente		condizionale passato	
comprender**ei**	comprender**emmo**	**avrei** compreso	**avremmo** compreso
comprender**esti**	comprender**este**	**avresti** compreso	**avreste** compreso
comprender**ebbe**	comprender**ebbero**	**avrebbe** compreso	**avrebbero** compreso
congiuntivo presente		congiuntivo passato	
comprend**a**	comprend**iamo**	**abbia** compreso	**abbiamo** compreso
comprend**a**	comprend**iate**	**abbia** compreso	**abbiate** compreso
comprend**a**	comprend**ano**	**abbia** compreso	**abbiano** compreso
congiuntivo imperfetto		congiuntivo trapassato	
comprend**essi**	comprend**essimo**	**avessi** compreso	**avessimo** compreso
comprend**essi**	comprend**este**	**avessi** compreso	**aveste** compreso
comprend**esse**	comprend**essero**	**avesse** compreso	**avessero** compreso
imperativo			
	comprendiamo		
comprendi; non comprendere	comprendete		
comprenda	comprendano		

comunicare — to communicate

gerundio **comunicando** — participio passato **comunicato**

SINGULAR	PLURAL
indicativo presente	
comunic**o**	comunich**iamo**
comunich**i**	comunic**ate**
comunic**a**	comunic**ano**
imperfetto	
comunica**vo**	comunica**vamo**
comunica**vi**	comunica**vate**
comunica**va**	comunica**vano**
passato remoto	
comunic**ai**	comunic**ammo**
comunic**asti**	comunic**aste**
comunic**ò**	comunic**arono**
futuro semplice	
comunicher**ò**	comunicher**emo**
comunicher**ai**	comunicher**ete**
comunicher**à**	comunicher**anno**
condizionale presente	
comunicher**ei**	comunicher**emmo**
comunicher**esti**	comunicher**este**
comunicher**ebbe**	comunicher**ebbero**
congiuntivo presente	
comunich**i**	comunich**iamo**
comunich**i**	comunich**iate**
comunich**i**	comunich**ino**
congiuntivo imperfetto	
comunic**assi**	comunic**assimo**
comunic**assi**	comunic**aste**
comunic**asse**	comunic**assero**
imperativo	
	comunichiamo
comunica; non comunicare	comunicate
comunichi	comunichino

SINGULAR	PLURAL
passato prossimo	
ho comunicato	**abbiamo** comunicato
hai comunicato	**avete** comunicato
ha comunicato	**hanno** comunicato
trapassato prossimo	
avevo comunicato	**avevamo** comunicato
avevi comunicato	**avevate** comunicato
aveva comunicato	**avevano** comunicato
trapassato remoto	
ebbi comunicato	**avemmo** comunicato
avesti comunicato	**aveste** comunicato
ebbe comunicato	**ebbero** comunicato
futuro anteriore	
avrò comunicato	**avremo** comunicato
avrai comunicato	**avrete** comunicato
avrà comunicato	**avranno** comunicato
condizionale passato	
avrei comunicato	**avremmo** comunicato
avresti comunicato	**avreste** comunicato
avrebbe comunicato	**avrebbero** comunicato
congiuntivo passato	
abbia comunicato	**abbiamo** comunicato
abbia comunicato	**abbiate** comunicato
abbia comunicato	**abbiano** comunicato
congiuntivo trapassato	
avessi comunicato	**avessimo** comunicato
avessi comunicato	**aveste** comunicato
avesse comunicato	**avessero** comunicato

to concede, to grant, to award **concedere**

gerundio **concedendo** participio passato **concesso**

SINGULAR	PLURAL
indicativo presente	
conced**o**	conced**iamo**
conced**i**	conced**ete**
conced**e**	conced**ono**
imperfetto	
concede**vo**	concede**vamo**
concede**vi**	concede**vate**
concede**va**	concede**vano**
passato remoto	
concess**i**	conced**emmo**
conced**esti**	conced**este**
concess**e**	concess**ero**
futuro semplice	
conceder**ò**	conceder**emo**
conceder**ai**	conceder**ete**
conceder**à**	conceder**anno**
condizionale presente	
conceder**ei**	conceder**emmo**
conceder**esti**	conceder**este**
conceder**ebbe**	conceder**ebbero**
congiuntivo presente	
conced**a**	conced**iamo**
conced**a**	conced**iate**
conced**a**	conced**ano**
congiuntivo imperfetto	
conced**essi**	conced**essimo**
conced**essi**	conced**este**
conced**esse**	conced**essero**
imperativo	
	concediamo
concedi; non concedere	concedete
conceda	concedano

SINGULAR	PLURAL
passato prossimo	
ho concesso	**abbiamo** concesso
hai concesso	**avete** concesso
ha concesso	**hanno** concesso
trapassato prossimo	
avevo concesso	**avevamo** concesso
avevi concesso	**avevate** concesso
aveva concesso	**avevano** concesso
trapassato remoto	
ebbi concesso	**avemmo** concesso
avesti concesso	**aveste** concesso
ebbe concesso	**ebbero** concesso
futuro anteriore	
avrò concesso	**avremo** concesso
avrai concesso	**avrete** concesso
avrà concesso	**avranno** concesso
condizionale passato	
avrei concesso	**avremmo** concesso
avresti concesso	**avreste** concesso
avrebbe concesso	**avrebbero** concesso
congiuntivo passato	
abbia concesso	**abbiamo** concesso
abbia concesso	**abbiate** concesso
abbia concesso	**abbiano** concesso
congiuntivo trapassato	
avessi concesso	**avessimo** concesso
avessi concesso	**aveste** concesso
avesse concesso	**avessero** concesso

concludere — to conclude, to end

gerundio **concludendo** participio passato **concluso**

indicativo presente

SINGULAR	PLURAL
conclud**o**	conclud**iamo**
conclud**i**	conclud**ete**
conclud**e**	conclud**ono**

imperfetto

SINGULAR	PLURAL
conclude**vo**	conclude**vamo**
conclude**vi**	conclude**vate**
conclude**va**	conclude**vano**

passato remoto

SINGULAR	PLURAL
conclus**i**	conclud**emmo**
conclud**esti**	conclud**este**
conclus**e**	conclus**ero**

futuro semplice

SINGULAR	PLURAL
concluder**ò**	concluder**emo**
concluder**ai**	concluder**ete**
concluder**à**	concluder**anno**

condizionale presente

SINGULAR	PLURAL
concluder**ei**	concluder**emmo**
concluder**esti**	concluder**este**
concluder**ebbe**	concluder**ebbero**

congiuntivo presente

SINGULAR	PLURAL
conclud**a**	conclud**iamo**
conclud**a**	conclud**iate**
conclud**a**	conclud**ano**

congiuntivo imperfetto

SINGULAR	PLURAL
conclud**essi**	conclud**essimo**
conclud**essi**	conclud**este**
conclud**esse**	conclud**essero**

imperativo

SINGULAR	PLURAL
	concludiamo
concludi; non concludere	concludete
concluda	concludano

passato prossimo

SINGULAR	PLURAL
ho concluso	**abbiamo** concluso
hai concluso	**avete** concluso
ha concluso	**hanno** concluso

trapassato prossimo

SINGULAR	PLURAL
avevo concluso	**avevamo** concluso
avevi concluso	**avevate** concluso
aveva concluso	**avevano** concluso

trapassato remoto

SINGULAR	PLURAL
ebbi concluso	**avemmo** concluso
avesti concluso	**aveste** concluso
ebbe concluso	**ebbero** concluso

futuro anteriore

SINGULAR	PLURAL
avrò concluso	**avremo** concluso
avrai concluso	**avrete** concluso
avrà concluso	**avranno** concluso

condizionale passato

SINGULAR	PLURAL
avrei concluso	**avremmo** concluso
avresti concluso	**avreste** concluso
avrebbe concluso	**avrebbero** concluso

congiuntivo passato

SINGULAR	PLURAL
abbia concluso	**abbiamo** concluso
abbia concluso	**abbiate** concluso
abbia concluso	**abbiano** concluso

congiuntivo trapassato

SINGULAR	PLURAL
avessi concluso	**avessimo** concluso
avessi concluso	**aveste** concluso
avesse concluso	**avessero** concluso

The jury **concluded** that there was enough evidence for a conviction.

gerundio **condendo** | participio passato **condito**

SINGULAR	PLURAL
indicativo presente	
condisc**o**	cond**iamo**
condisc**i**	cond**ite**
condisc**e**	condisc**ono**
imperfetto	
condi**vo**	condi**vamo**
condi**vi**	condi**vate**
condi**va**	condi**vano**
passato remoto	
cond**ii**	cond**immo**
cond**isti**	cond**iste**
cond**ì**	cond**irono**
futuro semplice	
condir**ò**	condir**emo**
condir**ai**	condir**ete**
condir**à**	condir**anno**
condizionale presente	
condir**ei**	condir**emmo**
condir**esti**	condir**este**
condir**ebbe**	condir**ebbero**
congiuntivo presente	
condisc**a**	cond**iamo**
condisc**a**	cond**iate**
condisc**a**	condisc**ano**
congiuntivo imperfetto	
cond**issi**	cond**issimo**
cond**issi**	cond**iste**
cond**isse**	cond**issero**
imperativo	
	condiamo
condisci; non condire	condite
condisca	condiscano

SINGULAR	PLURAL
passato prossimo	
ho condito	**abbiamo** condito
hai condito	**avete** condito
ha condito	**hanno** condito
trapassato prossimo	
avevo condito	**avevamo** condito
avevi condito	**avevate** condito
aveva condito	**avevano** condito
trapassato remoto	
ebbi condito	**avemmo** condito
avesti condito	**aveste** condito
ebbe condito	**ebbero** condito
futuro anteriore	
avrò condito	**avremo** condito
avrai condito	**avrete** condito
avrà condito	**avranno** condito
condizionale passato	
avrei condito	**avremmo** condito
avresti condito	**avreste** condito
avrebbe condito	**avrebbero** condito
congiuntivo passato	
abbia condito	**abbiamo** condito
abbia condito	**abbiate** condito
abbia condito	**abbiano** condito
congiuntivo trapassato	
avessi condito	**avessimo** condito
avessi condito	**aveste** condito
avesse condito	**avessero** condito

condurre — to conduct, to lead, to drive

gerundio **conducendo** participio passato **condotto**

SINGULAR	PLURAL
indicativo presente	
conduc**o**	conduc**iamo**
conduc**i**	conduc**ete**
conduc**e**	conduc**ono**
imperfetto	
conduce**vo**	conduce**vamo**
conduce**vi**	conduce**vate**
conduce**va**	conduce**vano**
passato remoto	
conduss**i**	conduc**emmo**
conduc**esti**	conduc**este**
conduss**e**	conduss**ero**
futuro semplice	
condurr**ò**	condurr**emo**
condurr**ai**	condurr**ete**
condurr**à**	condurr**anno**
condizionale presente	
condurr**ei**	condurr**emmo**
condurr**esti**	condurr**este**
condurr**ebbe**	condurr**ebbero**
congiuntivo presente	
conduc**a**	conduc**iamo**
conduc**a**	conduc**iate**
conduc**a**	conduc**ano**
congiuntivo imperfetto	
conduc**essi**	conduc**essimo**
conduc**essi**	conduc**este**
conduc**esse**	conduc**essero**
imperativo	
	conduciamo
conduci; non condurre	conducete
conduca	conducano

SINGULAR	PLURAL
passato prossimo	
ho condotto	**abbiamo** condotto
hai condotto	**avete** condotto
ha condotto	**hanno** condotto
trapassato prossimo	
avevo condotto	**avevamo** condotto
avevi condotto	**avevate** condotto
aveva condotto	**avevano** condotto
trapassato remoto	
ebbi condotto	**avemmo** condotto
avesti condotto	**aveste** condotto
ebbe condotto	**ebbero** condotto
futuro anteriore	
avrò condotto	**avremo** condotto
avrai condotto	**avrete** condotto
avrà condotto	**avranno** condotto
condizionale passato	
avrei condotto	**avremmo** condotto
avresti condotto	**avreste** condotto
avrebbe condotto	**avrebbero** condotto
congiuntivo passato	
abbia condotto	**abbiamo** condotto
abbia condotto	**abbiate** condotto
abbia condotto	**abbiano** condotto
congiuntivo trapassato	
avessi condotto	**avessimo** condotto
avessi condotto	**aveste** condotto
avesse condotto	**avessero** condotto

gerundio **confondendo** participio passato **confuso**

SINGULAR	PLURAL
indicativo presente	
confond**o**	confond**iamo**
confond**i**	confond**ete**
confond**e**	confond**ono**
imperfetto	
confonde**vo**	confonde**vamo**
confonde**vi**	confonde**vate**
confonde**va**	confonde**vano**
passato remoto	
confus**i**	confond**emmo**
confond**esti**	confond**este**
confus**e**	confus**ero**
futuro semplice	
confonder**ò**	confonder**emo**
confonder**ai**	confonder**ete**
confonder**à**	confonder**anno**
condizionale presente	
confonder**ei**	confonder**emmo**
confonder**esti**	confonder**este**
confonder**ebbe**	confonder**ebbero**
congiuntivo presente	
confond**a**	confond**iamo**
confond**a**	confond**iate**
confond**a**	confond**ano**
congiuntivo imperfetto	
confond**essi**	confond**essimo**
confond**essi**	confond**este**
confond**esse**	confond**essero**
imperativo	
	confondiamo
confondi; non confondere	confondete
confonda	confondano

SINGULAR	PLURAL
passato prossimo	
ho confuso	**abbiamo** confuso
hai confuso	**avete** confuso
ha confuso	**hanno** confuso
trapassato prossimo	
avevo confuso	**avevamo** confuso
avevi confuso	**avevate** confuso
aveva confuso	**avevano** confuso
trapassato remoto	
ebbi confuso	**avemmo** confuso
avesti confuso	**aveste** confuso
ebbe confuso	**ebbero** confuso
futuro anteriore	
avrò confuso	**avremo** confuso
avrai confuso	**avrete** confuso
avrà confuso	**avranno** confuso
condizionale passato	
avrei confuso	**avremmo** confuso
avresti confuso	**avreste** confuso
avrebbe confuso	**avrebbero** confuso
congiuntivo passato	
abbia confuso	**abbiamo** confuso
abbia confuso	**abbiate** confuso
abbia confuso	**abbiano** confuso
congiuntivo trapassato	
avessi confuso	**avessimo** confuso
avessi confuso	**aveste** confuso
avesse confuso	**avessero** confuso

Never confuse right and wrong.

conoscere — to know, to meet

gerundio **conoscendo** — participio passato **conosciuto**

C

SINGULAR	PLURAL	SINGULAR	PLURAL
indicativo presente		passato prossimo	
conosc**o**	conosc**iamo**	**ho** conosciuto	**abbiamo** conosciuto
conosc**i**	conosc**ete**	**hai** conosciuto	**avete** conosciuto
conosc**e**	conosc**ono**	**ha** conosciuto	**hanno** conosciuto
imperfetto		trapassato prossimo	
conosce**vo**	conosce**vamo**	**avevo** conosciuto	**avevamo** conosciuto
conosce**vi**	conosce**vate**	**avevi** conosciuto	**avevate** conosciuto
conosce**va**	conosce**vano**	**aveva** conosciuto	**avevano** conosciuto
passato remoto		trapassato remoto	
conobb**i**	conosc**emmo**	**ebbi** conosciuto	**avemmo** conosciuto
conosc**esti**	conosc**este**	**avesti** conosciuto	**aveste** conosciuto
conobb**e**	conobb**ero**	**ebbe** conosciuto	**ebbero** conosciuto
futuro semplice		futuro anteriore	
conoscer**ò**	conoscer**emo**	**avrò** conosciuto	**avremo** conosciuto
conoscer**ai**	conoscer**ete**	**avrai** conosciuto	**avrete** conosciuto
conoscer**à**	conoscer**anno**	**avrà** conosciuto	**avranno** conosciuto
condizionale presente		condizionale passato	
conoscer**ei**	conoscer**emmo**	**avrei** conosciuto	**avremmo** conosciuto
conoscer**esti**	conoscer**este**	**avresti** conosciuto	**avreste** conosciuto
conoscer**ebbe**	conoscer**ebbero**	**avrebbe** conosciuto	**avrebbero** conosciuto
congiuntivo presente		congiuntivo passato	
conosc**a**	conosc**iamo**	**abbia** conosciuto	**abbiamo** conosciuto
conosc**a**	conosc**iate**	**abbia** conosciuto	**abbiate** conosciuto
conosc**a**	conosc**ano**	**abbia** conosciuto	**abbiano** conosciuto
congiuntivo imperfetto		congiuntivo trapassato	
conosc**essi**	conosc**essimo**	**avessi** conosciuto	**avessimo** conosciuto
conosc**essi**	conosc**este**	**avessi** conosciuto	**aveste** conosciuto
conosc**esse**	conosc**essero**	**avesse** conosciuto	**avessero** conosciuto

imperativo

SINGULAR	PLURAL
	conosciamo
conosci; non conoscere	conoscete
conosca	conoscano

gerundio **consistendo** participio passato **consistito**

SINGULAR	PLURAL
indicativo presente	
consist**o**	consist**iamo**
consist**i**	consist**ete**
consist**e**	consist**ono**
imperfetto	
consiste**vo**	consiste**vamo**
consiste**vi**	consiste**vate**
consiste**va**	consiste**vano**
passato remoto	
consist**ei**, consist**etti**	consist**emmo**
consist**esti**	consist**este**
consist**é**, consist**ette**	consist**erono**, consist**ettero**
futuro semplice	
consister**ò**	consister**emo**
consister**ai**	consister**ete**
consister**à**	consister**anno**
condizionale presente	
consister**ei**	consister**emmo**
consister**esti**	consister**este**
consister**ebbe**	consister**ebbero**
congiuntivo presente	
consist**a**	consist**iamo**
consist**a**	consist**iate**
consist**a**	consist**ano**
congiuntivo imperfetto	
consist**essi**	consist**essimo**
consist**essi**	consist**este**
consist**esse**	consist**essero**
imperativo	
	consistiamo
consisti; non consistere	consistete
consista	consistano

SINGULAR	PLURAL
passato prossimo	
sono consistito(a)	**siamo** consistiti(e)
sei consistito(a)	**siete** consistiti(e)
è consistito(a)	**sono** consistiti(e)
trapassato prossimo	
ero consistito(a)	**eravamo** consistiti(e)
eri consistito(a)	**eravate** consistiti(e)
era consistito(a)	**erano** consistiti(e)
trapassato remoto	
fui consistito(a)	**fummo** consistiti(e)
fosti consistito(a)	**foste** consistiti(e)
fu consistito(a)	**furono** consistiti(e)
futuro anteriore	
sarò consistito(a)	**saremo** consistiti(e)
sarai consistito(a)	**sarete** consistiti(e)
sarà consistito(a)	**saranno** consistiti(e)
condizionale passato	
sarei consistito(a)	**saremmo** consistiti(e)
saresti consistito(a)	**sareste** consistiti(e)
sarebbe consistito(a)	**sarebbero** consistiti(e)
congiuntivo passato	
sia consistito(a)	**siamo** consistiti(e)
sia consistito(a)	**siate** consistiti(e)
sia consistito(a)	**siano** consistiti(e)
congiuntivo trapassato	
fossi consistito(a)	**fossimo** consistiti(e)
fossi consistito(a)	**foste** consistiti(e)
fosse consistito(a)	**fossero** consistiti(e)

consumare to consume, to use up, to wear out

gerundio **consumando** participio passato **consumato**

C

SINGULAR	PLURAL	SINGULAR	PLURAL
indicativo presente		passato prossimo	
consum**o**	consum**iamo**	**ho** consumato	**abbiamo** consumato
consum**i**	consuma**te**	**hai** consumato	**avete** consumato
consum**a**	consuma**no**	**ha** consumato	**hanno** consumato
imperfetto		trapassato prossimo	
consuma**vo**	consuma**vamo**	**avevo** consumato	**avevamo** consumato
consuma**vi**	consuma**vate**	**avevi** consumato	**avevate** consumato
consuma**va**	consuma**vano**	**aveva** consumato	**avevano** consumato
passato remoto		trapassato remoto	
consum**ai**	consum**ammo**	**ebbi** consumato	**avemmo** consumato
consum**asti**	consum**aste**	**avesti** consumato	**aveste** consumato
consum**ò**	consum**arono**	**ebbe** consumato	**ebbero** consumato
futuro semplice		futuro anteriore	
consumer**ò**	consumer**emo**	**avrò** consumato	**avremo** consumato
consumer**ai**	consumer**ete**	**avrai** consumato	**avrete** consumato
consumer**à**	consumer**anno**	**avrà** consumato	**avranno** consumato
condizionale presente		condizionale passato	
consumer**ei**	consumer**emmo**	**avrei** consumato	**avremmo** consumato
consumer**esti**	consumer**este**	**avresti** consumato	**avreste** consumato
consumer**ebbe**	consumer**ebbero**	**avrebbe** consumato	**avrebbero** consumato
congiuntivo presente		congiuntivo passato	
consum**i**	consum**iamo**	**abbia** consumato	**abbiamo** consumato
consum**i**	consum**iate**	**abbia** consumato	**abbiate** consumato
consum**i**	consum**ino**	**abbia** consumato	**abbiano** consumato
congiuntivo imperfetto		congiuntivo trapassato	
consum**assi**	consum**assimo**	**avessi** consumato	**avessimo** consumato
consum**assi**	consum**aste**	**avessi** consumato	**aveste** consumato
consum**asse**	consum**assero**	**avesse** consumato	**avessero** consumato
imperativo			
	consumiamo		
consuma; non consumare	consumate		
consumi	consumino		

gerundio **contando** participio passato **contato**

SINGULAR	PLURAL	SINGULAR	PLURAL
indicativo presente		passato prossimo	
cont**o**	conti**amo**	**ho** contato	**abbiamo** contato
cont**i**	cont**ate**	**hai** contato	**avete** contato
cont**a**	cont**ano**	**ha** contato	**hanno** contato
imperfetto		trapassato prossimo	
conta**vo**	conta**vamo**	**avevo** contato	**avevamo** contato
conta**vi**	conta**vate**	**avevi** contato	**avevate** contato
conta**va**	conta**vano**	**aveva** contato	**avevano** contato
passato remoto		trapassato remoto	
cont**ai**	cont**ammo**	**ebbi** contato	**avemmo** contato
cont**asti**	cont**aste**	**avesti** contato	**aveste** contato
cont**ò**	cont**arono**	**ebbe** contato	**ebbero** contato
futuro semplice		futuro anteriore	
conter**ò**	conter**emo**	**avrò** contato	**avremo** contato
conter**ai**	conter**ete**	**avrai** contato	**avrete** contato
conter**à**	conter**anno**	**avrà** contato	**avranno** contato
condizionale presente		condizionale passato	
conter**ei**	conter**emmo**	**avrei** contato	**avremmo** contato
conter**esti**	conter**este**	**avresti** contato	**avreste** contato
conter**ebbe**	conter**ebbero**	**avrebbe** contato	**avrebbero** contato
congiuntivo presente		congiuntivo passato	
cont**i**	cont**iamo**	**abbia** contato	**abbiamo** contato
cont**i**	cont**iate**	**abbia** contato	**abbiate** contato
cont**i**	cont**ino**	**abbia** contato	**abbiano** contato
congiuntivo imperfetto		congiuntivo trapassato	
cont**assi**	cont**assimo**	**avessi** contato	**avessimo** contato
cont**assi**	cont**aste**	**avessi** contato	**aveste** contato
cont**asse**	cont**assero**	**avesse** contato	**avessero** contato
imperativo			
	contiamo		
conta; non contare	contate		
conti	contino		

C

contendere to contend, to contest, to dispute

gerundio **contendendo** participio passato **conteso**

C

SINGULAR	PLURAL	SINGULAR	PLURAL
indicativo presente		passato prossimo	
contend**o**	contend**iamo**	**ho** conteso	**abbiamo** conteso
contend**i**	contend**ete**	**hai** conteso	**avete** conteso
contend**e**	contend**ono**	**ha** conteso	**hanno** conteso
imperfetto		trapassato prossimo	
contende**vo**	contende**vamo**	**avevo** conteso	**avevamo** conteso
contende**vi**	contende**vate**	**avevi** conteso	**avevate** conteso
contende**va**	contende**vano**	**aveva** conteso	**avevano** conteso
passato remoto		trapassato remoto	
contes**i**	contend**emmo**	**ebbi** conteso	**avemmo** conteso
contend**esti**	contend**este**	**avesti** conteso	**aveste** conteso
contes**e**	contes**ero**	**ebbe** conteso	**ebbero** conteso
futuro semplice		futuro anteriore	
contender**ò**	contender**emo**	**avrò** conteso	**avremo** conteso
contender**ai**	contender**ete**	**avrai** conteso	**avrete** conteso
contender**à**	contender**anno**	**avrà** conteso	**avranno** conteso
condizionale presente		condizionale passato	
contender**ei**	contender**emmo**	**avrei** conteso	**avremmo** conteso
contender**esti**	contender**este**	**avresti** conteso	**avreste** conteso
contender**ebbe**	contender**ebbero**	**avrebbe** conteso	**avrebbero** conteso
congiuntivo presente		congiuntivo passato	
contend**a**	contend**iamo**	**abbia** conteso	**abbiamo** conteso
contend**a**	contend**iate**	**abbia** conteso	**abbiate** conteso
contend**a**	contend**ano**	**abbia** conteso	**abbiano** conteso
congiuntivo imperfetto		congiuntivo trapassato	
contend**essi**	contend**essimo**	**avessi** conteso	**avessimo** conteso
contend**essi**	contend**este**	**avessi** conteso	**aveste** conteso
contend**esse**	contend**essero**	**avesse** conteso	**avessero** conteso
imperativo			
	contendiamo		
contendi; non contendere	contendete		
contenda	contendano		

to contain **contenere**

gerundio **contenendo** participio passato **contenuto**

SINGULAR	PLURAL
indicativo presente	
conteng**o**	conten**iamo**
contien**i**	conten**ete**
contien**e**	conteng**ono**
imperfetto	
contene**vo**	contene**vamo**
contene**vi**	contene**vate**
contene**va**	contene**vano**
passato remoto	
contenn**i**	conten**emmo**
conten**esti**	conten**este**
contenn**e**	contenn**ero**
futuro semplice	
conterr**ò**	conterr**emo**
conterr**ai**	conterr**ete**
conterr**à**	conterr**anno**
condizionale presente	
conterr**ei**	conterr**emmo**
conterr**esti**	conterr**este**
conterr**ebbe**	conterr**ebbero**
congiuntivo presente	
conteng**a**	conten**iamo**
conteng**a**	conten**iate**
conteng**a**	conteng**ano**
congiuntivo imperfetto	
conten**essi**	conten**essimo**
conten**essi**	conten**este**
conten**esse**	conten**essero**
imperativo	
	conteniamo
contieni; non contenere	contenete
contenga	contengano

SINGULAR	PLURAL
passato prossimo	
ho contenuto	**abbiamo** contenuto
hai contenuto	**avete** contenuto
ha contenuto	**hanno** contenuto
trapassato prossimo	
avevo contenuto	**avevamo** contenuto
avevi contenuto	**avevate** contenuto
aveva contenuto	**avevano** contenuto
trapassato remoto	
ebbi contenuto	**avemmo** contenuto
avesti contenuto	**aveste** contenuto
ebbe contenuto	**ebbero** contenuto
futuro anteriore	
avrò contenuto	**avremo** contenuto
avrai contenuto	**avrete** contenuto
avrà contenuto	**avranno** contenuto
condizionale passato	
avrei contenuto	**avremmo** contenuto
avresti contenuto	**avreste** contenuto
avrebbe contenuto	**avrebbero** contenuto
congiuntivo passato	
abbia contenuto	**abbiamo** contenuto
abbia contenuto	**abbiate** contenuto
abbia contenuto	**abbiano** contenuto
congiuntivo trapassato	
avessi contenuto	**avessimo** contenuto
avessi contenuto	**aveste** contenuto
avesse contenuto	**avessero** contenuto

continuare — to continue

gerundio **continuando** — participio passato **continuato**

SINGULAR	PLURAL
indicativo presente	
continu**o**	continu**iamo**
continu**i**	continu**ate**
continu**a**	continu**ano**
imperfetto	
continua**vo**	continua**vamo**
continua**vi**	continua**vate**
continua**va**	continua**vano**
passato remoto	
continu**ai**	continu**ammo**
continu**asti**	continu**aste**
continu**ò**	continu**arono**
futuro semplice	
continuer**ò**	continuer**emo**
continuer**ai**	continuer**ete**
continuer**à**	continuer**anno**
condizionale presente	
continuer**ei**	continuer**emmo**
continuer**esti**	continuer**este**
continuer**ebbe**	continuer**ebbero**
congiuntivo presente	
continu**i**	continu**iamo**
continu**i**	continu**iate**
continu**i**	continu**ino**
congiuntivo imperfetto	
continu**assi**	continu**assimo**
continu**assi**	continu**aste**
continu**asse**	continu**assero**
imperativo	
	continuiamo
continua; non continuare	continuate
continui	continuino

SINGULAR	PLURAL
passato prossimo	
ho continuato	**abbiamo** continuato
hai continuato	**avete** continuato
ha continuato	**hanno** continuato
trapassato prossimo	
avevo continuato	**avevamo** continuato
avevi continuato	**avevate** continuato
aveva continuato	**avevano** continuato
trapassato remoto	
ebbi continuato	**avemmo** continuato
avesti continuato	**aveste** continuato
ebbe continuato	**ebbero** continuato
futuro anteriore	
avrò continuato	**avremo** continuato
avrai continuato	**avrete** continuato
avrà continuato	**avranno** continuato
condizionale passato	
avrei continuato	**avremmo** continuato
avresti continuato	**avreste** continuato
avrebbe continuato	**avrebbero** continuato
congiuntivo passato	
abbia continuato	**abbiamo** continuato
abbia continuato	**abbiate** continuato
abbia continuato	**abbiano** continuato
congiuntivo trapassato	
avessi continuato	**avessimo** continuato
avessi continuato	**aveste** continuato
avesse continuato	**avessero** continuato

gerundio **contraddicendo** participio passato **contraddetto**

SINGULAR	PLURAL
indicativo presente	
contraddic**o**	contraddic**iamo**
contraddic**i**	contradd**ite**
contraddic**e**	contraddic**ono**
imperfetto	
contraddice**vo**	contraddice**vamo**
contraddice**vi**	contraddice**vate**
contraddice**va**	contraddice**vano**
passato remoto	
contraddiss**i**	contraddic**emmo**
contraddic**esti**	contraddic**este**
contraddiss**e**	contraddiss**ero**
futuro semplice	
contraddir**ò**	contraddir**emo**
contraddir**ai**	contraddir**ete**
contraddir**à**	contraddir**anno**
condizionale presente	
contraddir**ei**	contraddir**emmo**
contraddir**esti**	contraddir**este**
contraddir**ebbe**	contraddir**ebbero**
congiuntivo presente	
contraddic**a**	contraddic**iamo**
contraddic**a**	contraddic**iate**
contraddic**a**	contraddic**ano**
congiuntivo imperfetto	
contraddic**essi**	contraddic**essimo**
contraddic**essi**	contraddic**este**
contraddic**esse**	contraddic**essero**
imperativo	
	contraddiciamo
contraddici; non contraddire	contraddite
contraddica	contraddicano

SINGULAR	PLURAL
passato prossimo	
ho contraddetto	**abbiamo** contraddetto
hai contraddetto	**avete** contraddetto
ha contraddetto	**hanno** contraddetto
trapassato prossimo	
avevo contraddetto	**avevamo** contraddetto
avevi contraddetto	**avevate** contraddetto
aveva contraddetto	**avevano** contraddetto
trapassato remoto	
ebbi contraddetto	**avemmo** contraddetto
avesti contraddetto	**aveste** contraddetto
ebbe contraddetto	**ebbero** contraddetto
futuro anteriore	
avrò contraddetto	**avremo** contraddetto
avrai contraddetto	**avrete** contraddetto
avrà contraddetto	**avranno** contraddetto
condizionale passato	
avrei contraddetto	**avremmo** contraddetto
avresti contraddetto	**avreste** contraddetto
avrebbe contraddetto	**avrebbero** contraddetto
congiuntivo passato	
abbia contraddetto	**abbiamo** contraddetto
abbia contraddetto	**abbiate** contraddetto
abbia contraddetto	**abbiano** contraddetto
congiuntivo trapassato	
avessi contraddetto	**avessimo** contraddetto
avessi contraddetto	**aveste** contraddetto
avesse contraddetto	**avessero** contraddetto

contrarre — to contract, to incur, to catch

gerundio **contraendo** — participio passato **contratto**

SINGULAR	PLURAL
indicativo presente	
contraggo	contraiamo
contrai	contraete
contrae	contraggono
imperfetto	
contraevo	contraevamo
contraevi	contraevate
contraeva	contraevano
passato remoto	
contrassi	contraemmo
contraesti	contraeste
contrasse	contrassero
futuro semplice	
contrarrò	contrarremo
contrarrai	contrarrete
contrarrà	contrarranno
condizionale presente	
contrarrei	contrarremmo
contrarresti	contrarreste
contrarrebbe	contrarrebbero
congiuntivo presente	
contragga	contraiamo
contragga	contraiate
contragga	contraggano
congiuntivo imperfetto	
contraessi	contraessimo
contraessi	contraeste
contraesse	contraessero
imperativo	
	contraiamo
contrai; non contrarre	contraete
contragga	contraggano

SINGULAR	PLURAL
passato prossimo	
ho contratto	abbiamo contratto
hai contratto	avete contratto
ha contratto	hanno contratto
trapassato prossimo	
avevo contratto	avevamo contratto
avevi contratto	avevate contratto
aveva contratto	avevano contratto
trapassato remoto	
ebbi contratto	avemmo contratto
avesti contratto	aveste contratto
ebbe contratto	ebbero contratto
futuro anteriore	
avrò contratto	avremo contratto
avrai contratto	avrete contratto
avrà contratto	avranno contratto
condizionale passato	
avrei contratto	avremmo contratto
avresti contratto	avreste contratto
avrebbe contratto	avrebbero contratto
congiuntivo passato	
abbia contratto	abbiamo contratto
abbia contratto	abbiate contratto
abbia contratto	abbiano contratto
congiuntivo trapassato	
avessi contratto	avessimo contratto
avessi contratto	aveste contratto
avesse contratto	avessero contratto

gerundio **convenendo** participio passato **convenuto**

SINGULAR	PLURAL	SINGULAR	PLURAL
indicativo presente		passato prossimo	
convien**e**	conveng**ono**	**è** convenuto(a)	**sono** convenuti(e)
imperfetto		trapassato prossimo	
conveni**va**	conveni**vano**	**era** convenuto(a)	**erano** convenuti(e)
passato remoto		trapassato remoto	
convenn**e**	convenn**ero**	**fu** convenuto(a)	**furono** convenuti(e)
futuro semplice		futuro anteriore	
converr**à**	converr**anno**	**sarà** convenuto(a)	**saranno** convenuti(e)
condizionale presente		condizionale passato	
converr**ebbe**	converr**ebbero**	**sarebbe** convenuto(a)	**sarebbero** convenuti(e)
congiuntivo presente		congiuntivo passato	
conveng**a**	conveng**ano**	**sia** convenuto(a)	**siano** convenuti(e)
congiuntivo imperfetto		congiuntivo trapassato	
conven**isse**	conven**issero**	**fosse** convenuto(a)	**fossero** convenuti(e)

convertire — to convert

gerundio **convertendo** participio passato **convertito**

SINGULAR	PLURAL
indicativo presente	
converto	convertiamo
converti	convertite
converte	convertono
imperfetto	
convertivo	convertivamo
convertivi	convertivate
convertiva	convertivano
passato remoto	
convertii	convertimmo
convertisti	convertiste
convertì	convertirono
futuro semplice	
convertirò	convertiremo
convertirai	convertirete
convertirà	convertiranno
condizionale presente	
convertirei	convertiremmo
convertiresti	convertireste
convertirebbe	convertirebbero
congiuntivo presente	
converta	convertiamo
converta	convertiate
converta	convertano
congiuntivo imperfetto	
convertissi	convertissimo
convertissi	convertiste
convertisse	convertissero
imperativo	
	convertiamo
converti; non convertire	convertite
converta	convertano

SINGULAR	PLURAL
passato prossimo	
ho convertito	abbiamo convertito
hai convertito	avete convertito
ha convertito	hanno convertito
trapassato prossimo	
avevo convertito	avevamo convertito
avevi convertito	avevate convertito
aveva convertito	avevano convertito
trapassato remoto	
ebbi convertito	avemmo convertito
avesti convertito	aveste convertito
ebbe convertito	ebbero convertito
futuro anteriore	
avrò convertito	avremo convertito
avrai convertito	avrete convertito
avrà convertito	avranno convertito
condizionale passato	
avrei convertito	avremmo convertito
avresti convertito	avreste convertito
avrebbe convertito	avrebbero convertito
congiuntivo passato	
abbia convertito	abbiamo convertito
abbia convertito	abbiate convertito
abbia convertito	abbiano convertito
congiuntivo trapassato	
avessi convertito	avessimo convertito
avessi convertito	aveste convertito
avesse convertito	avessero convertito

to convince, to persuade convincere

gerundio **convincendo** participio passato **convinto**

SINGULAR	PLURAL	SINGULAR	PLURAL
indicativo presente		passato prossimo	
convinc**o**	convinc**iamo**	**ho** convinto	**abbiamo** convinto
convinc**i**	convinc**ete**	**hai** convinto	**avete** convinto
convinc**e**	convinc**ono**	**ha** convinto	**hanno** convinto
imperfetto		trapassato prossimo	
convince**vo**	convince**vamo**	**avevo** convinto	**avevamo** convinto
convince**vi**	convince**vate**	**avevi** convinto	**avevate** convinto
convince**va**	convince**vano**	**aveva** convinto	**avevano** convinto
passato remoto		trapassato remoto	
convins**i**	convinc**emmo**	**ebbi** convinto	**avemmo** convinto
convinc**esti**	convinc**este**	**avesti** convinto	**aveste** convinto
convins**e**	convins**ero**	**ebbe** convinto	**ebbero** convinto
futuro semplice		futuro anteriore	
convincer**ò**	convincer**emo**	**avrò** convinto	**avremo** convinto
convincer**ai**	convincer**ete**	**avrai** convinto	**avrete** convinto
convincer**à**	convincer**anno**	**avrà** convinto	**avranno** convinto
condizionale presente		condizionale passato	
convincer**ei**	convincer**emmo**	**avrei** convinto	**avremmo** convinto
convincer**esti**	convincer**este**	**avresti** convinto	**avreste** convinto
convincer**ebbe**	convincer**ebbero**	**avrebbe** convinto	**avrebbero** convinto
congiuntivo presente		congiuntivo passato	
convinc**a**	convinc**iamo**	**abbia** convinto	**abbiamo** convinto
convinc**a**	convinc**iate**	**abbia** convinto	**abbiate** convinto
convinc**a**	convinc**ano**	**abbia** convinto	**abbiano** convinto
congiuntivo imperfetto		congiuntivo trapassato	
convinc**essi**	convinc**essimo**	**avessi** convinto	**avessimo** convinto
convinc**essi**	convinc**este**	**avessi** convinto	**aveste** convinto
convinc**esse**	convinc**essero**	**avesse** convinto	**avessero** convinto
imperativo			
	convinciamo		
convinci; non convincere	convincete		
convinca	convincano		

C

copiare — to copy

gerundio **copiando** — participio passato **copiato**

SINGULAR	PLURAL
indicativo presente	
copi**o**	copi**amo**
cop**i**	copi**ate**
copi**a**	copi**ano**
imperfetto	
copia**vo**	copia**vamo**
copia**vi**	copia**vate**
copia**va**	copia**vano**
passato remoto	
copia**i**	copi**ammo**
copi**asti**	copi**aste**
copi**ò**	copiar**ono**
futuro semplice	
copier**ò**	copier**emo**
copier**ai**	copier**ete**
copier**à**	copier**anno**
condizionale presente	
copier**ei**	copier**emmo**
copier**esti**	copier**este**
copier**ebbe**	copier**ebbero**
congiuntivo presente	
cop**i**	copi**amo**
cop**i**	copi**ate**
cop**i**	cop**ino**
congiuntivo imperfetto	
copi**assi**	copi**assimo**
copi**assi**	copi**aste**
copi**asse**	copi**assero**
imperativo	
	copiamo
copia; non copiare	copiate
copi	copino

SINGULAR	PLURAL
passato prossimo	
ho copiato	**abbiamo** copiato
hai copiato	**avete** copiato
ha copiato	**hanno** copiato
trapassato prossimo	
avevo copiato	**avevamo** copiato
avevi copiato	**avevate** copiato
aveva copiato	**avevano** copiato
trapassato remoto	
ebbi copiato	**avemmo** copiato
avesti copiato	**aveste** copiato
ebbe copiato	**ebbero** copiato
futuro anteriore	
avrò copiato	**avremo** copiato
avrai copiato	**avrete** copiato
avrà copiato	**avranno** copiato
condizionale passato	
avrei copiato	**avremmo** copiato
avresti copiato	**avreste** copiato
avrebbe copiato	**avrebbero** copiato
congiuntivo passato	
abbia copiato	**abbiamo** copiato
abbia copiato	**abbiate** copiato
abbia copiato	**abbiano** copiato
congiuntivo trapassato	
avessi copiato	**avessimo** copiato
avessi copiato	**aveste** copiato
avesse copiato	**avessero** copiato

gerundio **coprendo** participio passato **coperto**

SINGULAR	PLURAL
indicativo presente	
copr**o**	copr**iamo**
copr**i**	copr**ite**
copr**e**	copr**ono**
imperfetto	
copri**vo**	copri**vamo**
copri**vi**	copri**vate**
copri**va**	copri**vano**
passato remoto	
copr**ii**	copr**immo**
copr**isti**	copr**iste**
copr**ì**	copri**rono**
futuro semplice	
copri**rò**	copri**remo**
copri**rai**	copri**rete**
copri**rà**	copri**ranno**
condizionale presente	
copri**rei**	copri**remmo**
copri**resti**	copri**reste**
copri**rebbe**	copri**rebbero**
congiuntivo presente	
copr**a**	copr**iamo**
copr**a**	copr**iate**
copr**a**	copr**ano**
congiuntivo imperfetto	
copr**issi**	copr**issimo**
copr**issi**	copr**iste**
copr**isse**	copr**issero**
imperativo	
	copriamo
copri; non coprire	coprite
copra	coprano

SINGULAR	PLURAL
passato prossimo	
ho coperto	**abbiamo** coperto
hai coperto	**avete** coperto
ha coperto	**hanno** coperto
trapassato prossimo	
avevo coperto	**avevamo** coperto
avevi coperto	**avevate** coperto
aveva coperto	**avevano** coperto
trapassato remoto	
ebbi coperto	**avemmo** coperto
avesti coperto	**aveste** coperto
ebbe coperto	**ebbero** coperto
futuro anteriore	
avrò coperto	**avremo** coperto
avrai coperto	**avrete** coperto
avrà coperto	**avranno** coperto
condizionale passato	
avrei coperto	**avremmo** coperto
avresti coperto	**avreste** coperto
avrebbe coperto	**avrebbero** coperto
congiuntivo passato	
abbia coperto	**abbiamo** coperto
abbia coperto	**abbiate** coperto
abbia coperto	**abbiano** coperto
congiuntivo trapassato	
avessi coperto	**avessimo** coperto
avessi coperto	**aveste** coperto
avesse coperto	**avessero** coperto

correggere — to correct

gerundio **correggendo** — participio passato **corretto**

C

SINGULAR	PLURAL
indicativo presente	
corregg**o**	corregg**iamo**
corregg**i**	corregg**ete**
corregg**e**	corregg**ono**
imperfetto	
corregge**vo**	corregge**vamo**
corregge**vi**	corregge**vate**
corregge**va**	corregge**vano**
passato remoto	
corress**i**	corregg**emmo**
corregg**esti**	corregg**este**
corress**e**	corress**ero**
futuro semplice	
corregger**ò**	corregger**emo**
corregger**ai**	corregger**ete**
corregger**à**	corregger**anno**
condizionale presente	
corregger**ei**	corregger**emmo**
corregger**esti**	corregger**este**
corregger**ebbe**	corregger**ebbero**
congiuntivo presente	
corregg**a**	corregg**iamo**
corregg**a**	corregg**iate**
corregg**a**	corregg**ano**
congiuntivo imperfetto	
corregg**essi**	corregg**essimo**
corregg**essi**	corregg**este**
corregg**esse**	corregg**essero**
imperativo	
	correggiamo
correggi; non correggere	correggete
corregga	correggano

SINGULAR	PLURAL
passato prossimo	
ho corretto	**abbiamo** corretto
hai corretto	**avete** corretto
ha corretto	**hanno** corretto
trapassato prossimo	
avevo corretto	**avevamo** corretto
avevi corretto	**avevate** corretto
aveva corretto	**avevano** corretto
trapassato remoto	
ebbi corretto	**avemmo** corretto
avesti corretto	**aveste** corretto
ebbe corretto	**ebbero** corretto
futuro anteriore	
avrò corretto	**avremo** corretto
avrai corretto	**avrete** corretto
avrà corretto	**avranno** corretto
condizionale passato	
avrei corretto	**avremmo** corretto
avresti corretto	**avreste** corretto
avrebbe corretto	**avrebbero** corretto
congiuntivo passato	
abbia corretto	**abbiamo** corretto
abbia corretto	**abbiate** corretto
abbia corretto	**abbiano** corretto
congiuntivo trapassato	
avessi corretto	**avessimo** corretto
avessi corretto	**aveste** corretto
avesse corretto	**avessero** corretto

to run **correre**

gerundio **correndo** participio passato **corso**

SINGULAR	PLURAL	SINGULAR	PLURAL
indicativo presente		passato prossimo	
corr**o**	corr**iamo**	**ho** corso	**abbiamo** corso
corr**i**	corr**ete**	**hai** corso	**avete** corso
corr**e**	corr**ono**	**ha** corso	**hanno** corso
imperfetto		trapassato prossimo	
corre**vo**	corre**vamo**	**avevo** corso	**avevamo** corso
corre**vi**	corre**vate**	**avevi** corso	**avevate** corso
corre**va**	corre**vano**	**aveva** corso	**avevano** corso
passato remoto		trapassato remoto	
cors**i**	corr**emmo**	**ebbi** corso	**avemmo** corso
corr**esti**	corr**este**	**avesti** corso	**aveste** corso
cors**e**	cors**ero**	**ebbe** corso	**ebbero** corso
futuro semplice		futuro anteriore	
correr**ò**	correr**emo**	**avrò** corso	**avremo** corso
correr**ai**	correr**ete**	**avrai** corso	**avrete** corso
correr**à**	correr**anno**	**avrà** corso	**avranno** corso
condizionale presente		condizionale passato	
correr**ei**	correr**emmo**	**avrei** corso	**avremmo** corso
correr**esti**	correr**este**	**avresti** corso	**avreste** corso
correr**ebbe**	correr**ebbero**	**avrebbe** corso	**avrebbero** corso
congiuntivo presente		congiuntivo passato	
corr**a**	corr**iamo**	**abbia** corso	**abbiamo** corso
corr**a**	corr**iate**	**abbia** corso	**abbiate** corso
corr**a**	corr**ano**	**abbia** corso	**abbiano** corso
congiuntivo imperfetto		congiuntivo trapassato	
corr**essi**	corr**essimo**	**avessi** corso	**avessimo** corso
corr**essi**	corr**este**	**avessi** corso	**aveste** corso
corr**esse**	corr**essero**	**avesse** corso	**avessero** corso
imperativo			
	corriamo		
corri; non correre	correte		
corra	corrano		

C

corrispondere — to correspond

gerundio **corrispondendo** — participio passato **corrisposto**

SINGULAR	PLURAL	SINGULAR	PLURAL
indicativo presente		passato prossimo	
corrispond**o**	corrispond**iamo**	**ho** corrisposto	**abbiamo** corrisposto
corrispond**i**	corrispond**ete**	**hai** corrisposto	**avete** corrisposto
corrispond**e**	corrispond**ono**	**ha** corrisposto	**hanno** corrisposto
imperfetto		trapassato prossimo	
corrisponde**vo**	corrisponde**vamo**	**avevo** corrisposto	**avevamo** corrisposto
corrisponde**vi**	corrisponde**vate**	**avevi** corrisposto	**avevate** corrisposto
corrisponde**va**	corrisponde**vano**	**aveva** corrisposto	**avevano** corrisposto
passato remoto		trapassato remoto	
corrispos**i**	corrispond**emmo**	**ebbi** corrisposto	**avemmo** corrisposto
corrispond**esti**	corrispond**este**	**avesti** corrisposto	**aveste** corrisposto
corrispos**e**	corrispos**ero**	**ebbe** corrisposto	**ebbero** corrisposto
futuro semplice		futuro anteriore	
corrisponder**ò**	corrisponder**emo**	**avrò** corrisposto	**avremo** corrisposto
corrisponder**ai**	corrisponder**ete**	**avrai** corrisposto	**avrete** corrisposto
corrisponder**à**	corrisponder**anno**	**avrà** corrisposto	**avranno** corrisposto
condizionale presente		condizionale passato	
corrisponder**ei**	corrisponder**emmo**	**avrei** corrisposto	**avremmo** corrisposto
corrisponder**esti**	corrisponder**este**	**avresti** corrisposto	**avreste** corrisposto
corrisponder**ebbe**	corrisponder**ebbero**	**avrebbe** corrisposto	**avrebbero** corrisposto
congiuntivo presente		congiuntivo passato	
corrispond**a**	corrispond**iamo**	**abbia** corrisposto	**abbiamo** corrisposto
corrispond**a**	corrispond**iate**	**abbia** corrisposto	**abbiate** corrisposto
corrispond**a**	corrispond**ano**	**abbia** corrisposto	**abbiano** corrisposto
congiuntivo imperfetto		congiuntivo trapassato	
corrispond**essi**	corrispond**essimo**	**avessi** corrisposto	**avessimo** corrisposto
corrispond**essi**	corrispond**este**	**avessi** corrisposto	**aveste** corrisposto
corrispond**esse**	corrispond**essero**	**avesse** corrisposto	**avessero** corrisposto
imperativo			
	corrispondiamo		
corrispondi; non corrispondere	corrispondete		
corrisponda	corrispondano		

to corrupt — corrompere

gerundio **corrompendo** participio passato **corrotto**

SINGULAR	PLURAL	SINGULAR	PLURAL
indicativo presente		passato prossimo	
corromp**o**	corromp**iamo**	**ho** corrotto	**abbiamo** corrotto
corromp**i**	corromp**ete**	**hai** corrotto	**avete** corrotto
corromp**e**	corromp**ono**	**ha** corrotto	**hanno** corrotto
imperfetto		trapassato prossimo	
corrompe**vo**	corrompe**vamo**	**avevo** corrotto	**avevamo** corrotto
corrompe**vi**	corrompe**vate**	**avevi** corrotto	**avevate** corrotto
corrompe**va**	corrompe**vano**	**aveva** corrotto	**avevano** corrotto
passato remoto		trapassato remoto	
corrupp**i**	corromp**emmo**	**ebbi** corrotto	**avemmo** corrotto
corromp**esti**	corromp**este**	**avesti** corrotto	**aveste** corrotto
corrupp**e**	corrupp**ero**	**ebbe** corrotto	**ebbero** corrotto
futuro semplice		futuro anteriore	
corromper**ò**	corromper**emo**	**avrò** corrotto	**avremo** corrotto
corromper**ai**	corromper**ete**	**avrai** corrotto	**avrete** corrotto
corromper**à**	corromper**anno**	**avrà** corrotto	**avranno** corrotto
condizionale presente		condizionale passato	
corromper**ei**	corromper**emmo**	**avrei** corrotto	**avremmo** corrotto
corromper**esti**	corromper**este**	**avresti** corrotto	**avreste** corrotto
corromper**ebbe**	corromper**ebbero**	**avrebbe** corrotto	**avrebbero** corrotto
congiuntivo presente		congiuntivo passato	
corromp**a**	corromp**iamo**	**abbia** corrotto	**abbiamo** corrotto
corromp**a**	corromp**iate**	**abbia** corrotto	**abbiate** corrotto
corromp**a**	corromp**ano**	**abbia** corrotto	**abbiano** corrotto
congiuntivo imperfetto		congiuntivo trapassato	
corromp**essi**	corromp**essimo**	**avessi** corrotto	**avessimo** corrotto
corromp**essi**	corromp**este**	**avessi** corrotto	**aveste** corrotto
corromp**esse**	corromp**essero**	**avesse** corrotto	**avessero** corrotto

imperativo

SINGULAR	PLURAL
	corrompiamo
corrompi; non corrompere	corrompete
corrompa	corrompano

C

cospargere — to spread, to sprinkle

gerundio **cospargendo** participio passato **cosparso**

SINGULAR	PLURAL	SINGULAR	PLURAL
indicativo presente		passato prossimo	
cosparg**o**	cosparg**iamo**	**ho** cosparso	**abbiamo** cosparso
cosparg**i**	cosparg**ete**	**hai** cosparso	**avete** cosparso
cosparg**e**	cosparg**ono**	**ha** cosparso	**hanno** cosparso
imperfetto		trapassato prossimo	
cosparge**vo**	cosparge**vamo**	**avevo** cosparso	**avevamo** cosparso
cosparge**vi**	cosparge**vate**	**avevi** cosparso	**avevate** cosparso
cosparge**va**	cosparge**vano**	**aveva** cosparso	**avevano** cosparso
passato remoto		trapassato remoto	
cospars**i**	cosparg**emmo**	**ebbi** cosparso	**avemmo** cosparso
cosparg**esti**	cosparg**este**	**avesti** cosparso	**aveste** cosparso
cospars**e**	cospars**ero**	**ebbe** cosparso	**ebbero** cosparso
futuro semplice		futuro anteriore	
cosparger**ò**	cosparger**emo**	**avrò** cosparso	**avremo** cosparso
cosparger**ai**	cosparger**ete**	**avrai** cosparso	**avrete** cosparso
cosparger**à**	cosparger**anno**	**avrà** cosparso	**avranno** cosparso
condizionale presente		condizionale passato	
cosparger**ei**	cosparger**emmo**	**avrei** cosparso	**avremmo** cosparso
cosparger**esti**	cosparger**este**	**avresti** cosparso	**avreste** cosparso
cosparger**ebbe**	cosparger**ebbero**	**avrebbe** cosparso	**avrebbero** cosparso
congiuntivo presente		congiuntivo passato	
cosparg**a**	cosparg**iamo**	**abbia** cosparso	**abbiamo** cosparso
cosparg**a**	cosparg**iate**	**abbia** cosparso	**abbiate** cosparso
cosparg**a**	cosparg**ano**	**abbia** cosparso	**abbiano** cosparso
congiuntivo imperfetto		congiuntivo trapassato	
cosparg**essi**	cosparg**essimo**	**avessi** cosparso	**avessimo** cosparso
cosparg**essi**	cosparg**este**	**avessi** cosparso	**aveste** cosparso
cosparg**esse**	cosparg**essero**	**avesse** cosparso	**avessero** cosparso
imperativo			
	cospargiamo		
cospargi; non cospargere	cospargete		
cosparga	cospargano		

to cost — costare

gerundio **costando** | participio passato **costato**

SINGULAR	PLURAL	SINGULAR	PLURAL
indicativo presente		passato prossimo	
cost**a**	cost**ano**	**è** costato(a)	**sono** costati(e)
imperfetto		trapassato prossimo	
costa**va**	costa**vano**	**era** costato(a)	**erano** costati(e)
passato remoto		trapassato remoto	
cost**ò**	cost**arono**	**fu** costato(a)	**furono** costati(e)
futuro semplice		futuro anteriore	
coster**à**	coster**anno**	**sarà** costato(a)	**saranno** costati(e)
condizionale presente		condizionale passato	
coster**ebbe**	coster**ebbero**	**sarebbe** costato(a)	**sarebbero** costati(e)
congiuntivo presente		congiuntivo passato	
cost**i**	cost**ino**	**sia** costato(a)	**siano** costati(e)
congiuntivo imperfetto		congiuntivo trapassato	
cost**asse**	cost**assero**	**fosse** costato(a)	**fossero** costati(e)

costringere — to force, to compel

gerundio **costringendo** — participio passato **costretto**

SINGULAR	PLURAL
indicativo presente	
costring**o**	costring**iamo**
costring**i**	costring**ete**
costring**e**	costring**ono**
imperfetto	
costringe**vo**	costringe**vamo**
costringe**vi**	costringe**vate**
costringe**va**	costringe**vano**
passato remoto	
costrins**i**	costring**emmo**
costring**esti**	costring**este**
costrins**e**	costrins**ero**
futuro semplice	
costringer**ò**	costringer**emo**
costringer**ai**	costringer**ete**
costringer**à**	costringer**anno**
condizionale presente	
costringer**ei**	costringer**emmo**
costringer**esti**	costringer**este**
costringer**ebbe**	costringer**ebbero**
congiuntivo presente	
costring**a**	costring**iamo**
costring**a**	costring**iate**
costring**a**	costring**ano**
congiuntivo imperfetto	
costring**essi**	costring**essimo**
costring**essi**	costring**este**
costring**esse**	costring**essero**
imperativo	
	costringiamo
costringi; non costringere	costringete
costringa	costringano

SINGULAR	PLURAL
passato prossimo	
ho costretto	**abbiamo** costretto
hai costretto	**avete** costretto
ha costretto	**hanno** costretto
trapassato prossimo	
avevo costretto	**avevamo** costretto
avevi costretto	**avevate** costretto
aveva costretto	**avevano** costretto
trapassato remoto	
ebbi costretto	**avemmo** costretto
avesti costretto	**aveste** costretto
ebbe costretto	**ebbero** costretto
futuro anteriore	
avrò costretto	**avremo** costretto
avrai costretto	**avrete** costretto
avrà costretto	**avranno** costretto
condizionale passato	
avrei costretto	**avremmo** costretto
avresti costretto	**avreste** costretto
avrebbe costretto	**avrebbero** costretto
congiuntivo passato	
abbia costretto	**abbiamo** costretto
abbia costretto	**abbiate** costretto
abbia costretto	**abbiano** costretto
congiuntivo trapassato	
avessi costretto	**avessimo** costretto
avessi costretto	**aveste** costretto
avesse costretto	**avessero** costretto

to build, to construct **costruire**

gerundio **costruendo** participio passato **costruito**

SINGULAR	PLURAL	SINGULAR	PLURAL
indicativo presente		passato prossimo	
costruisc**o**	costru**iamo**	**ho** costruito	**abbiamo** costruito
costruisc**i**	costru**ite**	**hai** costruito	**avete** costruito
costruisc**e**	costruisc**ono**	**ha** costruito	**hanno** costruito
imperfetto		trapassato prossimo	
costrui**vo**	costrui**vamo**	**avevo** costruito	**avevamo** costruito
costrui**vi**	costrui**vate**	**avevi** costruito	**avevate** costruito
costrui**va**	costrui**vano**	**aveva** costruito	**avevano** costruito
passato remoto		trapassato remoto	
costru**ii**	costru**immo**	**ebbi** costruito	**avemmo** costruito
costru**isti**	costru**iste**	**avesti** costruito	**aveste** costruito
costru**ì**	costrui**rono**	**ebbe** costruito	**ebbero** costruito
futuro semplice		futuro anteriore	
costruir**ò**	costruir**emo**	**avrò** costruito	**avremo** costruito
costruir**ai**	costruir**ete**	**avrai** costruito	**avrete** costruito
costruir**à**	costruir**anno**	**avrà** costruito	**avranno** costruito
condizionale presente		condizionale passato	
costruir**ei**	costruir**emmo**	**avrei** costruito	**avremmo** costruito
costruir**esti**	costruir**este**	**avresti** costruito	**avreste** costruito
costruir**ebbe**	costruir**ebbero**	**avrebbe** costruito	**avrebbero** costruito
congiuntivo presente		congiuntivo passato	
costruisc**a**	costru**iamo**	**abbia** costruito	**abbiamo** costruito
costruisc**a**	costru**iate**	**abbia** costruito	**abbiate** costruito
costruisc**a**	costruisc**ano**	**abbia** costruito	**abbiano** costruito
congiuntivo imperfetto		congiuntivo trapassato	
costru**issi**	costru**issimo**	**avessi** costruito	**avessimo** costruito
costru**issi**	costru**iste**	**avessi** costruito	**aveste** costruito
costru**isse**	costru**issero**	**avesse** costruito	**avessero** costruito
imperativo			
	costruiamo		
costruisci; non costruire	costruite		
costruisca	costruiscano		

C

credere — to believe

gerundio **credendo** — participio passato **creduto**

SINGULAR	PLURAL
indicativo presente	
cred**o**	cred**iamo**
cred**i**	cred**ete**
cred**e**	cred**ono**
imperfetto	
crede**vo**	crede**vamo**
crede**vi**	crede**vate**
crede**va**	crede**vano**
passato remoto	
cred**ei**, cred**etti**	cred**emmo**
cred**esti**	cred**este**
cred**é**, cred**ette**	cred**erono**, cred**ettero**
futuro semplice	
creder**ò**	creder**emo**
creder**ai**	creder**ete**
creder**à**	creder**anno**
condizionale presente	
creder**ei**	creder**emmo**
creder**esti**	creder**este**
creder**ebbe**	creder**ebbero**
congiuntivo presente	
cred**a**	cred**iamo**
cred**a**	cred**iate**
cred**a**	cred**ano**
congiuntivo imperfetto	
cred**essi**	cred**essimo**
cred**essi**	cred**este**
cred**esse**	cred**essero**
imperativo	
	crediamo
credi; non credere	credete
creda	credano

C

SINGULAR	PLURAL
passato prossimo	
ho creduto	**abbiamo** creduto
hai creduto	**avete** creduto
ha creduto	**hanno** creduto
trapassato prossimo	
avevo creduto	**avevamo** creduto
avevi creduto	**avevate** creduto
aveva creduto	**avevano** creduto
trapassato remoto	
ebbi creduto	**avemmo** creduto
avesti creduto	**aveste** creduto
ebbe creduto	**ebbero** creduto
futuro anteriore	
avrò creduto	**avremo** creduto
avrai creduto	**avrete** creduto
avrà creduto	**avranno** creduto
condizionale passato	
avrei creduto	**avremmo** creduto
avresti creduto	**avreste** creduto
avrebbe creduto	**avrebbero** creduto
congiuntivo passato	
abbia creduto	**abbiamo** creduto
abbia creduto	**abbiate** creduto
abbia creduto	**abbiano** creduto
congiuntivo trapassato	
avessi creduto	**avessimo** creduto
avessi creduto	**aveste** creduto
avesse creduto	**avessero** creduto

gerundio **crescendo** participio passato **cresciuto**

SINGULAR	PLURAL
indicativo presente	
cresc**o**	cresc**iamo**
cresc**i**	cresc**ete**
cresc**e**	cresc**ono**
imperfetto	
cresce**vo**	cresce**vamo**
cresce**vi**	cresce**vate**
cresce**va**	cresce**vano**
passato remoto	
crebb**i**	cresc**emmo**
cresc**esti**	cresc**este**
crebb**e**	crebb**ero**
futuro semplice	
crescer**ò**	crescer**emo**
crescer**ai**	crescer**ete**
crescer**à**	crescer**anno**
condizionale presente	
crescer**ei**	crescer**emmo**
crescer**esti**	crescer**este**
crescer**ebbe**	crescer**ebbero**
congiuntivo presente	
cresc**a**	cresc**iamo**
cresc**a**	cresc**iate**
cresc**a**	cresc**ano**
congiuntivo imperfetto	
cresc**essi**	cresc**essimo**
cresc**essi**	cresc**este**
cresc**esse**	cresc**essero**
imperativo	
	cresciamo
cresci; non crescere	crescete
cresca	crescano

SINGULAR	PLURAL
passato prossimo	
sono cresciuto(a)	**siamo** cresciuti(e)
sei cresciuto(a)	**siete** cresciuti(e)
è cresciuto(a)	**sono** cresciuti(e)
trapassato prossimo	
ero cresciuto(a)	**eravamo** cresciuti(e)
eri cresciuto(a)	**eravate** cresciuti(e)
era cresciuto(a)	**erano** cresciuti(e)
trapassato remoto	
fui cresciuto(a)	**fummo** cresciuti(e)
fosti cresciuto(a)	**foste** cresciuti(e)
fu cresciuto(a)	**furono** cresciuti(e)
futuro anteriore	
sarò cresciuto(a)	**saremo** cresciuti(e)
sarai cresciuto(a)	**sarete** cresciuti(e)
sarà cresciuto(a)	**saranno** cresciuti(e)
condizionale passato	
sarei cresciuto(a)	**saremmo** cresciuti(e)
saresti cresciuto(a)	**sareste** cresciuti(e)
sarebbe cresciuto(a)	**sarebbero** cresciuti(e)
congiuntivo passato	
sia cresciuto(a)	**siamo** cresciuti(e)
sia cresciuto(a)	**siate** cresciuti(e)
sia cresciuto(a)	**siano** cresciuti(e)
congiuntivo trapassato	
fossi cresciuto(a)	**fossimo** cresciuti(e)
fossi cresciuto(a)	**foste** cresciuti(e)
fosse cresciuto(a)	**fossero** cresciuti(e)

cucinare — to cook

gerundio **cucinando** participio passato **cucinato**

indicativo presente

SINGULAR	PLURAL
cucin**o**	cucin**iamo**
cucin**i**	cucin**ate**
cucin**a**	cucin**ano**

imperfetto

SINGULAR	PLURAL
cucina**vo**	cucina**vamo**
cucina**vi**	cucina**vate**
cucina**va**	cucina**vano**

passato remoto

SINGULAR	PLURAL
cucin**ai**	cucin**ammo**
cucin**asti**	cucin**aste**
cucin**ò**	cucin**arono**

futuro semplice

SINGULAR	PLURAL
cuciner**ò**	cuciner**emo**
cuciner**ai**	cuciner**ete**
cuciner**à**	cuciner**anno**

condizionale presente

SINGULAR	PLURAL
cuciner**ei**	cuciner**emmo**
cuciner**esti**	cuciner**este**
cuciner**ebbe**	cuciner**ebbero**

congiuntivo presente

SINGULAR	PLURAL
cucin**i**	cucin**iamo**
cucin**i**	cucin**iate**
cucin**i**	cucin**ino**

congiuntivo imperfetto

SINGULAR	PLURAL
cucin**assi**	cucin**assimo**
cucin**assi**	cucin**aste**
cucin**asse**	cucin**assero**

imperativo

SINGULAR	PLURAL
	cuciniamo
cucina; non cucinare	cucinate
cucini	cucinino

passato prossimo

SINGULAR	PLURAL
ho cucinato	**abbiamo** cucinato
hai cucinato	**avete** cucinato
ha cucinato	**hanno** cucinato

trapassato prossimo

SINGULAR	PLURAL
avevo cucinato	**avevamo** cucinato
avevi cucinato	**avevate** cucinato
aveva cucinato	**avevano** cucinato

trapassato remoto

SINGULAR	PLURAL
ebbi cucinato	**avemmo** cucinato
avesti cucinato	**aveste** cucinato
ebbe cucinato	**ebbero** cucinato

futuro anteriore

SINGULAR	PLURAL
avrò cucinato	**avremo** cucinato
avrai cucinato	**avrete** cucinato
avrà cucinato	**avranno** cucinato

condizionale passato

SINGULAR	PLURAL
avrei cucinato	**avremmo** cucinato
avresti cucinato	**avreste** cucinato
avrebbe cucinato	**avrebbero** cucinato

congiuntivo passato

SINGULAR	PLURAL
abbia cucinato	**abbiamo** cucinato
abbia cucinato	**abbiate** cucinato
abbia cucinato	**abbiano** cucinato

congiuntivo trapassato

SINGULAR	PLURAL
avessi cucinato	**avessimo** cucinato
avessi cucinato	**aveste** cucinato
avesse cucinato	**avessero** cucinato

gerundio **cucendo** participio passato **cucito**

SINGULAR	PLURAL	SINGULAR	PLURAL
indicativo presente		passato prossimo	
cuci**o**	cuc**iamo**	**ho** cucito	**abbiamo** cucito
cuc**i**	cuc**ite**	**hai** cucito	**avete** cucito
cuc**e**	cuc**iono**	**ha** cucito	**hanno** cucito
imperfetto		trapassato prossimo	
cuci**vo**	cuci**vamo**	**avevo** cucito	**avevamo** cucito
cuci**vi**	cuci**vate**	**avevi** cucito	**avevate** cucito
cuci**va**	cuci**vano**	**aveva** cucito	**avevano** cucito
passato remoto		trapassato remoto	
cuc**ii**	cuc**immo**	**ebbi** cucito	**avemmo** cucito
cuc**isti**	cuc**iste**	**avesti** cucito	**aveste** cucito
cuc**ì**	cuc**irono**	**ebbe** cucito	**ebbero** cucito
futuro semplice		futuro anteriore	
cucir**ò**	cucir**emo**	**avrò** cucito	**avremo** cucito
cucir**ai**	cucir**ete**	**avrai** cucito	**avrete** cucito
cucir**à**	cucir**anno**	**avrà** cucito	**avranno** cucito
condizionale presente		condizionale passato	
cucir**ei**	cucir**emmo**	**avrei** cucito	**avremmo** cucito
cucir**esti**	cucir**este**	**avresti** cucito	**avreste** cucito
cucir**ebbe**	cucir**ebbero**	**avrebbe** cucito	**avrebbero** cucito
congiuntivo presente		congiuntivo passato	
cuci**a**	cuc**iamo**	**abbia** cucito	**abbiamo** cucito
cuci**a**	cuc**iate**	**abbia** cucito	**abbiate** cucito
cuci**a**	cuci**ano**	**abbia** cucito	**abbiano** cucito
congiuntivo imperfetto		congiuntivo trapassato	
cuc**issi**	cuc**issimo**	**avessi** cucito	**avessimo** cucito
cuc**issi**	cuc**iste**	**avessi** cucito	**aveste** cucito
cuc**isse**	cuc**issero**	**avesse** cucito	**avessero** cucito
imperativo			
	cuciamo		
cuci; non cucire	cucite		
cucia	cuciano		

C

cuocere — to cook

gerundio **cuocendo** participio passato **cotto**

SINGULAR	PLURAL
indicativo presente	
cuoc**io**	cuoc**iamo**
cuoc**i**	cuoc**ete**
cuoc**e**	cuoc**iono**
imperfetto	
cuoce**vo**	cuoce**vamo**
cuoce**vi**	cuoce**vate**
cuoce**va**	cuoce**vano**
passato remoto	
coss**i**	cuoc**emmo**
cuoc**esti**	cuoc**este**
coss**e**	coss**ero**
futuro semplice	
cuocer**ò**	cuocer**emo**
cuocer**ai**	cuocer**ete**
cuocer**à**	cuocer**anno**
condizionale presente	
cuocer**ei**	cuocer**emmo**
cuocer**esti**	cuocer**este**
cuocer**ebbe**	cuocer**ebbero**
congiuntivo presente	
cuoci**a**	cuoc**iamo**
cuoci**a**	cuoc**iate**
cuoci**a**	cuoc**iano**
congiuntivo imperfetto	
cuoc**essi**	cuoc**essimo**
cuoc**essi**	cuoc**este**
cuoc**esse**	cuoc**essero**
imperativo	
	cuociamo
cuoci; non cuocere	cuocete
cuocia	cuociano

SINGULAR	PLURAL
passato prossimo	
ho cotto	**abbiamo** cotto
hai cotto	**avete** cotto
ha cotto	**hanno** cotto
trapassato prossimo	
avevo cotto	**avevamo** cotto
avevi cotto	**avevate** cotto
aveva cotto	**avevano** cotto
trapassato remoto	
ebbi cotto	**avemmo** cotto
avesti cotto	**aveste** cotto
ebbe cotto	**ebbero** cotto
futuro anteriore	
avrò cotto	**avremo** cotto
avrai cotto	**avrete** cotto
avrà cotto	**avranno** cotto
condizionale passato	
avrei cotto	**avremmo** cotto
avresti cotto	**avreste** cotto
avrebbe cotto	**avrebbero** cotto
congiuntivo passato	
abbia cotto	**abbiamo** cotto
abbia cotto	**abbiate** cotto
abbia cotto	**abbiano** cotto
congiuntivo trapassato	
avessi cotto	**avessimo** cotto
avessi cotto	**aveste** cotto
avesse cotto	**avessero** cotto

gerundio **curando** participio passato **curato**

SINGULAR	PLURAL
indicativo presente	
cur**o**	cur**iamo**
cur**i**	cur**ate**
cur**a**	cur**ano**
imperfetto	
cura**vo**	cura**vamo**
cura**vi**	cura**vate**
cura**va**	cura**vano**
passato remoto	
cur**ai**	cur**ammo**
cur**asti**	cur**aste**
cur**ò**	cur**arono**
futuro semplice	
curer**ò**	curer**emo**
curer**ai**	curer**ete**
curer**à**	curer**anno**
condizionale presente	
curer**ei**	curer**emmo**
curer**esti**	curer**este**
curer**ebbe**	curer**ebbero**
congiuntivo presente	
cur**i**	cur**iamo**
cur**i**	cur**iate**
cur**i**	cur**ino**
congiuntivo imperfetto	
cur**assi**	cur**assimo**
cur**assi**	cur**aste**
cur**asse**	cur**assero**
imperativo	
	curiamo
cura; non curare	curate
curi	curino

SINGULAR	PLURAL
passato prossimo	
ho curato	**abbiamo** curato
hai curato	**avete** curato
ha curato	**hanno** curato
trapassato prossimo	
avevo curato	**avevamo** curato
avevi curato	**avevate** curato
aveva curato	**avevano** curato
trapassato remoto	
ebbi curato	**avemmo** curato
avesti curato	**aveste** curato
ebbe curato	**ebbero** curato
futuro anteriore	
avrò curato	**avremo** curato
avrai curato	**avrete** curato
avrà curato	**avranno** curato
condizionale passato	
avrei curato	**avremmo** curato
avresti curato	**avreste** curato
avrebbe curato	**avrebbero** curato
congiuntivo passato	
abbia curato	**abbiamo** curato
abbia curato	**abbiate** curato
abbia curato	**abbiano** curato
congiuntivo trapassato	
avessi curato	**avessimo** curato
avessi curato	**aveste** curato
avesse curato	**avessero** curato

dare — to give

gerundio **dando** participio passato **dato**

SINGULAR	PLURAL	SINGULAR	PLURAL
indicativo presente		passato prossimo	
do	**diamo**	**ho** dato	**abbiamo** dato
dai	**date**	**hai** dato	**avete** dato
dà	**danno**	**ha** dato	**hanno** dato
imperfetto		trapassato prossimo	
da**vo**	da**vamo**	**avevo** dato	**avevamo** dato
da**vi**	da**vate**	**avevi** dato	**avevate** dato
da**va**	da**vano**	**aveva** dato	**avevano** dato
passato remoto		trapassato remoto	
died**i**, d**etti**	d**emmo**	**ebbi** dato	**avemmo** dato
d**esti**	d**este**	**avesti** dato	**aveste** dato
died**e**, d**ette**	died**ero**, d**ettero**	**ebbe** dato	**ebbero** dato
futuro semplice		futuro anteriore	
dar**ò**	dar**emo**	**avrò** dato	**avremo** dato
dar**ai**	dar**ete**	**avrai** dato	**avrete** dato
dar**à**	dar**anno**	**avrà** dato	**avranno** dato
condizionale presente		condizionale passato	
dar**ei**	dar**emmo**	**avrei** dato	**avremmo** dato
dar**esti**	dar**este**	**avresti** dato	**avreste** dato
dar**ebbe**	dar**ebbero**	**avrebbe** dato	**avrebbero** dato
congiuntivo presente		congiuntivo passato	
d**ia**	d**iamo**	**abbia** dato	**abbiamo** dato
d**ia**	d**iate**	**abbia** dato	**abbiate** dato
d**ia**	d**iano**	**abbia** dato	**abbiano** dato
congiuntivo imperfetto		congiuntivo trapassato	
d**essi**	d**essimo**	**avessi** dato	**avessimo** dato
d**essi**	d**este**	**avessi** dato	**aveste** dato
d**esse**	d**essero**	**avesse** dato	**avessero** dato

imperativo

	diamo
da'/dai; non dare	date
dia	diano

to decide — decidere

gerundio **decidendo** participio passato **deciso**

SINGULAR	PLURAL
indicativo presente	
decid**o**	decid**iamo**
decid**i**	decid**ete**
decid**e**	decid**ono**
imperfetto	
decide**vo**	decide**vamo**
decide**vi**	decide**vate**
decide**va**	decide**vano**
passato remoto	
decis**i**	decid**emmo**
decid**esti**	decid**este**
decis**e**	decis**ero**
futuro semplice	
decider**ò**	decider**emo**
decider**ai**	decider**ete**
decider**à**	decider**anno**
condizionale presente	
decider**ei**	decider**emmo**
decider**esti**	decider**este**
decider**ebbe**	decider**ebbero**
congiuntivo presente	
decid**a**	decid**iamo**
decid**a**	decid**iate**
decid**a**	decid**ano**
congiuntivo imperfetto	
decid**essi**	decid**essimo**
decid**essi**	decid**este**
decid**esse**	decid**essero**
imperativo	
	decidiamo
decidi; non decidere	decidete
decida	decidano

SINGULAR	PLURAL
passato prossimo	
ho deciso	**abbiamo** deciso
hai deciso	**avete** deciso
ha deciso	**hanno** deciso
trapassato prossimo	
avevo deciso	**avevamo** deciso
avevi deciso	**avevate** deciso
aveva deciso	**avevano** deciso
trapassato remoto	
ebbi deciso	**avemmo** deciso
avesti deciso	**aveste** deciso
ebbe deciso	**ebbero** deciso
futuro anteriore	
avrò deciso	**avremo** deciso
avrai deciso	**avrete** deciso
avrà deciso	**avranno** deciso
condizionale passato	
avrei deciso	**avremmo** deciso
avresti deciso	**avreste** deciso
avrebbe deciso	**avrebbero** deciso
congiuntivo passato	
abbia deciso	**abbiamo** deciso
abbia deciso	**abbiate** deciso
abbia deciso	**abbiano** deciso
congiuntivo trapassato	
avessi deciso	**avessimo** deciso
avessi deciso	**aveste** deciso
avesse deciso	**avessero** deciso

definire — to define

gerundio **definendo** participio passato **definito**

SINGULAR	PLURAL
indicativo presente	
defin**isco**	defin**iamo**
defin**isci**	defin**ite**
defin**isce**	defin**iscono**
imperfetto	
defini**vo**	defini**vamo**
defini**vi**	defini**vate**
defini**va**	defini**vano**
passato remoto	
defin**ii**	defin**immo**
defin**isti**	defin**iste**
defin**ì**	defin**irono**
futuro semplice	
definir**ò**	definir**emo**
definir**ai**	definir**ete**
definir**à**	definir**anno**
condizionale presente	
definir**ei**	definir**emmo**
definir**esti**	definir**este**
definir**ebbe**	definir**ebbero**
congiuntivo presente	
defin**isca**	defin**iamo**
defin**isca**	defin**iate**
defin**isca**	defin**iscano**
congiuntivo imperfetto	
defin**issi**	defin**issimo**
defin**issi**	defin**iste**
defin**isse**	defin**issero**
imperativo	
	definiamo
definisci; non definire	definite
definisca	definiscano

SINGULAR	PLURAL
passato prossimo	
ho definito	**abbiamo** definito
hai definito	**avete** definito
ha definito	**hanno** definito
trapassato prossimo	
avevo definito	**avevamo** definito
avevi definito	**avevate** definito
aveva definito	**avevano** definito
trapassato remoto	
ebbi definito	**avemmo** definito
avesti definito	**aveste** definito
ebbe definito	**ebbero** definito
futuro anteriore	
avrò definito	**avremo** definito
avrai definito	**avrete** definito
avrà definito	**avranno** definito
condizionale passato	
avrei definito	**avremmo** definito
avresti definito	**avreste** definito
avrebbe definito	**avrebbero** definito
congiuntivo passato	
abbia definito	**abbiamo** definito
abbia definito	**abbiate** definito
abbia definito	**abbiano** definito
congiuntivo trapassato	
avessi definito	**avessimo** definito
avessi definito	**aveste** definito
avesse definito	**avessero** definito

gerundio **deliberando** participio passato **deliberato**

SINGULAR	PLURAL
indicativo presente	
delibero	deliberiamo
deliberi	deliberate
delibera	deliberano
imperfetto	
deliberavo	deliberavamo
deliberavi	deliberavate
deliberava	deliberavano
passato remoto	
deliberai	deliberammo
deliberasti	deliberaste
deliberò	deliberarono
futuro semplice	
delibererò	delibereremo
delibererai	delibererete
delibererà	delibereranno
condizionale presente	
delibererei	delibereremmo
delibereresti	deliberereste
delibererebbe	delibererebbero
congiuntivo presente	
deliberi	deliberiamo
deliberi	deliberiate
deliberi	deliberino
congiuntivo imperfetto	
deliberassi	deliberassimo
deliberassi	deliberaste
deliberasse	deliberassero
imperativo	
	deliberiamo
delibera; non deliberare	deliberate
deliberi	deliberino

SINGULAR	PLURAL
passato prossimo	
ho deliberato	abbiamo deliberato
hai deliberato	avete deliberato
ha deliberato	hanno deliberato
trapassato prossimo	
avevo deliberato	avevamo deliberato
avevi deliberato	avevate deliberato
aveva deliberato	avevano deliberato
trapassato remoto	
ebbi deliberato	avemmo deliberato
avesti deliberato	aveste deliberato
ebbe deliberato	ebbero deliberato
futuro anteriore	
avrò deliberato	avremo deliberato
avrai deliberato	avrete deliberato
avrà deliberato	avranno deliberato
condizionale passato	
avrei deliberato	avremmo deliberato
avresti deliberato	avreste deliberato
avrebbe deliberato	avrebbero deliberato
congiuntivo passato	
abbia deliberato	abbiamo deliberato
abbia deliberato	abbiate deliberato
abbia deliberato	abbiano deliberato
congiuntivo trapassato	
avessi deliberato	avessimo deliberato
avessi deliberato	aveste deliberato
avesse deliberato	avessero deliberato

deludere to disappoint, to let down

gerundio **deludendo** participio passato **deluso**

SINGULAR	PLURAL	SINGULAR	PLURAL
indicativo presente		passato prossimo	
delud**o**	delud**iamo**	**ho** deluso	**abbiamo** deluso
delud**i**	delud**ete**	**hai** deluso	**avete** deluso
delud**e**	delud**ono**	**ha** deluso	**hanno** deluso
imperfetto		trapassato prossimo	
delude**vo**	delude**vamo**	**avevo** deluso	**avevamo** deluso
delude**vi**	delude**vate**	**avevi** deluso	**avevate** deluso
delude**va**	delude**vano**	**aveva** deluso	**avevano** deluso
passato remoto		trapassato remoto	
delus**i**	delud**emmo**	**ebbi** deluso	**avemmo** deluso
delud**esti**	delud**este**	**avesti** deluso	**aveste** deluso
delus**e**	delus**ero**	**ebbe** deluso	**ebbero** deluso
futuro semplice		futuro anteriore	
deluder**ò**	deluder**emo**	**avrò** deluso	**avremo** deluso
deluder**ai**	deluder**ete**	**avrai** deluso	**avrete** deluso
deluder**à**	deluder**anno**	**avrà** deluso	**avranno** deluso
condizionale presente		condizionale passato	
deluder**ei**	deluder**emmo**	**avrei** deluso	**avremmo** deluso
deluder**esti**	deluder**este**	**avresti** deluso	**avreste** deluso
deluder**ebbe**	deluder**ebbero**	**avrebbe** deluso	**avrebbero** deluso
congiuntivo presente		congiuntivo passato	
delud**a**	delud**iamo**	**abbia** deluso	**abbiamo** deluso
delud**a**	delud**iate**	**abbia** deluso	**abbiate** deluso
delud**a**	delud**ano**	**abbia** deluso	**abbiano** deluso
congiuntivo imperfetto		congiuntivo trapassato	
delud**essi**	delud**essimo**	**avessi** deluso	**avessimo** deluso
delud**essi**	delud**este**	**avessi** deluso	**aveste** deluso
delud**esse**	delud**essero**	**avesse** deluso	**avessero** deluso
imperativo			
	deludiamo		
deludi; non deludere	deludete		
deluda	deludano		

gerundio **denunciando** participio passato **denunciato**

SINGULAR	PLURAL	SINGULAR	PLURAL
indicativo presente		passato prossimo	
denunc**io**	denunc**iamo**	**ho** denunciato	**abbiamo** denunciato
denunc**i**	denunc**iate**	**hai** denunciato	**avete** denunciato
denunc**ia**	denunc**iano**	**ha** denunciato	**hanno** denunciato
imperfetto		trapassato prossimo	
denuncia**vo**	denuncia**vamo**	**avevo** denunciato	**avevamo** denunciato
denuncia**vi**	denuncia**vate**	**avevi** denunciato	**avevate** denunciato
denuncia**va**	denuncia**vano**	**aveva** denunciato	**avevano** denunciato
passato remoto		trapassato remoto	
denunci**ai**	denunci**ammo**	**ebbi** denunciato	**avemmo** denunciato
denunci**asti**	denunci**aste**	**avesti** denunciato	**aveste** denunciato
denunci**ò**	denunci**arono**	**ebbe** denunciato	**ebbero** denunciato
futuro semplice		futuro anteriore	
denuncer**ò**	denuncer**emo**	**avrò** denunciato	**avremo** denunciato
denuncer**ai**	denuncer**ete**	**avrai** denunciato	**avrete** denunciato
denuncer**à**	denuncer**anno**	**avrà** denunciato	**avranno** denunciato
condizionale presente		condizionale passato	
denuncer**ei**	denuncer**emmo**	**avrei** denunciato	**avremmo** denunciato
denuncer**esti**	denuncer**este**	**avresti** denunciato	**avreste** denunciato
denuncer**ebbe**	denuncer**ebbero**	**avrebbe** denunciato	**avrebbero** denunciato
congiuntivo presente		congiuntivo passato	
denunc**i**	denunc**iamo**	**abbia** denunciato	**abbiamo** denunciato
denunc**i**	denunc**iate**	**abbia** denunciato	**abbiate** denunciato
denunc**i**	denunc**ino**	**abbia** denunciato	**abbiano** denunciato
congiuntivo imperfetto		congiuntivo trapassato	
denuncia**ssi**	denuncia**ssimo**	**avessi** denunciato	**avessimo** denunciato
denuncia**ssi**	denuncia**ste**	**avessi** denunciato	**aveste** denunciato
denuncia**sse**	denuncia**ssero**	**avesse** denunciato	**avessero** denunciato

imperativo

	denunciamo
denuncia; non denunciare	denunciate
denunci	denuncino

D

depositare — to deposit

gerundio **depositando** participio passato **depositato**

SINGULAR	PLURAL
indicativo presente	
deposit**o**	deposit**iamo**
deposit**i**	deposit**ate**
deposit**a**	deposit**ano**
imperfetto	
deposita**vo**	deposita**vamo**
deposita**vi**	deposita**vate**
deposita**va**	deposita**vano**
passato remoto	
deposit**ai**	deposit**ammo**
deposit**asti**	deposit**aste**
deposit**ò**	deposit**arono**
futuro semplice	
depositer**ò**	depositer**emo**
depositer**ai**	depositer**ete**
depositer**à**	depositer**anno**
condizionale presente	
depositer**ei**	depositer**emmo**
depositer**esti**	depositer**este**
depositer**ebbe**	depositer**ebbero**
congiuntivo presente	
deposit**i**	deposit**iamo**
deposit**i**	deposit**iate**
deposit**i**	deposit**ino**
congiuntivo imperfetto	
deposit**assi**	deposit**assimo**
deposit**assi**	deposit**aste**
deposit**asse**	deposit**assero**
imperativo	
	depositiamo
deposita; non depositare	depositate
depositi	depositino

SINGULAR	PLURAL
passato prossimo	
ho depositato	**abbiamo** depositato
hai depositato	**avete** depositato
ha depositato	**hanno** depositato
trapassato prossimo	
avevo depositato	**avevamo** depositato
avevi depositato	**avevate** depositato
aveva depositato	**avevano** depositato
trapassato remoto	
ebbi depositato	**avemmo** depositato
avesti depositato	**aveste** depositato
ebbe depositato	**ebbero** depositato
futuro anteriore	
avrò depositato	**avremo** depositato
avrai depositato	**avrete** depositato
avrà depositato	**avranno** depositato
condizionale passato	
avrei depositato	**avremmo** depositato
avresti depositato	**avreste** depositato
avrebbe depositato	**avrebbero** depositato
congiuntivo passato	
abbia depositato	**abbiamo** depositato
abbia depositato	**abbiate** depositato
abbia depositato	**abbiano** depositato
congiuntivo trapassato	
avessi depositato	**avessimo** depositato
avessi depositato	**aveste** depositato
avesse depositato	**avessero** depositato

to describe — descrivere

gerundio **descrivendo** participio passato **descritto**

SINGULAR	PLURAL
indicativo presente	
descrivo	descriviamo
descrivi	descrivete
descrive	descrivono
imperfetto	
descrivevo	descrivevamo
descrivevi	descrivevate
descriveva	descrivevano
passato remoto	
descrissi	descrivemmo
descrivesti	descriveste
descrisse	descrissero
futuro semplice	
descriverò	descriveremo
descriverai	descriverete
descriverà	descriveranno
condizionale presente	
descriverei	descriveremmo
descriveresti	descrivereste
descriverebbe	descriverebbero
congiuntivo presente	
descriva	descriviamo
descriva	descriviate
descriva	descrivano
congiuntivo imperfetto	
descrivessi	descrivessimo
descrivessi	descriveste
descrivesse	descrivessero
imperativo	
	descriviamo
descrivi; non descrivere	descrivete
descriva	descrivano

SINGULAR	PLURAL
passato prossimo	
ho descritto	**abbiamo** descritto
hai descritto	**avete** descritto
ha descritto	**hanno** descritto
trapassato prossimo	
avevo descritto	**avevamo** descritto
avevi descritto	**avevate** descritto
aveva descritto	**avevano** descritto
trapassato remoto	
ebbi descritto	**avemmo** descritto
avesti descritto	**aveste** descritto
ebbe descritto	**ebbero** descritto
futuro anteriore	
avrò descritto	**avremo** descritto
avrai descritto	**avrete** descritto
avrà descritto	**avranno** descritto
condizionale passato	
avrei descritto	**avremmo** descritto
avresti descritto	**avreste** descritto
avrebbe descritto	**avrebbero** descritto
congiuntivo passato	
abbia descritto	**abbiamo** descritto
abbia descritto	**abbiate** descritto
abbia descritto	**abbiano** descritto
congiuntivo trapassato	
avessi descritto	**avessimo** descritto
avessi descritto	**aveste** descritto
avesse descritto	**avessero** descritto

desiderare — to desire, to wish, to want

gerundio **desiderando** participio passato **desiderato**

D

SINGULAR	PLURAL	SINGULAR	PLURAL
indicativo presente		passato prossimo	
desider**o**	desider**iamo**	**ho** desiderato	**abbiamo** desiderato
desider**i**	desider**ate**	**hai** desiderato	**avete** desiderato
desider**a**	desider**ano**	**ha** desiderato	**hanno** desiderato
imperfetto		trapassato prossimo	
desidera**vo**	desidera**vamo**	**avevo** desiderato	**avevamo** desiderato
desidera**vi**	desidera**vate**	**avevi** desiderato	**avevate** desiderato
desidera**va**	desidera**vano**	**aveva** desiderato	**avevano** desiderato
passato remoto		trapassato remoto	
desider**ai**	desider**ammo**	**ebbi** desiderato	**avemmo** desiderato
desider**asti**	desider**aste**	**avesti** desiderato	**aveste** desiderato
desider**ò**	desider**arono**	**ebbe** desiderato	**ebbero** desiderato
futuro semplice		futuro anteriore	
desiderer**ò**	desiderer**emo**	**avrò** desiderato	**avremo** desiderato
desiderer**ai**	desiderer**ete**	**avrai** desiderato	**avrete** desiderato
desiderer**à**	desiderer**anno**	**avrà** desiderato	**avranno** desiderato
condizionale presente		condizionale passato	
desiderer**ei**	desiderer**emmo**	**avrei** desiderato	**avremmo** desiderato
desiderer**esti**	desiderer**este**	**avresti** desiderato	**avreste** desiderato
desiderer**ebbe**	desiderer**ebbero**	**avrebbe** desiderato	**avrebbero** desiderato
congiuntivo presente		congiuntivo passato	
desider**i**	desider**iamo**	**abbia** desiderato	**abbiamo** desiderato
desider**i**	desider**iate**	**abbia** desiderato	**abbiate** desiderato
desider**i**	desider**ino**	**abbia** desiderato	**abbiano** desiderato
congiuntivo imperfetto		congiuntivo trapassato	
desider**assi**	desider**assimo**	**avessi** desiderato	**avessimo** desiderato
desider**assi**	desider**aste**	**avessi** desiderato	**aveste** desiderato
desider**asse**	desider**assero**	**avesse** desiderato	**avessero** desiderato
imperativo			
	desideriamo		
desidera; non desiderare	desiderate		
desideri	desiderino		

to determine, to resolve **determinare**

gerundio **determinando** participio passato **determinato**

SINGULAR	PLURAL	SINGULAR	PLURAL
indicativo presente		passato prossimo	
determin**o**	determin**iamo**	**ho** determinato	**abbiamo** determinato
determin**i**	determin**ate**	**hai** determinato	**avete** determinato
determin**a**	determin**ano**	**ha** determinato	**hanno** determinato
imperfetto		trapassato prossimo	
determina**vo**	determina**vamo**	**avevo** determinato	**avevamo** determinato
determina**vi**	determina**vate**	**avevi** determinato	**avevate** determinato
determina**va**	determina**vano**	**aveva** determinato	**avevano** determinato
passato remoto		trapassato remoto	
determin**ai**	determin**ammo**	**ebbi** determinato	**avemmo** determinato
determin**asti**	determin**aste**	**avesti** determinato	**aveste** determinato
determin**ò**	determin**arono**	**ebbe** determinato	**ebbero** determinato
futuro semplice		futuro anteriore	
determiner**ò**	determiner**emo**	**avrò** determinato	**avremo** determinato
determiner**ai**	determiner**ete**	**avrai** determinato	**avrete** determinato
determiner**à**	determiner**anno**	**avrà** determinato	**avranno** determinato
condizionale presente		condizionale passato	
determin**erei**	determin**eremmo**	**avrei** determinato	**avremmo** determinato
determin**eresti**	determin**ereste**	**avresti** determinato	**avreste** determinato
determin**erebbe**	determin**erebbero**	**avrebbe** determinato	**avrebbero** determinato
congiuntivo presente		congiuntivo passato	
determin**i**	determin**iamo**	**abbia** determinato	**abbiamo** determinato
determin**i**	determin**iate**	**abbia** determinato	**abbiate** determinato
determin**i**	determin**ino**	**abbia** determinato	**abbiano** determinato
congiuntivo imperfetto		congiuntivo trapassato	
determin**assi**	determin**assimo**	**avessi** determinato	**avessimo** determinato
determin**assi**	determin**aste**	**avessi** determinato	**aveste** determinato
determin**asse**	determin**assero**	**avesse** determinato	**avessero** determinato

imperativo

	determiniamo
determina; non determinare	determinate
determini	determinino

D

detestare — to hate, to loathe

gerundio **detestando** — participio passato **detestato**

SINGULAR	PLURAL
indicativo presente	
detest**o**	detest**iamo**
detest**i**	detest**ate**
detest**a**	detest**ano**
imperfetto	
detesta**vo**	detesta**vamo**
detesta**vi**	detesta**vate**
detesta**va**	detesta**vano**
passato remoto	
detest**ai**	detest**ammo**
detest**asti**	detest**aste**
detest**ò**	detest**arono**
futuro semplice	
detester**ò**	detester**emo**
detester**ai**	detester**ete**
detester**à**	detester**anno**
condizionale presente	
detester**ei**	detester**emmo**
detester**esti**	detester**este**
detester**ebbe**	detester**ebbero**
congiuntivo presente	
detest**i**	detest**iamo**
detest**i**	detest**iate**
detest**i**	detest**ino**
congiuntivo imperfetto	
detest**assi**	detest**assimo**
detest**assi**	detest**aste**
detest**asse**	detest**assero**
imperativo	
	detestiamo
detesta; non detestare	detestate
detesti	detestino

SINGULAR	PLURAL
passato prossimo	
ho detestato	**abbiamo** detestato
hai detestato	**avete** detestato
ha detestato	**hanno** detestato
trapassato prossimo	
avevo detestato	**avevamo** detestato
avevi detestato	**avevate** detestato
aveva detestato	**avevano** detestato
trapassato remoto	
ebbi detestato	**avemmo** detestato
avesti detestato	**aveste** detestato
ebbe detestato	**ebbero** detestato
futuro anteriore	
avrò detestato	**avremo** detestato
avrai detestato	**avrete** detestato
avrà detestato	**avranno** detestato
condizionale passato	
avrei detestato	**avremmo** detestato
avresti detestato	**avreste** detestato
avrebbe detestato	**avrebbero** detestato
congiuntivo passato	
abbia detestato	**abbiamo** detestato
abbia detestato	**abbiate** detestato
abbia detestato	**abbiano** detestato
congiuntivo trapassato	
avessi detestato	**avessimo** detestato
avessi detestato	**aveste** detestato
avesse detestato	**avessero** detestato

gerundio **dettando** participio passato **dettato**

SINGULAR	PLURAL	SINGULAR	PLURAL
indicativo presente		passato prossimo	
dett**o**	dett**iamo**	**ho** dettato	**abbiamo** dettato
dett**i**	dett**ate**	**hai** dettato	**avete** dettato
dett**a**	dett**ano**	**ha** dettato	**hanno** dettato
imperfetto		trapassato prossimo	
detta**vo**	detta**vamo**	**avevo** dettato	**avevamo** dettato
detta**vi**	detta**vate**	**avevi** dettato	**avevate** dettato
detta**va**	detta**vano**	**aveva** dettato	**avevano** dettato
passato remoto		trapassato remoto	
dett**ai**	dett**ammo**	**ebbi** dettato	**avemmo** dettato
dett**asti**	dett**aste**	**avesti** dettato	**aveste** dettato
dett**ò**	dett**arono**	**ebbe** dettato	**ebbero** dettato
futuro semplice		futuro anteriore	
detter**ò**	detter**emo**	**avrò** dettato	**avremo** dettato
detter**ai**	detter**ete**	**avrai** dettato	**avrete** dettato
detter**à**	detter**anno**	**avrà** dettato	**avranno** dettato
condizionale presente		condizionale passato	
detter**ei**	detter**emmo**	**avrei** dettato	**avremmo** dettato
detter**esti**	detter**este**	**avresti** dettato	**avreste** dettato
detter**ebbe**	detter**ebbero**	**avrebbe** dettato	**avrebbero** dettato
congiuntivo presente		congiuntivo passato	
dett**i**	dett**iamo**	**abbia** dettato	**abbiamo** dettato
dett**i**	dett**iate**	**abbia** dettato	**abbiate** dettato
dett**i**	dett**ino**	**abbia** dettato	**abbiano** dettato
congiuntivo imperfetto		congiuntivo trapassato	
dett**assi**	dett**assimo**	**avessi** dettato	**avessimo** dettato
dett**assi**	dett**aste**	**avessi** dettato	**aveste** dettato
dett**asse**	dett**assero**	**avesse** dettato	**avessero** dettato
imperativo			
	dettiamo		
detta; non dettare	dettate		
detti	dettino		

difendere — to defend

gerundio **difendendo** participio passato **difeso**

D

SINGULAR	PLURAL	SINGULAR	PLURAL
indicativo presente		passato prossimo	
difend**o**	difend**iamo**	**ho** difeso	**abbiamo** difeso
difend**i**	difend**ete**	**hai** difeso	**avete** difeso
difend**e**	difend**ono**	**ha** difeso	**hanno** difeso
imperfetto		trapassato prossimo	
difende**vo**	difende**vamo**	**avevo** difeso	**avevamo** difeso
difende**vi**	difende**vate**	**avevi** difeso	**avevate** difeso
difende**va**	difende**vano**	**aveva** difeso	**avevano** difeso
passato remoto		trapassato remoto	
difes**i**	difend**emmo**	**ebbi** difeso	**avemmo** difeso
difend**esti**	difend**este**	**avesti** difeso	**aveste** difeso
difes**e**	difes**ero**	**ebbe** difeso	**ebbero** difeso
futuro semplice		futuro anteriore	
difender**ò**	difender**emo**	**avrò** difeso	**avremo** difeso
difender**ai**	difender**ete**	**avrai** difeso	**avrete** difeso
difender**à**	difender**anno**	**avrà** difeso	**avranno** difeso
condizionale presente		condizionale passato	
difender**ei**	difender**emmo**	**avrei** difeso	**avremmo** difeso
difender**esti**	difender**este**	**avresti** difeso	**avreste** difeso
difender**ebbe**	difender**ebbero**	**avrebbe** difeso	**avrebbero** difeso
congiuntivo presente		congiuntivo passato	
difend**a**	difend**iamo**	**abbia** difeso	**abbiamo** difeso
difend**a**	difend**iate**	**abbia** difeso	**abbiate** difeso
difend**a**	difend**ano**	**abbia** difeso	**abbiano** difeso
congiuntivo imperfetto		congiuntivo trapassato	
difend**essi**	difend**essimo**	**avessi** difeso	**avessimo** difeso
difend**essi**	difend**este**	**avessi** difeso	**aveste** difeso
difend**esse**	difend**essero**	**avesse** difeso	**avessero** difeso
imperativo			
	difendiamo		
difendi; non difendere	difendete		
difenda	difendano		

gerundio **diffondendo** participio passato **diffuso**

SINGULAR	PLURAL
indicativo presente	
diffond**o**	diffond**iamo**
diffond**i**	diffond**ete**
diffond**e**	diffond**ono**
imperfetto	
diffonde**vo**	diffonde**vamo**
diffonde**vi**	diffonde**vate**
diffonde**va**	diffonde**vano**
passato remoto	
diffus**i**	diffond**emmo**
diffond**esti**	diffond**este**
diffus**e**	diffus**ero**
futuro semplice	
diffonder**ò**	diffonder**emo**
diffonder**ai**	diffonder**ete**
diffonder**à**	diffonder**anno**
condizionale presente	
diffonder**ei**	diffonder**emmo**
diffonder**esti**	diffonder**este**
diffonder**ebbe**	diffonder**ebbero**
congiuntivo presente	
diffond**a**	diffond**iamo**
diffond**a**	diffond**iate**
diffond**a**	diffond**ano**
congiuntivo imperfetto	
diffond**essi**	diffond**essimo**
diffond**essi**	diffond**este**
diffond**esse**	diffond**essero**
imperativo	
	diffondiamo
diffondi; non diffondere	diffondete
diffonda	diffondano

SINGULAR	PLURAL
passato prossimo	
ho diffuso	**abbiamo** diffuso
hai diffuso	**avete** diffuso
ha diffuso	**hanno** diffuso
trapassato prossimo	
avevo diffuso	**avevamo** diffuso
avevi diffuso	**avevate** diffuso
aveva diffuso	**avevano** diffuso
trapassato remoto	
ebbi diffuso	**avemmo** diffuso
avesti diffuso	**aveste** diffuso
ebbe diffuso	**ebbero** diffuso
futuro anteriore	
avrò diffuso	**avremo** diffuso
avrai diffuso	**avrete** diffuso
avrà diffuso	**avranno** diffuso
condizionale passato	
avrei diffuso	**avremmo** diffuso
avresti diffuso	**avreste** diffuso
avrebbe diffuso	**avrebbero** diffuso
congiuntivo passato	
abbia diffuso	**abbiamo** diffuso
abbia diffuso	**abbiate** diffuso
abbia diffuso	**abbiano** diffuso
congiuntivo trapassato	
avessi diffuso	**avessimo** diffuso
avessi diffuso	**aveste** diffuso
avesse diffuso	**avessero** diffuso

digerire — to digest, to tolerate

gerundio **digerendo** participio passato **digerito**

SINGULAR	PLURAL
indicativo presente	
digeris**co**	diger**iamo**
digeris**ci**	diger**ite**
digeris**ce**	digeris**cono**
imperfetto	
digeri**vo**	digeri**vamo**
digeri**vi**	digeri**vate**
digeri**va**	digeri**vano**
passato remoto	
diger**ii**	diger**immo**
diger**isti**	diger**iste**
diger**ì**	diger**irono**
futuro semplice	
digeri**rò**	digeri**remo**
digeri**rai**	digeri**rete**
digeri**rà**	digeri**ranno**
condizionale presente	
digeri**rei**	digeri**remmo**
digeri**resti**	digeri**reste**
digeri**rebbe**	digeri**rebbero**
congiuntivo presente	
digeris**ca**	diger**iamo**
digeris**ca**	diger**iate**
digeris**ca**	digeris**cano**
congiuntivo imperfetto	
diger**issi**	diger**issimo**
diger**issi**	diger**iste**
diger**isse**	diger**issero**
imperativo	
	digeriamo
digerisci; non digerire	digerite
digerisca	digeriscano

SINGULAR	PLURAL
passato prossimo	
ho digerito	**abbiamo** digerito
hai digerito	**avete** digerito
ha digerito	**hanno** digerito
trapassato prossimo	
avevo digerito	**avevamo** digerito
avevi digerito	**avevate** digerito
aveva digerito	**avevano** digerito
trapassato remoto	
ebbi digerito	**avemmo** digerito
avesti digerito	**aveste** digerito
ebbe digerito	**ebbero** digerito
futuro anteriore	
avrò digerito	**avremo** digerito
avrai digerito	**avrete** digerito
avrà digerito	**avranno** digerito
condizionale passato	
avrei digerito	**avremmo** digerito
avresti digerito	**avreste** digerito
avrebbe digerito	**avrebbero** digerito
congiuntivo passato	
abbia digerito	**abbiamo** digerito
abbia digerito	**abbiate** digerito
abbia digerito	**abbiano** digerito
congiuntivo trapassato	
avessi digerito	**avessimo** digerito
avessi digerito	**aveste** digerito
avesse digerito	**avessero** digerito

to forget — dimenticare

gerundio **dimenticando** participio passato **dimenticato**

SINGULAR	PLURAL
indicativo presente	
dimentic**o**	dimentic**hiamo**
dimentic**hi**	dimentic**ate**
dimentic**a**	dimentic**ano**
imperfetto	
dimentica**vo**	dimentica**vamo**
dimentica**vi**	dimentica**vate**
dimentica**va**	dimentica**vano**
passato remoto	
dimentic**ai**	dimentic**ammo**
dimentic**asti**	dimentic**aste**
dimentic**ò**	dimentic**arono**
futuro semplice	
dimentiche**rò**	dimentiche**remo**
dimentiche**rai**	dimentiche**rete**
dimentiche**rà**	dimentiche**ranno**
condizionale presente	
dimentiche**rei**	dimentiche**remmo**
dimentiche**resti**	dimentiche**reste**
dimentiche**rebbe**	dimentiche**rebbero**
congiuntivo presente	
dimentic**hi**	dimentic**hiamo**
dimentic**hi**	dimentic**hiate**
dimentic**hi**	dimentic**hino**
congiuntivo imperfetto	
dimentic**assi**	dimentic**assimo**
dimentic**assi**	dimentic**aste**
dimentic**asse**	dimentic**assero**
imperativo	
	dimentichiamo
dimentica; non dimenticare	dimenticate
dimentichi	dimentichino

SINGULAR	PLURAL
passato prossimo	
ho dimenticato	**abbiamo** dimenticato
hai dimenticato	**avete** dimenticato
ha dimenticato	**hanno** dimenticato
trapassato prossimo	
avevo dimenticato	**avevamo** dimenticato
avevi dimenticato	**avevate** dimenticato
aveva dimenticato	**avevano** dimenticato
trapassato remoto	
ebbi dimenticato	**avemmo** dimenticato
avesti dimenticato	**aveste** dimenticato
ebbe dimenticato	**ebbero** dimenticato
futuro anteriore	
avrò dimenticato	**avremo** dimenticato
avrai dimenticato	**avrete** dimenticato
avrà dimenticato	**avranno** dimenticato
condizionale passato	
avrei dimenticato	**avremmo** dimenticato
avresti dimenticato	**avreste** dimenticato
avrebbe dimenticato	**avrebbero** dimenticato
congiuntivo passato	
abbia dimenticato	**abbiamo** dimenticato
abbia dimenticato	**abbiate** dimenticato
abbia dimenticato	**abbiano** dimenticato
congiuntivo trapassato	
avessi dimenticato	**avessimo** dimenticato
avessi dimenticato	**aveste** dimenticato
avesse dimenticato	**avessero** dimenticato

gerundio **dimettendosi** participio passato **dimessosi**

SINGULAR	PLURAL	SINGULAR	PLURAL
indicativo presente		passato prossimo	
mi dimett**o**	**ci** dimett**iamo**	**mi sono** dimesso(a)	**ci siamo** dimessi(e)
ti dimett**i**	**vi** dimett**ete**	**ti sei** dimesso(a)	**vi siete** dimessi(e)
si dimett**e**	**si** dimett**ono**	**si è** dimesso(a)	**si sono** dimessi(e)
imperfetto		trapassato prossimo	
mi dimette**vo**	**ci** dimette**vamo**	**mi ero** dimesso(a)	**ci eravamo** dimessi(e)
ti dimette**vi**	**vi** dimette**vate**	**ti eri** dimesso(a)	**vi eravate** dimessi(e)
si dimette**va**	**si** dimette**vano**	**si era** dimesso(a)	**si erano** dimessi(e)
passato remoto		trapassato remoto	
mi dimis**i**	**ci** dimett**emmo**	**mi fui** dimesso(a)	**ci fummo** dimessi(e)
ti dimett**esti**	**vi** dimett**este**	**ti fosti** dimesso(a)	**vi foste** dimessi(e)
si dimis**e**	**si** dimis**ero**	**si fu** dimesso(a)	**si furono** dimessi(e)
futuro semplice		futuro anteriore	
mi dimetter**ò**	**ci** dimetter**emo**	**mi sarò** dimesso(a)	**ci saremo** dimessi(e)
ti dimetter**ai**	**vi** dimetter**ete**	**ti sarai** dimesso(a)	**vi sarete** dimessi(e)
si dimetter**à**	**si** dimetter**anno**	**si sarà** dimesso(a)	**si saranno** dimessi(e)
condizionale presente		condizionale passato	
mi dimetter**ei**	**ci** dimetter**emmo**	**mi sarei** dimesso(a)	**ci saremmo** dimessi(e)
ti dimetter**esti**	**vi** dimetter**este**	**ti saresti** dimesso(a)	**vi sareste** dimessi(e)
si dimetter**ebbe**	**si** dimetter**ebbero**	**si sarebbe** dimesso(a)	**si sarebbero** dimessi(e)
congiuntivo presente		congiuntivo passato	
mi dimett**a**	**ci** dimett**iamo**	**mi sia** dimesso(a)	**ci siamo** dimessi(e)
ti dimett**a**	**vi** dimett**iate**	**ti sia** dimesso(a)	**vi siate** dimessi(e)
si dimett**a**	**si** dimett**ano**	**si sia** dimesso(a)	**si siano** dimessi(e)
congiuntivo imperfetto		congiuntivo trapassato	
mi dimett**essi**	**ci** dimett**essimo**	**mi fossi** dimesso(a)	**ci fossimo** dimessi(e)
ti dimett**essi**	**vi** dimett**este**	**ti fossi** dimesso(a)	**vi foste** dimessi(e)
si dimett**esse**	**si** dimett**essero**	**si fosse** dimesso(a)	**si fossero** dimessi(e)

imperativo

	dimettiamoci
dimettiti; non dimetterti/ non ti dimettere	dimettetevi
si dimetta	si dimettano

D

to show, to demonstrate **dimostrare**

gerundio **dimostrando** participio passato **dimostrato**

SINGULAR	PLURAL
indicativo presente	
dimostr**o**	dimostr**iamo**
dimostr**i**	dimostr**ate**
dimostr**a**	dimostr**ano**
imperfetto	
dimostra**vo**	dimostra**vamo**
dimostra**vi**	dimostra**vate**
dimostra**va**	dimostra**vano**
passato remoto	
dimostr**ai**	dimostr**ammo**
dimostr**asti**	dimostr**aste**
dimostr**ò**	dimostr**arono**
futuro semplice	
dimostrer**ò**	dimostrer**emo**
dimostrer**ai**	dimostrer**ete**
dimostrer**à**	dimostrer**anno**
condizionale presente	
dimostrer**ei**	dimostrer**emmo**
dimostrer**esti**	dimostrer**este**
dimostrer**ebbe**	dimostrer**ebbero**
congiuntivo presente	
dimostr**i**	dimostr**iamo**
dimostr**i**	dimostr**iate**
dimostr**i**	dimostr**ino**
congiuntivo imperfetto	
dimostr**assi**	dimostr**assimo**
dimostr**assi**	dimostr**aste**
dimostr**asse**	dimostr**assero**
imperativo	
	dimostriamo
dimostra; non dimostrare	dimostrate
dimostri	dimostrino

SINGULAR	PLURAL
passato prossimo	
ho dimostrato	**abbiamo** dimostrato
hai dimostrato	**avete** dimostrato
ha dimostrato	**hanno** dimostrato
trapassato prossimo	
avevo dimostrato	**avevamo** dimostrato
avevi dimostrato	**avevate** dimostrato
aveva dimostrato	**avevano** dimostrato
trapassato remoto	
ebbi dimostrato	**avemmo** dimostrato
avesti dimostrato	**aveste** dimostrato
ebbe dimostrato	**ebbero** dimostrato
futuro anteriore	
avrò dimostrato	**avremo** dimostrato
avrai dimostrato	**avrete** dimostrato
avrà dimostrato	**avranno** dimostrato
condizionale passato	
avrei dimostrato	**avremmo** dimostrato
avresti dimostrato	**avreste** dimostrato
avrebbe dimostrato	**avrebbero** dimostrato
congiuntivo passato	
abbia dimostrato	**abbiamo** dimostrato
abbia dimostrato	**abbiate** dimostrato
abbia dimostrato	**abbiano** dimostrato
congiuntivo trapassato	
avessi dimostrato	**avessimo** dimostrato
avessi dimostrato	**aveste** dimostrato
avesse dimostrato	**avessero** dimostrato

dipendere — to depend

gerundio **dipendendo** participio passato **dipeso**

SINGULAR	PLURAL	SINGULAR	PLURAL
indicativo presente		passato prossimo	
dipend**o**	dipend**iamo**	**sono** dipeso(a)	**siamo** dipesi(e)
dipend**i**	dipend**ete**	**sei** dipeso(a)	**siete** dipesi(e)
dipend**e**	dipend**ono**	**è** dipeso(a)	**sono** dipesi(e)
imperfetto		trapassato prossimo	
dipende**vo**	dipende**vamo**	**ero** dipeso(a)	**eravamo** dipesi(e)
dipende**vi**	dipende**vate**	**eri** dipeso(a)	**eravate** dipesi(e)
dipende**va**	dipende**vano**	**era** dipeso(a)	**erano** dipesi(e)
passato remoto		trapassato remoto	
dipes**i**	dipend**emmo**	**fui** dipeso(a)	**fummo** dipesi(e)
dipend**esti**	dipend**este**	**fosti** dipeso(a)	**foste** dipesi(e)
dipes**e**	dipes**ero**	**fu** dipeso(a)	**furono** dipesi(e)
futuro semplice		futuro anteriore	
dipender**ò**	dipender**emo**	**sarò** dipeso(a)	**saremo** dipesi(e)
dipender**ai**	dipender**ete**	**sarai** dipeso(a)	**sarete** dipesi(e)
dipender**à**	dipender**anno**	**sarà** dipeso(a)	**saranno** dipesi(e)
condizionale presente		condizionale passato	
dipender**ei**	dipender**emmo**	**sarei** dipeso(a)	**saremmo** dipesi(e)
dipender**esti**	dipender**este**	**saresti** dipeso(a)	**sareste** dipesi(e)
dipender**ebbe**	dipender**ebbero**	**sarebbe** dipeso(a)	**sarebbero** dipesi(e)
congiuntivo presente		congiuntivo passato	
dipend**a**	dipend**iamo**	**sia** dipeso(a)	**siamo** dipesi(e)
dipend**a**	dipend**iate**	**sia** dipeso(a)	**siate** dipesi(e)
dipend**a**	dipend**ano**	**sia** dipeso(a)	**siano** dipesi(e)
congiuntivo imperfetto		congiuntivo trapassato	
dipend**essi**	dipend**essimo**	**fossi** dipeso(a)	**fossimo** dipesi(e)
dipend**essi**	dipend**este**	**fossi** dipeso(a)	**foste** dipesi(e)
dipend**esse**	dipend**essero**	**fosse** dipeso(a)	**fossero** dipesi(e)
imperativo			
	dipendiamo		
dipendi; non dipendere	dipendete		
dipenda	dipendano		

D

gerundio **dipingendo** participio passato **dipinto**

SINGULAR	PLURAL
indicativo presente	
dipingo	dipingiamo
dipingi	dipingete
dipinge	dipingono
imperfetto	
dipingevo	dipingevamo
dipingevi	dipingevate
dipingeva	dipingevano
passato remoto	
dipinsi	dipingemmo
dipingesti	dipingeste
dipinse	dipinsero
futuro semplice	
dipingerò	dipingeremo
dipingerai	dipingerete
dipingerà	dipingeranno
condizionale presente	
dipingerei	dipingeremmo
dipingeresti	dipingereste
dipingerebbe	dipingerebbero
congiuntivo presente	
dipinga	dipingiamo
dipinga	dipingiate
dipinga	dipingano
congiuntivo imperfetto	
dipingessi	dipingessimo
dipingessi	dipingeste
dipingesse	dipingessero
imperativo	
	dipingiamo
dipingi; non dipingere	dipingete
dipinga	dipingano

SINGULAR	PLURAL
passato prossimo	
ho dipinto	**abbiamo** dipinto
hai dipinto	**avete** dipinto
ha dipinto	**hanno** dipinto
trapassato prossimo	
avevo dipinto	**avevamo** dipinto
avevi dipinto	**avevate** dipinto
aveva dipinto	**avevano** dipinto
trapassato remoto	
ebbi dipinto	**avemmo** dipinto
avesti dipinto	**aveste** dipinto
ebbe dipinto	**ebbero** dipinto
futuro anteriore	
avrò dipinto	**avremo** dipinto
avrai dipinto	**avrete** dipinto
avrà dipinto	**avranno** dipinto
condizionale passato	
avrei dipinto	**avremmo** dipinto
avresti dipinto	**avreste** dipinto
avrebbe dipinto	**avrebbero** dipinto
congiuntivo passato	
abbia dipinto	**abbiamo** dipinto
abbia dipinto	**abbiate** dipinto
abbia dipinto	**abbiano** dipinto
congiuntivo trapassato	
avessi dipinto	**avessimo** dipinto
avessi dipinto	**aveste** dipinto
avesse dipinto	**avessero** dipinto

dire — to tell, to say

gerundio **dicendo** participio passato **detto**

SINGULAR	PLURAL	SINGULAR	PLURAL
indicativo presente		passato prossimo	
dic**o**	dic**iamo**	**ho** detto	**abbiamo** detto
dic**i**	dit**e**	**hai** detto	**avete** detto
dic**e**	dic**ono**	**ha** detto	**hanno** detto
imperfetto		trapassato prossimo	
dice**vo**	dice**vamo**	**avevo** detto	**avevamo** detto
dice**vi**	dice**vate**	**avevi** detto	**avevate** detto
dice**va**	dice**vano**	**aveva** detto	**avevano** detto
passato remoto		trapassato remoto	
diss**i**	dic**emmo**	**ebbi** detto	**avemmo** detto
dic**esti**	dic**este**	**avesti** detto	**aveste** detto
diss**e**	diss**ero**	**ebbe** detto	**ebbero** detto
futuro semplice		futuro anteriore	
dir**ò**	dir**emo**	**avrò** detto	**avremo** detto
dir**ai**	dir**ete**	**avrai** detto	**avrete** detto
dir**à**	dir**anno**	**avrà** detto	**avranno** detto
condizionale presente		condizionale passato	
dir**ei**	dir**emmo**	**avrei** detto	**avremmo** detto
dir**esti**	dir**este**	**avresti** detto	**avreste** detto
dir**ebbe**	dir**ebbero**	**avrebbe** detto	**avrebbero** detto
congiuntivo presente		congiuntivo passato	
dic**a**	dic**iamo**	**abbia** detto	**abbiamo** detto
dic**a**	dic**iate**	**abbia** detto	**abbiate** detto
dic**a**	dic**ano**	**abbia** detto	**abbiano** detto
congiuntivo imperfetto		congiuntivo trapassato	
dice**ssi**	dice**ssimo**	**avessi** detto	**avessimo** detto
dice**ssi**	dice**ste**	**avessi** detto	**aveste** detto
dice**sse**	dice**ssero**	**avesse** detto	**avessero** detto
imperativo			
	diciamo		
di'; non dire	dite		
dica	dicano		

D

gerundio **dirigendo** participio passato **diretto**

SINGULAR	PLURAL	SINGULAR	PLURAL
indicativo presente		passato prossimo	
dirig**o**	dirig**iamo**	**ho** diretto	**abbiamo** diretto
dirig**i**	dirig**ete**	**hai** diretto	**avete** diretto
dirig**e**	dirig**ono**	**ha** diretto	**hanno** diretto
imperfetto		trapassato prossimo	
dirige**vo**	dirige**vamo**	**avevo** diretto	**avevamo** diretto
dirige**vi**	dirige**vate**	**avevi** diretto	**avevate** diretto
dirige**va**	dirige**vano**	**aveva** diretto	**avevano** diretto
passato remoto		trapassato remoto	
diress**i**	dirig**emmo**	**ebbi** diretto	**avemmo** diretto
dirig**esti**	dirig**este**	**avesti** diretto	**aveste** diretto
diress**e**	diress**ero**	**ebbe** diretto	**ebbero** diretto
futuro semplice		futuro anteriore	
diriger**ò**	diriger**emo**	**avrò** diretto	**avremo** diretto
diriger**ai**	diriger**ete**	**avrai** diretto	**avrete** diretto
diriger**à**	diriger**anno**	**avrà** diretto	**avranno** diretto
condizionale presente		condizionale passato	
diriger**ei**	diriger**emmo**	**avrei** diretto	**avremmo** diretto
diriger**esti**	diriger**este**	**avresti** diretto	**avreste** diretto
diriger**ebbe**	diriger**ebbero**	**avrebbe** diretto	**avrebbero** diretto
congiuntivo presente		congiuntivo passato	
dirig**a**	dirig**iamo**	**abbia** diretto	**abbiamo** diretto
dirig**a**	dirig**iate**	**abbia** diretto	**abbiate** diretto
dirig**a**	dirig**ano**	**abbia** diretto	**abbiano** diretto
congiuntivo imperfetto		congiuntivo trapassato	
dirig**essi**	dirig**essimo**	**avessi** diretto	**avessimo** diretto
dirig**essi**	dirig**este**	**avessi** diretto	**aveste** diretto
dirig**esse**	dirig**essero**	**avesse** diretto	**avessero** diretto
imperativo			
	dirigiamo		
dirigi; non dirigere	dirigete		
diriga	dirigano		

D

disarmare — to disarm

gerundio **disarmando** participio passato **disarmato**

SINGULAR	PLURAL	SINGULAR	PLURAL
indicativo presente		passato prossimo	
disarm**o**	disarm**iamo**	**ho** disarmato	**abbiamo** disarmato
disarm**i**	disarm**ate**	**hai** disarmato	**avete** disarmato
disarm**a**	disarm**ano**	**ha** disarmato	**hanno** disarmato
imperfetto		trapassato prossimo	
disarma**vo**	disarma**vamo**	**avevo** disarmato	**avevamo** disarmato
disarma**vi**	disarma**vate**	**avevi** disarmato	**avevate** disarmato
disarma**va**	disarma**vano**	**aveva** disarmato	**avevano** disarmato
passato remoto		trapassato remoto	
disarm**ai**	disarm**ammo**	**ebbi** disarmato	**avemmo** disarmato
disarm**asti**	disarm**aste**	**avesti** disarmato	**aveste** disarmato
disarm**ò**	disarm**arono**	**ebbe** disarmato	**ebbero** disarmato
futuro semplice		futuro anteriore	
disarmer**ò**	disarmer**emo**	**avrò** disarmato	**avremo** disarmato
disarmer**ai**	disarmer**ete**	**avrai** disarmato	**avrete** disarmato
disarmer**à**	disarmer**anno**	**avrà** disarmato	**avranno** disarmato
condizionale presente		condizionale passato	
disarmer**ei**	disarmer**emmo**	**avrei** disarmato	**avremmo** disarmato
disarmer**esti**	disarmer**este**	**avresti** disarmato	**avreste** disarmato
disarmer**ebbe**	disarmer**ebbero**	**avrebbe** disarmato	**avrebbero** disarmato
congiuntivo presente		congiuntivo passato	
disarm**i**	disarm**iamo**	**abbia** disarmato	**abbiamo** disarmato
disarm**i**	disarm**iate**	**abbia** disarmato	**abbiate** disarmato
disarm**i**	disarm**ino**	**abbia** disarmato	**abbiano** disarmato
congiuntivo imperfetto		congiuntivo trapassato	
disarm**assi**	disarm**assimo**	**avessi** disarmato	**avessimo** disarmato
disarm**assi**	disarm**aste**	**avessi** disarmato	**aveste** disarmato
disarm**asse**	disarm**assero**	**avesse** disarmato	**avessero** disarmato

imperativo

	disarmiamo
disarma; non disarmare	disarmate
disarmi	disarmino

D

to descend, to do down discendere

gerundio **discendendo** participio passato **disceso**

SINGULAR	PLURAL
indicativo presente	
discend**o**	discend**iamo**
discend**i**	discend**ete**
discend**e**	discend**ono**
imperfetto	
discende**vo**	discende**vamo**
discende**vi**	discende**vate**
discende**va**	discende**vano**
passato remoto	
disces**i**	discend**emmo**
discend**esti**	discend**este**
disces**e**	disces**ero**
futuro semplice	
discender**ò**	discender**emo**
discender**ai**	discender**ete**
discender**à**	discender**anno**
condizionale presente	
discender**ei**	discender**emmo**
discender**esti**	discender**este**
discender**ebbe**	discender**ebbero**
congiuntivo presente	
discend**a**	discend**iamo**
discend**a**	discend**iate**
discend**a**	discend**ano**
congiuntivo imperfetto	
discend**essi**	discend**essimo**
discend**essi**	discend**este**
discend**esse**	discend**essero**
imperativo	
	discendiamo
discendi; non discendere	discendete
discenda	discendano

SINGULAR	PLURAL
passato prossimo	
sono disceso(a)	**siamo** discesi(e)
sei disceso(a)	**siete** discesi(e)
è disceso(a)	**sono** discesi(e)
trapassato prossimo	
ero disceso(a)	**eravamo** discesi(e)
eri disceso(a)	**eravate** discesi(e)
era disceso(a)	**erano** discesi(e)
trapassato remoto	
fui disceso(a)	**fummo** discesi(e)
fosti disceso(a)	**foste** discesi(e)
fu disceso(a)	**furono** discesi(e)
futuro anteriore	
sarò disceso(a)	**saremo** discesi(e)
sarai disceso(a)	**sarete** discesi(e)
sarà disceso(a)	**saranno** discesi(e)
condizionale passato	
sarei disceso(a)	**saremmo** discesi(e)
saresti disceso(a)	**sareste** discesi(e)
sarebbe disceso(a)	**sarebbero** discesi(e)
congiuntivo passato	
sia disceso(a)	**siamo** discesi(e)
sia disceso(a)	**siate** discesi(e)
sia disceso(a)	**siano** discesi(e)
congiuntivo trapassato	
fossi disceso(a)	**fossimo** discesi(e)
fossi disceso(a)	**foste** discesi(e)
fosse disceso(a)	**fossero** discesi(e)

discutere — to discuss, to argue

gerundio **discorrendo** participio passato **discusso**

SINGULAR	PLURAL	SINGULAR	PLURAL
indicativo presente		passato prossimo	
discut**o**	discut**iamo**	**ho** discusso	**abbiamo** discusso
discut**i**	discut**ete**	**hai** discusso	**avete** discusso
discut**e**	discut**ono**	**ha** discusso	**hanno** discusso
imperfetto		trapassato prossimo	
discute**vo**	discute**vamo**	**avevo** discusso	**avevamo** discusso
discute**vi**	discute**vate**	**avevi** discusso	**avevate** discusso
discute**va**	discute**vano**	**aveva** discusso	**avevano** discusso
passato remoto		trapassato remoto	
discuss**i**	discut**emmo**	**ebbi** discusso	**avemmo** discusso
discut**esti**	discut**este**	**avesti** discusso	**aveste** discusso
discuss**e**	discuss**ero**	**ebbe** discusso	**ebbero** discusso
futuro semplice		futuro anteriore	
discuter**ò**	discuter**emo**	**avrò** discusso	**avremo** discusso
discuter**ai**	discuter**ete**	**avrai** discusso	**avrete** discusso
discuter**à**	discuter**anno**	**avrà** discusso	**avranno** discusso
condizionale presente		condizionale passato	
discuter**ei**	discuter**emmo**	**avrei** discusso	**avremmo** discusso
discuter**esti**	discuter**este**	**avresti** discusso	**avreste** discusso
discuter**ebbe**	discuter**ebbero**	**avrebbe** discusso	**avrebbero** discusso
congiuntivo presente		congiuntivo passato	
discut**a**	discut**iamo**	**abbia** discusso	**abbiamo** discusso
discut**a**	discut**iate**	**abbia** discusso	**abbiate** discusso
discut**a**	discut**ano**	**abbia** discusso	**abbiano** discusso
congiuntivo imperfetto		congiuntivo trapassato	
discut**essi**	discut**essimo**	**avessi** discusso	**avessimo** discusso
discut**essi**	discut**este**	**avessi** discusso	**aveste** discusso
discut**esse**	discut**essero**	**avesse** discusso	**avessero** discusso
imperativo			
	discutiamo		
discuti; non discutere	discutete		
discuta	discutano		

D

gerundio **disfacendo** participio passato **disfatto**

SINGULAR	PLURAL	SINGULAR	PLURAL
indicativo presente		passato prossimo	
disfacci**o**, disf**o**	disfacc**iamo**	**ho** disfatto	**abbiamo** disfatto
disfa**i**	disf**ate**	**hai** disfatto	**avete** disfatto
disf**a**	disf**ano**	**ha** disfatto	**hanno** disfatto
imperfetto		trapassato prossimo	
disface**vo**	disface**vamo**	**avevo** disfatto	**avevamo** disfatto
disface**vi**	disface**vate**	**avevi** disfatto	**avevate** disfatto
disface**va**	disface**vano**	**aveva** disfatto	**avevano** disfatto
passato remoto		trapassato remoto	
disfec**i**	disfac**emmo**	**ebbi** disfatto	**avemmo** disfatto
disfac**esti**	disfac**este**	**avesti** disfatto	**aveste** disfatto
disfec**e**	disfec**ero**	**ebbe** disfatto	**ebbero** disfatto
futuro semplice		futuro anteriore	
disfar**ò**	disfar**emo**	**avrò** disfatto	**avremo** disfatto
disfar**ai**	disfar**ete**	**avrai** disfatto	**avrete** disfatto
disfar**à**	disfar**anno**	**avrà** disfatto	**avranno** disfatto
condizionale presente		condizionale passato	
disfar**ei**	disfar**emmo**	**avrei** disfatto	**avremmo** disfatto
disfar**esti**	disfar**este**	**avresti** disfatto	**avreste** disfatto
disfar**ebbe**	disfar**ebbero**	**avrebbe** disfatto	**avrebbero** disfatto
congiuntivo presente		congiuntivo passato	
disfacci**a**	disfacc**iamo**	**abbia** disfatto	**abbiamo** disfatto
disfacci**a**	disfacc**iate**	**abbia** disfatto	**abbiate** disfatto
disfacci**a**	disfacc**iano**	**abbia** disfatto	**abbiano** disfatto
congiuntivo imperfetto		congiuntivo trapassato	
disfac**essi**	disfac**essimo**	**avessi** disfatto	**avessimo** disfatto
disfac**essi**	disfac**este**	**avessi** disfatto	**aveste** disfatto
disfac**esse**	disfac**essero**	**avesse** disfatto	**avessero** disfatto
imperativo			
	disfacciamo		
disfai; non disfare	disfate		
disfaccia	disfacciano		

disgustare — to disgust

gerundio **disgustando** participio passato **disgustato**

D

SINGULAR	PLURAL
indicativo presente	
disgust**o**	disgust**iamo**
disgust**i**	disgust**ate**
disgust**a**	disgust**ano**
imperfetto	
disgusta**vo**	disgusta**vamo**
disgusta**vi**	disgusta**vate**
disgusta**va**	disgusta**vano**
passato remoto	
disgust**ai**	disgust**ammo**
disgust**asti**	disgust**aste**
disgust**ò**	disgust**arono**
futuro semplice	
disguster**ò**	disguster**emo**
disguster**ai**	disguster**ete**
disguster**à**	disguster**anno**
condizionale presente	
disguster**ei**	disguster**emmo**
disguster**esti**	disguster**este**
disguster**ebbe**	disguster**ebbero**
congiuntivo presente	
disgust**i**	disgust**iamo**
disgust**i**	disgust**iate**
disgust**i**	disgust**ino**
congiuntivo imperfetto	
disgust**assi**	disgust**assimo**
disgust**assi**	disgust**aste**
disgust**asse**	disgust**assero**
imperativo	
	disgustiamo
disgusta; non disgustare	disgustate
disgusti	disgustino

SINGULAR	PLURAL
passato prossimo	
ho disgustato	**abbiamo** disgustato
hai disgustato	**avete** disgustato
ha disgustato	**hanno** disgustato
trapassato prossimo	
avevo disgustato	**avevamo** disgustato
avevi disgustato	**avevate** disgustato
aveva disgustato	**avevano** disgustato
trapassato remoto	
ebbi disgustato	**avemmo** disgustato
avesti disgustato	**aveste** disgustato
ebbe disgustato	**ebbero** disgustato
futuro anteriore	
avrò disgustato	**avremo** disgustato
avrai disgustato	**avrete** disgustato
avrà disgustato	**avranno** disgustato
condizionale passato	
avrei disgustato	**avremmo** disgustato
avresti disgustato	**avreste** disgustato
avrebbe disgustato	**avrebbero** disgustato
congiuntivo passato	
abbia disgustato	**abbiamo** disgustato
abbia disgustato	**abbiate** disgustato
abbia disgustato	**abbiano** disgustato
congiuntivo trapassato	
avessi disgustato	**avessimo** disgustato
avessi disgustato	**aveste** disgustato
avesse disgustato	**avessero** disgustato

to despair — disperare

gerundio **disperando** participio passato **disperato**

SINGULAR	PLURAL	SINGULAR	PLURAL
indicativo presente		passato prossimo	
disper**o**	disper**iamo**	**ho** disperato	**abbiamo** disperato
disper**i**	disper**ate**	**hai** disperato	**avete** disperato
disper**a**	disper**ano**	**ha** disperato	**hanno** disperato
imperfetto		trapassato prossimo	
dispera**vo**	dispera**vamo**	**avevo** disperato	**avevamo** disperato
dispera**vi**	dispera**vate**	**avevi** disperato	**avevate** disperato
dispera**va**	dispera**vano**	**aveva** disperato	**avevano** disperato
passato remoto		trapassato remoto	
disper**ai**	disper**ammo**	**ebbi** disperato	**avemmo** disperato
disper**asti**	disper**aste**	**avesti** disperato	**aveste** disperato
disper**ò**	disper**arono**	**ebbe** disperato	**ebbero** disperato
futuro semplice		futuro anteriore	
disperer**ò**	disperer**emo**	**avrò** disperato	**avremo** disperato
disperer**ai**	disperer**ete**	**avrai** disperato	**avrete** disperato
disperer**à**	disperer**anno**	**avrà** disperato	**avranno** disperato
condizionale presente		condizionale passato	
disperer**ei**	disperer**emmo**	**avrei** disperato	**avremmo** disperato
disperer**esti**	disperer**este**	**avresti** disperato	**avreste** disperato
disperer**ebbe**	disperer**ebbero**	**avrebbe** disperato	**avrebbero** disperato
congiuntivo presente		congiuntivo passato	
disper**i**	disper**iamo**	**abbia** disperato	**abbiamo** disperato
disper**i**	disper**iate**	**abbia** disperato	**abbiate** disperato
disper**i**	disper**ino**	**abbia** disperato	**abbiano** disperato
congiuntivo imperfetto		congiuntivo trapassato	
disper**assi**	disper**assimo**	**avessi** disperato	**avessimo** disperato
disper**assi**	disper**aste**	**avessi** disperato	**aveste** disperato
disper**asse**	disper**assero**	**avesse** disperato	**avessero** disperato
imperativo			
	disperiamo		
dispera; non disperare	disperate		
disperi	disperino		

dispiacere — to be sorry, to dislike

gerundio **dispiacendo** — participio passato **dispiaciuto**

D

SINGULAR	PLURAL	SINGULAR	PLURAL
indicativo presente		passato prossimo	
dispiac**e**	dispiacci**ono**	**è** dispiaciuto(a)	**sono** dispiaciuti(e)
imperfetto		trapassato prossimo	
dispiac**eva**	dispiac**evano**	**era** dispiaciuto(a)	**erano** dispiaciuti(e)
passato remoto		trapassato remoto	
dispiacqu**e**	dispiacqu**ero**	**fu** dispiaciuto(a)	**furono** dispiaciuti(e)
futuro semplice		futuro anteriore	
dispiac**erà**	dispiac**eranno**	**sarà** dispiaciuto(a)	**saranno** dispiaciuti(e)
condizionale presente		condizionale passato	
dispiac**erebbe**	dispiac**erebbero**	**sarebbe** dispiaciuto(a)	**sarebbero** dispiaciuti(e)
congiuntivo presente		congiuntivo passato	
dispiacci**a**	dispiacci**ano**	**sia** dispiaciuto(a)	**siano** dispiaciuti(e)
congiuntivo imperfetto		congiuntivo trapassato	
dispiac**esse**	dispiac**essero**	**fosse** dispiaciuto(a)	**fossero** dispiaciuti(e)

imperativo

gerundio **dispiacendosi**

participio passato **dispiaciutosi**

SINGULAR	PLURAL
indicativo presente	
mi dispiac**cio**	**ci** dispiac**ciamo**
ti dispiac**i**	**vi** dispiac**ete**
si dispiac**e**	**si** dispiac**ciono**
imperfetto	
mi dispiace**vo**	**ci** dispiace**vamo**
ti dispiace**vi**	**vi** dispiace**vate**
si dispiace**va**	**si** dispiace**vano**
passato remoto	
mi dispiac**qui**	**ci** dispiac**emmo**
ti dispiac**esti**	**vi** dispiac**este**
si dispiac**que**	**si** dispiac**quero**
futuro semplice	
mi dispiacer**ò**	**ci** dispiacer**emo**
ti dispiacer**ai**	**vi** dispiacer**ete**
si dispiacer**à**	**si** dispiacer**anno**
condizionale presente	
mi dispiacer**ei**	**ci** dispiacer**emmo**
ti dispiacer**esti**	**vi** dispiacer**este**
si dispiacer**ebbe**	**si** dispiacer**ebbero**
congiuntivo presente	
mi dispiac**cia**	**ci** dispiac**ciamo**
ti dispiac**cia**	**vi** dispiac**ciate**
si dispiac**cia**	**si** dispiac**ciano**
congiuntivo imperfetto	
mi dispiac**essi**	**ci** dispiac**essimo**
ti dispiac**essi**	**vi** dispiac**este**
si dispiac**esse**	**si** dispiac**essero**
imperativo	
	dispiacciamoci
dispiaciti; non dispiacerti/ non ti dispiacere	dispiacetevi
si dispiaccia	si dispiacciano

SINGULAR	PLURAL
passato prossimo	
mi sono dispiaciuto(a)	**ci siamo** dispiaciuti(e)
ti sei dispiaciuto(a)	**vi siete** dispiaciuti(e)
si è dispiaciuto(a)	**si sono** dispiaciuti(e)
trapassato prossimo	
mi ero dispiaciuto(a)	**ci eravamo** dispiaciuti(e)
ti eri dispiaciuto(a)	**vi eravate** dispiaciuti(e)
si era dispiaciuto(a)	**si erano** dispiaciuti(e)
trapassato remoto	
mi fui dispiaciuto(a)	**ci fummo** dispiaciuti(e)
ti fosti dispiaciuto(a)	**vi foste** dispiaciuti(e)
si fu dispiaciuto(a)	**si furono** dispiaciuti(e)
futuro anteriore	
mi sarò dispiaciuto(a)	**ci saremo** dispiaciuti(e)
ti sarai dispiaciuto(a)	**vi sarete** dispiaciuti(e)
si sarà dispiaciuto(a)	**si saranno** dispiaciuti(e)
condizionale passato	
mi sarei dispiaciuto(a)	**ci saremmo** dispiaciuti(e)
ti saresti dispiaciuto(a)	**vi sareste** dispiaciuti(e)
si sarebbe dispiaciuto(a)	**si sarebbero** dispiaciuti(e)
congiuntivo passato	
mi sia dispiaciuto(a)	**ci siamo** dispiaciuti(e)
ti sia dispiaciuto(a)	**vi siate** dispiaciuti(e)
si sia dispiaciuto(a)	**si siano** dispiaciuti(e)
congiuntivo trapassato	
mi fossi dispiaciuto(a)	**ci fossimo** dispiaciuti(e)
ti fossi dispiaciuto(a)	**vi foste** dispiaciuti(e)
si fosse dispiaciuto(a)	**si fossero** dispiaciuti(e)

disporre — to arrange, to dispose

gerundio **disponendo** participio passato **disposto**

	SINGULAR	PLURAL
indicativo presente	dispong**o**	dispon**iamo**
	dispon**i**	dispon**ete**
	dispon**e**	dispong**ono**
imperfetto	dispone**vo**	dispone**vamo**
	dispone**vi**	dispone**vate**
	dispone**va**	dispone**vano**
passato remoto	dispos**i**	dispon**emmo**
	dispon**esti**	dispon**este**
	dispos**e**	dispos**ero**
futuro semplice	disporr**ò**	disporr**emo**
	disporr**ai**	disporr**ete**
	disporr**à**	disporr**anno**
condizionale presente	disporr**ei**	disporr**emmo**
	disporr**esti**	disporr**este**
	disporr**ebbe**	disporr**ebbero**
congiuntivo presente	dispong**a**	dispon**iamo**
	dispong**a**	dispon**iate**
	dispong**a**	dispong**ano**
congiuntivo imperfetto	dispon**essi**	dispon**essimo**
	dispon**essi**	dispon**este**
	dispon**esse**	dispon**essero**
imperativo		disponiamo
	disponi; non disporre	disponete
	disponga	dispongano

	SINGULAR	PLURAL
passato prossimo	**ho** disposto	**abbiamo** disposto
	hai disposto	**avete** disposto
	ha disposto	**hanno** disposto
trapassato prossimo	**avevo** disposto	**avevamo** disposto
	avevi disposto	**avevate** disposto
	aveva disposto	**avevano** disposto
trapassato remoto	**ebbi** disposto	**avemmo** disposto
	avesti disposto	**aveste** disposto
	ebbe disposto	**ebbero** disposto
futuro anteriore	**avrò** disposto	**avremo** disposto
	avrai disposto	**avrete** disposto
	avrà disposto	**avranno** disposto
condizionale passato	**avrei** disposto	**avremmo** disposto
	avresti disposto	**avreste** disposto
	avrebbe disposto	**avrebbero** disposto
congiuntivo passato	**abbia** disposto	**abbiamo** disposto
	abbia disposto	**abbiate** disposto
	abbia disposto	**abbiano** disposto
congiuntivo trapassato	**avessi** disposto	**avessimo** disposto
	avessi disposto	**aveste** disposto
	avesse disposto	**avessero** disposto

to dissolve — dissolvere

gerundio **dissolvendo** participio passato **dissolto**

SINGULAR	PLURAL	SINGULAR	PLURAL
indicativo presente		passato prossimo	
dissolv**o**	dissolv**iamo**	**ho** dissolto	**abbiamo** dissolto
dissolv**i**	dissolv**ete**	**hai** dissolto	**avete** dissolto
dissolv**e**	dissolv**ono**	**ha** dissolto	**hanno** dissolto
imperfetto		trapassato prossimo	
dissolve**vo**	dissolve**vamo**	**avevo** dissolto	**avevamo** dissolto
dissolve**vi**	dissolve**vate**	**avevi** dissolto	**avevate** dissolto
dissolve**va**	dissolve**vano**	**aveva** dissolto	**avevano** dissolto
passato remoto		trapassato remoto	
dissols**i**	dissolv**emmo**	**ebbi** dissolto	**avemmo** dissolto
dissolv**esti**	dissolv**este**	**avesti** dissolto	**aveste** dissolto
dissols**e**	dissols**ero**	**ebbe** dissolto	**ebbero** dissolto
futuro semplice		futuro anteriore	
dissolver**ò**	dissolver**emo**	**avrò** dissolto	**avremo** dissolto
dissolver**ai**	dissolver**ete**	**avrai** dissolto	**avrete** dissolto
dissolver**à**	dissolver**anno**	**avrà** dissolto	**avranno** dissolto
condizionale presente		condizionale passato	
dissolver**ei**	dissolver**emmo**	**avrei** dissolto	**avremmo** dissolto
dissolver**esti**	dissolver**este**	**avresti** dissolto	**avreste** dissolto
dissolver**ebbe**	dissolver**ebbero**	**avrebbe** dissolto	**avrebbero** dissolto
congiuntivo presente		congiuntivo passato	
dissolv**a**	dissolv**iamo**	**abbia** dissolto	**abbiamo** dissolto
dissolv**a**	dissolv**iate**	**abbia** dissolto	**abbiate** dissolto
dissolv**a**	dissolv**ano**	**abbia** dissolto	**abbiano** dissolto
congiuntivo imperfetto		congiuntivo trapassato	
dissolv**essi**	dissolv**essimo**	**avessi** dissolto	**avessimo** dissolto
dissolv**essi**	dissolv**este**	**avessi** dissolto	**aveste** dissolto
dissolv**esse**	dissolv**essero**	**avesse** dissolto	**avessero** dissolto
imperativo			
	dissolviamo		
dissolvi; non dissolvere	dissolvete		
dissolva	dissolvano		

D

distinguere — to distinguish

gerundio **distinguendo** participio passato **distinto**

SINGULAR	PLURAL	SINGULAR	PLURAL
indicativo presente		passato prossimo	
distingu**o**	distingu**iamo**	**ho** distinto	**abbiamo** distinto
distingu**i**	distingu**ete**	**hai** distinto	**avete** distinto
disting**ue**	distingu**ono**	**ha** distinto	**hanno** distinto
imperfetto		trapassato prossimo	
distingue**vo**	distingue**vamo**	**avevo** distinto	**avevamo** distinto
distingue**vi**	distingue**vate**	**avevi** distinto	**avevate** distinto
distingue**va**	distingue**vano**	**aveva** distinto	**avevano** distinto
passato remoto		trapassato remoto	
distins**i**	distingu**emmo**	**ebbi** distinto	**avemmo** distinto
distingu**esti**	distingu**este**	**avesti** distinto	**aveste** distinto
distins**e**	distins**ero**	**ebbe** distinto	**ebbero** distinto
futuro semplice		futuro anteriore	
distinguer**ò**	distinguer**emo**	**avrò** distinto	**avremo** distinto
distinguer**ai**	distinguer**ete**	**avrai** distinto	**avrete** distinto
distinguer**à**	distinguer**anno**	**avrà** distinto	**avranno** distinto
condizionale presente		condizionale passato	
distinguer**ei**	distinguer**emmo**	**avrei** distinto	**avremmo** distinto
distinguer**esti**	distinguer**este**	**avresti** distinto	**avreste** distinto
distinguer**ebbe**	distinguer**ebbero**	**avrebbe** distinto	**avrebbero** distinto
congiuntivo presente		congiuntivo passato	
distingu**a**	distingu**iamo**	**abbia** distinto	**abbiamo** distinto
distingu**a**	distingu**iate**	**abbia** distinto	**abbiate** distinto
distingu**a**	distingu**ano**	**abbia** distinto	**abbiano** distinto
congiuntivo imperfetto		congiuntivo trapassato	
distingu**essi**	distingu**essimo**	**avessi** distinto	**avessimo** distinto
distingu**essi**	distingu**este**	**avessi** distinto	**aveste** distinto
distingu**esse**	distingu**essero**	**avesse** distinto	**avessero** distinto
imperativo			
	distinguiamo		
distingui; non distinguere	distinguete		
distingua	distinguano		

D

gerundio **distraendo** participio passato **distratto**

SINGULAR	PLURAL	SINGULAR	PLURAL
indicativo presente		passato prossimo	
distr**aggo**	distr**aiamo**	**ho** distratto	**abbiamo** distratto
distr**ai**	distr**aete**	**hai** distratto	**avete** distratto
distr**ae**	distr**aggono**	**ha** distratto	**hanno** distratto
imperfetto		trapassato prossimo	
distrae**vo**	distrae**vamo**	**avevo** distratto	**avevamo** distratto
distrae**vi**	distrae**vate**	**avevi** distratto	**avevate** distratto
distrae**va**	distrae**vano**	**aveva** distratto	**avevano** distratto
passato remoto		trapassato remoto	
distr**assi**	distr**aemmo**	**ebbi** distratto	**avemmo** distratto
distr**aesti**	distr**aeste**	**avesti** distratto	**aveste** distratto
distr**asse**	distr**assero**	**ebbe** distratto	**ebbero** distratto
futuro semplice		futuro anteriore	
distrarr**ò**	distrarr**emo**	**avrò** distratto	**avremo** distratto
distrarr**ai**	distrarr**ete**	**avrai** distratto	**avrete** distratto
distrarr**à**	distrarr**anno**	**avrà** distratto	**avranno** distratto
condizionale presente		condizionale passato	
distrarr**ei**	distrarr**emmo**	**avrei** distratto	**avremmo** distratto
distrarr**esti**	distrarr**este**	**avresti** distratto	**avreste** distratto
distrarr**ebbe**	distrarr**ebbero**	**avrebbe** distratto	**avrebbero** distratto
congiuntivo presente		congiuntivo passato	
distr**agga**	distr**aiamo**	**abbia** distratto	**abbiamo** distratto
distr**agga**	distr**aiate**	**abbia** distratto	**abbiate** distratto
distr**agga**	distr**aggano**	**abbia** distratto	**abbiano** distratto
congiuntivo imperfetto		congiuntivo trapassato	
distr**aessi**	distr**aessimo**	**avessi** distratto	**avessimo** distratto
distr**aessi**	distr**aeste**	**avessi** distratto	**aveste** distratto
distr**aesse**	distr**aessero**	**avesse** distratto	**avessero** distratto
imperativo			
	distraiamo		
distrai; non distrarre	distraete		
distragga	distraggano		

D

distrarsi to amuse oneself, to divert one's mind

gerundio **distraendosi** participio passato **distrattosi**

SINGULAR	PLURAL

indicativo presente

SINGULAR	PLURAL
mi distr**aggo**	**ci** distr**aiamo**
ti distr**ai**	**vi** distr**aete**
si distr**ae**	**si** distr**aggono**

imperfetto

SINGULAR	PLURAL
mi distrae**vo**	**ci** distrae**vamo**
ti distrae**vi**	**vi** distrae**vate**
si distrae**va**	**si** distrae**vano**

passato remoto

SINGULAR	PLURAL
mi distr**assi**	**ci** distr**aemmo**
ti distr**aesti**	**vi** distr**aeste**
si distr**asse**	**si** distr**assero**

futuro semplice

SINGULAR	PLURAL
mi distrarr**ò**	**ci** distrarr**emo**
ti distrarr**ai**	**vi** distrarr**ete**
si distrarr**à**	**si** distrarr**anno**

condizionale presente

SINGULAR	PLURAL
mi distrarr**ei**	**ci** distrarr**emmo**
ti distrarr**esti**	**vi** distrarr**este**
si distrarr**ebbe**	**si** distrarr**ebbero**

congiuntivo presente

SINGULAR	PLURAL
mi distr**agga**	**ci** distr**aiamo**
ti distr**agga**	**vi** distr**aiate**
si distr**agga**	**si** distr**aggano**

congiuntivo imperfetto

SINGULAR	PLURAL
mi distr**aessi**	**ci** distr**aessimo**
ti distr**aessi**	**vi** distr**aeste**
si distr**aesse**	**si** distr**aessero**

imperativo

SINGULAR	PLURAL
	distraiamoci
distraiti; non distraerti/ non ti distrarre	distraetevi
si distragga	si distraggano

SINGULAR	PLURAL

passato prossimo

SINGULAR	PLURAL
mi sono distratto(ao)	**ci siamo** distratti(e)
ti sei distratto(a)	**vi siete** distratti(e)
si è distratto(a)	**si sono** distratto

trapassato prossimo

SINGULAR	PLURAL
mi ero distratto(a)	**ci eravamo** distratti(e)
ti eri distratto(a)	**vi eravate** distratti(e)
si era distratto(a)	**si erano** distratti(e)

trapassato remoto

SINGULAR	PLURAL
mi fui distratto(a)	**ci fummo** distratti(e)
ti fosti distratto(a)	**vi foste** distratti(e)
si fu distratto(a)	**si furono** distratti(e)

futuro anteriore

SINGULAR	PLURAL
mi sarò distratto(a)	**ci saremo** distratti(e)
ti sarai distratto(a)	**vi sarete** distratti(e)
si sarà distratto(a)	**si saranno** distratti(e)

condizionale passato

SINGULAR	PLURAL
mi sarei distratto(a)	**ci saremmo** distratti(e)
ti saresti distratto(a)	**vi sareste** distratti(e)
si sarebbe distratto(a)	**si sarebbero** distratti(e)

congiuntivo passato

SINGULAR	PLURAL
mi sia distratto	**ci siamo** distratti(e)
ti sia distratto	**vi siate** distratti(e)
si sia distratto	**si siano** distratti(e)

congiuntivo trapassato

SINGULAR	PLURAL
mi fossi distratto(a)	**ci fossimo** distratti(e)
ti fossi distratto(a)	**vi foste** distratti(e)
si fosse distratto(a)	**si fossero** distratti(e)

to destroy — distruggere

gerundio **distruggendo** participio passato **distrutto**

SINGULAR	PLURAL
indicativo presente	
distruggo	distruggiamo
distruggi	distruggete
distrugge	distruggono
imperfetto	
distruggevo	distruggevamo
distruggevi	distruggevate
distruggeva	distruggevano
passato remoto	
distrussi	distruggemmo
distruggesti	distruggeste
distrusse	distrussero
futuro semplice	
distruggerò	distruggeremo
distruggerai	distruggerete
distruggerà	distruggeranno
condizionale presente	
distruggerei	distruggeremmo
distruggeresti	distruggereste
distruggerebbe	distruggerebbero
congiuntivo presente	
distrugga	distruggiamo
distrugga	distruggiate
distrugga	distruggano
congiuntivo imperfetto	
distruggessi	distruggessimo
distruggessi	distruggeste
distruggesse	distruggessero
imperativo	
	distruggiamo
distruggi; non distruggere	distruggete
distrugga	distruggano

SINGULAR	PLURAL
passato prossimo	
ho distrutto	**abbiamo** distrutto
hai distrutto	**avete** distrutto
ha distrutto	**hanno** distrutto
trapassato prossimo	
avevo distrutto	**avevamo** distrutto
avevi distrutto	**avevate** distrutto
aveva distrutto	**avevano** distrutto
trapassato remoto	
ebbi distrutto	**avemmo** distrutto
avesti distrutto	**aveste** distrutto
ebbe distrutto	**ebbero** distrutto
futuro anteriore	
avrò distrutto	**avremo** distrutto
avrai distrutto	**avrete** distrutto
avrà distrutto	**avranno** distrutto
condizionale passato	
avrei distrutto	**avremmo** distrutto
avresti distrutto	**avreste** distrutto
avrebbe distrutto	**avrebbero** distrutto
congiuntivo passato	
abbia distrutto	**abbiamo** distrutto
abbia distrutto	**abbiate** distrutto
abbia distrutto	**abbiano** distrutto
congiuntivo trapassato	
avessi distrutto	**avessimo** distrutto
avessi distrutto	**aveste** distrutto
avesse distrutto	**avessero** distrutto

divenire — to become

gerundio **divenendo** — participio passato **divenuto**

SINGULAR	PLURAL
indicativo presente	
diveng**o**	diven**iamo**
divien**i**	diven**ite**
divien**e**	diveng**ono**
imperfetto	
diveni**vo**	diveni**vamo**
diveni**vi**	diveni**vate**
diveni**va**	diveni**vano**
passato remoto	
divenn**i**	diven**immo**
diven**isti**	diven**iste**
divenn**e**	divenn**ero**
futuro semplice	
diverr**ò**	diverr**emo**
diverr**ai**	diverr**ete**
diverr**à**	diverr**anno**
condizionale presente	
diverr**ei**	diverr**emmo**
diverr**esti**	diverr**este**
diverr**ebbe**	diverr**ebbero**
congiuntivo presente	
diveng**a**	diven**iamo**
diveng**a**	diven**iate**
diveng**a**	diveng**ano**
congiuntivo imperfetto	
diven**issi**	diven**issimo**
diven**issi**	diven**iste**
diven**isse**	diven**issero**
imperativo	
	diveniamo
divieni; non divenire	divenite
divenga	divengano

SINGULAR	PLURAL
passato prossimo	
sono divenuto(a)	**siamo** divenuti(e)
sei divenuto(a)	**siete** divenuti(e)
è divenuto(a)	**sono** divenuti(e)
trapassato prossimo	
ero divenuto(a)	**eravamo** divenuti(e)
eri divenuto(a)	**eravate** divenuti(e)
era divenuto(a)	**erano** divenuti(e)
trapassato remoto	
fui divenuto(a)	**fummo** divenuti(e)
fosti divenuto(a)	**foste** divenuti(e)
fu divenuto(a)	**furono** divenuti(e)
futuro anteriore	
sarò divenuto(a)	**saremo** divenuti(e)
sarai divenuto(a)	**sarete** divenuti(e)
sarà divenuto(a)	**saranno** divenuti(e)
condizionale passato	
sarei divenuto(a)	**saremmo** divenuti(e)
saresti divenuto(a)	**sareste** divenuti(e)
sarebbe divenuto(a)	**sarebbero** divenuti(e)
congiuntivo passato	
sia divenuto(a)	**siamo** divenuti(e)
sia divenuto(a)	**siate** divenuti(e)
sia divenuto(a)	**siano** divenuti(e)
congiuntivo trapassato	
fossi divenuto(a)	**fossimo** divenuti(e)
fossi divenuto(a)	**foste** divenuti(e)
fosse divenuto(a)	**fossero** divenuti(e)

gerundio **diventando** participio passato **diventato**

SINGULAR	PLURAL	SINGULAR	PLURAL
indicativo presente		passato prossimo	
divent**o**	divent**iamo**	**sono** diventato(a)	**siamo** diventati(e)
divent**i**	divent**ate**	**sei** diventato(a)	**siete** diventati(e)
divent**a**	divent**ano**	**è** diventato(a)	**sono** diventati(e)
imperfetto		trapassato prossimo	
diventa**vo**	diventa**vamo**	**ero** diventato(a)	**eravamo** diventati(e)
diventa**vi**	diventa**vate**	**eri** diventato(a)	**eravate** diventati(e)
diventa**va**	diventa**vano**	**era** diventato(a)	**erano** diventati(e)
passato remoto		trapassato remoto	
divent**ai**	divent**ammo**	**fui** diventato(a)	**fummo** diventati(e)
divent**asti**	divent**aste**	**fosti** diventato(a)	**foste** diventati(e)
divent**ò**	divent**arono**	**fu** diventato(a)	**furono** diventati(e)
futuro semplice		futuro anteriore	
divente**rò**	divente**remo**	**sarò** diventato(a)	**saremo** diventati(e)
divente**rai**	divente**rete**	**sarai** diventato(a)	**sarete** diventati(e)
divente**rà**	divente**ranno**	**sarà** diventato(a)	**saranno** diventati(e)
condizionale presente		condizionale passato	
divente**rei**	divente**remmo**	**sarei** diventato(a)	**saremmo** diventati(e)
divente**resti**	divente**reste**	**saresti** diventato(a)	**sareste** diventati(e)
divente**rebbe**	divente**rebbero**	**sarebbe** diventato(a)	**sarebbero** diventati(e)
congiuntivo presente		congiuntivo passato	
divent**i**	divent**iamo**	**sia** diventato(a)	**siamo** diventati(e)
divent**i**	divent**iate**	**sia** diventato(a)	**siate** diventati(e)
divent**i**	divent**ino**	**sia** diventato(a)	**siano** diventati(e)
congiuntivo imperfetto		congiuntivo trapassato	
divent**assi**	divent**assimo**	**fossi** diventato(a)	**fossimo** diventati(e)
divent**assi**	divent**aste**	**fossi** diventato(a)	**foste** diventati(e)
divent**asse**	divent**assero**	**fosse** diventato(a)	**fossero** diventati(e)

D

imperativo

	diventiamo
diventa; non diventare	diventate
diventi	diventino

divertirsi — to have fun, to enjoy oneself

gerundio **divertendosi** — participio passato **divertitosi**

D

SINGULAR	PLURAL	SINGULAR	PLURAL
indicativo presente		passato prossimo	
mi divert**o**	**ci** divert**iamo**	**mi sono** divertito(a)	**ci siamo** divertiti(e)
ti divert**i**	**vi** divert**ite**	**ti sei** divertito(a)	**vi siete** divertiti(e)
si divert**e**	**si** divert**ono**	**si è** divertito(a)	**si sono** divertiti(e)
imperfetto		trapassato prossimo	
mi diverti**vo**	**ci** diverti**vamo**	**mi ero** divertito(a)	**ci eravamo** divertiti(e)
ti diverti**vi**	**vi** diverti**vate**	**ti eri** divertito(a)	**vi eravate** divertiti(e)
si diverti**va**	**si** diverti**vano**	**si era** divertito(a)	**si erano** divertiti(e)
passato remoto		trapassato remoto	
mi diverti**i**	**ci** divert**immo**	**mi fui** divertito(a)	**ci fummo** divertiti(e)
ti divert**isti**	**vi** divert**iste**	**ti fosti** divertito(a)	**vi foste** divertiti(e)
si divert**ì**	**si** divert**irono**	**si fu** divertito(a)	**si furono** divertiti(e)
futuro semplice		futuro anteriore	
mi divertir**ò**	**ci** divertir**emo**	**mi sarò** divertito(a)	**ci saremo** divertiti(e)
ti divertir**ai**	**vi** divertir**ete**	**ti sarai** divertito(a)	**vi sarete** divertiti(e)
si divertir**à**	**si** divertir**anno**	**si sarà** divertito(a)	**si saranno** divertiti(e)
condizionale presente		condizionale passato	
mi divertir**ei**	**ci** divertir**emmo**	**mi sarei** divertito(a)	**ci saremmo** divertiti(e)
ti divertir**esti**	**vi** divertir**este**	**ti saresti** divertito(a)	**vi sareste** divertiti(e)
si divertir**ebbe**	**si** divertir**ebbero**	**si sarebbe** divertito(a)	**si sarebbero** divertiti(e)
congiuntivo presente		congiuntivo passato	
mi divert**a**	**ci** divert**iamo**	**mi sia** divertito(a)	**ci siamo** divertiti(e)
ti divert**a**	**vi** divert**iate**	**ti sia** divertito(a)	**vi siate** divertiti(e)
si divert**a**	**si** divert**ano**	**si sia** divertito(a)	**si siano** divertati(e)
congiuntivo imperfetto		congiuntivo trapassato	
mi divert**issi**	**ci** divert**issimo**	**mi fossi** divertato(a)	**ci fossimo** divertiti(e)
ti divert**issi**	**vi** divert**iste**	**ti fossi** divertato(a)	**vi foste** divertiti(e)
si divert**isse**	**si** divert**issero**	**si fosse** divertito(a)	**si fossero** divertiti(e)

imperativo

SINGULAR	PLURAL
	divertiamoci
divertiti; non divertirti/ non ti divertire	divertitevi
si diverta	si divertano

to divide **dividere**

gerundio **dividendo** participio passato **diviso**

SINGULAR	PLURAL
indicativo presente	
divid**o**	divid**iamo**
divid**i**	divid**ete**
divid**e**	divid**ono**
imperfetto	
divide**vo**	divide**vamo**
divide**vi**	divide**vate**
divide**va**	divide**vano**
passato remoto	
divis**i**	divid**emmo**
divid**esti**	divid**este**
divis**e**	divis**ero**
futuro semplice	
divider**ò**	divider**emo**
divider**ai**	divider**ete**
divider**à**	divider**anno**
condizionale presente	
divider**ei**	divider**emmo**
divider**esti**	divider**este**
divider**ebbe**	divider**ebbero**
congiuntivo presente	
divid**a**	divid**iamo**
divid**a**	divid**iate**
divid**a**	divid**ano**
congiuntivo imperfetto	
divid**essi**	divid**essimo**
divid**essi**	divid**este**
divid**esse**	divid**essero**
imperativo	
	dividiamo
dividi; non dividere	dividete
divida	dividano

SINGULAR	PLURAL
passato prossimo	
ho diviso	**abbiamo** diviso
hai diviso	**avete** diviso
ha diviso	**hanno** diviso
trapassato prossimo	
avevo diviso	**avevamo** diviso
avevi diviso	**avevate** diviso
aveva diviso	**avevano** diviso
trapassato remoto	
ebbi diviso	**avemmo** diviso
avesti diviso	**aveste** diviso
ebbe diviso	**ebbero** diviso
futuro anteriore	
avrò diviso	**avremo** diviso
avrai diviso	**avrete** diviso
avrà diviso	**avranno** diviso
condizionale passato	
avrei diviso	**avremmo** diviso
avresti diviso	**avreste** diviso
avrebbe diviso	**avrebbero** diviso
congiuntivo passato	
abbia diviso	**abbiamo** diviso
abbia diviso	**abbiate** diviso
abbia diviso	**abbiano** diviso
congiuntivo trapassato	
avessi diviso	**avessimo** diviso
avessi diviso	**aveste** diviso
avesse diviso	**avessero** diviso

domandare to ask, to inquire, to question

gerundio **domandando** participio passato **domandato**

D

SINGULAR	PLURAL	SINGULAR	PLURAL
indicativo presente		passato prossimo	
domand**o**	domand**iamo**	**ho** domandato	**abbiamo** domandato
domand**i**	domand**ate**	**hai** domandato	**avete** domandato
domand**a**	domand**ano**	**ha** domandato	**hanno** domandato
imperfetto		trapassato prossimo	
domanda**vo**	domanda**vamo**	**avevo** domandato	**avevamo** domandato
domanda**vi**	domanda**vate**	**avevi** domandato	**avevate** domandato
domanda**va**	domanda**vano**	**aveva** domandato	**avevano** domandato
passato remoto		trapassato remoto	
domand**ai**	domand**ammo**	**ebbi** domandato	**avemmo** domandato
domand**asti**	domand**aste**	**avesti** domandato	**aveste** domandato
domand**ò**	domand**arono**	**ebbe** domandato	**ebbero** domandato
futuro semplice		futuro anteriore	
domander**ò**	domander**emo**	**avrò** domandato	**avremo** domandato
domander**ai**	domander**ete**	**avrai** domandato	**avrete** domandato
domander**à**	domander**anno**	**avrà** domandato	**avranno** domandato
condizionale presente		condizionale passato	
domander**ei**	domander**emmo**	**avrei** domandato	**avremmo** domandato
domander**esti**	domander**este**	**avresti** domandato	**avreste** domandato
domander**ebbe**	domander**ebbero**	**avrebbe** domandato	**avrebbero** domandato
congiuntivo presente		congiuntivo passato	
domand**i**	domand**iamo**	**abbia** domandato	**abbiamo** domandato
domand**i**	domand**iate**	**abbia** domandato	**abbiate** domandato
domand**i**	domand**ino**	**abbia** domandato	**abbiano** domandato
congiuntivo imperfetto		congiuntivo trapassato	
domand**assi**	domand**assimo**	**avessi** domandato	**avessimo** domandato
domand**assi**	domand**aste**	**avessi** domandato	**aveste** domandato
domand**asse**	domand**assero**	**avesse** domandato	**avessero** domandato

imperativo

	domandiamo
domanda; non domandare	domandate
domandi	domandino

gerundio **dormendo** participio passato **dormito**

SINGULAR	PLURAL	SINGULAR	PLURAL
indicativo presente		passato prossimo	
dorm**o**	dorm**iamo**	**ho** dormito	**abbiamo** dormito
dorm**i**	dorm**ite**	**hai** dormito	**avete** dormito
dorm**e**	dorm**ono**	**ha** dormito	**hanno** dormito
imperfetto		trapassato prossimo	
dormi**vo**	dormi**vamo**	**avevo** dormito	**avevamo** dormito
dormi**vi**	dormi**vate**	**avevi** dormito	**avevate** dormito
dormi**va**	dormi**vano**	**aveva** dormito	**avevano** dormito
passato remoto		trapassato remoto	
dorm**ii**	dorm**immo**	**ebbi** dormito	**avemmo** dormito
dorm**isti**	dorm**iste**	**avesti** dormito	**aveste** dormito
dorm**ì**	dorm**irono**	**ebbe** dormito	**ebbero** dormito
futuro semplice		futuro anteriore	
dormir**ò**	dormir**emo**	**avrò** dormito	**avremo** dormito
dormir**ai**	dormir**ete**	**avrai** dormito	**avrete** dormito
dormir**à**	dormir**anno**	**avrà** dormito	**avranno** dormito
condizionale presente		condizionale passato	
dormir**ei**	dormir**emmo**	**avrei** dormito	**avremmo** dormito
dormir**esti**	dormir**este**	**avresti** dormito	**avreste** dormito
dormir**ebbe**	dormir**ebbero**	**avrebbe** dormito	**avrebbero** dormito
congiuntivo presente		congiuntivo passato	
dorm**a**	dorm**iamo**	**abbia** dormito	**abbiamo** dormito
dorm**a**	dorm**iate**	**abbia** dormito	**abbiate** dormito
dorm**a**	dorm**ano**	**abbia** dormito	**abbiano** dormito
congiuntivo imperfetto		congiuntivo trapassato	
dorm**issi**	dorm**issimo**	**avessi** dormito	**avessimo** dormito
dorm**issi**	dorm**iste**	**avessi** dormito	**aveste** dormito
dorm**isse**	dorm**issero**	**avesse** dormito	**avessero** dormito
imperativo			
	dormiamo		
dormi; non dormire	dormite		
dorma	dormano		

dovere must, to have to, should, to owe

gerundio **dovendo** participio passato **dovuto**

SINGULAR	PLURAL	SINGULAR	PLURAL
indicativo presente		passato prossimo	
dev**o (debbo)**	dobb**iamo**	**ho** dovuto	**abbiamo** dovuto
dev**i**	dov**ete**	**hai** dovuto	**avete** dovuto
dev**e**	dev**ono (debbono)**	**ha** dovuto	**hanno** dovuto
imperfetto		trapassato prossimo	
dove**vo**	dove**vamo**	**avevo** dovuto	**avevamo** dovuto
dove**vi**	dove**vate**	**avevi** dovuto	**avevate** dovuto
dove**va**	dove**vano**	**aveva** dovuto	**avevano** dovuto
passato remoto		trapassato remoto	
dov**ei (**dov**etti)**	dov**emmo**	**ebbi** dovuto	**avemmo** dovuto
dov**esti**	dov**este**	**avesti** dovuto	**aveste** dovuto
dov**ette**	dov**ettero**	**ebbe** dovuto	**ebbero** dovuto
futuro semplice		futuro anteriore	
dovr**ò**	dovr**emo**	**avrò** dovuto	**avremo** dovuto
dovr**ai**	dovr**ete**	**avrai** dovuto	**avrete** dovuto
dovr**à**	dovr**anno**	**avrà** dovuto	**avranno** dovuto
condizionale presente		condizionale passato	
dovr**ei**	dovr**emmo**	**avrei** dovuto	**avremmo** dovuto
dovr**esti**	dovr**este**	**avresti** dovuto	**avreste** dovuto
dovr**ebbe**	dovr**ebbero**	**avrebbe** dovuto	**avrebbero** dovuto
congiuntivo presente		congiuntivo passato	
dev**a (debba)**	dobb**iamo**	**abbia** dovuto	**abbiamo** dovuto
dev**a (debba)**	dobb**iate**	**abbia** dovuto	**abbiate** dovuto
dev**a (debba)**	dev**ano (debbano)**	**abbia** dovuto	**abbiano** dovuto
congiuntivo imperfetto		congiuntivo trapassato	
dov**essi**	dov**essimo**	**avessi** dovuto	**avessimo** dovuto
dov**essi**	dov**este**	**avessi** dovuto	**aveste** dovuto
dov**esse**	dov**essero**	**avesse** dovuto	**avessero** dovuto

imperativo

to elect, to choose **eleggere**

gerundio **eleggendo** participio passato **eletto**

SINGULAR	PLURAL
indicativo presente	
elegg**o**	elegg**iamo**
elegg**i**	elegg**ete**
elegg**e**	elegg**ono**
imperfetto	
elegge**vo**	elegge**vamo**
elegge**vi**	elegge**vate**
elegge**va**	elegge**vano**
passato remoto	
eless**i**	elegg**emmo**
elegg**esti**	elegg**este**
eless**e**	eless**ero**
futuro semplice	
elegger**ò**	elegger**emo**
elegger**ai**	elegger**ete**
elegger**à**	elegger**anno**
condizionale presente	
elegger**ei**	elegger**emmo**
elegger**esti**	elegger**este**
elegger**ebbe**	elegger**ebbero**
congiuntivo presente	
elegg**a**	elegg**iamo**
elegg**a**	elegg**iate**
elegg**a**	elegg**ano**
congiuntivo imperfetto	
elegg**essi**	elegg**essimo**
elegg**essi**	elegg**este**
elegg**esse**	elegg**essero**
imperativo	
	eleggiamo
eleggi; non eleggere	eleggete
elegga	eleggano

SINGULAR	PLURAL
passato prossimo	
ho eletto	**abbiamo** eletto
hai eletto	**avete** eletto
ha eletto	**hanno** eletto
trapassato prossimo	
avevo eletto	**avevamo** eletto
avevi eletto	**avevate** eletto
aveva eletto	**avevano** eletto
trapassato remoto	
ebbi eletto	**avemmo** eletto
avesti eletto	**aveste** eletto
ebbe eletto	**ebbero** eletto
futuro anteriore	
avrò eletto	**avremo** eletto
avrai eletto	**avrete** eletto
avrà eletto	**avranno** eletto
condizionale passato	
avrei eletto	**avremmo** eletto
avresti eletto	**avreste** eletto
avrebbe eletto	**avrebbero** eletto
congiuntivo passato	
abbia eletto	**abbiamo** eletto
abbia eletto	**abbiate** eletto
abbia eletto	**abbiano** eletto
congiuntivo trapassato	
avessi eletto	**avessimo** eletto
avessi eletto	**aveste** eletto
avesse eletto	**avessero** eletto

elevare — to raise, to lift up

gerundio **elevando** — participio passato **elevato**

SINGULAR	PLURAL
indicativo presente	
elev**o**	elev**iamo**
elev**i**	elev**ate**
elev**a**	elev**ano**
imperfetto	
eleva**vo**	eleva**vamo**
eleva**vi**	eleva**vate**
eleva**va**	eleva**vano**
passato remoto	
elev**ai**	elev**ammo**
elev**asti**	elev**aste**
elev**ò**	elev**arono**
futuro semplice	
elever**ò**	elever**emo**
elever**ai**	elever**ete**
elever**à**	elever**anno**
condizionale presente	
elev**erei**	elev**eremmo**
elev**eresti**	elev**ereste**
elev**erebbe**	elev**erebbero**
congiuntivo presente	
elev**i**	elev**iamo**
elev**i**	elev**iate**
elev**i**	elev**ino**
congiuntivo imperfetto	
elev**assi**	elev**assimo**
elev**assi**	elev**aste**
elev**asse**	elev**assero**
imperativo	
	eleviamo
eleva; non elevare	elevate
elevi	elevino

SINGULAR	PLURAL
passato prossimo	
ho elevato	**abbiamo** elevato
hai elevato	**avete** elevato
ha elevato	**hanno** elevato
trapassato prossimo	
avevo elevato	**avevamo** elevato
avevi elevato	**avevate** elevato
aveva elevato	**avevano** elevato
trapassato remoto	
ebbi elevato	**avemmo** elevato
avesti elevato	**aveste** elevato
ebbe elevato	**ebbero** elevato
futuro anteriore	
avrò elevato	**avremo** elevato
avrai elevato	**avrete** elevato
avrà elevato	**avranno** elevato
condizionale passato	
avrei elevato	**avremmo** elevato
avresti elevato	**avreste** elevato
avrebbe elevato	**avrebbero** elevato
congiuntivo passato	
abbia elevato	**abbiamo** elevato
abbia elevato	**abbiate** elevato
abbia elevato	**abbiano** elevato
congiuntivo trapassato	
avessi elevato	**avessimo** elevato
avessi elevato	**aveste** elevato
avesse elevato	**avessero** elevato

to eliminate, to delete — eliminare

gerundio **eliminando**

participio passato **eliminato**

SINGULAR	PLURAL
indicativo presente	
elimin**o**	elimin**iamo**
elimin**i**	elimina**te**
elimin**a**	elimina**no**
imperfetto	
elimina**vo**	elimina**vamo**
elimina**vi**	elimina**vate**
elimina**va**	elimina**vano**
passato remoto	
elimin**ai**	elimin**ammo**
elimina**sti**	elimin**aste**
elimin**ò**	elimin**arono**
futuro semplice	
eliminer**ò**	eliminer**emo**
eliminer**ai**	eliminer**ete**
eliminer**à**	eliminer**anno**
condizionale presente	
eliminer**ei**	eliminer**emmo**
eliminer**esti**	eliminer**este**
eliminer**ebbe**	eliminer**ebbero**
congiuntivo presente	
elimin**i**	elimin**iamo**
elimin**i**	elimin**iate**
elimin**i**	elimin**ino**
congiuntivo imperfetto	
elimin**assi**	elimin**assimo**
elimin**assi**	elimin**aste**
elimin**asse**	elimin**assero**
imperativo	
	eliminiamo
elimina; non eliminare	eliminate
elimini	eliminino

SINGULAR	PLURAL
passato prossimo	
ho eliminato	**abbiamo** eliminato
hai eliminato	**avete** eliminato
ha eliminato	**hanno** eliminato
trapassato prossimo	
avevo eliminato	**avevamo** eliminato
avevi eliminato	**avevate** eliminato
aveva eliminato	**avevano** eliminato
trapassato remoto	
ebbi eliminato	**avemmo** eliminato
avesti eliminato	**aveste** eliminato
ebbe eliminato	**ebbero** eliminato
futuro anteriore	
avrò eliminato	**avremo** eliminato
avrai eliminato	**avrete** eliminato
avrà eliminato	**avranno** eliminato
condizionale passato	
avrei eliminato	**avremmo** eliminato
avresti eliminato	**avreste** eliminato
avrebbe eliminato	**avrebbero** eliminato
congiuntivo passato	
abbia eliminato	**abbiamo** eliminato
abbia eliminato	**abbiate** eliminato
abbia eliminato	**abbiano** eliminato
congiuntivo trapassato	
avessi eliminato	**avessimo** eliminato
avessi eliminato	**aveste** eliminato
avesse eliminato	**avessero** eliminato

eludere — to elude, to avoid

gerundio **eludendo** participio passato **eluso**

SINGULAR	PLURAL	SINGULAR	PLURAL
indicativo presente		passato prossimo	
elud**o**	elud**iamo**	**ho** eluso	**abbiamo** eluso
elud**i**	elud**ete**	**hai** eluso	**avete** eluso
elud**e**	elud**ono**	**ha** eluso	**hanno** eluso
imperfetto		trapassato prossimo	
elud**evo**	elud**evamo**	**avevo** eluso	**avevamo** eluso
elud**evi**	elud**evate**	**avevi** eluso	**avevate** eluso
elud**eva**	elud**evano**	**aveva** eluso	**avevano** eluso
passato remoto		trapassato remoto	
elus**i**	elud**emmo**	**ebbi** eluso	**avemmo** eluso
elud**esti**	elud**este**	**avesti** eluso	**aveste** eluso
elus**e**	elus**ero**	**ebbe** eluso	**ebbero** eluso
futuro semplice		futuro anteriore	
eluder**ò**	eluder**emo**	**avrò** eluso	**avremo** eluso
eluder**ai**	eluder**ete**	**avrai** eluso	**avrete** eluso
eluder**à**	eluder**anno**	**avrà** eluso	**avranno** eluso
condizionale presente		condizionale passato	
eluder**ei**	eluder**emmo**	**avrei** eluso	**avremmo** eluso
eluder**esti**	eluder**este**	**avresti** eluso	**avreste** eluso
eluder**ebbe**	eluder**ebbero**	**avrebbe** eluso	**avrebbero** eluso
congiuntivo presente		congiuntivo passato	
elud**a**	elud**iamo**	**abbia** eluso	**abbiamo** eluso
elud**a**	elud**iate**	**abbia** eluso	**abbiate** eluso
elud**a**	elud**ano**	**abbia** eluso	**abbiano** eluso
congiuntivo imperfetto		congiuntivo trapassato	
elud**essi**	elud**essimo**	**avessi** eluso	**avessimo** eluso
elud**essi**	elud**este**	**avessi** eluso	**aveste** eluso
elud**esse**	elud**essero**	**avesse** eluso	**avessero** eluso
imperativo			
	eludiamo		
eludi; non eludere	eludete		
eluda	eludano		

E

gerundio **emergendo** participio passato **emerso**

SINGULAR	PLURAL
indicativo presente	
emerg**o**	emerg**iamo**
emerg**i**	emerg**ete**
emerg**e**	emerg**ono**
imperfetto	
emerge**vo**	emerge**vamo**
emerge**vi**	emerge**vate**
emerge**va**	emerge**vano**
passato remoto	
emers**i**	emerg**emmo**
emerg**esti**	emerg**este**
emers**e**	emers**ero**
futuro semplice	
emerger**ò**	emerger**emo**
emerger**ai**	emerger**ete**
emerger**à**	emerger**anno**
condizionale presente	
emerger**ei**	emerger**emmo**
emerger**esti**	emerger**este**
emerger**ebbe**	emerger**ebbero**
congiuntivo presente	
emerg**a**	emerg**iamo**
emerg**a**	emerg**iate**
emerg**a**	emerg**ano**
congiuntivo imperfetto	
emerg**essi**	emerg**essimo**
emerg**essi**	emerg**este**
emerg**esse**	emerg**essero**
imperativo	
	emergiamo
emergi; non emergere	emergete
emerga	emergano

SINGULAR	PLURAL
passato prossimo	
sono emerso(a)	**siamo** emersi(e)
sei emerso(a)	**siete** emersi(e)
è emerso(a)	**sono** emersi(e)
trapassato prossimo	
ero emerso(a)	**eravamo** emersi(e)
eri emerso(a)	**eravate** emersi(e)
era emerso(a)	**erano** emersi(e)
trapassato remoto	
fui emerso(a)	**fummo** emersi(e)
fosti emerso(a)	**foste** emersi(e)
fu emerso(a)	**furono** emersi(e)
futuro anteriore	
sarò emerso(a)	**saremo** emersi(e)
sarai emerso(a)	**sarete** emersi(e)
sarà emerso(a)	**saranno** emersi(e)
condizionale passato	
sarei emerso(a)	**saremmo** emersi(e)
saresti emerso(a)	**sareste** emersi(e)
sarebbe emerso(a)	**sarebbero** emersi(e)
congiuntivo passato	
sia emerso(a)	**siamo** emersi(e)
sia emerso(a)	**siate** emersi(e)
sia emerso(a)	**siano** emersi(e)
congiuntivo trapassato	
fossi emerso(a)	**fossimo** emersi(e)
fossi emerso(a)	**foste** emersi(e)
fosse emerso(a)	**fossero** emersi(e)

emettere — to emit, to give out

gerundio **emettendo** — participio passato **emesso**

SINGULAR	PLURAL
indicativo presente	
emett**o**	emett**iamo**
emett**i**	emett**ete**
emett**e**	emett**ono**
imperfetto	
emette**vo**	emette**vamo**
emette**vi**	emette**vate**
emette**va**	emette**vano**
passato remoto	
emis**i**	emett**emmo**
emett**esti**	emett**este**
emis**e**	emis**ero**
futuro semplice	
emetter**ò**	emetter**emo**
emetter**ai**	emetter**ete**
emetter**à**	emetter**anno**
condizionale presente	
emetter**ei**	emetter**emmo**
emetter**esti**	emetter**este**
emetter**ebbe**	emetter**ebbero**
congiuntivo presente	
emett**a**	emett**iamo**
emett**a**	emett**iate**
emett**a**	emett**ano**
congiuntivo imperfetto	
emett**essi**	emett**essimo**
emett**essi**	emett**este**
emett**esse**	emett**essero**
imperativo	
	emettiamo
emetti; non emettere	emettete
emetta	emettano

SINGULAR	PLURAL
passato prossimo	
ho emesso	**abbiamo** emesso
hai emesso	**avete** emesso
ha emesso	**hanno** emesso
trapassato prossimo	
avevo emesso	**avevamo** emesso
avevi emesso	**avevate** emesso
aveva emesso	**avevano** emesso
trapassato remoto	
ebbi emesso	**avemmo** emesso
avesti emesso	**aveste** emesso
ebbe emesso	**ebbero** emesso
futuro anteriore	
avrò emesso	**avremo** emesso
avrai emesso	**avrete** emesso
avrà emesso	**avranno** emesso
condizionale passato	
avrei emesso	**avremmo** emesso
avresti emesso	**avreste** emesso
avrebbe emesso	**avrebbero** emesso
congiuntivo passato	
abbia emesso	**abbiamo** emesso
abbia emesso	**abbiate** emesso
abbia emesso	**abbiano** emesso
congiuntivo trapassato	
avessi emesso	**avessimo** emesso
avessi emesso	**aveste** emesso
avesse emesso	**avessero** emesso

gerundio **emozionandosi** participio passato **emozionatosi**

SINGULAR	PLURAL
indicativo presente	
mi emoziono	**ci** emozioniamo
ti emozioni	**vi** emozionate
si emoziona	**si** emozionano
imperfetto	
mi emozionavo	**ci** emozionavamo
ti emozionavi	**vi** emozionavate
si emozionava	**si** emozionavano
passato remoto	
mi emozionai	**ci** emozionammo
ti emozionasti	**vi** emozionaste
si emozionò	**si** emozionarono
futuro semplice	
mi emozionerò	**ci** emozioneremo
ti emozionerai	**vi** emozionerete
si emozionerà	**si** emozioneranno
condizionale presente	
mi emozionerei	**ci** emozioneremmo
ti emozioneresti	**vi** emozionereste
si emozionerebbe	**si** emozionerebbero
congiuntivo presente	
mi emozioni	**ci** emozioniamo
ti emozioni	**vi** emozioniate
si emozioni	**si** emozionino
congiuntivo imperfetto	
mi emozionassi	**ci** emozionassimo
ti emozionassi	**vi** emozionaste
si emozionasse	**si** emozionassero
imperativo	
	emozioniamoci
emozionati; non emozionarti/ non ti emozionare	emozionatevi
si emozioni	si emozionino

SINGULAR	PLURAL
passato prossimo	
mi sono emozionato(a)	**ci siamo** emozionati(e)
ti sei emozionato(a)	**vi siete** emozionati(e)
si è emozionato(a)	**si sono** emozionati(e)
trapassato prossimo	
mi ero emozionato(a)	**ci eravamo** emozionati(e)
ti eri emozionato(a)	**vi eravate** emozionati(e)
si era emozionato(a)	**si erano** emozionati(e)
trapassato remoto	
mi fui emozionato(a)	**ci fummo** emozionati(e)
ti fosti emozionato(a)	**vi foste** emozionati(e)
si fu emozionato(a)	**si furono** emozionati(e)
futuro anteriore	
mi sarò emozionato(a)	**ci saremo** emozionati(e)
ti sarai emozionato(a)	**vi sarete** emozionati(e)
si sarà emozionato(a)	**si saranno** emozionati(e)
condizionale passato	
mi sarei emozionato(a)	**ci saremmo** emozionati(e)
ti saresti emozionato(a)	**vi sareste** emozionati(e)
si sarebbe emozionato(a)	**si sarebbero** emozionati(e)
congiuntivo passato	
mi sia emozionato(a)	**ci siamo** emozionati(e)
ti sia emozionato(a)	**vi siate** emozionati(e)
si sia emozionato(a)	**si siano** emozionati(e)
congiuntivo trapassato	
mi fossi emozionato(a)	**ci fossimo** emozionati(e)
ti fossi emozionato(a)	**vi foste** emozionati(e)
si fosse emozionato(a)	**si fossero** emozionati(e)

entrare — to enter

gerundio **entrando** participio passato **entrato**

SINGULAR	PLURAL	SINGULAR	PLURAL
indicativo presente		passato prossimo	
entr**o**	entr**iamo**	**sono** entrato(a)	**siamo** entrati(e)
entr**i**	entr**ate**	**sei** entrato(a)	**siete** entrati(e)
entr**a**	entr**ano**	**è** entrato(a)	**sono** entrati(e)
imperfetto		trapassato prossimo	
entra**vo**	entra**vamo**	**ero** entrato(a)	**eravamo** entrati(e)
entra**vi**	entra**vate**	**eri** entrato(a)	**eravate** entrati(e)
entra**va**	entra**vano**	**era** entrato(a)	**erano** entrati(e)
passato remoto		trapassato remoto	
entr**ai**	entr**ammo**	**fui** entrato(a)	**fummo** entrati(e)
entr**asti**	entr**aste**	**fosti** entrato(a)	**foste** entrati(e)
entr**ò**	entr**arono**	**fu** entrato(a)	**furono** entrati(e)
futuro semplice		futuro anteriore	
entrer**ò**	entrer**emo**	**sarò** entrato(a)	**saremo** entrati(e)
entrer**ai**	entrer**ete**	**sarai** entrato(a)	**sarete** entrati(e)
entrer**à**	entrer**anno**	**sarà** entrato(a)	**saranno** entrati(e)
condizionale presente		condizionale passato	
entrer**ei**	entrer**emmo**	**sarei** entrato(a)	**saremmo** entrati(e)
entrer**esti**	entrer**este**	**saresti** entrato(a)	**sareste** entrati(e)
entrer**ebbe**	entrer**ebbero**	**sarebbe** entrato(a)	**sarebbero** entrati(e)
congiuntivo presente		congiuntivo passato	
entr**i**	entr**iamo**	**sia** entrato(a)	**siamo** entrati(e)
entr**i**	entr**iate**	**sia** entrato(a)	**siate** entrati(e)
entr**i**	entr**ino**	**sia** entrato(a)	**siano** entrati(e)
congiuntivo imperfetto		congiuntivo trapassato	
entr**assi**	entr**assimo**	**fossi** entrato(a)	**fossimo** entrati(e)
entr**assi**	entr**aste**	**fossi** entrato(a)	**foste** entrati(e)
entr**asse**	entr**assero**	**fosse** entrato(a)	**fossero** entrati(e)
imperativo			
	entriamo		
entra; non entrare	entrate		
entri	entrino		

gerundio **esagerando** participio passato **esagerato**

SINGULAR	PLURAL	SINGULAR	PLURAL
indicativo presente		passato prossimo	
esager**o**	esager**iamo**	**ho** esagerato	**abbiamo** esagerato
esager**i**	esager**ate**	**hai** esagerato	**avete** esagerato
esager**a**	esager**ano**	**ha** esagerato	**hanno** esagerato
imperfetto		trapassato prossimo	
esagera**vo**	esagera**vamo**	**avevo** esagerato	**avevamo** esagerato
esagera**vi**	esagera**vate**	**avevi** esagerato	**avevate** esagerato
esagera**va**	esagera**vano**	**aveva** esagerato	**avevano** esagerato
passato remoto		trapassato remoto	
esager**ai**	esager**ammo**	**ebbi** esagerato	**avemmo** esagerato
esager**asti**	esager**aste**	**avesti** esagerato	**aveste** esagerato
esager**ò**	esager**arono**	**ebbe** esagerato	**ebbero** esagerato
futuro semplice		futuro anteriore	
esagerer**ò**	esagerer**emo**	**avrò** esagerato	**avremo** esagerato
esagerer**ai**	esagerer**ete**	**avrai** esagerato	**avrete** esagerato
esagerer**à**	esagerer**anno**	**avrà** esagerato	**avranno** esagerato
condizionale presente		condizionale passato	
esagerer**ei**	esagerer**emmo**	**avrei** esagerato	**avremmo** esagerato
esagerer**esti**	esagerer**este**	**avresti** esagerato	**avreste** esagerato
esagerer**ebbe**	esagerer**ebbero**	**avrebbe** esagerato	**avrebbero** esagerato
congiuntivo presente		congiuntivo passato	
esager**i**	esager**iamo**	**abbia** esagerato	**abbiamo** esagerato
esager**i**	esager**iate**	**abbia** esagerato	**abbiate** esagerato
esager**i**	esager**ino**	**abbia** esagerato	**abbiano** esagerato
congiuntivo imperfetto		congiuntivo trapassato	
esager**assi**	esager**assimo**	**avessi** esagerato	**avessimo** esagerato
esager**assi**	esager**aste**	**avessi** esagerato	**aveste** esagerato
esager**asse**	esager**assero**	**avesse** esagerato	**avessero** esagerato
imperativo			
	esageriamo		
esagera; non esagerare	esagerate		
esageri	esagerino		

esaminare — to examine, to consider

gerundio **esaminando** — participio passato **esaminato**

SINGULAR	PLURAL
indicativo presente	
esamin**o**	esamin**iamo**
esamin**i**	esamin**ate**
esamin**a**	esamin**ano**
imperfetto	
esamina**vo**	esamina**vamo**
esamina**vi**	esamina**vate**
esamina**va**	esamina**vano**
passato remoto	
esamin**ai**	esamin**ammo**
esamin**asti**	esamin**aste**
esamin**ò**	esamin**arono**
futuro semplice	
esaminer**ò**	esaminer**emo**
esaminer**ai**	esaminer**ete**
esaminer**à**	esaminer**anno**
condizionale presente	
esaminer**ei**	esaminer**emmo**
esaminer**esti**	esaminer**este**
esaminer**ebbe**	esaminer**ebbero**
congiuntivo presente	
esamin**i**	esamin**iamo**
esamin**i**	esamin**iate**
esamin**i**	esamin**ino**
congiuntivo imperfetto	
esamin**assi**	esamin**assimo**
esamin**assi**	esamin**aste**
esamin**asse**	esamin**assero**
imperativo	
	esaminiamo
esamina; non esaminare	esaminate
esamini	esaminino

SINGULAR	PLURAL
passato prossimo	
ho esaminato	**abbiamo** esaminato
hai esaminato	**avete** esaminato
ha esaminato	**hanno** esaminato
trapassato prossimo	
avevo esaminato	**avevamo** esaminato
avevi esaminato	**avevate** esaminato
aveva esaminato	**avevano** esaminato
trapassato remoto	
ebbi esaminato	**avemmo** esaminato
avesti esaminato	**aveste** esaminato
ebbe esaminato	**ebbero** esaminato
futuro anteriore	
avrò esaminato	**avremo** esaminato
avrai esaminato	**avrete** esaminato
avrà esaminato	**avranno** esaminato
condizionale passato	
avrei esaminato	**avremmo** esaminato
avresti esaminato	**avreste** esaminato
avrebbe esaminato	**avrebbero** esaminato
congiuntivo passato	
abbia esaminato	**abbiamo** esaminato
abbia esaminato	**abbiate** esaminato
abbia esaminato	**abbiano** esaminato
congiuntivo trapassato	
avessi esaminato	**avessimo** esaminato
avessi esaminato	**aveste** esaminato
avesse esaminato	**avessero** esaminato

to irritate, to exasperate **esasperare**

gerundio **esasperando** participio passato **esasperato**

SINGULAR	PLURAL

indicativo presente

esasper**o**	esasper**iamo**
esasper**i**	esasper**ate**
esasper**a**	esasper**ano**

imperfetto

esaspera**vo**	esaspera**vamo**
esaspera**vi**	esaspera**vate**
esaspera**va**	esaspera**vano**

passato remoto

esasper**ai**	esasper**ammo**
esasper**asti**	esasper**aste**
esasper**ò**	esasper**arono**

futuro semplice

esasperer**ò**	esasperer**emo**
esasperer**ai**	esasperer**ete**
esasperer**à**	esasperer**anno**

condizionale presente

esasperer**ei**	esasperer**emmo**
esasperer**esti**	esasperer**este**
esasperer**ebbe**	esasperer**ebbero**

congiuntivo presente

esasper**i**	esasper**iamo**
esasper**i**	esasper**iate**
esasper**i**	esasper**ino**

congiuntivo imperfetto

esasper**assi**	esasper**assimo**
esasper**assi**	esasper**aste**
esasper**asse**	esasper**assero**

imperativo

	esasperiamo
esaspera; non esasperare	esasperate
esasperi	esasperino

SINGULAR	PLURAL

passato prossimo

ho esasperato	**abbiamo** esasperato
hai esasperato	**avete** esasperato
ha esasperato	**hanno** esasperato

trapassato prossimo

avevo esasperato	**avevamo** esasperato
avevi esasperato	**avevate** esasperato
aveva esasperato	**avevano** esasperato

trapassato remoto

ebbi esasperato	**avemmo** esasperato
avesti esasperato	**aveste** esasperato
ebbe esasperato	**ebbero** esasperato

futuro anteriore

avrò esasperato	**avremo** esasperato
avrai esasperato	**avrete** esasperato
avrà esasperato	**avranno** esasperato

condizionale passato

avrei esasperato	**avremmo** esasperato
avresti esasperato	**avreste** esasperato
avrebbe esasperato	**avrebbero** esasperato

congiuntivo passato

abbia esasperato	**abbiamo** esasperato
abbia esasperato	**abbiate** esasperato
abbia esasperato	**abbiano** esasperato

congiuntivo trapassato

avessi esasperato	**avessimo** esasperato
avessi esasperato	**aveste** esasperato
avesse esasperato	**avessero** esasperato

esaurire — to use up, to wear out, to exhaust

gerundio **esaurendo** — participio passato **esaurito**

SINGULAR	PLURAL
indicativo presente	
esaur**isco**	esaur**iamo**
esaur**isci**	esaur**ite**
esaur**isce**	esaur**iscono**
imperfetto	
esauri**vo**	esauri**vamo**
esauri**vi**	esauri**vate**
esauri**va**	esauri**vano**
passato remoto	
esaur**ii**	esaur**immo**
esaur**isti**	esaur**iste**
esaur**ì**	esaur**irono**
futuro semplice	
esauri**rò**	esaurir**emo**
esaurir**ai**	esaurir**ete**
esaurir**à**	esaurir**anno**
condizionale presente	
esaurir**ei**	esaurir**emmo**
esaurir**esti**	esaurir**este**
esaurir**ebbe**	esaurir**ebbero**
congiuntivo presente	
esaur**isca**	esaur**iamo**
esaur**isca**	esaur**iate**
esaur**isca**	esaur**iscano**
congiuntivo imperfetto	
esaur**issi**	esaur**issimo**
esaur**issi**	esaur**iste**
esaur**isse**	esaur**issero**
imperativo	
	esauriamo
esaurisci; non esaurire	esaurite
esaurisca	esauriscano

SINGULAR	PLURAL
passato prossimo	
ho esaurito	**abbiamo** esaurito
hai esaurito	**avete** esaurito
ha esaurito	**hanno** esaurito
trapassato prossimo	
avevo esaurito	**avevamo** esaurito
avevi esaurito	**avevate** esaurito
aveva esaurito	**avevano** esaurito
trapassato remoto	
ebbi esaurito	**avemmo** esaurito
avesti esaurito	**aveste** esaurito
ebbe esaurito	**ebbero** esaurito
futuro anteriore	
avrò esaurito	**avremo** esaurito
avrai esaurito	**avrete** esaurito
avrà esaurito	**avranno** esaurito
condizionale passato	
avrei esaurito	**avremmo** esaurito
avresti esaurito	**avreste** esaurito
avrebbe esaurito	**avrebbero** esaurito
congiuntivo passato	
abbia esaurito	**abbiamo** esaurito
abbia esaurito	**abbiate** esaurito
abbia esaurito	**abbiano** esaurito
congiuntivo trapassato	
avessi esaurito	**avessimo** esaurito
avessi esaurito	**aveste** esaurito
avesse esaurito	**avessero** esaurito

gerundio **escludendo** participio passato **escluso**

SINGULAR	PLURAL	SINGULAR	PLURAL
indicativo presente		passato prossimo	
esclud**o**	esclud**iamo**	**ho** escluso	**abbiamo** escluso
esclud**i**	esclud**ete**	**hai** escluso	**avete** escluso
esclud**e**	esclud**ono**	**ha** escluso	**hanno** escluso
imperfetto		trapassato prossimo	
esclude**vo**	esclude**vamo**	**avevo** escluso	**avevamo** escluso
esclude**vi**	esclude**vate**	**avevi** escluso	**avevate** escluso
esclude**va**	esclude**vano**	**aveva** escluso	**avevano** escluso
passato remoto		trapassato remoto	
esclus**i**	esclud**emmo**	**ebbi** escluso	**avemmo** escluso
esclud**esti**	esclud**este**	**avesti** escluso	**aveste** escluso
esclus**e**	esclus**ero**	**ebbe** escluso	**ebbero** escluso
futuro semplice		futuro anteriore	
escluder**ò**	escluder**emo**	**avrò** escluso	**avremo** escluso
escluder**ai**	escluder**ete**	**avrai** escluso	**avrete** escluso
escluder**à**	escluder**anno**	**avrà** escluso	**avranno** escluso
condizionale presente		condizionale passato	
escluder**ei**	escluder**emmo**	**avrei** escluso	**avremmo** escluso
escluder**esti**	escluder**este**	**avresti** escluso	**avreste** escluso
escluder**ebbe**	escluder**ebbero**	**avrebbe** escluso	**avrebbero** escluso
congiuntivo presente		congiuntivo passato	
esclud**a**	esclud**iamo**	**abbia** escluso	**abbiamo** escluso
esclud**a**	esclud**iate**	**abbia** escluso	**abbiate** escluso
esclud**a**	esclud**ano**	**abbia** escluso	**abbiano** escluso
congiuntivo imperfetto		congiuntivo trapassato	
esclud**essi**	esclud**essimo**	**avessi** escluso	**avessimo** escluso
esclud**essi**	esclud**este**	**avessi** escluso	**aveste** escluso
esclud**esse**	esclud**essero**	**avesse** escluso	**avessero** escluso
imperativo			
	escludiamo		
escludi; non escludere	escludete		
escluda	escludano		

MEMORY TIP

I am sorry I **excluded** you from the party.

esibire — to show, to display

gerundio **esibendo** — participio passato **esibito**

E

SINGULAR	PLURAL
indicativo presente	
esibisc**o**	esibi**amo**
esibisc**i**	esibi**te**
esibisc**e**	esibisc**ono**
imperfetto	
esibi**vo**	esibi**vamo**
esibi**vi**	esibi**vate**
esibi**va**	esibi**vano**
passato remoto	
esibi**i**	esibi**mmo**
esibi**sti**	esibi**ste**
esib**ì**	esibi**rono**
futuro semplice	
esibir**ò**	esibir**emo**
esibir**ai**	esibir**ete**
esibir**à**	esibir**anno**
condizionale presente	
esibir**ei**	esibir**emmo**
esibir**esti**	esibir**este**
esibir**ebbe**	esibir**ebbero**
congiuntivo presente	
esibisc**a**	esibi**amo**
esibisc**a**	esibi**ate**
esibisc**a**	esibisc**ano**
congiuntivo imperfetto	
esibi**ssi**	esibi**ssimo**
esibi**ssi**	esibi**ste**
esibi**sse**	esibi**ssero**
imperativo	
	esibiamo
esibisci; non esibire	esibite
esibisca	esibiscano

SINGULAR	PLURAL
passato prossimo	
ho esibito	**abbiamo** esibito
hai esibito	**avete** esibito
ha esibito	**hanno** esibito
trapassato prossimo	
avevo esibito	**avevamo** esibito
avevi esibito	**avevate** esibito
aveva esibito	**avevano** esibito
trapassato remoto	
ebbi esibito	**avemmo** esibito
avesti esibito	**aveste** esibito
ebbe esibito	**ebbero** esibito
futuro anteriore	
avrò esibito	**avremo** esibito
avrai esibito	**avrete** esibito
avrà esibito	**avranno** esibito
condizionale passato	
avrei esibito	**avremmo** esibito
avresti esibito	**avreste** esibito
avrebbe esibito	**avrebbero** esibito
congiuntivo passato	
abbia esibito	**abbiamo** esibito
abbia esibito	**abbiate** esibito
abbia esibito	**abbiano** esibito
congiuntivo trapassato	
avessi esibito	**avessimo** esibito
avessi esibito	**aveste** esibito
avesse esibito	**avessero** esibito

gerundio **esistendo** participio passato **esistito**

SINGULAR	PLURAL	SINGULAR	PLURAL
indicativo presente		passato prossimo	
esist**o**	esist**iamo**	**sono** esistito(a)	**siamo** esistiti(e)
esist**i**	esist**ete**	**sei** esistito(a)	**siete** esistiti(e)
esist**e**	esist**ono**	**è** esistito(a)	**sono** esistiti(e)
imperfetto		trapassato prossimo	
esiste**vo**	esiste**vamo**	**ero** esistito(a)	**eravamo** esistiti(e)
esiste**vi**	esiste**vate**	**eri** esistito(a)	**eravate** esistiti(e)
esiste**va**	esiste**vano**	**era** esistito(a)	**erano** esistiti(e)
passato remoto		trapassato remoto	
esiste**i**, esist**etti**	esist**emmo**	**fui** esistito(a)	**fummo** esistiti(e)
esist**esti**	esist**este**	**fosti** esistito(a)	**foste** esistiti(e)
esist**é**, esist**ette**	esist**erono**, esist**ettero**	**fu** esistito(a)	**furono** esistiti(e)
futuro semplice		futuro anteriore	
esister**ò**	esister**emo**	**sarò** esistito(a)	**saremo** esistiti(e)
esister**ai**	esister**ete**	**sarai** esistito(a)	**sarete** esistiti(e)
esister**à**	esister**anno**	**sarà** esistito(a)	**saranno** esistiti(e)
condizionale presente		condizionale passato	
esister**ei**	esister**emmo**	**sarei** esistito(a)	**saremmo** esistiti(e)
esister**esti**	esister**este**	**saresti** esistito(a)	**sareste** esistiti(e)
esister**ebbe**	esister**ebbero**	**sarebbe** esistito(a)	**sarebbero** esistiti(e)
congiuntivo presente		congiuntivo passato	
esist**a**	esist**iamo**	**sia** esistito(a)	**siamo** esistiti(e)
esist**a**	esist**iate**	**sia** esistito(a)	**siate** esistiti(e)
esist**a**	esist**ano**	**sia** esistito(a)	**siano** esistiti(e)
congiuntivo imperfetto		congiuntivo trapassato	
esist**essi**	esist**essimo**	**fossi** esistito(a)	**fossimo** esistiti(e)
esist**essi**	esist**este**	**fossi** esistito(a)	**foste** esistiti(e)
esist**esse**	esist**essero**	**fosse** esistito(a)	**fossero** esistiti(e)

imperativo

	esistiamo
esisti; non esistere	esistete
esista	esistano

esprimere — to express

gerundio **esprimendo** participio passato **espresso**

SINGULAR	PLURAL	SINGULAR	PLURAL
indicativo presente		passato prossimo	
esprim**o**	esprim**iamo**	**ho** espresso	**abbiamo** espresso
esprim**i**	esprim**ete**	**hai** espresso	**avete** espresso
esprim**e**	esprim**ono**	**ha** espresso	**hanno** espresso
imperfetto		trapassato prossimo	
esprime**vo**	esprime**vamo**	**avevo** espresso	**avevamo** espresso
esprime**vi**	esprime**vate**	**avevi** espresso	**avevate** espresso
esprime**va**	esprime**vano**	**aveva** espresso	**avevano** espresso
passato remoto		trapassato remoto	
espress**i**	esprim**emmo**	**ebbi** espresso	**avemmo** espresso
esprim**esti**	esprim**este**	**avesti** espresso	**aveste** espresso
espress**e**	espress**ero**	**ebbe** espresso	**ebbero** espresso
futuro semplice		futuro anteriore	
esprimer**ò**	esprimer**emo**	**avrò** espresso	**avremo** espresso
esprimer**ai**	esprimer**ete**	**avrai** espresso	**avrete** espresso
esprimer**à**	esprimer**anno**	**avrà** espresso	**avranno** espresso
condizionale presente		condizionale passato	
esprimer**ei**	esprimer**emmo**	**avrei** espresso	**avremmo** espresso
esprimer**esti**	esprimer**este**	**avresti** espresso	**avreste** espresso
esprimer**ebbe**	esprimer**ebbero**	**avrebbe** espresso	**avrebbero** espresso
congiuntivo presente		congiuntivo passato	
esprim**a**	esprim**iamo**	**abbia** espresso	**abbiamo** espresso
esprim**a**	esprim**iate**	**abbia** espresso	**abbiate** espresso
esprim**a**	esprim**ano**	**abbia** espresso	**abbiano** espresso
congiuntivo imperfetto		congiuntivo trapassato	
esprim**essi**	esprim**essimo**	**avessi** espresso	**avessimo** espresso
esprim**essi**	esprim**este**	**avessi** espresso	**aveste** espresso
esprim**esse**	esprim**essero**	**avesse** espresso	**avessero** espresso
imperativo			
	esprimiamo		
esprimi; non esprimere	esprimete		
esprima	esprimano		

to be — essere

gerundio **essendo** participio passato **stato**

SINGULAR	PLURAL	SINGULAR	PLURAL
indicativo presente		passato prossimo	
son**o**	si**amo**	**sono** stato(a)	**siamo** stati(e)
se**i**	si**ete**	**sei** stato(a)	**siete** stati(e)
è	son**o**	**è** stato(a)	**sono** stati(e)
imperfetto		trapassato prossimo	
er**o**	er**avamo**	**ero** stato(a)	**eravamo** stati(e)
er**i**	er**avate**	**eri** stato(a)	**eravate** stati(e)
er**a**	er**ano**	**era** stato(a)	**erano** stati(e)
passato remoto		trapassato remoto	
fu**i**	fu**mmo**	**fui** stato(a)	**fummo** stati(e)
fos**ti**	fo**ste**	**fosti** stato(a)	**foste** stati(e)
f**u**	fur**ono**	**fu** stato(a)	**furono** stati(e)
futuro semplice		futuro anteriore	
sar**ò**	sar**emo**	**sarò** stato(a)	**saremo** stati(e)
sar**ai**	sar**ete**	**sarai** stato(a)	**sarete** stati(e)
sar**à**	sar**anno**	**sarà** stato(a)	**saranno** stati(e)
condizionale presente		condizionale passato	
sar**ei**	sar**emmo**	**sarei** stato(a)	**saremmo** stati(e)
sar**esti**	sar**este**	**saresti** stato(a)	**sareste** stati(e)
sar**ebbe**	sar**ebbero**	**sarebbe** stato(a)	**sarebbero** stati(e)
congiuntivo presente		congiuntivo passato	
si**a**	si**amo**	**sia** stato(a)	**siamo** stati(e)
si**a**	si**ate**	**sia** stato(a)	**siate** stati(e)
si**a**	si**ano**	**sia** stato(a)	**siano** stati(e)
congiuntivo imperfetto		congiuntivo trapassato	
fossi	fossi**mo**	**fossi** stato(a)	**fossimo** stati(e)
foss**i**	fost**e**	**fossi** stato(a)	**foste** stati(e)
foss**e**	foss**ero**	**fosse** stato(a)	**fossero** stati(e)
imperativo			
	siamo		
sii; non essere	siate		
sia	siano		

E

MUST KNOW VERB

estendere — to extend

gerundio **estendendo** — participio passato **esteso**

SINGULAR	PLURAL
indicativo presente	
estend**o**	estend**iamo**
estend**i**	estend**ete**
estend**e**	estend**ono**
imperfetto	
estende**vo**	estende**vamo**
estende**vi**	estende**vate**
estende**va**	estende**vano**
passato remoto	
este**si**	estend**emmo**
estend**esti**	estend**este**
este**se**	este**sero**
futuro semplice	
estender**ò**	estender**emo**
estender**ai**	estender**ete**
estender**à**	estender**anno**
condizionale presente	
estender**ei**	estender**emmo**
estender**esti**	estender**este**
estender**ebbe**	estender**ebbero**
congiuntivo presente	
estend**a**	estend**iamo**
estend**a**	estend**iate**
estend**a**	estend**ano**
congiuntivo imperfetto	
estend**essi**	estend**essimo**
estend**essi**	estend**este**
estend**esse**	estend**essero**
imperativo	
	estendiamo
estendi; non estendere	estendete
estenda	estendano

SINGULAR	PLURAL
passato prossimo	
ho esteso	**abbiamo** esteso
hai esteso	**avete** esteso
ha esteso	**hanno** esteso
trapassato prossimo	
avevo esteso	**avevamo** esteso
avevi esteso	**avevate** esteso
aveva esteso	**avevano** esteso
trapassato remoto	
ebbi esteso	**avemmo** esteso
avesti esteso	**aveste** esteso
ebbe esteso	**ebbero** esteso
futuro anteriore	
avrò esteso	**avremo** esteso
avrai esteso	**avrete** esteso
avrà esteso	**avranno** esteso
condizionale passato	
avrei esteso	**avremmo** esteso
avresti esteso	**avreste** esteso
avrebbe esteso	**avrebbero** esteso
congiuntivo passato	
abbia esteso	**abbiamo** esteso
abbia esteso	**abbiate** esteso
abbia esteso	**abbiano** esteso
congiuntivo trapassato	
avessi esteso	**avessimo** esteso
avessi esteso	**aveste** esteso
avesse esteso	**avessero** esteso

to avoid, to evade — evitare

gerundio **evitando** — participio passato **evitato**

SINGULAR	PLURAL	SINGULAR	PLURAL
indicativo presente		passato prossimo	
evit**o**	evit**iamo**	**ho** evitato	**abbiamo** evitato
evit**i**	evit**ate**	**hai** evitato	**avete** evitato
evit**a**	evit**ano**	**ha** evitato	**hanno** evitato
imperfetto		trapassato prossimo	
evita**vo**	evita**vamo**	**avevo** evitato	**avevamo** evitato
evita**vi**	evita**vate**	**avevi** evitato	**avevate** evitato
evita**va**	evita**vano**	**aveva** evitato	**avevano** evitato
passato remoto		trapassato remoto	
evit**ai**	evit**ammo**	**ebbi** evitato	**avemmo** evitato
evit**asti**	evit**aste**	**avesti** evitato	**aveste** evitato
evit**ò**	evit**arono**	**ebbe** evitato	**ebbero** evitato
futuro semplice		futuro anteriore	
eviter**ò**	eviter**emo**	**avrò** evitato	**avremo** evitato
eviter**ai**	eviter**ete**	**avrai** evitato	**avrete** evitato
eviter**à**	eviter**anno**	**avrà** evitato	**avranno** evitato
condizionale presente		condizionale passato	
eviter**ei**	eviter**emmo**	**avrei** evitato	**avremmo** evitato
eviter**esti**	eviter**este**	**avresti** evitato	**avreste** evitato
eviter**ebbe**	eviter**ebbero**	**avrebbe** evitato	**avrebbero** evitato
congiuntivo presente		congiuntivo passato	
evit**i**	evit**iamo**	**abbia** evitato	**abbiamo** evitato
evit**i**	evit**iate**	**abbia** evitato	**abbiate** evitato
evit**i**	evit**ino**	**abbia** evitato	**abbiano** evitato
congiuntivo imperfetto		congiuntivo trapassato	
evit**assi**	evit**assimo**	**avessi** evitato	**avessimo** evitato
evit**assi**	evit**aste**	**avessi** evitato	**aveste** evitato
evit**asse**	evit**assero**	**avesse** evitato	**avessero** evitato
imperativo			
	evitiamo		
evita; non evitare	evitate		
eviti	evitino		

E

facilitare — to facilitate, to make easier

gerundio **facilitando** participio passato **facilitato**

SINGULAR	PLURAL	SINGULAR	PLURAL
indicativo presente		passato prossimo	
facilit**o**	facilit**iamo**	**ho** facilitato	**abbiamo** facilitato
facilit**i**	facilit**ate**	**hai** facilitato	**avete** facilitato
facilit**a**	facilit**ano**	**ha** facilitato	**hanno** facilitato
imperfetto		trapassato prossimo	
facilita**vo**	facilita**vamo**	**avevo** facilitato	**avevamo** facilitato
facilita**vi**	facilita**vate**	**avevi** facilitato	**avevate** facilitato
facilita**va**	facilita**vano**	**aveva** facilitato	**avevano** facilitato
passato remoto		trapassato remoto	
facilit**ai**	facilit**ammo**	**ebbi** facilitato	**avemmo** facilitato
facilit**asti**	facilit**aste**	**avesti** facilitato	**aveste** facilitato
facilit**ò**	facilit**arono**	**ebbe** facilitato	**ebbero** facilitato
futuro semplice		futuro anteriore	
faciliter**ò**	faciliter**emo**	**avrò** facilitato	**avremo** facilitato
faciliter**ai**	faciliter**ete**	**avrai** facilitato	**avrete** facilitato
faciliter**à**	faciliter**anno**	**avrà** facilitato	**avranno** facilitato
condizionale presente		condizionale passato	
faciliter**ei**	faciliter**emmo**	**avrei** facilitato	**avremmo** facilitato
faciliter**esti**	faciliter**este**	**avresti** facilitato	**avreste** facilitato
faciliter**ebbe**	faciliter**ebbero**	**avrebbe** facilitato	**avrebbero** facilitato
congiuntivo presente		congiuntivo passato	
facilit**i**	facilit**iamo**	**abbia** facilitato	**abbiamo** facilitato
facilit**i**	facilit**iate**	**abbia** facilitato	**abbiate** facilitato
facilit**i**	facilit**ino**	**abbia** facilitato	**abbiano** facilitato
congiuntivo imperfetto		congiuntivo trapassato	
facilit**assi**	facilit**assimo**	**avessi** facilitato	**avessimo** facilitato
facilit**assi**	facilit**aste**	**avessi** facilitato	**aveste** facilitato
facilit**asse**	facilit**assero**	**avesse** facilitato	**avessero** facilitato
imperativo			
	facilitiamo		
facilita; non facilitare	facilitate		
faciliti	facilitino		

F

gerundio **fallendo** participio passato **fallito**

SINGULAR	PLURAL
indicativo presente	
fallisc**o**	fall**iamo**
fallisc**i**	fall**ite**
fallisc**e**	fallisc**ono**
imperfetto	
falli**vo**	falli**vamo**
falli**vi**	falli**vate**
falli**va**	falli**vano**
passato remoto	
fall**ii**	fall**immo**
fall**isti**	fall**iste**
fall**ì**	fall**irono**
futuro semplice	
fallir**ò**	fallir**emo**
fallir**ai**	fallir**ete**
fallir**à**	fallir**anno**
condizionale presente	
fallir**ei**	fallir**emmo**
fallir**esti**	fallir**este**
fallir**ebbe**	fallir**ebbero**
congiuntivo presente	
fallisc**a**	fall**iamo**
fallisc**a**	fall**iate**
fallisc**a**	fallisc**ano**
congiuntivo imperfetto	
fall**issi**	fall**issimo**
fall**issi**	fall**iste**
fall**isse**	fall**issero**
imperativo	
	falliamo
fallisci; non fallire	fallite
fallisca	falliscano

SINGULAR	PLURAL
passato prossimo	
sono fallito(a)	**siamo** falliti(e)
sei fallito(a)	**siete** falliti(e)
è fallito(a)	**sono** falliti(e)
trapassato prossimo	
ero fallito(a)	**eravamo** falliti(e)
eri fallito(a)	**eravate** falliti(e)
era fallito(a)	**erano** falliti(e)
trapassato remoto	
fui fallito(a)	**fummo** falliti(e)
fosti fallito(a)	**foste** falliti(e)
fu fallito(a)	**furono** falliti(e)
futuro anteriore	
sarò fallito(a)	**saremo** falliti(e)
sarai fallito(a)	**sarete** falliti(e)
sarà fallito(a)	**saranno** falliti(e)
condizionale passato	
sarei fallito(a)	**saremmo** falliti(e)
saresti fallito(a)	**sareste** falliti(e)
sarebbe fallito(a)	**sarebbero** falliti(e)
congiuntivo passato	
sia fallito(a)	**siamo** falliti(e)
sia fallito(a)	**siate** falliti(e)
sia fallito(a)	**siano** falliti(e)
congiuntivo trapassato	
fossi fallito(a)	**fossimo** falliti(e)
fossi fallito(a)	**foste** falliti(e)
fosse fallito(a)	**fossero** falliti(e)

falsificare — to falsify, to fake, to forge

gerundio **falsificando** — participio passato **falsificato**

SINGULAR	PLURAL	SINGULAR	PLURAL
indicativo presente		passato prossimo	
falsific**o**	falsifich**iamo**	**ho** falsificato	**abbiamo** falsificato
falsifich**i**	falsific**ate**	**hai** falsificato	**avete** falsificato
falsific**a**	falsific**ano**	**ha** falsificato	**hanno** falsificato
imperfetto		trapassato prossimo	
falsifica**vo**	falsifica**vamo**	**avevo** falsificato	**avevamo** falsificato
falsifica**vi**	falsifica**vate**	**avevi** falsificato	**avevate** falsificato
falsifica**va**	falsifica**vano**	**aveva** falsificato	**avevano** falsificato
passato remoto		trapassato remoto	
falsific**ai**	falsific**ammo**	**ebbi** falsificato	**avemmo** falsificato
falsific**asti**	falsific**aste**	**avesti** falsificato	**aveste** falsificato
falsific**ò**	falsific**arono**	**ebbe** falsificato	**ebbero** falsificato
futuro semplice		futuro anteriore	
falsificher**ò**	falsificher**emo**	**avrò** falsificato	**avremo** falsificato
falsificher**ai**	falsificher**ete**	**avrai** falsificato	**avrete** falsificato
falsificher**à**	falsificher**anno**	**avrà** falsificato	**avranno** falsificato
condizionale presente		condizionale passato	
falsificher**ei**	falsificher**emmo**	**avrei** falsificato	**avremmo** falsificato
falsificher**esti**	falsificher**este**	**avresti** falsificato	**avreste** falsificato
falsificher**ebbe**	falsificher**ebbero**	**avrebbe** falsificato	**avrebbero** falsificato
congiuntivo presente		congiuntivo passato	
falsifich**i**	falsifich**iamo**	**abbia** falsificato	**abbiamo** falsificato
falsifich**i**	falsifich**iate**	**abbia** falsificato	**abbiate** falsificato
falsifich**i**	falsifich**ino**	**abbia** falsificato	**abbiano** falsificato
congiuntivo imperfetto		congiuntivo trapassato	
falsific**assi**	falsific**assimo**	**avessi** falsificato	**avessimo** falsificato
falsific**assi**	falsific**aste**	**avessi** falsificato	**aveste** falsificato
falsific**asse**	falsific**assero**	**avesse** falsificato	**avessero** falsificato
imperativo			
	falsifichiamo		
falsifica; non falsificare	falsificate		
falsifichi	falsifichino		

F

to do, to make

gerundio **facendo** participio passato **fatto**

SINGULAR	PLURAL	SINGULAR	PLURAL
indicativo presente		passato prossimo	
faccio	**facciamo**	**ho** fatto	**abbiamo** fatto
fai	**fate**	**hai** fatto	**avete** fatto
fa	**fanno**	**ha** fatto	**hanno** fatto
imperfetto		trapassato prossimo	
facevo	**facevamo**	**avevo** fatto	**avevamo** fatto
facevi	**facevate**	**avevi** fatto	**avevate** fatto
faceva	**facevano**	**aveva** fatto	**avevano** fatto
passato remoto		trapassato remoto	
feci	**facemmo**	**ebbi** fatto	**avemmo** fatto
facesti	**faceste**	**avesti** fatto	**aveste** fatto
fece	**fecero**	**ebbe** fatto	**ebbero** fatto
futuro semplice		futuro anteriore	
farò	**faremo**	**avrò** fatto	**avremo** fatto
farai	**farete**	**avrai** fatto	**avrete** fatto
farà	**faranno**	**avrà** fatto	**avranno** fatto
condizionale presente		condizionale passato	
farei	**faremmo**	**avrei** fatto	**avremmo** fatto
faresti	**fareste**	**avresti** fatto	**avreste** fatto
farebbe	**farebbero**	**avrebbe** fatto	**avrebbero** fatto
congiuntivo presente		congiuntivo passato	
faccia	**facciamo**	**abbia** fatto	**abbiamo** fatto
faccia	**facciate**	**abbia** fatto	**abbiate** fatto
faccia	**facciano**	**abbia** fatto	**abbiano** fatto
congiuntivo imperfetto		congiuntivo trapassato	
facessi	**facessimo**	**avessi** fatto	**avessimo** fatto
facessi	**faceste**	**avessi** fatto	**aveste** fatto
facesse	**facessero**	**avesse** fatto	**avessero** fatto
imperativo			
	facciamo		
fa'/fai; non fare	fate		
faccia	facciano		

F

favorire — to favor

gerundio **favorendo** participio passato **favorito**

SINGULAR	PLURAL
indicativo presente	
favorisc**o**	favor**iamo**
favorisc**i**	favor**ite**
favorisc**e**	favorisc**ono**
imperfetto	
favori**vo**	favori**vamo**
favori**vi**	favori**vate**
favori**va**	favori**vano**
passato remoto	
favor**ii**	favor**immo**
favor**isti**	favor**iste**
favor**ì**	favor**irono**
futuro semplice	
favorir**ò**	favorir**emo**
favorir**ai**	favorir**ete**
favorir**à**	favorir**anno**
condizionale presente	
favorir**ei**	favorir**emmo**
favorir**esti**	favorir**este**
favorir**ebbe**	favorir**ebbero**
congiuntivo presente	
favorisc**a**	favor**iamo**
favorisc**a**	favor**iate**
favorisc**a**	favorisc**ano**
congiuntivo imperfetto	
favor**issi**	favor**issimo**
favor**issi**	favor**iste**
favor**isse**	favor**issero**
imperativo	
	favoriamo
favorisci; non favorire	favorite
favorisca	favoriscano

SINGULAR	PLURAL
passato prossimo	
ho favorito	**abbiamo** favorito
hai favorito	**avete** favorito
ha favorito	**hanno** favorito
trapassato prossimo	
avevo favorito	**avevamo** favorito
avevi favorito	**avevate** favorito
aveva favorito	**avevano** favorito
trapassato remoto	
ebbi favorito	**avemmo** favorito
avesti favorito	**aveste** favorito
ebbe favorito	**ebbero** favorito
futuro anteriore	
avrò favorito	**avremo** favorito
avrai favorito	**avrete** favorito
avrà favorito	**avranno** favorito
condizionale passato	
avrei favorito	**avremmo** favorito
avresti favorito	**avreste** favorito
avrebbe favorito	**avrebbero** favorito
congiuntivo passato	
abbia favorito	**abbiamo** favorito
abbia favorito	**abbiate** favorito
abbia favorito	**abbiano** favorito
congiuntivo trapassato	
avessi favorito	**avessimo** favorito
avessi favorito	**aveste** favorito
avesse favorito	**avessero** favorito

to wound **ferire**

gerundio **ferendo** participio passato **ferito**

SINGULAR	PLURAL	SINGULAR	PLURAL
indicativo presente		passato prossimo	
feris**co**	fer**iamo**	**ho** ferito	**abbiamo** ferito
feris**ci**	fer**ite**	**hai** ferito	**avete** ferito
feris**ce**	feris**cono**	**ha** ferito	**hanno** ferito
imperfetto		trapassato prossimo	
feri**vo**	feri**vamo**	**avevo** ferito	**avevamo** ferito
feri**vi**	feri**vate**	**avevi** ferito	**avevate** ferito
feri**va**	feri**vano**	**aveva** ferito	**avevano** ferito
passato remoto		trapassato remoto	
fer**ii**	fer**immo**	**ebbi** ferito	**avemmo** ferito
fer**isti**	fer**iste**	**avesti** ferito	**aveste** ferito
fer**ì**	fer**irono**	**ebbe** ferito	**ebbero** ferito
futuro semplice		futuro anteriore	
ferir**ò**	ferir**emo**	**avrò** ferito	**avremo** ferito
ferir**ai**	ferir**ete**	**avrai** ferito	**avrete** ferito
ferir**à**	ferir**anno**	**avrà** ferito	**avranno** ferito
condizionale presente		condizionale passato	
ferir**ei**	ferir**emmo**	**avrei** ferito	**avremmo** ferito
ferir**esti**	ferir**este**	**avresti** ferito	**avreste** ferito
ferir**ebbe**	ferir**ebbero**	**avrebbe** ferito	**avrebbero** ferito
congiuntivo presente		congiuntivo passato	
feris**ca**	fer**iamo**	**abbia** ferito	**abbiamo** ferito
feris**ca**	fer**iate**	**abbia** ferito	**abbiate** ferito
feris**ca**	feris**cano**	**abbia** ferito	**abbiano** ferito
congiuntivo imperfetto		congiuntivo trapassato	
fer**issi**	fer**issimo**	**avessi** ferito	**avessimo** ferito
fer**issi**	fer**iste**	**avessi** ferito	**aveste** ferito
fer**isse**	fer**issero**	**avesse** ferito	**avessero** ferito
imperativo			
	feriamo		
ferisci; non ferire	ferite		
ferisca	feriscano		

F

fermare — to stop, to hold

gerundio **fermando** participio passato **fermato**

SINGULAR	PLURAL	SINGULAR	PLURAL
indicativo presente		passato prossimo	
ferm**o**	ferm**iamo**	**ho** fermato	**abbiamo** fermato
ferm**i**	ferm**ate**	**hai** fermato	**avete** fermato
ferm**a**	ferm**ano**	**ha** fermato	**hanno** fermato
imperfetto		trapassato prossimo	
ferma**vo**	ferma**vamo**	**avevo** fermato	**avevamo** fermato
ferma**vi**	ferma**vate**	**avevi** fermato	**avevate** fermato
ferma**va**	ferma**vano**	**aveva** fermato	**avevano** fermato
passato remoto		trapassato remoto	
ferm**ai**	ferm**ammo**	**ebbi** fermato	**avemmo** fermato
ferm**asti**	ferm**aste**	**avesti** fermato	**aveste** fermato
ferm**ò**	ferm**arono**	**ebbe** fermato	**ebbero** fermato
futuro semplice		futuro anteriore	
fermer**ò**	fermer**emo**	**avrò** fermato	**avremo** fermato
fermer**ai**	fermer**ete**	**avrai** fermato	**avrete** fermato
fermer**à**	fermer**anno**	**avrà** fermato	**avranno** fermato
condizionale presente		condizionale passato	
fermer**ei**	fermer**emmo**	**avrei** fermato	**avremmo** fermato
fermer**esti**	fermer**este**	**avresti** fermato	**avreste** fermato
fermer**ebbe**	fermer**ebbero**	**avrebbe** fermato	**avrebbero** fermato
congiuntivo presente		congiuntivo passato	
ferm**i**	ferm**iamo**	**abbia** fermato	**abbiamo** fermato
ferm**i**	ferm**iate**	**abbia** fermato	**abbiate** fermato
ferm**i**	ferm**ino**	**abbia** fermato	**abbiano** fermato
congiuntivo imperfetto		congiuntivo trapassato	
ferm**assi**	ferm**assimo**	**avessi** fermato	**avessimo** fermato
ferm**assi**	ferm**aste**	**avessi** fermato	**aveste** fermato
ferm**asse**	ferm**assero**	**avesse** fermato	**avessero** fermato
imperativo			
	fermiamo		
ferma; non fermare	fermate		
fermi	fermino		

F

gerundio **fermandosi** participio passato **fermatosi**

SINGULAR	PLURAL
indicativo presente	
mi ferm**o**	**ci** ferm**iamo**
ti ferm**i**	**vi** ferm**ate**
si ferm**a**	**si** ferm**ano**
imperfetto	
mi ferma**vo**	**ci** ferma**vamo**
ti ferma**vi**	**vi** ferma**vate**
si ferma**va**	**si** ferma**vano**
passato remoto	
mi ferm**ai**	**ci** ferm**ammo**
ti ferm**asti**	**vi** ferm**aste**
si ferm**ò**	**si** ferm**arono**
futuro semplice	
mi fermer**ò**	**ci** fermer**emo**
ti fermer**ai**	**vi** fermer**ete**
si fermer**à**	**si** fermer**anno**
condizionale presente	
mi fermer**ei**	**ci** fermer**emmo**
ti fermer**esti**	**vi** fermer**este**
si fermer**ebbe**	**si** fermer**ebbero**
congiuntivo presente	
mi ferm**i**	**ci** ferm**iamo**
ti ferm**i**	**vi** ferm**iate**
si ferm**i**	**si** ferm**ino**
congiuntivo imperfetto	
mi ferm**assi**	**ci** ferm**assimo**
ti ferm**assi**	**vi** ferm**aste**
si ferm**asse**	**si** ferm**assero**
imperativo	
	fermiamoci
fermati; non fermarti/ non ti fermare	fermatevi
si fermi	si fermino

SINGULAR	PLURAL
passato prossimo	
mi sono fermato(a)	**ci siamo** fermati(e)
ti sei fermato(a)	**vi siete** fermati(e)
si è fermato(a)	**si sono** fermati(e)
trapassato prossimo	
mi ero fermato(a)	**ci eravamo** fermati(e)
ti eri fermato(a)	**vi eravate** fermati(e)
si era fermato(a)	**si erano** fermati(e)
trapassato remoto	
mi fui fermato(a)	**ci fummo** fermati(e)
ti fosti fermato(a)	**vi foste** fermati(e)
si fu fermato(a)	**si furono** fermati(e)
futuro anteriore	
mi sarò fermato(a)	**ci saremo** fermati(e)
ti sarai fermato(a)	**vi sarete** fermati(e)
si sarà fermato(a)	**si saranno** fermati(e)
condizionale passato	
mi sarei fermato(a)	**ci saremmo** fermati(e)
ti saresti fermato(a)	**vi sareste** fermati(e)
si sarebbe fermato(a)	**si sarebbero** fermati(e)
congiuntivo passato	
mi sia fermato(a)	**ci siamo** fermati(e)
ti sia fermato(a)	**vi siate** fermati(e)
si sia fermato(a)	**si siano** fermati(e)
congiuntivo trapassato	
mi fossi fermato(a)	**ci fossimo** fermati(e)
ti fossi fermato(a)	**vi foste** fermati(e)
si fosse fermato(a)	**si fossero** fermati(e)

festeggiare — to celebrate

gerundio **festeggiando** — participio passato **festeggiato**

SINGULAR	PLURAL	SINGULAR	PLURAL
indicativo presente		passato prossimo	
festeggi**o**	festegg**iamo**	**ho** festeggiato	**abbiamo** festeggiato
festegg**i**	festeggi**ate**	**hai** festeggiato	**avete** festeggiato
festeggi**a**	festeggi**ano**	**ha** festeggiato	**hanno** festeggiato
imperfetto		trapassato prossimo	
festeggia**vo**	festeggia**vamo**	**avevo** festeggiato	**avevamo** festeggiato
festeggia**vi**	festeggia**vate**	**avevi** festeggiato	**avevate** festeggiato
festeggia**va**	festeggia**vano**	**aveva** festeggiato	**avevano** festeggiato
passato remoto		trapassato remoto	
festeggi**ai**	festeggi**ammo**	**ebbi** festeggiato	**avemmo** festeggiato
festeggi**asti**	festeggi**aste**	**avesti** festeggiato	**aveste** festeggiato
festegg**iò**	festeggi**arono**	**ebbe** festeggiato	**ebbero** festeggiato
futuro semplice		futuro anteriore	
festegger**ò**	festegger**emo**	**avrò** festeggiato	**avremo** festeggiato
festegger**ai**	festegger**ete**	**avrai** festeggiato	**avrete** festeggiato
festegger**à**	festegger**anno**	**avrà** festeggiato	**avranno** festeggiato
condizionale presente		condizionale passato	
festegger**ei**	festegger**emmo**	**avrei** festeggiato	**avremmo** festeggiato
festegger**esti**	festegger**este**	**avresti** festeggiato	**avreste** festeggiato
festegger**ebbe**	festegger**ebbero**	**avrebbe** festeggiato	**avrebbero** festeggiato
congiuntivo presente		congiuntivo passato	
festegg**i**	festegg**iamo**	**abbia** festeggiato	**abbiamo** festeggiato
festegg**i**	festegg**iate**	**abbia** festeggiato	**abbiate** festeggiato
festegg**i**	festegg**ino**	**abbia** festeggiato	**abbiano** festeggiato
congiuntivo imperfetto		congiuntivo trapassato	
festeggi**assi**	festeggi**assimo**	**avessi** festeggiato	**avessimo** festeggiato
festeggi**assi**	festeggi**aste**	**avessi** festeggiato	**aveste** festeggiato
festeggi**asse**	festeggi**assero**	**avesse** festeggiato	**avessero** festeggiato
imperativo			
	festeggiamo		
festeggia; non festeggiare	festeggiate		
festeggi	festeggino		

F

gerundio **fidandosi** participio passato **fidatosi**

SINGULAR	PLURAL	SINGULAR	PLURAL
indicativo presente		passato prossimo	
mi fid**o**	**ci** fid**iamo**	**mi sono** fidato(a)	**ci siamo** fidati(e)
ti fid**i**	**vi** fid**ate**	**ti sei** fidato(a)	**vi siete** fidati(e)
si fid**a**	**si** fid**ano**	**si è** fidato(a)	**si sono** fidati(e)
imperfetto		trapassato prossimo	
mi fida**vo**	**ci** fida**vamo**	**mi ero** fidato(a)	**ci eravamo** fidati(e)
ti fida**vi**	**vi** fida**vate**	**ti eri** fidato(a)	**vi eravate** fidati(e)
si fida**va**	**si** fida**vano**	**si era** fidato(a)	**si erano** fidati(e)
passato remoto		trapassato remoto	
mi fid**ai**	**ci** fid**ammo**	**mi fui** fidato(a)	**ci fummo** fidati(e)
ti fid**asti**	**vi** fid**aste**	**ti fosti** fidato(a)	**vi foste** fidati(e)
si fid**ò**	**si** fid**arono**	**si fu** fidato(a)	**si furono** fidati(e)
futuro semplice		futuro anteriore	
mi fider**ò**	**ci** fider**emo**	**mi sarò** fidato(a)	**ci saremo** fidati(e)
ti fider**ai**	**vi** fider**ete**	**ti sarai** fidato(a)	**vi sarete** fidati(e)
si fider**à**	**si** fider**anno**	**si sarà** fidato(a)	**si saranno** fidati(e)
condizionale presente		condizionale passato	
mi fider**ei**	**ci** fider**emmo**	**mi sarei** fidato(a)	**ci saremmo** fidati(e)
ti fider**esti**	**vi** fider**este**	**ti saresti** fidato(a)	**vi sareste** fidati(e)
si fider**ebbe**	**si** fider**ebbero**	**si sarebbe** fidato(a)	**si sarebbero** fidati(e)
congiuntivo presente		congiuntivo passato	
mi fid**i**	**ci** fid**iamo**	**mi sia** fidato(a)	**ci siamo** fidati(e)
ti fid**i**	**vi** fid**iate**	**ti sia** fidato(a)	**vi siate** fidati(e)
si fid**i**	**si** fid**ino**	**si sia** fidato(a)	**si siano** fidati(e)
congiuntivo imperfetto		congiuntivo trapassato	
mi fid**assi**	**ci** fid**assimo**	**mi fossi** fidato(a)	**ci fossimo** fidati(e)
ti fid**assi**	**vi** fid**aste**	**ti fossi** fidato(a)	**vi foste** fidati(e)
si fid**asse**	**si** fid**assero**	**si fosse** fidato(a)	**si fossero** fidati(e)

imperativo

	fidiamoci
fidati; non fidarti/ non ti fidare	fidatevi
si fidi	si fidino

F

figgere — to fix

gerundio **figgendo** participio passato **fitto**

SINGULAR	PLURAL	SINGULAR	PLURAL
indicativo presente		passato prossimo	
figg**o**	figg**iamo**	**ho** fitto	**abbiamo** fitto
figg**i**	figg**ete**	**hai** fitto	**avete** fitto
figg**e**	figg**ono**	**ha** fitto	**hanno** fitto
imperfetto		trapassato prossimo	
figge**vo**	figge**vamo**	**avevo** fitto	**avevamo** fitto
figge**vi**	figge**vate**	**avevi** fitto	**avevate** fitto
figge**va**	figge**vano**	**aveva** fitto	**avevano** fitto
passato remoto		trapassato remoto	
fiss**i**	figg**emmo**	**ebbi** fitto	**avemmo** fitto
figg**esti**	figg**este**	**avesti** fitto	**aveste** fitto
fiss**e**	fiss**ero**	**ebbe** fitto	**ebbero** fitto
futuro semplice		futuro anteriore	
figger**ò**	figger**emo**	**avrò** fitto	**avremo** fitto
figger**ai**	figger**ete**	**avrai** fitto	**avrete** fitto
figger**à**	figger**anno**	**avrà** fitto	**avranno** fitto
condizionale presente		condizionale passato	
figger**ei**	figger**emmo**	**avrei** fitto	**avremmo** fitto
figger**esti**	figger**este**	**avresti** fitto	**avreste** fitto
figger**ebbe**	figger**ebbero**	**avrebbe** fitto	**avrebbero** fitto
congiuntivo presente		congiuntivo passato	
figg**a**	figg**iamo**	**abbia** fitto	**abbiamo** fitto
figg**a**	figg**iate**	**abbia** fitto	**abbiate** fitto
figg**a**	figg**ano**	**abbia** fitto	**abbiano** fitto
congiuntivo imperfetto		congiuntivo trapassato	
figg**essi**	figg**essimo**	**avessi** fitto	**avessimo** fitto
figg**essi**	figg**este**	**avessi** fitto	**aveste** fitto
figg**esse**	figg**essero**	**avesse** fitto	**avessero** fitto

imperativo

	figgiamo
figgi; non figgere	figgete
figga	figgano

gerundio **fingendo** participio passato **finto**

SINGULAR	PLURAL
indicativo presente	
ling**o**	fing**iamo**
fing**i**	fing**ete**
fing**e**	fing**ono**
imperfetto	
finge**vo**	finge**vamo**
finge**vi**	finge**vate**
finge**va**	finge**vano**
passato remoto	
fins**i**	fing**emmo**
fing**esti**	fing**este**
fins**e**	fins**ero**
futuro semplice	
finger**ò**	finger**emo**
finger**ai**	finger**ete**
finger**à**	finger**anno**
condizionale presente	
finger**ei**	finger**emmo**
finger**esti**	finger**este**
finger**ebbe**	finger**ebbero**
congiuntivo presente	
fing**a**	fing**iamo**
fing**a**	fing**iate**
fing**a**	fing**ano**
congiuntivo imperfetto	
fing**essi**	fing**essimo**
fing**essi**	fing**este**
fing**esse**	fing**essero**
imperativo	
	fingiamo
fingi; non fingere	fingete
finga	fingano

SINGULAR	PLURAL
passato prossimo	
ho finto	**abbiamo** finto
hai finto	**avete** finto
ha finto	**hanno** finto
trapassato prossimo	
avevo finto	**avevamo** finto
avevi finto	**avevate** finto
aveva finto	**avevano** finto
trapassato remoto	
ebbi finto	**avemmo** finto
avesti finto	**aveste** finto
ebbe finto	**ebbero** finto
futuro anteriore	
avrò finto	**avremo** finto
avrai finto	**avrete** finto
avrà finto	**avranno** finto
condizionale passato	
avrei finto	**avremmo** finto
avresti finto	**avreste** finto
avrebbe finto	**avrebbero** finto
congiuntivo passato	
abbia finto	**abbiamo** finto
abbia finto	**abbiate** finto
abbia finto	**abbiano** finto
congiuntivo trapassato	
avessi finto	**avessimo** finto
avessi finto	**aveste** finto
avesse finto	**avessero** finto

finire — to end, to finish

gerundio **finendo** participio passato **finito**

SINGULAR	PLURAL	SINGULAR	PLURAL
indicativo presente		passato prossimo	
finisc**o**	fin**iamo**	**ho** finito	**abbiamo** finito
finisc**i**	fin**ite**	**hai** finito	**avete** finito
finisc**e**	finisc**ono**	**ha** finito	**hanno** finito
imperfetto		trapassato prossimo	
fini**vo**	fini**vamo**	**avevo** finito	**avevamo** finito
fini**vi**	fini**vate**	**avevi** finito	**avevate** finito
fini**va**	fini**vano**	**aveva** finito	**avevano** finito
passato remoto		trapassato remoto	
fin**ii**	fin**immo**	**ebbi** finito	**avemmo** finito
fin**isti**	fin**iste**	**avesti** finito	**aveste** finito
finì	fin**irono**	**ebbe** finito	**ebbero** finito
futuro semplice		futuro anteriore	
finir**ò**	finir**emo**	**avrò** finito	**avremo** finito
finir**ai**	finir**ete**	**avrai** finito	**avrete** finito
finir**à**	finir**anno**	**avrà** finito	**avranno** finito
condizionale presente		condizionale passato	
finir**ei**	finir**emmo**	**avrei** finito	**avremmo** finito
finir**esti**	finir**este**	**avresti** finito	**avreste** finito
finir**ebbe**	finir**ebbero**	**avrebbe** finito	**avrebbero** finito
congiuntivo presente		congiuntivo passato	
finisc**a**	fin**iamo**	**abbia** finito	**abbiamo** finito
finisc**a**	fin**iate**	**abbia** finito	**abbiate** finito
finisc**a**	finisc**ano**	**abbia** finito	**abbiano** finito
congiuntivo imperfetto		congiuntivo trapassato	
fin**issi**	fin**issimo**	**avessi** finito	**avessimo** finito
fin**issi**	fin**iste**	**avessi** finito	**aveste** finito
fin**isse**	fin**issero**	**avesse** finito	**avessero** finito
imperativo			
	finiamo		
finisci; non finire	finite		
finisca	finiscano		

MUST KNOW VERB

gerundio **firmando** participio passato **firmato**

SINGULAR	PLURAL	SINGULAR	PLURAL
indicativo presente		passato prossimo	
firm**o**	firm**iamo**	**ho** firmato	**abbiamo** firmato
firm**i**	firm**ate**	**hai** firmato	**avete** firmato
firm**a**	firm**ano**	**ha** firmato	**hanno** firmato
imperfetto		trapassato prossimo	
firma**vo**	firma**vamo**	**avevo** firmato	**avevamo** firmato
firma**vi**	firma**vate**	**avevi** firmato	**avevate** firmato
firma**va**	firma**vano**	**aveva** firmato	**avevano** firmato
passato remoto		trapassato remoto	
firm**ai**	firm**ammo**	**ebbi** firmato	**avemmo** firmato
firm**asti**	firm**aste**	**avesti** firmato	**aveste** firmato
firm**ò**	firm**arono**	**ebbe** firmato	**ebbero** firmato
futuro semplice		futuro anteriore	
firmer**ò**	firmer**emo**	**avrò** firmato	**avremo** firmato
firmer**ai**	firmer**ete**	**avrai** firmato	**avrete** firmato
firmer**à**	firemer**anno**	**avrà** firmato	**avranno** firmato
condizionale presente		condizionale passato	
firmer**ei**	firmer**emmo**	**avrei** firmato	**avremmo** firmato
firmer**esti**	firmer**este**	**avresti** firmato	**avreste** firmato
firmer**ebbe**	firmer**ebbero**	**avrebbe** firmato	**avrebbero** firmato
congiuntivo presente		congiuntivo passato	
firm**i**	firm**iamo**	**abbia** firmato	**abbiamo** firmato
firm**i**	firm**iate**	**abbia** firmato	**abbiate** firmato
firm**i**	firm**ino**	**abbia** firmato	**abbiano** firmato
congiuntivo imperfetto		congiuntivo trapassato	
firm**assi**	firm**assimo**	**avessi** firmato	**avessimo** firmato
firm**assi**	firm**aste**	**avessi** firmato	**aveste** firmato
firm**asse**	firm**assero**	**avesse** firmato	**avessero** firmato

imperativo

	firmiamo
firma; non firmare	firmate
firmi	firmino

F

MUST KNOW VERB

fondere — to melt

gerundio **fondendo** participio passato **fuso**

SINGULAR	PLURAL
indicativo presente	
fond**o**	fond**iamo**
fond**i**	fond**ete**
fond**e**	fond**ono**
imperfetto	
fonde**vo**	fonde**vamo**
fonde**vi**	fonde**vate**
fonde**va**	fonde**vano**
passato remoto	
fus**i**	fond**emmo**
fond**esti**	fond**este**
fus**e**	fus**ero**
futuro semplice	
fonder**ò**	fonder**emo**
fonder**ai**	fonder**ete**
fonder**à**	fonder**anno**
condizionale presente	
fonder**ei**	fonder**emmo**
fonder**esti**	fonder**este**
fonder**ebbe**	fonder**ebbero**
congiuntivo presente	
fond**a**	fond**iamo**
fond**a**	fond**iate**
fond**a**	fond**ano**
congiuntivo imperfetto	
fond**essi**	fond**essimo**
fond**essi**	fond**este**
fond**esse**	fond**essero**
imperativo	
	fondiamo
fondi; non fondere	fondate
fonda	fondano

SINGULAR	PLURAL
passato prossimo	
ho fuso	**abbiamo** fuso
hai fuso	**avete** fuso
ha fuso	**hanno** fuso
trapassato prossimo	
avevo fuso	**avevamo** fuso
avevi fuso	**avevate** fuso
aveva fuso	**avevano** fuso
trapassato remoto	
ebbi fuso	**avemmo** fuso
avesti fuso	**aveste** fuso
ebbe fuso	**ebbero** fuso
futuro anteriore	
avrò fuso	**avremo** fuso
avrai fuso	**avrete** fuso
avrà fuso	**avranno** fuso
condizionale passato	
avrei fuso	**avremmo** fuso
avresti fuso	**avreste** fuso
avrebbe fuso	**avrebbero** fuso
congiuntivo passato	
abbia fuso	**abbiamo** fuso
abbia fuso	**abbiate** fuso
abbia fuso	**abbiano** fuso
congiuntivo trapassato	
avessi fuso	**avessimo** fuso
avessi fuso	**aveste** fuso
avesse fuso	**avessero** fuso

to create, to form **formare**

gerundio **formando** participio passato **formato**

SINGULAR	PLURAL	SINGULAR	PLURAL
indicativo presente		passato prossimo	
form**o**	form**iamo**	**ho** formato	**abbiamo** formato
form**i**	form**ate**	**hai** formato	**avete** formato
form**a**	form**ano**	**ha** formato	**hanno** formato
imperfetto		trapassato prossimo	
forma**vo**	forma**vamo**	**avevo** formato	**avevamo** formato
forma**vi**	forma**vate**	**avevi** formato	**avevate** formato
forma**va**	forma**vano**	**aveva** formato	**avevano** formato
passato remoto		trapassato remoto	
form**ai**	form**ammo**	**ebbi** formato	**avemmo** formato
form**asti**	form**aste**	**avesti** formato	**aveste** formato
form**ò**	form**arono**	**ebbe** formato	**ebbero** formato
futuro semplice		futuro anteriore	
former**ò**	former**emo**	**avrò** formato	**avremo** formato
former**ai**	former**ete**	**avrai** formato	**avrete** formato
former**à**	former**anno**	**avrà** formato	**avranno** formato
condizionale presente		condizionale passato	
former**ei**	former**emmo**	**avrei** formato	**avremmo** formato
former**esti**	former**este**	**avresti** formato	**avreste** formato
former**ebbe**	former**ebbero**	**avrebbe** formato	**avrebbero** formato
congiuntivo presente		congiuntivo passato	
form**i**	form**iamo**	**abbia** formato	**abbiamo** formato
form**i**	form**iate**	**abbia** formato	**abbiate** formato
form**i**	form**ino**	**abbia** formato	**abbiano** formato
congiuntivo imperfetto		congiuntivo trapassato	
form**assi**	form**assimo**	**avessi** formato	**avessimo** formato
form**assi**	form**aste**	**avessi** formato	**aveste** formato
form**asse**	form**assero**	**avesse** formato	**avessero** formato

imperativo

	formiamo
forma; non formare	formate
formi	formino

F

fornire — to provide, to supply

gerundio **fornendo** participio passato **fornito**

SINGULAR	PLURAL	SINGULAR	PLURAL
indicativo presente		*passato prossimo*	
fornisc**o**	forn**iamo**	**ho** fornito	**abbiamo** fornito
fornisc**i**	forn**ite**	**hai** fornito	**avete** fornito
fornisc**e**	fornisc**ono**	**ha** fornito	**hanno** fornito
imperfetto		*trapassato prossimo*	
forni**vo**	forni**vamo**	**avevo** fornito	**avevamo** fornito
forni**vi**	forni**vate**	**avevi** fornito	**avevate** fornito
forni**va**	forni**vano**	**aveva** fornito	**avevano** fornito
passato remoto		*trapassato remoto*	
forn**ii**	forn**immo**	**ebbi** fornito	**avemmo** fornito
forn**isti**	forn**iste**	**avesti** fornito	**aveste** fornito
forn**ì**	forn**irono**	**ebbe** fornito	**ebbero** fornito
futuro semplice		*futuro anteriore*	
fornir**ò**	fornir**emo**	**avrò** fornito	**avremo** fornito
fornir**ai**	fornir**ete**	**avrai** fornito	**avrete** fornito
fornir**à**	fornir**anno**	**avrà** fornito	**avranno** fornito
condizionale presente		*condizionale passato*	
fornir**ei**	fornir**emmo**	**avrei** fornito	**avremmo** fornito
fornir**esti**	fornir**este**	**avresti** fornito	**avreste** fornito
fornir**ebbe**	fornir**ebbero**	**avrebbe** fornito	**avrebbero** fornito
congiuntivo presente		*congiuntivo passato*	
fornisc**a**	forn**iamo**	**abbia** fornito	**abbiamo** fornito
fornisc**a**	forn**iate**	**abbia** fornito	**abbiate** fornito
fornisc**a**	fornisc**ano**	**abbia** fornito	**abbiano** fornito
congiuntivo imperfetto		*congiuntivo trapassato*	
forn**issi**	forn**issimo**	**avessi** fornito	**avessimo** fornito
forn**issi**	forn**iste**	**avessi** fornito	**aveste** fornito
forn**isse**	forn**issero**	**avesse** fornito	**avessero** fornito
imperativo			
	forniamo		
fornisci; non fornire	fornite		
fornisca	forniscano		

F

to associate with, to attend **frequentare**

gerundio **frequentando** participio passato **frequentato**

SINGULAR	PLURAL	SINGULAR	PLURAL
indicativo presente		passato prossimo	
frequent**o**	frequent**iamo**	**ho** frequentato	**abbiamo** frequentato
frequent**i**	frequent**ate**	**hai** frequentato	**avete** frequentato
frequent**a**	frequent**ano**	**ha** frequentato	**hanno** frequentato
imperfetto		trapassato prossimo	
frequenta**vo**	frequenta**vamo**	**avevo** frequentato	**avevamo** frequentato
frequenta**vi**	frequenta**vate**	**avevi** frequentato	**avevate** frequentato
frequenta**va**	frequenta**vano**	**aveva** frequentato	**avevano** frequentato
passato remoto		trapassato remoto	
frequent**ai**	frequent**ammo**	**ebbi** frequentato	**avemmo** frequentato
frequent**asti**	frequent**aste**	**avesti** frequentato	**aveste** frequentato
frequent**ò**	frequent**arono**	**ebbe** frequentato	**ebbero** frequentato
futuro semplice		futuro anteriore	
frequenter**ò**	frequenter**emo**	**avrò** frequentato	**avremo** frequentato
frequenter**ai**	frequenter**ete**	**avrai** frequentato	**avrete** frequentato
frequenter**à**	frequenter**anno**	**avrà** frequentato	**avranno** frequentato
condizionale presente		condizionale passato	
frequenter**ei**	frequenter**emmo**	**avrei** frequentato	**avremmo** frequentato
frequenter**esti**	frequenter**este**	**avresti** frequentato	**avreste** frequentato
frequenter**ebbe**	frequenter**ebbero**	**avrebbe** frequentato	**avrebbero** frequentato
congiuntivo presente		congiuntivo passato	
frequent**i**	frequent**iamo**	**abbia** frequentato	**abbiamo** frequentato
frequient**i**	frequent**iate**	**abbia** frequentato	**abbiate** frequentato
frequent**i**	frequent**ino**	**abbia** frequentato	**abbiano** frequentato
congiuntivo imperfetto		congiuntivo trapassato	
frequent**assi**	frequent**assimo**	**avessi** frequentato	**avessimo** frequentato
frequent**assi**	frequent**aste**	**avessi** frequentato	**aveste** frequentato
frequent**asse**	frequent**assero**	**avesse** frequentato	**avessero** frequentato
imperativo			
	frequentiamo		
frequenta; non frequentare	frequentate		
frequenti	frequentino		

F

friggere — to fry

gerundio **friggendo** participio passato **fritto**

indicativo presente

SINGULAR	PLURAL
frigg**o**	frigg**iamo**
frigg**i**	frigg**ete**
frigg**e**	frigg**ono**

imperfetto

SINGULAR	PLURAL
frigge**vo**	frigge**vamo**
frigge**vi**	frigge**vate**
frigge**va**	frigge**vano**

passato remoto

SINGULAR	PLURAL
friss**i**	frigg**emmo**
frigg**esti**	frigg**este**
friss**e**	friss**ero**

futuro semplice

SINGULAR	PLURAL
frigger**ò**	frigger**emo**
frigger**ai**	frigger**ete**
frigger**à**	frigger**anno**

condizionale presente

SINGULAR	PLURAL
frigger**ei**	frigger**emmo**
frigger**esti**	frigger**este**
frigger**ebbe**	frigger**ebbero**

congiuntivo presente

SINGULAR	PLURAL
frigg**a**	frigg**iamo**
frigg**a**	frigg**iate**
frigg**a**	frigg**ano**

congiuntivo imperfetto

SINGULAR	PLURAL
frigg**essi**	frigg**essimo**
frigg**essi**	frigg**este**
frigg**esse**	frigg**essero**

imperativo

SINGULAR	PLURAL
	friggiamo
friggi; non friggere	friggete
frigga	friggano

passato prossimo

SINGULAR	PLURAL
ho fritto	**abbiamo** fritto
hai fritto	**avete** fritto
ha fritto	**hanno** fritto

trapassato prossimo

SINGULAR	PLURAL
avevo fritto	**avevamo** fritto
avevi fritto	**avevate** fritto
aveva fritto	**avevano** fritto

trapassato remoto

SINGULAR	PLURAL
ebbi fritto	**avemmo** fritto
avesti fritto	**aveste** fritto
ebbe fritto	**ebbero** fritto

futuro anteriore

SINGULAR	PLURAL
avrò fritto	**avremo** fritto
avrai fritto	**avrete** fritto
avrà fritto	**avranno** fritto

condizionale passato

SINGULAR	PLURAL
avrei fritto	**avremmo** fritto
avresti fritto	**avreste** fritto
avrebbe fritto	**avrebbero** fritto

congiuntivo passato

SINGULAR	PLURAL
abbia fritto	**abbiamo** fritto
abbia fritto	**abbiate** fritto
abbia fritto	**abbiano** fritto

congiuntivo trapassato

SINGULAR	PLURAL
avessi fritto	**avessimo** fritto
avessi fritto	**aveste** fritto
avesse fritto	**avessero** fritto

to escape, to flee **fuggire**

gerundio **fuggendo** participio passato **fuggito**

SINGULAR	PLURAL
indicativo presente	
fugg**o**	fugg**iamo**
fugg**i**	fugg**ite**
fugg**e**	fugg**ono**
imperfetto	
fuggi**vo**	fuggi**vamo**
fuggi**vi**	fuggi**vate**
fuggi**va**	fuggi**vano**
passato remoto	
fugg**ii**	fugg**immo**
fugg**isti**	fugg**iste**
fugg**ì**	fugg**irono**
futuro semplice	
fuggir**ò**	fuggir**emo**
fuggir**ai**	fuggir**ete**
fuggir**à**	fuggir**anno**
condizionale presente	
fuggir**ei**	fuggir**emmo**
fuggir**esti**	fuggir**este**
fuggir**ebbe**	fuggir**ebbero**
congiuntivo presente	
fugg**a**	fugg**iamo**
fugg**a**	fugg**iate**
fugg**a**	fugg**ano**
congiuntivo imperfetto	
fugg**issi**	fugg**issimo**
fugg**issi**	fugg**iste**
fugg**isse**	fugg**issero**
imperativo	
	fuggiamo
fuggi; non fuggire	fuggite
fugga	fuggano

SINGULAR	PLURAL
passato prossimo	
sono fuggito(a)	**siamo** fuggiti(e)
sei fuggito(a)	**siete** fuggiti(e)
è fuggito(a)	**sono** fuggiti(e)
trapassato prossimo	
ero fuggito(a)	**eravamo** fuggiti(e)
eri fuggito(a)	**eravate** fuggiti(e)
era fuggito(a)	**erano** fuggiti(e)
trapassato remoto	
fui fuggito(a)	**fummo** fuggiti(e)
fosti fuggito(a)	**foste** fuggiti(e)
fu fuggito(a)	**furono** fuggiti(e)
futuro anteriore	
sarò fuggito(a)	**saremo** fuggiti(e)
sarai fuggito(a)	**sarete** fuggiti(e)
sarà fuggito(a)	**saranno** fuggiti(e)
condizionale passato	
sarei fuggito(a)	**saremmo** fuggiti(e)
saresti fuggito(a)	**sareste** fuggiti(e)
sarebbe fuggito(a)	**sarebbero** fuggiti(e)
congiuntivo passato	
sia fuggito(a)	**siamo** fuggiti(e)
sia fuggito(a)	**siate** fuggiti(e)
sia fuggito(a)	**siano** fuggiti(e)
congiuntivo trapassato	
fossi fuggito(a)	**fossimo** fuggiti(e)
fossi fuggito(a)	**foste** fuggiti(e)
fosse fuggito(a)	**fossero** fuggiti(e)

fumare — to smoke

gerundio **fumando** — participio passato **fumato**

SINGULAR	PLURAL
indicativo presente	
fum**o**	fum**iamo**
fum**i**	fum**ate**
fum**a**	fum**ano**
imperfetto	
fuma**vo**	fuma**vamo**
fuma**vi**	fuma**vate**
fuma**va**	fuma**vano**
passato remoto	
fum**ai**	fum**ammo**
fum**asti**	fum**aste**
fum**ò**	fum**arono**
futuro semplice	
fumer**ò**	fumer**emo**
fumer**ai**	fumer**ete**
fumer**à**	fumer**anno**
condizionale presente	
fumer**ei**	fumer**emmo**
fumer**esti**	fumer**este**
fumer**ebbe**	fumer**ebbero**
congiuntivo presente	
fum**i**	fum**iamo**
fum**i**	fum**iate**
fum**i**	fum**ino**
congiuntivo imperfetto	
fum**assi**	fum**assimo**
fum**assi**	fum**aste**
fum**asse**	fum**assero**
imperativo	
	fumiamo
fuma; non fumare	fumate
fumi	fumino

SINGULAR	PLURAL
passato prossimo	
ho fumato	**abbiamo** fumato
hai fumato	**avete** fumato
ha fumato	**hanno** fumato
trapassato prossimo	
avevo fumato	**avevamo** fumato
avevi fumato	**avevate** fumato
aveva fumato	**avevano** fumato
trapassato remoto	
ebbi fumato	**avemmo** fumato
avesti fumato	**aveste** fumato
ebbe fumato	**ebbero** fumato
futuro anteriore	
avrò fumato	**avremo** fumato
avrai fumato	**avrete** fumato
avrà fumato	**avranno** fumato
condizionale passato	
avrei fumato	**avremmo** fumato
avresti fumato	**avreste** fumato
avrebbe fumato	**avrebbero** fumato
congiuntivo passato	
abbia fumato	**abbiamo** fumato
abbia fumato	**abbiate** fumato
abbia fumato	**abbiano** fumato
congiuntivo trapassato	
avessi fumato	**avessimo** fumato
avessi fumato	**aveste** fumato
avesse fumato	**avessero** fumato

to act, to function **funzionare**

gerundio **funzionando** participio passato **funzionato**

SINGULAR	PLURAL	SINGULAR	PLURAL
indicativo presente		passato prossimo	
funzion**o**	funzion**iamo**	**ho** funzionato	**abbiamo** funzionato
funzion**i**	funzion**ate**	**hai** funzionato	**avete** funzionato
funzion**a**	funzion**ano**	**ha** funzionato	**hanno** funzionato
imperfetto		trapassato prossimo	
funziona**vo**	funziona**vamo**	**avevo** funzionato	**avevamo** funzionato
funziona**vi**	funziona**vate**	**avevi** funzionato	**avevate** funzionato
funziona**va**	funziona**vano**	**aveva** funzionato	**avevano** funzionato
passato remoto		trapassato remoto	
funzion**ai**	funzion**ammo**	**ebbi** funzionato	**avemmo** funzionato
funzion**asti**	funzion**aste**	**avesti** funzionato	**aveste** funzionato
funzion**ò**	funzion**arono**	**ebbe** funzionato	**ebbero** funzionato
futuro semplice		futuro anteriore	
funzioner**ò**	funzioner**emo**	**avrò** funzionato	**avremo** funzionato
funzioner**ai**	funzioner**ete**	**avrai** funzionato	**avrete** funzionato
funzioner**à**	funzioner**anno**	**avrà** funzionato	**avranno** funzionato
condizionale presente		condizionale passato	
funzioner**ei**	funzioner**emmo**	**avrei** funzionato	**avremmo** funzionato
funzioner**esti**	funzioner**este**	**avresti** funzionato	**avreste** funzionato
funzioner**ebbe**	funzioner**ebbero**	**avrebbe** funzionato	**avrebbero** funzionato
congiuntivo presente		congiuntivo passato	
funzion**i**	funzion**iamo**	**abbia** funzionato	**abbiano** funzionato
funzion**i**	funzion**iate**	**abbia** funzionato	**abbiate** funzionato
funzion**i**	funzion**ino**	**abbia** funzionato	**abbiano** funzionato
congiuntivo imperfetto		congiuntivo trapassato	
funzion**assi**	funzion**assimo**	**avessi** funzionato	**avessimo** funzionato
funzion**assi**	funzion**aste**	**avessi** funzionato	**aveste** funzionato
frunzion**asse**	funzion**assero**	**avesse** funzionato	**avessero** funzionato
imperativo			
	funzioniamo		
funziona; non funzionare	funzionate		
funzioni	funzionino		

F

garantire — to guarantee

gerundio **garantendo** participio passato **garantito**

SINGULAR	PLURAL	SINGULAR	PLURAL
indicativo presente		passato prossimo	
garantisc**o**	garant**iamo**	**ho** garantito	**abbiamo** garantito
garantisc**i**	garant**ite**	**hai** garantito	**avete** garantito
garantisc**e**	garantisc**ono**	**ha** garantito	**hanno** garantito
imperfetto		trapassato prossimo	
garanti**vo**	garanti**vamo**	**avevo** garantito	**avevamo** garantito
garanti**vi**	garanti**vate**	**avevi** garantito	**avevate** garantito
garanti**va**	garanti**vano**	**aveva** garantito	**avevano** garantito
passato remoto		trapassato remoto	
garanti**i**	garanti**mmo**	**ebbi** garantito	**avemmo** garantito
garanti**sti**	garanti**ste**	**avesti** garantito	**aveste** garantito
garant**ì**	garanti**rono**	**ebbe** garantito	**ebbero** garantito
futuro semplice		futuro anteriore	
garantir**ò**	garantir**emo**	**avrò** garantito	**avremo** garantito
garantir**ai**	garantir**ete**	**avrai** garantito	**avrete** garantito
garantir**à**	garantir**anno**	**avrà** garantito	**avranno** garantito
condizionale presente		condizionale passato	
garantir**ei**	garantir**emmo**	**avrei** garantito	**avremmo** garantito
garantir**esti**	garantir**este**	**avresti** garantito	**avreste** garantito
garantir**ebbe**	garantir**ebbero**	**avrebbe** garantito	**avrebbero** garantito
congiuntivo presente		congiuntivo passato	
garantisc**a**	garant**iamo**	**abbia** garantito	**abbiamo** garantito
garantisc**a**	garant**iate**	**abbia** garantito	**abbiate** garantito
garantisc**a**	garantisc**ano**	**abbia** garantito	**abbiano** garantito
congiuntivo imperfetto		congiuntivo trapassato	
garanti**ssi**	garanti**ssimo**	**avessi** garantito	**avessimo** garantito
garanti**ssi**	garanti**ste**	**avessi** garantito	**aveste** garantito
garanti**sse**	garanti**ssero**	**avesse** garantito	**avessero** garantito
imperativo			
	garantiamo		
garantisci; non garantire	garantite		
garantisca	garantiscano		

G

to generate — generare

gerundio **generando** — participio passato **generato**

SINGULAR	PLURAL
indicativo presente	
gener**o**	gener**iamo**
gener**i**	gener**ate**
gener**a**	gener**ano**
imperfetto	
genera**vo**	genera**vamo**
genera**vi**	genera**vate**
genera**va**	genera**vano**
passato remoto	
genera**i**	genera**mmo**
genera**sti**	genera**ste**
gener**ò**	genera**rono**
futuro semplice	
generer**ò**	generer**emo**
generer**ai**	generer**ete**
generer**à**	generer**anno**
condizionale presente	
generer**ei**	generer**emmo**
generer**esti**	generer**este**
generer**ebbe**	generer**ebbero**
congiuntivo presente	
gener**i**	gener**iamo**
gener**i**	gener**iate**
gener**i**	gener**ino**
congiuntivo imperfetto	
genera**ssi**	genera**ssimo**
genera**ssi**	genera**ste**
genera**sse**	genera**ssero**
imperativo	
	generiamo
genera; non generare	generate
generi	generino

SINGULAR	PLURAL
passato prossimo	
ho generato	**abbiamo** generato
hai generato	**avete** generato
ha generato	**hanno** generato
trapassato prossimo	
avevo generato	**avevamo** generato
avevi generato	**avevate** generato
aveva generato	**avevano** generato
trapassato remoto	
ebbi generato	**avemmo** generato
avesti generato	**aveste** generato
ebbe generato	**ebbero** generato
futuro anteriore	
avrò generato	**avremo** generato
avrai generato	**avrete** generato
avrà generato	**avranno** generato
condizionale passato	
avrei generato	**avremmo** generato
avresti generato	**avreste** generato
avrebbe generato	**avrebbero** generato
congiuntivo passato	
abbia generato	**abbiamo** generato
abbia generato	**abbiate** generato
abbia generato	**abbiano** generato
congiuntivo trapassato	
avessi generato	**avessimo** generato
avessi generato	**aveste** generato
avesse generato	**avessero** generato

gestire — to manage

gerundio **gestendo** participio passato **gestito**

SINGULAR	PLURAL
indicativo presente	
gestisc**o**	gest**iamo**
gestisc**i**	gest**ite**
gestisc**e**	gestisc**ono**
imperfetto	
gesti**vo**	gesti**vamo**
gesti**vi**	gesti**vate**
gesti**va**	gesti**vano**
passato remoto	
gest**ii**	gest**immo**
gest**isti**	gest**iste**
gest**ì**	gest**irono**
futuro semplice	
gestir**ò**	gestir**emo**
gestir**ai**	gestir**ete**
gestir**à**	gestir**anno**
condizionale presente	
gestir**ei**	gestir**emmo**
gestir**esti**	gestir**este**
gestir**ebbe**	gestir**ebbero**
congiuntivo presente	
gestisc**a**	gest**iamo**
gestisc**a**	gest**iate**
gestisc**a**	gestisc**ano**
congiuntivo imperfetto	
gest**issi**	gest**issimo**
gest**issi**	gest**iste**
gest**isse**	gest**issero**
imperativo	
	gestiamo
gestisci; non gestire	gestite
gestisca	gestiscano

SINGULAR	PLURAL
passato prossimo	
ho gestito	**abbiamo** gestito
hai gestito	**avete** gestito
ha gestito	**hanno** gestito
trapassato prossimo	
avevo gestito	**avevamo** gestito
avevi gestito	**avevate** gestito
aveva gestito	**avevano** gestito
trapassato remoto	
ebbi gestito	**avemmo** gestito
avesti gestito	**aveste** gestito
ebbe gestito	**ebbero** gestito
futuro anteriore	
avrò gestito	**avremo** gestito
avrai gestito	**avrete** gestito
avrà gestito	**avranno** gestito
condizionale passato	
avrei gestito	**avremmo** gestito
avresti gestito	**avreste** gestito
avrebbe gestito	**avrebbero** gestito
congiuntivo passato	
abbia gestito	**abbiamo** gestito
abbia gestito	**abbiate** gestito
abbia gestito	**abbiano** gestito
congiuntivo trapassato	
avessi gestito	**avessimo** gestito
avessi gestito	**aveste** gestito
avesse gestito	**avessero** gestito

to throw — gettare

gerundio **gettando** — participio passato **gettato**

SINGULAR	PLURAL
indicativo presente	
gett**o**	gett**iamo**
gett**i**	gett**ate**
gett**a**	gett**ano**
imperfetto	
getta**vo**	getta**vamo**
getta**vi**	getta**vate**
getta**va**	getta**vano**
passato remoto	
gett**ai**	gett**ammo**
gett**asti**	gett**aste**
gett**ò**	gett**arono**
futuro semplice	
getter**ò**	getter**emo**
getter**ai**	getter**ete**
getter**à**	getter**anno**
condizionale presente	
gett**erei**	gett**eremmo**
gett**eresti**	gett**ereste**
gett**erebbe**	gett**erebbero**
congiuntivo presente	
gett**i**	gett**iamo**
gett**i**	gett**iate**
gett**i**	gett**ino**
congiuntivo imperfetto	
getta**ssi**	getta**ssimo**
getta**ssi**	getta**ste**
getta**sse**	getta**ssero**
imperativo	
	gettiamo
getta; non gettare	gettate
getti	gettino

SINGULAR	PLURAL
passato prossimo	
ho gettato	**abbiamo** gettato
hai gettato	**avete** gettato
ha gettato	**hanno** gettato
trapassato prossimo	
avevo gettato	**avevamo** gettato
avevi gettato	**avevate** gettato
aveva gettato	**avevano** gettato
trapassato remoto	
ebbi gettato	**avemmo** gettato
avesti gettato	**aveste** gettato
ebbe gettato	**ebbero** gettato
futuro anteriore	
avrò gettato	**avremo** gettato
avrai gettato	**avrete** gettato
avrà gettato	**avranno** gettato
condizionale passato	
avrei gettato	**avremmo** gettato
avresti gettato	**avreste** gettato
avrebbe gettato	**avrebbero** gettato
congiuntivo passato	
abbia gettato	**abbiamo** gettato
abbia gettato	**abbiate** gettato
abbia gettato	**abbiano** gettato
congiuntivo trapassato	
avessi gettato	**avessimo** gettato
avessi gettato	**aveste** gettato
avesse gettato	**avessero** gettato

giacere — to lie

gerundio **giacendo** participio passato **giaciuto**

SINGULAR	PLURAL	SINGULAR	PLURAL
indicativo presente		passato prossimo	
giac**cio**	giac(c)**iamo**	**sono** giaciuto(a)	**siamo** giaciuti(e)
giac**i**	giac**ete**	**sei** giaciuto(a)	**siete** giaciuti(e)
giac**e**	giac**ciono**	**è** giaciuto(a)	**sono** giaciuti(e)
imperfetto		trapassato prossimo	
giace**vo**	giace**vamo**	**ero** giaciuto(a)	**eravamo** giaciuti(e)
giace**vi**	giace**vate**	**eri** giaciuto(a)	**eravate** giaciuti(e)
giace**va**	giace**vano**	**era** giaciuto(a)	**erano** giaciuti(e)
passato remoto		trapassato remoto	
giac**qui**	giac**emmo**	**fui** giaciuto(a)	**fummo** giaciuti(e)
giac**esti**	giac**este**	**fosti** giaciuto(a)	**foste** giaciuti(e)
giac**que**	giac**quero**	**fu** giaciuto(a)	**furono** giaciuti(e)
futuro semplice		futuro anteriore	
giacer**ò**	giacer**emo**	**sarò** giaciuto(a)	**saremo** giaciuti(e)
giacer**ai**	giacer**ete**	**sarai** giaciuto(a)	**sarete** giaciuti(e)
giacer**à**	giacer**anno**	**sarà** giaciuto(a)	**saranno** giaciuti(e)
condizionale presente		condizionale passato	
giac**erei**	giac**eremmo**	**sarei** giaciuto(a)	**saremmo** giaciuti(e)
giac**eresti**	giac**ereste**	**saresti** giaciuto(a)	**sareste** giaciuti(e)
giac**erebbe**	giac**erebbero**	**sarebbe** giaciuto(a)	**sarebbero** giaciuti(e)
congiuntivo presente		congiuntivo passato	
giac**cia**	giac(c)**iamo**	**sia** giaciuto(a)	**siamo** giaciuti(e)
giac**cia**	giac(c)**iate**	**sia** giaciuto(a)	**siate** giaciuti(e)
giac**cia**	giac**ciano**	**sia** giaciuto(a)	**siano** giaciuti(e)
congiuntivo imperfetto		congiuntivo trapassato	
giace**ssi**	giace**ssimo**	**fossi** giaciuto(a)	**fossimo** giaciuti(e)
giace**ssi**	giace**ste**	**fossi** giaciuto(a)	**foste** giaciuti(e)
giace**sse**	giace**ssero**	**fosse** giaciuto(a)	**fossero** giaciuti(e)

imperativo

	giac(c)iamo
giaci; non giacere	giacete
giaccia	giacciano

G

to play (a game) **giocare**

gerundio **giocando** participio passato **giocato**

SINGULAR	PLURAL	SINGULAR	PLURAL
indicativo presente		passato prossimo	
gioc**o**	gioch**iamo**	**ho** giocato	**abbiamo** giocato
gioch**i**	gioc**ate**	**hai** giocato	**avete** giocato
gioc**a**	gioc**ano**	**ha** giocato	**hanno** giocato
imperfetto		trapassato prossimo	
gioca**vo**	gioca**vamo**	**avevo** giocato	**avevamo** giocato
gioca**vi**	gioca**vate**	**avevi** giocato	**avevate** giocato
gioca**va**	gioca**vano**	**aveva** giocato	**avevano** giocato
passato remoto		trapassato remoto	
gioc**ai**	gioc**ammo**	**ebbi** giocato	**avemmo** giocato
gioc**asti**	gioc**aste**	**avesti** giocato	**aveste** giocato
gioc**ò**	gioc**arono**	**ebbe** giocato	**ebbero** giocato
futuro semplice		futuro anteriore	
giocher**ò**	giocher**emo**	**avrò** giocato	**avremo** giocato
giocher**ai**	giocher**ete**	**avrai** giocato	**avrete** giocato
giocher**à**	giocher**anno**	**avrà** giocato	**avranno** giocato
condizionale presente		condizionale passato	
gioch**erei**	gioch**eremmo**	**avrei** giocato	**avremmo** giocato
gioch**eresti**	gioch**ereste**	**avresti** giocato	**avreste** giocato
gioch**erebbe**	gioch**erebbero**	**avrebbe** giocato	**avrebbero** giocato
congiuntivo presente		congiuntivo passato	
gioch**i**	gioch**iamo**	**abbia** giocato	**abbiamo** giocato
gioch**i**	gioch**iate**	**abbia** giocato	**abbiate** giocato
gioch**i**	gioch**ino**	**abbia** giocato	**abbiano** giocato
congiuntivo imperfetto		congiuntivo trapassato	
gioca**ssi**	gioca**ssimo**	**avessi** giocato	**avessimo** giocato
gioca**ssi**	gioca**ste**	**avessi** giocato	**aveste** giocato
gioca**sse**	gioca**ssero**	**avesse** giocato	**avessero** giocato
imperativo			
	giochiamo		
gioca; non giocare	giocate		
giochi	giochino		

G

girare — to turn

gerundio **girando** participio passato **girato**

SINGULAR	PLURAL
indicativo presente	
gir**o**	gir**iamo**
gir**i**	gir**ate**
gir**a**	gir**ano**
imperfetto	
gira**vo**	gira**vamo**
gira**vi**	gira**vate**
gira**va**	gira**vano**
passato remoto	
gir**ai**	gir**ammo**
gir**asti**	gir**aste**
gir**ò**	gir**arono**
futuro semplice	
girer**ò**	girer**emo**
girer**ai**	girer**ete**
girer**à**	girer**anno**
condizionale presente	
gir**erei**	gir**eremmo**
gir**eresti**	gir**ereste**
gir**erebbe**	gir**erebbero**
congiuntivo presente	
gir**i**	gir**iamo**
gir**i**	gir**iate**
gir**i**	gir**ino**
congiuntivo imperfetto	
gira**ssi**	gira**ssimo**
gira**ssi**	gira**ste**
gira**sse**	gira**ssero**
imperativo	
	giriamo
gira; non girare	girate
giri	girino

SINGULAR	PLURAL
passato prossimo	
ho girato	**abbiamo** girato
hai girato	**avete** girato
ha girato	**hanno** girato
trapassato prossimo	
avevo girato	**avevamo** girato
avevi girato	**avevate** girato
aveva girato	**avevano** girato
trapassato remoto	
ebbi girato	**avemmo** girato
avesti girato	**aveste** girato
ebbe girato	**ebbero** girato
futuro anteriore	
avrò girato	**avremo** girato
avrai girato	**avrete** girato
avrà girato	**avranno** girato
condizionale passato	
avrei girato	**avremmo** girato
avresti girato	**avreste** girato
avrebbe girato	**avrebbero** girato
congiuntivo passato	
abbia girato	**abbiamo** girato
abbia girato	**abbiate** girato
abbia girato	**abbiano** girato
congiuntivo trapassato	
avessi girato	**avessimo** girato
avessi girato	**aveste** girato
avesse girato	**avessero** girato

to judge giudicare

gerundio **giudicando** participio passato **giudicato**

SINGULAR	PLURAL
indicativo presente	
giudic**o**	giudich**iamo**
giudich**i**	giudic**ate**
giudic**a**	giudic**ano**
imperfetto	
giudica**vo**	giudica**vamo**
giudica**vi**	giudica**vate**
giudica**va**	giudica**vano**
passato remoto	
giudic**ai**	giudic**ammo**
giudic**asti**	giudic**aste**
giudic**ò**	giudic**arono**
futuro semplice	
giudicher**ò**	gudicher**emo**
giudicher**ai**	giudicher**ete**
giudicher**à**	giudicher**anno**
condizionale presente	
giudich**erei**	giudich**eremmo**
giudich**eresti**	giudich**ereste**
giudich**erebbe**	giudich**erebbero**
congiuntivo presente	
giudich**i**	giudich**iamo**
giudich**i**	giudich**iate**
giudich**i**	giudich**ino**
congiuntivo imperfetto	
giudica**ssi**	giudica**ssimo**
giudica**ssi**	giudica**ste**
giudica**sse**	giudica**ssero**
imperativo	
	giudichiamo
giudica; non giudicare	giudicate
giudichi	giudichino

SINGULAR	PLURAL
passato prossimo	
ho giudicato	**abbiamo** giudicato
hai giudicato	**avete** giudicato
ha giudicato	**hanno** giudicato
trapassato prossimo	
avevo giudicato	**avevamo** giudicato
avevi giudicato	**avevate** giudicato
aveva giudicato	**avevano** giudicato
trapassato remoto	
ebbi giudicato	**avemmo** giudicato
avesti giudicato	**aveste** giudicato
ebbe giudicato	**ebbero** giudicato
futuro anteriore	
avrò giudicato	**avremo** giudicato
avrai giudicato	**avrete** giudicato
avrà giudicato	**avranno** giudicato
condizionale passato	
avrei giudicato	**avremmo** giudicato
avresti giudicato	**avreste** giudicato
avrebbe giudicato	**avrebbero** giudicato
congiuntivo passato	
abbia giudicato	**abbiamo** giudicato
abbia giudicato	**abbiate** giudicato
abbia giudicato	**abbiano** giudicato
congiuntivo trapassato	
avessi giudicato	**avessimo** giudicato
avessi giudicato	**aveste** giudicato
avesse giudicato	**avessero** giudicato

giungere — to arrive

gerundio **giungendo** — participio passato **giunto**

	SINGULAR	PLURAL
indicativo presente	giung**o**	giung**iamo**
	giung**i**	giung**ete**
	giung**e**	giung**ono**
imperfetto	giunge**vo**	giunge**vamo**
	giunge**vi**	giunge**vate**
	giunge**va**	giunge**vano**
passato remoto	giun**si**	giung**emmo**
	giung**esti**	giung**este**
	giun**se**	giun**sero**
futuro semplice	giunger**ò**	giunger**emo**
	giunger**ai**	giunger**ete**
	giunger**à**	giunger**anno**
condizionale presente	giung**erei**	giung**eremmo**
	giung**eresti**	giung**ereste**
	giung**erebbe**	giung**erebbero**
congiuntivo presente	giung**a**	giung**iamo**
	giung**a**	giung**iate**
	giung**a**	giung**ano**
congiuntivo imperfetto	giunge**ssi**	giunge**ssimo**
	giunge**ssi**	giunge**ste**
	giunge**sse**	giunge**ssero**
imperativo		giungiamo
	giungi; non giungere	giungete
	giunga	giungano

	SINGULAR	PLURAL
passato prossimo	**sono** giunto(a)	**siamo** giunti(e)
	sei giunto(a)	**siete** giunti(e)
	è giunto(a)	**sono** giunti(e)
trapassato prossimo	**ero** giunto(a)	**eravamo** giunti(e)
	eri giunto(a)	**eravate** giunti(e)
	era giunto(a)	**erano** giunti(e)
trapassato remoto	**fui** giunto(a)	**fummo** giunti(e)
	fosti giunto(a)	**foste** giunti(e)
	fu giunto(a)	**furono** giunti(e)
futuro anteriore	**sarò** giunto(a)	**saremo** giunti(e)
	sarai giunto(a)	**sarete** giunti(e)
	sarà giunto(a)	**saranno** giunti(e)
condizionale passato	**sarei** giunto(a)	**saremmo** giunti(e)
	saresti giunto(a)	**sareste** giunti(e)
	sarebbe giunto(a)	**sarebbero** giunti(e)
congiuntivo passato	**sia** giunto(a)	**siamo** giunti(e)
	sia giunto(a)	**siate** giunti(e)
	sia giunto(a)	**siano** giunti(e)
congiuntivo trapassato	**fossi** giunto(a)	**fossimo** giunti(e)
	fossi giunto(a)	**foste** giunti(e)
	fosse giunto(a)	**fossero** giunti(e)

gerundio **giurando** participio passato **giurato**

SINGULAR	PLURAL
indicativo presente	
giur**o**	giur**iamo**
giur**i**	giur**ate**
giur**a**	giur**ano**
imperfetto	
giura**vo**	giura**vamo**
giura**vi**	giura**vate**
giura**va**	giura**vano**
passato remoto	
giur**ai**	giur**ammo**
giur**asti**	giur**aste**
giur**ò**	giur**arono**
futuro semplice	
giurer**ò**	giurer**emo**
giurer**ai**	giurer**ete**
giurer**à**	giurer**anno**
condizionale presente	
giur**erei**	giur**eremmo**
giur**eresti**	giur**ereste**
giur**erebbe**	giur**erebbero**
congiuntivo presente	
giur**i**	giur**iamo**
giur**i**	giur**iate**
giur**i**	giur**ino**
congiuntivo imperfetto	
giura**ssi**	giura**ssimo**
giura**ssi**	giura**ste**
giura**sse**	giura**ssero**
imperativo	
	giuriamo
giura; non giurare	giurate
giuri	giurino

SINGULAR	PLURAL
passato prossimo	
ho giurato	**abbiamo** giurato
hai giurato	**avete** giurato
ha giurato	**hanno** giurato
trapassato prossimo	
avevo giurato	**avevamo** giurato
avevi giurato	**avevate** giurato
aveva giurato	**avevano** giurato
trapassato remoto	
ebbi giurato	**avemmo** giurato
avesti giurato	**aveste** giurato
ebbe giurato	**ebbero** giurato
futuro anteriore	
avrò giurato	**avremo** giurato
avrai giurato	**avrete** giurato
avrà giurato	**avranno** giurato
condizionale passato	
avrei giurato	**avremmo** giurato
avresti giurato	**avreste** giurato
avrebbe giurato	**avrebbero** giurato
congiuntivo passato	
abbia giurato	**abbiamo** giurato
abbia giurato	**abbiate** giurato
abbia giurato	**abbiano** giurato
congiuntivo trapassato	
avessi giurato	**avessimo** giurato
avessi giurato	**aveste** giurato
avesse giurato	**avessero** giurato

giustificare — to justify

gerundio **giustificando** participio passato **giustificato**

SINGULAR	PLURAL	SINGULAR	PLURAL
indicativo presente		passato prossimo	
giustific**o**	giustifich**iamo**	**ho** giustificato	**abbiamo** giustificato
giustifich**i**	giustific**ate**	**hai** giustificato	**avete** giustificato
giustific**a**	giustific**ano**	**ha** giustificato	**hanno** giustificato
imperfetto		trapassato prossimo	
giustifica**vo**	giustifica**vamo**	**avevo** giustificato	**avevamo** giustificato
giustifica**vi**	giustifica**vate**	**avevi** giustificato	**avevate** giustificato
giustifica**va**	giustifica**vano**	**aveva** giustificato	**avevano** giustificato
passato remoto		trapassato remoto	
giustific**ai**	giustific**ammo**	**ebbi** giustificato	**avemmo** giustificato
giustific**asti**	giustific**aste**	**avesti** giustificato	**aveste** giustificato
giustific**ò**	giustific**arono**	**ebbe** giustificato	**ebbero** giustificato
futuro semplice		futuro anteriore	
giustificher**ò**	giustificher**emo**	**avrò** giustificato	**avremo** giustificato
giustificher**ai**	giustificher**ete**	**avrai** giustificato	**avrete** giustificato
giustificher**à**	giustificher**anno**	**avrà** giustificato	**avranno** giustificato
condizionale presente		condizionale passato	
giustifich**erei**	giustifich**eremmo**	**avrei** giustificato	**avremmo** giustificato
giustifich**eresti**	giustifich**ereste**	**avresti** giustificato	**avreste** giustificato
giustifich**erebbe**	giustifich**erebbero**	**avrebbe** giustificato	**avrebbero** giustificato
congiuntivo presente		congiuntivo passato	
giustifich**i**	giustifich**iamo**	**abbia** giustificato	**abbiamo** giustificato
giustifich**i**	giustifich**iate**	**abbia** giustificato	**abbiate** giustificato
giustifich**i**	giustifich**ino**	**abbia** giustificato	**abbiano** giustificato
congiuntivo imperfetto		congiuntivo trapassato	
giustifica**ssi**	giustifica**ssimo**	**avessi** giustificato	**avessimo** giustificato
giustifica**ssi**	giustifica**ste**	**avessi** giustificato	**aveste** giustificato
giustifica**sse**	giustifica**ssero**	**avesse** giustificato	**avessero** giustificato
imperativo			
	giustifichiamo		
giustifica; non giustificare	giustificate		
giustifichi	giustifichino		

G

to praise, to glorify **glorificare**

gerundio **glorificando** participio passato **glorificato**

SINGULAR	PLURAL	SINGULAR	PLURAL
indicativo presente		passato prossimo	
glorific**o**	glorifich**iamo**	**ho** glorificato	**abbiamo** glorificato
glorifich**i**	glorific**ate**	**hai** glorificato	**avete** glorificato
glorific**a**	glorific**ano**	**ha** glorificato	**hanno** glorificato
imperfetto		trapassato prossimo	
glorifica**vo**	glorifica**vamo**	**avevo** glorificato	**avevamo** glorificato
glorifica**vi**	glorifica**vate**	**avevi** glorificato	**avevate** glorificato
glorifica**va**	glorifica**vano**	**aveva** glorificato	**avevano** glorificato
passato remoto		trapassato remoto	
glorific**ai**	glorific**ammo**	**ebbi** glorificato	**avemmo** glorificato
glorific**asti**	glorific**aste**	**avesti** glorificato	**aveste** glorificato
glorific**ò**	glorific**arono**	**ebbe** glorificato	**ebbero** glorificato
futuro semplice		futuro anteriore	
glorificher**ò**	glorificher**emo**	**avrò** glorificato	**avremo** glorificato
glorificher**ai**	glorificher**ete**	**avrai** glorificato	**avrete** glorificato
glorificher**à**	glorificher**anno**	**avrà** glorificato	**avranno** glorificato
condizionale presente		condizionale passato	
glorifich**erei**	glorifich**eremmo**	**avrei** glorificato	**avremmo** glorificato
glorifich**eresti**	glorifich**ereste**	**avresti** glorificato	**avreste** glorificato
glorifich**erebbe**	glorifich**erebbero**	**avrebbe** glorificato	**avrebbero** glorificato
congiuntivo presente		congiuntivo passato	
glorifich**i**	glorifich**iamo**	**abbia** glorificato	**abbiamo** glorificato
glorifich**i**	glorifich**iate**	**abbia** glorificato	**abbiate** glorificato
glorifich**i**	glorifich**ino**	**abbia** glorificato	**abbiano** glorificato
congiuntivo imperfetto		congiuntivo trapassato	
glorifica**ssi**	glorifica**ssimo**	**avessi** glorificato	**avessimo** glorificato
glorifica**ssi**	glorifica**ste**	**avessi** glorificato	**aveste** glorificato
glorifica**sse**	glorifica**ssero**	**avesse** glorificato	**avessero** glorificato
imperativo			
	glorifichiamo		
glorifica; non glorificare	glorificate		
glorifichi	glorifichino		

G

godere — to enjoy

gerundio **godendo** participio passato **goduto**

SINGULAR	PLURAL
indicativo presente	
god**o**	god**iamo**
god**i**	god**ete**
god**e**	god**ono**
imperfetto	
gode**vo**	gode**vamo**
gode**vi**	gode**vate**
gode**va**	gode**vano**
passato remoto	
god**ei**, god**etti**	god**emmo**
god**esti**	god**este**
god**é**, god**ette**	god**erono**, god**ettero**
futuro semplice	
godr**ò**	godr**emo**
godr**ai**	godr**ete**
godr**à**	godr**anno**
condizionale presente	
godr**ei**	godr**emmo**
godr**esti**	godr**este**
godr**ebbe**	godr**ebbero**
congiuntivo presente	
god**a**	god**iamo**
god**a**	god**iate**
god**a**	god**ano**
congiuntivo imperfetto	
gode**ssi**	gode**ssimo**
gode**ssi**	gode**ste**
gode**sse**	gode**ssero**
imperativo	
	godiamo
godi; non godere	godete
goda	godano

SINGULAR	PLURAL
passato prossimo	
ho goduto	**abbiamo** goduto
hai goduto	**avete** goduto
ha goduto	**hanno** goduto
trapassato prossimo	
avevo goduto	**avevamo** goduto
avevi goduto	**avevate** goduto
aveva goduto	**avevano** goduto
trapassato remoto	
ebbi goduto	**avemmo** goduto
avesti goduto	**aveste** goduto
ebbe goduto	**ebbero** goduto
futuro anteriore	
avrò goduto	**avremo** goduto
avrai goduto	**avrete** goduto
avrà goduto	**avranno** goduto
condizionale passato	
avrei goduto	**avremmo** goduto
avresti goduto	**avreste** goduto
avrebbe goduto	**avrebbero** goduto
congiuntivo passato	
abbia goduto	**abbiamo** goduto
abbia goduto	**abbiate** goduto
abbia goduto	**abbiano** goduto
congiuntivo trapassato	
avessi goduto	**avessimo** goduto
avessi goduto	**aveste** goduto
avesse goduto	**avessero** goduto

gerundio **governando** participio passato **governato**

SINGULAR	PLURAL	SINGULAR	PLURAL
indicativo presente		passato prossimo	
govern**o**	govern**iamo**	**ho** governato	**abbiamo** governato
govern**i**	govern**ate**	**hai** governato	**avete** governato
govern**a**	govern**ano**	**ha** governato	**hanno** governato
imperfetto		trapassato prossimo	
governa**vo**	governa**vamo**	**avevo** governato	**avevamo** governato
governa**vi**	governa**vate**	**avevi** governato	**avevate** governato
governa**va**	governa**vano**	**aveva** governato	**avevano** governato
passato remoto		trapassato remoto	
govern**ai**	govern**ammo**	**ebbi** governato	**avemmo** governato
govern**asti**	govern**aste**	**avesti** governato	**aveste** governato
govern**ò**	govern**arono**	**ebbe** governato	**ebbero** governato
futuro semplice		futuro anteriore	
governer**ò**	governer**emo**	**avrò** governato	**avremo** governato
governer**ai**	governer**ete**	**avrai** governato	**avrete** governato
governer**à**	governer**anno**	**avrà** governato	**avranno** governato
condizionale presente		condizionale passato	
govern**erei**	govern**eremmo**	**avrei** governato	**avremmo** governato
govern**eresti**	govern**ereste**	**avresti** governato	**avreste** governato
govern**erebbe**	govern**erebbero**	**avrebbe** governato	**avrebbero** governato
congiuntivo presente		congiuntivo passato	
govern**i**	govern**iamo**	**abbia** governato	**abbiamo** governato
govern**i**	govern**iate**	**abbia** governato	**abbiate** governato
govern**i**	govern**ino**	**abbia** governato	**abbiano** governato
congiuntivo imperfetto		congiuntivo trapassato	
governa**ssi**	governa**ssimo**	**avessi** governato	**avessimo** governato
governa**ssi**	governa**ste**	**avessi** governato	**aveste** governato
governa**sse**	governa**ssero**	**avesse** governato	**avessero** governato
imperativo			
	governiamo		
governa; non governare	governate		
governi	governino		

G

gridare — to shout, to scream

gerundio **gridando** — participio passato **gridato**

SINGULAR	PLURAL
indicativo presente	
grid**o**	grid**iamo**
grid**i**	grid**ate**
grid**a**	grid**ano**
imperfetto	
grida**vo**	grida**vamo**
grida**vi**	grida**vate**
grida**va**	grida**vano**
passato remoto	
grid**ai**	grid**ammo**
grid**asti**	grid**aste**
grid**ò**	grid**arono**
futuro semplice	
grider**ò**	grider**emo**
grider**ai**	grider**ete**
grider**à**	grider**anno**
condizionale presente	
grid**erei**	grid**eremmo**
grid**eresti**	grid**ereste**
grid**erebbe**	grid**erebbero**
congiuntivo presente	
grid**i**	grid**iamo**
grid**i**	grid**iate**
grid**i**	grid**ino**
congiuntivo imperfetto	
grid**assi**	grid**assimo**
grid**assi**	grid**aste**
grid**asse**	grid**assero**
imperativo	
	gridiamo
grida; non gridare	gridate
gridi	gridino

SINGULAR	PLURAL
passato prossimo	
ho gridato	**abbiamo** gridato
hai gridato	**avete** gridato
ha gridato	**hanno** gridato
trapassato prossimo	
avevo gridato	**avevamo** gridato
avevi gridato	**avevate** gridato
aveva gridato	**avevano** gridato
trapassato remoto	
ebbi gridato	**avemmo** gridato
avesti gridato	**aveste** gridato
ebbe gridato	**ebbero** gridato
futuro anteriore	
avrò gridato	**avremo** gridato
avrai gridato	**avrete** gridato
avrà gridato	**avranno** gridato
condizionale passato	
avrei gridato	**avremmo** gridato
avresti gridato	**avreste** gridato
avrebbe gridato	**avrebbero** gridato
congiuntivo passato	
abbia gridato	**abbiamo** gridato
abbia gridato	**abbiate** gridato
abbia gridato	**abbiano** gridato
congiuntivo trapassato	
avessi gridato	**avessimo** gridato
avessi gridato	**aveste** gridato
avesse gridato	**avessero** gridato

to gain, to earn — guadagnare

gerundio **guadagnando** participio passato **guadagnato**

SINGULAR	PLURAL
indicativo presente	
guadagn**o**	guadagn**iamo**
guadagn**i**	guadagn**ate**
guadagn**a**	guadagn**ano**
imperfetto	
guadagna**vo**	guadagna**vamo**
guadagna**vi**	guadagna**vate**
guadagna**va**	guadagna**vano**
passato remoto	
guadagn**ai**	guadagn**ammo**
guadagn**asti**	guadagn**aste**
guadagn**ò**	guadagn**arono**
futuro semplice	
guadagner**ò**	guadagner**emo**
guadagner**ai**	guadagner**ete**
guadagner**à**	guadagner**anno**
condizionale presente	
guadagn**erei**	guadagn**eremmo**
guadagn**eresti**	guadagn**ereste**
guadagn**erebbe**	guadagn**erebbero**
congiuntivo presente	
guadagn**i**	guadagn**iamo**
guadagn**i**	guadagn**iate**
guadagn**i**	guadagn**ino**
congiuntivo imperfetto	
guadagna**ssi**	guadagna**ssimo**
guadagna**ssi**	guadagna**ste**
guadagna**sse**	guadagna**ssero**
imperativo	
	guadagniamo
guadagna; non guadagnare	guadagnate
guadagni	guadagnino

SINGULAR	PLURAL
passato prossimo	
ho guadagnato	**abbiamo** guadagnato
hai guadagnato	**avete** guadagnato
ha guadagnato	**hanno** guadagnato
trapassato prossimo	
avevo guadagnato	**avevamo** guadagnato
avevi guadagnato	**avevate** guadagnato
aveva guadagnato	**avevano** guadagnato
trapassato remoto	
ebbi guadagnato	**avemmo** guadagnato
avesti guadagnato	**aveste** guadagnato
ebbe guadagnato	**ebbero** guadagnato
futuro anteriore	
avrò guadagnato	**avremo** guadagnato
avrai guadagnato	**avrete** guadagnato
avrà guadagnato	**avranno** guadagnato
condizionale passato	
avrei guadagnato	**avremmo** guadagnato
avresti guadagnato	**avreste** guadagnato
avrebbe guadagnato	**avrebbero** guadagnato
congiuntivo passato	
abbia guadagnato	**abbiamo** guadagnato
abbia guadagnato	**abbiate** guadagnato
abbia guadagnato	**abbiano** guadagnato
congiuntivo trapassato	
avessi guadagnato	**avessimo** guadagnato
avessi guadagnato	**aveste** guadagnato
avesse guadagnato	**avessero** guadagnato

guardare — to look at, to watch

gerundio **guardando** participio passato **guardato**

SINGULAR	PLURAL	SINGULAR	PLURAL
indicativo presente		passato prossimo	
guard**o**	guard**iamo**	**ho** guardato	**abbiamo** guardato
guard**i**	guard**ate**	**hai** guardato	**avete** guardato
guard**a**	guard**ano**	**ha** guardato	**hanno** guardato
imperfetto		trapassato prossimo	
guarda**vo**	guarda**vamo**	**avevo** guardato	**avevamo** guardato
guarda**vi**	guarda**vate**	**avevi** guardato	**avevate** guardato
guarda**va**	guarda**vano**	**aveva** guardato	**avevano** guardato
passato remoto		trapassato remoto	
guard**ai**	guard**ammo**	**ebbi** guardato	**avemmo** guardato
guard**asti**	guard**aste**	**avesti** guardato	**aveste** guardato
guard**ò**	guard**arono**	**ebbe** guardato	**ebbero** guardato
futuro semplice		futuro anteriore	
guarder**ò**	guarder**emo**	**avrò** guardato	**avremo** guardato
guarder**ai**	guarder**ete**	**avrai** guardato	**avrete** guardato
guarder**à**	guarder**anno**	**avrà** guardato	**avranno** guardato
condizionale presente		condizionale passato	
guard**erei**	guard**eremmo**	**avrei** guardato	**avremmo** guardato
guard**eresti**	guard**ereste**	**avresti** guardato	**avreste** guardato
guard**erebbe**	guard**erebbero**	**avrebbe** guardato	**avrebbero** guardato
congiuntivo presente		congiuntivo passato	
guard**i**	guard**iamo**	**abbia** guardato	**abbiamo** guardato
guard**i**	guard**iate**	**abbia** guardato	**abbiate** guardato
guard**i**	guard**ino**	**abbia** guardato	**abbiano** guardato
congiuntivo imperfetto		congiuntivo trapassato	
guarda**ssi**	guarda**ssimo**	**avessi** guardato	**avessimo** guardato
guarda**ssi**	guarda**ste**	**avessi** guardato	**aveste** guardato
guarda**sse**	guarda**ssero**	**avesse** guardato	**avessero** guardato

imperativo

	guardiamo
guarda; non guardare	guardate
guardi	guardino

G

MUST KNOW VERB

to heal, to recover — guarire

gerundio **guarendo** participio passato **guarito**

SINGULAR	PLURAL
indicativo presente	
guarisc**o**	guar**iamo**
guarisc**i**	guar**ite**
guarisc**e**	guarisc**ono**
imperfetto	
guari**vo**	guari**vamo**
guari**vi**	guari**vate**
guari**va**	guari**vano**
passato remoto	
guar**ii**	guar**immo**
guar**isti**	guar**iste**
guar**ì**	guar**irono**
futuro semplice	
guarir**ò**	guarir**emo**
guarir**ai**	guarir**ete**
guarir**à**	guarir**anno**
condizionale presente	
guar**irei**	guar**iremmo**
guar**iresti**	guar**ireste**
guar**irebbe**	guar**irebbero**
congiuntivo presente	
guarisc**a**	guar**iamo**
guarisc**a**	guar**iate**
guarisc**a**	guarisc**ano**
congiuntivo imperfetto	
guari**ssi**	guari**ssimo**
guari**ssi**	guari**ste**
guari**sse**	guari**ssero**
imperativo	
	guariamo
guarisci; non guarire	guarite
guarisca	guariscano

SINGULAR	PLURAL
passato prossimo	
sono guarito(a)	**siamo** guariti(e)
sei guarito(a)	**siete** guariti(e)
è guarito(a)	**sono** guariti(e)
trapassato prossimo	
ero guarito(a)	**eravamo** guariti(e)
eri guarito(a)	**eravate** guariti(e)
era guarito(a)	**erano** guariti(e)
trapassato remoto	
fui guarito(a)	**fummo** guariti(e)
fosti guarito(a)	**foste** guariti(e)
fu guarito(a)	**furono** guariti(e)
futuro anteriore	
sarò guarito(a)	**saremo** guariti(e)
sarai guarito(a)	**sarete** guariti(e)
sarà guarito(a)	**saranno** guariti(e)
condizionale passato	
sarei guarito(a)	**saremmo** guariti(e)
saresti guarito(a)	**sareste** guariti(e)
sarebbe guarito(a)	**sarebbero** guariti(e)
congiuntivo passato	
sia guarito(a)	**siamo** guariti(e)
sia guarito(a)	**siate** guariti(e)
sia guarito(a)	**siano** guariti(e)
congiuntivo trapassato	
fossi guarito(a)	**fossimo** guariti(e)
fossi guarito(a)	**foste** guariti(e)
fosse guarito(a)	**fossero** guariti(e)

guidare — to drive, to guide

gerundio **guidando** — participio passato **guidato**

SINGULAR	PLURAL	SINGULAR	PLURAL
indicativo presente		passato prossimo	
guid**o**	guid**iamo**	**ho** guidato	**abbiamo** guidato
guid**i**	guid**ate**	**hai** guidato	**avete** guidato
guid**a**	guid**ano**	**ha** guidato	**hanno** guidato
imperfetto		trapassato prossimo	
guida**vo**	guida**vamo**	**avevo** guidato	**avevamo** guidato
guida**vi**	guida**vate**	**avevi** guidato	**avevate** guidato
guida**va**	guida**vano**	**aveva** guidato	**avevano** guidato
passato remoto		trapassato remoto	
guid**ai**	guid**ammo**	**ebbi** guidato	**avemmo** guidato
guid**asti**	guid**aste**	**avesti** guidato	**aveste** guidato
guid**ò**	guid**arono**	**ebbe** guidato	**ebbero** guidato
futuro semplice		futuro anteriore	
guider**ò**	guider**emo**	**avrò** guidato	**avremo** guidato
guider**ai**	guider**ete**	**avrai** guidato	**avrete** guidato
guider**à**	guider**anno**	**avrà** guidato	**avranno** guidato
condizionale presente		condizionale passato	
guid**erei**	guid**eremmo**	**avrei** guidato	**avremmo** guidato
guid**eresti**	guid**ereste**	**avresti** guidato	**avreste** guidato
guid**erebbe**	guid**erebbero**	**avrebbe** guidato	**avrebbero** guidato
congiuntivo presente		congiuntivo passato	
guid**i**	guid**iamo**	**abbia** guidato	**abbiamo** guidato
guid**i**	guid**iate**	**abbia** guidato	**abbiate** guidato
guid**i**	guid**ino**	**abbia** guidato	**abbiano** guidato
congiuntivo imperfetto		congiuntivo trapassato	
guida**ssi**	guida**ssimo**	**avessi** guidato	**avessimo** guidato
guida**ssi**	guida**ste**	**avessi** guidato	**aveste** guidato
guida**sse**	guida**ssero**	**avesse** guidato	**avessero** guidato

imperativo

	guidiamo
guida; non guidare	guidate
guidi	guidino

G

to taste, to enjoy **gustare**

gerundio **gustando** participio passato **gustato**

SINGULAR	PLURAL	SINGULAR	PLURAL
indicativo presente		passato prossimo	
gust**o**	gust**iamo**	**ho** gustato	**abbiamo** gustato
gust**i**	gust**ate**	**hai** gustato	**avete** gustato
gust**a**	gust**ano**	**ha** gustato	**hanno** gustato
imperfetto		trapassato prossimo	
gusta**vo**	gusta**vamo**	**avevo** gustato	**avevamo** gustato
gusta**vi**	gusta**vate**	**avevi** gustato	**avevate** gustato
gusta**va**	gusta**vano**	**aveva** gustato	**avevano** gustato
passato remoto		trapassato remoto	
gust**ai**	gust**ammo**	**ebbi** gustato	**avemmo** gustato
gust**asti**	gust**aste**	**avesti** gustato	**aveste** gustato
gust**ò**	gust**arono**	**ebbe** gustato	**ebbero** gustato
futuro semplice		futuro anteriore	
guster**ò**	guster**emo**	**avrò** gustato	**avremo** gustato
guster**ai**	guster**ete**	**avrai** gustato	**avrete** gustato
guster**à**	guster**anno**	**avrà** gustato	**avranno** gustato
condizionale presente		condizionale passato	
gust**erei**	gust**eremmo**	**avrei** gustato	**avremmo** gustato
gust**eresti**	gust**ereste**	**avresti** gustato	**avreste** gustato
gust**erebbe**	gust**erebbero**	**avrebbe** gustato	**avrebbero** gustato
congiuntivo presente		congiuntivo passato	
gust**i**	gust**iamo**	**abbia** gustato	**abbiamo** gustato
gust**i**	gust**iate**	**abbia** gustato	**abbiate** gustato
gust**i**	gust**ino**	**abbia** gustato	**abbiano** gustato
congiuntivo imperfetto		congiuntivo trapassato	
gusta**ssi**	gusta**ssimo**	**avessi** gustato	**avessimo** gustato
gusta**ssi**	gusta**ste**	**avessi** gustato	**aveste** gustato
gusta**sse**	gusta**ssero**	**avesse** gustato	**avessero** gustato
imperativo			
	gustiamo		
gusta; non gustare	gustate		
gusti	gustino		

G

illudere — to deceive, to delude

gerundio **illudendo** — participio passato **illuso**

SINGULAR	PLURAL
indicativo presente	
illud**o**	illud**iamo**
illud**i**	illud**ete**
illud**e**	illud**ono**
imperfetto	
illude**vo**	illude**vamo**
illude**vi**	illude**vate**
illude**va**	illude**vano**
passato remoto	
illu**si**	illud**emmo**
illud**esti**	illud**este**
illu**se**	illu**sero**
futuro semplice	
illuder**ò**	illuder**emo**
illuder**ai**	illuder**ete**
illuder**à**	illuder**anno**
condizionale presente	
illud**erei**	illud**eremmo**
illud**eresti**	illud**ereste**
illud**erebbe**	illud**erebbero**
congiuntivo presente	
illud**a**	illud**iamo**
illud**a**	illud**iate**
illud**a**	illud**ano**
congiuntivo imperfetto	
illude**ssi**	illude**ssimo**
illude**ssi**	illude**ste**
illude**sse**	illude**ssero**
imperativo	
	illudiamo
illudi; non illudere	illudete
illuda	illudano

SINGULAR	PLURAL
passato prossimo	
ho illuso	**abbiamo** illuso
hai illuso	**avete** illuso
ha illuso	**hanno** illuso
trapassato prossimo	
avevo illuso	**avevamo** illuso
avevi illuso	**avevate** illuso
aveva illuso	**avevano** illuso
trapassato remoto	
ebbi illuso	**avemmo** illuso
avesti illuso	**aveste** illuso
ebbe illuso	**ebbero** illuso
futuro anteriore	
avrò illuso	**avremo** illuso
avrai illuso	**avrete** illuso
avrà illuso	**avranno** illuso
condizionale passato	
avrei illuso	**avremmo** illuso
avresti illuso	**avreste** illuso
avrebbe illuso	**avrebbero** illuso
congiuntivo passato	
abbia illuso	**abbiamo** illuso
abbia illuso	**abbiate** illuso
abbia illuso	**abbiano** illuso
congiuntivo trapassato	
avessi illuso	**avessimo** illuso
avessi illuso	**aveste** illuso
avesse illuso	**avessero** illuso

to mail a letter — imbucare

gerundio **imbucando** participio passato **imbucato**

SINGULAR	PLURAL	SINGULAR	PLURAL
indicativo presente		passato prossimo	
imbuc**o**	imbuch**iamo**	**ho** imbucato	**abbiamo** imbucato
imbuch**i**	imbuc**ate**	**hai** imbucato	**avete** imbucato
imbuc**a**	imbuc**ano**	**ha** imbucato	**hanno** imbucato
imperfetto		trapassato prossimo	
imbuca**vo**	imbuca**vamo**	**avevo** imbucato	**avevamo** imbucato
imbuca**vi**	imbuca**vate**	**avevi** imbucato	**avevate** imbucato
imbuca**va**	imbuca**vano**	**aveva** imbucato	**avevano** imbucato
passato remoto		trapassato remoto	
imbuc**ai**	imbuc**ammo**	**ebbi** imbucato	**avemmo** imbucato
imbuc**asti**	imbuc**aste**	**avesti** imbucato	**aveste** imbucato
imbuc**ò**	imbuc**arono**	**ebbe** imbucato	**ebbero** imbucato
futuro semplice		futuro anteriore	
imbucher**ò**	imbucher**emo**	**avrò** imbucato	**avremo** imbucato
imbucher**ai**	imbucher**ete**	**avrai** imbucato	**avrete** imbucato
imbucher**à**	imbucher**anno**	**avrà** imbucato	**avranno** imbucato
condizionale presente		condizionale passato	
imbuch**erei**	imbuch**eremmo**	**avrei** imbucato	**avremmo** imbucato
imbuch**eresti**	imbuch**ereste**	**avresti** imbucato	**avreste** imbucato
imbuch**erebbe**	imbuch**erebbero**	**avrebbe** imbucato	**avrebbero** imbucato
congiuntivo presente		congiuntivo passato	
imbuch**i**	imbuch**iamo**	**abbia** imbucato	**abbiamo** imbucato
imbuch**i**	imbuch**iate**	**abbia** imbucato	**abbiate** imbucato
imbuch**i**	imbuch**ino**	**abbia** imbucato	**abbiano** imbucato
congiuntivo imperfetto		congiuntivo trapassato	
imbuca**ssi**	imbuca**ssimo**	**avessi** imbucato	**avessimo** imbucato
imbuca**ssi**	imbuca**ste**	**avessi** imbucato	**aveste** imbucato
imbuca**sse**	imbuca**ssero**	**avesse** imbucato	**avessero** imbucato

imperativo

	imbuchiamo
imbuca; non imbucare	imbucate
imbuchi	imbuchino

I

immaginare — to imagine

gerundio **immaginando** — participio passato **immaginato**

SINGULAR	PLURAL	SINGULAR	PLURAL
indicativo presente		passato prossimo	
immagin**o**	immagin**iamo**	**ho** immaginato	**abbiamo** immaginato
immagin**i**	immagin**ate**	**hai** immaginato	**avete** immaginato
immagin**a**	immagin**ano**	**ha** immaginato	**hanno** immaginato
imperfetto		trapassato prossimo	
immagina**vo**	immagina**vamo**	**avevo** immaginato	**avevamo** immaginato
immagina**vi**	immagina**vate**	**avevi** immaginato	**avevate** immaginato
immagina**va**	immagina**vano**	**aveva** immaginato	**avevano** immaginato
passato remoto		trapassato remoto	
immagin**ai**	immagin**ammo**	**ebbi** immaginato	**avemmo** immaginato
immagin**asti**	immagin**aste**	**avesti** immaginato	**aveste** immaginato
immagin**ò**	immagin**arono**	**ebbe** immaginato	**ebbero** immaginato
futuro semplice		futuro anteriore	
immaginer**ò**	immaginer**emo**	**avrò** immaginato	**avremo** immaginato
immaginer**ai**	immaginer**ete**	**avrai** immaginato	**avrete** immaginato
immaginer**à**	immaginer**anno**	**avrà** immaginato	**avranno** immaginato
condizionale presente		condizionale passato	
immaginer**ei**	immaginer**emmo**	**avrei** immaginato	**avremmo** immaginato
immaginer**esti**	immaginer**este**	**avresti** immaginato	**avreste** immaginato
immaginer**ebbe**	immaginer**ebbero**	**avrebbe** immaginato	**avrebbero** immaginato
congiuntivo presente		congiuntivo passato	
immagin**i**	immagin**iamo**	**abbia** immaginato	**abbiamo** immaginato
immagin**i**	immagin**iate**	**abbia** immaginato	**abbiate** immaginato
immagin**i**	immagin**ino**	**abbia** immaginato	**abbiano** immaginato
congiuntivo imperfetto		congiuntivo trapassato	
immagina**ssi**	immagina**ssimo**	**avessi** immaginato	**avessimo** immaginato
immagina**ssi**	immagina**ste**	**avessi** immaginato	**aveste** immaginato
immagina**sse**	immagina**ssero**	**avesse** immaginato	**avessero** immaginato

imperativo

SINGULAR	PLURAL
	immaginiamo
immagina; non immaginare	immaginate
immagini	immaginino

gerundio **immergendo** participio passato **immerso**

SINGULAR	PLURAL	SINGULAR	PLURAL
indicativo presente		passato prossimo	
immerg**o**	immerg**iamo**	**ho** immerso	**abbiamo** immerso
immerg**i**	immerg**ete**	**hai** immerso	**avete** immerso
immerg**e**	immerg**ono**	**ha** immerso	**hanno** immerso
imperfetto		trapassato prossimo	
immerge**vo**	immerge**vamo**	**avevo** immerso	**avevamo** immerso
immerge**vi**	immerge**vate**	**avevi** immerso	**avevate** immerso
immerge**va**	immerge**vano**	**aveva** immerso	**avevano** immerso
passato remoto		trapassato remoto	
immer**si**	immerg**emmo**	**ebbi** immerso	**avemmo** immerso
immerg**esti**	immerg**este**	**avesti** immerso	**aveste** immerso
immer**se**	immer**sero**	**ebbe** immerso	**ebbero** immerso
futuro semplice		futuro anteriore	
immerger**ò**	immerger**emo**	**avrò** immerso	**avremo** immerso
immerger**ai**	immerger**ete**	**avrai** immerso	**avrete** immerso
immerger**à**	immerger**anno**	**avrà** immerso	**avranno** immerso
condizionale presente		condizionale passato	
immerg**erei**	immerg**eremmo**	**avrei** immerso	**avremmo** immerso
immerg**eresti**	immerg**ereste**	**avresti** immerso	**avreste** immerso
immerg**erebbe**	immerg**erebbero**	**avrebbe** immerso	**avrebbero** immerso
congiuntivo presente		congiuntivo passato	
immerg**a**	immerg**iamo**	**abbia** immerso	**abbiamo** immerso
immerg**a**	immerg**iate**	**abbia** immerso	**abbiate** immerso
immerg**a**	immerg**ano**	**abbia** immerso	**abbiano** immerso
congiuntivo imperfetto		congiuntivo trapassato	
immerge**ssi**	immerge**ssimo**	**avessi** immerso	**avessimo** immerso
immerge**ssi**	immerge**ste**	**avessi** immerso	**aveste** immerso
immerge**sse**	immerge**ssero**	**avesse** immerso	**avessero** immerso
imperativo			
	immergiamo		
immergi; non immergere	immergete		
immerga	immergano		

I

imparare — to learn

gerundio **imparando** participio passato **imparato**

SINGULAR	PLURAL
indicativo presente	
impar**o**	impar**iamo**
impar**i**	impar**ate**
impar**a**	impar**ano**
imperfetto	
impara**vo**	impara**vamo**
impara**vi**	impara**vate**
impara**va**	impara**vano**
passato remoto	
impar**ai**	impar**ammo**
impar**asti**	impar**aste**
impar**ò**	impar**arono**
futuro semplice	
imparer**ò**	imparer**emo**
imparer**ai**	imparer**ete**
imparer**à**	imparer**anno**
condizionale presente	
impar**erei**	impar**eremmo**
impar**eresti**	impar**ereste**
impar**erebbe**	impar**erebbero**
congiuntivo presente	
impar**i**	impar**iamo**
impar**i**	impar**iate**
impar**i**	impar**ino**
congiuntivo imperfetto	
impara**ssi**	impara**ssimo**
impara**ssi**	impara**ste**
impara**sse**	impara**ssero**
imperativo	
	impariamo
impara; non imparare	imparate
impari	imparino

SINGULAR	PLURAL
passato prossimo	
ho imparato	**abbiamo** imparato
hai imparato	**avete** imparato
ha imparato	**hanno** imparato
trapassato prossimo	
avevo imparato	**avevamo** imparato
avevi imparato	**avevate** imparato
aveva imparato	**avevano** imparato
trapassato remoto	
ebbi imparato	**avemmo** imparato
avesti imparato	**aveste** imparato
ebbe imparato	**ebbero** imparato
futuro anteriore	
avrò imparato	**avremo** imparato
avrai imparato	**avrete** imparato
avrà imparato	**avranno** imparato
condizionale passato	
avrei imparato	**avremmo** imparato
avresti imparato	**avreste** imparato
avrebbe imparato	**avrebbero** imparato
congiuntivo passato	
abbia imparato	**abbiamo** imparato
abbia imparato	**abbiate** imparato
abbia imparato	**abbiano** imparato
congiuntivo trapassato	
avessi imparato	**avessimo** imparato
avessi imparato	**aveste** imparato
avesse imparato	**avessero** imparato

gerundio **impaurendosi** participio passato **impauritosi**

SINGULAR	PLURAL
indicativo presente	
mi impauris**co**	**ci** impaur**iamo**
ti impauris**ci**	**vi** impaur**ite**
si impauris**ce**	**si** impauris**cono**
imperfetto	
mi impauri**vo**	**ci** impauri**vamo**
ti impauri**vi**	**vi** impauri**vate**
si impauri**va**	**si** impauri**vano**
passato remoto	
mi impaur**ii**	**ci** impaur**immo**
ti impaur**isti**	**vi** impaur**iste**
si impaur**ì**	**si** impaur**irono**
futuro semplice	
mi impaurir**ò**	**ci** impaurir**emo**
ti impaurir**ai**	**vi** impaurir**ete**
si impaurir**à**	**si** impaurir**anno**
condizionale presente	
mi impaur**irei**	**ci** impaur**iremmo**
ti impaur**iresti**	**vi** impaur**ireste**
si impaur**irebbe**	**si** impaur**irebbero**
congiuntivo presente	
mi impauris**ca**	**ci** impaur**iamo**
ti impauris**ca**	**vi** impaur**iate**
si impauris**ca**	**si** impaur**iscano**
congiuntivo imperfetto	
mi impauri**ssi**	**ci** impauri**ssimo**
ti impauri**ssi**	**vi** impauri**ste**
si impauri**sse**	**si** impauri**ssero**
imperativo	
	impauriamoci
impaurisciti; non impaurirti/ non ti impaurire	impauritevi
si impaurisca	si impauriscano

SINGULAR	PLURAL
passato prossimo	
mi sono impaurito(a)	**ci siamo** impauriti(e)
ti sei impaurito(a)	**vi siete** impauriti(e)
si è impaurito(a)	**si sono** impauriti(e)
trapassato prossimo	
mi ero impaurito(a)	**ci eravamo** impauriti(e)
ti eri impaurito(a)	**vi eravate** impauriti(e)
si era impaurito(a)	**si erano** impauriti(e)
trapassato remoto	
mi fui impaurito(a)	**ci fummo** impauriti(e)
ti fosti impaurito(a)	**vi foste** impauriti(e)
si fu impaurito(a)	**si furono** impauriti(e)
futuro anteriore	
mi sarò impaurito(a)	**ci saremo** impauriti(e)
ti sarai impaurito(a)	**vi sarete** impauriti(e)
si sarà impaurito(a)	**si saranno** impauriti(e)
condizionale passato	
mi sarei impaurito(a)	**ci saremmo** impauriti(e)
ti saresti impaurito(a)	**vi sareste** impauriti(e)
si sarebbe impaurito(a)	**si sarebbero** impauriti(e)
congiuntivo passato	
mi sia impaurito(a)	**ci siamo** impauriti(e)
ti sia impaurito(a)	**vi siate** impauriti(e)
si sia impaurito(a)	**si siano** impauriti(e)
congiuntivo trapassato	
mi fossi impaurito(a)	**ci fossimo** impauriti(e)
ti fossi impaurito(a)	**vi foste** impauriti(e)
si fosse impaurito(a)	**si fossero** impauriti(e)

impazzire — to go insane

gerundio **impazzendo** participio passato **impazzito**

SINGULAR	PLURAL	SINGULAR	PLURAL
indicativo presente		passato prossimo	
impazzisc**o**	impazz**iamo**	**sono** impazzito(a)	**siamo** impazziti(e)
impazzisc**i**	impazz**ite**	**sei** impazzito(a)	**siete** impazziti(e)
impazzisc**e**	impazz**iscono**	**è** impazzito(a)	**sono** impazziti(e)
imperfetto		trapassato prossimo	
impazzi**vo**	impazzi**vamo**	**ero** impazzito(a)	**eravamo** impazziti(e)
impazzi**vi**	impazzi**vate**	**eri** impazzito(a)	**eravate** impazziti(e)
impazzi**va**	impazzi**vano**	**era** impazzito(a)	**erano** impazziti(e)
passato remoto		trapassato remoto	
impazz**ii**	impazz**immo**	**fui** impazzito(a)	**fummo** impazziti(e)
impazz**isti**	impazz**iste**	**fosti** impazzito(a)	**foste** impazziti(e)
impazz**ì**	impazz**irono**	**fu** impazzito(a)	**furono** impazziti(e)
futuro semplice		futuro anteriore	
impazzir**ò**	impazzir**emo**	**sarò** impazzito(a)	**saremo** impazziti(e)
impazzir**ai**	impazzir**ete**	**sarai** impazzito(a)	**sarete** impazziti(e)
impazzir**à**	impazzir**anno**	**sarà** impazzito(a)	**saranno** impazziti(e)
condizionale presente		condizionale passato	
impazzir**ei**	impazzir**emmo**	**sarei** impazzito(a)	**saremmo** impazziti(e)
impazzir**esti**	impazzir**este**	**saresti** impazzito(a)	**sareste** impazziti(e)
impazzir**ebbe**	impazzir**ebbero**	**sarebbe** impazzito(a)	**sarebbero** impazziti(e)
congiuntivo presente		congiuntivo passato	
impazzisc**a**	impazz**iamo**	**sia** impazzito(a)	**siamo** impazziti(e)
impazzisc**a**	impazz**iate**	**sia** impazzito(a)	**siate** impazziti(e)
impazzisc**a**	impazz**iscano**	**sia** impazzito(a)	**siano** impazziti(e)
congiuntivo imperfetto		congiuntivo trapassato	
impazzi**ssi**	impazzi**ssimo**	**fossi** impazzito(a)	**fossimo** impazziti(e)
impazzi**ssi**	impazzi**ste**	**fossi** impazzito(a)	**foste** impazziti(e)
impazzi**sse**	impazzi**ssero**	**fosse** impazzito(a)	**fossero** impazziti(e)

imperativo

	impazziamo
impazzisci; non impazzire	impazzite
impazzisca	impazziscano

I

gerundio **impersonando** participio passato **impersonato**

SINGULAR	PLURAL	SINGULAR	PLURAL
indicativo presente		passato prossimo	
imperson**o**	imperson**iamo**	**ho** impersonato	**abbiamo** impersonato
imperson**i**	imperson**ate**	**hai** impersonato	**avete** impersonato
imperson**a**	imperson**ano**	**ha** impersonato	**hanno** impersonato
imperfetto		trapassato prossimo	
imperson**avo**	imperson**avamo**	**avevo** impersonato	**avevamo** impersonato
imperson**avi**	imperson**avate**	**avevi** impersonato	**avevate** impersonato
imperson**ava**	imperson**avano**	**aveva** impersonato	**avevano** impersonato
passato remoto		trapassato remoto	
imperson**ai**	imperson**ammo**	**ebbi** impersonato	**avemmo** impersonato
imperson**asti**	imperson**aste**	**avesti** impersonato	**aveste** impersonato
imperson**ò**	imperson**arono**	**ebbe** impersonato	**ebbero** impersonato
futuro semplice		futuro anteriore	
imperson**erò**	imperson**eremo**	**avrò** impersonato	**avremo** impersonato
imperson**erai**	imperson**erete**	**avrai** impersonato	**avrete** impersonato
imperson**erà**	imperson**eranno**	**avrà** impersonato	**avranno** impersonato
condizionale presente		condizionale passato	
imperson**erei**	imperson**eremmo**	**avrei** impersonato	**avremmo** impersonato
imperson**eresti**	imperson**ereste**	**avresti** impersonato	**avreste** impersonato
imperson**erebbe**	imperson**erebbero**	**avresti** impersonato	**avrebbero** impersonato
congiuntivo presente		congiuntivo passato	
imperson**i**	imperson**iamo**	**abbia** impersonato	**abbiamo** impersonato
imperson**i**	imperson**iate**	**abbia** impersonato	**abbiate** impersonato
imperson**i**	imperson**ino**	**abbia** impersonato	**abbiano** impersonato
congiuntivo imperfetto		congiuntivo trapassato	
imperson**assi**	imperson**assimo**	**avessi** impersonato	**avessimo** impersonato
imperson**assi**	imperson**aste**	**avessi** impersonato	**aveste** impersonato
imperson**asse**	imperson**assero**	**avesse** impersonato	**avessero** impersonato
imperativo			
	impersoniamo		
impersona; non impersonare	impersonate		
impersoni	impersonino		

I

impiegare — to employ, to engage

gerundio **impiegando** participio passato **impiegato**

SINGULAR	PLURAL	SINGULAR	PLURAL
indicativo presente		passato prossimo	
impieg**o**	impiegh**iamo**	**ho** impiegato	**abbiamo** impiegato
impiegh**i**	impieg**ate**	**hai** impiegato	**avete** impiegato
impieg**a**	impieg**ano**	**ha** impiegato	**hanno** impiegato
imperfetto		trapassato prossimo	
impiega**vo**	impiega**vamo**	**avevo** impiegato	**avevamo** impiegato
impiega**vi**	impiega**vate**	**avevi** impiegato	**avevate** impiegato
impiega**va**	impiega**vano**	**aveva** impiegato	**avevano** impiegato
passato remoto		trapassato remoto	
impieg**ai**	impieg**ammo**	**ebbi** impiegato	**avemmo** impiegato
impieg**asti**	impieg**aste**	**avesti** impiegato	**aveste** impiegato
impieg**ò**	impieg**arono**	**ebbe** impiegato	**ebbero** impiegato
futuro semplice		futuro anteriore	
impiegher**ò**	impiegher**emo**	**avrò** impiegato	**avremo** impiegato
impiegher**ai**	impiegher**ete**	**avrai** impiegato	**avrete** impiegato
impiegher**à**	impiegher**anno**	**avrà** impiegato	**avranno** impiegato
condizionale presente		condizionale passato	
impiegh**erei**	impiegh**eremmo**	**avrei** impiegato	**avremmo** impiegato
impiegh**eresti**	impiegh**ereste**	**avresti** impiegato	**avreste** impiegato
impiegh**erebbe**	impiegh**erebbero**	**avrebbe** impiegato	**avrebbero** impiegato
congiuntivo presente		congiuntivo passato	
impiegh**i**	impiegh**iamo**	**abbia** impiegato	**abbiamo** impiegato
impiegh**i**	impiegh**iate**	**abbia** impiegato	**abbiate** impiegato
impiegh**i**	impiegh**ino**	**abbia** impiegato	**abbiano** impiegato
congiuntivo imperfetto		congiuntivo trapassato	
impiega**ssi**	impiega**ssimo**	**avessi** impiegato	**avessimo** impiegato
impiega**ssi**	impiega**ste**	**avessi** impiegato	**aveste** impiegato
impiega**sse**	impiega**ssero**	**avesse** impiegato	**avessero** impiegato

imperativo

	impieghiamo
impiega; non impiegare	impiegate
impieghi	impieghino

I

to implicate, to involve **implicare**

gerundio **implicando** participio passato **implicato**

SINGULAR	PLURAL
indicativo presente	
implic**o**	implich**iamo**
implich**i**	implic**ate**
implic**a**	implic**ano**
imperfetto	
implica**vo**	implica**vamo**
implica**vi**	implica**vate**
implica**va**	implica**vano**
passato remoto	
implic**ai**	implic**ammo**
implic**asti**	implic**aste**
implic**ò**	implic**arono**
futuro semplice	
impliche**rò**	impliche**remo**
impliche**rai**	impliche**rete**
impliche**rà**	impliche**ranno**
condizionale presente	
implich**erei**	implich**eremmo**
implich**eresti**	implich**ereste**
implich**erebbe**	implich**erebbero**
congiuntivo presente	
implich**i**	implich**iamo**
implich**i**	implich**iate**
implich**i**	implich**ino**
congiuntivo imperfetto	
implica**ssi**	implica**ssimo**
implica**ssi**	implica**ste**
implica**sse**	implica**ssero**
imperativo	
	implichiamo
implica; non implicare	implicate
implichi	implichino

SINGULAR	PLURAL
passato prossimo	
ho implicato	**abbiamo** implicato
hai implicato	**avete** implicato
ha implicato	**hanno** implicato
trapassato prossimo	
avevo implicato	**avevamo** implicato
avevi implicato	**avevate** implicato
aveva implicato	**avevano** implicato
trapassato remoto	
ebbi implicato	**avemmo** implicato
avesti implicato	**aveste** implicato
ebbe implicato	**ebbero** implicato
futuro anteriore	
avrò implicato	**avremo** implicato
avrai implicato	**avrete** implicato
avrà implicato	**avranno** implicato
condizionale passato	
avrei implicato	**avremmo** implicato
avresti implicato	**avreste** implicato
avrebbe implicato	**avrebbero** implicato
congiuntivo passato	
abbia implicato	**abbiamo** implicato
abbia implicato	**abbiate** implicato
abbia implicato	**abbiano** implicato
congiuntivo trapassato	
avessi implicato	**avessimo** implicato
avessi implicato	**aveste** implicato
avesse implicato	**avessero** implicato

imporre — to impose

gerundio **imponendo** — participio passato **imposto**

SINGULAR	PLURAL	SINGULAR	PLURAL
indicativo presente		passato prossimo	
impong**o**	impon**iamo**	**ho** imposto	**abbiamo** imposto
impon**i**	impon**ete**	**hai** imposto	**avete** imposto
impon**e**	impong**ono**	**ha** imposto	**hanno** imposto
imperfetto		trapassato prossimo	
impone**vo**	impone**vamo**	**avevo** imposto	**avevamo** imposto
impone**vi**	impone**vate**	**avevi** imposto	**avevate** imposto
impone**va**	impone**vano**	**aveva** imposto	**avevano** imposto
passato remoto		trapassato remoto	
impos**i**	impon**emmo**	**ebbi** imposto	**avemmo** imposto
impon**esti**	impon**este**	**avesti** imposto	**aveste** imposto
impos**e**	impos**ero**	**ebbe** imposto	**ebbero** imposto
futuro semplice		futuro anteriore	
imporr**ò**	imporr**emo**	**avrò** imposto	**avremo** imposto
imporr**ai**	imporr**ete**	**avrai** imposto	**avrete** imposto
imporr**à**	imporr**anno**	**avrà** imposto	**avranno** imposto
condizionale presente		condizionale passato	
imporr**ei**	imporr**emmo**	**avrei** imposto	**avremmo** imposto
imporr**esti**	imporr**este**	**avresti** imposto	**avreste** imposto
imporr**ebbe**	imporr**ebbero**	**avrebbe** imposto	**avrebbero** imposto
congiuntivo presente		congiuntivo passato	
impong**a**	impon**iamo**	**abbia** imposto	**abbiamo** imposto
impong**a**	impon**iate**	**abbia** imposto	**abbiate** imposto
impong**a**	impong**ano**	**abbia** imposto	**abbiano** imposto
congiuntivo imperfetto		congiuntivo trapassato	
impon**essi**	impon**essimo**	**avessi** imposto	**avessimo** imposto
impon**essi**	impon**este**	**avessi** imposto	**aveste** imposto
impon**esse**	impon**essero**	**avesse** imposto	**avessero** imposto

imperativo

	imponiamo
imponi; non imporre	imponete
imponga	impongano

I

gerundio **imprimendo** participio passato **impressso**

SINGULAR	PLURAL	SINGULAR	PLURAL
indicativo presente		passato prossimo	
imprim**o**	imprim**iamo**	**ho** impresso	**abbiamo** impresso
imprim**i**	imprim**ete**	**hai** impresso	**avete** impresso
imprim**e**	imprim**ono**	**ha** impresso	**hanno** impresso
imperfetto		trapassato prossimo	
imprime**vo**	imprime**vamo**	**avevo** impresso	**avevamo** impresso
imprime**vi**	imprime**vate**	**avevi** impresso	**avevate** impresso
imprime**va**	imprime**vano**	**aveva** impresso	**avevano** impresso
passato remoto		trapassato remoto	
impress**i**	imprim**emmo**	**ebbi** impresso	**avemmo** impresso
imprim**esti**	imprim**este**	**avesti** impresso	**aveste** impresso
impress**e**	impress**ero**	**ebbe** impresso	**ebbero** impresso
futuro semplice		futuro anteriore	
imprimer**ò**	imprimer**emo**	**avrò** impresso	**avremo** impresso
imprimer**ai**	imprimer**ete**	**avrai** impresso	**avrete** impresso
imprimer**à**	imprimer**anno**	**avrà** impresso	**avranno** impresso
condizionale presente		condizionale passato	
imprim**erei**	imprim**eremmo**	**avrei** impresso	**avremmo** impresso
imprim**eresti**	imprim**ereste**	**avresti** impresso	**avreste** impresso
imprim**erebbe**	imprim**erebbero**	**avrebbe** impresso	**avrebbero** impresso
congiuntivo presente		congiuntivo passato	
imprim**a**	imprim**iamo**	**abbia** impresso	**abbiamo** impresso
imprim**a**	imprim**iate**	**abbia** impresso	**abbiate** impresso
imprim**a**	imprim**ano**	**abbia** impresso	**abbiano** impresso
congiuntivo imperfetto		congiuntivo trapassato	
imprime**ssi**	imprime**ssimo**	**avessi** impresso	**avessimo** impresso
imprime**ssi**	imprime**ste**	**avessi** impresso	**aveste** impresso
imprime**sse**	imprime**ssero**	**avesse** impresso	**avessero** impresso
imperativo			
	imprimiamo		
imprimi; non imprimere	imprimete		
imprima	imprimano		

I

incassare — to cash, to take in

gerundio **incassando** participio passato **incassato**

SINGULAR	PLURAL
indicativo presente	
incass**o**	incass**iamo**
incass**i**	incass**ate**
incass**a**	incass**ano**
imperfetto	
incassa**vo**	incassa**vamo**
incassa**vi**	incassa**vate**
incassa**va**	incassa**vano**
passato remoto	
incass**ai**	incass**ammo**
incass**asti**	incass**aste**
incass**ò**	incass**arono**
futuro semplice	
incasser**ò**	incasser**emo**
incasser**ai**	incasser**ete**
incasser**à**	incasser**anno**
condizionale presente	
incasser**ei**	incasser**emmo**
incasser**esti**	incasser**este**
incasser**ebbe**	incasser**ebbero**
congiuntivo presente	
incass**i**	incass**iamo**
incass**i**	incass**iate**
incass**i**	incass**ino**
congiuntivo imperfetto	
incassa**ssi**	incassa**ssimo**
incassa**ssi**	incassa**ste**
incassa**sse**	incassa**ssero**
imperativo	
	incassiamo
incassa; non incassare	incassate
incassi	incassino

SINGULAR	PLURAL
passato prossimo	
ho incassato	**abbiamo** incassato
hai incassato	**avete** incassato
ha incassato	**hanno** incassato
trapassato prossimo	
avevo incassato	**avevamo** incassato
avevi incassato	**avevate** incassato
aveva incassato	**avevano** incassato
trapassato remoto	
ebbi incassato	**avemmo** incassato
avesti incassato	**aveste** incassaio
ebbe incassato	**ebbero** incassato
futuro anteriore	
avrò incassato	**avremo** incassato
avrai incassato	**avrete** incassato
avrà incassato	**avranno** incassato
condizionale passato	
avrei incassato	**avremmo** incassato
avresti incassato	**avreste** incassato
avrebbe incassato	**avrebbero** incassato
congiuntivo passato	
abbia incassato	**abbiamo** incassato
abbia incassato	**abbiate** incassato
abbia incassato	**abbiano** incassato
congiuntivo trapassato	
avessi incassato	**avessimo** incassato
avessi incassato	**aveste** incassato
avesse incassato	**avessero** incassato

gerundio **includendo** participio passato **incluso**

SINGULAR	PLURAL	SINGULAR	PLURAL
indicativo presente		passato prossimo	
includ**o**	includ**iamo**	**ho** incluso	**abbiamo** incluso
includ**i**	includ**ete**	**hai** incluso	**avete** incluso
includ**e**	includ**ono**	**ha** incluso	**hanno** incluso
imperfetto		trapassato prossimo	
include**vo**	include**vamo**	**avevo** incluso	**avevamo** incluso
include**vi**	include**vate**	**avevi** incluso	**avevate** incluso
include**va**	include**vano**	**aveva** incluso	**avevano** incluso
passato remoto		trapassato remoto	
inclus**i**	includ**emmo**	**ebbi** incluso	**avemmo** incluso
includ**esti**	includ**este**	**avesti** incluso	**aveste** incluso
inclus**e**	inclus**ero**	**ebbe** incluso	**ebbero** incluso
futuro semplice		futuro anteriore	
includer**ò**	includer**emo**	**avrò** incluso	**avremo** incluso
includer**ai**	includer**ete**	**avrai** incluso	**avrete** incluso
includer**à**	includer**anno**	**avrà** incluso	**avranno** incluso
condizionale presente		condizionale passato	
includ**erei**	includ**eremmo**	**avrei** incluso	**avremmo** incluso
includ**eresti**	includ**ereste**	**avresti** incluso	**avreste** incluso
includ**erebbe**	includ**erebbero**	**avrebbe** incluso	**avrebbero** incluso
congiuntivo presente		congiuntivo passato	
includ**a**	includ**iamo**	**abbia** incluso	**abbiamo** incluso
includ**a**	includ**iate**	**abbia** incluso	**abbiate** incluso
includ**a**	includ**ano**	**abbia** incluso	**abbiano** incluso
congiuntivo imperfetto		congiuntivo trapassato	
includ**essi**	includ**essimo**	**avessi** incluso	**avessimo** incluso
includ**essi**	includ**este**	**avessi** incluso	**aveste** incluso
includ**esse**	includ**essero**	**avesse** incluso	**avessero** incluso
imperativo			
	includiamo		
includi; non includere	includete		
includa	includano		

I

incomodare — to inconvenience, to annoy

gerundio **incomodando** — participio passato **incomodato**

SINGULAR	PLURAL	SINGULAR	PLURAL
indicativo presente		*passato prossimo*	
incomod**o**	incomod**iamo**	**ho** incomodato	**abbiamo** incomodato
incomod**i**	incomod**ate**	**hai** incomodato	**avete** incomodato
incomod**a**	incomod**ano**	**ha** incomodato	**hanno** incomodato
imperfetto		*trapassato prossimo*	
incomoda**vo**	incomoda**vamo**	**avevo** incomodato	**avevamo** incomodato
incomoda**vi**	incomoda**vate**	**avevi** incomodato	**avevate** incomodato
incomoda**va**	incomoda**vano**	**aveva** incomodato	**avevano** incomodato
passato remoto		*trapassato remoto*	
incomod**ai**	incomod**ammo**	**ebbi** incomodato	**avemmo** incomodato
incomod**asti**	incomod**aste**	**avesti** incomodato	**aveste** incomodato
incomod**ò**	incomod**arono**	**ebbe** incomodato	**ebbero** incomodato
futuro semplice		*futuro anteriore*	
incomoder**ò**	incomoder**emo**	**avrò** incomodato	**avremo** incomodato
incomoder**ai**	incomoder**ete**	**avrai** incomodato	**avrete** incomodato
incomoder**à**	incomoder**anno**	**avrà** incomodato	**avranno** incomodato
condizionale presente		*condizionale passato*	
incomod**erei**	incomod**eremmo**	**avrei** incomodato	**avremmo** incomodato
incomod**eresti**	incomod**ereste**	**avresti** incomodato	**avreste** incomodato
incomod**erebbe**	incomod**erebbero**	**avrebbe** incomodato	**avrebbero** incomodato
congiuntivo presente		*congiuntivo passato*	
incomod**i**	incomod**iamo**	**abbia** incomodato	**abbiamo** incomodato
incomod**i**	incomod**iate**	**abbia** incomodato	**abbiate** incomodato
incomod**i**	incomod**ino**	**abbia** incomodato	**abbiano** incomodato
congiuntivo imperfetto		*congiuntivo trapassato*	
incomoda**ssi**	incomoda**ssimo**	**avessi** incomodato	**avessimo** incomodato
incomoda**ssi**	incomoda**ste**	**avessi** incomodato	**aveste** incomodato
incomoda**sse**	incomoda**ssero**	**avesse** incomodato	**avessero** incomodato
imperativo			
	incomodiamo		
incomoda; non incomodare	incomodate		
incomodi	incomodino		

I

to meet, to encounter — incontrare

gerundio **incontrando** participio passato **incontrato**

SINGULAR	PLURAL	SINGULAR	PLURAL
indicativo presente		passato prossimo	
incontr**o**	incontr**iamo**	**ho** incontrato	**abbiamo** incontrato
incontr**i**	incontr**ate**	**hai** incontrato	**avete** incontrato
incontr**a**	incontr**ano**	**ha** incontrato	**hanno** incontrato
imperfetto		trapassato prossimo	
incontra**vo**	incontra**vamo**	**avevo** incontrato	**avevamo** incontrato
incontra**vi**	incontra**vate**	**avevi** incontrato	**avevate** incontrato
incontra**va**	incontra**vano**	**aveva** incontrato	**avevano** incontrato
passato remoto		trapassato remoto	
incontr**ai**	incontr**ammo**	**ebbi** incontrato	**avemmo** incontrato
incontr**asti**	incontr**aste**	**avesti** incontrato	**aveste** incontrato
incontr**ò**	incontr**arono**	**ebbe** incontrato	**ebbero** incontrato
futuro semplice		futuro anteriore	
incontrer**ò**	incontrer**emo**	**avrò** incontrato	**avremo** incontrato
incontrer**ai**	incontrer**ete**	**avrai** incontrato	**avrete** incontrato
incontrer**à**	incontrer**anno**	**avrà** incontrato	**avranno** incontrato
condizionale presente		condizionale passato	
incontr**erei**	incontr**eremmo**	**avrei** incontrato	**avremmo** incontrato
incontr**eresti**	incontr**ereste**	**avresti** incontrato	**avreste** incontrato
incontr**erebbe**	incontr**erebbero**	**avrebbe** incontrato	**avrebbero** incontrato
congiuntivo presente		congiuntivo passato	
incontr**i**	incontr**iamo**	**abbia** incontrato	**abbiamo** incontrato
incontr**i**	incontr**iate**	**abbia** incontrato	**abbiate** incontrato
incontr**i**	incontr**ino**	**abbia** incontrato	**abbiano** incontrato
congiuntivo imperfetto		congiuntivo trapassato	
incontra**ssi**	incontra**ssimo**	**avessi** incontrato	**avessimo** incontrato
incontra**ssi**	incontra**ste**	**avessi** incontrato	**aveste** incontrato
incontra**sse**	incontra**ssero**	**avesse** incontrato	**avessero** incontrato
imperativo			
	incontriamo		
incontra; non incontrare	incontrate		
incontri	incontrino		

indagare — to investigate, to inquire

gerundio **indagando** — participio passato **indagato**

SINGULAR	PLURAL
indicativo presente	
indag**o**	indagh**iamo**
indagh**i**	indag**ate**
indag**a**	indag**ano**
imperfetto	
indaga**vo**	indaga**vamo**
indaga**vi**	indaga**vate**
indaga**va**	indaga**vano**
passato remoto	
indag**ai**	indag**ammo**
indag**asti**	indag**aste**
indag**ò**	indag**arono**
futuro semplice	
indagher**ò**	indagher**emo**
indagher**ai**	indagher**ete**
indagher**à**	indagher**anno**
condizionale presente	
indagher**ei**	indagher**emmo**
indagher**esti**	indagher**este**
indagher**ebbe**	indagher**ebbero**
congiuntivo presente	
indagh**i**	indagh**iamo**
indagh**i**	indagh**iate**
indagh**i**	indagh**ino**
congiuntivo imperfetto	
indaga**ssi**	indaga**ssimo**
indaga**ssi**	indaga**ste**
indaga**sse**	indaga**ssero**
imperativo	
	indaghiamo
indaga; non indagare	indagate
indaghi	indaghino

SINGULAR	PLURAL
passato prossimo	
ho indagato	**abbiamo** indagato
hai indagato	**avete** indagato
ha indagato	**hanno** indagato
trapassato prossimo	
avevo indagato	**avevamo** indagato
avevi indagato	**avevate** indagato
aveva indagato	**avevano** indagato
trapassato remoto	
ebbi indagato	**avemmo** indagato
avesti indagato	**aveste** indagato
ebbe indagato	**ebbero** indagato
futuro anteriore	
avrò indagato	**avremo** indagato
avrai indagato	**avrete** indagato
avrà indagato	**avranno** indagato
condizionale passato	
avrei indagato	**avremmo** indagato
avresti indagato	**avreste** indagato
avrebbe indagato	**avrebbero** indagato
congiuntivo passato	
abbia indagato	**abbiamo** indagato
abbia indagato	**abbiate** indagato
abbia indagato	**abbiano** indagato
congiuntivo trapassato	
avessi indagato	**avessimo** indagato
avessi indagato	**aveste** indagato
avesse indagato	**avessero** indagato

gerundio **indicando** participio passato **indicato**

SINGULAR	PLURAL
indicativo presente	
indic**o**	indich**iamo**
indich**i**	indic**ate**
indic**a**	indic**ano**
imperfetto	
indica**vo**	indica**vamo**
indica**vi**	indica**vate**
indica**va**	indica**vano**
passato remoto	
indic**ai**	indic**ammo**
indic**asti**	indic**aste**
indic**ò**	indic**arono**
futuro semplice	
indicher**ò**	indicher**emo**
indicher**ai**	indicher**ete**
indicher**à**	indicher**anno**
condizionale presente	
indich**erei**	indich**eremmo**
indich**eresti**	indich**ereste**
indich**erebbe**	indich**erebbero**
congiuntivo presente	
indich**i**	indich**iamo**
indich**i**	indich**iate**
indich**i**	indich**ino**
congiuntivo imperfetto	
indica**ssi**	indica**ssimo**
indica**ssi**	indica**ste**
indica**sse**	indica**ssero**
imperativo	
	indichiamo
indica; non indicare	indicate
indichi	indichino

SINGULAR	PLURAL
passato prossimo	
ho indicato	**abbiamo** indicato
hai indicato	**avete** indicato
ha indicato	**hanno** indicato
trapassato prossimo	
avevo indicato	**avevamo** indicato
avevi indicato	**avevate** indicato
aveva indicato	**avevano** indicato
trapassato remoto	
ebbi indicato	**avemmo** indicato
avesti indicato	**aveste** indicato
ebbe indicato	**ebbero** indicato
futuro anteriore	
avrò indicato	**avremo** indicato
avrai indicato	**avrete** indicato
avrà indicato	**avranno** indicato
condizionale passato	
avrei indicato	**avremmo** indicato
avresti indicato	**avreste** indicato
avrebbe indicato	**avrebbero** indicato
congiuntivo passato	
abbia indicato	**abbiamo** indicato
abbia indicato	**abbiate** indicato
abbia indicato	**abbiano** indicato
congiuntivo trapassato	
avessi indicato	**avessimo** indicato
avessi indicato	**aveste** indicato
avesse indicato	**avessero** indicato

infliggere — to inflict

gerundio **infliggendo** — participio passato **inflitto**

SINGULAR	PLURAL
indicativo presente	
inflig**go**	inflig**giamo**
inflig**gi**	inflig**gete**
inflig**ge**	inflig**gono**
imperfetto	
infligge**vo**	infligge**vamo**
infligge**vi**	infligge**vate**
infligge**va**	infligge**vano**
passato remoto	
infli**ssi**	inflig**gemmo**
inflig**gesti**	inflig**geste**
infli**sse**	infli**ssero**
futuro semplice	
inflig**gerò**	inflig**geremo**
inflig**gerai**	inflig**gerete**
inflig**gerà**	inflig**geranno**
condizionale presente	
inflig**gerei**	inflig**geremmo**
inflig**geresti**	inflig**gereste**
inflig**gerebbe**	inflig**gerebbero**
congiuntivo presente	
inflig**ga**	inflig**giamo**
inflig**ga**	inflig**giate**
inflig**ga**	inflig**gano**
congiuntivo imperfetto	
infligge**ssi**	infligge**ssimo**
infligge**ssi**	infligge**ste**
infligge**sse**	infligge**ssero**
imperativo	
	infliggiamo
infliggi; non infliggere	infliggete
infligga	infliggano

SINGULAR	PLURAL
passato prossimo	
ho inflitto	**abbiamo** inflitto
hai inflitto	**avete** inflitto
ha inflitto	**hanno** inflitto
trapassato prossimo	
avevo inflitto	**avevamo** inflitto
avevi inflitto	**avevate** inflitto
aveva inflitto	**avevano** inflitto
trapassato remoto	
ebbi inflitto	**avemmo** inflitto
avesti inflitto	**aveste** inflitto
ebbe inflitto	**ebbero** inflitto
futuro anteriore	
avrò inflitto	**avremo** inflitto
avrai inflitto	**avrete** inflitto
avrà inflitto	**avranno** inflitto
condizionale passato	
avrei inflitto	**avremmo** inflitto
avresti inflitto	**avreste** inflitto
avrebbe inflitto	**avrebbero** inflitto
congiuntivo passato	
abbia inflitto	**abbiamo** inflitto
abbia inflitto	**abbiate** inflitto
abbia inflitto	**abbiano** inflitto
congiuntivo trapassato	
avessi inflitto	**avessimo** inflitto
avessi inflitto	**aveste** inflitto
avesse inflitto	**avessero** inflitto

to inform, to notify **informare**

gerundio **informando** participio passato **informato**

SINGULAR	PLURAL	SINGULAR	PLURAL
indicativo presente		passato prossimo	
inform**o**	inform**iamo**	**ho** informato	**abbiamo** informato
inform**i**	inform**ate**	**hai** informato	**avete** informato
inform**a**	inform**ano**	**ha** informato	**hanno** informato
imperfetto		trapassato prossimo	
informa**vo**	informa**vamo**	**avevo** informato	**avevamo** informato
informa**vi**	informa**vate**	**avevi** informato	**avevate** informato
informa**va**	informa**vano**	**aveva** informato	**avevano** informato
passato remoto		trapassato remoto	
inform**ai**	inform**ammo**	**ebbi** informato	**avemmo** informato
inform**asti**	inform**aste**	**avesti** informato	**aveste** informato
inform**ò**	inform**arono**	**ebbe** informato	**ebbero** informato
futuro semplice		futuro anteriore	
informer**ò**	informer**emo**	**avrò** informato	**avremo** informato
informer**ai**	informer**ete**	**avrai** informato	**avrete** informato
informer**à**	informer**anno**	**avrà** informato	**avranno** informato
condizionale presente		condizionale passato	
inform**erei**	inform**eremmo**	**avrei** informato	**avremmo** informato
inform**eresti**	inform**ereste**	**avresti** informato	**avreste** informato
inform**erebbe**	inform**erebbero**	**avrebbe** informato	**avrebbero** informato
congiuntivo presente		congiuntivo passato	
inform**i**	inform**iamo**	**abbia** informato	**abbiamo** informato
inform**i**	inform**iate**	**abbia** informato	**abbiate** informato
inform**i**	inform**ino**	**abbia** informato	**abbiano** informato
congiuntivo imperfetto		congiuntivo trapassato	
informa**ssi**	informa**ssimo**	**avessi** informato	**avessimo** informato
informa**ssi**	informa**ste**	**avessi** informato	**aveste** informato
informa**sse**	informa**ssero**	**avesse** informato	**avessero** informato

imperativo

	informiamo
informa; non informare	informate
informi	informino

I

iniziare — to begin, to start

gerundio **iniziando** — participio passato **iniziato**

SINGULAR	PLURAL
indicativo presente	
inizi**o**	inizi**amo**
inizi**i**	inizi**ate**
inizi**a**	inizi**ano**
imperfetto	
inizia**vo**	inizia**vamo**
inizia**vi**	inizia**vate**
inizia**va**	inizia**vano**
passato remoto	
inizi**ai**	inizi**ammo**
inizi**asti**	inizi**aste**
inizi**ò**	inizi**arono**
futuro semplice	
inizier**ò**	inizier**emo**
inizier**ai**	inizier**ete**
inizier**à**	inizier**anno**
condizionale presente	
inizi**erei**	inizi**eremmo**
inizi**eresti**	inizi**ereste**
inizi**erebbe**	inizi**erebbero**
congiuntivo presente	
inizi**i**	inizi**amo**
inizi**i**	inizi**ate**
inizi**i**	inizi**no**
congiuntivo imperfetto	
inizia**ssi**	inizia**ssimo**
inizia**ssi**	inizia**ste**
inizia**sse**	inizia**ssero**
imperativo	
	iniziamo
inizia; non iniziare	iniziate
inizi	inizino

SINGULAR	PLURAL
passato prossimo	
ho iniziato	**abbiamo** iniziato
hai iniziato	**avete** iniziato
ha iniziato	**hanno** iniziato
trapassato prossimo	
avevo iniziato	**avevamo** iniziato
avevi iniziato	**avevate** iniziato
aveva iniziato	**avevano** iniziato
trapassato remoto	
ebbi iniziato	**avemmo** iniziato
avesti iniziato	**aveste** iniziato
ebbe iniziato	**ebbero** iniziato
futuro anteriore	
avrò iniziato	**avremo** iniziato
avrai iniziato	**avrete** iniziato
avrà iniziato	**avranno** iniziato
condizionale passato	
avrei iniziato	**avremmo** iniziato
avresti iniziato	**avreste** iniziato
avrebbe iniziato	**avrebbero** iniziato
congiuntivo passato	
abbia iniziato	**abbiamo** iniziato
abbia iniziato	**abbiate** iniziato
abbia iniziato	**abbiano** iniziato
congiuntivo trapassato	
avessi iniziato	**avessimo** iniziato
avessi iniziato	**aveste** iniziato
avesse iniziato	**avessero** iniziato

to fall in love with **innamorarsi**

gerundio **innamorandosi** participio passato **innamoratosi**

indicativo presente

SINGULAR	PLURAL
mi innamor**o**	**ci** innamor**iamo**
ti innamor**i**	**vi** innamor**ate**
si innamor**a**	**si** innamor**ano**

imperfetto

SINGULAR	PLURAL
mi innamora**vo**	**ci** innamora**vamo**
ti innamora**vi**	**vi** innamora**vate**
si innamora**va**	**si** innamora**vano**

passato remoto

SINGULAR	PLURAL
mi innamor**ai**	**ci** innamor**ammo**
ti innamor**asti**	**vi** innamor**aste**
si innamor**ò**	**si** innamor**arono**

futuro semplice

SINGULAR	PLURAL
mi innamorer**ò**	**ci** innamorer**emo**
ti innamorer**ai**	**vi** innamorer**ete**
si innamorer**à**	**si** innamorer**anno**

condizionale presente

SINGULAR	PLURAL
mi innamor**erei**	**ci** innamor**eremmo**
ti innamor**eresti**	**vi** innamor**ereste**
si innamor**erebbe**	**si** innamor**erebbero**

congiuntivo presente

SINGULAR	PLURAL
mi innamor**i**	**ci** innamor**iamo**
ti innamor**i**	**vi** innamor**iate**
si innamor**i**	**si** innamor**ino**

congiuntivo imperfetto

SINGULAR	PLURAL
mi innamora**ssi**	**ci** innamora**ssimo**
ti innamora**ssi**	**vi** innamora**ste**
si innamora**sse**	**si** innamora**ssero**

imperativo

SINGULAR	PLURAL
	innamoriamoci
innamorati; non innamorarti/ non ti innamorare	innamoratevi
si innamori	si innamorino

passato prossimo

SINGULAR	PLURAL
mi sono innamorato(a)	**ci siamo** innamorati(e)
ti sei innamorato(a)	**vi siete** innamorati(e)
si è innamorato(a)	**si sono** innamorati(e)

trapassato prossimo

SINGULAR	PLURAL
mi ero innamorato(a)	**ci eravamo** innamorati(e)
ti eri innamorato(a)	**vi eravate** innamorati(e)
si era innamorato(a)	**si erano** innamorati(e)

trapassato remoto

SINGULAR	PLURAL
mi fui innamorato(a)	**ci fummo** innamorati(e)
ti fosti innamorato(a)	**vi foste** innamorati(e)
si fu innamorato(a)	**si furono** innamorati(e)

futuro anteriore

SINGULAR	PLURAL
mi sarò innamorato(a)	**ci saremo** innamorati(e)
ti sarai innamorato(a)	**vi sarete** innamorati(e)
si sarà innamorato(a)	**si saranno** innamorati(e)

condizionale passato

SINGULAR	PLURAL
mi sarei innamorato(a)	**ci saremmo** innamorati(e)
ti saresti innamorato(a)	**vi sareste** innamorati(e)
si sarebbe innamorato(a)	**si sarebbero** innamorati(e)

congiuntivo passato

SINGULAR	PLURAL
mi sia innamorato(a)	**ci siamo** innamorati(e)
ti sia innamorato(a)	**vi siate** innamorati(e)
si sia innamorato(a)	**si siano** innamorati(e)

congiuntivo trapassato

SINGULAR	PLURAL
mi fossi innamorato(a)	**ci fossimo** innamorati(e)
ti fossi innamorato(a)	**vi foste** innamorati(e)
si fosse innamorato(a)	**si fossero** innamorati(e)

inquinare — to pollute

gerundio **inquinando** participio passato **inquinato**

SINGULAR	PLURAL
indicativo presente	
inquin**o**	inquin**iamo**
inquin**i**	inquin**ate**
inquin**a**	inquin**ano**
imperfetto	
inquina**vo**	inquina**vamo**
inquina**vi**	inquina**vate**
inquina**va**	inquina**vano**
passato remoto	
inquin**ai**	inquin**ammo**
inquin**asti**	inquin**aste**
inquin**ò**	inquin**arono**
futuro semplice	
inquiner**ò**	inquiner**emo**
inquiner**ai**	inquiner**ete**
inquiner**à**	inquiner**anno**
condizionale presente	
inquin**erei**	inquin**eremmo**
inquin**eresti**	inquin**ereste**
inquin**erebbe**	inquin**erebbero**
congiuntivo presente	
inquin**i**	inquin**iamo**
inquin**i**	inquin**iate**
inquin**i**	inquin**ino**
congiuntivo imperfetto	
inquina**ssi**	inquina**ssimo**
inquina**ssi**	inquina**ste**
inquina**sse**	inquina**ssero**
imperativo	
	inquiniamo
inquina; non inquinare	inquinate
inquini	inquinino

SINGULAR	PLURAL
passato prossimo	
ho inquinato	**abbiamo** inquinato
hai inquinato	**avete** inquinato
ha inquinato	**hanno** inquinato
trapassato prossimo	
avevo inquinato	**avevamo** inquinato
avevi inquinato	**avevate** inquinato
aveva inquinato	**avevano** inquinato
trapassato remoto	
ebbi inquinato	**avemmo** inquinato
avesti inquinato	**aveste** inquinato
ebbe inquinato	**ebbero** inquinato
futuro anteriore	
avrò inquinato	**avremo** inquinato
avrai inquinato	**avrete** inquinato
avrà inquinato	**avranno** inquinato
condizionale passato	
avrei inquinato	**avremmo** inquinato
avresti inquinato	**avreste** inquinato
avrebbe inquinato	**avrebbero** inquinato
congiuntivo passato	
abbia inquinato	**abbiamo** inquinato
abbia inquinato	**abbiate** inquinato
abbia inquinato	**abbiano** inquinato
congiuntivo trapassato	
avessi inquinato	**avessimo** inquinato
avessi inquinato	**aveste** inquinato
avesse inquinato	**avessero** inquinato

gerundio **insegnando** participio passato **insegnato**

SINGULAR	PLURAL	SINGULAR	PLURAL
indicativo presente		passato prossimo	
insegn**o**	insegn**iamo**	**ho** insegnato	**abbiamo** insegnato
insegn**i**	insegn**ate**	**hai** insegnato	**avete** insegnato
insegn**a**	insegn**ano**	**ha** insegnato	**hanno** insegnato
imperfetto		trapassato prossimo	
insegna**vo**	insegna**vamo**	**avevo** insegnato	**avevamo** insegnato
insegna**vi**	insegna**vate**	**avevi** insegnato	**avevate** insegnato
insegna**va**	insegna**vano**	**aveva** insegnato	**avevano** insegnato
passato remoto		trapassato remoto	
insegn**ai**	insegn**ammo**	**ebbi** insegnato	**avemmo** insegnato
insegn**asti**	insegn**aste**	**avesti** insegnato	**aveste** insegnato
insegn**ò**	insegn**arono**	**ebbe** insegnato	**ebbero** insegnato
futuro semplice		futuro anteriore	
insegner**ò**	insegner**emo**	**avrò** insegnato	**avremo** insegnato
insegner**ai**	insegner**ete**	**avrai** insegnato	**avrete** insegnato
insegner**à**	insegner**anno**	**avrà** insegnato	**avranno** insegnato
condizionale presente		condizionale passato	
insegner**ei**	insegner**emmo**	**avrei** insegnato	**avremmo** insegnato
insegner**esti**	insegner**este**	**avresti** insegnato	**avreste** insegnato
insegner**ebbe**	insegner**ebbero**	**avrebbe** insegnato	**avrebbero** insegnato
congiuntivo presente		congiuntivo passato	
insegn**i**	insegn**iamo**	**abbia** insegnato	**abbiamo** insegnato
insegn**i**	insegn**iate**	**abbia** insegnato	**abbiate** insegnato
insegn**i**	insegn**ino**	**abbia** insegnato	**abbiano** insegnato
congiuntivo imperfetto		congiuntivo trapassato	
insegna**ssi**	insegna**ssimo**	**avessi** insegnato	**avessimo** insegnato
insegna**ssi**	insegna**ste**	**avessi** insegnato	**aveste** insegnato
insegna**sse**	insegna**ssero**	**avesse** insegnato	**avessero** insegnato
imperativo			
	insegniamo		
insegna; non insegnare	insegnate		
insegni	insegnino		

I

insistere — to insist

gerundio **insistendo** participio passato **insistito**

SINGULAR	PLURAL
indicativo presente	
insist**o**	insist**iamo**
insist**i**	insist**ete**
insist**e**	insist**ono**
imperfetto	
insiste**vo**	insiste**vamo**
insiste**vi**	insiste**vate**
insiste**va**	insiste**vano**
passato remoto	
insist**ei**, insist**etti**	insist**emmo**
insist**esti**	insist**este**
insist**é**, insist**ette**	insist**erono**, insist**ettero**
futuro semplice	
insister**ò**	insister**emo**
insister**ai**	insister**ete**
insister**à**	insister**anno**
condizionale presente	
insist**erei**	insist**eremmo**
insist**eresti**	insist**ereste**
insist**erebbe**	insist**erebbero**
congiuntivo presente	
insist**a**	insist**iamo**
insist**a**	insist**iate**
insist**a**	insist**ano**
congiuntivo imperfetto	
insiste**ssi**	insiste**ssimo**
insiste**ssi**	insiste**ste**
insiste**sse**	insiste**ssero**
imperativo	
	insistiamo
insisti; non insistere	insistete
insista	insistano

SINGULAR	PLURAL
passato prossimo	
ho insistito	**abbiamo** insistito
hai insistito	**avete** insistito
ha insistito	**hanno** insistito
trapassato prossimo	
avevo insistito	**avevamo** insistito
avevi insistito	**avevate** insistito
aveva insistito	**avevano** insistito
trapassato remoto	
ebbi insistito	**avemmo** insistito
avesti insistito	**aveste** insistito
ebbe insistito	**ebbero** insistito
futuro anteriore	
avrò insistito	**avremo** insistito
avrai insistito	**avrete** insistito
avrà insistito	**avranno** insistito
condizionale passato	
avrei insistito	**avremmo** insistito
avresti insistito	**avreste** insistito
avrebbe insistito	**avrebbero** insistito
congiuntivo passato	
abbia insistito	**abbiamo** insistito
abbia insistito	**abbiate** insistito
abbia insistito	**abbiano** insistito
congiuntivo trapassato	
avessi insistito	**avessimo** insistito
avessi insistito	**aveste** insistito
avesse insistito	**avessero** insistito

to insult — insultare

gerundio **insultando** participio passato **insultato**

SINGULAR	PLURAL	SINGULAR	PLURAL
indicativo presente		passato prossimo	
insult**o**	insult**iamo**	**ho** insultato	**abbiamo** insultato
insult**i**	insult**ate**	**hai** insultato	**avete** insultato
insult**a**	insult**ano**	**ha** insultato	**hanno** insultato
imperfetto		trapassato prossimo	
insulta**vo**	insulta**vamo**	**avevo** insultato	**avevamo** insultato
insulta**vi**	insulta**vate**	**avevi** insultato	**avevate** insultato
insulta**va**	insulta**vano**	**aveva** insultato	**avevano** insultato
passato remoto		trapassato remoto	
insult**ai**	insult**ammo**	**ebbi** insultato	**avemmo** insultato
insult**asti**	insult**aste**	**avesti** insultato	**aveste** insultato
insult**ò**	insult**arono**	**ebbe** insultato	**ebbero** insultato
futuro semplice		futuro anteriore	
insulter**ò**	insulter**emo**	**avrò** insultato	**avremo** insultato
insulter**ai**	insulter**ete**	**avrai** insultato	**avrete** insultato
insulter**à**	insulter**anno**	**avrà** insultato	**avranno** insultato
condizionale presente		condizionale passato	
insulter**ei**	insulter**emmo**	**avrei** insultato	**avremmo** insultato
insulter**esti**	insulter**este**	**avresti** insultato	**avreste** insultato
insulter**ebbe**	insulter**ebbero**	**avrebbe** insultato	**avrebbero** insultato
congiuntivo presente		congiuntivo passato	
insult**i**	insult**iamo**	**abbia** insultato	**abbiamo** insultato
insult**i**	insult**iate**	**abbia** insultato	**abbiate** insultato
insult**i**	insult**ino**	**abbia** insultato	**abbiano** insultato
congiuntivo imperfetto		congiuntivo trapassato	
insulta**ssi**	insulta**ssimo**	**avessi** insultato	**avessimo** insultato
insulta**ssi**	insulta**ste**	**avessi** insultato	**aveste** insultato
insulta**sse**	insulta**ssero**	**avesse** insultato	**avessero** insultato
imperativo			
	insultiamo		
insulta; non insultare	insultate		
insulti	insultino		

I

intendere to understand, to mean, to intend

gerundio **intendendo** participio passato **inteso**

SINGULAR	PLURAL
indicativo presente	
intend**o**	intend**iamo**
intend**i**	intend**ete**
intend**e**	intend**ono**
imperfetto	
intende**vo**	intende**vamo**
intende**vi**	intende**vate**
intende**va**	intende**vano**
passato remoto	
intes**i**	intend**emmo**
intend**esti**	intend**este**
intes**e**	intes**ero**
futuro semplice	
intender**ò**	intender**emo**
intender**ai**	intender**ete**
intender**à**	intender**anno**
condizionale presente	
intender**ei**	intender**emmo**
intender**esti**	intender**este**
intender**ebbe**	intender**ebbero**
congiuntivo presente	
intend**a**	intend**iamo**
intend**a**	intend**iate**
intend**a**	intend**ano**
congiuntivo imperfetto	
intende**ssi**	intende**ssimo**
intende**ssi**	intende**ste**
intende**sse**	intende**ssero**
imperativo	
	intendiamo
intendi; non intendere	intendete
intenda	intendano

SINGULAR	PLURAL
passato prossimo	
ho inteso	**abbiamo** inteso
hai inteso	**avete** inteso
ha inteso	**hanno** inteso
trapassato prossimo	
avevo inteso	**avevamo** inteso
avevi inteso	**avevate** inteso
aveva inteso	**avevano** inteso
trapassato remoto	
ebbi inteso	**avemmo** inteso
avesti inteso	**aveste** inteso
ebbe inteso	**ebbero** inteso
futuro anteriore	
avrò inteso	**avremo** inteso
avrai inteso	**avrete** inteso
avrà inteso	**avranno** inteso
condizionale passato	
avrei inteso	**avremmo** inteso
avresti inteso	**avreste** inteso
avrebbe inteso	**avrebbero** inteso
congiuntivo passato	
abbia inteso	**abbiamo** inteso
abbia inteso	**abbiate** inteso
abbia inteso	**abbiano** inteso
congiuntivo trapassato	
avessi inteso	**avessimo** inteso
avessi inteso	**aveste** inteso
avesse inteso	**avessero** inteso

gerundio **interrompendo** participio passato **interrotto**

SINGULAR	PLURAL
indicativo presente	
interromp**o**	interromp**iamo**
interromp**i**	interromp**ete**
interromp**e**	interromp**ono**
imperfetto	
interrompe**vo**	interrompe**vamo**
interrompe**vi**	interrompe**vate**
interrompe**va**	interrompe**vano**
passato remoto	
interrupp**i**	interromp**emmo**
interromp**esti**	interromp**este**
interrupp**e**	interrupp**ero**
futuro semplice	
interromper**ò**	interromper**emo**
interromper**ai**	interromper**ete**
interromper**à**	interromper**anno**
condizionale presente	
interromp**erei**	interromp**eremmo**
interromp**eresti**	interromp**ereste**
interromp**erebbe**	interromp**erebbero**
congiuntivo presente	
interromp**a**	interromp**iamo**
interromp**a**	interromp**iate**
interromp**a**	interromp**ano**
congiuntivo imperfetto	
interrompe**ssi**	interrompe**ssimo**
interrompe**ssi**	interrompe**ste**
interrompe**sse**	interrompe**ssero**
imperativo	
	interrompiamo
interrompi; non interrompere	interrompete
interrompa	interrompano

SINGULAR	PLURAL
passato prossimo	
ho interrotto	**abbiamo** interrotto
hai interrotto	**avete** interrotto
ha interrotto	**hanno** interrotto
trapassato prossimo	
avevo interrotto	**avevamo** interrotto
avevi interrotto	**avevate** interrotto
aveva interrotto	**avevano** interrotto
trapassato remoto	
ebbi interrotto	**avemmo** interrotto
avesti interrotto	**aveste** interrotto
ebbe interrotto	**ebbero** interrotto
futuro anteriore	
avrò interrotto	**avremo** interrotto
avrai interrotto	**avrete** interrotto
avrà interrotto	**avranno** interrotto
condizionale passato	
avrei interrotto	**avremmo** interrotto
avresti interrotto	**avreste** interrotto
avrebbe interrotto	**avrebbero** interrotto
congiuntivo passato	
abbia interrotto	**abbiamo** interrotto
abbia interrotto	**abbiate** interrotto
abbia interrotto	**abbiano** interrotto
congiuntivo trapassato	
avessi interrotto	**avessimo** interrotto
avessi interrotto	**aveste** interrotto
avesse interrotto	**avessero** interrotto

intervenire — to intervene

gerundio **intervenendo** — participio passato **intervenuto**

SINGULAR	PLURAL	SINGULAR	PLURAL
indicativo presente		*passato prossimo*	
interveng**o**	interven**iamo**	**sono** intervenuto(a)	**siamo** intervenuti(e)
intervien**i**	interven**ite**	**sei** intervenuto(a)	**siete** intervenuti(e)
intervien**e**	interveng**ono**	**è** intervenuto(a)	**sono** intervenuti(e)
imperfetto		*trapassato prossimo*	
interveni**vo**	interveni**vamo**	**ero** intervenuto(a)	**eravamo** intervenuti(e)
interveni**vi**	interveni**vate**	**eri** intervenuto(a)	**eravate** intervenuti(e)
interveni**va**	interveni**vano**	**era** intervenuto(a)	**erano** intervenuti(e)
passato remoto		*trapassato remoto*	
intervenn**i**	interven**immo**	**fui** intervenuto(a)	**fummo** intervenuti(e)
interven**isti**	interven**iste**	**fosti** intervenuto(a)	**foste** intervenuti(e)
intervenn**e**	intervenn**ero**	**fu** intervenuto(a)	**furono** intervenuti(e)
futuro semplice		*futuro anteriore*	
interverr**ò**	interverr**emo**	**sarò** intervenuto(a)	**saremo** intervenuti(e)
interverr**ai**	interverr**ete**	**sarai** intervenuto(a)	**sarete** intervenuti(e)
interverr**à**	interverr**anno**	**sarà** intervenuto(a)	**saranno** intervenuti(e)
condizionale presente		*condizionale passato*	
interverr**ei**	interverr**emmo**	**sarei** intervenuto(a)	**saremmo** intervenuti(e)
interverr**esti**	interverr**este**	**saresti** intervenuto(a)	**sareste** intervenuti(e)
interverr**ebbe**	interverr**ebbero**	**sarebbe** intervenuto(a)	**sarebbero** intervenuti(e)
congiuntivo presente		*congiuntivo passato*	
interveng**a**	interven**iamo**	**sia** intervenuto(a)	**siamo** intervenuti(e)
interveng**a**	interven**iate**	**sia** intervenuto(a)	**siate** intervenuti(e)
interveng**a**	interveng**ano**	**sia** intervenuto(a)	**siano** intervenuti(e)
congiuntivo imperfetto		*congiuntivo trapassato*	
interveni**ssi**	interveni**ssimo**	**fossi** intervenuto(a)	**fossimo** intervenuti(e)
interveni**ssi**	interveni**ste**	**fossi** intervenuto(a)	**foste** intervenuti(e)
interveni**sse**	interveni**ssero**	**fosse** intervenuto(a)	**fossero** intervenuti(e)
imperativo			
	interveniamo		
intervieni; non intervenire	intervenite		
intervenga	intervengano		

I

to introduce, to insert — introdurre

gerundio **introducendo** participio passato **introdotto**

SINGULAR	PLURAL	SINGULAR	PLURAL
indicativo presente		passato prossimo	
introduc**o**	introduc**iamo**	**ho** introdotto	**abbiamo** introdotto
introduc**i**	introduc**ete**	**hai** introdotto	**avete** introdotto
introduc**e**	introduc**ono**	**ha** introdotto	**hanno** introdotto
imperfetto		trapassato prossimo	
introduce**vo**	introduce**vamo**	**avevo** introdotto	**avevamo** introdotto
introduce**vi**	introduce**vate**	**avevi** introdotto	**avevate** introdotto
introduce**va**	introduce**vano**	**aveva** introdotto	**avevano** introdotto
passato remoto		trapassato remoto	
introdus**si**	introduc**emmo**	**ebbi** introdotto	**avemmo** introdotto
introduc**esti**	introduc**este**	**avesti** introdotto	**aveste** introdotto
introdus**se**	introdu**ssero**	**ebbe** introdotto	**ebbero** introdotto
futuro semplice		futuro anteriore	
introdurr**ò**	introdurr**emo**	**avrò** introdotto	**avremo** introdotto
introdurr**ai**	introdurr**ete**	**avrai** introdotto	**avrete** introdotto
introdurr**à**	introdurr**anno**	**avrà** introdotto	**avranno** introdotto
condizionale presente		condizionale passato	
introdurr**ei**	introdurr**emmo**	**avrei** introdotto	**avremmo** introdotto
introdurr**esti**	introdurr**este**	**avresti** introdotto	**avreste** introdotto
introdurr**ebbe**	introdurr**ebbero**	**avrebbe** introdotto	**avrebbero** introdotto
congiuntivo presente		congiuntivo passato	
introduc**a**	introduc**iamo**	**abbia** introdotto	**abbiamo** introdotto
introduc**a**	introduc**iate**	**abbia** introdotto	**abbiate** introdotto
introduc**a**	introduc**ano**	**abbia** introdotto	**abbiano** introdotto
congiuntivo imperfetto		congiuntivo trapassato	
introduce**ssi**	introduce**ssimo**	**avessi** introdotto	**avessimo** introdotto
introduce**ssi**	introduce**ste**	**avessi** introdotto	**aveste** introdotto
introduce**sse**	introduce**ssero**	**avesse** introdotto	**avessero** introdotto
imperativo			
	introduciamo		
introduci; non introdurre	introducete		
introduca	introducano		

I

invadere — to invade

gerundio **invadendo** participio passato **invaso**

indicativo presente

SINGULAR	PLURAL
invad**o**	invad**iamo**
invad**i**	invad**ete**
invad**e**	invad**ono**

imperfetto

SINGULAR	PLURAL
invade**vo**	invade**vamo**
invade**vi**	invade**vate**
invade**va**	invade**vano**

passato remoto

SINGULAR	PLURAL
invas**i**	invad**emmo**
invad**esti**	invad**este**
invas**e**	invas**ero**

futuro semplice

SINGULAR	PLURAL
invader**ò**	invader**emo**
invader**ai**	invader**ete**
invader**à**	invader**anno**

condizionale presente

SINGULAR	PLURAL
invad**erei**	invad**eremmo**
invad**eresti**	invad**ereste**
invad**erebbe**	invad**erebbero**

congiuntivo presente

SINGULAR	PLURAL
invad**a**	invad**iamo**
invad**a**	invad**iate**
invad**a**	invad**ano**

congiuntivo imperfetto

SINGULAR	PLURAL
invade**ssi**	invade**ssimo**
invade**ssi**	invade**ste**
invade**sse**	invade**ssero**

imperativo

SINGULAR	PLURAL
	invadiamo
invadi; non invadere	invadete
invada	invadano

passato prossimo

SINGULAR	PLURAL
ho invaso	**abbiamo** invaso
hai invaso	**avete** invaso
ha invaso	**hanno** invaso

trapassato prossimo

SINGULAR	PLURAL
avevo invaso	**avevamo** invaso
avevi invaso	**avevate** invaso
aveva invaso	**avevano** invaso

trapassato remoto

SINGULAR	PLURAL
ebbi invaso	**avemmo** invaso
avesti invaso	**aveste** invaso
ebbe invaso	**ebbero** invaso

futuro anteriore

SINGULAR	PLURAL
avrò invaso	**avremo** invaso
avrai invaso	**avrete** invaso
avrà invaso	**avranno** invaso

condizionale passato

SINGULAR	PLURAL
avrei invaso	**avremmo** invaso
avresti invaso	**avreste** invaso
avrebbe invaso	**avrebbero** invaso

congiuntivo passato

SINGULAR	PLURAL
abbia invaso	**abbiamo** invaso
abbia invaso	**abbiate** invaso
abbia invaso	**abbiano** invaso

congiuntivo trapassato

SINGULAR	PLURAL
avessi invaso	**avessimo** invaso
avessi invaso	**aveste** invaso
avesse invaso	**avessero** invaso

gerundio **inviando** participio passato **inviato**

SINGULAR	PLURAL	SINGULAR	PLURAL
indicativo presente		passato prossimo	
invi**o**	invi**amo**	**ho** inviato	**abbiamo** inviato
invi**i**	invi**ate**	**hai** inviato	**avete** inviato
invi**a**	invi**ano**	**ha** inviato	**hanno** inviato
imperfetto		trapassato prossimo	
invia**vo**	invia**vamo**	**avevo** inviato	**avevamo** inviato
invia**vi**	invia**vate**	**avevi** inviato	**avevate** inviato
invia**va**	invia**vano**	**aveva** inviato	**avevano** inviato
passato remoto		trapassato remoto	
invi**ai**	invi**ammo**	**ebbi** inviato	**avemmo** inviato
invi**asti**	invi**aste**	**avesti** inviato	**aveste** inviato
invi**ò**	invi**arono**	**ebbe** inviato	**ebbero** inviato
futuro semplice		futuro anteriore	
invier**ò**	invier**emo**	**avrò** inviato	**avremo** inviato
invier**ai**	invier**ete**	**avrai** inviato	**avrete** inviato
invier**à**	invier**anno**	**avrà** inviato	**avranno** inviato
condizionale presente		condizionale passato	
invier**ei**	invier**emmo**	**avrei** inviato	**avremmo** inviato
invier**esti**	invier**este**	**avresti** inviato	**avreste** inviato
invier**ebbe**	invier**ebbero**	**avrebbe** inviato	**avrebbero** inviato
congiuntivo presente		congiuntivo passato	
invi**i**	invi**amo**	**abbia** inviato	**abbiamo** inviato
invi**i**	invi**ate**	**abbia** inviato	**abbiate** inviato
invi**i**	invi**ino**	**abbia** inviato	**abbiano** inviato
congiuntivo imperfetto		congiuntivo trapassato	
invia**ssi**	invia**ssimo**	**avessi** inviato	**avessimo** inviato
invia**ssi**	invia**ste**	**avessi** inviato	**aveste** inviato
invia**sse**	invia**ssero**	**avesse** inviato	**avessero** inviato
imperativo			
	inviamo		
invia; non invitare	inviate		
invii	inviino		

I

invidiare — to envy

gerundio **invidiando** participio passato **invidiato**

SINGULAR	PLURAL	SINGULAR	PLURAL
indicativo presente		passato prossimo	
invidi**o**	invidi**amo**	**ho** invidiato	**abbiamo** invidiato
invid**i**	invidi**ate**	**hai** invidiato	**avete** invidiato
invidi**a**	invidi**ano**	**ha** invidiato	**hanno** invidiato
imperfetto		trapassato prossimo	
invidia**vo**	invidia**vamo**	**avevo** invidiato	**avevamo** invidiato
invidia**vi**	invidia**vate**	**avevi** invidiato	**avevate** invidiato
invidia**va**	invidia**vano**	**aveva** invidiato	**avevano** invidiato
passato remoto		trapassato remoto	
invidi**ai**	invidi**ammo**	**ebbi** invidiato	**avemmo** invidiato
invidi**asti**	invidi**aste**	**avesti** invidiato	**aveste** invidiato
invidi**ò**	invidi**arono**	**ebbe** invidiato	**ebbero** invidiato
futuro semplice		futuro anteriore	
invidier**ò**	invidier**emo**	**avrò** invidiato	**avremo** invidiato
invidier**ai**	invidier**ete**	**avrai** invidiato	**avrete** invidiato
invidier**à**	invidier**anno**	**avrà** invidiato	**avranno** invidiato
condizionale presente		condizionale passato	
invidier**ei**	invidier**emmo**	**avrei** invidiato	**avremmo** invidiato
invidier**esti**	invidier**este**	**avresti** invidiato	**avreste** invidiato
invidier**ebbe**	invidier**ebbero**	**avrebbe** invidiato	**avrebbero** invidiato
congiuntivo presente		congiuntivo passato	
invid**i**	invidi**amo**	**abbia** invidiato	**abbiamo** invidiato
invid**i**	invidi**ate**	**abbia** invidiato	**abbiate** invidiato
invid**i**	invid**ino**	**abbia** invidiato	**abbiano** invidiato
congiuntivo imperfetto		congiuntivo trapassato	
invidia**ssi**	invidia**ssimo**	**avessi** invidiato	**avessimo** invidiato
invidia**ssi**	invidia**ste**	**avessi** invidiato	**aveste** invidiato
invidia**sse**	invidia**ssero**	**avesse** invidiato	**avessero** invidiato
imperativo			
	invidiamo		
invidia; non invidiare	invidiate		
invidi	invidino		

gerundio **invitando** participio passato **invitato**

SINGULAR	PLURAL	SINGULAR	PLURAL
indicativo presente		passato prossimo	
invit**o**	invit**iamo**	**ho** invitato	**abbiamo** invitato
invit**i**	invit**ate**	**hai** invitato	**avete** invitato
invit**a**	invit**ano**	**ha** invitato	**hanno** invitato
imperfetto		trapassato prossimo	
invita**vo**	invita**vamo**	**avevo** invitato	**avevamo** invitato
invita**vi**	invita**vate**	**avevi** invitato	**avevate** invitato
invita**va**	invita**vano**	**aveva** invitato	**avevano** invitato
passato remoto		trapassato remoto	
invit**ai**	invit**ammo**	**ebbi** invitato	**avemmo** invitato
invit**asti**	invit**aste**	**avesti** invitato	**aveste** invitato
invit**ò**	invit**arono**	**ebbe** invitato	**ebbero** invitato
futuro semplice		futuro anteriore	
inviter**ò**	inviter**emo**	**avrò** invitato	**avremo** invitato
inviter**ai**	inviter**ete**	**avrai** invitato	**avrete** invitato
inviter**à**	inviter**anno**	**avrà** invitato	**avranno** invitato
condizionale presente		condizionale passato	
invit**erei**	invit**eremmo**	**avrei** invitato	**avremmo** invitato
invit**eresti**	invit**ereste**	**avresti** invitato	**avreste** invitato
invit**erebbe**	invit**erebbero**	**avrebbe** invitato	**avrebbero** invitato
congiuntivo presente		congiuntivo passato	
invit**i**	invit**iamo**	**abbia** invitato	**abbiamo** invitato
invit**i**	invit**iate**	**abbia** invitato	**abbiate** invitato
invit**i**	invit**ino**	**abbia** invitato	**abbiano** invitato
congiuntivo imperfetto		congiuntivo trapassato	
invita**ssi**	invita**ssimo**	**avessi** invitato	**avessimo** invitato
invita**ssi**	invita**ste**	**avessi** invitato	**aveste** invitato
invita**sse**	invita**ssero**	**avesse** invitato	**avessero** invitato
imperativo			
	invitiamo		
invita; non invitare	invitate		
inviti	invitino		

MUST KNOW VERB

involgere — to wrap (up), to envelop

gerundio **involgendo** — participio passato **involto**

indicativo presente

SINGULAR	PLURAL
involg**o**	involg**iamo**
involg**i**	involg**ete**
involg**e**	involg**ono**

imperfetto

SINGULAR	PLURAL
involge**vo**	involge**vamo**
involge**vi**	involge**vate**
involge**va**	involge**vano**

passato remoto

SINGULAR	PLURAL
invols**i**	involg**emmo**
involg**esti**	involg**este**
invols**e**	invols**ero**

futuro semplice

SINGULAR	PLURAL
involger**ò**	involger**emo**
involger**ai**	involger**ete**
involger**à**	involger**anno**

condizionale presente

SINGULAR	PLURAL
involger**ei**	involger**emmo**
involger**esti**	involger**este**
involger**ebbe**	involger**ebbero**

congiuntivo presente

SINGULAR	PLURAL
involg**a**	involg**iamo**
involg**a**	involg**iate**
involg**a**	involg**ano**

congiuntivo imperfetto

SINGULAR	PLURAL
involge**ssi**	involge**ssimo**
involge**ssi**	involge**ste**
involge**sse**	involge**ssero**

imperativo

SINGULAR	PLURAL
	involgiamo
involgi; non involgere	involgete
involga	involgano

passato prossimo

SINGULAR	PLURAL
ho involto	**abbiamo** involto
hai involto	**avete** involto
ha involto	**hanno** involto

trapassato prossimo

SINGULAR	PLURAL
avevo involto	**avevamo** involto
avevi involto	**avevate** involto
aveva involto	**avevano** involto

trapassato remoto

SINGULAR	PLURAL
ebbi involto	**avemmo** involto
avesti involto	**aveste** involto
ebbe involto	**ebbero** involto

futuro anteriore

SINGULAR	PLURAL
avrò involto	**avremo** involto
avrai involto	**avrete** involto
avrà involto	**avranno** involto

condizionale passato

SINGULAR	PLURAL
avrei involto	**avremmo** involto
avresti involto	**avreste** involto
avrebbe involto	**avrebbero** involto

congiuntivo passato

SINGULAR	PLURAL
abbia involto	**abbiamo** involto
abbia involto	**abbiate** involto
abbia involto	**abbiano** involto

congiuntivo trapassato

SINGULAR	PLURAL
avessi involto	**avessimo** involto
avessi involto	**aveste** involto
avesse involto	**avessero** involto

to teach, to instruct **istruire**

gerundio **istruendo** participio passato **istruito**

SINGULAR	PLURAL	SINGULAR	PLURAL
indicativo presente		passato prossimo	
istruisc**o**	istru**iamo**	**ho** istruito	**abbiamo** istruito
istruisc**i**	istru**ite**	**hai** istruito	**avete** istruito
istruisc**e**	istruisc**ono**	**ha** istruito	**hanno** istruito
imperfetto		trapassato prossimo	
istrui**vo**	istru**vamo**	**avevo** istruito	**avevamo** istruito
istrui**vi**	istrui**vate**	**avevi** istruito	**avevate** istruito
istrui**va**	istrui**vano**	**aveva** istruito	**avevano** istruito
passato remoto		trapassato remoto	
istru**ii**	istru**immo**	**ebbi** istruito	**avemmo** istruito
istru**isti**	istru**iste**	**avesti** istruito	**aveste** istruito
istrù**ì**	istru**irono**	**ebbe** istruito	**ebbero** istruito
futuro semplice		futuro anteriore	
istruir**ò**	istruir**emo**	**avrò** istruito	**avremo** istruito
istruir**ai**	istruir**ete**	**avrai** istruito	**avrete** istruito
istruir**à**	istruir**anno**	**avrà** istruito	**avranno** istruito
condizionale presente		condizionale passato	
istru**irei**	istru**iremmo**	**avrei** istruito	**avremmo** istruito
istru**iresti**	istru**ireste**	**avresti** istruito	**avreste** istruito
istru**irebbe**	istru**irebbero**	**avrebbe** istruito	**avrebbero** istruito
congiuntivo presente		congiuntivo passato	
istruisc**a**	istru**iamo**	**abbia** istruito	**abbiamo** istruito
istruisc**a**	istru**iate**	**abbia** istruito	**abbiate** istruito
istruisc**a**	istruisc**ano**	**abbia** istruito	**abbiano** istruito
congiuntivo imperfetto		congiuntivo trapassato	
istrui**ssi**	istrui**ssimo**	**avessi** istruito	**avessimo** istruito
istrui**ssi**	istrui**ste**	**avessi** istruito	**aveste** istruito
istrui**sse**	istrui**ssero**	**avesse** istruito	**avessero** istruito

imperativo

	istruiamo
istruisci; non istruire	istruite
istruisca	istruiscano

I

lagnarsi

to complain, to lament

gerundio **lagnandosi** participio passato **lagnatosi**

SINGULAR	PLURAL
indicativo presente	
mi lagn**o**	**ci** lagn**iamo**
ti lagn**i**	**vi** lagn**ate**
si lagn**a**	**si** lagn**ano**
imperfetto	
mi lagna**vo**	**ci** lagna**vamo**
ti lagna**vi**	**vi** lagna**vate**
si lagna**va**	**si** lagna**vano**
passato remoto	
mi lagn**ai**	**ci** lagn**ammo**
ti lagn**asti**	**vi** lagn**aste**
si lagn**ò**	**si** lagnar**ono**
futuro semplice	
mi lagner**ò**	**ci** lagner**emo**
ti lagner**ai**	**vi** lagner**ete**
si lagner**à**	**si** lagner**anno**
condizionale presente	
mi lagn**erei**	**ci** lagn**eremmo**
ti lagn**eresti**	**vi** lagn**ereste**
si lagn**erebbe**	**si** lagn**erebbero**
congiuntivo presente	
mi lagn**i**	**ci** lagn**iamo**
ti lagn**i**	**vi** lagn**iate**
si lagn**i**	**si** lagn**ino**
congiuntivo imperfetto	
mi lagna**ssi**	**ci** lagna**ssimo**
ti lagna**ssi**	**vi** lagna**ste**
si lagna**sse**	**si** lagna**ssero**
imperativo	
	lagniamoci
lagnati; non lagnarti/ non ti lagnare	lagnatevi
si lagni	si lagnino

SINGULAR	PLURAL
passato prossimo	
mi sono lagnato(a)	**ci siamo** lagnati(e)
ti sei lagnato(a)	**vi siete** lagnati(e)
si è lagnato(a)	**si sono** lagnati(e)
trapassato prossimo	
mi ero lagnato(a)	**ci eravamo** lagnati(e)
ti eri lagnato(a)	**vi eravate** lagnati(e)
si era lagnato(a)	**si erano** lagnati(e)
trapassato remoto	
mi fui lagnato(a)	**ci fummo** lagnati(e)
ti fosti lagnato(a)	**vi foste** lagnati(e)
si fu lagnato(a)	**si furono** lagnati(e)
futuro anteriore	
mi sarò lagnato(a)	**ci saremo** lagnati(e)
ti sarai lagnato(a)	**vi sarete** lagnati(e)
si sarà lagnato(a)	**si saranno** lagnati(e)
condizionale passato	
mi sarei lagnato(a)	**ci saremmo** lagnati(e)
ti saresti lagnato(a)	**vi sareste** lagnati(e)
si sarebbe lagnato(a)	**si sarebbero** lagnati(e)
congiuntivo passato	
mi sia lagnato(a)	**ci siamo** lagnati(e)
ti sia lagnato(a)	**vi siate** lagnati(e)
si sia lagnato(a)	**si siano** lagnati(e)
congiuntivo trapassato	
mi fossi lagnato(a)	**ci fossimo** lagnati(e)
ti fossi lagnato(a)	**vi foste** lagnati(e)
si fosse lagnato(a)	**si fossero** lagnati(e)

to throw **lanciare**

gerundio **lanciando** participio passato **lanciato**

SINGULAR	PLURAL	SINGULAR	PLURAL
indicativo presente		passato prossimo	
lanc**io**	lanc**iamo**	**ho** lanciato	**abbiamo** lanciato
lanc**i**	lanc**iate**	**hai** lanciato	**avete** lanciato
lanc**ia**	lanc**iano**	**ha** lanciato	**hanno** lanciato
imperfetto		trapassato prossimo	
lancia**vo**	lancia**vamo**	**avevo** lanciato	**avevamo** lanciato
lancia**vi**	lancia**vate**	**avevi** lanciato	**avevate** lanciato
lancia**va**	lancia**vano**	**aveva** lanciato	**avevano** lanciato
passato remoto		trapassato remoto	
lanc**iai**	lanc**iammo**	**ebbi** lanciato	**avemmo** lanciato
lanc**iasti**	lanc**iaste**	**avesti** lanciato	**aveste** lanciato
lanc**iò**	lanc**iarono**	**ebbe** lanciato	**ebbero** lanciato
futuro semplice		futuro anteriore	
lancer**ò**	lancer**emo**	**avrò** lanciato	**avremo** lanciato
lancer**ai**	lancer**ete**	**avrai** lanciato	**avrete** lanciato
lancer**à**	lancer**anno**	**avrà** lanciato	**avranno** lanciato
condizionale presente		condizionale passato	
lanc**erei**	lanc**eremmo**	**avrei** lanciato	**avremmo** lanciato
lanc**eresti**	lanc**ereste**	**avresti** lanciato	**avreste** lanciato
lanc**erebbe**	lanc**erebbero**	**avrebbe** lanciato	**avrebbero** lanciato
congiuntivo presente		congiuntivo passato	
lanc**i**	lanc**iamo**	**abbia** lanciato	**abbiamo** lanciato
lanc**i**	lanc**iate**	**abbia** lanciato	**abbiate** lanciato
lanc**i**	lanc**ino**	**abbia** lanciato	**abbiano** lanciato
congiuntivo imperfetto		congiuntivo trapassato	
lancia**ssi**	lancia**ssimo**	**avessi** lanciato	**avessimo** lanciato
lancia**ssi**	lancia**ste**	**avessi** lanciato	**aveste** lanciato
lancia**sse**	lancia**ssero**	**avesse** lanciato	**avessero** lanciato
imperativo			
	lanciamo		
lancia; non lanciare	lanciate		
lanci	lancino		

L

lasciare — to leave, to let

gerundio **lasciando** — participio passato **lasciato**

SINGULAR	PLURAL	SINGULAR	PLURAL
indicativo presente		passato prossimo	
lasc**io**	lasc**iamo**	**ho** lasciato	**abbiamo** lasciato
lasc**i**	lasc**iate**	**hai** lasciato	**avete** lasciato
lasc**ia**	lasc**iano**	**ha** lasciato	**hanno** lasciato
imperfetto		trapassato prossimo	
lascia**vo**	lascia**vamo**	**avevo** lasciato	**avevamo** lasciato
lascia**vi**	lascia**vate**	**avevi** lasciato	**avevate** lasciato
lascia**va**	lascia**vano**	**aveva** lasciato	**avevano** lasciato
passato remoto		trapassato remoto	
lasc**iai**	lasc**iammo**	**ebbi** lasciato	**avemmo** lasciato
lasc**iasti**	lasc**iaste**	**avesti** lasciato	**aveste** lasciato
lasc**iò**	lasc**iarono**	**ebbe** lasciato	**ebbero** lasciato
futuro semplice		futuro anteriore	
lascer**ò**	lascer**emo**	**avrò** lasciato	**avremo** lasciato
lascer**ai**	lascer**ete**	**avrai** lasciato	**avrete** lasciato
lascer**à**	lascer**anno**	**avrà** lasciato	**avranno** lasciato
condizionale presente		condizionale passato	
lasc**erei**	lasc**eremmo**	**avrei** lasciato	**avremmo** lasciato
lasc**eresti**	lasc**ereste**	**avresti** lasciato	**avreste** lasciato
lasc**erebbe**	lasc**erebbero**	**avrebbe** lasciato	**avrebbero** lasciato
congiuntivo presente		congiuntivo passato	
lasc**i**	lasc**iamo**	**abbia** lasciato	**abbiamo** lasciato
lasc**i**	lasc**iate**	**abbia** lasciato	**abbiate** lasciato
lasc**i**	lasc**ino**	**abbia** lasciato	**abbiano** lasciato
congiuntivo imperfetto		congiuntivo trapassato	
lascia**ssi**	lascia**ssimo**	**avessi** lasciato	**avessimo** lasciato
lascia**ssi**	lascia**ste**	**avessi** lasciato	**aveste** lasciato
lascia**sse**	lascia**ssero**	**avesse** lasciato	**avessero** lasciato

imperativo

	lasciamo
lascia; non lasciare	lasciate
lasci	lascino

L

gerundio **laureandosi** participio passato **laureatosi**

SINGULAR	PLURAL
indicativo presente	
mi laure**o**	**ci** laure**iamo**
ti laure**i**	**vi** laure**ate**
si laure**a**	**si** laure**ano**
imperfetto	
mi laurea**vo**	**ci** laurea**vamo**
ti laurea**vi**	**vi** laurea**vate**
si laurea**va**	**si** laurea**vano**
passato remoto	
mi laure**ai**	**ci** laure**ammo**
ti laure**asti**	**vi** laure**aste**
si laure**ò**	**si** laure**arono**
futuro semplice	
mi laureer**ò**	**ci** laureer**emo**
ti laureer**ai**	**vi** laureer**ete**
si laureer**à**	**si** laureer**anno**
condizionale presente	
mi laure**erei**	**ci** laure**eremmo**
ti laure**eresti**	**vi** laure**ereste**
si laure**erebbe**	**si** laure**erebbero**
congiuntivo presente	
mi laure**i**	**ci** laure**iamo**
ti laure**i**	**vi** laure**iate**
si laure**i**	**si** laure**ino**
congiuntivo imperfetto	
mi laurea**ssi**	**ci** laurea**ssimo**
ti laurea**ssi**	**vi** laurea**ste**
si laurea**sse**	**si** laurea**ssero**
imperativo	
	laureiamoci
laureati; non laurearti/ non ti laureare	laureatevi
si laurei	si laureino

SINGULAR	PLURAL
passato prossimo	
mi sono laureato(a)	**ci siamo** laureati(e)
ti sei laureato(a)	**vi siete** laureati(e)
si è laureato(a)	**si sono** laureati(e)
trapassato prossimo	
mi ero laureato(a)	**ci eravamo** laureati(e)
ti eri laureato(a)	**vi eravate** laureati(e)
si era laureato(a)	**si erano** laureati(e)
trapassato remoto	
mi fui laureato(a)	**ci fummo** laureati(e)
ti fosti laureato(a)	**vi foste** laureati(e)
si fu laureato(a)	**si furono** laureati(e)
futuro anteriore	
mi sarò laureato(a)	**ci saremo** laureati(e)
ti sarai laureato(a)	**vi sarete** laureati(e)
si sarà laureato(a)	**si saranno** laureati(e)
condizionale passato	
mi sarei laureato(a)	**ci saremmo** laureati(e)
ti saresti laureato(a)	**vi sareste** laureati(e)
si sarebbe laureato(a)	**si sarebbero** laureati(e)
congiuntivo passato	
mi sia laureato(a)	**ci siamo** laureati(e)
ti sia laureato(a)	**vi siate** laureati(e)
si sia laureato(a)	**si siano** laureati(e)
congiuntivo trapassato	
mi fossi laureato(a)	**ci fossimo** laureati(e)
ti fossi laureato(a)	**vi foste** laureati(e)
si fosse laureato(a)	**si fossero** laureati(e)

lavare — to wash, to clean

gerundio **lavando** participio passato **lavato**

SINGULAR	PLURAL
indicativo presente	
lav**o**	lav**iamo**
lav**i**	lav**ate**
lav**a**	lav**ano**
imperfetto	
lava**vo**	lava**vamo**
lava**vi**	lava**vate**
lava**va**	lava**vano**
passato remoto	
lav**ai**	lav**ammo**
lav**asti**	lav**aste**
lav**ò**	lav**arono**
futuro semplice	
laver**ò**	laver**emo**
laver**ai**	laver**ete**
laver**à**	laver**anno**
condizionale presente	
lav**erei**	lav**eremmo**
lav**eresti**	lav**ereste**
lav**erebbe**	lav**erebbero**
congiuntivo presente	
lav**i**	lav**iamo**
lav**i**	lav**iate**
lav**i**	lav**ino**
congiuntivo imperfetto	
lava**ssi**	lava**ssimo**
lava**ssi**	lava**ste**
lava**sse**	lava**ssero**
imperativo	
	laviamo
lava; non lavare	lavate
lavi	lavino

SINGULAR	PLURAL
passato prossimo	
ho lavato	**abbiamo** lavato
hai lavato	**avete** lavato
ha lavato	**hanno** lavato
trapassato prossimo	
avevo lavato	**avevamo** lavato
avevi lavato	**avevate** lavato
aveva lavato	**avevano** lavato
trapassato remoto	
ebbi lavato	**avemmo** lavato
avesti lavato	**aveste** lavato
ebbe lavato	**ebbero** lavato
futuro anteriore	
avrò lavato	**avremo** lavato
avrai lavato	**avrete** lavato
avrà lavato	**avranno** lavato
condizionale passato	
avrei lavato	**avremmo** lavato
avresti lavato	**avreste** lavato
avrebbe lavato	**avrebbero** lavato
congiuntivo passato	
abbia lavato	**abbiamo** lavato
abbia lavato	**abbiate** lavato
abbia lavato	**abbiano** lavato
congiuntivo trapassato	
avessi lavato	**avessimo** lavato
avessi lavato	**aveste** lavato
avesse lavato	**avessero** lavato

to wash oneself — lavarsi

gerundio lavandosi   **participio passato** lavatosi

SINGULAR	PLURAL	SINGULAR	PLURAL
indicativo presente		*passato prossimo*	
mi lav**o**	**ci** lav**iamo**	**mi sono** lavato(a)	**ci siamo** lavati(e)
ti lav**i**	**vi** lav**ate**	**ti sei** lavato(a)	**vi siete** lavati(e)
si lav**a**	**si** lav**ano**	**si è** lavato(a)	**si sono** lavati(e)
imperfetto		*trapassato prossimo*	
mi lava**vo**	**ci** lava**vamo**	**mi ero** lavato(a)	**ci eravamo** lavati(e)
ti lava**vi**	**vi** lava**vate**	**ti eri** lavato(a)	**vi eravate** lavati(e)
si lava**va**	**si** lava**vano**	**si era** lavato(a)	**si erano** lavati(e)
passato remoto		*trapassato remoto*	
mi lav**ai**	**ci** lav**ammo**	**mi fui** lavato(a)	**ci fummo** lavati(e)
ti lav**asti**	**vi** lav**aste**	**ti fosti** lavato(a)	**vi foste** lavati(e)
si lav**ò**	**si** lav**arono**	**si fu** lavato(a)	**si furono** lavati(e)
futuro semplice		*futuro anteriore*	
mi laver**ò**	**ci** laver**emo**	**mi sarò** lavato(a)	**ci saremo** lavati(e)
ti laver**ai**	**vi** laver**ete**	**ti sarai** lavato(a)	**vi sarete** lavati(e)
si laver**à**	**si** laver**anno**	**si sarà** lavato(a)	**si saranno** lavati(e)
condizionale presente		*condizionale passato*	
mi lav**erei**	**ci** lav**eremmo**	**mi sarei** lavato(a)	**ci saremmo** lavati(e)
ti lav**eresti**	**vi** lav**ereste**	**ti saresti** lavato(a)	**vi sareste** lavati(e)
si lav**erebbe**	**si** lav**erebbero**	**si sarebbe** lavato(a)	**si sarebbero** lavati(e)
congiuntivo presente		*congiuntivo passato*	
mi lav**i**	**ci** lav**iamo**	**mi sia** lavato(a)	**ci siamo** lavati(e)
ti lav**i**	**vi** lav**iate**	**ti sia** lavato(a)	**vi siate** lavati(e)
si lav**i**	**si** lav**ino**	**si sia** lavato(a)	**si siano** lavati(e)
congiuntivo imperfetto		*congiuntivo trapassato*	
mi lava**ssi**	**ci** lava**ssimo**	**mi fossi** lavato(a)	**ci fossimo** lavati(e)
ti lava**ssi**	**vi** lava**ste**	**ti fossi** lavato(a)	**vi foste** lavati(e)
si lava**sse**	**si** lava**ssero**	**si fosse** lavato(a)	**si fossero** lavati(e)
imperativo			
	laviamoci		
lavati; non lavarti/ non ti lavare	lavatevi		
si lavi	si lavino		

lavorare — to work

gerundio **lavorando** participio passato **lavorato**

SINGULAR	PLURAL	SINGULAR	PLURAL
indicativo presente		passato prossimo	
lavor**o**	lavor**iamo**	**ho** lavorato	**abbiamo** lavorato
lavor**i**	lavor**ate**	**hai** lavorato	**avete** lavorato
lavor**a**	lavor**ano**	**ha** lavorato	**hanno** lavorato
imperfetto		trapassato prossimo	
lavora**vo**	lavora**vamo**	**avevo** lavorato	**avevamo** lavorato
lavora**vi**	lavora**vate**	**avevi** lavorato	**avevate** lavorato
lavora**va**	lavora**vano**	**aveva** lavorato	**avevano** lavorato
passato remoto		trapassato remoto	
lavor**ai**	lavor**ammo**	**ebbi** lavorato	**avemmo** lavorato
lavor**asti**	lavor**aste**	**avesti** lavorato	**aveste** lavorato
lavor**ò**	lavor**arono**	**ebbe** lavorato	**ebbero** lavorato
futuro semplice		futuro anteriore	
lavorer**ò**	lavorer**emo**	**avrò** lavorato	**avremo** lavorato
lavorer**ai**	lavorer**ete**	**avrai** lavorato	**avrete** lavorato
lavorer**à**	lavorer**anno**	**avrà** lavorato	**avranno** lavorato
condizionale presente		condizionale passato	
lavor**erei**	lavor**eremmo**	**avrei** lavorato	**avremmo** lavorato
lavor**eresti**	lavor**ereste**	**avresti** lavorato	**avreste** lavorato
lavor**erebbe**	lavor**erebbero**	**avrebbe** lavorato	**avrebbero** lavorato
congiuntivo presente		congiuntivo passato	
lavor**i**	lavor**iamo**	**abbia** lavorato	**abbiamo** lavorato
lavor**i**	lavor**iate**	**abbia** lavorato	**abbiate** lavorato
lavor**i**	lavor**ino**	**abbia** lavorato	**abbiano** lavorato
congiuntivo imperfetto		congiuntivo trapassato	
lavora**ssi**	lavora**ssimo**	**avessi** lavorato	**avessimo** lavorato
lavora**ssi**	lavora**ste**	**avessi** lavorato	**aveste** lavorato
lavora**sse**	lavora**ssero**	**avesse** lavorato	**avessero** lavorato
imperativo			
	lavoriamo		
lavora; non lavorare	lavorate		
lavori	lavorino		

L

gerundio **legando** participio passato **legato**

SINGULAR	PLURAL
indicativo presente	
leg**o**	legh**iamo**
legh**i**	leg**ate**
leg**a**	leg**ano**
imperfetto	
lega**vo**	lega**vamo**
lega**vi**	lega**vate**
lega**va**	lega**vano**
passato remoto	
leg**ai**	leg**ammo**
leg**asti**	leg**aste**
leg**ò**	leg**arono**
futuro semplice	
legher**ò**	legher**emo**
legher**ai**	legher**ete**
legher**à**	legher**anno**
condizionale presente	
legh**erei**	legh**eremmo**
legh**eresti**	legh**ereste**
legh**erebbe**	legh**erebbero**
congiuntivo presente	
legh**i**	legh**iamo**
legh**i**	legh**iate**
legh**i**	legh**ino**
congiuntivo imperfetto	
lega**ssi**	lega**ssimo**
lega**ssi**	lega**ste**
lega**sse**	lega**ssero**
imperativo	
	leghiamo
lega; non legare	legate
leghi	leghino

SINGULAR	PLURAL
passato prossimo	
ho legato	**abbiamo** legato
hai legato	**avete** legato
ha legato	**hanno** legato
trapassato prossimo	
avevo legato	**avevamo** legato
avevi legato	**avevate** legato
aveva legato	**avevano** legato
trapassato remoto	
ebbi legato	**avemmo** legato
avesti legato	**aveste** legato
ebbe legato	**ebbero** legato
futuro anteriore	
avrò legato	**avremo** legato
avrai legato	**avrete** legato
avrà legato	**avranno** legato
condizionale passato	
avrei legato	**avremmo** legato
avresti legato	**avreste** legato
avrebbe legato	**avrebbero** legato
congiuntivo passato	
abbia legato	**abbiamo** legato
abbia legato	**abbiate** legato
abbia legato	**abbiano** legato
congiuntivo trapassato	
avessi legato	**avessimo** legato
avessi legato	**aveste** legato
avesse legato	**avessero** legato

leggere — to read

gerundio **leggendo** — participio passato **letto**

SINGULAR	PLURAL	SINGULAR	PLURAL
indicativo presente		passato prossimo	
legg**o**	legg**iamo**	**ho** letto	**abbiamo** letto
legg**i**	legg**ete**	**hai** letto	**avete** letto
legg**e**	legg**ono**	**ha** letto	**hanno** letto
imperfetto		trapassato prossimo	
legge**vo**	legge**vamo**	**avevo** letto	**avevamo** letto
legge**vi**	legge**vate**	**avevi** letto	**avevate** letto
legge**va**	legge**vano**	**aveva** letto	**avevano** letto
passato remoto		trapassato remoto	
less**i**	legg**emmo**	**ebbi** letto	**avemmo** letto
legg**esti**	legg**este**	**avesti** letto	**aveste** letto
less**e**	less**ero**	**ebbe** letto	**ebbero** letto
futuro semplice		futuro anteriore	
legger**ò**	legger**emo**	**avrò** letto	**avremo** letto
legger**ai**	legger**ete**	**avrai** letto	**avrete** letto
legger**à**	legger**anno**	**avrà** letto	**avranno** letto
condizionale presente		condizionale passato	
legg**erei**	legg**eremmo**	**avrei** letto	**avremmo** letto
legg**eresti**	legg**ereste**	**avresti** letto	**avreste** letto
legg**erebbe**	legg**erebbero**	**avrebbe** letto	**avrebbero** letto
congiuntivo presente		congiuntivo passato	
legg**a**	legg**iamo**	**abbia** letto	**abbiamo** letto
legg**a**	legg**iate**	**abbia** letto	**abbiate** letto
legg**a**	legg**ano**	**abbia** letto	**abbiano** letto
congiuntivo imperfetto		congiuntivo trapassato	
legge**ssi**	legge**ssimo**	**avessi** letto	**avessimo** letto
legge**ssi**	legge**ste**	**avessi** letto	**aveste** letto
legge**sse**	legge**ssero**	**avesse** letto	**avessero** letto
imperativo			
	leggiamo		
leggi; non leggere	leggete		
legga	leggano		

L

to free, to liberate **liberare**

gerundio **liberando** participio passato **liberato**

SINGULAR	PLURAL	SINGULAR	PLURAL
indicativo presente		passato prossimo	
liber**o**	liber**iamo**	**ho** liberato	**abbiamo** liberato
liber**i**	liber**ate**	**hai** liberato	**avete** liberato
liber**a**	liber**ano**	**ha** liberato	**hanno** liberato
imperfetto		trapassato prossimo	
libera**vo**	libera**vamo**	**avevo** liberato	**avevamo** liberato
libera**vi**	libera**vate**	**avevi** liberato	**avevate** liberato
libera**va**	libera**vano**	**aveva** liberato	**avevano** liberato
passato remoto		trapassato remoto	
liber**ai**	liber**ammo**	**ebbi** liberato	**avemmo** liberato
liber**asti**	liber**aste**	**avesti** liberato	**aveste** liberato
liber**ò**	liber**arono**	**ebbe** liberato	**ebbero** liberato
futuro semplice		futuro anteriore	
libere**rò**	libere**remo**	**avrò** liberato	**avremo** liberato
libere**rai**	libere**rete**	**avrai** liberato	**avrete** liberato
libere**rà**	libere**ranno**	**avrà** liberato	**avranno** liberato
condizionale presente		condizionale passato	
liber**erei**	liber**eremmo**	**avrei** liberato	**avremmo** liberato
liber**eresti**	liber**ereste**	**avresti** liberato	**avreste** liberato
liber**erebbe**	liber**erebbero**	**avrebbe** liberato	**avrebbero** liberato
congiuntivo presente		congiuntivo passato	
liber**i**	liber**iamo**	**abbia** liberato	**abbiamo** liberato
liber**i**	liber**iate**	**abbia** liberato	**abbiate** liberato
liber**i**	liber**ino**	**abbia** liberato	**abbiano** liberato
congiuntivo imperfetto		congiuntivo trapassato	
libera**ssi**	libera**ssimo**	**avessi** liberato	**avessimo** liberato
libera**ssi**	libera**ste**	**avessi** liberato	**aveste** liberato
libera**sse**	libera**ssero**	**avesse** liberato	**avessero** liberato
imperativo			
	liberiamo		
libera; non liberare	liberate		
liberi	liberino		

L

limitare

to limit, to restrict

gerundio **limitando** participio passato **limitato**

SINGULAR	PLURAL	SINGULAR	PLURAL
indicativo presente		passato prossimo	
limit**o**	limit**iamo**	**ho** limitato	**abbiamo** limitato
limit**i**	limit**ate**	**hai** limitato	**avete** limitato
limit**a**	limit**ano**	**ha** limitato	**hanno** limitato
imperfetto		trapassato prossimo	
limita**vo**	limita**vamo**	**avevo** limitato	**avevamo** limitato
limita**vi**	limita**vate**	**avevi** limitato	**avevate** limitato
limita**va**	limita**vano**	**aveva** limitato	**avevano** limitato
passato remoto		trapassato remoto	
limit**ai**	limit**ammo**	**ebbi** limitato	**avemmo** limitato
limit**asti**	limit**aste**	**avesti** limitato	**aveste** limitato
limit**ò**	limit**arono**	**ebbe** limitato	**ebbero** limitato
futuro semplice		futuro anteriore	
limiter**ò**	limiter**emo**	**avrò** limitato	**avremo** limitato
limiter**ai**	limiter**ete**	**avrai** limitato	**avrete** limitato
limiter**à**	limiter**anno**	**avrà** limitato	**avranno** limitato
condizionale presente		condizionale passato	
limit**erei**	limit**eremmo**	**avrei** limitato	**avremmo** limitato
limit**eresti**	limit**ereste**	**avresti** limitato	**avreste** limitato
limit**erebbe**	limit**erebbero**	**avrebbe** limitato	**avrebbero** limitato
congiuntivo presente		congiuntivo passato	
limit**i**	limit**iamo**	**abbia** limitato	**abbiamo** limitato
limit**i**	limit**iate**	**abbia** limitato	**abbiate** limitato
limit**i**	limit**ino**	**abbia** limitato	**abbiano** limitato
congiuntivo imperfetto		congiuntivo trapassato	
limita**ssi**	limita**ssimo**	**avessi** limitato	**avessimo** limitato
limita**ssi**	limita**ste**	**avessi** limitato	**aveste** limitato
limita**sse**	limita**ssero**	**avesse** limitato	**avessero** limitato

imperativo

	limitiamo
limita; non limitare	limitate
limiti	limitino

to liquidate, to settle **liquidare**

gerundio **liquidando** participio passato **liquidato**

SINGULAR	PLURAL	SINGULAR	PLURAL
indicativo presente		passato prossimo	
liquid**o**	liquid**iamo**	**ho** liquidato	**abbiamo** liquidato
liquid**i**	liquid**ate**	**hai** liquidato	**avete** liquidato
liquid**a**	liquid**ano**	**ha** liquidato	**hanno** liquidato
imperfetto		trapassato prossimo	
liquida**vo**	liquida**vamo**	**avevo** liquidato	**avevamo** liquidato
liquida**vi**	liquida**vate**	**avevi** liquidato	**avevate** liquidato
liquida**va**	liquida**vano**	**aveva** liquidato	**avevano** liquidato
passato remoto		trapassato remoto	
liquid**ai**	liquid**ammo**	**ebbi** liquidato	**avemmo** liquidato
liquid**asti**	liquid**aste**	**avesti** liquidato	**aveste** liquidato
liquid**ò**	liquid**arono**	**ebbe** liquidato	**ebbero** liquidato
futuro semplice		futuro anteriore	
liquider**ò**	liquider**emo**	**avrò** liquidato	**avremo** liquidato
liquider**ai**	liquider**ete**	**avrai** liquidato	**avrete** liquidato
liquider**à**	liquider**anno**	**avrà** liquidato	**avranno** liquidato
condizionale presente		condizionale passato	
liquid**erei**	liquid**eremmo**	**avrei** liquidato	**avremmo** liquidato
liquid**eresti**	liquid**ereste**	**avresti** liquidato	**avreste** liquidato
liquid**erebbe**	liquid**erebbero**	**avrebbe** liquidato	**avrebbero** liquidato
congiuntivo presente		congiuntivo passato	
liquid**i**	liquid**iamo**	**abbia** liquidato	**abbiamo** liquidato
liquid**i**	liquid**iate**	**abbia** liquidato	**abbiate** liquidato
liquid**i**	liquid**ino**	**abbia** liquidato	**abbiano** liquidato
congiuntivo imperfetto		congiuntivo trapassato	
liquida**ssi**	liquida**ssimo**	**avessi** liquidato	**avessimo** liquidato
liquida**ssi**	liquida**ste**	**avessi** liquidato	**aveste** liquidato
liquida**sse**	liquida**ssero**	**avesse** liquidato	**avessero** liquidato

imperativo

	liquidiamo
liquida; non liquidare	liquidate
liquidi	liquidino

lodare — to praise, to commend

gerundio **lodando** participio passato **lodato**

SINGULAR	PLURAL	SINGULAR	PLURAL
indicativo presente		passato prossimo	
lod**o**	lod**iamo**	**ho** lodato	**abbiamo** lodato
lod**i**	lod**ate**	**hai** lodato	**avete** lodato
lod**a**	lod**ano**	**ha** lodato	**hanno** lodato
imperfetto		trapassato prossimo	
loda**vo**	loda**vamo**	**avevo** lodato	**avevamo** lodato
loda**vi**	loda**vate**	**avevi** lodato	**avevate** lodato
loda**va**	loda**vano**	**aveva** lodato	**avevano** lodato
passato remoto		trapassato remoto	
lod**ai**	lod**ammo**	**ebbi** lodato	**avemmo** lodato
lod**asti**	lod**aste**	**avesti** lodato	**aveste** lodato
lod**ò**	lod**arono**	**ebbe** lodato	**ebbero** lodato
futuro semplice		futuro anteriore	
loder**ò**	loder**emo**	**avrò** lodato	**avremo** lodato
loder**ai**	loder**ete**	**avrai** lodato	**avrete** lodato
loder**à**	loder**anno**	**avrà** lodato	**avranno** lodato
condizionale presente		condizionale passato	
lod**erei**	lod**eremmo**	**avrei** lodato	**avremmo** lodato
lod**eresti**	lod**ereste**	**avresti** lodato	**avreste** lodato
lod**erebbe**	lod**erebbero**	**avrebbe** lodato	**avrebbero** lodato
congiuntivo presente		congiuntivo passato	
lod**i**	lod**iamo**	**abbia** lodato	**abbiamo** lodato
lod**i**	lod**iate**	**abbia** lodato	**abbiate** lodato
lod**i**	lod**ino**	**abbia** lodato	**abbiano** lodato
congiuntivo imperfetto		congiuntivo trapassato	
loda**ssi**	loda**ssimo**	**avessi** lodato	**avessimo** lodato
loda**ssi**	loda**ste**	**avessi** lodato	**aveste** lodato
loda**sse**	loda**ssero**	**avesse** lodato	**avessero** lodato
imperativo			
	lodiamo		
loda; non lodare	lodate		
lodi	lodino		

L

to struggle, to fight **lottare**

gerundio **lottando** participio passato **lottato**

SINGULAR	PLURAL	SINGULAR	PLURAL
indicativo presente		passato prossimo	
lott**o**	lott**iamo**	**ho** lottato	**abbiamo** lottato
lott**i**	lott**ate**	**hai** lottato	**avete** lottato
lott**a**	lott**ano**	**ha** lottato	**hanno** lottato
imperfetto		trapassato prossimo	
lotta**vo**	lotta**vamo**	**avevo** lottato	**avevamo** lottato
lotta**vi**	lotta**vate**	**avevi** lottato	**avevate** lottato
lotta**va**	lotta**vano**	**aveva** lottato	**avevano** lottato
passato remoto		trapassato remoto	
lott**ai**	lott**ammo**	**ebbi** lottato	**avemmo** lottato
lott**asti**	lott**aste**	**avesti** lottato	**aveste** lottato
lott**ò**	lott**arono**	**ebbe** lottato	**ebbero** lottato
futuro semplice		futuro anteriore	
lotter**ò**	lotter**emo**	**avrò** lottato	**avremo** lottato
lotter**ai**	lotter**ete**	**avrai** lottato	**avrete** lottato
lotter**à**	lotter**anno**	**avrà** lottato	**avranno** lottato
condizionale presente		condizionale passato	
lott**erei**	lott**eremmo**	**avrei** lottato	**avremmo** lottato
lott**eresti**	lott**ereste**	**avresti** lottato	**avreste** lottato
lott**erebbe**	lott**erebbero**	**avrebbe** lottato	**avrebbero** lottato
congiuntivo presente		congiuntivo passato	
lott**i**	lott**iamo**	**abbia** lottato	**abbiamo** lottato
lott**i**	lott**iate**	**abbia** lottato	**abbiate** lottato
lott**i**	lott**ino**	**abbia** lottato	**abbiano** lottato
congiuntivo imperfetto		congiuntivo trapassato	
lotta**ssi**	lotta**ssimo**	**avessi** lottato	**avessimo** lottato
lotta**ssi**	lotta**ste**	**avessi** lottato	**aveste** lottato
lotta**sse**	lotta**ssero**	**avesse** lottato	**avessero** lottato
imperativo			
	lottiamo		
lotta; non lottare	lottate		
lotti	lottino		

L

lusingare — to allure, to flatter

gerundio **lusingando** — participio passato **lusingato**

SINGULAR	PLURAL
indicativo presente	
lusing**o**	lusingh**iamo**
lusingh**i**	lusing**ate**
lusing**a**	lusing**ano**
imperfetto	
lusinga**vo**	lusinga**vamo**
lusinga**vi**	lusinga**vate**
lusinga**va**	lusinga**vano**
passato remoto	
lusing**ai**	lusing**ammo**
lusing**asti**	lusing**aste**
lusing**ò**	lusing**arono**
futuro semplice	
lusingher**ò**	lusingher**emo**
lusingher**ai**	lusingher**ete**
lusingher**à**	lusingher**anno**
condizionale presente	
lusingh**erei**	lusingh**eremmo**
lusingh**eresti**	lusingh**ereste**
lusingh**erebbe**	lusingh**erebbero**
congiuntivo presente	
lusingh**i**	lusingh**iamo**
lusingh**i**	lusingh**iate**
lusingh**i**	lusingh**ino**
congiuntivo imperfetto	
lusinga**ssi**	lusinga**ssimo**
lusinga**ssi**	lusinga**ste**
lusinga**sse**	lusinga**ssero**
imperativo	
	lusinghiamo
lusinga; non lusingare	lusingate
lusinghi	lusinghino

SINGULAR	PLURAL
passato prossimo	
ho lusingato	**abbiamo** lusingato
hai lusingato	**avete** lusingato
ha lusingato	**hanno** lusingato
trapassato prossimo	
avevo lusingato	**avevamo** lusingato
avevi lusingato	**avevate** lusingato
aveva lusingato	**avevano** lusingato
trapassato remoto	
ebbi lusingato	**avemmo** lusingato
avesti lusingato	**aveste** lusingato
ebbe lusingato	**ebbero** lusingato
futuro anteriore	
avrò lusingato	**avremo** lusingato
avrai lusingato	**avrete** lusingato
avrà lusingato	**avranno** lusingato
condizionale passato	
avrei lusingato	**avremmo** lusingato
avresti lusingato	**avreste** lusingato
avrebbe lusingato	**avrebbero** lusingato
congiuntivo passato	
abbia lusingato	**abbiamo** lusingato
abbia lusingato	**abbiate** lusingato
abbia lusingato	**abbiano** lusingato
congiuntivo trapassato	
avessi lusingato	**avessimo** lusingato
avessi lusingato	**aveste** lusingato
avesse lusingato	**avessero** lusingato

gerundio **macchiando** participio passato **macchiato**

SINGULAR	PLURAL	SINGULAR	PLURAL
indicativo presente		passato prossimo	
macchi**o**	macchi**amo**	**ho** macchiato	**abbiamo** macchiato
macchi**i**	macchi**ate**	**hai** macchiato	**avete** macchiato
macchi**a**	macchi**ano**	**ha** macchiato	**hanno** macchiato
imperfetto		trapassato prossimo	
macchia**vo**	macchia**vamo**	**avevo** macchiato	**avevamo** macchiato
macchia**vi**	macchia**vate**	**avevi** macchiato	**avevate** macchiato
macchia**va**	macchia**vano**	**aveva** macchiato	**avevano** macchiato
passato remoto		trapassato remoto	
macchi**ai**	macchi**ammo**	**ebbi** macchiato	**avemmo** macchiato
macchi**asti**	macchi**aste**	**avesti** macchiato	**aveste** macchiato
macchi**ò**	macchi**arono**	**ebbe** macchiato	**ebbero** macchiato
futuro semplice		futuro anteriore	
macchier**ò**	macchier**emo**	**avrò** macchiato	**avremo** macchiato
macchier**ai**	macchier**ete**	**avrai** macchiato	**avrete** macchiato
macchier**à**	macchier**anno**	**avrà** macchiato	**avranno** macchiato
condizionale presente		condizionale passato	
macchi**erei**	macchi**eremmo**	**avrei** macchiato	**avremmo** macchiato
macchi**eresti**	macchi**ereste**	**avresti** macchiato	**avreste** macchiato
macchi**erebbe**	macchi**erebbero**	**avrebbe** macchiato	**avrebbero** macchiato
congiuntivo presente		congiuntivo passato	
macchi**i**	macchi**amo**	**abbia** macchiato	**abbiamo** macchiato
macchi**i**	macchi**ate**	**abbia** macchiato	**abbiate** macchiato
macchi**i**	macchi**no**	**abbia** macchiato	**abbiano** macchiato
congiuntivo imperfetto		congiuntivo trapassato	
macchia**ssi**	macchia**ssimo**	**avessi** macchiato	**avessimo** macchiato
macchia**ssi**	macchia**ste**	**avessi** macchiato	**aveste** macchiato
macchia**sse**	macchia**ssero**	**avesse** macchiato	**avessero** macchiato
imperativo			
	macchiamo		
macchia; non macchiare	macchiate		
macchi	macchino		

maledire — to curse

gerundio **maledicendo** — participio passato **maledetto**

SINGULAR	PLURAL
indicativo presente	
maledic**o**	maledic**iamo**
maledic**i**	maledi**te**
maledic**e**	maledic**ono**
imperfetto	
maledice**vo**	maledice**vamo**
maledice**vi**	maledice**vate**
maledice**va**	maledice**vano**
passato remoto	
malediss**i**	maledic**emmo**
maledic**esti**	maledic**este**
malediss**e**	malediss**ero**
futuro semplice	
maledir**ò**	maledir**emo**
maledir**ai**	maledir**ete**
maledir**à**	maledir**anno**
condizionale presente	
maledir**ei**	maledir**emmo**
maledir**esti**	maledir**este**
maledir**ebbe**	maledir**ebbero**
congiuntivo presente	
maledi**ca**	maledi**ciamo**
maledi**ca**	maledi**ciate**
maledi**ca**	maledi**cano**
congiuntivo imperfetto	
maledice**ssi**	maledice**ssimo**
maledice**ssi**	malediceste
maledice**sse**	maledice**ssero**
imperativo	
	malediciamo
maledici; non maledire	maledite
maledica	maledicano

SINGULAR	PLURAL
passato prossimo	
ho maledetto	**abbiamo** maledetto
hai maledetto	**avete** maledetto
ha maledetto	**hanno** maledetto
trapassato prossimo	
avevo maledetto	**avevamo** maledetto
avevi maledetto	**avevate** maledetto
aveva maledetto	**avevano** maledetto
trapassato remoto	
ebbi maledetto	**avemmo** maledetto
avesti maledetto	**aveste** maledetto
ebbe maledetto	**ebbero** maledetto
futuro anteriore	
avrò maledetto	**avremo** maledetto
avrai maledetto	**avrete** maledetto
avrà maledetto	**avranno** maledetto
condizionale passato	
avrei maledetto	**avremmo** maledetto
avresti maledetto	**avreste** maledetto
avrebbe maledetto	**avrebbero** maledetto
congiuntivo passato	
abbia maledetto	**abbiamo** maledetto
abbia maledetto	**abbiate** maledetto
abbia maledetto	**abbiano** maledetto
congiuntivo trapassato	
avessi maledetto	**avessimo** maledetto
avessi maledetto	**aveste** maledetto
avesse maledetto	**avessero** maledetto

gerundio **maltrattando** participio passato **maltrattato**

SINGULAR	PLURAL
indicativo presente	
maltratt**o**	maltratt**iamo**
maltratt**i**	maltratt**ate**
maltratt**a**	maltratt**ano**
imperfetto	
maltratta**vo**	maltratta**vamo**
maltratta**vi**	maltratta**vate**
maltratta**va**	maltratta**vano**
passato remoto	
maltratt**ai**	maltratt**ammo**
maltratt**asti**	maltratt**aste**
maltratt**ò**	maltratt**arono**
futuro semplice	
maltratter**ò**	maltratter**emo**
maltratter**ai**	maltratter**ete**
maltratter**à**	maltratter**anno**
condizionale presente	
maltratt**erei**	maltratt**eremmo**
maltratt**eresti**	maltratt**ereste**
maltratt**erebbe**	maltratt**erebbero**
congiuntivo presente	
maltratt**i**	maltratt**iamo**
maltratt**i**	maltratt**iate**
maltratt**i**	maltratt**ino**
congiuntivo imperfetto	
maltratta**ssi**	maltratta**ssimo**
maltratta**ssi**	maltratta**ste**
maltratta**sse**	maltratta**ssero**
imperativo	
	maltrattiamo
maltratta; non maltrattare	maltrattate
maltratti	maltrattino

SINGULAR	PLURAL
passato prossimo	
ho maltrattato	**abbiamo** maltrattato
hai maltrattato	**avete** maltrattato
ha maltrattato	**hanno** maltrattato
trapassato prossimo	
avevo maltrattato	**avevamo** maltrattato
avevi maltrattato	**avevate** maltrattato
aveva maltrattato	**avevano** maltrattato
trapassato remoto	
ebbi maltrattato	**avemmo** maltrattato
avesti maltrattato	**aveste** maltrattato
ebbe maltrattato	**ebbero** maltrattato
futuro anteriore	
avrò maltrattato	**avremo** maltrattato
avrai maltrattato	**avrete** maltrattato
avrà maltrattato	**avranno** maltrattato
condizionale passato	
avrei maltrattato	**avremmo** maltrattato
avresti maltrattato	**avreste** maltrattato
avrebbe maltrattato	**avrebbero** maltrattato
congiuntivo passato	
abbia maltrattato	**abbiamo** maltrattato
abbia maltrattato	**abbiate** maltrattato
abbia maltrattato	**abbiano** maltrattato
congiuntivo trapassato	
avessi maltrattato	**avessimo** maltrattato
avessi maltrattato	**aveste** maltrattato
avesse maltrattato	**avessero** maltrattato

gerundio **mancando** participio passato **mancato**

SINGULAR	PLURAL	SINGULAR	PLURAL
indicativo presente		passato prossimo	
manc**o**	manc**hiamo**	**sono** mancato(a)	**siamo** mancati(e)
manc**hi**	manc**ate**	**sei** mancato(a)	**siete** mancati(e)
manc**a**	manc**ano**	**è** mancato(a)	**sono** mancati(e)
imperfetto		trapassato prossimo	
manca**vo**	manca**vamo**	**ero** mancato(a)	**eravamo** mancati(e)
manca**vi**	manca**vate**	**eri** mancato(a)	**eravate** mancati(e)
manca**va**	manca**vano**	**era** mancato(a)	**erano** mancati(e)
passato remoto		trapassato remoto	
manc**ai**	manc**ammo**	**fui** mancato(a)	**fummo** mancati(e)
manc**asti**	manc**aste**	**fosti** mancato(a)	**foste** mancati(e)
manc**ò**	manc**arono**	**fu** mancato(a)	**furono** mancati(e)
futuro semplice		futuro anteriore	
mancher**ò**	mancher**emo**	**sarò** mancato(a)	**saremo** mancati(e)
mancher**ai**	mancher**ete**	**sarai** mancato(a)	**sarete** mancati(e)
mancher**à**	mancher**anno**	**sarà** mancato(a)	**saranno** mancati(e)
condizionale presente		condizionale passato	
manc**herei**	manc**heremmo**	**sarei** mancato(a)	**saremmo** mancati(e)
manc**heresti**	manc**hereste**	**saresti** mancato(a)	**sareste** mancati(e)
manc**herebbe**	manc**herebbero**	**sarebbe** mancato(a)	**sarebbero** mancati(e)
congiuntivo presente		congiuntivo passato	
manc**hi**	manc**hiamo**	**sia** mancato(a)	**siamo** mancati(e)
manc**hi**	manc**hiate**	**sia** mancato(a)	**siate** mancati(e)
manc**hi**	manc**hino**	**sia** mancato(a)	**siano** mancati(e)
congiuntivo imperfetto		congiuntivo trapassato	
manca**ssi**	manca**ssimo**	**fossi** mancato(a)	**fossimo** mancati(e)
manca**ssi**	manca**ste**	**fossi** mancato(a)	**foste** mancati(e)
manca**sse**	manca**ssero**	**fosse** mancato(a)	**fossero** mancati(e)
imperativo			
	manchiamo		
manca; non mancare	mancate		
manchi	manchino		

gerundio **mandando** participio passato **mandato**

SINGULAR	PLURAL	SINGULAR	PLURAL
indicativo presente		passato prossimo	
mand**o**	mand**iamo**	**ho** mandato	**abbiamo** mandato
mand**i**	mand**ate**	**hai** mandato	**avete** mandato
mand**a**	mand**ano**	**ha** mandato	**hanno** mandato
imperfetto		trapassato prossimo	
manda**vo**	manda**vamo**	**avevo** mandato	**avevamo** mandato
manda**vi**	manda**vate**	**avevi** mandato	**avevate** mandato
manda**va**	manda**vano**	**aveva** mandato	**avevano** mandato
passato remoto		trapassato remoto	
mand**ai**	mand**ammo**	**ebbi** mandato	**avemmo** mandato
mand**asti**	mand**aste**	**avesti** mandato	**aveste** mandato
mand**ò**	mand**arono**	**ebbe** mandato	**ebbero** mandato
futuro semplice		futuro anteriore	
mander**ò**	mander**emo**	**avrò** mandato	**avremo** mandato
mander**ai**	mander**ete**	**avrai** mandato	**avrete** mandato
mander**à**	mander**anno**	**avrà** mandato	**avranno** mandato
condizionale presente		condizionale passato	
mand**erei**	mand**eremmo**	**avrei** mandato	**avremmo** mandato
mand**eresti**	mand**ereste**	**avresti** mandato	**avreste** mandato
mand**erebbe**	mand**erebbero**	**avrebbe** mandato	**avrebbero** mandato
congiuntivo presente		congiuntivo passato	
mand**i**	mand**iamo**	**abbia** mandato	**abbiamo** mandato
mand**i**	mand**iate**	**abbia** mandato	**abbiate** mandato
mand**i**	mand**ino**	**abbia** mandato	**abbiano** mandato
congiuntivo imperfetto		congiuntivo trapassato	
manda**ssi**	manda**ssimo**	**avessi** mandato	**avessimo** mandato
manda**ssi**	manda**ste**	**avessi** mandato	**aveste** mandato
manda**sse**	manda**ssero**	**avesse** mandato	**avessero** mandato
imperativo			
	mandiamo		
manda; non mandare	mandate		
mandi	mandino		

M

mangiare — to eat

gerundio **mangiando** participio passato **mangiato**

SINGULAR	PLURAL	SINGULAR	PLURAL
indicativo presente		passato prossimo	
mangi**o**	mangi**amo**	**ho** mangiato	**abbiamo** mangiato
mangi	mangi**ate**	**hai** mangiato	**avete** mangiato
mangi**a**	mangi**ano**	**ha** mangiato	**hanno** mangiato
imperfetto		trapassato prossimo	
mangia**vo**	mangia**vamo**	**avevo** mangiato	**avevamo** mangiato
mangia**vi**	mangia**vate**	**avevi** mangiato	**avevate** mangiato
mangia**va**	mangia**vano**	**aveva** mangiato	**avevano** mangiato
passato remoto		trapassato remoto	
mangi**ai**	mangi**ammo**	**ebbi** mangiato	**avemmo** mangiato
mangi**asti**	mangi**aste**	**avesti** mangiato	**aveste** mangiato
mangi**ò**	mangi**arono**	**ebbe** mangiato	**ebbero** mangiato
futuro semplice		futuro anteriore	
manger**ò**	manger**emo**	**avrò** mangiato	**avremo** mangiato
manger**ai**	manger**ete**	**avrai** mangiato	**avrete** mangiato
manger**à**	manger**anno**	**avrà** mangiato	**avranno** mangiato
condizionale presente		condizionale passato	
mang**erei**	mang**eremmo**	**avrei** mangiato	**avremmo** mangiato
mang**eresti**	mang**ereste**	**avresti** mangiato	**avreste** mangiato
mang**erebbe**	mang**erebbero**	**avrebbe** mangiato	**avrebbero** mangiato
congiuntivo presente		congiuntivo passato	
mang**i**	mangi**amo**	**abbia** mangiato	**abbiamo** mangiato
mang**i**	mangi**ate**	**abbia** mangiato	**abbiate** mangiato
mang**i**	mang**ino**	**abbia** mangiato	**abbiano** mangiato
congiuntivo imperfetto		congiuntivo trapassato	
mangia**ssi**	mangia**ssimo**	**avessi** mangiato	**avessimo** mangiato
mangia**ssi**	mangia**ste**	**avessi** mangiato	**aveste** mangiato
mangia**sse**	mangia**ssero**	**avesse** mangiato	**avessero** mangiato

imperativo

	mangiamo
mangia;	mangiate
non mangiare	
mangi	mangino

M

to maintain, to keep, to preserve **mantenere**

gerundio **mantenendo** participio passato **mantenuto**

SINGULAR	PLURAL	SINGULAR	PLURAL
indicativo presente		passato prossimo	
manteng**o**	manten**iamo**	**ho** mantenuto	**abbiamo** mantenuto
mantien**i**	manten**ete**	**hai** mantenuto	**avete** mantenuto
mantien**e**	manteng**ono**	**ha** mantenuto	**hanno** mantenuto
imperfetto		trapassato prossimo	
mantene**vo**	mantene**vamo**	**avevo** mantenuto	**avevamo** mantenuto
mantene**vi**	mantene**vate**	**avevi** mantenuto	**avevate** mantenuto
mantene**va**	mantene**vano**	**aveva** mantenuto	**avevano** mantenuto
passato remoto		trapassato remoto	
mant**enni**	mant**enemmo**	**ebbi** mantenuto	**avemmo** mantenuto
mant**enesti**	mant**eneste**	**avesti** mantenuto	**aveste** mantenuto
mant**enne**	mant**ennero**	**ebbe** mantenuto	**ebbero** mantenuto
futuro semplice		futuro anteriore	
manterr**ò**	manterr**emo**	**avrò** mantenuto	**avremo** mantenuto
manterr**ai**	manterr**ete**	**avrai** mantenuto	**avrete** mantenuto
manterr**à**	manterr**anno**	**avrà** mantenuto	**avranno** mantenuto
condizionale presente		condizionale passato	
mant**errei**	mant**erremmo**	**avrei** mantenuto	**avremmo** mantenuto
mant**erresti**	mant**erreste**	**avresti** mantenuto	**avreste** mantenuto
mant**errebbe**	mant**errebbero**	**avrebbe** mantenuto	**avrebbero** mantenuto
congiuntivo presente		congiuntivo passato	
manteng**a**	manten**iamo**	**abbia** mantenuto	**abbiamo** mantenuto
manteng**a**	manten**iate**	**abbia** mantenuto	**abbiate** mantenuto
manteng**a**	manteng**ano**	**abbia** mantenuto	**abbiano** mantenuto
congiuntivo imperfetto		congiuntivo trapassato	
mantene**ssi**	mantene**ssimo**	**avessi** mantenuto	**avessimo** mantenuto
mantene**ssi**	mantene**ste**	**avessi** mantenuto	**aveste** mantenuto
mantene**sse**	mantene**ssero**	**avesse** mantenuto	**avessero** mantenuto
imperativo			
	manteniamo		
mantieni; non mantenere	mantenete		
mantenga	mantengano		

M

mascherare — to mask

gerundio **mascherando** — participio passato **mascherato**

SINGULAR	PLURAL
indicativo presente	
maschero	mascheri**amo**
mascher**i**	mascher**ate**
mascher**a**	mascher**ano**
imperfetto	
maschera**vo**	maschera**vamo**
maschera**vi**	maschera**vate**
maschera**va**	maschera**vano**
passato remoto	
mascher**ai**	mascher**ammo**
mascher**asti**	mascher**aste**
mascher**ò**	mascher**arono**
futuro semplice	
maschere**rò**	maschere**remo**
maschere**rai**	maschere**rete**
maschere**rà**	maschere**ranno**
condizionale presente	
mascher**erei**	mascher**eremmo**
mascher**eresti**	mascher**ereste**
mascher**erebbe**	mascher**erebbero**
congiuntivo presente	
mascher**i**	mascher**iamo**
mascher**i**	mascher**iate**
mascher**i**	mascher**ino**
congiuntivo imperfetto	
maschera**ssi**	maschera**ssimo**
maschera**ssi**	maschera**ste**
maschera**sse**	maschera**ssero**
imperativo	
	mascheriamo
maschera; non mascherare	mascherate
mascheri	mascherino

SINGULAR	PLURAL
passato prossimo	
ho mascherato	**abbiamo** mascherato
hai mascherato	**avete** mascherato
ha mascherato	**hanno** mascherato
trapassato prossimo	
avevo mascherato	**avevamo** mascherato
avevi mascherato	**avevate** mascherato
aveva mascherato	**avevano** mascherato
trapassato remoto	
ebbi mascherato	**avemmo** mascherato
avesti mascherato	**aveste** mascherato
ebbe mascherato	**ebbero** mascherato
futuro anteriore	
avrò mascherato	**avremo** mascherato
avrai mascherato	**avrete** mascherato
avrà mascherato	**avranno** mascherato
condizionale passato	
avrei mascherato	**avremmo** mascherato
avresti mascherato	**avreste** mascherato
avrebbe mascherato	**avrebbero** mascherato
congiuntivo passato	
abbia mascherato	**abbiamo** mascherato
abbia mascherato	**abbiate** mascherato
abbia mascherato	**abbiano** mascherato
congiuntivo trapassato	
avessi mascherato	**avessimo** mascherato
avessi mascherato	**aveste** mascherato
avesse mascherato	**avessero** mascherato

gerundio **medicando** participio passato **medicato**

SINGULAR	PLURAL	SINGULAR	PLURAL
indicativo presente		passato prossimo	
medic**o**	medic**hiamo**	**ho** medicato	**abbiamo** medicato
medic**hi**	medic**ate**	**hai** medicato	**avete** medicato
medic**a**	medic**ano**	**ha** medicato	**hanno** medicato
imperfetto		trapassato prossimo	
medica**vo**	medica**vamo**	**avevo** medicato	**avevamo** medicato
medica**vi**	medica**vate**	**avevi** medicato	**avevate** medicato
medica**va**	medica**vano**	**aveva** medicato	**avevano** medicato
passato remoto		trapassato remoto	
medic**ai**	medic**ammo**	**ebbi** medicato	**avemmo** medicato
medic**asti**	medic**aste**	**avesti** medicato	**aveste** medicato
medic**ò**	medic**arono**	**ebbe** medicato	**ebbero** medicato
futuro semplice		futuro anteriore	
mediche**rò**	medicher**emo**	**avrò** medicato	**avremo** medicato
medicher**ai**	medicher**ete**	**avrai** medicato	**avrete** medicato
mediche**rà**	medicher**anno**	**avrà** medicato	**avranno** medicato
condizionale presente		condizionale passato	
medic**herei**	medic**heremmo**	**avrei** medicato	**avremmo** medicato
medic**heresti**	medic**hereste**	**avresti** medicato	**avreste** medicato
medic**herebbe**	medic**herebbero**	**avrebbe** medicato	**avrebbero** medicato
congiuntivo presente		congiuntivo passato	
medic**hi**	medic**hiamo**	**abbia** medicato	**abbiamo** medicato
medic**hi**	medic**hiate**	**abbia** medicato	**abbiate** medicato
medic**hi**	medic**hino**	**abbia** medicato	**abbiano** medicato
congiuntivo imperfetto		congiuntivo trapassato	
medica**ssi**	medica**ssimo**	**avessi** medicato	**avessimo** medicato
medica**ssi**	medica**ste**	**avessi** medicato	**aveste** medicato
medica**sse**	medica**ssero**	**avesse** medicato	**avessero** medicato
imperativo			
	medichiamo		
medica; non medicare	medicate		
medichi	medichino		

M

meditare — to meditate, to ponder

gerundio **meditando** — participio passato **meditato**

SINGULAR	PLURAL
indicativo presente	
medit**o**	medit**iamo**
medit**i**	medit**ate**
medit**a**	medit**ano**
imperfetto	
medita**vo**	medita**vamo**
medita**vi**	medita**vate**
medita**va**	medita**vano**
passato remoto	
medit**ai**	medit**ammo**
medit**asti**	medit**aste**
medit**ò**	medit**arono**
futuro semplice	
mediter**ò**	mediter**emo**
mediter**ai**	mediter**ete**
mediter**à**	mediter**anno**
condizionale presente	
medit**erei**	medit**eremmo**
medit**eresti**	medit**ereste**
medit**erebbe**	medit**erebbero**
congiuntivo presente	
medit**i**	medit**iamo**
medit**i**	medit**iate**
medit**i**	medit**ino**
congiuntivo imperfetto	
medita**ssi**	medita**ssimo**
medita**ssi**	medita**ste**
medita**sse**	medita**ssero**
imperativo	
	meditiamo
medita; non meditare	meditate
mediti	meditino

SINGULAR	PLURAL
passato prossimo	
ho meditato	**abbiamo** meditato
hai meditato	**avete** meditato
ha meditato	**hanno** meditato
trapassato prossimo	
avevo meditato	**avevamo** meditato
avevi meditato	**avevate** meditato
aveva meditato	**avevano** meditato
trapassato remoto	
ebbi meditato	**avemmo** meditato
avesti meditato	**aveste** meditato
ebbe meditato	**ebbero** meditato
futuro anteriore	
avrò meditato	**avremo** meditato
avrai meditato	**avrete** meditato
avrà meditato	**avranno** meditato
condizionale passato	
avrei meditato	**avremmo** meditato
avresti meditato	**avreste** meditato
avrebbe meditato	**avrebbero** meditato
congiuntivo passato	
abbia meditato	**abbiamo** meditato
abbia meditato	**abbiate** meditato
abbia meditato	**abbiano** meditato
congiuntivo trapassato	
avessi meditato	**avessimo** meditato
avessi meditato	**aveste** meditato
avesse meditato	**avessero** meditato

to lie — mentire

gerundio **mentendo** participio passato **mentito**

SINGULAR	PLURAL	SINGULAR	PLURAL
indicativo presente		passato prossimo	
ment**o**	ment**iamo**	**ho** mentito	**abbiamo** mentito
ment**i**	ment**ite**	**hai** mentito	**avete** mentito
ment**e**	ment**ono**	**ha** mentito	**hanno** mentito
imperfetto		trapassato prossimo	
menti**vo**	menti**vamo**	**avevo** mentito	**avevamo** mentito
menti**vi**	menti**vate**	**avevi** mentito	**avevate** mentito
menti**va**	menti**vano**	**aveva** mentito	**avevano** mentito
passato remoto		trapassato remoto	
ment**ii**	ment**immo**	**ebbi** mentito	**avemmo** mentito
ment**isti**	ment**iste**	**avesti** mentito	**aveste** mentito
ment**ì**	ment**irono**	**ebbe** mentito	**ebbero** mentito
futuro semplice		futuro anteriore	
mentir**ò**	mentir**emo**	**avrò** mentito	**avremo** mentito
mentir**ai**	mentir**ete**	**avrai** mentito	**avrete** mentito
mentir**à**	mentir**anno**	**avrà** mentito	**avranno** mentito
condizionale presente		condizionale passato	
ment**irei**	ment**iremmo**	**avrei** mentito	**avremmo** mentito
ment**iresti**	ment**ireste**	**avresti** mentito	**avreste** mentito
ment**irebbe**	ment**irebbero**	**avrebbe** mentito	**avrebbero** mentito
congiuntivo presente		congiuntivo passato	
ment**a**	ment**iamo**	**abbia** mentito	**abbiamo** mentito
ment**a**	ment**iate**	**abbia** mentito	**abbiate** mentito
ment**a**	ment**ano**	**abbia** mentito	**abbiano** mentito
congiuntivo imperfetto		congiuntivo trapassato	
menti**ssi**	menti**ssimo**	**avessi** mentito	**avessimo** mentito
menti**ssi**	menti**ste**	**avessi** mentito	**aveste** mentito
menti**sse**	menti**ssero**	**avesse** mentito	**avessero** mentito
imperativo			
	mentiamo		
menti; non mentire	mentite		
menta	mentano		

M

meraviglare — to astonish

gerundio **meravigliando** participio passato **meravigliato**

SINGULAR	PLURAL
indicativo presente	
meraviglio	meravigliamo
meravigli	meravigliate
meraviglia	meravigliano
imperfetto	
meravigliavo	meravigliavamo
meravigliavi	meravigliavate
meravigliava	meravigliavano
passato remoto	
meravigliai	meravigliammo
meravigliasti	meravigliaste
meravigliò	meravigliarono
futuro semplice	
meraviglierò	meraviglieremo
meraviglierai	meraviglierete
meraviglierà	meraviglieranno
condizionale presente	
meraviglierei	meraviglieremmo
meraviglieresti	meravigliereste
meraviglierebbe	meraviglierebbero
congiuntivo presente	
meravigli	meravigliamo
meravigli	meravigliate
meravigli	meraviglino
congiuntivo imperfetto	
meravigliassi	meravigliassimo
meravigliassi	meravigliaste
meravigliasse	meravigliassero
imperativo	
	meravigliamo
meraviglia; non meravigliare	meravigliate
meravigli	meraviglino

SINGULAR	PLURAL
passato prossimo	
ho meravigliato	**abbiamo** meravigliato
hai meravigliato	**avete** meravigliato
ha meravigliato	**hanno** meravigliato
trapassato prossimo	
avevo meravigliato	**avevamo** meravigliato
avevi meravigliato	**avevate** meravigliato
aveva meravigliato	**avevano** meravigliato
trapassato remoto	
ebbi meravigliato	**avemmo** meravigliato
avesti meravigliato	**aveste** meravigliato
ebbe meravigliato	**ebbero** meravigliato
futuro anteriore	
avrò meravigliato	**avremo** meravigliato
avrai meravigliato	**avrete** meravigliato
avrà meravigliato	**avranno** meravigliato
condizionale passato	
avrei meravigliato	**avremmo** meravigliato
avresti meravigliato	**avreste** meravigliato
avrebbe meravigliato	**avrebbero** meravigliato
congiuntivo passato	
abbia meravigliato	**abbiamo** meravigliato
abbia meravigliato	**abbiate** meravigliato
abbia meravigliato	**abbiano** meravigliato
congiuntivo trapassato	
avessi meravigliato	**avessimo** meravigliato
avessi meravigliato	**aveste** meravigliato
avesse meravigliato	**avessero** meravigliato

gerundio **meritando**

participio passato **meritato**

SINGULAR	PLURAL
indicativo presente	
merit**o**	merit**iamo**
merit**i**	merit**ate**
merit**a**	merit**ano**
imperfetto	
merita**vo**	merita**vamo**
merita**vi**	merita**vate**
merita**va**	merita**vano**
passato remoto	
merit**ai**	merit**ammo**
merit**asti**	merit**aste**
merit**ò**	merit**arono**
futuro semplice	
meriter**ò**	meriter**emo**
meriter**ai**	meriter**ete**
meriter**à**	meriter**anno**
condizionale presente	
merit**erei**	merit**eremmo**
merit**eresti**	merit**ereste**
merit**erebbe**	merit**erebbero**
congiuntivo presente	
merit**i**	merit**iamo**
merit**i**	merit**iate**
merit**i**	merit**ino**
congiuntivo imperfetto	
merita**ssi**	merita**ssimo**
merita**ssi**	merita**ste**
merita**sse**	merita**ssero**
imperativo	
	meritiamo
merita; non meritare	meritate
meriti	meritino

SINGULAR	PLURAL
passato prossimo	
ho meritato	**abbiamo** meritato
hai meritato	**avete** meritato
ha meritato	**hanno** meritato
trapassato prossimo	
avevo meritato	**avevamo** meritato
avevi meritato	**avevate** meritato
aveva meritato	**avevano** meritato
trapassato remoto	
ebbi meritato	**avemmo** meritato
avesti meritato	**aveste** meritato
ebbe meritato	**ebbero** meritato
futuro anteriore	
avrò meritato	**avremo** meritato
avrai meritato	**avrete** meritato
avrà meritato	**avranno** meritato
condizionale passato	
avrei meritato	**avremmo** meritato
avresti meritato	**avreste** meritato
avrebbe meritato	**avrebbero** meritato
congiuntivo passato	
abbia meritato	**abbiamo** meritato
abbia meritato	**abbiate** meritato
abbia meritato	**abbiano** meritato
congiuntivo trapassato	
avessi meritato	**avessimo** meritato
avessi meritato	**aveste** meritato
avesse meritato	**avessero** meritato

mettere — to place, to put

gerundio **mettendo** participio passato **messo**

SINGULAR	PLURAL	SINGULAR	PLURAL
indicativo presente		passato prossimo	
mett**o**	mett**iamo**	**ho** messo	**abbiamo** messo
mett**i**	mett**ete**	**hai** messo	**avete** messo
mett**e**	mett**ono**	**ha** messo	**hanno** messo
imperfetto		trapassato prossimo	
mette**vo**	mette**vamo**	**avevo** messo	**avevamo** messo
mette**vi**	mette**vate**	**avevi** messo	**avevate** messo
mette**va**	mette**vano**	**aveva** messo	**avevano** messo
passato remoto		trapassato remoto	
mis**i**	mett**emmo**	**ebbi** messo	**avemmo** messo
mett**esti**	mett**este**	**avesti** messo	**aveste** messo
mis**e**	mis**ero**	**ebbe** messo	**ebbero** messo
futuro semplice		futuro anteriore	
metter**ò**	metter**emo**	**avrò** messo	**avremo** messo
metter**ai**	metter**ete**	**avrai** messo	**avrete** messo
metter**à**	metter**anno**	**avrà** messo	**avranno** messo
condizionale presente		condizionale passato	
mett**erei**	mett**eremmo**	**avrei** messo	**avremmo** messo
mett**eresti**	mett**ereste**	**avresti** messo	**avreste** messo
mett**erebbe**	mett**erebbero**	**avrebbe** messo	**avrebbero** messo
congiuntivo presente		congiuntivo passato	
mett**a**	mett**iamo**	**abbia** messo	**abbiamo** messo
mett**a**	mett**iate**	**abbia** messo	**abbiate** messo
mett**a**	mett**ano**	**abbia** messo	**abbiano** messo
congiuntivo imperfetto		congiuntivo trapassato	
mette**ssi**	mette**ssimo**	**avessi** messo	**avessimo** messo
mette**ssi**	mette**ste**	**avessi** messo	**aveste** messo
mette**sse**	mette**ssero**	**avesse** messo	**avessero** messo
imperativo			
	mettiamo		
metti; non mettere	mettete		
metta	mettano		

to put on (clothing), to place oneself **mettersi**

gerundio **mettendosi** participio passato **messosi**

SINGULAR	PLURAL
indicativo presente	
mi mett**o**	**ci** mett**iamo**
ti mett**i**	**vi** mett**ete**
si mett**e**	**si** mett**ono**
imperfetto	
mi mette**vo**	**ci** mette**vamo**
ti mette**vi**	**vi** mette**vate**
si mette**va**	**si** mette**vano**
passato remoto	
mi mis**i**	**ci** mett**emmo**
ti mett**esti**	**vi** mett**este**
si mis**e**	**si** mis**ero**
futuro semplice	
mi metter**ò**	**ci** metter**emo**
ti metter**ai**	**vi** metter**ete**
si metter**à**	**si** metter**anno**
condizionale presente	
mi metter**ei**	**ci** metter**emmo**
ti metter**esti**	**vi** metter**este**
si metter**ebbe**	**si** metter**ebbero**
congiuntivo presente	
mi mett**a**	**ci** mett**iamo**
ti mett**a**	**vi** mett**iate**
si mett**a**	**si** mett**ano**
congiuntivo imperfetto	
mi mett**essi**	**ci** mett**essimo**
ti mett**essi**	**vi** mett**este**
si mett**esse**	**si** mett**essero**
imperativo	
	mettiamoci
mettiti; non metterti/ non ti mettere	mettetevi
si metta	si mettano

SINGULAR	PLURAL
passato prossimo	
mi sono messo(a)	**ci siamo** messi(e)
ti sei messo(a)	**vi siete** messi(e)
si è messo(a)	**si sono** messi(e)
trapassato prossimo	
mi ero messo(a)	**ci eravamo** messi(e)
ti eri messo(a)	**vi eravate** messi(e)
si era messo(a)	**si erano** messi(e)
trapassato remoto	
mi fui messo(a)	**ci fummo** messi(e)
ti fosti messo(a)	**vi foste** messi(e)
si fu messo(a)	**si furono** messi(e)
futuro anteriore	
mi sarò messo(a)	**ci saremo** messi(e)
ti sarai messo(a)	**vi sarete** messi(e)
si sarà messo(a)	**si saranno** messi(e)
condizionale passato	
mi sarei messo(a)	**ci saremmo** messi(e)
ti saresti messo(a)	**vi sareste** messi(e)
si sarebbe messo(a)	**si sarebbero** messi(e)
congiuntivo passato	
mi sia messo(a)	**ci siamo** messi(e)
ti sia messo(a)	**vi siate** messi(e)
si sia messo(a)	**si siano** messi(e)
congiuntivo trapassato	
mi fossi messo(a)	**ci fossimo** messi(e)
ti fossi messo(a)	**vi foste** messi(e)
si fosse messo(a)	**si fossero** messi(e)

migliorare — to better, to improve

gerundio **migliorando** — participio passato **migliorato**

SINGULAR	PLURAL
indicativo presente	
miglior**o**	miglior**iamo**
miglior**i**	miglior**ate**
miglior**a**	miglior**ano**
imperfetto	
migliora**vo**	migliora**vamo**
migliora**vi**	migliora**vate**
migliora**va**	migliora**vano**
passato remoto	
miglior**ai**	miglior**ammo**
miglior**asti**	miglior**aste**
miglior**ò**	miglior**arono**
futuro semplice	
migliorer**ò**	migliorer**emo**
migliorer**ai**	migliorer**ete**
migliorer**à**	migliorer**anno**
condizionale presente	
miglior**erei**	miglior**eremmo**
miglior**eresti**	miglior**ereste**
miglior**erebbe**	miglior**erebbero**
congiuntivo presente	
miglior**i**	miglior**iamo**
miglior**i**	miglior**iate**
miglior**i**	miglior**ino**
congiuntivo imperfetto	
miglior**assi**	miglior**assimo**
miglior**assi**	miglior**aste**
miglior**asse**	miglior**assero**
imperativo	
	miglioriamo
migliora; non migliorare	migliorate
migliori	migliorino

SINGULAR	PLURAL
passato prossimo	
ho migliorato	**abbiamo** migliorato
hai migliorato	**avete** migliorato
ha migliorato	**hanno** migliorato
trapassato prossimo	
avevo migliorato	**avevamo** migliorato
avevi migliorato	**avevate** migliorato
aveva migliorato	**avevano** migliorato
trapassato remoto	
ebbi migliorato	**avemmo** migliorato
avesti migliorato	**aveste** migliorato
ebbe migliorato	**ebbero** migliorato
futuro anteriore	
avrò migliorato	**avremo** migliorato
avrai migliorato	**avrete** migliorato
avrà migliorato	**avranno** migliorato
condizionale passato	
avrei migliorato	**avremmo** migliorato
avresti migliorato	**avreste** migliorato
avrebbe migliorato	**avrebbero** migliorato
congiuntivo passato	
abbia migliorato	**abbiamo** migliorato
abbia migliorato	**abbiate** migliorato
abbia migliorato	**abbiano** migliorato
congiuntivo trapassato	
avessi migliorato	**avessimo** migliorato
avessi migliorato	**aveste** migliorato
avesse migliorato	**avessero** migliorato

gerundio **mischiando** participio passato **mischiato**

SINGULAR	PLURAL
indicativo presente	
mischi**o**	mischi**amo**
mischi**i**	mischi**ate**
mischi**a**	mischi**ano**
imperfetto	
mischia**vo**	mischia**vamo**
mischia**vi**	mischia**vate**
mischia**va**	mischia**vano**
passato remoto	
mischi**ai**	mischi**ammo**
mischi**asti**	mischi**aste**
mischi**ò**	mischi**arono**
futuro semplice	
mìschier**ò**	mischier**emo**
mischier**ai**	mischier**ete**
mischier**à**	mischier**anno**
condizionale presente	
mischi**erei**	mischi**eremmo**
mischi**eresti**	mischi**ereste**
mischi**erebbe**	mischi**erebbero**
congiuntivo presente	
mischi**i**	mischi**amo**
mischi**i**	mischi**ate**
mischi**i**	mischi**no**
congiuntivo imperfetto	
mischia**ssi**	mischia**ssimo**
mischia**ssi**	mischia**ste**
mischia**sse**	mischia**ssero**
imperativo	
	mischiamo
mischia; non mischiare	mischiate
mischi	mischino

SINGULAR	PLURAL
passato prossimo	
ho mischiato	**abbiamo** mischiato
hai mischiato	**avete** mischiato
ha mischiato	**hanno** mischiato
trapassato prossimo	
avevo mischiato	**avevamo** mischiato
avevi mischiato	**avevate** mischiato
aveva mischiato	**avevano** mischiato
trapassato remoto	
ebbi mischiato	**avemmo** mischiato
avesti mischiato	**aveste** mischiato
ebbe mischiato	**ebbero** mischiato
futuro anteriore	
avrò mischiato	**avremo** mischiato
avrai mischiato	**avrete** mischiato
avrà mischiato	**avranno** mischiato
condizionale passato	
avrei mischiato	**avremmo** mischiato
avresti mischiato	**avreste** mischiato
avrebbe mischiato	**avrebbero** mischiato
congiuntivo passato	
abbia mischiato	**abbiamo** mischiato
abbia mischiato	**abbiate** mischiato
abbia mischiato	**abbiano** mischiato
congiuntivo trapassato	
avessi mischiato	**avessimo** mischiato
avessi mischiato	**aveste** mischiato
avesse mischiato	**avessero** mischiato

misurare — to measure

gerundio **misurando** participio passato **misurato**

SINGULAR	PLURAL
indicativo presente	
misur**o**	misur**iamo**
misur**i**	misur**ate**
misur**a**	misur**ano**
imperfetto	
misura**vo**	misura**vamo**
misura**vi**	misura**vate**
misura**va**	misura**vano**
passato remoto	
misur**ai**	misur**ammo**
misur**asti**	misur**aste**
misur**ò**	misur**arono**
futuro semplice	
misurer**ò**	misurer**emo**
misurer**ai**	misurer**ete**
misurer**à**	misurer**anno**
condizionale presente	
misur**erei**	misur**eremmo**
misur**eresti**	misur**ereste**
misur**erebbe**	misur**erebbero**
congiuntivo presente	
misur**i**	misur**iamo**
misur**i**	misur**iate**
misur**i**	misur**ino**
congiuntivo imperfetto	
misura**ssi**	misura**ssimo**
misura**ssi**	misura**ste**
misura**sse**	misura**ssero**
imperativo	
	misuriamo
misura; non misurare	misurate
misuri	misurino

SINGULAR	PLURAL
passato prossimo	
ho misurato	**abbiamo** misurato
hai misurato	**avete** misurato
ha misurato	**hanno** misurato
trapassato prossimo	
avevo misurato	**avevamo** misurato
avevi misurato	**avevate** misurato
aveva misurato	**avevano** misurato
trapassato remoto	
ebbi misurato	**avemmo** misurato
avesti misurato	**aveste** misurato
ebbe misurato	**ebbero** misurato
futuro anteriore	
avrò misurato	**avremo** misurato
avrai misurato	**avrete** misurato
avrà misurato	**avranno** misurato
condizionale passato	
avrei misurato	**avremmo** misurato
avresti misurato	**avreste** misurato
avrebbe misurato	**avrebbero** misurato
congiuntivo passato	
abbia misurato	**abbiamo** misurato
abbia misurato	**abbiate** misurato
abbia misurato	**abbiano** misurato
congiuntivo trapassato	
avessi misurato	**avessimo** misurato
avessi misurato	**aveste** misurato
avesse misurato	**avessero** misurato

to moderate, to curb **moderare**

gerundio **moderando** participio passato **moderato**

SINGULAR	PLURAL
indicativo presente	
moder**o**	moder**iamo**
moder**i**	moder**ate**
moder**a**	moder**ano**
imperfetto	
modera**vo**	modera**vamo**
modera**vi**	modera**vate**
modera**va**	modera**vano**
passato remoto	
moder**ai**	moder**ammo**
moder**asti**	moder**aste**
moder**ò**	moder**arono**
futuro semplice	
modere**rò**	modere**remo**
modere**rai**	modere**rete**
modere**rà**	modere**ranno**
condizionale presente	
moder**erei**	moder**eremmo**
moder**eresti**	moder**ereste**
moder**erebbe**	moder**erebbero**
congiuntivo presente	
moder**i**	moder**iamo**
moder**i**	moder**iate**
moder**i**	moder**ino**
congiuntivo imperfetto	
modera**ssi**	modera**ssimo**
modera**ssi**	modera**ste**
modera**sse**	modera**ssero**
imperativo	
	moderiamo
modera; non moderare	moderate
moderi	moderino

SINGULAR	PLURAL
passato prossimo	
ho moderato	**abbiamo** moderato
hai moderato	**avete** moderato
ha moderato	**hanno** moderato
trapassato prossimo	
avevo moderato	**avevamo** moderato
avevi moderato	**avevate** moderato
aveva moderato	**avevano** moderato
trapassato remoto	
ebbi moderato	**avemmo** moderato
avesti moderato	**aveste** moderato
ebbe moderato	**ebbero** moderato
futuro anteriore	
avrò moderato	**avremo** moderato
avrai moderato	**avrete** moderato
avrà moderato	**avranno** moderato
condizionale passato	
avrei moderato	**avremmo** moderato
avresti moderato	**avreste** moderato
avrebbe moderato	**avrebbero** moderato
congiuntivo passato	
abbia moderato	**abbiamo** moderato
abbia moderato	**abbiate** moderato
abbia moderato	**abbiano** moderato
congiuntivo trapassato	
avessi moderato	**avessimo** moderato
avessi moderato	**aveste** moderato
avesse moderato	**avessero** moderato

modificare — to modify, to alter

gerundio **modificando** participio passato **modificato**

SINGULAR	PLURAL
indicativo presente	
modifico	modifichiamo
modifichi	modificate
modifica	modificano
imperfetto	
modificavo	modificavamo
modificavi	modificavate
modificava	modificavano
passato remoto	
modificai	modificammo
modificasti	modificaste
modificò	modificarono
futuro semplice	
modificherò	modificheremo
modificherai	modificherete
modificherà	modificheranno
condizionale presente	
modificherei	modificheremmo
modificheresti	modifichereste
modificherebbe	modificherebbero
congiuntivo presente	
modifichi	modifichiamo
modifichi	modifichiate
modifichi	modifichino
congiuntivo imperfetto	
modificassi	modificassimo
modificassi	modificaste
modificasse	modificassero
imperativo	
	modifichiamo
modifica; non modificare	modificate
modifichi	modifichino

SINGULAR	PLURAL
passato prossimo	
ho modificato	abbiamo modificato
hai modificato	avete modificato
ha modificato	hanno modificato
trapassato prossimo	
avevo modificato	avevamo modificato
avevi modificato	avevate modificato
aveva modificato	avevano modificato
trapassato remoto	
ebbi modificato	avemmo modificato
avesti modificato	aveste modificato
ebbe modificato	ebbero modificato
futuro anteriore	
avrò modificato	avremo modificato
avrai modificato	avrete modificato
avrà modificato	avranno modificato
condizionale passato	
avrei modificato	avremmo modificato
avresti modificato	avreste modificato
avrebbe modificato	avrebbero modificato
congiuntivo passato	
abbia modificato	abbiamo modificato
abbia modificato	abbiate modificato
abbia modificato	abbiano modificato
congiuntivo trapassato	
avessi modificato	avessimo modificato
avessi modificato	aveste modificato
avesse modificato	avessero modificato

gerundio **mordendo** participio passato **morso**

SINGULAR	PLURAL	SINGULAR	PLURAL
indicativo presente		passato prossimo	
mord**o**	mord**iamo**	**ho** morso	**abbiamo** morso
mord**i**	mord**ete**	**hai** morso	**avete** morso
mord**e**	mord**ono**	**ha** morso	**hanno** morso
imperfetto		trapassato prossimo	
morde**vo**	morde**vamo**	**avevo** morso	**avevamo** morso
morde**vi**	morde**vate**	**avevi** morso	**avevate** morso
morde**va**	morde**vano**	**aveva** morso	**avevano** morso
passato remoto		trapassato remoto	
mor**si**	mord**emmo**	**ebbi** morso	**avemmo** morso
mord**esti**	mord**este**	**avesti** morso	**aveste** morso
mor**se**	mor**sero**	**ebbe** morso	**ebbero** morso
futuro semplice		futuro anteriore	
morder**ò**	morder**emo**	**avrò** morso	**avremo** morso
morder**ai**	morder**ete**	**avrai** morso	**avrete** morso
morder**à**	morder**anno**	**avrà** morso	**avranno** morso
condizionale presente		condizionale passato	
mord**erei**	mord**eremmo**	**avrei** morso	**avremmo** morso
mord**eresti**	mord**ereste**	**avresti** morso	**avreste** morso
mord**erebbe**	mord**erebbero**	**avrebbe** morso	**avrebbero** morso
congiuntivo presente		congiuntivo passato	
mord**a**	mord**iamo**	**abbia** morso	**abbiamo** morso
mord**a**	mord**iate**	**abbia** morso	**abbiate** morso
mord**a**	mord**ano**	**abbia** morso	**abbiano** morso
congiuntivo imperfetto		congiuntivo trapassato	
morde**ssi**	morde**ssimo**	**avessi** morso	**avessimo** morso
morde**ssi**	morde**ste**	**avessi** morso	**aveste** morso
morde**sse**	morde**ssero**	**avesse** morso	**avessero** morso
imperativo			
	mordiamo		
mordi; non mordere	mordete		
morda	mordano		

morire — to die

gerundio **morendo** participio passato **morto**

SINGULAR	PLURAL	SINGULAR	PLURAL
indicativo presente		passato prossimo	
muoi**o**	mor**iamo**	**sono** morto(a)	**siamo** morti(e)
muor**i**	mori**te**	**sei** morto(a)	**siete** morti(e)
muor**e**	muoi**ono**	**è** morto(a)	**sono** morti(e)
imperfetto		trapassato prossimo	
mori**vo**	mori**vamo**	**ero** morto(a)	**eravamo** morti(e)
mori**vi**	mori**vate**	**eri** morto(a)	**eravate** morti(e)
mori**va**	mori**vano**	**era** morto(a)	**erano** morti(e)
passato remoto		trapassato remoto	
mori**i**	mor**immo**	**fui** morto(a)	**fummo** morti(e)
mori**sti**	mori**ste**	**fosti** morto(a)	**foste** morti(e)
mor**ì**	mor**irono**	**fu** morto(a)	**furono** morti(e)
futuro semplice		futuro anteriore	
morir**ò**	morir**emo**	**sarò** morto(a)	**saremo** morti(e)
morir**ai**	morir**ete**	**sarai** morto(a)	**sarete** morti(e)
morir**à**	morir**anno**	**sarà** morto(a)	**saranno** morti(e)
condizionale presente		condizionale passato	
mori**rei**	mori**remmo**	**sarei** morto(a)	**saremmo** morti(e)
mori**resti**	mori**reste**	**saresti** morto(a)	**sareste** morti(e)
mori**rebbe**	mori**rebbero**	**sarebbe** morto(a)	**sarebbero** morti(e)
congiuntivo presente		congiuntivo passato	
muoi**a**	mor**iamo**	**sia** morto(a)	**siamo** morti(e)
muoi**a**	mor**iate**	**sia** morto(a)	**siate** morti(e)
muoi**a**	muoi**ano**	**sia** morto(a)	**siano** morti(e)
congiuntivo imperfetto		congiuntivo trapassato	
mori**ssi**	mori**ssimo**	**fossi** morto(a)	**fossimo** morti(e)
mori**ssi**	mori**ste**	**fossi** morto(a)	**foste** morti(e)
mori**sse**	mori**ssero**	**fosse** morto(a)	**fossero** morti(e)
imperativo			
	moriamo		
muori; non morire	morite		
muoia	muoiano		

M

gerundio **mostrando** participio passato **mostrato**

SINGULAR	PLURAL
indicativo presente	
mostr**o**	mostr**iamo**
mostr**i**	mostr**ate**
mostr**a**	mostr**ano**
imperfetto	
mostra**vo**	mostra**vamo**
mostra**vi**	mostra**vate**
mostra**va**	mostra**vano**
passato remoto	
mostr**ai**	mostr**ammo**
mostr**asti**	mostr**aste**
mostr**ò**	mostr**arono**
futuro semplice	
mostrer**ò**	mostrer**emo**
mostrer**ai**	mostrer**ete**
mostrer**à**	mostrer**anno**
condizionale presente	
mostr**erei**	mostr**eremmo**
mostr**eresti**	mostr**ereste**
mostr**erebbe**	mostr**erebbero**
congiuntivo presente	
mostr**i**	mostr**iamo**
mostr**i**	mostr**iate**
mostr**i**	mostr**ino**
congiuntivo imperfetto	
mostra**ssi**	mostra**ssimo**
mostra**ssi**	mostra**ste**
mostra**sse**	mostra**ssero**
imperativo	
	mostriamo
mostra; non mostrare	mostrate
mostri	mostrino

SINGULAR	PLURAL
passato prossimo	
ho mostrato	**abbiamo** mostrato
hai mostrato	**avete** mostrato
ha mostrato	**hanno** mostrato
trapassato prossimo	
avevo mostrato	**avevamo** mostrato
avevi mostrato	**avevate** mostrato
aveva mostrato	**avevano** mostrato
trapassato remoto	
ebbi mostrato	**avemmo** mostrato
avesti mostrato	**aveste** mostrato
ebbe mostrato	**ebbero** mostrato
futuro anteriore	
avrò mostrato	**avremo** mostrato
avrai mostrato	**avrete** mostrato
avrà mostrato	**avranno** mostrato
condizionale passato	
avrei mostrato	**avremmo** mostrato
avresti mostrato	**avreste** mostrato
avrebbe mostrato	**avrebbero** mostrato
congiuntivo passato	
abbia mostrato	**abbiamo** mostrato
abbia mostrato	**abbiate** mostrato
abbia mostrato	**abbiano** mostrato
congiuntivo trapassato	
avessi mostrato	**avessimo** mostrato
avessi mostrato	**aveste** mostrato
avesse mostrato	**avessero** mostrato

MEMORY TIP

When you demonstrate, you show someone how to do something.

muovere — to move

gerundio **muovendo** participio passato **mosso**

SINGULAR	PLURAL	SINGULAR	PLURAL
indicativo presente		passato prossimo	
muov**o**	muov**iamo**	**ho** mosso	**abbiamo** mosso
muov**i**	muov**ete**	**hai** mosso	**avete** mosso
muov**e**	muov**ono**	**ha** mosso	**hanno** mosso
imperfetto		trapassato prossimo	
muove**vo**	muove**vamo**	**avevo** mosso	**avevamo** mosso
muove**vi**	muove**vate**	**avevi** mosso	**avevate** mosso
muove**va**	muove**vano**	**aveva** mosso	**avevano** mosso
passato remoto		trapassato remoto	
moss**i**	muov**emmo**	**ebbi** mosso	**avemmo** mosso
muov**esti**	muov**este**	**avesti** mosso	**aveste** mosso
moss**e**	moss**ero**	**ebbe** mosso	**ebbero** mosso
futuro semplice		futuro anteriore	
muover**ò**	muover**emo**	**avrò** mosso	**avremo** mosso
muover**ai**	muover**ete**	**avrai** mosso	**avrete** mosso
muover**à**	muover**anno**	**avrà** mosso	**avranno** mosso
condizionale presente		condizionale passato	
muover**ei**	muover**emmo**	**avrei** mosso	**avremmo** mosso
muover**esti**	muover**este**	**avresti** mosso	**avreste** mosso
muover**ebbe**	muover**ebbero**	**avrebbe** mosso	**avrebbero** mosso
congiuntivo presente		congiuntivo passato	
muov**a**	muov**iamo**	**abbia** mosso	**abbiamo** mosso
muov**a**	muov**iate**	**abbia** mosso	**abbiate** mosso
muov**a**	muov**ano**	**abbia** mosso	**abbiano** mosso
congiuntivo imperfetto		congiuntivo trapassato	
muove**ssi**	muove**ssimo**	**avessi** mosso	**avessimo** mosso
muove**ssi**	muove**ste**	**avessi** mosso	**aveste** mosso
muove**sse**	muove**ssero**	**avesse** mosso	**avessero** mosso

imperativo

	muoviamo
muovi; non muovere	muovete
muova	muovano

M

gerundio **mutando** participio passato **mutato**

SINGULAR	PLURAL
indicativo presente	
mut**o**	mut**iamo**
mut**i**	mut**ate**
mut**a**	mut**ano**
imperfetto	
muta**vo**	muta**vamo**
muta**vi**	muta**vate**
muta**va**	muta**vano**
passato remoto	
mut**ai**	mut**ammo**
mut**asti**	mut**aste**
mut**ò**	mut**arono**
futuro semplice	
muter**ò**	muter**emo**
muter**ai**	muter**ete**
muter**à**	muter**anno**
condizionale presente	
mut**erei**	mut**eremmo**
mut**eresti**	mut**ereste**
mut**erebbe**	mut**erebbero**
congiuntivo presente	
mut**i**	mut**iamo**
mut**i**	mut**iate**
mut**i**	mut**ino**
congiuntivo imperfetto	
muta**ssi**	muta**ssimo**
muta**ssi**	muta**ste**
muta**sse**	muta**ssero**
imperativo	
	mutiamo
muta; non mutare	mutate
muti	mutino

SINGULAR	PLURAL
passato prossimo	
ho mutato	**abbiamo** mutato
hai mutato	**avete** mutato
ha mutato	**hanno** mutato
trapassato prossimo	
avevo mutato	**avevamo** mutato
avevi mutato	**avevate** mutato
aveva mutato	**avevano** mutato
trapassato remoto	
ebbi mutato	**avemmo** mutato
avesti mutato	**aveste** mutato
ebbe mutato	**ebbero** mutato
futuro anteriore	
avrò mutato	**avremo** mutato
avrai mutato	**avrete** mutato
avrà mutato	**avranno** mutato
condizionale passato	
avrei mutato	**avremmo** mutato
avresti mutato	**avreste** mutato
avrebbe mutato	**avrebbero** mutato
congiuntivo passato	
abbia mutato	**abbiamo** mutato
abbia mutato	**abbiate** mutato
abbia mutato	**abbiano** mutato
congiuntivo trapassato	
avessi mutato	**avessimo** mutato
avessi mutato	**aveste** mutato
avesse mutato	**avessero** mutato

nascere — to be born

gerundio **nascendo** participio passato **nato**

SINGULAR	PLURAL	SINGULAR	PLURAL
indicativo presente		passato prossimo	
nasc**o**	nasc**iamo**	**sono** nato(a)	**siamo** nati(e)
nasc**i**	nasc**ete**	**sei** nato(a)	**siete** nati(e)
nasc**e**	nasc**ono**	**è** nato(a)	**sono** nati(e)
imperfetto		trapassato prossimo	
nasce**vo**	nasce**vamo**	**ero** nato(a)	**eravamo** nati(e)
nasce**vi**	nasce**vate**	**eri** nato(a)	**eravate** nati(e)
nasce**va**	nasce**vano**	**era** nato(a)	**erano** nati(e)
passato remoto		trapassato remoto	
nacqui	nasc**emmo**	**fui** nato(a)	**fummo** nati(e)
nasc**esti**	nasc**este**	**fosti** nato(a)	**foste** nati(e)
nacque	**nacquero**	**fu** nato(a)	**furono** nati(e)
futuro semplice		futuro anteriore	
nascer**ò**	nascer**emo**	**sarò** nato(a)	**saremo** nati(e)
nascer**ai**	nascer**ete**	**sarai** nato(a)	**sarete** nati(e)
nascer**à**	nascer**anno**	**sarà** nato(a)	**saranno** nati(e)
condizionale presente		condizionale passato	
nasc**erei**	nasc**eremmo**	**sarei** nato(a)	**saremmo** nati(e)
nasc**eresti**	nasc**ereste**	**saresti** nato(a)	**sareste** nati(e)
nasc**erebbe**	nasc**erebbero**	**sarebbe** nato(a)	**sarebbero** nati(e)
congiuntivo presente		congiuntivo passato	
nasc**a**	nasc**iamo**	**sia** nato(a)	**siamo** nati(e)
nasc**a**	nasc**iate**	**sia** nato(a)	**siate** nati(e)
nasc**a**	nasc**ano**	**sia** nato(a)	**siano** nati(e)
congiuntivo imperfetto		congiuntivo trapassato	
nasc**essi**	nasc**essimo**	**fossi** nato(a)	**fossimo** nati(e)
nasc**essi**	nasc**este**	**fossi** nato(a)	**foste** nati(e)
nasc**esse**	nasc**essero**	**fosse** nato(a)	**fossero** nati(e)
imperativo			
	nasciamo		
nasci; non nascere	nascete		
nasca	nascano		

N

MUST KNOW VERB

to hide, to conceal **nascondere**

gerundio **nascondendo** participio passato **nascosto**

SINGULAR	PLURAL
indicativo presente	
nascond**o**	nascond**iamo**
nascond**i**	nascond**ete**
nascond**e**	nascond**ono**
imperfetto	
nasconde**vo**	nasconde**vamo**
nasconde**vi**	nasconde**vate**
nasconde**va**	nasconde**vano**
passato remoto	
nascosi	nascond**emmo**
nascond**esti**	nascond**este**
nascose	**nascosero**
futuro semplice	
nasconder**ò**	nasconder**emo**
nasconder**ai**	nasconder**ete**
nasconder**à**	nasconder**anno**
condizionale presente	
nascond**erei**	nascond**eremmo**
nascond**eresti**	nascond**ereste**
nascond**erebbe**	nascond**erebbero**
congiuntivo presente	
nascond**a**	nascond**iamo**
nascond**a**	nascond**iate**
nascond**a**	nascond**ano**
congiuntivo imperfetto	
nascond**essi**	nascond**essimo**
nascond**essi**	nascond**este**
nascond**esse**	nascond**essero**
imperativo	
	nascondiamo
nascondi; non nascondere	nascondete
nasconda	nascondano

SINGULAR	PLURAL
passato prossimo	
ho nascosto	**abbiamo** nascosto
hai nascosto	**avete** nascosto
ha nascosto	**hanno** nascosto
trapassato prossimo	
avevo nascosto	**avevamo** nascosto
avevi nascosto	**avevate** nascosto
aveva nascosto	**avevano** nascosto
trapassato remoto	
ebbi nascosto	**avemmo** nascosto
avesti nascosto	**aveste** nascosto
ebbe nascosto	**ebbero** nascosto
futuro anteriore	
avrò nascosto	**avremo** nascosto
avrai nascosto	**avrete** nascosto
avrà nascosto	**avranno** nascosto
condizionale passato	
avrei nascosto	**avremmo** nascosto
avresti nascosto	**avreste** nascosto
avrebbe nascosto	**avrebbero** nascosto
congiuntivo passato	
abbia nascosto	**abbiamo** nascosto
abbia nascosto	**abbiate** nascosto
abbia nascosto	**abbiano** nascosto
congiuntivo trapassato	
avessi nascosto	**avessimo** nascosto
avessi nascosto	**aveste** nascosto
avesse nascosto	**avessero** nascosto

navigare — to sail

gerundio **navigando** participio passato **navigato**

indicativo presente

SINGULAR	PLURAL
navig**o**	navigh**iamo**
navigh**i**	navig**ate**
navig**a**	navig**ano**

imperfetto

SINGULAR	PLURAL
naviga**vo**	naviga**vamo**
naviga**vi**	naviga**vate**
naviga**va**	naviga**vano**

passato remoto

SINGULAR	PLURAL
navig**ai**	navig**ammo**
navig**asti**	navig**aste**
navig**ò**	navig**arono**

futuro semplice

SINGULAR	PLURAL
navigher**ò**	navigher**emo**
navigher**ai**	navigher**ete**
navigher**à**	navigher**anno**

condizionale presente

SINGULAR	PLURAL
navigh**erei**	navigh**eremmo**
navigh**eresti**	navigh**ereste**
navigh**erebbe**	navigh**erebbero**

congiuntivo presente

SINGULAR	PLURAL
navigh**i**	navigh**iamo**
navigh**i**	navigh**iate**
navigh**i**	navigh**ino**

congiuntivo imperfetto

SINGULAR	PLURAL
navig**assi**	navig**assimo**
navig**assi**	navig**aste**
navig**asse**	navig**assero**

imperativo

SINGULAR	PLURAL
	navighiamo
naviga; non navigare	navigate
navighi	navighino

passato prossimo

SINGULAR	PLURAL
ho navigato	**abbiamo** navigato
hai navigato	**avete** navigato
ha navigato	**hanno** navigato

trapassato prossimo

SINGULAR	PLURAL
avevo navigato	**avevamo** navigato
avevi navigato	**avevate** navigato
aveva navigato	**avevano** navigato

trapassato remoto

SINGULAR	PLURAL
ebbi navigato	**avemmo** navigato
avesti navigato	**aveste** navigato
ebbe navigato	**ebbero** navigato

futuro anteriore

SINGULAR	PLURAL
avrò navigato	**avremo** navigato
avrai navigato	**avrete** navigato
avrà navigato	**avranno** navigato

condizionale passato

SINGULAR	PLURAL
avrei navigato	**avremmo** navigato
avresti navigato	**avreste** navigato
avrebbe navigato	**avrebbero** navigato

congiuntivo passato

SINGULAR	PLURAL
abbia navigato	**abbiamo** navigato
abbia navigato	**abbiate** navigato
abbia navigato	**abbiano** navigato

congiuntivo trapassato

SINGULAR	PLURAL
avessi navigato	**avessimo** navigato
avessi navigato	**aveste** navigato
avesse navigato	**avessero** navigato

gerundio **negando** participio passato **negato**

SINGULAR	PLURAL
indicativo presente	
nego	neghiamo
neghi	negate
nega	negano
imperfetto	
negavo	negavamo
negavi	negavate
negava	negavano
passato remoto	
negai	negammo
negasti	negaste
negò	negarono
futuro semplice	
negherò	negheremo
negherai	negherete
negherà	negheranno
condizionale presente	
negherei	negheremmo
negheresti	neghereste
negherebbe	negherebbero
congiuntivo presente	
neghi	neghiamo
neghi	neghiate
neghi	neghino
congiuntivo imperfetto	
negassi	negassimo
negassi	negaste
negasse	negassero
imperativo	
	neghiamo
nega; non negare	negate
neghi	neghino

SINGULAR	PLURAL
passato prossimo	
ho negato	**abbiamo** negato
hai negato	**avete** negato
ha negato	**hanno** negato
trapassato prossimo	
avevo negato	**avevamo** negato
avevi negato	**avevate** negato
aveva negato	**avevano** negato
trapassato remoto	
ebbi negato	**avemmo** negato
avesti negato	**aveste** negato
ebbe negato	**ebbero** negato
futuro anteriore	
avrò negato	**avremo** negato
avrai negato	**avrete** negato
avrà negato	**avranno** negato
condizionale passato	
avrei negato	**avremmo** negato
avresti negato	**avreste** negato
avrebbe negato	**avrebbero** negato
congiuntivo passato	
abbia negato	**abbiamo** negato
abbia negato	**abbiate** negato
abbia negato	**abbiano** negato
congiuntivo trapassato	
avessi negato	**avessimo** negato
avessi negato	**aveste** negato
avesse negato	**avessero** negato

negoziare — to negotiate

gerundio **negoziando** participio passato **negoziato**

SINGULAR	PLURAL
indicativo presente	
negozi**o**	negozi**amo**
negozi	negozi**ate**
negozi**a**	negozi**ano**
imperfetto	
negozia**vo**	negozia**vamo**
negozia**vi**	negozia**vate**
negozia**va**	negozia**vano**
passato remoto	
negozi**ai**	negozi**ammo**
negozi**asti**	negozi**aste**
negozi**ò**	negozi**arono**
futuro semplice	
negozier**ò**	negozier**emo**
negozier**ai**	negozier**ete**
negozier**à**	negozier**anno**
condizionale presente	
negozi**erei**	negozi**eremmo**
negozi**eresti**	negozi**ereste**
negozi**erebbe**	negozi**erebbero**
congiuntivo presente	
negoz**i**	negozi**amo**
negoz**i**	negozi**ate**
negoz**i**	negoz**ino**
congiuntivo imperfetto	
negozi**assi**	negozi**assimo**
negozi**assi**	negozi**aste**
negozi**asse**	negozi**assero**
imperativo	
	negoziamo
negozia; non negoziare	negoziate
negozi	negozino

SINGULAR	PLURAL
passato prossimo	
ho negoziato	**abbiamo** negoziato
hai negoziato	**avete** negoziato
ha negoziato	**hanno** negoziato
trapassato prossimo	
avevo negoziato	**avevamo** negoziato
avevi negoziato	**avevate** negoziato
aveva negoziato	**avevano** negoziato
trapassato remoto	
ebbi negoziato	**avemmo** negoziato
avesti negoziato	**aveste** negoziato
ebbe negoziato	**ebbero** negoziato
futuro anteriore	
avrò negoziato	**avremo** negoziato
avrai negoziato	**avrete** negoziato
avrà negoziato	**avranno** negoziato
condizionale passato	
avrei negoziato	**avremmo** negoziato
avresti negoziato	**avreste** negoziato
avrebbe negoziato	**avrebbero** negoziato
congiuntivo passato	
abbia negoziato	**abbiamo** negoziato
abbia negoziato	**abbiate** negoziato
abbia negoziato	**abbiano** negoziato
congiuntivo trapassato	
avessi negoziato	**avessimo** negoziato
avessi negoziato	**aveste** negoziato
avesse negoziato	**avessero** negoziato

to snow **nevicare**

gerundio **nevicando** participio passato **nevicato**

SINGULAR PLURAL

indicativo presente
nevic**a**

imperfetto
nevica**va**

passato remoto
nevic**ò**

futuro semplice
neviche**rà**

condizionale presente
nevich**erebbe**

congiuntivo presente
nevich**i**

congiuntivo imperfetto
nevica**sse**

SINGULAR PLURAL

passato prossimo
è/ha nevicato

trapassato prossimo
era/aveva nevicato

trapassato remoto
fu/ebbe nevicato

futuro anteriore
sarà/avrà nevicato

condizionale passato
sarebbe/avrebbe nevicato

congiuntivo passato
sia/abbia nevicato

congiuntivo trapassato
fosse/avesse nevicato

gerundio **noleggiando** participio passato **noleggiato**

SINGULAR	PLURAL
indicativo presente	
noleggi**o**	noleggi**amo**
noleggi	noleggi**ate**
noleggi**a**	noleggi**ano**
imperfetto	
noleggia**vo**	noleggia**vamo**
noleggia**vi**	noleggia**vate**
noleggia**va**	noleggia**vano**
passato remoto	
noleggi**ai**	noleggi**ammo**
noleggi**asti**	noleggi**aste**
noleggi**ò**	noleggi**arono**
futuro semplice	
nolegger**ò**	nolegger**emo**
nolegger**ai**	nolegger**ete**
nolegger**à**	nolegger**anno**
condizionale presente	
nolegg**erei**	nolegg**eremmo**
nolegg**eresti**	nolegg**ereste**
nolegg**erebbe**	nolegg**erebbero**
congiuntivo presente	
noleggi	noleggi**amo**
noleggi	noleggi**ate**
noleggi	nolegg**ino**
congiuntivo imperfetto	
noleggi**assi**	noleggi**assimo**
noleggi**assi**	noleggi**aste**
noleggi**asse**	noleggi**assero**
imperativo	
	noleggiamo
noleggia; non noleggiare	noleggiate
noleggi	noleggino

SINGULAR	PLURAL
passato prossimo	
ho noleggiato	**abbiamo** noleggiato
hai noleggiato	**avete** noleggiato
ha noleggiato	**hanno** noleggiato
trapassato prossimo	
avevo noleggiato	**avevamo** noleggiato
avevi noleggiato	**avevate** noleggiato
aveva noleggiato	**avevano** noleggiato
trapassato remoto	
ebbi noleggiato	**avemmo** noleggiato
avesti noleggiato	**aveste** noleggiato
ebbe noleggiato	**ebbero** noleggiato
futuro anteriore	
avrò noleggiato	**avremo** noleggiato
avrai noleggiato	**avrete** noleggiato
avrà noleggiato	**avranno** noleggiato
condizionale passato	
avrei noleggiato	**avremmo** noleggiato
avresti noleggiato	**avreste** noleggiato
avrebbe noleggiato	**avrebbero** noleggiato
congiuntivo passato	
abbia noleggiato	**abbiamo** noleggiato
abbia noleggiato	**abbiate** noleggiato
abbia noleggiato	**abbiano** noleggiato
congiuntivo trapassato	
avessi noleggiato	**avessimo** noleggiato
avessi noleggiato	**aveste** noleggiato
avesse noleggiato	**avessero** noleggiato

to name, to call **nominare**

gerundio **nominando** participio passato **nominato**

SINGULAR	PLURAL	SINGULAR	PLURAL
indicativo presente		passato prossimo	
nomin**o**	nomin**iamo**	**ho** nominato	**abbiamo** nominato
nomin**i**	nomin**ate**	**hai** nominato	**avete** nominato
nomin**a**	nomin**ano**	**ha** nominato	**hanno** nominato
imperfetto		trapassato prossimo	
nomina**vo**	nomina**vamo**	**avevo** nominato	**avevamo** nominato
nomina**vi**	nomina**vate**	**avevi** nominato	**avevate** nominato
nomina**va**	nomina**vano**	**aveva** nominato	**avevano** nominato
passato remoto		trapassato remoto	
nomin**ai**	nomin**ammo**	**ebbi** nominato	**avemmo** nominato
nomin**asti**	nomin**aste**	**avesti** nominato	**aveste** nominato
nomin**ò**	nomin**arono**	**ebbe** nominato	**ebbero** nominato
futuro semplice		futuro anteriore	
nominer**ò**	nominer**emo**	**avrò** nominato	**avremo** nominato
nominer**ai**	nominer**ete**	**avrai** nominato	**avrete** nominato
nominer**à**	nominer**anno**	**avrà** nominato	**avranno** nominato
condizionale presente		condizionale passato	
nomin**erei**	nomin**eremmo**	**avrei** nominato	**avremmo** nominato
nomin**eresti**	nomin**ereste**	**avresti** nominato	**avreste** nominato
nomin**erebbe**	nomin**erebbero**	**avrebbe** nominato	**avrebbero** nominato
congiuntivo presente		congiuntivo passato	
nomin**i**	nomin**iamo**	**abbia** nominato	**abbiamo** nominato
nomin**i**	nomin**iate**	**abbia** nominato	**abbiate** nominato
nomin**i**	nomin**ino**	**abbia** nominato	**abbiano** nominato
congiuntivo imperfetto		congiuntivo trapassato	
nomin**assi**	nomin**assimo**	**avessi** nominato	**avessimo** nominato
nomin**assi**	nomin**aste**	**avessi** nominato	**aveste** nominato
nomin**asse**	nomin**assero**	**avesse** nominato	**avessero** nominato

imperativo

	nominiamo
nomina; non nominare	nominate
nomini	nominino

N

notare — to note, to write down

gerundio **notando** — participio passato **notato**

SINGULAR	PLURAL	SINGULAR	PLURAL
indicativo presente		passato prossimo	
not**o**	not**iamo**	**ho** notato	**abbiamo** notato
not**i**	not**ate**	**hai** notato	**avete** notato
not**a**	not**ano**	**ha** notato	**hanno** notato
imperfetto		trapassato prossimo	
nota**vo**	nota**vamo**	**avevo** notato	**avevamo** notato
nota**vi**	nota**vate**	**avevi** notato	**avevate** notato
nota**va**	nota**vano**	**aveva** notato	**avevano** notato
passato remoto		trapassato remoto	
not**ai**	not**ammo**	**ebbi** notato	**avemmo** notato
not**asti**	not**aste**	**avesti** notato	**aveste** notato
not**ò**	not**arono**	**ebbe** notato	**ebbero** notato
futuro semplice		futuro anteriore	
noter**ò**	noter**emo**	**avrò** notato	**avremo** notato
noter**ai**	noter**ete**	**avrai** notato	**avrete** notato
noter**à**	noter**anno**	**avrà** notato	**avranno** notato
condizionale presente		condizionale passato	
not**erei**	not**eremmo**	**avrei** notato	**avremmo** notato
not**eresti**	not**ereste**	**avresti** notato	**avreste** notato
not**erebbe**	not**erebbero**	**avrebbe** notato	**avrebbero** notato
congiuntivo presente		congiuntivo passato	
not**i**	not**iamo**	**abbia** notato	**abbiamo** notato
not**i**	not**iate**	**abbia** notato	**abbiate** notato
not**i**	not**ino**	**abbia** notato	**abbiano** notato
congiuntivo imperfetto		congiuntivo trapassato	
not**assi**	not**assimo**	**avessi** notato	**avessimo** notato
not**assi**	not**aste**	**avessi** notato	**aveste** notato
not**asse**	not**assero**	**avesse** notato	**avessero** notato
imperativo			
	notiamo		
nota; non notare	notate		
noti	notino		

gerundio **notificando** participio passato **notificato**

SINGULAR	PLURAL	SINGULAR	PLURAL
indicativo presente		passato prossimo	
notific**o**	notifich**iamo**	**ho** notificato	**abbiamo** notificato
notifich**i**	notific**ate**	**hai** notificato	**avete** notificato
notific**a**	notific**ano**	**ha** notificato	**hanno** notificato
imperfetto		trapassato prossimo	
notifica**vo**	notifica**vamo**	**avevo** notificato	**avevamo** notificato
notifica**vi**	notifica**vate**	**avevi** notificato	**avevate** notificato
notifica**va**	notifica**vano**	**aveva** notificato	**avevano** notificato
passato remoto		trapassato remoto	
notific**ai**	notific**ammo**	**ebbi** notificato	**avemmo** notificato
notific**asti**	notific**aste**	**avesti** notificato	**aveste** notificato
notific**ò**	notific**arono**	**ebbe** notificato	**ebbero** notificato
futuro semplice		futuro anteriore	
notificher**ò**	notificher**emo**	**avrò** notificato	**avremo** notificato
notificher**ai**	notificher**ete**	**avrai** notificato	**avrete** notificato
notificher**à**	notificher**anno**	**avrà** notificato	**avranno** notificato
condizionale presente		condizionale passato	
notifich**erei**	notifich**eremmo**	**avrei** notificato	**avremmo** notificato
notifich**eresti**	notifich**ereste**	**avresti** notificato	**avreste** notificato
notifich**erebbe**	notifich**erebbero**	**avrebbe** notificato	**avrebbero** notificato
congiuntivo presente		congiuntivo passato	
notifich**i**	notifich**iamo**	**abbia** notificato	**abbiamo** notificato
notifich**i**	notifich**iate**	**abbia** notificato	**abbiate** notificato
notifich**i**	notifich**ino**	**abbia** notificato	**abbiano** notificato
congiuntivo imperfetto		congiuntivo trapassato	
notific**assi**	notific**assimo**	**avessi** notificato	**avessimo** notificato
notific**assi**	notific**aste**	**avessi** notificato	**aveste** notificato
notific**asse**	notific**assero**	**avesse** notificato	**avessero** notificato
imperativo			
	notifichiamo		
notifica; non notificare	notificate		
notifichi	notifichino		

N

nuocere — to hurt, to harm

gerundio **noucendo** participio passato **nuociuto**

SINGULAR	PLURAL	SINGULAR	PLURAL
indicativo presente		passato prossimo	
n(u)occi**o**	n(u)oc**iamo**	**ho** nuociuto	**abbiamo** nuociuto
nuoc**i**	n(u)oc**ete**	**hai** nuociuto	**avete** nuociuto
nuoc**e**	n(u)occ**iono**	**ha** nuociuto	**hanno** nuociuto
imperfetto		trapassato prossimo	
n(u)oce**vo**	n(u)oce**vamo**	**avevo** nuociuto	**avevamo** nuociuto
n(u)oce**vi**	n(u)oce**vate**	**avevi** nuociuto	**avevate** nuociuto
n(u)oce**va**	n(u)oce**vano**	**aveva** nuociuto	**avevano** nuociuto
passato remoto		trapassato remoto	
nocqui	n(u)oc**emmo**	**ebbi** nuociuto	**avemmo** nuociuto
n(u)oc**esti**	n(u)oc**este**	**avesti** nuociuto	**aveste** nuociuto
nocque	**nocquero**	**ebbe** nuociuto	**ebbero** nuociuto
futuro semplice		futuro anteriore	
n(u)ocer**ò**	n(u)ocer**emo**	**avrò** nuociuto	**avremo** nuociuto
n(u)ocer**ai**	n(u)ocer**ete**	**avrai** nuociuto	**avrete** nuociuto
n(u)ocer**à**	n(u)ocer**anno**	**avrà** nuociuto	**avranno** nuociuto
condizionale presente		condizionale passato	
n(u)oc**erei**	n(u)oc**eremmo**	**avrei** nuociuto	**avremmo** nuociuto
n(u)oc**eresti**	n(u)oc**ereste**	**avresti** nuociuto	**avreste** nuociuto
n(u)oc**erebbe**	n(u)oc**erebbero**	**avrebbe** nuociuto	**avrebbero** nuociuto
congiuntivo presente		congiuntivo passato	
nuocc**ia**	nuoc**iamo**	**abbia** nuociuto	**abbiamo** nuociuto
nuocc**ia**	nuoc**iate**	**abbia** nuociuto	**abbiate** nuociuto
nuocc**ia**	nuocc**iano**	**abbia** nuociuto	**abbiano** nuociuto
congiuntivo imperfetto		congiuntivo trapassato	
n(u)oc**essi**	n(u)oc**essimo**	**avessi** nuociuto	**avessimo** nuociuto
n(u)oc**essi**	n(u)oc**este**	**avessi** nuociuto	**aveste** nuociuto
n(u)oc**esse**	n(u)oc**essero**	**avesse** nuociuto	**avessero** nuociuto
imperativo			
	n(u)ociamo		
nuoci; non nuocere	n(u)ocete		
nuoccia	n(u)occiano		

gerundio **nuotando** participio passato **nuotato**

SINGULAR	PLURAL	SINGULAR	PLURAL
indicativo presente		passato prossimo	
nuot**o**	nuot**iamo**	**ho** nuotato	**abbiamo** nuotato
nuot**i**	nuot**ate**	**hai** nuotato	**avete** nuotato
nuot**a**	nuot**ano**	**ha** nuotato	**hanno** nuotato
imperfetto		trapassato prossimo	
nuota**vo**	nuota**vamo**	**avevo** nuotato	**avevamo** nuotato
nuota**vi**	nuota**vate**	**avevi** nuotato	**avevate** nuotato
nuota**va**	nuota**vano**	**aveva** nuotato	**avevano** nuotato
passato remoto		trapassato remoto	
nuot**ai**	nuot**ammo**	**ebbi** nuotato	**avemmo** nuotato
nuot**asti**	nuot**aste**	**avesti** nuotato	**aveste** nuotato
nuot**ò**	nuot**arono**	**ebbe** nuotato	**ebbero** nuotato
futuro semplice		futuro anteriore	
nuoter**ò**	nuoter**emo**	**avrò** nuotato	**avremo** nuotato
nuoter**ai**	nuoter**ete**	**avrai** nuotato	**avrete** nuotato
nuoter**à**	nuoter**anno**	**avrà** nuotato	**avranno** nuotato
condizionale presente		condizionale passato	
nuot**erei**	nuot**eremmo**	**avrei** nuotato	**avremmo** nuotato
nuot**eresti**	nuot**ereste**	**avresti** nuotato	**avreste** nuotato
nuot**erebbe**	nuot**erebbero**	**avrebbe** nuotato	**avrebbero** nuotato
congiuntivo presente		congiuntivo passato	
nuot**i**	nuoti**amo**	**abbia** nuotato	**abbiamo** nuotato
nuot**i**	nuoti**ate**	**abbia** nuotato	**abbiate** nuotato
nuot**i**	nuot**ino**	**abbia** nuotato	**abbiano** nuotato
congiuntivo imperfetto		congiuntivo trapassato	
nuot**assi**	nuot**assimo**	**avessi** nuotato	**avessimo** nuotato
nuot**assi**	nuot**aste**	**avessi** nuotato	**aveste** nuotato
nuot**asse**	nuot**assero**	**avesse** nuotato	**avessero** nuotato
imperativo			
	nuotiamo		
nuota; non nuotare	nuotate		
nuoti	nuotino		

nutrire — to feed

gerundio **nutrendo** participio passato **nutrito**

SINGULAR	PLURAL
indicativo presente	
nutr**o**	nutr**iamo**
nutr**i**	nutr**ite**
nutr**e**	nutr**ono**
imperfetto	
nutri**vo**	nutri**vamo**
nutri**vi**	nutri**vate**
nutri**va**	nutri**vano**
passato remoto	
nutr**ii**	nutr**immo**
nutr**isti**	nutr**iste**
nutr**ì**	nutr**irono**
futuro semplice	
nutrir**ò**	nutrir**emo**
nutrir**ai**	nutrir**ete**
nutrir**à**	nutrir**anno**
condizionale presente	
nutr**irei**	nutr**iremmo**
nutr**iresti**	nutr**ireste**
nutr**irebbe**	nutr**irebbero**
congiuntivo presente	
nutr**a**	nutr**iamo**
nutr**a**	nutr**iate**
nutr**a**	nutr**ano**
congiuntivo imperfetto	
nutr**issi**	nutr**issimo**
nutr**issi**	nutr**iste**
nutr**isse**	nutr**issero**
imperativo	
	nutriamo
nutri; non nutrire	nutrite
nutra	nutrano

SINGULAR	PLURAL
passato prossimo	
ho nutrito	**abbiamo** nutrito
hai nutrito	**avete** nutrito
ha nutrito	**hanno** nutrito
trapassato prossimo	
avevo nutrito	**avevamo** nutrito
avevi nutrito	**avevate** nutrito
aveva nutrito	**avevano** nutrito
trapassato remoto	
ebbi nutrito	**avemmo** nutrito
avesti nutrito	**aveste** nutrito
ebbe nutrito	**ebbero** nutrito
futuro anteriore	
avrò nutrito	**avremo** nutrito
avrai nutrito	**avrete** nutrito
avrà nutrito	**avranno** nutrito
condizionale passato	
avrei nutrito	**avremmo** nutrito
avresti nutrito	**avreste** nutrito
avrebbe nutrito	**avrebbero** nutrito
congiuntivo passato	
abbia nutrito	**abbiamo** nutrito
abbia nutrito	**abbiate** nutrito
abbia nutrito	**abbiano** nutrito
congiuntivo trapassato	
avessi nutrito	**avessimo** nutrito
avessi nutrito	**aveste** nutrito
avesse nutrito	**avessero** nutrito

to obey **obbedire**

gerundio **obbedendo** participio passato **obbedito**

SINGULAR	PLURAL
indicativo presente	
obbedisc**o**	obbed**iamo**
obbedisc**i**	obbed**ite**
obbedisc**e**	obbedisc**ono**
imperfetto	
obbedi**vo**	obbedi**vamo**
obbedi**vi**	obbedi**vate**
obbedi**va**	obbedi**vano**
passato remoto	
obbed**ii**	obbed**immo**
obbed**isti**	obbed**iste**
obbed**ì**	obbed**irono**
futuro semplice	
obbedir**ò**	obbedir**emo**
obbedir**ai**	obbedir**ete**
obbedir**à**	obbedir**anno**
condizionale presente	
obbed**irei**	obbed**iremmo**
obbed**iresti**	obbed**ireste**
obbed**irebbe**	obbed**irebbero**
congiuntivo presente	
obbedisc**a**	obbed**iamo**
obbedisc**a**	obbed**iate**
obbedisc**a**	obbedisc**ano**
congiuntivo imperfetto	
obbed**issi**	obbed**issimo**
obbed**issi**	obbed**iste**
obbed**isse**	obbed**issero**
imperativo	
	obbediamo
obbedisci; non obbedire	obbedite
obbedisca	obbediscano

SINGULAR	PLURAL
passato prossimo	
ho obbedito	**abbiamo** obbedito
hai obbedito	**avete** obbedito
ha obbedito	**hanno** obbedito
trapassato prossimo	
avevo obbedito	**avevamo** obbedito
avevi obbedito	**avevate** obbedito
aveva obbedito	**avevano** obbedito
trapassato remoto	
ebbi obbedito	**avemmo** obbedito
avesti obbedito	**aveste** obbedito
ebbe obbedito	**ebbero** obbedito
futuro anteriore	
avrò obbedito	**avremo** obbedito
avrai obbedito	**avrete** obbedito
avrà obbedito	**avranno** obbedito
condizionale passato	
avrei obbedito	**avremmo** obbedito
avresti obbedito	**avreste** obbedito
avrebbe obbedito	**avrebbero** obbedito
congiuntivo passato	
abbia obbedito	**abbiamo** obbedito
abbia obbedito	**abbiate** obbedito
abbia obbedito	**abbiano** obbedito
congiuntivo trapassato	
avessi obbedito	**avessimo** obbedito
avessi obbedito	**aveste** obbedito
avesse obbedito	**avessero** obbedito

obbligare — to oblige

gerundio **obbligando** participio passato **obbligato**

SINGULAR	PLURAL	SINGULAR	PLURAL
indicativo presente		passato prossimo	
obblig**o**	obblig**hiamo**	**ho** obbligato	**abbiamo** obbligato
obblig**hi**	obblig**ate**	**hai** obbligato	**avete** obbligato
obblig**a**	obblig**ano**	**ha** obbligato	**hanno** obbligato
imperfetto		trapassato prossimo	
obbliga**vo**	obbliga**vamo**	**avevo** obbligato	**avevamo** obbligato
obbliga**vi**	obbliga**vate**	**avevi** obbligato	**avevate** obbligato
obbliga**va**	obbliga**vano**	**aveva** obbligato	**avevano** obbligato
passato remoto		trapassato remoto	
obblig**ai**	obblig**ammo**	**ebbi** obbligato	**avemmo** obbligato
obblig**asti**	obblig**aste**	**avesti** obbligato	**aveste** obbligato
obblig**ò**	obblig**arono**	**ebbe** obbligato	**ebbero** obbligato
futuro semplice		futuro anteriore	
obbligher**ò**	obbligher**emo**	**avrò** obbligato	**avremo** obbligato
obbligher**ai**	obbligher**ete**	**avrai** obbligato	**avrete** obbligato
obbligher**à**	obbligher**anno**	**avrà** obbligato	**avranno** obbligato
condizionale presente		condizionale passato	
obblig**herei**	obblig**heremmo**	**avrei** obbligato	**avremmo** obbligato
obblig**heresti**	obblig**hereste**	**avresti** obbligato	**avreste** obbligato
obblig**herebbe**	obblig**herebbero**	**avrebbe** obbligato	**avrebbero** obbligato
congiuntivo presente		congiuntivo passato	
obblig**hi**	obblig**hiamo**	**abbia** obbligato	**abbiamo** obbligato
obblig**hi**	obblig**hiate**	**abbia** obbligato	**abbiate** obbligato
obblig**hi**	obblig**hino**	**abbia** obbligato	**abbiano** obbligato
congiuntivo imperfetto		congiuntivo trapassato	
obblig**assi**	obblig**assimo**	**avessi** obbligato	**avessimo** obbligato
obblig**assi**	obblig**aste**	**avessi** obbligato	**aveste** obbligato
obblig**asse**	obblig**assero**	**avesse** obbligato	**avessero** obbligato

imperativo

	obblighiamo
obbliga; non obbligare	obbligate
obblighi	obblighino

to be necessary — occorrere

gerundio **occorrendo** participio passato **occorso**

SINGULAR	PLURAL	SINGULAR	PLURAL
indicativo presente		passato prossimo	
occor**re**	occor**rono**	**è** occorso(a)	**sono** occorsi(e)
imperfetto		trapassato prossimo	
occor**reva**	occor**revano**	**era** occorso(a)	**erano** occorsi(e)
passato remoto		trapassato remoto	
occor**se**	occor**sero**	**fu** occorso(a)	**furono** occorsi(e)
futuro semplice		futuro anteriore	
occorrer**à**	occorrer**anno**	**sarà** occorso(a)	**saranno** occorsi(e)
condizionale presente		condizionale passato	
occor**rerebbe**	occor**rerebbero**	**sarebbe** occorso(a)	**sarebbero** occorsi(e)
congiuntivo presente		congiuntivo passato	
occor**ra**	occor**rano**	**sia** occorso(a)	**siano** occorsi(e)
congiuntivo imperfetto		congiuntivo trapassato	
occor**resse**	occor**ressero**	**fosse** occorso(a)	**fossero** occorsi(e)

occupare — to occupy

gerundio **occupando** participio passato **occupato**

SINGULAR	PLURAL	SINGULAR	PLURAL
indicativo presente		passato prossimo	
occup**o**	occup**iamo**	**ho** occupato	**abbiamo** occupato
occup**i**	occup**ate**	**hai** occupato	**avete** occupato
occup**a**	occup**ano**	**ha** occupato	**hanno** occupato
imperfetto		trapassato prossimo	
occupa**vo**	occupa**vamo**	**avevo** occupato	**avevamo** occupato
occupa**vi**	occupa**vate**	**avevi** occupato	**avevate** occupato
occupa**va**	occupa**vano**	**aveva** occupato	**avevano** occupato
passato remoto		trapassato remoto	
occup**ai**	occup**ammo**	**ebbi** occupato	**avemmo** occupato
occup**asti**	occup**aste**	**avesti** occupato	**aveste** occupato
occup**ò**	occup**arono**	**ebbe** occupato	**ebbero** occupato
futuro semplice		futuro anteriore	
occuper**ò**	occuper**emo**	**avrò** occupato	**avremo** occupato
occuper**ai**	occuper**ete**	**avrai** occupato	**avrete** occupato
occuper**à**	occuper**anno**	**avrà** occupato	**avranno** occupato
condizionale presente		condizionale passato	
occup**erei**	occup**eremmo**	**avrei** occupato	**avremmo** occupato
occup**eresti**	occup**ereste**	**avresti** occupato	**avreste** occupato
occup**erebbe**	occup**erebbero**	**avrebbe** occupato	**avrebbero** occupato
congiuntivo presente		congiuntivo passato	
occup**i**	occup**iamo**	**abbia** occupato	**abbiamo** occupato
occup**i**	occup**iate**	**abbia** occupato	**abbiate** occupato
occup**i**	occup**ino**	**abbia** occupato	**abbiano** occupato
congiuntivo imperfetto		congiuntivo trapassato	
occup**assi**	occup**assimo**	**avessi** occupato	**avessimo** occupato
occup**assi**	occup**aste**	**avessi** occupato	**aveste** occupato
occup**asse**	occup**assero**	**avesse** occupato	**avessero** occupato
imperativo			
	occupiamo		
occupa; non occupare	occupate		
occupi	occupino		

O

gerundio **odiando** participio passato **odiato**

SINGULAR	PLURAL	SINGULAR	PLURAL
indicativo presente		passato prossimo	
odi**o**	odi**amo**	**ho** odiato	**abbiamo** odiato
odi**i**	odi**ate**	**hai** odiato	**avete** odiato
odi**a**	odi**ano**	**ha** odiato	**hanno** odiato
imperfetto		trapassato prossimo	
odia**vo**	odia**vamo**	**avevo** odiato	**avevamo** odiato
odia**vi**	odia**vate**	**avevi** odiato	**avevate** odiato
odia**va**	odia**vano**	**aveva** odiato	**avevano** odiato
passato remoto		trapassato remoto	
odi**ai**	odi**ammo**	**ebbi** odiato	**avemmo** odiato
odi**asti**	odi**aste**	**avesti** odiato	**aveste** odiato
odi**ò**	odi**arono**	**ebbe** odiato	**ebbero** odiato
futuro semplice		futuro anteriore	
odier**ò**	odier**emo**	**avrò** odiato	**avremo** odiato
odier**ai**	odier**ete**	**avrai** odiato	**avrete** odiato
odier**à**	odier**anno**	**avrà** odiato	**avranno** odiato
condizionale presente		condizionale passato	
odi**erei**	odi**eremmo**	**avrei** odiato	**avremmo** odiato
odi**eresti**	odi**ereste**	**avresti** odiato	**avreste** odiato
odi**erebbe**	odi**erebbero**	**avrebbe** odiato	**avrebbero** odiato
congiuntivo presente		congiuntivo passato	
odi	odi**amo**	**abbia** odiato	**abbiamo** odiato
odi	odi**ate**	**abbia** odiato	**abbiate** odiato
odi	odi**no**	**abbia** odiato	**abbiano** odiato
congiuntivo imperfetto		congiuntivo trapassato	
odi**assi**	odi**assimo**	**avessi** odiato	**avessimo** odiato
odi**assi**	odi**aste**	**avessi** odiato	**aveste** odiato
odi**asse**	odi**assero**	**avesse** odiato	**avessero** odiato
imperativo			
	odiamo		
odia; non odiare	odiate		
odi	odino		

offendere — to offend

gerundio **offendendo** participio passato **offeso**

SINGULAR	PLURAL	SINGULAR	PLURAL
indicativo presente		passato prossimo	
offend**o**	offend**iamo**	**ho** offeso	**abbiamo** offeso
offend**i**	offend**ete**	**hai** offeso	**avete** offeso
offend**e**	offend**ono**	**ha** offeso	**hanno** offeso
imperfetto		trapassato prossimo	
offende**vo**	offende**vamo**	**avevo** offeso	**avevamo** offeso
offende**vi**	offende**vate**	**avevi** offeso	**avevate** offeso
offende**va**	offende**vano**	**aveva** offeso	**avevano** offeso
passato remoto		trapassato remoto	
offes**i**	offend**emmo**	**ebbi** offeso	**avemmo** offeso
offend**esti**	offend**este**	**avesti** offeso	**aveste** offeso
offes**e**	offes**ero**	**ebbe** offeso	**ebbero** offeso
futuro semplice		futuro anteriore	
offender**ò**	offender**emo**	**avrò** offeso	**avremo** offeso
offender**ai**	offender**ete**	**avrai** offeso	**avrete** offeso
offender**à**	offender**anno**	**avrà** offeso	**avranno** offeso
condizionale presente		condizionale passato	
offend**erei**	offend**eremmo**	**avrei** offeso	**avremmo** offeso
offend**eresti**	offend**ereste**	**avresti** offeso	**avreste** offeso
offend**erebbe**	offend**erebbero**	**avrebbe** offeso	**avrebbero** offeso
congiuntivo presente		congiuntivo passato	
offend**a**	offend**iamo**	**abbia** offeso	**abbiamo** offeso
offend**a**	offend**iate**	**abbia** offeso	**abbiate** offeso
offend**a**	offend**ano**	**abbia** offeso	**abbiano** offeso
congiuntivo imperfetto		congiuntivo trapassato	
offend**essi**	offend**essimo**	**avessi** offeso	**avessimo** offeso
offend**essi**	offend**este**	**avessi** offeso	**aveste** offeso
offend**esse**	offend**essero**	**avesse** offeso	**avessero** offeso
imperativo			
	offendiamo		
offendi; non offendere	offendete		
offenda	offendano		

O

gerundio **offrendo** participio passato **offerto**

SINGULAR	PLURAL	SINGULAR	PLURAL
indicativo presente		passato prossimo	
offr**o**	offr**iamo**	**ho** offerto	**abbiamo** offerto
offr**i**	offr**ite**	**hai** offerto	**avete** offerto
offr**e**	offr**ono**	**ha** offerto	**hanno** offerto
imperfetto		trapassato prossimo	
offri**vo**	offri**vamo**	**avevo** offerto	**avevamo** offerto
offri**vi**	offri**vate**	**avevi** offerto	**avevate** offerto
offri**va**	offri**vano**	**aveva** offerto	**avevano** offerto
passato remoto		trapassato remoto	
offr**ii**, offers**i**	offr**immo**	**ebbi** offerto	**avemmo** offerto
offr**isti**	offr**iste**	**avesti** offerto	**aveste** offerto
offr**ì**, offers**e**	offr**irono**, offers**ero**	**ebbe** offerto	**ebbero** offerto
futuro semplice		futuro anteriore	
offrir**ò**	offrir**emo**	**avrò** offerto	**avremo** offerto
offrir**ai**	offrir**ete**	**avrai** offerto	**avrete** offerto
offrir**à**	offrir**anno**	**avrà** offerto	**avranno** offerto
condizionale presente		condizionale passato	
offr**irei**	offr**iremmo**	**avrei** offerto	**avremmo** offerto
offr**iresti**	offr**ireste**	**avresti** offerto	**avreste** offerto
offr**irebbe**	offr**irebbero**	**avrebbe** offerto	**avrebbero** offerto
congiuntivo presente		congiuntivo passato	
offr**a**	offr**iamo**	**abbia** offerto	**abbiamo** offerto
offr**a**	offr**iate**	**abbia** offerto	**abbiate** offerto
offr**a**	offr**ano**	**abbia** offerto	**abbiano** offerto
congiuntivo imperfetto		congiuntivo trapassato	
offr**issi**	offr**issimo**	**avessi** offerto	**avessimo** offerto
offr**issi**	offr**iste**	**avessi** offerto	**aveste** offerto
offr**isse**	offr**issero**	**avesse** offerto	**avessero** offerto

imperativo

	offriamo
offri; non offrire	offrite
offra	offrano

O

omettere — to omit

gerundio **omettendo** — participio passato **omesso**

SINGULAR	PLURAL
indicativo presente	
ometto	omettiamo
ometti	omettete
omette	omettono
imperfetto	
omettevo	omettevamo
omettevi	omettevate
ometteva	omettevano
passato remoto	
omisi	omettemmo
omettesti	ometteste
omise	omisero
futuro semplice	
ometterò	ometteremo
ometterai	ometterete
ometterà	ometteranno
condizionale presente	
ometterei	ometteremo
ometteresti	omettereste
ometterebbe	ometterebbero
congiuntivo presente	
ometta	omettiamo
ometta	omettiate
ometta	omettano
congiuntivo imperfetto	
omettessi	omettessimo
omettessi	ometteste
omettesse	omettessero
imperativo	
	omettiamo
ometti; non omettere	omettete
ometta	omettano

SINGULAR	PLURAL
passato prossimo	
ho omesso	**abbiamo** omesso
hai omesso	**avete** omesso
ha omesso	**hanno** omesso
trapassato prossimo	
avevo omesso	**avevamo** omesso
avevi omesso	**avevate** omesso
aveva omesso	**avevano** omesso
trapassato remoto	
ebbi omesso	**avemmo** omesso
avesti omesso	**aveste** omesso
ebbe omesso	**ebbero** omesso
futuro anteriore	
avrò omesso	**avremo** omesso
avrai omesso	**avrete** omesso
avrà omesso	**avranno** omesso
condizionale passato	
avrei omesso	**avremmo** omesso
avresti omesso	**avreste** omesso
avrebbe omesso	**avrebbero** omesso
congiuntivo passato	
abbia omesso	**abbiamo** omesso
abbia omesso	**abbiate** omesso
abbia omesso	**abbiano** omesso
congiuntivo trapassato	
avessi omesso	**avessimo** omesso
avessi omesso	**aveste** omesso
avesse omesso	**avessero** omesso

gerundio **onorando** participio passato **onorato**

SINGULAR	PLURAL	SINGULAR	PLURAL
indicativo presente		passato prossimo	
onor**o**	onor**iamo**	**ho** onorato	**abbiamo** onorato
onor**i**	onor**ate**	**hai** onorato	**avete** onorato
onor**a**	onor**ano**	**ha** onorato	**hanno** onorato
imperfetto		trapassato prossimo	
onora**vo**	onora**vamo**	**avevo** onorato	**avevamo** onorato
onora**vi**	onora**vate**	**avevi** onorato	**avevate** onorato
onora**va**	onora**vano**	**aveva** onorato	**avevano** onorato
passato remoto		trapassato remoto	
onor**ai**	onor**ammo**	**ebbi** onorato	**avemmo** onorato
onor**asti**	onor**aste**	**avesti** onorato	**aveste** onorato
onor**ò**	onor**arono**	**ebbe** onorato	**ebbero** onorato
futuro semplice		futuro anteriore	
onorer**ò**	onorer**emo**	**avrò** onorato	**avremo** onorato
onorer**ai**	onorer**ete**	**avrai** onorato	**avrete** onorato
onorer**à**	onorer**anno**	**avrà** onorato	**avranno** onorato
condizionale presente		condizionale passato	
onor**erei**	onor**eremmo**	**avrei** onorato	**avremmo** onorato
onor**eresti**	onor**ereste**	**avresti** onorato	**avreste** onorato
onor**erebbe**	onor**erebbero**	**avrebbe** onorato	**avrebbero** onorato
congiuntivo presente		congiuntivo passato	
onor**i**	onor**iamo**	**abbia** onorato	**abbiamo** onorato
onor**i**	onor**iate**	**abbia** onorato	**abbiate** onorato
onor**i**	onor**ino**	**abbia** onorato	**abbiano** onorato
congiuntivo imperfetto		congiuntivo trapassato	
onor**assi**	onor**assimo**	**avessi** onorato	**avessimo** onorato
onor**assi**	onor**aste**	**avessi** onorato	**aveste** onorato
onor**asse**	onor**assero**	**avesse** onorato	**avessero** onorato
imperativo			
	onoriamo		
onora; non onorare	onorate		
onori	onorino		

operare — to operate, to perform

gerundio **operando** — participio passato **operato**

SINGULAR	PLURAL	SINGULAR	PLURAL
indicativo presente		passato prossimo	
oper**o**	oper**iamo**	**ho** operato	**abbiamo** operato
oper**i**	oper**ate**	**hai** operato	**avete** operato
oper**a**	oper**ano**	**ha** operato	**hanno** operato
imperfetto		trapassato prossimo	
opera**vo**	opera**vamo**	**avevo** operato	**avevamo** operato
opera**vi**	opera**vate**	**avevi** operato	**avevate** operato
opera**va**	opera**vano**	**aveva** operato	**avevano** operato
passato remoto		trapassato remoto	
oper**ai**	oper**ammo**	**ebbi** operato	**avemmo** operato
oper**asti**	oper**aste**	**avesti** operato	**aveste** operato
oper**ò**	oper**arono**	**ebbe** operato	**ebbero** operato
futuro semplice		futuro anteriore	
operer**ò**	operer**emo**	**avrò** operato	**avremo** operato
operer**ai**	operer**ete**	**avrai** operato	**avrete** operato
operer**à**	operer**anno**	**avrà** operato	**avranno** operato
condizionale presente		condizionale passato	
oper**erei**	oper**eremmo**	**avrei** operato	**avremmo** operato
oper**eresti**	oper**ereste**	**avresti** operato	**avreste** operato
oper**erebbe**	oper**erebbero**	**avrebbe** operato	**avrebbero** operato
congiuntivo presente		congiuntivo passato	
oper**i**	oper**iamo**	**abbia** operato	**abbiamo** operato
oper**i**	oper**iate**	**abbia** operato	**abbiate** operato
oper**i**	oper**ino**	**abbia** operato	**abbiano** operato
congiuntivo imperfetto		congiuntivo trapassato	
oper**assi**	oper**assimo**	**avessi** operato	**avessimo** operato
oper**assi**	oper**aste**	**avessi** operato	**aveste** operato
oper**asse**	oper**assero**	**avesse** operato	**avessero** operato
imperativo			
	operiamo		
opera; non operare	operate		
operi	operino		

O

gerundio **opponendo** participio passato **opposto**

SINGULAR	PLURAL
indicativo presente	
oppon**go**	oppon**iamo**
oppon**i**	oppon**ete**
oppon**e**	oppon**gono**
imperfetto	
oppone**vo**	oppone**vamo**
oppone**vi**	oppone**vate**
oppone**va**	oppone**vano**
passato remoto	
oppo**si**	oppo**nemmo**
oppo**nesti**	oppo**neste**
oppo**se**	oppo**sero**
futuro semplice	
opporr**ò**	opporr**emo**
opporr**ai**	opporr**ete**
opporr**à**	opporr**anno**
condizionale presente	
opporr**ei**	opporr**emmo**
opporr**esti**	opporr**este**
opporr**ebbe**	opporr**ebbero**
congiuntivo presente	
oppon**ga**	oppon**iamo**
oppon**ga**	oppon**iate**
oppon**ga**	oppon**gano**
congiuntivo imperfetto	
oppon**essi**	oppon**essimo**
oppon**essi**	oppon**este**
oppon**esse**	oppon**essero**
imperativo	
	opponiamo
opponi; non opporre	opponete
opponga	oppongano

SINGULAR	PLURAL
passato prossimo	
ho opposto	**abbiamo** opposto
hai opposto	**avete** opposto
ha opposto	**hanno** opposto
trapassato prossimo	
avevo opposto	**avevamo** opposto
avevi opposto	**avevate** opposto
aveva opposto	**avevano** opposto
trapassato remoto	
ebbi opposto	**avemmo** opposto
avesti opposto	**aveste** opposto
ebbe opposto	**ebbero** opposto
futuro anteriore	
avrò opposto	**avremo** opposto
avrai opposto	**avrete** opposto
avrà opposto	**avranno** opposto
condizionale passato	
avrei opposto	**avremmo** opposto
avresti opposto	**avreste** opposto
avrebbe opposto	**avrebbero** opposto
congiuntivo passato	
abbia opposto	**abbiamo** opposto
abbia opposto	**abbiate** opposto
abbia opposto	**abbiano** opposto
congiuntivo trapassato	
avessi opposto	**avessimo** opposto
avessi opposto	**aveste** opposto
avesse opposto	**avessero** opposto

opprimere — to oppress, to overwhelm

gerundio **opprimendo** participio passato **oppresso**

SINGULAR	PLURAL
indicativo presente	
opprim**o**	opprim**iamo**
opprim**i**	opprim**ete**
opprim**e**	opprim**ono**
imperfetto	
opprime**vo**	opprime**vamo**
opprime**vi**	opprime**vate**
opprime**va**	opprime**vano**
passato remoto	
oppress**i**	opprim**emmo**
opprim**esti**	opprim**este**
oppress**e**	oppress**ero**
futuro semplice	
opprimer**ò**	opprimer**emo**
opprimer**ai**	opprimer**ete**
opprimer**à**	opprimer**anno**
condizionale presente	
opprim**erei**	opprim**eremmo**
opprim**eresti**	opprim**ereste**
opprim**erebbe**	opprim**erebbero**
congiuntivo presente	
opprim**a**	opprim**iamo**
opprim**a**	opprim**iate**
opprim**a**	opprim**ano**
congiuntivo imperfetto	
opprim**essi**	opprim**essimo**
opprim**essi**	opprim**este**
opprim**esse**	opprim**essero**
imperativo	
	opprimiamo
opprimi; non opprimere	opprimete
opprima	opprimano

SINGULAR	PLURAL
passato prossimo	
ho oppresso	**abbiamo** oppresso
hai oppresso	**avete** oppresso
ha oppresso	**hanno** oppresso
trapassato prossimo	
avevo oppresso	**avevamo** oppresso
avevi oppresso	**avevate** oppresso
aveva oppresso	**avevano** oppresso
trapassato remoto	
ebbi oppresso	**avemmo** oppresso
avesti oppresso	**aveste** oppresso
ebbe oppresso	**ebbero** oppresso
futuro anteriore	
avrò oppresso	**avremo** oppresso
avrai oppresso	**avrete** oppresso
avrà oppresso	**avranno** oppresso
condizionale passato	
avrei oppresso	**avremmo** oppresso
avresti oppresso	**avreste** oppresso
avrebbe oppresso	**avrebbero** oppresso
congiuntivo passato	
abbia oppresso	**abbiamo** oppresso
abbia oppresso	**abbiate** oppresso
abbia oppresso	**abbiano** oppresso
congiuntivo trapassato	
avessi oppresso	**avessimo** oppresso
avessi oppresso	**aveste** oppresso
avesse oppresso	**avessero** oppresso

gerundio **ordinando** participio passato **ordinato**

SINGULAR	PLURAL
indicativo presente	
ordin**o**	ordin**iamo**
ordin**i**	ordin**ate**
ordin**a**	ordin**ano**
imperfetto	
ordina**vo**	ordina**vamo**
ordina**vi**	ordina**vate**
ordina**va**	ordina**vano**
passato remoto	
ordin**ai**	ordin**ammo**
ordin**asti**	ordin**aste**
ordin**ò**	ordin**arono**
futuro semplice	
ordiner**ò**	ordiner**emo**
ordiner**ai**	ordiner**ete**
ordiner**à**	ordiner**anno**
condizionale presente	
ordin**erei**	ordin**eremmo**
ordin**eresti**	ordin**ereste**
ordin**erebbe**	ordin**erebbero**
congiuntivo presente	
ordin**i**	ordin**iamo**
ordin**i**	ordin**iate**
ordin**i**	ordin**ino**
congiuntivo imperfetto	
ordin**assi**	ordin**assimo**
ordin**assi**	ordin**aste**
ordin**asse**	ordin**assero**
imperativo	
	ordiniamo
ordina; non ordinare	ordinate
ordini	ordinino

SINGULAR	PLURAL
passato prossimo	
ho ordinato	**abbiamo** ordinato
hai ordinato	**avete** ordinato
ha ordinato	**hanno** ordinato
trapassato prossimo	
avevo ordinato	**avevamo** ordinato
avevi ordinato	**avevate** ordinato
aveva ordinato	**avevano** ordinato
trapassato remoto	
ebbi ordinato	**avemmo** ordinato
avesti ordinato	**aveste** ordinato
ebbe ordinato	**ebbero** ordinato
futuro anteriore	
avrò ordinato	**avremo** ordinato
avrai ordinato	**avrete** ordinato
avrà ordinato	**avranno** ordinato
condizionale passato	
avrei ordinato	**avremmo** ordinato
avresti ordinato	**avreste** ordinato
avrebbe ordinato	**avrebbero** ordinato
congiuntivo passato	
abbia ordinato	**abbiamo** ordinato
abbia ordinato	**abbiate** ordinato
abbia ordinato	**abbiano** ordinato
congiuntivo trapassato	
avessi ordinato	**avessimo** ordinato
avessi ordinato	**aveste** ordinato
avesse ordinato	**avessero** ordinato

organizzare — to organize

gerundio **organizzando** participio passato **organizzato**

indicativo presente

SINGULAR	PLURAL
organizz**o**	organizz**iamo**
organizz**i**	organizz**ate**
organizz**a**	organizz**ano**

imperfetto

SINGULAR	PLURAL
organizza**vo**	organizza**vamo**
organizza**vi**	organizza**vate**
organizza**va**	organizza**vano**

passato remoto

SINGULAR	PLURAL
organizz**ai**	organizz**ammo**
organizz**asti**	organizz**aste**
organizz**ò**	organizz**arono**

futuro semplice

SINGULAR	PLURAL
organizzer**ò**	organizzer**emo**
organizzer**ai**	organizzer**ete**
organizzer**à**	organizzer**anno**

condizionale presente

SINGULAR	PLURAL
organizz**erei**	organizz**eremmo**
organizz**eresti**	organizz**ereste**
organizz**erebbe**	organizz**erebbero**

congiuntivo presente

SINGULAR	PLURAL
organizz**i**	organizz**iamo**
organizz**i**	organizz**iate**
organizz**i**	organizz**ino**

congiuntivo imperfetto

SINGULAR	PLURAL
organizz**assi**	organizz**assimo**
organizz**assi**	organizz**aste**
organizz**asse**	organizz**assero**

imperativo

SINGULAR	PLURAL
	organizziamo
organizza; non organizzare	organizzate
organizzi	organizzino

passato prossimo

SINGULAR	PLURAL
ho organizzato	**abbiamo** organizzato
hai organizzato	**avete** organizzato
ha organizzato	**hanno** organizzato

trapassato prossimo

SINGULAR	PLURAL
avevo organizzato	**avevamo** organizzato
avevi organizzato	**avevate** organizzato
aveva organizzato	**avevano** organizzato

trapassato remoto

SINGULAR	PLURAL
ebbi organizzato	**avemmo** organizzato
avesti organizzato	**aveste** organizzato
ebbe organizzato	**ebbero** organizzato

futuro anteriore

SINGULAR	PLURAL
avrò organizzato	**avremo** organizzato
avrai organizzato	**avrete** organizzato
avrà organizzato	**avranno** organizzato

condizionale passato

SINGULAR	PLURAL
avrei organizzato	**avremmo** organizzato
avresti organizzato	**avreste** organizzato
avrebbe organizzato	**avrebbero** organizzato

congiuntivo passato

SINGULAR	PLURAL
abbia organizzato	**abbiamo** organizzato
abbia organizzato	**abbiate** organizzato
abbia organizzato	**abbiano** organizzato

congiuntivo trapassato

SINGULAR	PLURAL
avessi organizzato	**avessimo** organizzato
avessi organizzato	**aveste** organizzato
avesse organizzato	**avessero** organizzato

gerundio **osando** participio passato **osato**

SINGULAR	PLURAL	SINGULAR	PLURAL
indicativo presente		passato prossimo	
os**o**	os**iamo**	**ho** osato	**abbiamo** osato
os**i**	os**ate**	**hai** osato	**avete** osato
os**a**	os**ano**	**ha** osato	**hanno** osato
imperfetto		trapassato prossimo	
osa**vo**	osa**vamo**	**avevo** osato	**avevamo** osato
osa**vi**	osa**vate**	**avevi** osato	**avevate** osato
osa**va**	osa**vano**	**aveva** osato	**avevano** osato
passato remoto		trapassato remoto	
os**ai**	os**ammo**	**ebbi** osato	**avemmo** osato
os**asti**	os**aste**	**avesti** osato	**aveste** osato
os**ò**	os**arono**	**ebbe** osato	**ebbero** osato
futuro semplice		futuro anteriore	
oser**ò**	oser**emo**	**avrò** osato	**avremo** osato
oser**ai**	oser**ete**	**avrai** osato	**avrete** osato
oser**à**	oser**anno**	**avrà** osato	**avranno** osato
condizionale presente		condizionale passato	
os**erei**	os**eremmo**	**avrei** osato	**avremmo** osato
os**eresti**	os**ereste**	**avresti** osato	**avreste** osato
os**erebbe**	os**erebbero**	**avrebbe** osato	**avrebbero** osato
congiuntivo presente		congiuntivo passato	
os**i**	os**iamo**	**abbia** osato	**abbiamo** osato
os**i**	os**iate**	**abbia** osato	**abbiate** osato
os**i**	os**ino**	**abbia** osato	**abbiano** osato
congiuntivo imperfetto		congiuntivo trapassato	
os**assi**	os**assimo**	**avessi** osato	**avessimo** osato
os**assi**	os**aste**	**avessi** osato	**aveste** osato
os**asse**	os**assero**	**avesse** osato	**avessero** osato
imperativo			
	osiamo		
osa; non osare	osate		
osi	osino		

O

oscurare — to darken

gerundio **oscurando** participio passato **oscurato**

SINGULAR	PLURAL	SINGULAR	PLURAL
indicativo presente		passato prossimo	
oscur**o**	oscur**iamo**	**ho** oscurato	**abbiamo** oscurato
oscur**i**	oscur**ate**	**hai** oscurato	**avete** oscurato
oscur**a**	oscur**ano**	**ha** oscurato	**hanno** oscurato
imperfetto		trapassato prossimo	
oscura**vo**	oscura**vamo**	**avevo** oscurato	**avevamo** oscurato
oscura**vi**	oscura**vate**	**avevi** oscurato	**avevate** oscurato
oscura**va**	oscura**vano**	**aveva** oscurato	**avevano** oscurato
passato remoto		trapassato remoto	
oscur**ai**	oscur**ammo**	**ebbi** oscurato	**avemmo** oscurato
oscur**asti**	oscur**aste**	**avesti** oscurato	**aveste** oscurato
oscur**ò**	oscur**arono**	**ebbe** oscurato	**ebbero** oscurato
futuro semplice		futuro anteriore	
oscurer**ò**	oscurer**emo**	**avrò** oscurato	**avremo** oscurato
oscurer**ai**	oscurer**ete**	**avrai** oscurato	**avrete** oscurato
oscurer**à**	oscurer**anno**	**avrà** oscurato	**avranno** oscurato
condizionale presente		condizionale passato	
oscur**erei**	oscur**eremmo**	**avrei** oscurato	**avremmo** oscurato
oscur**eresti**	oscur**ereste**	**avresti** oscurato	**avreste** oscurato
oscur**erebbe**	oscur**erebbero**	**avrebbe** oscurato	**avrebbero** oscurato
congiuntivo presente		congiuntivo passato	
oscur**i**	oscur**iamo**	**abbia** oscurato	**abbiamo** oscurato
oscur**i**	oscur**iate**	**abbia** oscurato	**abbiate** oscurato
oscur**i**	oscur**ino**	**abbia** oscurato	**abbiano** oscurato
congiuntivo imperfetto		congiuntivo trapassato	
oscur**assi**	oscur**assimo**	**avessi** oscurato	**avessimo** oscurato
oscur**assi**	oscur**aste**	**avessi** oscurato	**aveste** oscurato
oscur**asse**	oscur**assero**	**avesse** oscurato	**avessero** oscurato
imperativo			
	oscuriamo		
oscura; non oscurare	oscurate		
oscuri	oscurino		

O

gerundio **ospitando** participio passato **ospitato**

SINGULAR	PLURAL
indicativo presente	
ospit**o**	ospit**iamo**
ospit**i**	ospit**ate**
ospit**a**	ospit**ano**
imperfetto	
ospita**vo**	ospita**vamo**
ospita**vi**	ospita**vate**
ospita**va**	ospita**vano**
passato remoto	
ospit**ai**	ospit**ammo**
ospit**asti**	ospit**aste**
ospit**ò**	ospit**arono**
futuro semplice	
ospiter**ò**	ospiter**emo**
ospiter**ai**	ospiter**ete**
ospiter**à**	ospiter**anno**
condizionale presente	
ospit**erei**	ospit**eremmo**
ospit**eresti**	ospit**ereste**
ospit**erebbe**	ospit**erebbero**
congiuntivo presente	
ospit**i**	ospit**iamo**
ospit**i**	ospit**iate**
ospit**i**	ospit**ino**
congiuntivo imperfetto	
ospit**assi**	ospit**assimo**
ospit**assi**	ospit**aste**
ospit**asse**	ospit**assero**
imperativo	
	ospita
ospiti; non ospitare	ospitiamo
ospitate	ospitino

SINGULAR	PLURAL
passato prossimo	
ho ospitato	**abbiamo** ospitato
hai ospitato	**avete** ospitato
ha ospitato	**hanno** ospitato
trapassato prossimo	
avevo ospitato	**avevamo** ospitato
avevi ospitato	**avevate** ospitato
aveva ospitato	**avevano** ospitato
trapassato remoto	
ebbi ospitato	**avemmo** ospitato
avesti ospitato	**aveste** ospitato
ebbe ospitato	**ebbero** ospitato
futuro anteriore	
avrò ospitato	**avremo** ospitato
avrai ospitato	**avrete** ospitato
avrà ospitato	**avranno** ospitato
condizionale passato	
avrei ospitato	**avremmo** ospitato
avresti ospitato	**avreste** ospitato
avrebbe ospitato	**avrebbero** ospitato
congiuntivo passato	
abbia ospitato	**abbiamo** ospitato
abbia ospitato	**abbiate** ospitato
abbia ospitato	**abbiano** ospitato
congiuntivo trapassato	
avessi ospitato	**avessimo** ospitato
avessi ospitato	**aveste** ospitato
avesse ospitato	**avessero** ospitato

osservare — to observe, to watch

gerundio **osservando** participio passato **osservato**

SINGULAR	PLURAL	SINGULAR	PLURAL
indicativo presente		passato prossimo	
osserv**o**	osserv**iamo**	**ho** osservato	**abbiamo** osservato
osserv**i**	osserv**ate**	**hai** osservato	**avete** osservato
osserv**a**	osserv**ano**	**ha** osservato	**hanno** osservato
imperfetto		trapassato prossimo	
osserva**vo**	osserva**vamo**	**avevo** osservato	**avevamo** osservato
osserva**vi**	osserva**vate**	**avevi** osservato	**avevate** osservato
osserva**va**	osserva**vano**	**aveva** osservato	**avevano** osservato
passato remoto		trapassato remoto	
osserv**ai**	osserv**ammo**	**ebbi** osservato	**avemmo** osservato
osserv**asti**	osserv**aste**	**avesti** osservato	**aveste** osservato
osserv**ò**	osserv**arono**	**ebbe** osservato	**ebbero** osservato
futuro semplice		futuro anteriore	
osserver**ò**	osserver**emo**	**avrò** osservato	**avremo** osservato
osserver**ai**	osserver**ete**	**avrai** osservato	**avrete** osservato
osserver**à**	osserver**anno**	**avrà** osservato	**avranno** osservato
condizionale presente		condizionale passato	
osserv**erei**	osserv**eremmo**	**avrei** osservato	**avremmo** osservato
osserv**eresti**	osserv**ereste**	**avresti** osservato	**avreste** osservato
osserv**erebbe**	osserv**erebbero**	**avrebbe** osservato	**avrebbero** osservato
congiuntivo presente		congiuntivo passato	
osserv**i**	osserv**iamo**	**abbia** osservato	**abbiamo** osservato
osserv**i**	osserv**iate**	**abbia** osservato	**abbiate** osservato
osserv**i**	osserv**ino**	**abbia** osservato	**abbiano** osservato
congiuntivo imperfetto		congiuntivo trapassato	
osserv**assi**	osserv**assimo**	**avessi** osservato	**avessimo** osservato
osserv**assi**	osserv**aste**	**avessi** osservato	**aveste** osservato
osserv**asse**	osserv**assero**	**avesse** osservato	**avessero** osservato
imperativo			
	osserviamo		
osserva; non osservare	osservate		
osservi	osservino		

O

to insist, to persist **ostinarsi**

gerundio **ostinandosi** participio passato **ostinatosi**

SINGULAR	PLURAL
indicativo presente	
mi ostin**o**	**ci** ostin**iamo**
ti ostin**i**	**vi** ostin**ate**
si ostin**a**	**si** ostin**ano**
imperfetto	
mi ostina**vo**	**ci** ostina**vamo**
ti ostina**vi**	**vi** ostina**vate**
si ostina**va**	**si** ostina**vano**
passato remoto	
mi ostin**ai**	**ci** ostin**ammo**
ti ostin**asti**	**vi** ostin**aste**
si ostin**ò**	**si** ostin**arono**
futuro semplice	
mi ostiner**ò**	**ci** ostiner**emo**
ti ostiner**ai**	**vi** ostiner**ete**
si ostiner**à**	**si** ostiner**anno**
condizionale presente	
mi ostin**erei**	**ci** ostin**eremmo**
ti ostin**eresti**	**vi** ostin**ereste**
si ostin**erebbe**	**si** ostin**erebbero**
congiuntivo presente	
mi ostin**i**	**ci** ostin**iamo**
ti ostin**i**	**vi** ostin**iate**
si ostin**i**	**si** ostin**ino**
congiuntivo imperfetto	
mi ostin**assi**	**ci** ostin**assimo**
ti ostin**assi**	**vi** ostin**aste**
si ostin**asse**	**si** ostin**assero**
imperativo	
	ostiniamoci
ostinati; non ostinarti/ non ti ostinare	ostinatevi
si ostini	si ostinino

SINGULAR	PLURAL
passato prossimo	
mi sono ostinato(a)	**ci siamo** ostinati(e)
ti sei ostinato(a)	**vi siete** ostinati(e)
si è ostinato(a)	**si sono** ostinati(e)
trapassato prossimo	
mi ero ostinato(a)	**ci eravamo** ostinati(e)
ti eri ostinato(a)	**vi eravate** ostinati(e)
si era ostinato(a)	**si erano** ostinati(e)
trapassato remoto	
mi fui ostinato(a)	**ci fummo** ostinati(e)
ti fosti ostinato(a)	**vi foste** ostinati(e)
si fu ostinato(a)	**si furono** ostinati(e)
futuro anteriore	
mi sarò ostinato(a)	**ci saremo** ostinati(e)
ti sarai ostinato(a)	**vi sarete** ostinati(e)
si sarà ostinato(a)	**si saranno** ostinati(e)
condizionale passato	
mi sarei ostinato(a)	**ci saremmo** ostinati(e)
ti saresti ostinato(a)	**vi sareste** ostinati(e)
si sarebbe ostinato(a)	**si sarebbero** ostinati(e)
congiuntivo passato	
mi sia ostinato(a)	**ci siamo** ostinati(e)
ti sia ostinato(a)	**vi siate** ostinati(e)
si sia ostinato(a)	**si siano** ostinati(e)
congiuntivo trapassato	
mi fossi ostinato(a)	**ci fossimo** ostinati(e)
ti fossi ostinato(a)	**vi foste** ostinati(e)
si fosse ostinato(a)	**si fossero** ostinati(e)

ottenere — to obtain, to get

gerundio **ottenendo** participio passato **ottenuto**

SINGULAR	PLURAL	SINGULAR	PLURAL
indicativo presente		passato prossimo	
otteng**o**	otten**iamo**	**ho** ottenuto	**abbiamo** ottenuto
ottien**i**	otten**ete**	**hai** ottenuto	**avete** ottenuto
ottien**e**	otteng**ono**	**ha** ottenuto	**hanno** ottenuto
imperfetto		trapassato prossimo	
ottene**vo**	ottene**vamo**	**avevo** ottenuto	**avevamo** ottenuto
ottene**vi**	ottene**vate**	**avevi** ottenuto	**avevate** ottenuto
ottene**va**	ottene**vano**	**aveva** ottenuto	**avevano** ottenuto
passato remoto		trapassato remoto	
otte**nni**	otte**nemmo**	**ebbi** ottenuto	**avemmo** ottenuto
otte**nesti**	otte**neste**	**avesti** ottenuto	**aveste** ottenuto
otte**nne**	otte**nnero**	**ebbe** ottenuto	**ebbero** ottenuto
futuro semplice		futuro anteriore	
otterr**ò**	otterr**emo**	**avrò** ottenuto	**avremo** ottenuto
otterr**ai**	otterr**ete**	**avrai** ottenuto	**avrete** ottenuto
otterr**à**	otterr**anno**	**avrà** ottenuto	**avranno** ottenuto
condizionale presente		condizionale passato	
ott**errei**	ott**erremmo**	**avrei** ottenuto	**avremmo** ottenuto
ott**erresti**	ott**erreste**	**avresti** ottenuto	**avreste** ottenuto
ott**errebbe**	ott**errebbero**	**avrebbe** ottenuto	**avrebbero** ottenuto
congiuntivo presente		congiuntivo passato	
otteng**a**	otten**iamo**	**abbia** ottenuto	**abbiamo** ottenuto
otteng**a**	otten**iate**	**abbia** ottenuto	**abbiate** ottenuto
otteng**a**	otteng**ano**	**abbia** ottenuto	**abbiano** ottenuto
congiuntivo imperfetto		congiuntivo trapassato	
otten**essi**	otten**essimo**	**avessi** ottenuto	**avessimo** ottenuto
otten**essi**	otten**este**	**avessi** ottenuto	**aveste** ottenuto
otten**esse**	otten**essero**	**avesse** ottenuto	**avessero** ottenuto
imperativo			
	otteniamo		
ottieni; non ottenere	ottenete		
ottenga	ottengano		

gerundio **pagando** participio passato **pagato**

SINGULAR	PLURAL	SINGULAR	PLURAL
indicativo presente		passato prossimo	
pag**o**	pagh**iamo**	**ho** pagato	**abbiamo** pagato
pagh**i**	pag**ate**	**hai** pagato	**avete** pagato
pag**a**	pag**ano**	**ha** pagato	**hanno** pagato
imperfetto		trapassato prossimo	
paga**vo**	paga**vamo**	**avevo** pagato	**avevamo** pagato
paga**vi**	paga**vate**	**avevi** pagato	**avevate** pagato
paga**va**	paga**vano**	**aveva** pagato	**avevano** pagato
passato remoto		trapassato remoto	
pag**ai**	pag**ammo**	**ebbi** pagato	**avemmo** pagato
pag**asti**	pag**aste**	**avesti** pagato	**aveste** pagato
pag**ò**	pag**arono**	**ebbe** pagato	**ebbero** pagato
futuro semplice		futuro anteriore	
pagher**ò**	pagher**emo**	**avrò** pagato	**avremo** pagato
pagher**ai**	pagher**ete**	**avrai** pagato	**avrete** pagato
pagher**à**	pagher**anno**	**avrà** pagato	**avranno** pagato
condizionale presente		condizionale passato	
pagh**erei**	pagh**eremmo**	**avrei** pagato	**avremmo** pagato
pagh**eresti**	pagh**ereste**	**avresti** pagato	**avreste** pagato
pagh**erebbe**	pagh**erebbero**	**avrebbe** pagato	**avrebbero** pagato
congiuntivo presente		congiuntivo passato	
pagh**i**	pagh**iamo**	**abbia** pagato	**abbiamo** pagato
pagh**i**	pagh**iate**	**abbia** pagato	**abbiate** pagato
pagh**i**	pagh**ino**	**abbia** pagato	**abbiano** pagato
congiuntivo imperfetto		congiuntivo trapassato	
pag**assi**	pag**assimo**	**avessi** pagato	**avessimo** pagato
pag**assi**	pag**aste**	**avessi** pagato	**aveste** pagato
pag**asse**	pag**assero**	**avesse** pagato	**avessero** pagato
imperativo			
	paghiamo		
paga; non pagare	pagate		
paghi	paghino		

P

parcheggiare — to park

gerundio **parcheggiando** participio passato **parcheggiato**

indicativo presente

SINGULAR	PLURAL
parcheggi**o**	parchegg**iamo**
parcheggi**i**	parchegg**iate**
parcheggi**a**	parchegg**iano**

imperfetto

SINGULAR	PLURAL
parcheggia**vo**	parcheggia**vamo**
parcheggia**vi**	parcheggia**vate**
parcheggia**va**	parcheggia**vano**

passato remoto

SINGULAR	PLURAL
parcheggi**ai**	parcheggi**ammo**
parcheggi**asti**	parcheggi**aste**
parcheggi**ò**	parcheggi**arono**

futuro semplice

SINGULAR	PLURAL
parchegger**ò**	parchegg**eremo**
parchegger**ai**	parchegg**erete**
parchegger**à**	parchegg**eranno**

condizionale presente

SINGULAR	PLURAL
pareheggg**erei**	parchegg**eremmo**
parchegg**eresti**	parchegg**ereste**
parchegg**erebbe**	parchegg**erebbero**

congiuntivo presente

SINGULAR	PLURAL
parchegg**i**	parchegg**iamo**
parchegg**i**	parchegg**iate**
parchegg**i**	parchegg**ino**

congiuntivo imperfetto

SINGULAR	PLURAL
parcheggi**assi**	parcheggi**assimo**
parcheggi**assi**	parcheggi**aste**
parcheggi**asse**	parcheggi**assero**

imperativo

SINGULAR	PLURAL
	parcheggiamo
parcheggia; non parcheggiare	parcheggiate
parcheggi	parcheggino

passato prossimo

SINGULAR	PLURAL
ho parcheggiato	**abbiamo** parcheggiato
hai parcheggiato	**avete** parcheggiato
ha parcheggiato	**hanno** parcheggiato

trapassato prossimo

SINGULAR	PLURAL
avevo parcheggiato	**avevamo** parcheggiato
avevi parcheggiato	**avevate** parcheggiato
aveva parcheggiato	**avevano** parcheggiato

trapassato remoto

SINGULAR	PLURAL
ebbi parcheggiato	**avemmo** parcheggiato
avesti parcheggiato	**aveste** parcheggiato
ebbe parcheggiato	**ebbero** parcheggiato

futuro anteriore

SINGULAR	PLURAL
avrò parcheggiato	**avremo** parcheggiato
avrai parcheggiato	**avrete** parcheggiato
avrà parcheggiato	**avranno** parcheggiato

condizionale passato

SINGULAR	PLURAL
avrei parcheggiato	**avremmo** parcheggiato
avresti parcheggiato	**avreste** parcheggiato
avrebbe parcheggiato	**avrebbero** parcheggiato

congiuntivo passato

SINGULAR	PLURAL
abbia parcheggiato	**abbiamo** parcheggiato
abbia parcheggiato	**abbiate** parcheggiato
abbia parcheggiato	**abbiano** parcheggiato

congiuntivo trapassato

SINGULAR	PLURAL
avessi parcheggiato	**avessimo** parcheggiato
avessi parcheggiato	**aveste** parcheggiato
avesse parcheggiato	**avessero** parcheggiato

to appear, to seem **parere**

gerundio **parendo** participio passato **parso**

SINGULAR	PLURAL	SINGULAR	PLURAL
indicativo presente		passato prossimo	
pai**o**	pa**iamo**	**sono** parso(a)	**siamo** parsi(e)
par**i**	par**ete**	**sei** parso(a)	**siete** parsi(e)
par**e**	pai**ono**	**è** parso(a)	**sono** parsi(e)
imperfetto		trapassato prossimo	
pare**vo**	pare**vamo**	**ero** parso(a)	**eravamo** parsi(e)
pare**vi**	pare**vate**	**eri** parso(a)	**eravate** parsi(e)
pare**va**	pare**vano**	**era** parso(a)	**erano** parsi(e)
passato remoto		trapassato remoto	
parvi	par**emmo**	**fui** parso(a)	**fummo** parsi(e)
par**esti**	par**este**	**fosti** parso(a)	**foste** parsi(e)
parve	**parvero**	**fu** parso(a)	**furono** parsi(e)
futuro semplice		futuro anteriore	
parr**ò**	parr**emo**	**sarò** parso(a)	**saremo** parsi(e)
parr**ai**	parr**ete**	**sarai** parso(a)	**sarete** parsi(e)
parr**à**	parr**anno**	**sarà** parso(a)	**saranno** parsi(e)
condizionale presente		condizionale passato	
parr**ei**	parr**emmo**	**sarei** parso(a)	**saremmo** parsi(e)
parr**esti**	parr**este**	**saresti** parso(a)	**sareste** parsi(e)
parr**ebbe**	parr**ebbero**	**sarebbe** parso(a)	**sarebbero** parsi(e)
congiuntivo presente		congiuntivo passato	
pai**a**	pa**iamo**	**sia** parso(a)	**siamo** parsi(e)
pai**a**	pa**iate**	**sia** parso(a)	**siate** parsi(e)
pai**a**	pa**iano**	**sia** parso(a)	**siano** parsi(e)
congiuntivo imperfetto		congiuntivo trapassato	
par**essi**	par**essimo**	**fossi** parso(a)	**fossimo** parsi(e)
par**essi**	par**este**	**fossi** parso(a)	**foste** parsi(e)
par**esse**	par**essero**	**fosse** parso(a)	**fossero** parsi(e)

parlare — to speak, to talk

gerundio **parlando** participio passato **parlato**

SINGULAR	PLURAL	SINGULAR	PLURAL
indicativo presente		passato prossimo	
parl**o**	parl**iamo**	**ho** parlato	**abbiamo** parlato
parl**i**	parl**ate**	**hai** parlato	**avete** parlato
parl**a**	parl**ano**	**ha** parlato	**hanno** parlato
imperfetto		trapassato prossimo	
parla**vo**	parla**vamo**	**avevo** parlato	**avevamo** parlato
parla**vi**	parla**vate**	**avevi** parlato	**avevate** parlato
parla**va**	parla**vano**	**aveva** parlato	**avevano** parlato
passato remoto		trapassato remoto	
parl**ai**	parl**ammo**	**ebbi** parlato	**avemmo** parlato
parl**asti**	parl**aste**	**avesti** parlato	**aveste** parlato
parl**ò**	parl**arono**	**ebbe** parlato	**ebbero** parlato
futuro semplice		futuro anteriore	
parler**ò**	parler**emo**	**avrò** parlato	**avremo** parlato
parler**ai**	parler**ete**	**avrai** parlato	**avrete** parlato
parler**à**	parler**anno**	**avrà** parlato	**avranno** parlato
condizionale presente		condizionale passato	
parl**erei**	parl**eremmo**	**avrei** parlato	**avremmo** parlato
parl**eresti**	parl**ereste**	**avresti** parlato	**avreste** parlato
parl**erebbe**	parl**erebbero**	**avrebbe** parlato	**avrebbero** parlato
congiuntivo presente		congiuntivo passato	
parl**i**	parl**iamo**	**abbia** parlato	**abbiamo** parlato
parl**i**	parl**iate**	**abbia** parlato	**abbiate** parlato
parl**i**	parl**ino**	**abbia** parlato	**abbiano** parlato
congiuntivo imperfetto		congiuntivo trapassato	
parl**assi**	parl**assimo**	**avessi** parlato	**avessimo** parlato
parl**assi**	parl**aste**	**avessi** parlato	**aveste** parlato
parl**asse**	parl**assero**	**avesse** parlato	**avessero** parlato
imperativo			
	parliamo		
parla; non parlare	parlate		
parli	parlino		

P

to participate **partecipare**

gerundio **partecipando** participio passato **partecipato**

SINGULAR	PLURAL	SINGULAR	PLURAL
indicativo presente		passato prossimo	
partecip**o**	partecip**iamo**	**ho** partecipato	**abbiamo** partecipato
partecip**i**	partecip**ate**	**hai** partecipato	**avete** partecipato
partecip**a**	partecip**ano**	**ha** partecipato	**hanno** partecipato
imperfetto		trapassato prossimo	
partecipa**vo**	partecipa**vamo**	**avevo** partecipato	**avevamo** partecipato
partecipa**vi**	partecipa**vate**	**avevi** partecipato	**avevate** partecipato
partecipa**va**	partecipa**vano**	**aveva** partecipato	**avevano** partecipato
passato remoto		trapassato remoto	
partecip**ai**	partecip**ammo**	**ebbi** partecipato	**avemmo** partecipato
partecip**asti**	partecip**aste**	**avesti** partecipato	**aveste** partecipato
partecip**ò**	partecip**arono**	**ebbe** partecipato	**ebbero** partecipato
futuro semplice		futuro anteriore	
parteciper**ò**	parteciper**emo**	**avrò** partecipato	**avremo** partecipato
parteciper**ai**	parteciper**ete**	**avrai** partecipato	**avrete** partecipato
parteciper**à**	parteciper**anno**	**avrà** partecipato	**avranno** partecipato
condizionale presente		condizionale passato	
partecip**erei**	partecip**eremmo**	**avrei** partecipato	**avremmo** partecipato
partecip**eresti**	partecip**ereste**	**avresti** partecipato	**avreste** partecipato
partecip**erebbe**	partecip**erebbero**	**avrebbe** partecipato	**avrebbero** partecipato
congiuntivo presente		congiuntivo passato	
partecip**i**	partecip**iamo**	**abbia** partecipato	**abbiamo** partecipato
partecip**i**	partecip**iate**	**abbia** partecipato	**abbiate** partecipato
partecip**i**	partecip**ino**	**abbia** partecipato	**abbiano** partecipato
congiuntivo imperfetto		congiuntivo trapassato	
partecip**assi**	partecip**assimo**	**avessi** partecipato	**avessimo** partecipato
partecip**assi**	partecip**aste**	**avessi** partecipato	**aveste** partecipato
partecip**asse**	partecip**assero**	**avesse** partecipato	**avessero** partecipato
imperativo			
	partecipiamo		
partecipa; non partecipare	partecipate		
partecipi	partecipino		

P

partire — to leave

gerundio **partendo** — participio passato **partito**

SINGULAR	PLURAL	SINGULAR	PLURAL
indicativo presente		passato prossimo	
part**o**	part**iamo**	**sono** partito(a)	**siamo** partiti(e)
part**i**	part**ite**	**sei** partito(a)	**siete** partiti(e)
part**e**	part**ono**	**è** partito(a)	**sono** partiti(e)
imperfetto		trapassato prossimo	
parti**vo**	parti**vamo**	**ero** partito(a)	**eravamo** partiti(e)
parti**vi**	parti**vate**	**eri** partito(a)	**eravate** partiti(e)
parti**va**	parti**vano**	**era** partito(a)	**erano** partiti(e)
passato remoto		trapassato remoto	
part**ii**	part**immo**	**fui** partito(a)	**fummo** partiti(e)
part**isti**	part**iste**	**fosti** partito(a)	**foste** partiti(e)
part**ì**	part**irono**	**fu** partito(a)	**furono** partiti(e)
futuro semplice		futuro anteriore	
partir**ò**	partir**emo**	**sarò** partito(a)	**saremo** partiti(e)
partir**ai**	partir**ete**	**sarai** partito(a)	**sarete** partiti(e)
partir**à**	partir**anno**	**sarà** partito(a)	**saranno** partiti(e)
condizionale presente		condizionale passato	
part**irei**	part**iremmo**	**sarei** partito(a)	**saremmo** partiti(e)
part**iresti**	part**ireste**	**saresti** partito(a)	**sareste** partiti(e)
part**irebbe**	part**irebbero**	**sarebbe** partito(a)	**sarebbero** partiti(e)
congiuntivo presente		congiuntivo passato	
part**a**	part**iamo**	**sia** partito(a)	**siamo** partiti(e)
part**a**	part**iate**	**sia** partito(a)	**siate** partiti(e)
part**a**	part**ano**	**sia** partito(a)	**siano** partiti(e)
congiuntivo imperfetto		congiuntivo trapassato	
part**issi**	part**issimo**	**fossi** partito(a)	**fossimo** partiti(e)
part**issi**	part**iste**	**fossi** partito(a)	**foste** partiti(e)
part**isse**	part**issero**	**fosse** partito(a)	**fossero** partiti(e)

P

imperativo

	partiamo
parti; non partire	partite
parta	partano

to pass, to proceed — passare

gerundio **passando** participio passato **passato**

SINGULAR	PLURAL
indicativo presente	
pass**o**	pass**iamo**
pass**i**	pass**ate**
pass**a**	pass**ano**
imperfetto	
passa**vo**	passa**vamo**
passa**vi**	passa**vate**
passa**va**	passa**vano**
passato remoto	
pass**ai**	pass**ammo**
pass**asti**	pass**aste**
pass**ò**	passar**ono**
futuro semplice	
passer**ò**	passer**emo**
passer**ai**	passer**ete**
passer**à**	passer**anno**
condizionale presente	
pass**erei**	pass**eremmo**
pass**eresti**	pass**ereste**
pass**erebbe**	pass**erebbero**
congiuntivo presente	
pass**i**	pass**iamo**
pass**i**	pass**iate**
pass**i**	pass**ino**
congiuntivo imperfetto	
pass**assi**	pass**assimo**
pass**assi**	pass**aste**
pass**asse**	pass**assero**
imperativo	
	passiamo
passa; non passare	passiate
passi	passino

SINGULAR	PLURAL
passato prossimo	
ho passato	**abbiamo** passato
hai passato	**avete** passato
ha passato	**hanno** passato
trapassato prossimo	
avevo passato	**avevamo** passato
avevi passato	**avevate** passato
aveva passato	**avevano** passato
trapassato remoto	
ebbi passato	**avemmo** passato
avesti passato	**aveste** passato
ebbe passato	**ebbero** passato
futuro anteriore	
avrò passato	**avremo** passato
avrai passato	**avrete** passato
avrà passato	**avranno** passato
condizionale passato	
avrei passato	**avremmo** passato
avresti passato	**avreste** passato
avrebbe passato	**avrebbero** passato
congiuntivo passato	
abbia passato	**abbiamo** passato
abbia passato	**abbiate** passato
abbia passato	**abbiano** passato
congiuntivo trapassato	
avessi passato	**avessimo** passato
avessi passato	**aveste** passato
avesse passato	**avessero** passato

passeggiare — to walk, to stroll

gerundio **passeggiando** participio passato **passeggiato**

SINGULAR	PLURAL	SINGULAR	PLURAL
indicativo presente		passato prossimo	
passeggi**o**	passeggi**amo**	**ho** passeggiato	**abbiamo** passeggiato
passegg**i**	passeggi**ate**	**hai** passeggiato	**avete** passeggiato
passeggi**a**	passeggi**ano**	**ha** passeggiato	**hanno** passeggiato
imperfetto		trapassato prossimo	
passeggia**vo**	passeggia**vamo**	**avevo** passeggiato	**avevamo** passeggiato
passeggia**vi**	passeggia**vate**	**avevi** passeggiato	**avevate** passeggiato
passeggia**va**	passeggia**vano**	**aveva** passeggiato	**avevano** passeggiato
passato remoto		trapassato remoto	
passeggi**ai**	passeggi**ammo**	**ebbi** passeggiato	**avemmo** passeggiato
passeggi**asti**	passeggi**aste**	**avesti** passeggiato	**aveste** passeggiato
passeggi**ò**	passeggiar**ono**	**ebbe** passeggiato	**ebbero** passeggiato
futuro semplice		futuro anteriore	
passegger**ò**	passegger**emo**	**avrò** passeggiato	**avremo** passeggiato
passegger**ai**	passegger**ete**	**avrai** passeggiato	**avrete** passeggiato
passegger**à**	passegger**anno**	**avrà** passeggiato	**avranno** passeggiato
condizionale presente		condizionale passato	
passegg**erei**	passegg**eremmo**	**avrei** passeggiato	**avremmo** passeggiato
passegg**eresti**	passegg**ereste**	**avresti** passeggiato	**avreste** passeggiato
passegg**erebbe**	passegg**erebbero**	**avrebbe** passeggiato	**avrebbero** passeggiato
congiuntivo presente		congiuntivo passato	
passegg**i**	passegg**iamo**	**abbia** passeggiato	**abbiamo** passeggiato
passegg**i**	passegg**iate**	**abbia** passeggiato	**abbiate** passeggiato
passegg**i**	passegg**ino**	**abbia** passeggiato	**abbiano** passeggiato
congiuntivo imperfetto		congiuntivo trapassato	
passeggi**assi**	passeggi**assimo**	**avessi** passeggiato	**avessimo** passeggiato
passeggi**assi**	passeggi**aste**	**avessi** passeggiato	**aveste** passeggiato
passeggi**asse**	passeggi**assero**	**avesse** passeggiato	**avessero** passeggiato

imperativo

	passeggiamo
passeggia; non passeggiare	passeggiate
passeggi	passeggino

P

to suffer, to endure **patire**

gerundio **patendo** participio passato **patito**

SINGULAR	PLURAL	SINGULAR	PLURAL
indicativo presente		passato prossimo	
patisc**o**	pat**iamo**	**ho** patito	**abbiamo** patito
partisc**i**	pat**ite**	**hai** patito	**avete** patito
patisc**e**	patisc**ono**	**ha** patito	**hanno** patito
imperfetto		trapassato prossimo	
pati**vo**	pati**vamo**	**avevo** patito	**avevamo** patito
pati**vi**	pati**vate**	**avevi** patito	**avevate** patito
pati**va**	pati**vano**	**aveva** patito	**avevano** patito
passato remoto		trapassato remoto	
pat**ii**	pat**immo**	**ebbi** patito	**avemmo** patito
pat**isti**	pat**iste**	**avesti** patito	**aveste** patito
pat**ì**	patir**ono**	**ebbe** patito	**ebbero** patito
futuro semplice		futuro anteriore	
patir**ò**	patir**emo**	**avrò** patito	**avremo** patito
patir**ai**	patir**ete**	**avrai** patito	**avrete** patito
patir**à**	patir**anno**	**avrà** patito	**avranno** patito
condizionale presente		condizionale passato	
pat**irei**	pat**iremmo**	**avrei** patito	**avremmo** patito
pat**iresti**	pat**ireste**	**avresti** patito	**avreste** patito
pat**irebbe**	pat**irebbero**	**avrebbe** patito	**avrebbero** patito
congiuntivo presente		congiuntivo passato	
patisc**a**	pat**iamo**	**abbia** patito	**abbiamo** patito
patisc**a**	pat**iate**	**abbia** patito	**abbiate** patito
patisc**a**	patisc**ano**	**abbia** patito	**abbiano** patito
congiuntivo imperfetto		congiuntivo trapassato	
pat**issi**	pat**issimo**	**avessi** patito	**avessimo** patito
pat**issi**	pat**iste**	**avessi** patito	**aveste** patito
pat**isse**	pat**issero**	**avesse** patito	**avessero** patito

imperativo

SINGULAR	PLURAL
	patiamo
patisci; non patire	patite
patisca	patiscano

pendere — to hang

gerundio **pendendo** participio passato **penduto**

SINGULAR	PLURAL	SINGULAR	PLURAL
indicativo presente		passato prossimo	
pend**o**	pend**iamo**	**ho** penduto	**abbiamo** penduto
pend**i**	pend**ete**	**hai** penduto	**avete** penduto
pend**e**	pend**ono**	**ha** penduto	**hanno** penduto
imperfetto		trapassato prossimo	
pende**vo**	pende**vamo**	**avevo** penduto	**avevamo** penduto
pende**vi**	pende**vate**	**avevi** penduto	**avevate** penduto
pende**va**	pende**vano**	**aveva** penduto	**avevano** penduto
passato remoto		trapassato remoto	
pend**ei** (pend**etti**)	pend**emmo**	**ebbi** penduto	**avemmo** penduto
pend**esti**	pend**este**	**avesti** penduto	**aveste** penduto
pend**é** (pendet**te**)	pender**ono** (pendett**ero**)	**ebbe** penduto	**ebbero** penduto
futuro semplice		futuro anteriore	
pender**ò**	pender**emo**	**avrò** penduto	**avremo** penduto
pender**ai**	pender**ete**	**avrai** penduto	**avrete** penduto
pender**à**	pender**anno**	**avrà** penduto	**avranno** penduto
condizionale presente		condizionale passato	
pend**erei**	pend**eremmo**	**avrei** penduto	**avremmo** penduto
pend**eresti**	pend**ereste**	**avresti** penduto	**avreste** penduto
pend**erebbe**	pend**erebbero**	**avrebbe** penduto	**avrebbero** penduto
congiuntivo presente		congiuntivo passato	
pend**a**	pend**iamo**	**abbia** penduto	**abbiamo** penduto
pend**a**	pend**iate**	**abbia** penduto	**abbiate** penduto
pend**a**	pend**ano**	**abbia** penduto	**abbiano** penduto
congiuntivo imperfetto		congiuntivo trapassato	
pend**essi**	pend**essimo**	**avessi** penduto	**avessimo** penduto
pend**essi**	pend**este**	**avessi** penduto	**aveste** penduto
pend**esse**	pend**essero**	**avesse** penduto	**avessero** penduto

imperativo

	pendiamo
pendi; non pendere	pendete
penda	pendano

P

gerundio **penetrando** participio passato **penetrato**

SINGULAR	PLURAL	SINGULAR	PLURAL
indicativo presente		passato prossimo	
penetr**o**	penetr**iamo**	**ho** penetrato	**abbiamo** penetrato
penetr**i**	penetr**ate**	**hai** penetrato	**avete** penetrato
penetr**a**	penetr**ano**	**ha** penetrato	**hanno** penetrato
imperfetto		trapassato prossimo	
penetra**vo**	penetra**vamo**	**avevo** penetrato	**avevamo** penetrato
penetra**vi**	penetra**vate**	**avevi** penetrato	**avevate** penetrato
penetra**va**	penetra**vano**	**aveva** penetrato	**avevano** penetrato
passato remoto		trapassato remoto	
penetr**ai**	penetr**ammo**	**ebbi** penetrato	**avemmo** penetrato
penetr**asti**	penetr**aste**	**avesti** penetrato	**aveste** penetrato
penetr**ò**	penetr**arono**	**ebbe** penetrato	**ebbero** penetrato
futuro semplice		futuro anteriore	
penetrer**ò**	penetrer**emo**	**avrò** penetrato	**avremo** penetrato
penetrer**ai**	penetrer**ete**	**avrai** penetrato	**avrete** penetrato
penetrer**à**	penetrer**anno**	**avrà** penetrato	**avranno** penetrato
condizionale presente		condizionale passato	
penetr**erei**	penetr**eremmo**	**avrei** penetrato	**avremmo** penetrato
penetr**eresti**	penetr**ereste**	**avresti** penetrato	**avreste** penetrato
penetr**erebbe**	penetr**erebbero**	**avrebbe** penetrato	**avrebbero** penetrato
congiuntivo presente		congiuntivo passato	
penetr**i**	penetr**iamo**	**abbia** penetrato	**abbiamo** penetrato
penetr**i**	penetr**iate**	**abbia** penetrato	**abbiate** penetrato
penetr**i**	penetr**ino**	**abbia** penetrato	**abbiano** penetrato
congiuntivo imperfetto		congiuntivo trapassato	
penetr**assi**	penetr**assimo**	**avessi** penetrato	**avessimo** penetrato
penetr**assi**	penetr**aste**	**avessi** penetrato	**aveste** penetrato
penetr**asse**	penetr**assero**	**avesse** penetrato	**avessero** penetrato
imperativo			
	penetriamo		
penetra; non penetrare	penetrate		
penetri	penetrino		

pensare — to think

gerundio **pensando**   participio passato **pensato**

	SINGULAR	PLURAL
indicativo presente	pens**o**	pens**iamo**
	pens**i**	pens**ate**
	pens**a**	pens**ano**
imperfetto	pensa**vo**	pansa**vamo**
	pensa**vi**	pensa**vate**
	pensa**va**	pensa**vano**
passato remoto	pens**ai**	pens**ammo**
	pens**asti**	pens**aste**
	pens**ò**	pens**arono**
futuro semplice	penser**ò**	penser**emo**
	penser**ai**	penser**ete**
	penser**à**	penser**anno**
condizionale presente	pens**erei**	pens**eremmo**
	pens**eresti**	pens**ereste**
	pens**erebbe**	pens**erebbero**
congiuntivo presente	pens**i**	pens**iamo**
	pens**i**	pens**iate**
	pens**i**	pens**ino**
congiuntivo imperfetto	pens**assi**	pens**assimo**
	pens**assi**	pens**aste**
	pens**asse**	pens**assero**
imperativo		pensiamo
	pensa; non pensare	pensate
	pensi	pensino

	SINGULAR	PLURAL
passato prossimo	**ho** pensato	**abbiamo** pensato
	hai pensato	**avete** pensato
	ha pensato	**hanno** pensato
trapassato prossimo	**avevo** pensato	**avevamo** pensato
	avevi pensato	**avevate** pensato
	aveva pensato	**avevano** pensato
trapassato remoto	**ebbi** pensato	**avemmo** pensato
	avesti pensato	**aveste** pensato
	ebbe pensato	**ebbero** pensato
futuro anteriore	**avrò** pensato	**avremo** pensato
	avrai pensato	**avrete** pensato
	avrà pensato	**avranno** pensato
condizionale passato	**avrei** pensato	**avremmo** pensato
	avresti pensato	**avreste** pensato
	avrebbe pensato	**avrebbero** pensato
congiuntivo passato	**abbia** pensato	**abbiamo** pensato
	abbia pensato	**abbiate** pensato
	abbia pensato	**abbiano** pensato
congiuntivo trapassato	**avessi** pensato	**avessimo** pensato
	avessi pensato	**aveste** pensato
	avesse pensato	**avessero** pensato

gerundio **percuotendo** participio passato **percosso**

SINGULAR	PLURAL
indicativo presente	
percuot**o**	percuot**iamo**
percuot**i**	percuot**ete**
percuot**e**	percuot**ono**
imperfetto	
percuote**vo**	percuote**vamo**
percuote**vi**	percuote**vate**
percuote**va**	percuote**vano**
passato remoto	
percoss**i**	percuot**emmo**
percuot**esti**	percuot**este**
percoss**e**	percoss**ero**
futuro semplice	
percuoter**ò**	percuoter**emo**
percuoter**ai**	percuoter**ete**
percuoter**à**	percuoter**anno**
condizionale presente	
percuot**erei**	percuot**eremmo**
percuot**eresti**	percuot**ereste**
percuot**erebbe**	percuot**erebbero**
congiuntivo presente	
percuot**a**	percuot**iamo**
percuot**a**	percuot**iate**
percuot**a**	percuot**ano**
congiuntivo imperfetto	
percuot**essi**	percuot**essimo**
percuot**essi**	percuot**este**
percuot**esse**	percuot**essero**
imperativo	
	percuotiamo
percuoti; non percuotere	percuotete
percuota	percuotano

SINGULAR	PLURAL
passato prossimo	
ho percosso	**abbiamo** percosso
hai percosso	**avete** percosso
ha percosso	**hanno** percosso
trapassato prossimo	
avevo percosso	**avevamo** percosso
avevi percosso	**avevate** percosso
aveva percosso	**avevano** percosso
trapassato remoto	
ebbi percosso	**avemmo** percosso
avesti percosso	**aveste** percosso
ebbe percosso	**ebbero** percosso
futuro anteriore	
avrò percosso	**avremo** percosso
avrai percosso	**avrete** percosso
avrà percosso	**avranno** percosso
condizionale passato	
avrei percosso	**avremmo** percosso
avresti percosso	**avreste** percosso
avrebbe percosso	**avrebbero** percosso
congiuntivo passato	
abbia percosso	**abbiamo** percosso
abbia percosso	**abbiate** percosso
abbia percosso	**abbiano** percosso
congiuntivo trapassato	
avessi percosso	**avessimo** percosso
avessi percosso	**aveste** percosso
avesse percosso	**avessero** percosso

perdere — to lose, to miss, to waste

gerundio **perdendo** participio passato **perso**

SINGULAR	PLURAL	SINGULAR	PLURAL
indicativo presente		passato prossimo	
perd**o**	perd**iamo**	**ho** perso	**abbiamo** perso
perd**i**	perd**ete**	**hai** perso	**avete** perso
perd**e**	perd**ono**	**ha** perso	**hanno** perso
imperfetto		trapassato prossimo	
perde**vo**	perde**vamo**	**avevo** perso	**avevamo** perso
perde**vi**	perde**vate**	**avevi** perso	**avevate** perso
perde**va**	perde**vano**	**aveva** perso	**avevano** perso
passato remoto		trapassato remoto	
pers**i**	perd**emmo**	**ebbi** perso	**avemmo** perso
perd**esti**	perd**este**	**avesti** perso	**aveste** perso
pers**e**	pers**ero**	**ebbe** perso	**ebbero** perso
futuro semplice		futuro anteriore	
perder**ò**	perder**emo**	**avrò** perso	**avremo** perso
perder**ai**	perder**ete**	**avrai** perso	**avrete** perso
perder**à**	perder**anno**	**avrà** perso	**avranno** perso
condizionale presente		condizionale passato	
perd**erei**	perd**eremmo**	**avrei** perso	**avremmo** perso
perd**eresti**	perd**ereste**	**avresti** perso	**avreste** perso
perd**erebbe**	perd**erebbero**	**avrebbe** perso	**avrebbero** perso
congiuntivo presente		congiuntivo passato	
perd**a**	perd**iamo**	**abbia** perso	**abbiamo** perso
perd**a**	perd**iate**	**abbia** perso	**abbiate** perso
perd**a**	perd**ano**	**abbia** perso	**abbiano** perso
congiuntivo imperfetto		congiuntivo trapassato	
perd**essi**	perd**essimo**	**avessi** perso	**avessimo** perso
perd**essi**	perd**este**	**avessi** perso	**aveste** perso
perd**esse**	perd**essero**	**avesse** perso	**avessero** perso

P

imperativo

	perdiamo
perdi; non perdere	perdete
perda	perdano

gerundio **permettendo** participio passato **permesso**

SINGULAR	PLURAL	SINGULAR	PLURAL
indicativo presente		passato prossimo	
permett**o**	permett**iamo**	**ho** permesso	**abbiamo** permesso
permett**i**	permett**ete**	**hai** permesso	**avete** permesso
permett**e**	permett**ono**	**ha** permesso	**hanno** permesso
imperfetto		trapassato prossimo	
permette**vo**	permette**vamo**	**avevo** permesso	**avevamo** permesso
permette**vi**	permette**vate**	**avevi** permesso	**avevate** permesso
permette**va**	permette**vano**	**aveva** permesso	**avevano** permesso
passato remoto		trapassato remoto	
permis**i**	permett**emmo**	**ebbi** permesso	**avemmo** permesso
permett**esti**	permett**este**	**avesti** permesso	**aveste** permesso
permis**e**	permis**ero**	**ebbe** permesso	**ebbero** permesso
futuro semplice		futuro anteriore	
permetter**ò**	permetter**emo**	**avrò** permesso	**avremo** permesso
permetter**ai**	permetter**ete**	**avrai** permesso	**avrete** permesso
permetter**à**	permetter**anno**	**avrà** permesso	**avranno** permesso
condizionale presente		condizionale passato	
permett**erei**	permett**eremmo**	**avrei** permesso	**avremmo** permesso
permett**eresti**	permett**ereste**	**avresti** permesso	**avreste** permesso
permett**erebbe**	permett**erebbero**	**avrebbe** permesso	**avrebbero** permesso
congiuntivo presente		congiuntivo passato	
permett**a**	permett**iamo**	**abbia** permesso	**abbiamo** permesso
permett**a**	permett**iate**	**abbia** permesso	**abbiate** permesso
permett**a**	permett**ano**	**abbia** permesso	**abbiano** permesso
congiuntivo imperfetto		congiuntivo trapassato	
permett**essi**	permett**essimo**	**avessi** permesso	**avessimo** permesso
permett**essi**	permett**este**	**avessi** permesso	**aveste** permesso
permett**esse**	permett**essero**	**avesse** permesso	**avessero** permesso
imperativo			
	permettiamo		
permetti; non permettere	permettete		
permetta	permettano		

P

perseverare

to persevere

gerundio **perseverando** participio passato **perseverato**

SINGULAR	PLURAL	SINGULAR	PLURAL
indicativo presente		passato prossimo	
persever**o**	persever**iamo**	**ho** perseverato	**abbiamo** perseverato
persever**i**	persever**ate**	**hai** perseverato	**avete** perseverato
persever**a**	persever**ano**	**ha** perseverato	**hanno** perseverato
imperfetto		trapassato prossimo	
persevera**vo**	persevera**vamo**	**avevo** perseverato	**avevamo** perseverato
persevera**vi**	persevera**vate**	**avevi** perseverato	**avevate** perseverato
persevera**va**	persevera**vano**	**aveva** perseverato	**avevano** perseverato
passato remoto		trapassato remoto	
persever**ai**	persever**ammo**	**ebbi** perseverato	**avemmo** perseverato
persever**asti**	persever**aste**	**avesti** perseverato	**aveste** perseverato
persever**ò**	persever**arono**	**ebbe** perseverato	**ebbero** perseverato
futuro semplice		futuro anteriore	
persevere**rò**	persevere**remo**	**avrò** perseverato	**avremo** perseverato
persevere**rai**	persevere**rete**	**avrai** perseverato	**avrete** perseverato
persevere**rà**	persevere**ranno**	**avrà** perseverato	**avranno** perseverato
condizionale presente		condizionale passato	
persever**erei**	persever**eremmo**	**avrei** perseverato	**avremmo** perseverato
persever**eresti**	persever**ereste**	**avresti** perseverato	**avreste** perseverato
persever**erebbe**	persever**erebbero**	**avrebbe** perseverato	**avrebbero** perseverato
congiuntivo presente		congiuntivo passato	
persever**i**	persever**iamo**	**abbia** perseverato	**abbiamo** perseverato
persever**i**	persever**iate**	**abbia** perseverato	**abbiate** perseverato
persever**i**	persever**ino**	**abbia** perseverato	**abbiano** perseverato
congiuntivo imperfetto		congiuntivo trapassato	
persever**assi**	persever**assimo**	**avessi** perseverato	**avessimo** perseverato
persever**assi**	persever**aste**	**avessi** perseverato	**aveste** perseverato
persever**asse**	persever**assero**	**avesse** perseverato	**avessero** perseverato

imperativo

	perseveriamo
persevera; non perseverare	perseverate
perseveri	perseverino

P

to persuade **persuadere**

gerundio **persuadendo** participio passato **persuaso**

SINGULAR	PLURAL	SINGULAR	PLURAL
indicativo presente		passato prossimo	
persuad**o**	persuad**iamo**	**ho** persuaso	**abbiamo** persuaso
persuad**i**	persuad**ete**	**hai** persuaso	**avete** persuaso
persuad**e**	persuad**ono**	**ha** persuaso	**hanno** persuaso
imperfetto		trapassato prossimo	
persuade**vo**	persuade**vamo**	**avevo** persuaso	**avevamo** persuaso
persuade**vi**	persuade**vate**	**avevi** persuaso	**avevate** persuaso
persuade**va**	persuade**vano**	**aveva** persuaso	**avevano** persuaso
passato remoto		trapassato remoto	
persuas**i**	persuad**emmo**	**ebbi** persuaso	**avemmo** persuaso
persuad**esti**	persuad**este**	**avesti** persuaso	**aveste** persuaso
persuas**e**	persuas**ero**	**ebbe** persuaso	**ebbero** persuaso
futuro semplice		futuro anteriore	
persuader**ò**	persuader**emo**	**avrò** persuaso	**avremo** persuaso
persuader**ai**	persuader**ete**	**avrai** persuaso	**avrete** persuaso
persuader**à**	persuader**anno**	**avrà** persuaso	**avranno** persuaso
condizionale presente		condizionale passato	
persuad**erei**	persuad**eremmo**	**avrei** persuaso	**avremmo** persuaso
persuad**eresti**	persuad**ereste**	**avresti** persuaso	**avreste** persuaso
persuad**erebbe**	persuad**erebbero**	**avrebbe** persuaso	**avrebbero** persuaso
congiuntivo presente		congiuntivo passato	
persuad**a**	persuad**iamo**	**abbia** persuaso	**abbiamo** persuaso
persuad**a**	persuad**iate**	**abbia** persuaso	**abbiate** persuaso
persuad**a**	persuad**ano**	**abbia** persuaso	**abbiano** persuaso
congiuntivo imperfetto		congiuntivo trapassato	
persuad**essi**	persuad**essimo**	**avessi** persuaso	**avessimo** persuaso
persuad**essi**	persuad**este**	**avessi** persuaso	**aveste** persuaso
persuad**esse**	persuad**essero**	**avesse** persuaso	**avessero** persuaso
imperativo			
	persuadiamo		
persuadi; non persuadere	persuadete		
persuada	persuadano		

P

pesare — to weigh

gerundio **pesando** — participio passato **pesato**

SINGULAR	PLURAL	SINGULAR	PLURAL
indicativo presente		passato prossimo	
pes**o**	pes**iamo**	**ho** pesato	**abbiamo** pesato
pes**i**	pes**ate**	**hai** pesato	**avete** pesato
pes**a**	pes**ano**	**ha** pesato	**hanno** pesato
imperfetto		trapassato prossimo	
pesa**vo**	pesa**vamo**	**avevo** pesato	**avevamo** pesato
pesa**vi**	pesa**vate**	**avevi** pesato	**avevate** pesato
pesa**va**	pesa**vano**	**aveva** pesato	**avevano** pesato
passato remoto		trapassato remoto	
pes**ai**	pes**ammo**	**ebbi** pesato	**avemmo** pesato
pes**asti**	pes**aste**	**avesti** pesato	**aveste** pesato
pes**ò**	pes**arono**	**ebbe** pesato	**ebbero** pesato
futuro semplice		futuro anteriore	
peser**ò**	peser**emo**	**avrò** pesato	**avremo** pesato
peser**ai**	peser**ete**	**avrai** pesato	**avrete** pesato
peser**à**	peser**anno**	**avrà** pesato	**avranno** pesato
condizionale presente		condizionale passato	
pes**erei**	pes**eremmo**	**avrei** pesato	**avremmo** pesato
pes**eresti**	pes**ereste**	**avresti** pesato	**avreste** pesato
pes**erebbe**	pes**erebbero**	**avrebbe** pesato	**avrebbero** pesato
congiuntivo presente		congiuntivo passato	
pes**i**	pes**iamo**	**abbia** pesato	**abbiamo** pesato
pes**i**	pes**iate**	**abbia** pesato	**abbiate** pesato
pes**i**	pes**ino**	**abbia** pesato	**abbiano** pesato
congiuntivo imperfetto		congiuntivo trapassato	
pes**assi**	pes**assimo**	**avessi** pesato	**avessimo** pesato
pes**assi**	pes**aste**	**avessi** pesato	**aveste** pesato
pes**asse**	pes**assero**	**avesse** pesato	**avessero** pesato
imperativo			
	pesiamo		
pesa; non pesare	pesate		
pesi	pesino		

P

gerundio **pettinando** participio passato **pettinato**

SINGULAR	PLURAL
indicativo presente	
pettin**o**	pettin**iamo**
pettin**i**	pettin**ate**
pettin**a**	pettin**ano**
imperfetto	
pettina**vo**	pettina**vamo**
pettina**vi**	pettina**vate**
pettina**va**	pettina**vano**
passato remoto	
pettin**ai**	pettin**ammo**
pettin**asti**	pettin**aste**
pettin**ò**	pettin**arono**
futuro semplice	
pettiner**ò**	pettiner**emo**
pettiner**ai**	pettiner**ete**
pettiner**à**	pettiner**anno**
condizionale presente	
pettin**erei**	pettin**eremmo**
pettin**eresti**	pettin**ereste**
pettin**erebbe**	pettin**erebbero**
congiuntivo presente	
pettin**i**	pettin**iamo**
pettin**i**	pettin**iate**
pettin**i**	pettin**ino**
congiuntivo imperfetto	
pettin**assi**	pettin**assimo**
pettin**assi**	pettin**aste**
pettin**asse**	pettin**assero**
imperativo	
	pettiniamo
pettina; non pettinare	pettinate
pettini	pettinino

SINGULAR	PLURAL
passato prossimo	
ho pettinato	**abbiamo** pettinato
hai pettinato	**avete** pettinato
ha pettinato	**hanno** pettinato
trapassato prossimo	
avevo pettinato	**avevamo** pettinato
avevi pettinato	**avevate** pettinato
aveva pettinato	**avevano** pettinato
trapassato remoto	
ebbi pettinato	**avemmo** pettinato
avesti pettinato	**aveste** pettinato
ebbe pettinato	**ebbero** pettinato
futuro anteriore	
avrò pettinato	**avremo** pettinato
avrai pettinato	**avrete** pettinato
avrà pettinato	**avranno** pettinato
condizionale passato	
avrei pettinato	**avremmo** pettinato
avresti pettinato	**avreste** pettinato
avrebbe pettinato	**avrebbero** pettinato
congiuntivo passato	
abbia pettinato	**abbiamo** pettinato
abbia pettinato	**abbiate** pettinato
abbia pettinato	**abbiano** pettinato
congiuntivo trapassato	
avessi pettinato	**avessimo** pettinato
avessi pettinato	**aveste** pettinato
avesse pettinato	**avessero** pettinato

pettinarsi — to comb one's hair

gerundio **pettinandosi** participio passato **pettinatosi**

SINGULAR	PLURAL
indicativo presente	
mi pettin**o**	**ci** pettin**iamo**
ti pettin**i**	**vi** pettin**ate**
si pettin**a**	**si** pettin**ano**
imperfetto	
mi pettina**vo**	**ci** pettina**vamo**
ti pettina**vi**	**vi** pettina**vate**
si pettina**va**	**si** pettina**vano**
passato remoto	
mi pettin**ai**	**ci** pettin**ammo**
ti pettin**asti**	**vi** pettin**aste**
si pettin**ò**	**si** pettin**arono**
futuro semplice	
mi pettiner**ò**	**ci** pettiner**emo**
ti pettiner**ai**	**vi** pettiner**ete**
si pettiner**à**	**si** pettiner**anno**
condizionale presente	
mi pettin**erei**	**ci** pettin**eremmo**
ti pettin**eresti**	**vi** pettin**ereste**
si pettin**erebbe**	**si** pettin**erebbero**
congiuntivo presente	
mi pettin**i**	**ci** pettin**iamo**
ti pettin**i**	**vi** pettin**iate**
si pettin**i**	**si** pettin**ino**
congiuntivo imperfetto	
mi pettin**assi**	**ci** pettin**assimo**
ti pettin**assi**	**vi** pettin**aste**
si pettin**asse**	**si** pettin**assero**
imperativo	
	pettiniamoci
pettinati; non pettinarti/non ti pettinare	pettinatevi
si pettini	si pettinino

SINGULAR	PLURAL
passato prossimo	
mi sono pettinato(a)	**ci siamo** pettinati(e)
ti sei pettinato(a)	**vi siete** pettinati(e)
si è pettinato(a)	**si sono** pettinati(e)
trapassato prossimo	
mi ero pettinato(a)	**ci eravamo** pettinati(e)
ti eri pettinato(a)	**vi eravate** pettinati(e)
si era pettinato(a)	**si erano** pettinati(e)
trapassato remoto	
mi fui pettinato(a)	**ci fummo** pettinati(e)
ti fosti pettinato(a)	**vi foste** pettinati(e)
si fu pettinato(a)	**si furono** pettinati(e)
futuro anteriore	
mi sarò pettinato(a)	**ci saremo** pettinati(e)
ti sarai pettinato(a)	**vi sarete** pettinati(e)
si sarà pettinato(a)	**si saranno** pettinati(e)
condizionale passato	
mi sarei pettinato(a)	**ci saremmo** pettinati(e)
ti saresti pettinato(a)	**vi sareste** pettinati(e)
si sarebbe pettinato(a)	**si sarebbero** pettinati(e)
congiuntivo passato	
mi sia pettinato(a)	**ci siamo** pettinati(e)
ti sia pettinato(a)	**vi siate** pettinati(e)
si sia pettinato(a)	**si siano** pettinati(e)
congiuntivo trapassato	
mi fossi pettinato(a)	**ci fossimo** pettinati(e)
ti fossi pettinato(a)	**vi foste** pettinati(e)
si fosse pettinato(a)	**si fossero** pettinati(e)

to like, to please, to be pleasing to **piacere**

gerundio **piacendo** participio passato **piaciuto**

SINGULAR	PLURAL	SINGULAR	PLURAL
indicativo presente		passato prossimo	
piacci**o**	piacc**iamo**	**sono** piaciuto(a)	**siamo** piaciuti(e)
piac**i**	piac**ete**	**sei** piaciuto(a)	**siete** piaciuti(e)
piac**e**	piacc**iono**	**è** piaciuto(a)	**sono** piaciuti(e)
imperfetto		trapassato prossimo	
piace**vo**	piace**vamo**	**ero** piaciuto(a)	**eravamo** piaciuti(e)
piace**vi**	piace**vate**	**eri** piaciuto(a)	**eravate** piaciuti(e)
piace**va**	piace**vano**	**era** piaciuto(a)	**erano** piaciuti(e)
passato remoto		trapassato remoto	
piacqui	piac**emmo**	**fui** piaciuto(a)	**fummo** piaciuti(e)
piac**esti**	piac**este**	**fosti** piaciuto(a)	**foste** piaciuti(e)
piacque	**piacquero**	**fu** piaciuto(a)	**furono** piaciuti(e)
futuro semplice		futuro anteriore	
piacer**ò**	piacer**emo**	**sarò** piaciuto(a)	**saremo** piaciuti(e)
piacer**ai**	piacer**ete**	**sarai** piaciuto(a)	**sarete** piaciuti(e)
piacer**à**	piacer**anno**	**sarà** piaciuto(a)	**saranno** piaciuti(e)
condizionale presente		condizionale passato	
piac**erei**	piac**eremmo**	**sarei** piaciuto(a)	**saremmo** piaciuti(e)
piac**eresti**	piac**ereste**	**saresti** piaciuto(a)	**sareste** piaciuti(e)
piac**erebbe**	piac**erebbero**	**sarebbe** piaciuto(a)	**sarebbero** piaciuti(e)
congiuntivo presente		congiuntivo passato	
piacci**a**	piac(c)**iamo**	**sia** piaciuto(a)	**siamo** piaciuti(e)
piacci**a**	pia(c)**iate**	**sia** piaciuto(a)	**siate** piaciuti(e)
piacci**a**	piacci**ano**	**sia** piaciuto(a)	**siano** piaciuti(e)
congiuntivo imperfetto		congiuntivo trapassato	
piac**essi**	piac**essimo**	**fossi** piaciuto(a)	**fossimo** piaciuti(e)
piac**essi**	piac**este**	**fossi** piaciuto(a)	**foste** piaciuti(e)
piac**esse**	piac**essero**	**fosse** piaciuto(a)	**fossero** piaciuti(e)

imperativo

	piacciamo
piaci; non piacere	piacete
piaccia	piacciano

P

piangere — to cry, to weep

gerundio **piangendo** — participio passato **pianto**

SINGULAR	PLURAL
indicativo presente	
piang**o**	piang**iamo**
piang**i**	piang**ete**
piang**e**	piang**ono**
imperfetto	
piange**vo**	piange**vamo**
piange**vi**	piange**vate**
piange**va**	piange**vano**
passato remoto	
piansi	piang**emmo**
piang**esti**	piang**este**
pianse	**piansero**
futuro semplice	
pianger**ò**	pianger**emo**
pianger**ai**	pianger**ete**
pianger**à**	pianger**anno**
condizionale presente	
pianger**ei**	pianger**emmo**
pianger**esti**	pianger**este**
pianger**ebbe**	pianger**ebbero**
congiuntivo presente	
piang**a**	piang**iamo**
piang**a**	piang**iate**
piang**a**	piang**ano**
congiuntivo imperfetto	
piang**essi**	piang**essimo**
piang**essi**	piang**este**
piang**esse**	piang**essero**
imperativo	
	piangiamo
piangi; non piangere	piangete
pianga	piangano

SINGULAR	PLURAL
passato prossimo	
ho pianto	**abbiamo** pianto
hai pianto	**avete** pianto
ha pianto	**hanno** pianto
trapassato prossimo	
avevo pianto	**avevamo** pianto
avevi pianto	**avevate** pianto
aveva pianto	**avevano** pianto
trapassato remoto	
ebbi pianto	**avemmo** pianto
avesti pianto	**aveste** pianto
ebbe pianto	**ebbero** pianto
futuro anteriore	
avrò pianto	**avremo** pianto
avrai pianto	**avrete** pianto
avrà pianto	**avranno** pianto
condizionale passato	
avrei pianto	**avremmo** pianto
avresti pianto	**avreste** pianto
avrebbe pianto	**avrebbero** pianto
congiuntivo passato	
abbia pianto	**abbiamo** pianto
abbia pianto	**abbiate** pianto
abbia pianto	**abbiano** pianto
congiuntivo trapassato	
avessi pianto	**avessimo** pianto
avessi pianto	**aveste** pianto
avesse pianto	**avessero** pianto

gerundio **piegando** participio passato **piegato**

SINGULAR	PLURAL	SINGULAR	PLURAL
indicativo presente		passato prossimo	
pieg**o**	pieghi**amo**	**ho** piegato	**abbiamo** piegato
piegh**i**	pieg**ate**	**hai** piegato	**avete** piegato
pieg**a**	pieg**ano**	**ha** piegato	**hanno** piegato
imperfetto		trapassato prossimo	
piega**vo**	piega**vamo**	**avevo** piegato	**avevamo** piegato
piega**vi**	piega**vate**	**avevi** piegato	**avevate** piegato
piega**va**	piega**vano**	**aveva** piegato	**avevano** toccato
passato remoto		trapassato remoto	
pieg**ai**	pieg**ammo**	**ebbi** piegato	**avemmo** piegato
pieg**asti**	pieg**aste**	**avesti** piegato	**aveste** piegato
pieg**ò**	pieg**arono**	**ebbe** piegato	**ebbero** piegato
futuro semplice		futuro anteriore	
piegher**ò**	piegher**emo**	**avrò** piegato	**avremo** piegato
piegher**ai**	piegher**ete**	**avrai** piegato	**avrete** piegato
piegher**à**	piegher**anno**	**avrà** piegato	**avranno** piegato
condizionale presente		condizionale passato	
piegh**erei**	piegh**eremmo**	**avrei** piegato	**avremmo** piegato
piegh**eresti**	piegh**ereste**	**avresti** piegato	**avreste** piegato
piegh**erebbe**	piegh**erebbero**	**avrebbe** piegato	**avrebbero** piegato
congiuntivo presente		congiuntivo passato	
piegh**i**	piegh**iamo**	**abbia** piegato	**abbiamo** piegato
piegh**i**	piegh**iate**	**abbia** piegato	**abbiate** piegato
piegh**i**	piegh**ino**	**abbia** piegato	**abbiano** piegato
congiuntivo imperfetto		congiuntivo trapassato	
pieg**assi**	pieg**assimo**	**avessi** piegato	**avessimo** piegato
pieg**assi**	pieg**aste**	**avessi** piegato	**aveste** piegato
pieg**asse**	pieg**assero**	**avesse** piegato	**avessero** piegato

imperativo

SINGULAR	PLURAL
	pieghiamo
piega; non piegare	piegate
pieghi	pieghino

piovere — to rain

gerundio **piovendo** participio passato **piovuto**

SINGULAR	PLURAL	SINGULAR	PLURAL
indicativo presente		passato prossimo	
piov**e**	piov**ono**	**ha** piovuto/**è** piovuto(a)	**sono** piovuti(e)
imperfetto		trapassato prossimo	
piove**va**	piove**vano**	**aveva** piovuto/**era** piovuto(a)	**sono** piovuti(e)
passato remoto		trapassato remoto	
piovv**e**	piovv**ero**	**ebbe** piovuto/**fu** piovuto(a)	**furono** piovuti(e)
futuro semplice		futuro anteriore	
piover**à**	piover**anno**	**avrà** piovuto/**sarà** piovuto(a)	**saranno** piovuti(e)
condizionale presente		condizionale passato	
piov**erebbe**	piover**ebbero**	**avrebbe** piovuto/**sarebbe** piovuto(a)	**sarebbero** piovuti(e)
congiuntivo presente		congiuntivo passato	
piov**a**	piov**ano**	**abbia** piovuto/**sia** piovuto(a)	**siano** piovuti(e)
congiuntivo imperfetto		congiuntivo trapassato	
piov**esse**	piov**essero**	**avesse** piovuto/**fosse** piovuto(a)	**fossero** piovuti(e)

gerundio **poltrendo** participio passato **poltrito**

SINGULAR	PLURAL	SINGULAR	PLURAL
indicativo presente		passato prossimo	
poltrisc**o**	poltr**iamo**	**ho** poltrito	**abbiamo** poltrito
poltrisc**i**	poltr**ite**	**hai** poltrito	**avete** poltrito
poltrisc**e**	poltrisc**ono**	**ha** poltrito	**hanno** poltrito
imperfetto		trapassato prossimo	
poltri**vo**	poltri**vamo**	**avevo** poltrito	**avevamo** poltrito
poltri**vi**	poltri**vate**	**avevi** poltrito	**avevate** poltrito
poltri**va**	poltri**vano**	**aveva** poltrito	**avevano** poltrito
passato remoto		trapassato remoto	
poltr**ii**	poltr**immo**	**ebbi** poltrito	**avemmo** poltrito
poltr**isti**	poltr**iste**	**avesti** poltrito	**aveste** poltrito
poltr**ì**	poltr**irono**	**ebbe** poltrito	**ebbero** poltrito
futuro semplice		futuro anteriore	
poltrir**ò**	poltrir**emo**	**avrò** poltrito	**avremo** poltrito
poltrir**ai**	poltrir**ete**	**avrai** poltrito	**avrete** poltrito
poltrir**à**	poltrir**anno**	**avrà** poltrito	**avranno** poltrito
condizionale presente		condizionale passato	
poltr**irei**	poltr**iremmo**	**avrei** poltrito	**avremmo** poltrito
poltr**iresti**	poltr**ireste**	**avresti** poltrito	**avreste** poltrito
poltr**irebbe**	poltr**irebbero**	**avrebbe** poltrito	**avrebbero** poltrito
congiuntivo presente		congiuntivo passato	
poltrisc**a**	poltr**iamo**	**abbia** poltrito	**abbiamo** poltrito
poltrisc**a**	poltr**iate**	**abbia** poltrito	**abbiate** poltrito
poltrisc**a**	poltrisc**ano**	**abbia** poltrito	**abbiano** poltrito
congiuntivo imperfetto		congiuntivo trapassato	
poltr**issi**	poltr**issimo**	**avessi** poltrito	**avessimo** poltrito
poltr**issi**	poltr**iste**	**avessi** poltrito	**aveste** poltrito
poltr**isse**	poltr**issero**	**avesse** poltrito	**avessero** poltrito
imperativo			
	poltriamo		
poltrisci; non poltrire	poltrite		
poltrisca	poltriscano		

porgere — to hand, to give

gerundio **porgendo** — participio passato **porto**

SINGULAR	PLURAL
indicativo presente	
porg**o**	porg**iamo**
porg**i**	porg**ete**
porg**e**	porg**ono**
imperfetto	
porge**vo**	porge**vamo**
porge**vi**	porge**vate**
porge**va**	porge**vano**
passato remoto	
porsi	porg**emmo**
porg**esti**	porg**este**
porse	**porsero**
futuro semplice	
porger**ò**	porger**emo**
porger**ai**	porger**ete**
porger**à**	porger**anno**
condizionale presente	
porg**erei**	porg**eremmo**
porg**eresti**	porg**ereste**
porg**erebbe**	porg**erebbero**
congiuntivo presente	
porg**a**	porg**iamo**
porg**a**	porg**iate**
porg**a**	porg**ano**
congiuntivo imperfetto	
porg**essi**	porg**essimo**
porg**essi**	porg**este**
porg**esse**	porg**essero**
imperativo	
	porgiamo
porgi; non porgere	porgete
porga	porgano

SINGULAR	PLURAL
passato prossimo	
ho porto	**abbiamo** porto
hai porto	**avete** porto
ha porto	**hanno** porto
trapassato prossimo	
avevo porto	**avevamo** porto
avevi porto	**avevate** porto
aveva porto	**avevano** porto
trapassato remoto	
ebbi porto	**avemmo** porto
avesti porto	**aveste** porto
ebbe porto	**ebbero** porto
futuro anteriore	
avrò porto	**avremo** porto
avrai porto	**avrete** porto
avrà porto	**avranno** porto
condizionale passato	
avrei porto	**avremmo** porto
avresti porto	**avreste** porto
avrebbe porto	**avrebbero** porto
congiuntivo passato	
abbia porto	**abbiamo** porto
abbia porto	**abbiate** porto
abbia porto	**abbiano** porto
congiuntivo trapassato	
avessi porto	**avessimo** porto
avessi porto	**aveste** porto
avesse porto	**avessero** porto

to put down, to place — porre

gerundio **ponendo** participio passato **posto**

SINGULAR	PLURAL

indicativo presente

SINGULAR	PLURAL
pong**o**	pon**iamo**
pon**i**	pon**ete**
pon**e**	pong**ono**

imperfetto

SINGULAR	PLURAL
pone**vo**	pone**vamo**
pone**vi**	pone**vate**
pone**va**	pone**vano**

passato remoto

SINGULAR	PLURAL
pos**i**	pon**emmo**
pon**esti**	pon**este**
pos**e**	pos**ero**

futuro semplice

SINGULAR	PLURAL
porr**ò**	porr**emo**
porr**ai**	porr**ete**
porr**à**	porr**anno**

condizionale presente

SINGULAR	PLURAL
porr**ei**	porr**emmo**
porr**esti**	porr**este**
porr**ebbe**	porr**ebbero**

congiuntivo presente

SINGULAR	PLURAL
pong**a**	pon**iamo**
pong**a**	pon**iate**
pong**a**	pong**ano**

congiuntivo imperfetto

SINGULAR	PLURAL
pon**essi**	pon**essimo**
pon**essi**	pon**este**
pon**esse**	pon**essero**

imperativo

SINGULAR	PLURAL
	poniamo
poni; non porre	ponete
ponga	pongano

SINGULAR	PLURAL

passato prossimo

SINGULAR	PLURAL
ho posto	**abbiamo** posto
hai posto	**avete** posto
ha posto	**hanno** posto

trapassato prossimo

SINGULAR	PLURAL
avevo posto	**avevamo** posto
avevi posto	**avevate** posto
aveva posto	**avevano** posto

trapassato remoto

SINGULAR	PLURAL
ebbi posto	**avemmo** posto
avesti posto	**aveste** posto
ebbe posto	**ebbero** posto

futuro anteriore

SINGULAR	PLURAL
avrò posto	**avremo** posto
avrai posto	**avrete** posto
avrà posto	**avranno** posto

condizionale passato

SINGULAR	PLURAL
avrei posto	**avremmo** posto
avresti posto	**avreste** posto
avrebbe posto	**avrebbero** posto

congiuntivo passato

SINGULAR	PLURAL
abbia posto	**abbiamo** posto
abbia posto	**abbiate** posto
abbia posto	**abbiano** posto

congiuntivo trapassato

SINGULAR	PLURAL
avessi posto	**avessimo** posto
avessi posto	**aveste** posto
avesse posto	**avessero** posto

porsi — to place oneself

gerundio **ponendosi** participio passato **postosi**

SINGULAR	PLURAL
indicativo presente	
mi pong**o**	**ci** pon**iamo**
ti pon**i**	**vi** pon**ete**
si pon**e**	**si** pong**ono**
imperfetto	
mi pone**vo**	**ci** pone**vamo**
ti pone**vi**	**vi** pone**vate**
si pone**va**	**si** pone**vano**
passato remoto	
mi pos**i**	**ci** pon**emmo**
ti pon**esti**	**vi** pon**este**
si pos**e**	**si** pos**ero**
futuro semplice	
mi porr**ò**	**ci** porr**emo**
ti porr**ai**	**vi** porr**ete**
si porr**à**	**si** porr**anno**
condizionale presente	
mi porr**ei**	**ci** porr**emmo**
ti porr**esti**	**vi** porr**este**
si porr**ebbe**	**si** porr**ebbero**
congiuntivo presente	
mi pong**a**	**ci** pon**iamo**
ti pong**a**	**vi** pon**iate**
si pong**a**	**si** pong**ano**
congiuntivo imperfetto	
mi pon**essi**	**ci** pon**essimo**
ti pon**essi**	**vi** pon**este**
si pon**esse**	**si** pon**essero**
imperativo	
	poniamoci
poniti; non porti/ non ti porre	ponetevi
si ponga	si pongano

SINGULAR	PLURAL
passato prossimo	
mi sono posto(a)	**ci siamo** posti(e)
ti sei posto(a)	**vi siete** posti(e)
si è posto(a)	**si sono** posti(e)
trapassato prossimo	
mi ero posto(a)	**ci eravamo** posti(e)
ti eri posto(a)	**vi eravate** posti(e)
si era posto(a)	**si erano** posti(e)
trapassato remoto	
mi fui posto(a)	**ci fummo** posti(e)
ti fosti posto(a)	**vi foste** posti(e)
si fu posto(a)	**si furono** posti(e)
futuro anteriore	
mi sarò posto(a)	**ci saremo** posti(e)
ti sarai posto(a)	**vi sarete** posti(e)
si sarà posto(a)	**si saranno** posti(e)
condizionale passato	
mi sarei posto(a)	**ci saremmo** posti(e)
ti saresti posto(a)	**vi sareste** posti(e)
si sarebbe posto(a)	**so sarebbero** posti(e)
congiuntivo passato	
mi sia posto(a)	**ci siamo** posti(e)
ti sia posto(a)	**vi siate** posti(e)
si sia posto(a)	**si siano** posti(e)
congiuntivo trapassato	
mi fossi posto(a)	**ci fossimo** posti(e)
ti fossi posto(a)	**vi foste** posti(e)
si fosse posto(a)	**si fossero** posti(e)

gerundio **portando** participio passato **portato**

SINGULAR	PLURAL	SINGULAR	PLURAL
indicativo presente		passato prossimo	
port**o**	port**iamo**	**ho** portato	**abbiamo** portato
port**i**	port**ate**	**hai** portato	**avete** portato
port**a**	port**ano**	**ha** portato	**hanno** portato
imperfetto		trapassato prossimo	
porta**vo**	porta**vamo**	**avevo** portato	**avevamo** portato
porta**vi**	porta**vate**	**avevi** portato	**avevate** portato
porta**va**	porta**vano**	**aveva** portato	**avevano** portato
passato remoto		trapassato remoto	
port**ai**	port**ammo**	**ebbi** portato	**avemmo** portato
port**asti**	port**aste**	**avesti** portato	**aveste** portato
port**ò**	port**arono**	**ebbe** portato	**ebbero** portato
futuro semplice		futuro anteriore	
porter**ò**	porter**emo**	**avrò** portato	**avremo** portato
porter**ai**	porter**ete**	**avrai** portato	**avrete** portato
porter**à**	porter**anno**	**avrà** portato	**avranno** portato
condizionale presente		condizionale passato	
port**erei**	port**eremmo**	**avrei** portato	**avremmo** portato
port**eresti**	port**ereste**	**avresti** portato	**avreste** portato
port**erebbe**	port**erebbero**	**avrebbe** portato	**avrebbero** portato
congiuntivo presente		congiuntivo passato	
port**i**	port**iamo**	**abbia** portato	**abbiamo** portato
port**i**	port**iate**	**abbia** portato	**abbiate** portato
port**i**	port**ino**	**abbia** portato	**abbiano** portato
congiuntivo imperfetto		congiuntivo trapassato	
port**assi**	port**assimo**	**avessi** portato	**avessimo** portato
port**assi**	port**aste**	**avessi** portato	**aveste** portato
port**asse**	port**assero**	**avesse** portato	**avessero** portato

imperativo

	portiamo
porta; non portare	portate
porti	portino

P

possedere

to possess

gerundio **possedendo**

participio passato **posseduto**

indicativo presente

SINGULAR	PLURAL
possied**o** (posseg**go**)	possed**iamo**
possied**i**	possed**ete**
possied**e**	possied**ono** (posseg**gono**)

imperfetto

SINGULAR	PLURAL
possede**vo**	possede**vamo**
possede**vi**	possede**vate**
possede**va**	possede**vano**

passato remoto

SINGULAR	PLURAL
possed**ei**, possed**etti**	possed**emmo**
possed**esti**	possed**este**
posse**dé**, possed**ette**	posseder**ono**, possed**ettero**

futuro semplice

SINGULAR	PLURAL
posseder**ò**	posseder**emo**
posseder**ai**	posseder**ete**
posseder**à**	posseder**anno**

condizionale presente

SINGULAR	PLURAL
possed**erei**	possed**eremmo**
possed**eresti**	possed**ereste**
possed**erebbe**	possed**erebbero**

congiuntivo presente

SINGULAR	PLURAL
possied**a**, possegg**a**	possed**iamo**
possied**a**, possegg**a**	possed**iate**
possied**a**, possegg**a**	possied**ano**, possegg**ano**

congiuntivo imperfetto

SINGULAR	PLURAL
possed**essi**	possed**essimo**
possed**essi**	possed**este**
possed**esse**	possed**essero**

imperativo

SINGULAR	PLURAL
	possediamo
possiedi; non possedere	possedete
possieda	possiedano

passato prossimo

SINGULAR	PLURAL
ho posseduto	**abbiamo** posseduto
hai posseduto	**avete** posseduto
ha posseduto	**hanno** posseduto

trapassato prossimo

SINGULAR	PLURAL
avevo posseduto	**avevamo** posseduto
avevi posseduto	**avevate** posseduto
aveva posseduto	**avevano** posseduto

trapassato remoto

SINGULAR	PLURAL
ebbi posseduto	**avemmo** posseduto
avesti posseduto	**aveste** posseduto
ebbe posseduto	**ebbero** posseduto

futuro anteriore

SINGULAR	PLURAL
avrò posseduto	**avremo** posseduto
avrai posseduto	**avrete** posseduto
avrà posseduto	**avranno** posseduto

condizionale passato

SINGULAR	PLURAL
avrei posseduto	**avremmo** posseduto
avresti posseduto	**avreste** posseduto
avrebbe posseduto	**avrebbero** posseduto

congiuntivo passato

SINGULAR	PLURAL
abbia posseduto	**abbiamo** posseduto
abbia posseduto	**abbiate** posseduto
abbia posseduto	**abbiano** posseduto

congiuntivo trapassato

SINGULAR	PLURAL
avessi posseduto	**avessimo** posseduto
avessi posseduto	**aveste** posseduto
avesse posseduto	**avessero** posseduto

can, to be able — potere

gerundio **potendo** participio passato **potuto**

SINGULAR	PLURAL	SINGULAR	PLURAL
indicativo presente		passato prossimo	
poss**o**	poss**iamo**	**ho** potuto	**abbiamo** potuto
puo**i**	pot**ete**	**hai** potuto	**avete** potuto
pu**ò**	poss**ono**	**ha** potuto	**hanno** potuto
imperfetto		trapassato prossimo	
pote**vo**	pote**vamo**	**avevo** potuto	**avevamo** potuto
pote**vi**	pote**vate**	**avevi** potuto	**avevate** potuto
pote**va**	pote**vano**	**aveva** potuto	**avevano** potuto
passato remoto		trapassato remoto	
pot**ei**, pot**etti**	pot**emmo**	**ebbi** potuto	**avemmo** potuto
pot**esti**	pot**este**	**avesti** potuto	**aveste** potuto
pot**é**, pot**ette**	pot**erono**, pot**ettero**	**ebbe** potuto	**ebbero** potuto
futuro semplice		futuro anteriore	
potr**ò**	potr**emo**	**avrò** potuto	**avremo** potuto
potr**ai**	potr**ete**	**avrai** potuto	**avrete** potuto
potr**à**	potr**anno**	**avrà** potuto	**avranno** potuto
condizionale presente		condizionale passato	
potr**ei**	potr**emmo**	**avrei** potuto	**avremmo** potuto
potr**esti**	potr**este**	**avresti** potuto	**avreste** potuto
potr**ebbe**	potr**ebbero**	**avrebbe** potuto	**avrebbero** potuto
congiuntivo presente		congiuntivo passato	
poss**a**	poss**iamo**	**abbia** potuto	**abbiamo** potuto
poss**a**	poss**iate**	**abbia** potuto	**abbiate** potuto
poss**a**	poss**ano**	**abbia** potuto	**abbiano** potuto
congiuntivo imperfetto		congiuntivo trapassato	
pot**essi**	pot**essimo**	**avessi** potuto	**avessimo** potuto
pot**essi**	pot**este**	**avessi** potuto	**aveste** potuto
pot**esse**	pot**essero**	**avesse** potuto	**avessero** potuto

pranzare — to eat lunch

gerundio **pranzando** participio passato **pranzato**

SINGULAR	PLURAL
indicativo presente	
pranz**o**	pranz**iamo**
pranz**i**	pranz**ate**
pranz**a**	pranz**ano**
imperfetto	
pranza**vo**	pranza**vamo**
pranza**vi**	pranza**vate**
pranza**va**	pranza**vano**
passato remoto	
pranz**ai**	pranz**ammo**
pranz**asti**	pranz**aste**
pranz**ò**	pranz**arono**
futuro semplice	
pranzer**ò**	pranzer**emo**
pranzer**ai**	pranzer**ete**
pranzer**à**	pranzer**anno**
condizionale presente	
pranz**erei**	pranz**eremmo**
pranz**eresti**	pranz**ereste**
pranz**erebbe**	pranz**erebbero**
congiuntivo presente	
pranz**i**	pranz**iamo**
pranz**i**	pranz**iate**
pranz**i**	pranz**ino**
congiuntivo imperfetto	
pranz**assi**	pranz**assimo**
pranz**assi**	pranz**aste**
pranz**asse**	pranz**assero**
imperativo	
	pranziamo
pranza; non pranzare	pranzate
pranzi	pranzino

SINGULAR	PLURAL
passato prossimo	
ho pranzato	**abbiamo** pranzato
hai pranzato	**avete** pranzato
ha pranzato	**hanno** pranzato
trapassato prossimo	
avevo pranzato	**avevamo** pranzato
avevi pranzato	**avevate** pranzato
aveva pranzato	**avevano** pranzato
trapassato remoto	
ebbi pranzato	**avemmo** pranzato
avesti pranzato	**aveste** pranzato
ebbe pranzato	**ebbero** pranzato
futuro anteriore	
avrò pranzato	**avremo** pranzato
avrai pranzato	**avrete** pranzato
avrà pranzato	**avranno** pranzato
condizionale passato	
avrei pranzato	**avremmo** pranzato
avresti pranzato	**avreste** pranzato
avrebbe pranzato	**avrebbero** pranzato
congiuntivo passato	
abbia pranzato	**abbiamo** pranzato
abbia pranzato	**abbiate** pranzato
abbia pranzato	**abbiano** pranzato
congiuntivo trapassato	
avessi pranzato	**avessimo** pranzato
avessi pranzato	**aveste** pranzato
avesse pranzato	**avessero** pranzato

gerundio **predicendo** participio passato **predetto**

SINGULAR	PLURAL
indicativo presente	
predic**o**	predic**iamo**
predic**i**	pred**ite**
predic**e**	predic**ono**
imperfetto	
predice**vo**	predice**vamo**
predice**vi**	predice**vate**
predice**va**	predice**vano**
passato remoto	
prediss**i**	predic**emmo**
predic**esti**	predic**este**
prediss**e**	prediss**ero**
futuro semplice	
predir**ò**	predir**emo**
predir**ai**	predir**ete**
predir**à**	predir**anno**
condizionale presente	
pred**irei**	pred**iremmo**
pred**iresti**	pred**ireste**
pred**irebbe**	pred**irebbero**
congiuntivo presente	
predic**a**	predic**iamo**
predic**a**	predic**iate**
predic**a**	predic**ano**
congiuntivo imperfetto	
predic**essi**	predic**essimo**
predic**essi**	predic**este**
predic**esse**	predic**essero**
imperativo	
	prediciamo
predici; non predire	predite
predica	predicano

SINGULAR	PLURAL
passato prossimo	
ho predetto	**abbiamo** predetto
hai predetto	**avete** predetto
ha predetto	**hanno** predetto
trapassato prossimo	
avevo predetto	**avevamo** predetto
avevi predetto	**avevate** predetto
aveva predetto	**avevano** predetto
trapassato remoto	
ebbi predetto	**avemmo** predetto
avesti predetto	**aveste** predetto
ebbe predetto	**ebbero** predetto
futuro anteriore	
avrò predetto	**avremo** predetto
avrai predetto	**avrete** predetto
avrà predetto	**avranno** predetto
condizionale passato	
avrei predetto	**avremmo** predetto
avresti predetto	**avreste** predetto
avrebbe predetto	**avrebbero** predetto
congiuntivo passato	
abbia predetto	**abbiamo** predetto
abbia predetto	**abbiate** predetto
abbia predetto	**abbiano** predetto
congiuntivo trapassato	
avessi predetto	**avessimo** predetto
avessi predetto	**aveste** predetto
avesse predetto	**avessero** predetto

preferire — to prefer

gerundio **preferendo** participio passato **preferito**

SINGULAR	PLURAL	SINGULAR	PLURAL
indicativo presente		passato prossimo	
preferisc**o**	prefer**iamo**	**ho** preferito	**abbiamo** preferito
preferisc**i**	prefer**ite**	**hai** preferito	**avete** preferito
preferisc**e**	preferisc**ono**	**ha** preferito	**hanno** preferito
imperfetto		trapassato prossimo	
preferi**vo**	preferi**vamo**	**avevo** preferito	**avevamo** preferito
preferi**vi**	preferi**vate**	**avevi** preferito	**avevate** preferito
preferi**va**	preferi**vano**	**aveva** preferito	**avevano** preferito
passato remoto		trapassato remoto	
prefer**ii**	prefer**immo**	**ebbi** preferito	**avemmo** preferito
prefer**isti**	prefer**iste**	**avesti** preferito	**aveste** preferito
prefer**ì**	prefer**irono**	**ebbe** preferito	**ebbero** preferito
futuro semplice		futuro anteriore	
preferir**ò**	preferir**emo**	**avrò** preferito	**avremo** preferito
preferir**ai**	preferir**ete**	**avrai** preferito	**avrete** preferito
preferir**à**	preferir**anno**	**avrà** preferito	**avranno** preferito
condizionale presente		condizionale passato	
prefer**irei**	prefer**iremmo**	**avrei** preferito	**avremmo** preferito
prefer**iresti**	prefer**ireste**	**avresti** preferito	**avreste** preferito
prefer**irebbe**	prefer**irebbero**	**avrebbe** preferito	**avrebbero** preferito
congiuntivo presente		congiuntivo passato	
prefer**isca**	prefer**iamo**	**abbia** preferito	**abbiamo** preferito
prefer**isca**	prefer**iate**	**abbia** preferito	**abbiate** preferito
prefer**isca**	prefer**iscano**	**abbia** preferito	**abbiano** preferito
congiuntivo imperfetto		congiuntivo trapassato	
prefer**issi**	prefer**issimo**	**avessi** preferito	**avessimo** preferito
prefer**issi**	prefer**iste**	**avessi** preferito	**aveste** preferito
prefer**isse**	prefer**issero**	**avesse** preferito	**avessero** preferito

imperativo

SINGULAR	PLURAL
	preferiamo
preferisci; non preferire	preferite
preferisca	preferiscano

P

to pray — pregare

gerundio **pregando** — participio passato **pregato**

SINGULAR	PLURAL
indicativo presente	
preg**o**	pregh**iamo**
pregh**i**	preg**ate**
preg**a**	preg**ano**
imperfetto	
prega**vo**	prega**vamo**
prega**vi**	prega**vate**
prega**va**	prega**vano**
passato remoto	
preg**ai**	preg**ammo**
preg**asti**	preg**aste**
preg**ò**	preg**arono**
futuro semplice	
pregher**ò**	pregher**emo**
pregher**ai**	pregher**ete**
pregher**à**	pregher**anno**
condizionale presente	
pregh**erei**	pregh**eremmo**
pregh**eresti**	pregh**ereste**
pregh**erebbe**	pregh**erebbero**
congiuntivo presente	
pregh**i**	pregh**iamo**
pregh**i**	pregh**iate**
pregh**i**	pregh**ino**
congiuntivo imperfetto	
preg**assi**	preg**assimo**
preg**assi**	preg**aste**
preg**asse**	preg**assero**
imperativo	
	preghiamo
prega; non pregare	pregate
preghi	preghino

SINGULAR	PLURAL
passato prossimo	
ho pregato	**abbiamo** pregato
hai pregato	**avete** pregato
ha pregato	**hanno** pregato
trapassato prossimo	
avevo pregato	**avevamo** pregato
avevi pregato	**avevate** pregato
aveva pregato	**avevano** pregato
trapassato remoto	
ebbi pregato	**avemmo** pregato
avesti pregato	**aveste** pregato
ebbe pregato	**ebbero** pregato
futuro anteriore	
avrò pregato	**avremo** pregato
avrai pregato	**avrete** pregato
avrà pregato	**avranno** pregato
condizionale passato	
avrei pregato	**avremmo** pregato
avresti pregato	**avreste** pregato
avrebbe pregato	**avrebbero** pregato
congiuntivo passato	
abbia pregato	**abbiamo** pregato
abbia pregato	**abbiate** pregato
abbia pregato	**abbiano** pregato
congiuntivo trapassato	
avessi pregato	**avessimo** pregato
avessi pregato	**aveste** pregato
avesse pregato	**avessero** pregato

premere — to press, to squeeze

gerundio **premendo** participio passato **premuto**

SINGULAR	PLURAL	SINGULAR	PLURAL
indicativo presente		passato prossimo	
prem**o**	prem**iamo**	**ho** premuto	**abbiamo** premuto
prem**i**	prem**ete**	**hai** premuto	**avete** premuto
prem**e**	prem**ono**	**ha** premuto	**hanno** premuto
imperfetto		trapassato prossimo	
preme**vo**	preme**vamo**	**avevo** premuto	**avevamo** premuto
preme**vi**	preme**vate**	**avevi** premuto	**avevate** premuto
preme**va**	preme**vano**	**aveva** premuto	**avevano** premuto
passato remoto		trapassato remoto	
prem**ei**, prem**etti**	prem**emmo**	**ebbi** premuto	**avemmo** premuto
prem**esti**	prem**este**	**avesti** premuto	**aveste** premuto
prem**é**, prem**ette**	prem**erono**, prem**ettero**	**ebbe** premuto	**ebbero** premuto
futuro semplice		futuro anteriore	
premer**ò**	premer**emo**	**avrò** premuto	**avremo** premuto
premer**ai**	premer**ete**	**avrai** premuto	**avrete** premuto
premer**à**	premer**anno**	**avrà** premuto	**avranno** premuto
condizionale presente		condizionale passato	
prem**erei**	prem**eremmo**	**avrei** premuto	**avremmo** premuto
prem**eresti**	prem**ereste**	**avresti** premuto	**avreste** premuto
prem**erebbe**	prem**erebbero**	**avrebbe** premuto	**avrebbero** premuto
congiuntivo presente		congiuntivo passato	
prem**a**	prem**iamo**	**abbia** premuto	**abbiamo** premuto
prem**a**	prem**iate**	**abbia** premuto	**abbiate** premuto
prem**a**	prem**ano**	**abbia** premuto	**abbiano** premuto
congiuntivo imperfetto		congiuntivo trapassato	
prem**essi**	prem**essimo**	**avessi** premuto	**avessimo** premuto
prem**essi**	prem**este**	**avessi** premuto	**aveste** premuto
prem**esse**	prem**essero**	**avesse** premuto	**avessero** premuto
imperativo			
	premiamo		
premi; non premere	premete		
prema	premano		

P

gerundio **prendendo** participio passato **preso**

SINGULAR	PLURAL	SINGULAR	PLURAL
indicativo presente		passato prossimo	
prend**o**	prend**iamo**	**ho** preso	**abbiamo** preso
prend**i**	prend**ete**	**hai** preso	**avete** preso
prend**e**	prend**ono**	**ha** preso	**hanno** preso
imperfetto		trapassato prossimo	
prende**vo**	prende**vamo**	**avevo** preso	**avevamo** preso
prende**vi**	prende**vate**	**avevi** preso	**avevate** preso
prende**va**	prende**vano**	**aveva** preso	**avevano** preso
passato remoto		trapassato remoto	
presi	prend**emmo**	**ebbi** preso	**avemmo** preso
prend**esti**	prend**este**	**avesti** preso	**aveste** preso
prese	**presero**	**ebbe** preso	**ebbero** preso
futuro semplice		futuro anteriore	
prender**ò**	prender**emo**	**avrò** preso	**avremo** preso
prender**ai**	prender**ete**	**avrai** preso	**avrete** preso
prender**à**	prender**anno**	**avrà** preso	**avranno** preso
condizionale presente		condizionale passato	
prend**erei**	prend**eremmo**	**avrei** preso	**avremmo** preso
prend**eresti**	prend**ereste**	**avresti** preso	**avreste** preso
prend**erebbe**	prend**erebbero**	**avrebbe** preso	**avrebbero** preso
congiuntivo presente		congiuntivo passato	
prend**a**	prend**iamo**	**abbia** preso	**abbiamo** preso
prend**a**	prend**iate**	**abbia** preso	**abbiate** preso
prend**a**	prend**ano**	**abbia** preso	**abbiano** preso
congiuntivo imperfetto		congiuntivo trapassato	
prend**essi**	prend**essimo**	**avessi** preso	**avessimo** preso
prend**essi**	prend**este**	**avessi** preso	**aveste** preso
prend**esse**	prend**essero**	**avesse** preso	**avessero** preso
imperativo			
	prendiamo		
prendi; non prendere	prendete		
prenda	prendano		

prenotare — to reserve

gerundio **prenotando** participio passato **prenotato**

SINGULAR	PLURAL	SINGULAR	PLURAL
indicativo presente		passato prossimo	
preno**to**	preno**tiamo**	**ho** prenotato	**abbiamo** prenotato
preno**ti**	preno**tate**	**hai** prenotato	**avete** prenotato
preno**ta**	preno**tano**	**ha** prenotato	**hanno** prenotato
imperfetto		trapassato prossimo	
prenota**vo**	prenota**vamo**	**avevo** prenotato	**avevamo** prenotato
prenota**vi**	prenota**vate**	**avevi** prenotato	**avevate** prenotato
prenota**va**	prenota**vano**	**aveva** prenotato	**avevano** prenotato
passato remoto		trapassato remoto	
prenot**ai**	prenot**ammo**	**ebbi** prenotato	**avemmo** prenotato
prenot**asti**	prenot**aste**	**avesti** prenotato	**aveste** prenotato
prenot**ò**	prenot**arono**	**ebbe** prenotato	**ebbero** prenotato
futuro semplice		futuro anteriore	
prenoter**ò**	prenoter**emo**	**avrò** prenotato	**avremo** prenotato
prenoter**ai**	prenoter**ete**	**avrai** prenotato	**avrete** prenotato
prenoter**à**	prenoter**anno**	**avrà** prenotato	**avranno** prenotato
condizionale presente		condizionale passato	
prenot**erei**	prenot**eremmo**	**avrei** prenotato	**avremmo** prenotato
prenot**eresti**	prenot**ereste**	**avresti** prenotato	**avreste** prenotato
prenot**erebbe**	prenot**erebbero**	**avrebbe** prenotato	**avrebbero** prenotato
congiuntivo presente		congiuntivo passato	
prenot**i**	prenot**iamo**	**abbia** prenotato	**abbiamo** prenotato
prenot**i**	prenot**iate**	**abbia** prenotato	**abbiate** prenotato
prenot**i**	prenot**ino**	**abbia** prenotato	**abbiano** prenotato
congiuntivo imperfetto		congiuntivo trapassato	
prenot**assi**	prenot**assimo**	**avessi** prenotato	**avessimo** prenotato
prenot**assi**	prenot**aste**	**avessi** prenotato	**aveste** prenotato
prenot**asse**	prenot**assero**	**avesse** prenotato	**avessero** prenotato
imperativo			
	prenotiamo		
prenota; non prenotare	prenotate		
prenoti	prenotino		

to worry (about something) preoccuparsi

gerundio **preoccupandosi** participio passato **preoccupatosi**

indicativo presente

SINGULAR	PLURAL
mi preoccup**o**	**ci** preoccup**iamo**
ti preoccup**i**	**vi** preoccup**ate**
si preoccup**a**	**si** preoccup**ano**

imperfetto

SINGULAR	PLURAL
mi preoccupa**vo**	**ci** preoccupa**vamo**
ti preoccupa**vi**	**vi** preoccupa**vate**
si preoccupa**va**	**si** preoccupa**vano**

passato remoto

SINGULAR	PLURAL
mi preoccup**ai**	**ci** preoccup**ammo**
ti preoccup**asti**	**vi** preoccup**aste**
si preoccup**ò**	**si** preoccup**arono**

futuro semplice

SINGULAR	PLURAL
mi preoccuper**ò**	**ci** preoccuper**emo**
ti preoccuper**ai**	**vi** preoccuper**ete**
si preoccuper**à**	**si** preoccuper**anno**

condizionale presente

SINGULAR	PLURAL
mi preoccup**erei**	**ci** preoccup**eremmo**
ti preoccup**eresti**	**vi** preoccup**ereste**
si preoccup**erebbe**	**si** preoccup**erebbero**

congiuntivo presente

SINGULAR	PLURAL
mi preoccup**i**	**ci** preoccup**iamo**
ti preoccup**i**	**vi** preoccup**iate**
si preoccup**i**	**si** preoccup**ino**

congiuntivo imperfetto

SINGULAR	PLURAL
mi preoccup**assi**	**ci** preoccup**assimo**
ti preoccup**assi**	**vi** preoccup**aste**
si preoccup**asse**	**si** preoccup**assero**

imperativo

SINGULAR	PLURAL
	preoccupiamoci
preoccupati; non preoccuparti/non ti preoccupare	preoccupatevi
si preoccupi	si preoccupino

passato prossimo

SINGULAR	PLURAL
mi sono preoccupato(a)	**ci siamo** preoccupati(e)
ti sei preoccupato(a)	**vi siete** preoccupati(e)
si è preoccupato(a)	**si sono** preoccupati(e)

trapassato prossimo

SINGULAR	PLURAL
mi ero preoccupato(a)	**ci eravamo** preoccupati(e)
ti eri preoccupato(a)	**vi eravate** preoccupati(e)
si era preoccupato(a)	**si erano** preoccupati(e)

trapassato remoto

SINGULAR	PLURAL
mi fui preoccupato(a)	**ci fummo** preoccupati(e)
ti fosti preoccupato(a)	**vi foste** preoccupati(e)
si fu preoccupato(a)	**si furono** preoccupati(e)

futuro anteriore

SINGULAR	PLURAL
mi sarò preoccupato(a)	**ci saremo** preoccupati(e)
ti sarai preoccupato(a)	**vi sarete** preoccupati(e)
si sarà preoccupato(a)	**si saranno** preoccupati(e)

condizionale passato

SINGULAR	PLURAL
mi sarei preoccupato(a)	**ci saremmo** preoccupati(e)
ti saresti preoccupato(a)	**vi sareste** preoccupati(e)
si sarebbe preoccupato(a)	**si sarebbero** preoccupati(e)

congiuntivo passato

SINGULAR	PLURAL
mi sia preoccupato(a)	**ci siamo** preoccupati(e)
ti sia preoccupato(a)	**vi siate** preoccupati(e)
si sia preoccupato(a)	**si siano** preoccupati(e)

congiuntivo trapassato

SINGULAR	PLURAL
mi fossi preoccupato(a)	**ci fossimo** preoccupati(e)
ti fossi preoccupato(a)	**vi foste** preoccupati(e)
si fosse preoccupato(a)	**si fossero** preoccupati(e)

preparare — to prepare

gerundio **preparando** participio passato **preparato**

SINGULAR	PLURAL	SINGULAR	PLURAL
indicativo presente		passato prossimo	
prepar**o**	prepar**iamo**	**ho** preparato	**abbiamo** preparato
prepar**i**	prepar**ate**	**hai** preparato	**avete** preparato
prepar**a**	prepar**ano**	**ha** preparato	**hanno** preparato
imperfetto		trapassato prossimo	
prepara**vo**	prepara**vamo**	**avevo** preparato	**avevamo** preparato
prepara**vi**	prepara**vate**	**avevi** preparato	**avevate** preparato
prepara**va**	prepara**vano**	**aveva** preparato	**avevano** preparato
passato remoto		trapassato remoto	
prepar**ai**	prepar**ammo**	**ebbi** preparato	**avemmo** preparato
prepar**asti**	prepar**aste**	**avesti** preparato	**aveste** preparato
prepar**ò**	prepar**arono**	**ebbe** preparato	**ebbero** preparato
futuro semplice		futuro anteriore	
preparer**ò**	preparer**emo**	**avrò** preparato	**avremo** preparato
preparer**ai**	preparer**ete**	**avrai** preparato	**avrete** preparato
preparer**à**	preparer**anno**	**avrà** preparato	**avranno** preparato
condizionale presente		condizionale passato	
prepar**erei**	prepar**eremmo**	**avrei** preparato	**avremmo** preparato
prepar**eresti**	prepar**ereste**	**avresti** preparato	**avreste** preparato
prepar**erebbe**	prepar**erebbero**	**avrebbe** preparato	**avrebbero** preparato
congiuntivo presente		congiuntivo passato	
prepar**i**	prepar**iamo**	**abbia** preparato	**abbiamo** preparato
prepar**i**	prepar**iate**	**abbia** preparato	**abbiate** preparato
prepar**i**	prepar**ino**	**abbia** preparato	**abbiano** preparato
congiuntivo imperfetto		congiuntivo trapassato	
prepar**assi**	prepar**assimo**	**avessi** preparato	**avessimo** preparato
prepar**assi**	prepar**aste**	**avessi** preparato	**aveste** preparato
prepar**asse**	prepar**assero**	**avesse** preparato	**avessero** preparato
imperativo			
	prepariamo		
prepara; non preparare	preparate		
prepari	preparino		

P

to present, to introduce — presentare

gerundio **presentando** participio passato **presentato**

SINGULAR	PLURAL
indicativo presente	
present**o**	present**iamo**
present**i**	present**ate**
present**a**	present**ano**
imperfetto	
presenta**vo**	presenta**vamo**
presenta**vi**	presenta**vate**
presenta**va**	presenta**vano**
passato remoto	
present**ai**	present**ammo**
present**asti**	present**aste**
present**ò**	present**arono**
futuro semplice	
presenter**ò**	presenter**emo**
presenter**ai**	presenter**ete**
presenter**à**	presenter**anno**
condizionale presente	
present**erei**	present**eremmo**
present**eresti**	present**ereste**
present**erebbe**	present**erebbero**
congiuntivo presente	
present**i**	present**iamo**
present**i**	present**iate**
present**i**	present**ino**
congiuntivo imperfetto	
present**assi**	present**assimo**
present**assi**	present**aste**
present**asse**	present**assero**
imperativo	
	presentiamo
presenta; non presentare	presentate
presenti	presentino

SINGULAR	PLURAL
passato prossimo	
ho presentato	**abbiamo** presentato
hai presentato	**avete** presentato
ha presentato	**hanno** presentato
trapassato prossimo	
avevo presentato	**avevamo** presentato
avevi presentato	**avevate** presentato
aveva presentato	**avevano** presentato
trapassato remoto	
ebbi presentato	**avemmo** presentato
avesti presentato	**aveste** presentato
ebbe presentato	**ebbero** presentato
futuro anteriore	
avrò presentato	**avremo** presentato
avrai presentato	**avrete** presentato
avrà presentato	**avranno** presentato
condizionale passato	
avrei presentato	**avremmo** presentato
avresti presentato	**avreste** presentato
avrebbe presentato	**avrebbero** presentato
congiuntivo passato	
abbia presentato	**abbiamo** presentato
abbia presentato	**abbiate** presentato
abbia presentato	**abbiano** presentato
congiuntivo trapassato	
avessi presentato	**avessimo** presentato
avessi presentato	**aveste** presentato
avesse presentato	**avessero** presentato

prestare — to lend

gerundio **prestando** participio passato **prestato**

SINGULAR	PLURAL	SINGULAR	PLURAL
indicativo presente		passato prossimo	
prest**o**	prest**iamo**	**ho** prestato	**abbiamo** prestato
prest**i**	prest**ate**	**hai** prestato	**avete** prestato
prest**a**	prest**ano**	**ha** prestato	**hanno** prestato
imperfetto		trapassato prossimo	
presta**vo**	presta**vamo**	**avevo** prestato	**avevamo** prestato
presta**vi**	presta**vate**	**avevi** prestato	**avevate** prestato
presta**va**	presta**vano**	**aveva** prestato	**avevano** prestato
passato remoto		trapassato remoto	
prest**ai**	prest**ammo**	**ebbi** prestato	**avemmo** prestato
prest**asti**	prest**aste**	**avesti** prestato	**aveste** prestato
prest**ò**	prest**arono**	**ebbe** prestato	**ebbero** prestato
futuro semplice		futuro anteriore	
prester**ò**	prester**emo**	**avrò** prestato	**avremo** prestato
prester**ai**	prester**ete**	**avrai** prestato	**avrete** prestato
prester**à**	prester**anno**	**avrà** prestato	**avranno** prestato
condizionale presente		condizionale passato	
prest**erei**	prest**eremmo**	**avrei** prestato	**avremmo** prestato
prest**eresti**	prest**ereste**	**avresti** prestato	**avreste** prestato
prest**erebbe**	prest**erebbero**	**avrebbe** prestato	**avrebbero** prestato
congiuntivo presente		congiuntivo passato	
prest**i**	prest**iamo**	**abbia** prestato	**abbiamo** prestato
prest**i**	prest**iate**	**abbia** prestato	**abbiate** prestato
prest**i**	prest**ino**	**abbia** prestato	**abbiano** prestato
congiuntivo imperfetto		congiuntivo trapassato	
prest**assi**	prest**assimo**	**avessi** prestato	**avessimo** prestato
prest**assi**	prest**aste**	**avessi** prestato	**aveste** prestato
prest**asse**	prest**assero**	**avesse** prestato	**avessero** prestato
imperativo			
	prestiamo		
presta; non prestare	prestate		
presti	prestino		

P

to demand, to pretend **pretendere**

gerundio **pretendendo** participio passato **preteso**

SINGULAR	PLURAL	SINGULAR	PLURAL
indicativo presente		passato prossimo	
pretend**o**	pretend**iamo**	**ho** preteso	**abbiamo** preteso
pretend**i**	pretend**ete**	**hai** preteso	**avete** preteso
pretend**e**	pretend**ono**	**ha** preteso	**hanno** preteso
imperfetto		trapassato prossimo	
pretende**vo**	pretende**vamo**	**avevo** preteso	**avevamo** preteso
pretende**vi**	pretende**vate**	**avevi** preteso	**avevate** preteso
pretende**va**	pretende**vano**	**aveva** preteso	**avevano** preteso
passato remoto		trapassato remoto	
pretes**i**	pretend**emmo**	**ebbi** preteso	**avemmo** preteso
pretend**esti**	pretend**este**	**avesti** preteso	**aveste** preteso
pretes**e**	pretes**ero**	**ebbe** preteso	**ebbero** preteso
futuro semplice		futuro anteriore	
pretender**ò**	pretender**emo**	**avrò** preteso	**avremo** preteso
pretender**ai**	pretender**ete**	**avrai** preteso	**avrete** preteso
pretender**à**	pretender**anno**	**avrà** preteso	**avranno** preteso
condizionale presente		condizionale passato	
pretend**erei**	pretend**eremmo**	**avrei** preteso	**avremmo** preteso
pretend**eresti**	pretend**ereste**	**avresti** preteso	**avreste** preteso
pretend**erebbe**	pretend**erebbero**	**avrebbe** preteso	**avrebbero** preteso
congiuntivo presente		congiuntivo passato	
pretend**a**	pretend**iamo**	**abbia** preteso	**abbiamo** preteso
pretend**a**	pretend**iate**	**abbia** preteso	**abbiate** preteso
pretend**a**	pretend**ano**	**abbia** preteso	**abbiano** preteso
congiuntivo imperfetto		congiuntivo trapassato	
pretend**essi**	pretend**essimo**	**avessi** preteso	**avessimo** preteso
pretend**essi**	pretend**este**	**avessi** preteso	**aveste** preteso
pretend**esse**	pretend**essero**	**avesse** preteso	**avessero** preteso
imperativo			
	pretendiamo		
pretendi; non pretendere	pretendete		
pretenda	pretendano		

P

prevalere

to prevail

gerundio **prevalendo**

participio passato **prevalso**

SINGULAR	PLURAL
indicativo presente	
prevalg**o**	preval**iamo**
preval**i**	preval**ete**
preval**e**	prevalg**ono**
imperfetto	
prevale**vo**	prevale**vamo**
prevale**vi**	prevale**vate**
prevale**va**	prevale**vano**
passato remoto	
prevalsi	preval**emmo**
preval**esti**	preval**este**
prevalse	**prevalsero**
futuro semplice	
prevarr**ò**	prevarr**emo**
prevarr**ai**	prevarr**ete**
prevarr**à**	prevarr**anno**
condizionale presente	
prev**arrei**	prev**arremmo**
prev**arresti**	prev**arreste**
prev**arrebbe**	prev**arrebbero**
congiuntivo presente	
prevalg**a**	preval**iamo**
prevalg**a**	preval**iate**
prevalg**a**	prevalg**ano**
congiuntivo imperfetto	
preval**essi**	preval**essimo**
preval**essi**	preval**este**
preval**esse**	preval**essero**
imperativo	
	prevaliamo
prevali; non prevalere	prevalete
prevalga	prevalgano

SINGULAR	PLURAL
passato prossimo	
ho prevalso	**abbiamo** prevalso
hai prevalso	**avete** prevalso
ha prevalso	**hanno** prevalso
trapassato prossimo	
avevo prevalso	**avevamo** prevalso
avevi prevalso	**avevate** prevalso
aveva prevalso	**avevano** prevalso
trapassato remoto	
ebbi prevalso	**avemmo** prevalso
avesti prevalso	**aveste** prevalso
ebbe prevalso	**ebbero** prevalso
futuro anteriore	
avrò prevalso	**avremo** prevalso
avrai prevalso	**avrete** prevalso
avrà prevalso	**avranno** prevalso
condizionale passato	
avrei prevalso	**avremmo** prevalso
avresti prevalso	**avreste** prevalso
avrebbe prevalso	**avrebbero** prevalso
congiuntivo passato	
abbia prevalso	**abbiamo** prevalso
abbia prevalso	**abbiate** prevalso
abbia prevalso	**abbiano** prevalso
congiuntivo trapassato	
avessi prevalso	**avessimo** prevalso
avessi prevalso	**aveste** prevalso
avesse prevalso	**avessero** prevalso

gerundio **prevedendo** participio passato **previsto**

SINGULAR	PLURAL
indicativo presente	
preved**o**	preved**iamo**
preved**i**	preved**ete**
preved**e**	preved**ono**
imperfetto	
prevede**vo**	prevede**vamo**
prevede**vi**	prevede**vate**
prevede**va**	prevede**vano**
passato remoto	
previd**i**	preved**emmo**
preved**esti**	preved**este**
previd**e**	previd**ero**
futuro semplice	
preveder**ò**	preveder**emo**
preveder**ai**	preveder**ete**
preveder**à**	preveder**anno**
condizionale presente	
preved**erei**	preved**eremmo**
preved**eresti**	preved**ereste**
preved**erebbe**	preved**erebbero**
congiuntivo presente	
preved**a**	preved**iamo**
preved**a**	preved**iate**
preved**a**	preved**ano**
congiuntivo imperfetto	
preved**essi**	preved**essimo**
preved**essi**	preved**este**
preved**esse**	preved**essero**
imperativo	
	prevediamo
prevedi; non prevedere	prevedete
preveda	prevedano

SINGULAR	PLURAL
passato prossimo	
ho previsto	**abbiamo** previsto
hai previsto	**avete** previsto
ha previsto	**hanno** previsto
trapassato prossimo	
avevo previsto	**avevamo** previsto
avevi previsto	**avevate** previsto
aveva previsto	**avevano** previsto
trapassato remoto	
ebbi previsto	**avemmo** previsto
avesti previsto	**aveste** previsto
ebbe previsto	**ebbero** previsto
futuro anteriore	
avrò previsto	**avremo** previsto
avrai previsto	**avrete** previsto
avrà previsto	**avranno** previsto
condizionale passato	
avrei previsto	**avremmo** previsto
avresti previsto	**avreste** previsto
avrebbe previsto	**avrebbero** previsto
congiuntivo passato	
abbia previsto	**abbiamo** previsto
abbia previsto	**abbiate** previsto
abbia previsto	**abbiano** previsto
congiuntivo trapassato	
avessi previsto	**avessimo** previsto
avessi previsto	**aveste** previsto
avesse previsto	**avessero** previsto

prevenire to anticipate, to precede, to prevent

gerundio **prevenendo** participio passato **prevenuto**

SINGULAR	PLURAL	SINGULAR	PLURAL
indicativo presente		passato prossimo	
preveng**o**	preven**iamo**	**ho** prevenuto	**abbiamo** prevenuto
previen**i**	preven**ite**	**hai** prevenuto	**avete** prevenuto
previen**e**	preveng**ono**	**ha** prevenuto	**hanno** prevenuto
imperfetto		trapassato prossimo	
preveni**vo**	preveni**vamo**	**avevo** prevenuto	**avevamo** prevenuto
preveni**vi**	preveni**vate**	**avevi** prevenuto	**avevate** prevenuto
preveni**va**	preveni**vano**	**aveva** prevenuto	**avevano** prevenuto
passato remoto		trapassato remoto	
prevenn**i**	preven**immo**	**ebbi** prevenuto	**avemmo** prevenuto
preven**isti**	preven**iste**	**avesti** prevenuto	**aveste** prevenuto
prevenn**e**	prevenn**ero**	**ebbe** prevenuto	**ebbero** prevenuto
futuro semplice		futuro anteriore	
preverr**ò**	preverr**emo**	**avrò** prevenuto	**avremo** prevenuto
preverr**ai**	preverr**ete**	**avrai** prevenuto	**avrete** prevenuto
preverr**à**	preverr**anno**	**avrà** prevenuto	**avranno** prevenuto
condizionale presente		condizionale passato	
prev**errei**	prev**erremmo**	**avrei** prevenuto	**avremmo** prevenuto
prev**erresti**	prev**erreste**	**avresti** prevenuto	**avreste** prevenuto
prev**errebbe**	prev**errebbero**	**avrebbe** prevenuto	**avrebbero** prevenuto
congiuntivo presente		congiuntivo passato	
preveng**a**	preven**iamo**	**abbia** prevenuto	**abbiamo** prevenuto
preveng**a**	preven**iate**	**abbia** prevenuto	**abbiate** prevenuto
preveng**a**	preveng**ano**	**abbia** prevenuto	**abbiano** prevenuto
congiuntivo imperfetto		congiuntivo trapassato	
preven**issi**	preven**issimo**	**avessi** prevenuto	**avessimo** prevenuto
preven**issi**	preven**iste**	**avessi** prevenuto	**aveste** prevenuto
preven**isse**	preven**issero**	**avesse** prevenuto	**avessero** prevenuto
imperativo			
	preveniamo		
previeni; non prevenire	prevenite		
prevenga	prevengano		

P

gerundio **producendo** participio passato **prodotto**

SINGULAR	PLURAL	SINGULAR	PLURAL
indicativo presente		passato prossimo	
produc**o**	produc**iamo**	**ho** prodotto	**abbiamo** prodotto
produc**i**	produc**ete**	**hai** prodotto	**avete** prodotto
produc**e**	produc**ono**	**ha** prodotto	**hanno** prodotto
imperfetto		trapassato prossimo	
produce**vo**	produce**vamo**	**avevo** prodotto	**avevamo** prodotto
produce**vi**	produce**vate**	**avevi** prodotto	**avevate** prodotto
produce**va**	produce**vano**	**aveva** prodotto	**avevano** prodotto
passato remoto		trapassato remoto	
produssi	produc**emmo**	**ebbi** prodotto	**avemmo** prodotto
produc**esti**	produc**este**	**avesti** prodotto	**aveste** prodotto
produsse	**produssero**	**ebbe** prodotto	**ebbero** prodotto
futuro semplice		futuro anteriore	
produrr**ò**	produrr**emo**	**avrò** prodotto	**avremo** prodotto
produrr**ai**	produrr**ete**	**avrai** prodotto	**avrete** prodotto
produrr**à**	produrr**anno**	**avrà** prodotto	**avranno** prodotto
condizionale presente		condizionale passato	
produrr**ei**	produrr**emmo**	**avrei** prodotto	**avremmo** prodotto
produrr**esti**	produrr**este**	**avresti** prodotto	**avreste** prodotto
produrr**ebbe**	produrr**ebbero**	**avrebbe** prodotto	**avrebbero** prodotto
congiuntivo presente		congiuntivo passato	
produc**a**	produc**iamo**	**abbia** prodotto	**abbiamo** prodotto
produc**a**	produc**iate**	**abbia** prodotto	**abbiate** prodotto
produc**a**	produc**ano**	**abbia** prodotto	**abbiano** prodotto
congiuntivo imperfetto		congiuntivo trapassato	
produc**essi**	produc**essimo**	**avessi** prodotto	**avessimo** prodotto
produc**essi**	produc**este**	**avessi** prodotto	**aveste** prodotto
produc**esse**	produc**essero**	**avesse** prodotto	**avessero** prodotto
imperativo			
	produciamo		
produci; non produrre	producete		
produca	producano		

P

progettare — to plan

gerundio **progettando** participio passato **progettato**

SINGULAR	PLURAL
indicativo presente	
progett**o**	progett**iamo**
progett**i**	progett**ate**
progett**a**	progett**ano**
imperfetto	
progetta**vo**	progetta**vamo**
progetta**vi**	progetta**vate**
progetta**va**	progetta**vano**
passato remoto	
progett**ai**	progett**ammo**
progett**asti**	progett**aste**
progett**ò**	progett**arono**
futuro semplice	
progetter**ò**	progetter**emo**
progetter**ai**	progetter**ete**
progetter**à**	progetter**anno**
condizionale presente	
progett**erei**	progett**eremmo**
progett**eresti**	progett**ereste**
progett**erebbe**	progett**erebbero**
congiuntivo presente	
progett**i**	progett**iamo**
progett**i**	progett**iate**
progett**i**	progett**ino**
congiuntivo imperfetto	
progett**assi**	progett**assimo**
progett**assi**	progett**aste**
progett**asse**	progett**assero**
imperativo	
	progettiamo
progetta; non progettare	progettate
progetti	progettino

SINGULAR	PLURAL
passato prossimo	
ho progettato	**abbiamo** progettato
hai progettato	**avete** progettato
ha progettato	**hanno** progettato
trapassato prossimo	
avevo progettato	**avevamo** progettato
avevi progettato	**avevate** progettato
aveva progettato	**avevano** progettato
trapassato remoto	
ebbi progettato	**avemmo** progettato
avesti progettato	**aveste** progettato
ebbe progettato	**ebbero** progettato
futuro anteriore	
avrò progettato	**avremo** progettato
avrai progettato	**avrete** progettato
avrà progettato	**avranno** progettato
condizionale passato	
avrei progettato	**avremmo** progettato
avresti progettato	**avreste** progettato
avrebbe progettato	**avrebbero** progettato
congiuntivo passato	
abbia progettato	**abbiamo** progettato
abbia progettato	**abbiate** progettato
abbia progettato	**abbiano** progettato
congiuntivo trapassato	
avessi progettato	**avessimo** progettato
avessi progettato	**aveste** progettato
avesse progettato	**avessero** progettato

to program **programmare**

gerundio **programmando**

participio passato **programmato**

indicativo presente

SINGULAR	PLURAL
programm**o**	programm**iamo**
programm**i**	programm**ate**
programm**a**	programm**ano**

imperfetto

SINGULAR	PLURAL
programma**vo**	programma**vamo**
programma**vi**	programma**vate**
programma**va**	programma**vano**

passato remoto

SINGULAR	PLURAL
programm**ai**	programm**ammo**
programm**asti**	programm**aste**
programm**ò**	programm**arono**

futuro semplice

SINGULAR	PLURAL
programmer**ò**	programmer**emo**
programmer**ai**	programmer**ete**
programmer**à**	programmer**anno**

condizionale presente

SINGULAR	PLURAL
programm**erei**	programm**eremmo**
programm**eresti**	programm**ereste**
programm**erebbe**	programm**erebbero**

congiuntivo presente

SINGULAR	PLURAL
programm**i**	programm**iamo**
programm**i**	programm**iate**
programm**i**	programm**ino**

congiuntivo imperfetto

SINGULAR	PLURAL
programm**assi**	programm**assimo**
programm**assi**	programm**aste**
programm**asse**	programm**assero**

imperativo

SINGULAR	PLURAL
	programmiamo
programma; non programmare	programmate
programmi	programmino

passato prossimo

SINGULAR	PLURAL
ho programmato	**abbiamo** programmato
hai programmato	**avete** programmato
ha programmato	**hanno** programmato

trapassato prossimo

SINGULAR	PLURAL
avevo programmato	**avevamo** programmato
avevi programmato	**aveva** programmato
aveva programmato	**avevano** programmato

trapassato remoto

SINGULAR	PLURAL
ebbi programmato	**avemmo** programmato
avesti programmato	**aveste** programmato
ebbe programmato	**ebbero** programmato

futuro anteriore

SINGULAR	PLURAL
avrò programmato	**avremo** programmato
avrai programmato	**avrete** programmato
avrà programmato	**avranno** programmato

condizionale passato

SINGULAR	PLURAL
avrei programmato	**avremmo** programmato
avresti programmato	**avreste** programmato
avrebbe programmato	**avrebbero** programmato

congiuntivo passato

SINGULAR	PLURAL
abbia programmato	**abbiamo** programmato
abbia programmato	**abbiate** programmato
abbia programmato	**abbiano** programmato

congiuntivo trapassato

SINGULAR	PLURAL
avessi programmato	**avessimo** programmato
avessi programmato	**aveste** programmato
avesse programmato	**avessero** programmato

proibire — to forbid

gerundio **proibendo** — participio passato **proibito**

SINGULAR	PLURAL	SINGULAR	PLURAL
indicativo presente		passato prossimo	
proibisc**o**	proib**iamo**	**ho** proibito	**abbiamo** proibito
proibisc**i**	proib**ite**	**hai** proibito	**avete** proibito
proibisc**e**	proibisc**ono**	**ha** proibito	**hanno** proibito
imperfetto		trapassato prossimo	
proibi**vo**	proibi**vamo**	**avevo** proibito	**avevamo** proibito
proibi**vi**	proibi**vate**	**avevi** proibito	**avevate** proibito
proibi**va**	proibi**vano**	**aveva** proibito	**avevano** proibito
passato remoto		trapassato remoto	
proib**ii**	proib**immo**	**ebbi** proibito	**avemmo** proibito
proib**isti**	proib**iste**	**avesti** proibito	**aveste** proibito
proib**ì**	proib**irono**	**ebbe** proibito	**ebbero** proibito
futuro semplice		futuro anteriore	
proibir**ò**	proibir**emo**	**avrò** proibito	**avremo** proibito
proibir**ai**	proibir**ete**	**avrai** proibito	**avrete** proibito
proibir**à**	proibir**anno**	**avrà** proibito	**avranno** proibito
condizionale presente		condizionale passato	
proib**irei**	proib**iremmo**	**avrei** proibito	**avremmo** proibito
proib**iresti**	proib**ireste**	**avresti** proibito	**avreste** proibito
proib**irebbe**	proib**irebbero**	**avrebbe** proibito	**avrebbero** proibito
congiuntivo presente		congiuntivo passato	
proibisc**a**	proib**iamo**	**abbia** proibito	**abbiamo** proibito
proibisc**a**	proib**iate**	**abbia** proibito	**abbiate** proibito
proibisc**a**	proibisc**ano**	**abbia** proibito	**abbiano** proibito
congiuntivo imperfetto		congiuntivo trapassato	
proib**issi**	proib**issimo**	**avessi** proibito	**avessimo** proibito
proib**issi**	proib**iste**	**avessi** proibito	**aveste** proibito
proib**isse**	proib**issero**	**avesse** proibito	**avessero** proibito

imperativo

SINGULAR	PLURAL
	proibiamo
proibisci; non proibire	proibite
proibisca	proibiscano

P

to promise **promettere**

gerundio **promettendo** participio passato **promesso**

SINGULAR	PLURAL	SINGULAR	PLURAL
indicativo presente		passato prossimo	
prometto	promettiamo	**ho** promesso	**abbiamo** promesso
prometti	promettete	**hai** promesso	**avete** promesso
promette	promettono	**ha** promesso	**hanno** promesso
imperfetto		trapassato prossimo	
promettevo	promettevamo	**avevo** promesso	**avevamo** promesso
promettevi	promettevate	**avevi** promesso	**avevate** promesso
prometteva	promettevano	**aveva** promesso	**avevano** promesso
passato remoto		trapassato remoto	
promisi	promettemmo	**ebbi** promesso	**avemmo** promesso
promettesti	prometteste	**avesti** promesso	**aveste** promesso
promise	**permisero**	**ebbe** promesso	**ebbero** promesso
futuro semplice		futuro anteriore	
prometterò	prometteremo	**avrò** promesso	**avremo** promesso
prometterai	prometterete	**avrai** promesso	**avrete** promesso
prometterà	prometteranno	**avrà** promesso	**avranno** promesso
condizionale presente		condizionale passato	
prometterei	prometteremmo	**avrei** promesso	**avremmo** promesso
prometteresti	promettereste	**avresti** promesso	**avreste** promesso
prometterebbe	prometterebbero	**avrebbe** promesso	**avrebbero** promesso
congiuntivo presente		congiuntivo passato	
prometta	promettiamo	**abbia** promesso	**abbiamo** promesso
prometta	promettiate	**abbia** promesso	**abbiate** promesso
prometta	promettano	**abbia** promesso	**abbiano** promesso
congiuntivo imperfetto		congiuntivo trapassato	
promettessi	promettessimo	**avessi** promesso	**avessimo** promesso
promettessi	prometteste	**avessi** promesso	**aveste** promesso
promettesse	promettessero	**avesse** promesso	**avessero** promesso
imperativo			
	promettiamo		
prometti; non promettere	promettete		
prometta	promettano		

P

promuovere — to promote

gerundio **promuovendo** participio passato **promosso**

SINGULAR	PLURAL
indicativo presente	
promuov**o**	promuov**iamo**
promuov**i**	promuov**ete**
promuov**e**	promuov**ono**
imperfetto	
promuove**vo**	promuove**vamo**
promuove**vi**	promuove**vate**
promuove**va**	promuove**vano**
passato remoto	
promossi	promuov**emmo**
promuov**esti**	promuov**este**
promosse	**promossero**
futuro semplice	
promuover**ò**	promuover**emo**
promuover**ai**	promuover**ete**
promuover**à**	promuover**anno**
condizionale presente	
promuov**erei**	promuov**eremmo**
promuov**eresti**	promuov**ereste**
promuov**erebbe**	promuov**erebbero**
congiuntivo presente	
promuov**a**	promuov**iamo**
promuov**a**	promuov**iate**
promuov**a**	promuov**ano**
congiuntivo imperfetto	
promuov**essi**	promuov**essimo**
promuov**essi**	promuov**este**
promuov**esse**	promuov**essero**
imperativo	
	promuoviamo
promuovi; non promuovere	promuovete
promuova	promuovano

SINGULAR	PLURAL
passato prossimo	
ho promosso	**abbiamo** promosso
hai promosso	**avete** promosso
ha promosso	**hanno** promosso
trapassato prossimo	
avevo promosso	**avevamo** promosso
avevi promosso	**avevate** promosso
aveva promosso	**avevano** promosso
trapassato remoto	
ebbi promosso	**avemmo** promosso
avesti promosso	**aveste** promosso
ebbe promosso	**ebbero** promosso
futuro anteriore	
avrò promosso	**avremo** promosso
avrai promosso	**avrete** promosso
avrà promosso	**avranno** promosso
condizionale passato	
avrei promosso	**avremmo** promosso
avresti promosso	**avreste** promosso
avrebbe promosso	**avrebbero** promosso
congiuntivo passato	
abbia promosso	**abbiamo** promosso
abbia promosso	**abbiate** promosso
abbia promosso	**abbiano** promosso
congiuntivo trapassato	
avessi promosso	**avessimo** promosso
avessi promosso	**aveste** promosso
avesse promosso	**avessero** promosso

gerundio **pronunciando** participio passato **pronunciato**

SINGULAR	PLURAL	SINGULAR	PLURAL
indicativo presente		passato prossimo	
pronunci**o**	pronunc**iamo**	**ho** pronunciato	**abbiamo** pronunciato
pronunc**i**	pronunc**iate**	**hai** pronunciato	**avete** pronunciato
pronunci**a**	pronunc**iano**	**ha** pronunciato	**hanno** pronunciato
imperfetto		trapassato prossimo	
pronuncia**vo**	pronuncia**vamo**	**avevo** pronunciato	**avevamo** pronunciato
pronuncia**vi**	pronuncia**vate**	**avevi** pronunciato	**avevate** pronunciato
pronuncia**va**	pronuncia**vano**	**aveva** pronunciato	**avevano** pronunciato
passato remoto		trapassato remoto	
pronunci**ai**	pronunci**ammo**	**ebbi** pronunciato	**avemmo** pronunciato
pronunci**asti**	pronunci**aste**	**avesti** pronunciato	**aveste** pronunciato
pronunci**ò**	pronunci**arono**	**ebbe** pronunciato	**ebbero** pronunciato
futuro semplice		futuro anteriore	
pronuncer**ò**	pronuncer**emo**	**avrò** pronunciato	**avremo** pronunciato
pronuncer**ai**	pronuncer**ete**	**avrai** pronunciato	**avrete** pronunciato
pronuncer**à**	pronuncer**anno**	**avrà** pronunciato	**avranno** pronunciato
condizionale presente		condizionale passato	
pronunc**erei**	pronunc**eremmo**	**avrei** pronunciato	**avremmo** pronunciato
pronunc**eresti**	pronunc**ereste**	**avresti** pronunciato	**avreste** pronunciato
pronunc**erebbe**	pronunc**erebbero**	**avrebbe** pronunciato	**avrebbero** pronunciato
congiuntivo presente		congiuntivo passato	
pronunc**i**	pronunc**iamo**	**abbia** pronunciato	**abbiamo** pronunciato
pronunc**i**	pronunc**iate**	**abbia** pronunciato	**abbiate** pronunciato
pronunc**i**	pronunc**ino**	**abbia** pronunciato	**abbiano** pronunciato
congiuntivo imperfetto		congiuntivo trapassato	
pronunci**assi**	pronunci**assimo**	**avessi** pronunciato	**avessimo** pronunciato
pronunci**assi**	pronunci**aste**	**avessi** pronunciato	**aveste** pronunciato
pronunci**asse**	pronunci**assero**	**avesse** pronunciato	**avessero** pronunciato
imperativo			
	pronunciamo		
pronuncia; non pronunciare	pronunciate		
pronunci	pronuncino		

P

proporre — to propose

gerundio **proponendo** participio passato **proposto**

SINGULAR	PLURAL	SINGULAR	PLURAL
indicativo presente		passato prossimo	
propong**o**	propon**iamo**	**ho** proposto	**abbiamo** proposto
propon**i**	propon**ete**	**hai** proposto	**avete** proposto
propon**e**	propong**ono**	**ha** proposto	**hanno** proposto
imperfetto		trapassato prossimo	
propone**vo**	propone**vamo**	**avevo** proposto	**avevamo** proposto
propone**vi**	propone**vate**	**avevi** proposto	**avevate** proposto
propone**va**	propone**vano**	**aveva** proposto	**avevano** proposto
passato remoto		trapassato remoto	
proposi	propon**emmo**	**ebbi** proposto	**avemmo** proposto
propon**esti**	propon**este**	**avesti** proposto	**aveste** proposto
propose	**proposero**	**ebbe** proposto	**ebbero** proposto
futuro semplice		futuro anteriore	
propor**rò**	propor**remo**	**avrò** proposto	**avremo** proposto
propor**rai**	propor**rete**	**avrai** proposto	**avrete** proposto
propor**rà**	propor**ranno**	**avrà** proposto	**avranno** proposto
condizionale presente		condizionale passato	
prop**orrei**	prop**orremmo**	**avrei** proposto	**avremmo** proposto
prop**orresti**	prop**orreste**	**avresti** proposto	**avreste** proposto
prop**orrebbe**	prop**orrebbero**	**avrebbe** proposto	**avrebbero** proposto
congiuntivo presente		congiuntivo passato	
propong**a**	propon**iamo**	**abbia** proposto	**abbiamo** proposto
propong**a**	propon**iate**	**abbia** proposto	**abbiate** proposto
propong**a**	propong**ano**	**abbia** proposto	**abbiano** proposto
congiuntivo imperfetto		congiuntivo trapassato	
propon**essi**	propon**essimo**	**avessi** proposto	**avessimo** proposto
propon**essi**	propon**este**	**avessi** proposto	**aveste** proposto
propon**esse**	propon**essero**	**avesse** proposto	**avessero** proposto

imperativo

SINGULAR	PLURAL
	proponiamo
proponi; non proporre	proponete
proponga	propongano

P

to protect **proteggere**

gerundio **proteggendo** participio passato **protetto**

SINGULAR	PLURAL	SINGULAR	PLURAL
indicativo presente		passato prossimo	
protegg**o**	protegg**iamo**	**ho** protetto	**abbiamo** protetto
protegg**i**	protegg**ete**	**hai** protetto	**avete** protetto
protegg**e**	protegg**ono**	**ha** protetto	**hanno** protetto
imperfetto		trapassato prossimo	
protegge**vo**	protegge**vamo**	**avevo** protetto	**avevamo** protetto
protegge**vi**	protegge**vate**	**avevi** protetto	**avevate** protetto
protegge**va**	protegge**vano**	**aveva** protetto	**avevano** protetto
passato remoto		trapassato remoto	
protessi	protegg**emmo**	**ebbi** protetto	**avemmo** protetto
protegg**esti**	protegg**este**	**avesti** protetto	**aveste** protetto
protesse	**protessero**	**ebbe** protetto	**ebbero** protetto
futuro semplice		futuro anteriore	
protegger**ò**	protegger**emo**	**avrò** protetto	**avremo** protetto
protegger**ai**	protegger**ete**	**avrai** protetto	**avrete** protetto
protegger**à**	protegger**anno**	**avrà** protetto	**avranno** protetto
condizionale presente		condizionale passato	
protegg**erei**	protegg**eremmo**	**avrei** protetto	**avremmo** protetto
protegg**eresti**	protegg**ereste**	**avresti** protetto	**avreste** protetto
protegg**erebbe**	protegg**erebbero**	**avrebbe** protetto	**avrebbero** protetto
congiuntivo presente		congiuntivo passato	
protegg**a**	protegg**iamo**	**abbia** protetto	**abbiamo** protetto
protegg**a**	protegg**iate**	**abbia** protetto	**abbiate** protetto
protegg**a**	protegg**ano**	**abbia** protetto	**abbiano** protetto
congiuntivo imperfetto		congiuntivo trapassato	
protegg**essi**	protegg**essimo**	**avessi** protetto	**avessimo** protetto
protegg**essi**	protegg**este**	**avessi** protetto	**aveste** protetto
protegg**esse**	protegg**essero**	**avesse** protetto	**avessero** protetto
imperativo			
	proteggiamo		
proteggi; non proteggere	proteggete		
protegga	proteggano		

P

protestare — to complain, to protest

gerundio **protestando** — participio passato **protestato**

SINGULAR	PLURAL	SINGULAR	PLURAL
indicativo presente		*passato prossimo*	
protest**o**	protest**iamo**	**ho** protestato	**abbiamo** protestato
protest**i**	protest**ate**	**hai** protestato	**avete** protestato
protest**a**	protest**ano**	**ha** protestato	**hanno** protestato
imperfetto		*trapassato prossimo*	
protesta**vo**	protesta**vamo**	**avevo** protestato	**avevamo** protestato
protesta**vi**	protesta**vate**	**avevi** protestato	**avevate** protestato
protesta**va**	protesta**vano**	**aveva** protestato	**avevano** protestato
passato remoto		*trapassato remoto*	
protest**ai**	protest**ammo**	**ebbi** protestato	**avemmo** protestato
protest**asti**	protest**aste**	**avesti** protestato	**aveste** protestato
protest**ò**	protest**arono**	**ebbe** protestato	**ebbero** protestato
futuro semplice		*futuro anteriore*	
protester**ò**	protester**emo**	**avrò** protestato	**avremo** protestato
protester**ai**	protester**ete**	**avrai** protestato	**avrete** protestato
protester**à**	protester**anno**	**avrà** protestato	**avranno** protestato
condizionale presente		*condizionale passato*	
protest**erei**	protest**eremmo**	**avrei** protestato	**avremmo** protestato
protest**eresti**	protest**ereste**	**avresti** protestato	**avreste** protestato
protest**erebbe**	protest**erebbero**	**avrebbe** protestato	**avrebbero** protestato
congiuntivo presente		*congiuntivo passato*	
protest**i**	protest**iamo**	**abbia** protestato	**abbiamo** protestato
protest**i**	protest**iate**	**abbia** protestato	**abbiate** protestato
protest**i**	protest**ino**	**abbia** protestato	**abbiano** protestato
congiuntivo imperfetto		*congiuntivo trapassato*	
protest**assi**	protest**assimo**	**avessi** protestato	**avessimo** protestato
protest**assi**	protest**aste**	**avessi** protestato	**aveste** protestato
protest**asse**	protest**assero**	**avesse** protestato	**avessero** protestato
imperativo			
	protestiamo		
protesta; non protestare	protestate		
protesti	protestino		

P

to try, to attempt — provare

gerundio **provando** | participio passato **provato**

SINGULAR	PLURAL
indicativo presente	
prov**o**	prov**iamo**
prov**i**	prov**ate**
prov**a**	prov**ano**
imperfetto	
prova**vo**	prova**vamo**
prova**vi**	prova**vate**
prova**va**	prova**vano**
passato remoto	
prov**ai**	prov**ammo**
prov**asti**	prov**aste**
prov**ò**	prov**arono**
futuro semplice	
prover**ò**	prover**emo**
prover**ai**	prover**ete**
prover**à**	prover**anno**
condizionale presente	
prov**erei**	prov**eremmo**
prov**eresti**	prov**ereste**
prov**erebbe**	prov**erebbero**
congiuntivo presente	
prov**i**	prov**iamo**
prov**i**	prov**iate**
prov**i**	prov**ino**
congiuntivo imperfetto	
prov**assi**	prov**assimo**
prov**assi**	prov**aste**
prov**asse**	prov**assero**
imperativo	
	proviamo
prova; non provare	provate
provi	provino

SINGULAR	PLURAL
passato prossimo	
ho provato	**abbiamo** provato
hai provato	**avete** provato
ha provato	**hanno** provato
trapassato prossimo	
avevo provato	**avevamo** provato
avevi provato	**avevate** provato
aveva provato	**avevano** provato
trapassato remoto	
ebbi provato	**avemmo** provato
avesti provato	**aveste** provato
ebbe provato	**ebbero** provato
futuro anteriore	
avrò provato	**avremo** provato
avrai provato	**avrete** provato
avrà provato	**avranno** provato
condizionale passato	
avrei provato	**avremmo** provato
avresti provato	**avreste** provato
avrebbe provato	**avrebbero** provato
congiuntivo passato	
abbia provato	**abbiamo** provato
abbia provato	**abbiate** provato
abbia provato	**abbiano** provato
congiuntivo trapassato	
avessi provato	**avessimo** provato
avessi provato	**aveste** provato
avesse provato	**avessero** provato

provvedere — to provide

gerundio **provvedendo** participio passato **provvisto**

SINGULAR	PLURAL	SINGULAR	PLURAL
indicativo presente		**passato prossimo**	
provved**o**	provved**iamo**	**ho** provvisto	**abbiamo** provvisto
provved**i**	provved**ete**	**hai** provvisto	**avete** provvisto
provved**e**	provved**ono**	**ha** provvisto	**hanno** provvisto
imperfetto		**trapassato prossimo**	
provvede**vo**	provvede**vamo**	**avevo** provvisto	**avevamo** provvisto
provvede**vi**	provvede**vate**	**avevi** provvisto	**avevate** provvisto
provvede**va**	provvede**vano**	**aveva** provvisto	**avevano** provvisto
passato remoto		**trapassato remoto**	
provvid**i**	provved**emmo**	**ebbi** provvisto	**avemmo** provvisto
provved**esti**	provved**este**	**avesti** provvisto	**aveste** provvisto
provvid**e**	provvid**ero**	**ebbe** provvisto	**ebbero** provvisto
futuro semplice		**futuro anteriore**	
provveder**ò**	provveder**emo**	**avrò** provvisto	**avremo** provvisto
provveder**ai**	provveder**ete**	**avrai** provvisto	**avrete** provvisto
provveder**à**	provveder**anno**	**avrà** provvisto	**avranno** provvisto
condizionale presente		**condizionale passato**	
provved**erei**	provved**eremmo**	**avrei** provvisto	**avremmo** provvisto
provved**eresti**	provved**ereste**	**avresti** provvisto	**avreste** provvisto
provved**erebbe**	provved**erebbero**	**avrebbe** provvisto	**avrebbero** provvisto
congiuntivo presente		**congiuntivo passato**	
provved**a**	provved**iamo**	**abbia** provvisto	**abbiamo** provvisto
provved**a**	provved**iate**	**abbia** provvisto	**abbiate** provvisto
provved**a**	provved**ano**	**abbia** provvisto	**abbiano** provvisto
congiuntivo imperfetto		**congiuntivo trapassato**	
provved**essi**	provved**essimo**	**avessi** provvisto	**avessimo** provvisto
provved**essi**	provved**este**	**avessi** provvisto	**aveste** provvisto
provved**esse**	provved**essero**	**avesse** provvisto	**avessero** provvisto
imperativo			
	provvediamo		
provvedi; non provvedere	provvedete		
provveda	provvedano		

P

gerundio **pulendo** participio passato **pulito**

SINGULAR	PLURAL	SINGULAR	PLURAL
indicativo presente		passato prossimo	
pulisc**o**	pul**iamo**	**ho** pulito	**abbiamo** pulito
pulisc**i**	pul**ite**	**hai** pulito	**avete** pulito
pulisc**e**	pulisc**ono**	**ha** pulito	**hanno** pulito
imperfetto		trapassato prossimo	
puli**vo**	puli**vamo**	**avevo** pulito	**avevamo** pulito
puli**vi**	puli**vate**	**avevi** pulito	**avevate** pulito
puli**va**	puli**vano**	**aveva** pulito	**avevano** pulito
passato remoto		trapassato remoto	
pul**ii**	pul**immo**	**ebbi** pulito	**avemmo** pulito
pul**isti**	pul**iste**	**avesti** pulito	**aveste** pulito
pul**ì**	pul**irono**	**ebbe** pulito	**ebbero** pulito
futuro semplice		futuro anteriore	
pulir**ò**	pulir**emo**	**avrò** pulito	**avremo** pulito
pulir**ai**	pulir**ete**	**avrai** pulito	**avrete** pulito
pulir**à**	pulir**anno**	**avrà** pulito	**avranno** pulito
condizionale presente		condizionale passato	
pul**irei**	pul**iremmo**	**avrei** pulito	**avremmo** pulito
pul**iresti**	pul**ireste**	**avresti** pulito	**avreste** pulito
pul**irebbe**	pul**irebbero**	**avrebbe** pulito	**avrebbero** pulito
congiuntivo presente		congiuntivo passato	
pulisc**a**	pul**iamo**	**abbia** pulito	**abbiamo** pulito
pulisc**a**	pul**iate**	**abbia** pulito	**abbiate** pulito
pulisc**a**	pulisc**ano**	**abbia** pulito	**abbiano** pulito
congiuntivo imperfetto		congiuntivo trapassato	
pul**issi**	pul**issimo**	**avessi** pulito	**avessimo** pulito
pul**issi**	pul**iste**	**avessi** pulito	**aveste** pulito
pul**isse**	pul**issero**	**avesse** pulito	**avessero** pulito

imperativo

	puliamo
pulisci; non pulire	pulite
pulisca	puliscano

P

gerundio **pungendo** participio passato **punto**

SINGULAR	PLURAL	SINGULAR	PLURAL
indicativo presente		passato prossimo	
pung**o**	pung**iamo**	**ho** punto	**abbiamo** punto
pung**i**	pung**ete**	**hai** punto	**avete** punto
pung**e**	pung**ono**	**ha** punto	**hanno** punto
imperfetto		trapassato prossimo	
punge**vo**	punge**vamo**	**avevo** punto	**avevamo** punto
punge**vi**	punge**vate**	**avevi** punto	**avevate** punto
punge**va**	punge**vano**	**aveva** punto	**avevano** punto
passato remoto		trapassato remoto	
punsi	pung**emmo**	**ebbi** punto	**avemmo** punto
pung**esti**	pung**este**	**avesti** punto	**aveste** punto
punse	**punsero**	**ebbe** punto	**ebbero** punto
futuro semplice		futuro anteriore	
punger**ò**	punger**emo**	**avrò** punto	**avremo** punto
punger**ai**	punger**ete**	**avrai** punto	**avrete** punto
punger**à**	punger**anno**	**avrà** punto	**avranno** punto
condizionale presente		condizionale passato	
pung**erei**	pung**eremmo**	**avrei** punto	**avremmo** punto
pung**eresti**	pung**ereste**	**avresti** punto	**avreste** punto
pung**erebbe**	pung**erebbero**	**avrebbe** punto	**avrebbero** punto
congiuntivo presente		congiuntivo passato	
pung**a**	pung**iamo**	**abbia** punto	**abbiamo** punto
pung**a**	pung**iate**	**abbia** punto	**abbiate** punto
pung**a**	pung**ano**	**abbia** punto	**abbiano** punto
congiuntivo imperfetto		congiuntivo trapassato	
pung**essi**	pung**essimo**	**avessi** punto	**avessimo** punto
pung**essi**	pung**este**	**avessi** punto	**aveste** punto
pung**esse**	pung**essero**	**avesse** punto	**avessero** punto
imperativo			
	pungiamo		
pungi; non pungere	pungete		
punga	pungano		

to punish — punire

gerundio **punendo** — participio passato **punito**

SINGULAR	PLURAL
indicativo presente	
punisc**o**	puni**amo**
punisc**i**	pun**ite**
punisc**e**	punisc**ono**
imperfetto	
puni**vo**	puni**vamo**
puni**vi**	puni**vate**
puni**va**	puni**vano**
passato remoto	
pun**ii**	pun**immo**
pun**isti**	pun**iste**
pun**ì**	pun**irono**
futuro semplice	
punir**ò**	punir**emo**
punir**ai**	punir**ete**
punir**à**	punir**anno**
condizionale presente	
pun**irei**	pun**iremmo**
pun**iresti**	pun**ireste**
pun**irebbe**	pun**irebbero**
congiuntivo presente	
punisc**a**	puni**amo**
punisc**a**	puni**ate**
punisc**a**	punisc**ano**
congiuntivo imperfetto	
pun**issi**	pun**issimo**
pun**issi**	pun**iste**
pun**isse**	pun**issero**
imperativo	
	puniamo
punisci; non punire	punite
punisca	puniscano

SINGULAR	PLURAL
passato prossimo	
ho punito	**abbiamo** punito
hai punito	**avete** punito
ha punito	**hanno** punito
trapassato prossimo	
avevo punito	**avevamo** punito
avevi punito	**avevate** punito
aveva punito	**avevano** punito
trapassato remoto	
ebbi punito	**avemmo** punito
avesti punito	**aveste** punito
ebbe punito	**ebbero** punito
futuro anteriore	
avrò punito	**avremo** punito
avrai punito	**avrete** punito
avrà punito	**avranno** punito
condizionale passato	
avrei punito	**avremmo** punito
avresti punito	**avreste** punito
avrebbe punito	**avrebbero** punito
congiuntivo passato	
abbia punito	**abbiamo** punito
abbia punito	**abbiate** punito
abbia punito	**abbiano** punito
congiuntivo trapassato	
avessi punito	**avessimo** punito
avessi punito	**aveste** punito
avesse punito	**avessero** punito

gerundio **quietando** participio passato **quietato**

SINGULAR	PLURAL	SINGULAR	PLURAL
indicativo presente		passato prossimo	
quiet**o**	quiet**iamo**	**ho** quietato	**abbiamo** quietato
quiet**i**	quiet**ate**	**hai** quietato	**avete** quietato
quiet**a**	quiet**ano**	**ha** quietato	**hanno** quietato
imperfetto		trapassato prossimo	
quieta**vo**	quieta**vamo**	**avevo** quietato	**avevamo** quietato
quieta**vi**	quieta**vate**	**avevi** quietato	**avevate** quietato
quieta**va**	quieta**vano**	**aveva** quietato	**avevano** quietato
passato remoto		trapassato remoto	
quiet**ai**	quiet**ammo**	**ebbi** quietato	**avemmo** quietato
quiet**asti**	quiet**aste**	**avesti** quietato	**aveste** quietato
quiet**ò**	quiet**arono**	**ebbe** quietato	**ebbero** quietato
futuro semplice		futuro anteriore	
quieter**ò**	quieter**emo**	**avrò** quietato	**avremo** quietato
quieter**ai**	quieter**ete**	**avrai** quietato	**avrete** quietato
quieter**à**	quieter**anno**	**avrà** quietato	**avranno** quietato
condizionale presente		condizionale passato	
quiet**erei**	quiet**eremmo**	**avrei** quietato	**avremmo** quietato
quiet**eresti**	quiet**ereste**	**avresti** quietato	**avreste** quietato
quiet**erebbe**	quiet**erebbero**	**avrebbe** quietato	**avrebbero** quietato
congiuntivo presente		congiuntivo passato	
quiet**i**	quiet**iamo**	**abbia** quietato	**abbiamo** quietato
quiet**i**	quiet**iate**	**abbia** quietato	**abbiate** quietato
quiet**i**	quiet**ino**	**abbia** quietato	**abbiano** quietato
congiuntivo imperfetto		congiuntivo trapassato	
quiet**assi**	quiet**assimo**	**avessi** quietato	**avessimo** quietato
quiet**assi**	quiet**aste**	**avessi** quietato	**aveste** quietato
quiet**asse**	quiet**assero**	**avesse** quietato	**avessero** quietato
imperativo			
	quietiamo		
quieta; non quietare	quietate		
quieti	quietino		

to recommend **raccomandare**

gerundio **raccomandando** participio passato **raccomandato**

SINGULAR	PLURAL
indicativo presente	
raccomand**o**	raccomand**iamo**
raccomand**i**	raccomand**ate**
raccomand**a**	raccomand**ano**
imperfetto	
raccomanda**vo**	raccomanda**vamo**
raccomanda**vi**	raccomanda**vate**
raccomanda**va**	raccomanda**vano**
passato remoto	
raccomand**ai**	raccomand**ammo**
raccomand**asti**	raccomand**aste**
raccomand**ò**	raccomand**arono**
futuro semplice	
raccomander**ò**	raccomander**emo**
raccomander**ai**	raccomander**ete**
raccomander**à**	raccomander**anno**
condizionale presente	
raccomander**ei**	raccomander**emmo**
raccomander**esti**	raccomander**este**
raccomander**ebbe**	raccomander**ebbero**
congiuntivo presente	
raccomand**i**	raccomand**iamo**
raccomand**i**	raccomand**iate**
raccomand**i**	raccomand**ino**
congiuntivo imperfetto	
raccomand**assi**	raccomand**assimo**
raccomand**assi**	raccomand**aste**
raccomand**asse**	raccomand**assero**
imperativo	
	raccomandiamo
raccomanda; non raccomandare	raccomandate
raccomandi	raccomandino

SINGULAR	PLURAL
passato prossimo	
ho raccomandato	**abbiamo** raccomandato
hai raccomandato	**avete** raccomandato
ha raccomandato	**hanno** raccomandato
trapassato prossimo	
avevo raccomandato	**avevamo** raccomandato
avevi raccomandato	**avevate** raccomandato
aveva raccomandato	**avevano** raccomandato
trapassato remoto	
ebbi raccomandato	**avemmo** raccomandato
avesti raccomandato	**aveste** raccomandato
ebbe raccomandato	**ebbero** raccomandato
futuro anteriore	
avrò raccomandato	**avremo** raccomandato
avrai raccomandato	**avrete** raccomandato
avrà raccomandato	**avranno** raccomandato
condizionale passato	
avrei raccomandato	**avremmo** raccomandato
avresti raccomandato	**avreste** raccomandato
avrebbe raccomandato	**avrebbero** raccomandato
congiuntivo passato	
abbia raccomandato	**abbiamo** raccomandato
abbia raccomandato	**abbiate** raccomandato
abbia raccomandato	**abbiano** raccomandato
congiuntivo trapassato	
avessi raccomandato	**avessimo** raccomandato
avessi raccomandato	**aveste** raccomandato
avesse raccomandato	**avessero** raccomandato

raccontare — to tell

gerundio **raccontando** participio passato **raccontato**

indicativo presente

SINGULAR	PLURAL
raccont**o**	raccont**iamo**
raccont**i**	raccont**ate**
raccont**a**	raccont**ano**

imperfetto

SINGULAR	PLURAL
raccontа**vo**	raccontа**vamo**
raccontа**vi**	raccontа**vate**
raccontа**va**	raccontа**vano**

passato remoto

SINGULAR	PLURAL
raccont**ai**	raccont**ammo**
raccont**asti**	raccont**aste**
raccont**ò**	raccont**arono**

futuro semplice

SINGULAR	PLURAL
racconter**ò**	racconter**emo**
racconter**ai**	racconter**ete**
racconter**à**	racconter**anno**

condizionale presente

SINGULAR	PLURAL
raccont**erei**	raccont**eremmo**
raccont**eresti**	raccont**ereste**
raccont**erebbe**	raccont**erebbero**

congiuntivo presente

SINGULAR	PLURAL
raccont**i**	raccont**iamo**
raccont**i**	raccont**iate**
raccont**i**	raccont**ino**

congiuntivo imperfetto

SINGULAR	PLURAL
raccont**assi**	raccont**assimo**
raccont**assi**	raccont**aste**
raccont**asse**	raccont**assero**

imperativo

SINGULAR	PLURAL
	raccontiamo
racconta; non raccontare	raccontate
racconti	raccontino

passato prossimo

SINGULAR	PLURAL
ho raccontato	**abbiamo** raccontato
hai raccontato	**avete** raccontato
ha raccontato	**hanno** raccontato

trapassato prossimo

SINGULAR	PLURAL
avevo raccontato	**avevamo** raccontato
avevi raccontato	**avevate** raccontato
aveva raccontato	**avevano** raccontato

trapassato remoto

SINGULAR	PLURAL
ebbi raccontato	**avemmo** raccontato
avesti raccontato	**aveste** raccontato
ebbe raccontato	**ebbero** raccontato

futuro anteriore

SINGULAR	PLURAL
avrò raccontato	**avremo** raccontato
avrai raccontato	**avrete** raccontato
avrà raccontato	**avranno** raccontato

condizionale passato

SINGULAR	PLURAL
avrei raccontato	**avremmo** raccontato
avresti racconato	**avreste** raccontato
avrebbe raccontato	**avrebbero** raccontato

congiuntivo passato

SINGULAR	PLURAL
abbia raccontato	**abbiamo** raccontato
abbia raccontato	**abbiate** raccontato
abbia raccontato	**abbiano** raccontato

congiuntivo trapassato

SINGULAR	PLURAL
avessi raccontato	**avessimo** raccontato
avessi raccontato	**aveste** raccontato
avesse raccontato	**avessero** raccontato

to shave **radersi**

gerundio **radendosi** participio passato **rasosi**

SINGULAR	PLURAL
indicativo presente	
mi rad**o**	**ci** rad**iamo**
ti rad**i**	**vi** rad**ete**
si rad**e**	**si** rad**ono**
imperfetto	
mi rade**vo**	**ci** rade**vamo**
ti rade**vi**	**vi** rade**vate**
si rade**va**	**si** rade**vano**
passato remoto	
mi ras**i**	**ci** rad**emmo**
ti rad**esti**	**vi** rad**este**
si ras**e**	**si** ras**ero**
futuro semplice	
mi rader**ò**	**ci** rader**emo**
ti rader**ai**	**vi** rader**ete**
si rader**à**	**si** rader**anno**
condizionale presente	
mi rad**erei**	**ci** rad**eremmo**
ti rad**eresti**	**vi** rad**ereste**
si rad**erebbe**	**si** rad**erebbero**
congiuntivo presente	
mi rad**a**	**ci** rad**iamo**
ti rad**a**	**vi** rad**iate**
si rad**a**	**si** rad**ano**
congiuntivo imperfetto	
mi rad**essi**	**ci** rad**essimo**
ti rad**essi**	**vi** rad**este**
si rad**esse**	**si** rad**essero**
imperativo	
	radiamoci
raditi; non raderti/ non ti radere	radetevi
si rada	si radano

SINGULAR	PLURAL
passato prossimo	
mi sono raso(a)	**ci siamo** rasi(e)
ti sei raso(a)	**vi siete** rasi(e)
si è raso(a)	**si sono** rasi(e)
trapassato prossimo	
mi ero raso(a)	**ci eravamo** rasi(e)
ti eri raso(a)	**vi eravate** rasi(e)
si era raso(a)	**si erano** rasi(e)
trapassato remoto	
mi fui raso(a)	**ci fummo** rasi(e)
ti fosti raso(a)	**vi foste** rasi(e)
si fu raso(a)	**si furono** rasi(e)
futuro anteriore	
mi sarò raso(a)	**ci saremo** rasi(e)
ti sarai raso(a)	**vi sarete** rasi(e)
si sarà raso(a)	**si saranno** rasi(e)
condizionale passato	
mi sarei raso(a)	**ci saremmo** rasi(e)
ti saresti raso(a)	**vi sareste** rasi(e)
si sarebbe raso(a)	**si sarebbero** rasi(e)
congiuntivo passato	
mi sia raso(a)	**ci siamo** rasi(e)
ti sia raso(a)	**vi siate** rasi(e)
si sia raso(a)	**si siano** rasi(e)
congiuntivo trapassato	
mi fossi raso(a)	**ci fossimo** rasi(e)
ti fossi raso(a)	**vi foste** rasi(e)
si fosse raso(a)	**si fossero** rasi(e)

raggiungere — to reach, to catch up to

gerundio **raggiungendo** — participio passato **raggiunto**

SINGULAR	PLURAL	SINGULAR	PLURAL
indicativo presente		passato prossimo	
raggiung**o**	raggiung**iamo**	**ho** raggiunto	**abbiamo** raggiunto
raggiung**i**	raggiung**ete**	**hai** raggiunto	**avete** raggiunto
raggiung**e**	raggiung**ono**	**ha** raggiunto	**hanno** raggiunto
imperfetto		trapassato prossimo	
raggiunge**vo**	raggiunge**vamo**	**avevo** raggiunto	**avevamo** raggiunto
raggiunge**vi**	raggiunge**vate**	**avevi** raggiunto	**avevate** raggiunto
raggiunge**va**	raggiunge**vano**	**aveva** raggiunto	**avevano** raggiunto
passato remoto		trapassato remoto	
raggiuns**i**	raggiung**emmo**	**ebbi** raggiunto	**avemmo** raggiunto
raggiung**esti**	raggiung**este**	**avesti** raggiunto	**aveste** raggiunto
raggiuns**e**	raggiuns**erono**	**ebbe** raggiunto	**ebbero** raggiunto
futuro semplice		futuro anteriore	
raggiunger**ò**	raggiunger**emo**	**avrò** raggiunto	**avremo** raggiunto
raggiunger**ai**	raggiunger**ete**	**avrai** raggiunto	**avrete** raggiunto
raggiunger**à**	raggiunger**anno**	**avrà** raggiunto	**avranno** raggiunto
condizionale presente		condizionale passato	
raggiung**erei**	raggiung**eremmo**	**avrei** raggiunto	**avremmo** raggiunto
raggiung**eresti**	raggiung**ereste**	**avresti** raggiunto	**avreste** raggiunto
raggiung**erebbe**	raggiung**erebbero**	**avrebbe** raggiunto	**avrebbero** raggiunto
congiuntivo presente		congiuntivo passato	
raggiung**a**	raggiung**iamo**	**abbia** raggiunto	**abbiamo** raggiunto
raggiung**a**	raggiung**iate**	**abbia** raggiunto	**abbiate** raggiunto
raggiung**a**	raggiung**ano**	**abbia** raggiunto	**abbiano** raggiunto
congiuntivo imperfetto		congiuntivo trapassato	
raggiung**essi**	raggiung**essimo**	**avessi** raggiunto	**avessimo** raggiunto
raggiung**essi**	raggiung**este**	**avessi** raggiunto	**aveste** raggiunto
raggiung**esse**	raggiung**essero**	**avesse** raggiunto	**avessero** raggiunto

imperativo

	raggiungiamo
raggiungi; non raggiungere	raggiungete
raggiunga	raggiungano

to reason, to discuss ragionare

gerundio **ragionando** participio passato **ragionato**

SINGULAR	PLURAL	SINGULAR	PLURAL
indicativo presente		passato prossimo	
ragion**o**	ragion**iamo**	**ho** ragionato	**abbiamo** ragionato
ragion**i**	ragion**ate**	**hai** ragionato	**avete** ragionato
ragion**a**	ragion**ano**	**ha** ragionato	**hanno** ragionato
imperfetto		trapassato prossimo	
ragiona**vo**	ragiona**vamo**	**avevo** ragionato	**avevamo** ragionato
ragiona**vi**	ragiona**vate**	**avevi** ragionato	**avevate** ragionato
ragiona**va**	ragiona**vano**	**aveva** ragionato	**avevano** ragionato
passato remoto		trapassato remoto	
ragion**ai**	ragion**ammo**	**ebbi** ragionato	**avemmo** ragionato
ragion**asti**	ragion**aste**	**avesti** ragionato	**aveste** ragionato
ragion**ò**	ragion**arono**	**ebbe** ragionato	**ebbero** ragionato
futuro semplice		futuro anteriore	
ragioner**ò**	ragioner**emo**	**avrò** ragionato	**avremo** ragionato
ragioner**ai**	ragioner**ete**	**avrai** ragionato	**avrete** ragionato
ragioner**à**	ragioner**anno**	**avrà** ragionato	**avranno** ragionato
condizionale presente		condizionale passato	
ragion**erei**	ragion**eremmo**	**avrei** ragionato	**avremmo** ragionato
ragion**eresti**	ragion**ereste**	**avresti** ragionato	**avreste** ragionato
ragion**erebbe**	ragion**erebbero**	**avrebbe** ragionato	**avrebbero** ragionato
congiuntivo presente		congiuntivo passato	
ragion**i**	ragion**iamo**	**abbia** ragionato	**abbiamo** ragionato
ragion**i**	ragion**iate**	**abbia** ragionato	**abbiate** ragionato
ragion**i**	ragion**ino**	**abbia** ragionato	**abbiano** ragionato
congiuntivo imperfetto		congiuntivo trapassato	
ragion**assi**	ragion**assimo**	**avessi** ragionato	**avessimo** ragionato
ragion**assi**	ragion**aste**	**avessi** ragionato	**aveste** ragionato
ragion**asse**	ragion**assero**	**avesse** ragionato	**avessero** ragionato

imperativo

SINGULAR	PLURAL
	ragioniamo
ragiona; non ragionare	ragionate
ragioni	ragionino

R

rallentare — to slow down

gerundio **rallentando** participio passato **rallentato**

SINGULAR	PLURAL
indicativo presente	
rallent**o**	rallent**iamo**
rallent**i**	rallent**ate**
rallent**a**	rallent**ano**
imperfetto	
rallenta**vo**	rallenta**vamo**
rallenta**vi**	rallenta**vate**
rallenta**va**	rallenta**vano**
passato remoto	
rallent**ai**	rallent**ammo**
rallent**asti**	rallent**aste**
rallent**ò**	rallent**arono**
futuro semplice	
rallenter**ò**	rallenter**emo**
rallenter**ai**	rallenter**ete**
rallenter**à**	rallenter**anno**
condizionale presente	
rallent**erei**	rallent**eremmo**
rallent**eresti**	rallent**ereste**
rallent**erebbe**	rallent**erebbero**
congiuntivo presente	
rallent**i**	rallent**iamo**
rallent**i**	rallent**iate**
rallent**i**	rallent**ino**
congiuntivo imperfetto	
rallent**assi**	rallent**assimo**
rallent**assi**	rallent**aste**
rallent**asse**	rallent**assero**
imperativo	
	rallentiamo
rallenta; non rallentare	rallentate
rallenti	rallentino

SINGULAR	PLURAL
passato prossimo	
ho rallentato	**abbiamo** rallentato
hai rallentato	**avete** rallentato
ha rallentato	**hanno** rallentato
trapassato prossimo	
avevo rallentato	**avevamo** rallentato
avevi rallentato	**avevate** rallentato
aveva rallentato	**avevano** rallentato
trapassato remoto	
ebbi rallentato	**avemmo** rallentato
avesti rallentato	**aveste** rallentato
ebbe rallentato	**ebbero** rallentato
futuro anteriore	
avrò rallentato	**avremo** rallentato
avrai rallentato	**avrete** rallentato
avrà ralìentato	**avranno** rallentato
condizionale passato	
avrei rallentato	**avremmo** rallentato
avresti rallentato	**avreste** rallentato
avrebbe rallentato	**avrebbero** rallentato
congiuntivo passato	
abbia rallentato	**abbiamo** rallentato
abbia rallentato	**abbiate** rallentato
abbia rallentato	**abbiano** rallentato
congiuntivo trapassato	
avessi rallentato	**avessimo** rallentato
avessi rallentato	**aveste** rallentato
avesse rallentato	**avessero** rallentato

to represent, to show, to perform **rappresentare**

gerundio **rappresentando** participio passato **rappresentato**

SINGULAR	PLURAL	SINGULAR	PLURAL
indicativo presente		**passato prossimo**	
rappresent**o**	rappresent**iamo**	**ho** rappresentato	**abbiamo** rappresentato
rappresent**i**	rappresent**ate**	**hai** rappresentato	**avete** rappresentato
rappresent**a**	rappresent**ano**	**ha** rappresentato	**hanno** rappresentato
imperfetto		**trapassato prossimo**	
rappresenta**vo**	rappresenta**vamo**	**avevo** rappresentato	**avevamo** rappresentato
rappresenta**vi**	rappresenta**vate**	**avevi** rappresentato	**avevate** rappresentato
rappresenta**va**	rappresenta**vano**	**aveva** rappresentato	**avevano** rappresentato
passato remoto		**trapassato remoto**	
rappresent**ai**	rappresent**ammo**	**ebbi** rappresentato	**avemmo** rappresentato
rappresent**asti**	rappresent**aste**	**avesti** rappresentato	**aveste** rappresentato
rappresent**ò**	rappresent**arono**	**ebbe** rappresentato	**ebbero** rappresentato
futuro semplice		**futuro anteriore**	
rappresenter**ò**	rappresenter**emo**	**avrò** rappresentato	**avremo** rappresentato
rappresenter**ai**	rappresenter**ete**	**avrai** rappresentato	**avrete** rappresentato
rappresenter**à**	rappresenter**anno**	**avrà** rappresentato	**avranno** rappresentato
condizionale presente		**condizionale passato**	
rappresent**erei**	rappresent**eremmo**	**avrei** rappresentato	**avremmo** rappresentato
rappresent**eresti**	rappresent**ereste**	**avresti** rappresentato	**avreste** rappresentato
rappresent**erebbe**	rappresent**erebbero**	**avrebbe** rappresentato	**avrebbero** rappresentato
congiuntivo presente		**congiuntivo passato**	
rappresent**i**	rappresent**iamo**	**abbia** rappresentato	**abbiamo** rappresentato
rappresent**i**	rappresent**iate**	**abbia** rappresentato	**abbiate** rappresentato
rappresent**i**	rappresent**ino**	**abbia** rappresentato	**abbiano** rappresentato
congiuntivo imperfetto		**congiuntivo trapassato**	
rappresent**assi**	rappresent**assimo**	**avessi** rappresentato	**avessimo** rappresentato
rappresent**assi**	rappresent**aste**	**avessi** rappresentato	**aveste** rappresentato
rappresent**asse**	rappresent**assero**	**avesse** rappresentato	**avessero** rappresentato
imperativo			
	rappresentiamo		
rappresenta; non rappresentare	rappresentate		
rappresenti	rappresentino		

R

rassegnarsi — to resign oneself

gerundio **rassegnandosi** participio passato **rassegnatosi**

SINGULAR	PLURAL
indicativo presente	
mi rassegn**o**	**ci** rassegn**iamo**
ti rassegn**i**	**vi** rassegn**ate**
si rassegn**a**	**si** rassegn**ano**
imperfetto	
mi rassegna**vo**	**ci** rassegna**vamo**
ti rassegna**vi**	**vi** rassegna**vate**
si rassegna**va**	**si** rassegna**vano**
passato remoto	
mi rassegn**ai**	**ci** rassegn**ammo**
ti rassegn**asti**	**vi** rassegn**aste**
si rassegn**ò**	**si** rassegnar**ono**
futuro semplice	
mi rassegner**ò**	**ci** rassegner**emo**
ti rassegner**ai**	**vi** rassegner**ete**
si rassegner**à**	**si** rassegner**anno**
condizionale presente	
mi rassegn**erei**	**ci** rassegn**eremmo**
ti rassegn**eresti**	**vi** rassegn**ereste**
si rassegn**erebbe**	**si** rassegn**erebbero**
congiuntivo presente	
mi rassegn**i**	**ci** rassegn**iamo**
ti rassegn**i**	**vi** rassegn**iate**
si rassegn**i**	**si** rassegn**ino**
congiuntivo imperfetto	
mi rassegn**assi**	**ci** rassegn**assimo**
ti rassegn**assi**	**vi** rassegn**aste**
si rassegn**asse**	**si** rassegn**assero**
imperativo	
	rassegniamoci
rassegnati; non rassegnarti/ non ti rassegnare	rassegnatevi
si rassegni	si rassegnino

SINGULAR	PLURAL
passato prossimo	
mi sono rassegnato(a)	**ci siamo** rassegnati(e)
ti sei rassegnato(a)	**vi siete** rassegnati(e)
si è rassegnato(a)	**si sono** rassegnati(e)
trapassato prossimo	
mi ero rassegnato(a)	**ci eravamo** rassegnati(e)
ti eri rassegnato(a)	**vi eravate** rassegnati(e)
si era rassegnato(a)	**si erano** rassegnati(e)
trapassato remoto	
mi fui rassegnato(a)	**ci fummo** rassegnati(e)
ti fosti rassegnato(a)	**vi foste** rassegnati(e)
si fu rassegnato(a)	**si furono** rassegnati(e)
futuro anteriore	
mi sarò rassegnato(a)	**ci saremo** rassegnati(e)
ti sarai rassegnato(a)	**vi sarete** rassegnati(e)
si sarà rassegnato(a)	**si saranno** rassegnati(e)
condizionale passato	
mi sarei rassegnato(a)	**ci saremmo** rassegnati(e)
ti saresti rassegnato(a)	**vi sareste** rassegnati(e)
si sarebbe rassegnato(a)	**si sarebbero** rassegnati(e)
congiuntivo passato	
mi sia rassegnato(a)	**ci siamo** rassegnati(e)
ti sia rassegnato(a)	**vi siate** rassegnati(e)
si sia rassegnato(a)	**si siano** rassegnati(e)
congiuntivo trapassato	
mi fossi rassegnato(a)	**ci fossimo** rassegnati(e)
ti fossi rassegnato(a)	**vi foste** rassegnati(e)
si fosse rassegnato(a)	**si fossero** rassegnati(e)

to encourage, to reassure **rassicurare**

gerundio **rassicurando** participio passato **rassicurato**

SINGULAR	PLURAL	SINGULAR	PLURAL
indicativo presente		passato prossimo	
rassicur**o**	rassicur**iamo**	**ho** rassicurato	**abbiamo** rassicurato
rassicur**i**	rassicur**ate**	**hai** rassicurato	**avete** rassicurato
rassicur**a**	rassicur**ano**	**ha** rassicurato	**hanno** rassicurato
imperfetto		trapassato prossimo	
rassicura**vo**	rassicura**vamo**	**avevo** rassicurato	**avevamo** rassicurato
rassicura**vi**	rassicura**vate**	**avevi** rassicurato	**avevate** rassicurato
rassicura**va**	rassicura**vano**	**aveva** rassicurato	**avevano** rassicurato
passato remoto		trapassato remoto	
rassicur**ai**	rassicur**ammo**	**ebbi** rassicurato	**avemmo** rassicurato
rassicur**aste**	rassicur**aste**	**avesti** rassicurato	**aveste** rassicurato
rassicur**ò**	rassicur**arono**	**ebbe** rassicurato	**ebbero** rassicurato
futuro semplice		futuro anteriore	
rassicurer**ò**	rassicurer**emo**	**avrò** rassicurato	**avremo** rassicurato
rassicurer**ai**	rassicurer**ete**	**avrai** rassicurato	**avrete** rassicurato
rassicurer**à**	rassicurer**anno**	**avrà** rassicurato	**avranno** rassicurato
condizionale presente		condizionale passato	
rassicur**erei**	rassicur**eremmo**	**avrei** rassicurato	**avremmo** rassicurato
rassicur**eresti**	rassicur**ereste**	**avresti** rassicurato	**avreste** rassicurato
rassicur**erebbe**	rassicur**erebbero**	**avrebbe** rassicurato	**avrebbero** rassicurato
congiuntivo presente		congiuntivo passato	
rassicur**i**	rassicur**iamo**	**abbia** rassicurato	**abbiamo** rassicurato
rassicur**i**	rassicur**iate**	**abbia** rassicurato	**abbiate** rassicurato
rassicur**i**	rassicur**ino**	**abbia** rassicurato	**abbiano** rassicurato
congiuntivo imperfetto		congiuntivo trapassato	
rassicur**assi**	rassicur**assimo**	**avessi** rassicurato	**avessimo** rassicurato
rassicur**assi**	rassicur**aste**	**avessi** rassicurato	**aveste** rassicurato
rassicur**asse**	rassicur**assero**	**avesse** rassicurato	**avessero** rassicurato
imperativo			
	rassicuriamo		
rassicura; non rassicurare	rassicurate		
rassicuri	rassicurino		

reagire

to react

gerundio **reagendo**

participio passato **reagito**

SINGULAR	PLURAL
indicativo presente	
reagisc**o**	reag**iamo**
reagisc**i**	reag**ite**
reagisc**e**	reagisc**ono**
imperfetto	
reagi**vo**	reagi**vamo**
reagi**vi**	reagi**vate**
reagi**va**	reagi**vano**
passato remoto	
reag**ii**	reag**immo**
reag**isti**	reag**iste**
reag**ì**	reag**irono**
futuro semplice	
reagir**ò**	reagir**emo**
reagir**ai**	reagir**ete**
reagir**à**	reagir**anno**
condizionale presente	
reag**irei**	reag**iremmo**
reag**iresti**	reag**ireste**
reag**irebbe**	reag**irebbero**
congiuntivo presente	
reagisc**a**	reag**iamo**
reagisc**a**	reag**iate**
reagisc**a**	reagisc**ano**
congiuntivo imperfetto	
reag**issi**	reag**issimo**
reag**issi**	reag**iste**
reag**isse**	reag**issero**
imperativo	
	reagiamo
reagisci; non reagire	reagite
reagisca	reagiscano

SINGULAR	PLURAL
passato prossimo	
ho reagito	**abbiamo** reagito
hai reagito	**avete** reagito
ha reagito	**hanno** reagito
trapassato prossimo	
avevo reagito	**avevamo** reagito
avevi reagito	**avevate** reagito
aveva reagito	**avevano** reagito
trapassato remoto	
ebbi reagito	**avemmo** reagito
avesti reagito	**aveste** reagito
ebbe reagito	**ebbero** reagito
futuro anteriore	
avrò reagito	**avremo** reagito
avrai reagito	**avrete** reagito
avrà reagito	**avranno** reagito
condizionale passato	
avrei reagito	**avremmo** reagito
avresti reagito	**avreste** reagito
avrebbe reagito	**avrebbero** reagito
congiuntivo passato	
abbia reagito	**abbiamo** reagito
abbia reagito	**abbiate** reagito
abbia reagito	**abbiano** reagito
congiuntivo trapassato	
avessi reagito	**avessimo** reagito
avessi reagito	**aveste** reagito
avesse reagito	**avessero** reagito

gerundio **recitando** participio passato **recitato**

SINGULAR	PLURAL	SINGULAR	PLURAL
indicativo presente		*passato prossimo*	
recit**o**	recit**iamo**	**ho** recitato	**abbiamo** recitato
recit**i**	recit**ate**	**hai** recitato	**avete** recitato
recit**a**	recit**ano**	**ha** recitato	**hanno** recitato
imperfetto		*trapassato prossimo*	
recita**vo**	recita**vamo**	**avevo** recitato	**avevamo** recitato
recita**vi**	recita**vate**	**avevi** recitato	**avevate** recitato
recita**va**	recita**vano**	**aveva** recitato	**avevano** recitato
passato remoto		*trapassato remoto*	
recit**ai**	recit**ammo**	**ebbi** recitato	**avemmo** recitato
recit**asti**	recit**aste**	**avesti** recitato	**aveste** recitato
recit**ò**	recit**arono**	**ebbe** recitato	**ebbero** recitato
futuro semplice		*futuro anteriore*	
reciter**ò**	reciter**emo**	**avrò** recitato	**avremo** recitato
reciter**ai**	reciter**ete**	**avrai** recitato	**avrete** recitato
reciter**à**	reciter**anno**	**avrà** recitato	**avranno** recitato
condizionale presente		*condizionale passato*	
recit**erei**	recit**eremmo**	**avrei** recitato	**avremmo** recitato
recit**eresti**	recit**ereste**	**avresti** recitato	**avreste** recitato
recit**erebbe**	recit**erebbero**	**avrebbe** recitato	**avrebbero** recitato
congiuntivo presente		*congiuntivo passato*	
recit**i**	recit**iamo**	**abbia** recitato	**abbiamo** recitato
recit**i**	recit**iate**	**abbia** recitato	**abbiate** recitato
recit**i**	recit**ino**	**abbia** recitato	**abbiano** recitato
congiuntivo imperfetto		*congiuntivo trapassato*	
recit**assi**	recit**assimo**	**avessi** recitato	**avessimo** recitato
recit**assi**	recit**aste**	**avessi** recitato	**aveste** recitato
recit**asse**	recit**assero**	**avesse** recitato	**avessero** recitato
imperativo			
	recitiamo		
recita; non recitare	recitate		
reciti	recitino		

R

redigere — to edit, to draw up

gerundio **redigendo** participio passato **redatto**

SINGULAR	PLURAL	SINGULAR	PLURAL
indicativo presente		passato prossimo	
redig**o**	redig**iamo**	**ho** redatto	**abbiamo** redatto
redig**i**	redig**ete**	**hai** redatto	**avete** redatto
redig**e**	redig**ono**	**ha** redatto	**hanno** redatto
imperfetto		trapassato prossimo	
redige**vo**	redige**vamo**	**avevo** redatto	**avevamo** redatto
redige**vi**	redige**vate**	**avevi** redatto	**avevate** redatto
redige**va**	redige**vano**	**aveva** redatto	**avevano** redatto
passato remoto		trapassato remoto	
redass**i**	redig**emmo**	**ebbi** redatto	**avemmo** redatto
redig**esti**	redig**este**	**avesti** redatto	**aveste** redatto
redass**e**	redass**ero**	**ebbe** redatto	**ebbero** redatto
futuro semplice		futuro anteriore	
rediger**ò**	rediger**emo**	**avrò** redatto	**avremo** redatto
rediger**ai**	rediger**ete**	**avrai** redatto	**avrete** redatto
rediger**à**	rediger**anno**	**avrà** redatto	**avranno** redatto
condizionale presente		condizionale passato	
redig**erei**	redig**eremmo**	**avrei** redatto	**avremmo** redatto
redig**eresti**	redig**ereste**	**avresti** redatto	**avreste** redatto
redig**erebbe**	redig**erebbero**	**avrebbe** redatto	**avrebbero** redatto
congiuntivo presente		congiuntivo passato	
redig**a**	redig**iamo**	**abbia** redatto	**abbiamo** redatto
redig**a**	redig**iate**	**abbia** redatto	**abbiate** redatto
redig**a**	redig**ano**	**abbia** redatto	**abbiano** redatto
congiuntivo imperfetto		congiuntivo trapassato	
redig**essi**	redig**essimo**	**avessi** redatto	**avessimo** redatto
redig**essi**	redig**este**	**avessi** redatto	**aveste** redatto
redig**esse**	redig**essero**	**avesse** redatto	**avessero** redatto

imperativo

	redigiamo
redigi; non redigere	redigete
rediga	redigano

to give as a present — regalare

gerundio **regalando** participio passato **regalato**

SINGULAR	PLURAL	SINGULAR	PLURAL
indicativo presente		passato prossimo	
regal**o**	regal**iamo**	**ho** regalato	**abbiamo** regalato
regal**i**	regal**ate**	**hai** regalato	**avete** regalato
regal**a**	regal**ano**	**ha** regalato	**hanno** regalato
imperfetto		trapassato prossimo	
regala**vo**	regala**vamo**	**avevo** regalato	**avevamo** regalato
regala**vi**	regala**vate**	**avevi** regalato	**avevate** regalato
regala**va**	regala**vano**	**aveva** regalato	**avevano** regalato
passato remoto		trapassato remoto	
regal**ai**	regal**ammo**	**ebbi** regalato	**avemmo** regalato
regal**asti**	regal**aste**	**avesti** regalato	**aveste** regalato
regal**ò**	regal**arono**	**ebbe** regalato	**ebbero** regalato
futuro semplice		futuro anteriore	
regaler**ò**	regaler**emo**	**avrò** regalato	**avremo** regalato
regaler**ai**	regaler**ete**	**avrai** regalato	**avrete** regalato
regaler**à**	regaler**anno**	**avrà** regalato	**avranno** regalato
condizionale presente		condizionale passato	
regal**erei**	regal**eremmo**	**avrei** regalato	**avremmo** regalato
regal**eresti**	regal**ereste**	**avresti** regalato	**avreste** regalato
regal**erebbe**	regal**erebbero**	**avrebbe** regalato	**avrebbero** regalato
congiuntivo presente		congiuntivo passato	
regal**i**	regal**iamo**	**abbia** regalato	**abbiamo** regalato
regal**i**	regal**iate**	**abbia** regalato	**abbiate** regalato
regal**i**	regal**ino**	**abbia** regalato	**abbiano** regalato
congiuntivo imperfetto		congiuntivo trapassato	
regal**assi**	regal**assimo**	**avessi** regalato	**avessimo** regalato
regal**assi**	regal**aste**	**avessi** regalato	**aveste** regalato
regal**asse**	regal**assero**	**avesse** regalato	**avessero** regalato
imperativo			
	regaliamo		
regala; non regalare	regalate		
regali	regalino		

reggere

to support, to hold

gerundio **reggendo** participio passato **retto**

SINGULAR	PLURAL	SINGULAR	PLURAL
indicativo presente		passato prossimo	
regg**o**	regg**iamo**	**ho** retto	**abbiamo** retto
regg**i**	regg**ete**	**hai** retto	**avete** retto
regg**e**	regg**ono**	**ha** retto	**hanno** retto
imperfetto		trapassato prossimo	
regge**vo**	regge**vamo**	**avevo** retto	**avevamo** retto
regge**vi**	regge**vate**	**avevi** retto	**avevate** retto
regge**va**	regge**vano**	**aveva** retto	**avevano** retto
passato remoto		trapassato remoto	
ress**i**	regg**emmo**	**ebbi** retto	**avemmo** retto
regg**esti**	regg**este**	**avesti** retto	**aveste** retto
ress**e**	ress**ero**	**ebbe** retto	**ebbero** retto
futuro semplice		futuro anteriore	
regger**ò**	regger**emo**	**avrò** retto	**avremo** retto
regger**ai**	regger**ete**	**avrai** retto	**avrete** retto
regger**à**	regger**anno**	**avrà** retto	**avranno** retto
condizionale presente		condizionale passato	
regg**erei**	regg**eremmo**	**avrei** retto	**avremmo** retto
regg**eresti**	regg**ereste**	**avresti** retto	**avreste** retto
regg**erebbe**	regg**erebbero**	**avrebbe** retto	**avrebbero** retto
congiuntivo presente		congiuntivo passato	
regg**a**	regg**iamo**	**abbia** retto	**abbiamo** retto
regg**a**	regg**iate**	**abbia** retto	**abbiate** retto
regg**a**	regg**ano**	**abbia** retto	**abbiano** retto
congiuntivo imperfetto		congiuntivo trapassato	
regg**essi**	regg**essimo**	**avessi** retto	**avessimo** retto
regg**essi**	regg**este**	**avessi** retto	**aveste** retto
regg**esse**	regg**essero**	**avesse** retto	**avessero** retto
imperativo			
	reggiamo		
reggi; non reggere	reggete		
regga	reggano		

gerundio **registrandosi** participio passato **registratosi**

SINGULAR	PLURAL	SINGULAR	PLURAL
indicativo presente		passato prossimo	
mi registr**o**	**ci** registr**iamo**	**mi sono** registrato(a)	**ci siamo** registrati(e)
ti registr**i**	**vi** registr**ate**	**ti sei** registrato(a)	**vi siete** registrati(e)
si registr**a**	**si** registr**ano**	**si è** registrato(a)	**si sono** registrati(e)
imperfetto		trapassato prossimo	
mi registra**vo**	**ci** registra**vamo**	**mi ero** registrato(a)	**ci eravamo** registrati(e)
ti registra**vi**	**vi** registra**vate**	**ti eri** registrato(a)	**vi eravate** registrati(e)
si registra**va**	**si** registra**vano**	**si era** registrato(a)	**si erano** registrati(e)
passato remoto		trapassato remoto	
mi registr**ai**	**ci** registra**mmo**	**mi fui** registrato(a)	**ci fummo** registrati(e)
ti registra**sti**	**vi** registra**ste**	**ti fosti** registrato(a)	**vi foste** registrati(e)
si registr**ò**	**si** registr**arono**	**si fu** registrato(a)	**si furono** registrati(e)
futuro semplice		futuro anteriore	
mi registrer**ò**	**ci** registrer**emo**	**mi sarò** registrato(a)	**ci saremo** registrati(e)
ti registrer**ai**	**vi** registrer**ete**	**ti sarai** registrato(a)	**vi sarete** registrati(e)
si registrer**à**	**si** registrer**anno**	**si sarà** registrato(a)	**si saranno** registrati(e)
condizionale presente		condizionale passato	
mi registrer**ei**	**ci** registrer**emmo**	**mi sarei** registrato(a)	**ci saremmo** registrati(e)
ti registrer**esti**	**vi** registrer**este**	**ti saresti** registrato(a)	**vi sareste** registrati(e)
si registrer**ebbe**	**si** registrer**ebbero**	**si sarebbe** registrato(a)	**si sarebbero** registrati(e)
congiuntivo presente		congiuntivo passato	
mi registr**i**	**ci** registr**iamo**	**mi sia** registrato(a)	**ci siamo** registrati(e)
ti registr**i**	**vi** registr**iate**	**ti sia** registrato(a)	**vi siate** registrati(e)
si registr**i**	**si** registr**ino**	**si sia** registrato(a)	**si siano** registrati(e)
congiuntivo imperfetto		congiuntivo trapassato	
mi registra**ssi**	**ci** registra**ssimo**	**mi fossi** registrato(a)	**ci fossimo** registrati(e)
ti registra**ssi**	**vi** registra**ste**	**ti fossi** registrato(a)	**vi foste** registrati(e)
si registra**sse**	**si** registra**ssero**	**si fosse** registrato(a)	**si fossero** registrati(e)

imperativo

	registriamoci
registrati; non registrarti	registratevi
si registri	si registrino

R

regolare — to regulate, to adjust

gerundio **regolando** — participio passato **regolato**

SINGULAR	PLURAL	SINGULAR	PLURAL
indicativo presente		passato prossimo	
regol**o**	regol**iamo**	**ho** regolato	**abbiamo** regolato
regol**i**	regol**ate**	**hai** regolato	**avete** regolato
regol**a**	regol**ano**	**ha** regolato	**hanno** regolato
imperfetto		trapassato prossimo	
regola**vo**	regola**vamo**	**avevo** regolato	**avevamo** regolato
regola**vi**	regola**vate**	**avevi** regolato	**avevate** regolato
regola**va**	regola**vano**	**aveva** regolato	**avevano** regolato
passato remoto		trapassato remoto	
regol**ai**	regol**ammo**	**ebbi** regolato	**avemmo** regolato
regol**asti**	regol**aste**	**avesti** regolato	**aveste** regolato
regol**ò**	regol**arono**	**ebbe** regolato	**ebbero** regolato
futuro semplice		futuro anteriore	
regoler**ò**	regoler**emmo**	**avrò** regolato	**avremo** regolato
regoler**ai**	regoler**ete**	**avrai** regolato	**avrete** regolato
regoler**à**	regoler**anno**	**avrà** regolato	**avranno** regolato
condizionale presente		condizionale passato	
regol**erei**	regol**eremmo**	**avrei** regolato	**avremmo** regolato
regol**eresti**	regol**ereste**	**avresti** regolato	**avreste** regolato
regol**erebbe**	regol**erebbero**	**avrebbe** regolato	**avrebbero** regolato
congiuntivo presente		congiuntivo passato	
regol**i**	regol**iamo**	**abbia** regolato	**abbiamo** regolato
regol**i**	regol**iate**	**abbia** regolato	**abbiate** regolato
regol**i**	regol**ino**	**abbia** regolato	**abbiano** regolato
congiuntivo imperfetto		congiuntivo trapassato	
regol**assi**	regol**assimo**	**avessi** regolato	**avessimo** regolato
regol**assi**	regol**aste**	**avessi** regolato	**aveste** regolato
regol**asse**	regol**assero**	**avesse** regolato	**avessero** regolato
imperativo			
	regoliamo		
regola; non regolare	regolate		
regoli	regolino		

to render, to give back **rendere**

gerundio **rendendo** participio passato **reso**

SINGULAR	PLURAL
indicativo presente	
rend**o**	rend**iamo**
rend**i**	rend**ete**
rend**e**	rend**ono**
imperfetto	
rende**vo**	rende**vamo**
rende**vi**	rende**vate**
rende**va**	rende**vano**
passato remoto	
res**i**	rend**emmo**
rend**esti**	rend**este**
res**e**	res**ero**
futuro semplice	
render**ò**	render**emo**
render**ai**	render**ete**
render**à**	render**anno**
condizionale presente	
rend**erei**	rend**eremmo**
rend**eresti**	rend**ereste**
rend**erebbe**	rend**erebbero**
congiuntivo presente	
rend**a**	rend**iamo**
rend**a**	rend**iate**
rend**a**	rend**ano**
congiuntivo imperfetto	
rend**essi**	rend**essimo**
rend**essi**	rend**este**
rend**esse**	rend**essero**
imperativo	
	rendiamo
rendi; non rendere	rendete
renda	rendano

SINGULAR	PLURAL
passato prossimo	
ho reso	**abbiamo** reso
hai reso	**avete** reso
ha reso	**hanno** reso
trapassato prossimo	
avevo reso	**avevamo** reso
avevi reso	**avevate** reso
aveva reso	**avevano** reso
trapassato remoto	
ebbi reso	**avemmo** reso
avesti reso	**aveste** reso
ebbe reso	**ebbero** reso
futuro anteriore	
avrò reso	**avremo** reso
avrai reso	**avrete** reso
avrà reso	**avranno** reso
condizionale passato	
avrei reso	**avremmo** reso
avresti reso	**avreste** reso
avrebbe reso	**avrebbero** reso
congiuntivo passato	
abbia reso	**abbiamo** reso
abbia reso	**abbiate** reso
abbia reso	**abbiano** reso
congiuntivo trapassato	
avessi reso	**avessimo** reso
avessi reso	**aveste** reso
avesse reso	**avessero** reso

resistere — to resist

gerundio **resistendo** participio passato **resistito**

SINGULAR	PLURAL	SINGULAR	PLURAL
indicativo presente		passato prossimo	
resist**o**	resist**iamo**	**ho** resistito	**abbiamo** resistito
resist**i**	resist**ete**	**hai** resistito	**avete** resistito
resist**e**	resist**ono**	**ha** resistito	**hanno** resistito
imperfetto		trapassato prossimo	
resiste**vo**	resiste**vamo**	**avevo** resistito	**avevamo** resistito
resiste**vi**	resiste**vate**	**avevi** resistito	**avevate** resistito
resiste**va**	resiste**vano**	**aveva** resistito	**avevano** resistito
passato remoto		trapassato remoto	
resist**ei** (resistetti)	resist**emmo**	**ebbi** resistito	**avemmo** resistito
resist**esti**	resist**este**	**avesti** resistito	**aveste** resistito
resist**é** (resistette)	resist**erono** (resistettero)	**ebbe** resistito	**ebbero** resistito
futuro semplice		futuro anteriore	
resister**ò**	resister**emo**	**avrò** resistito	**avremo** resistito
resister**ai**	resister**ete**	**avrai** resistito	**avrete** resistito
resister**à**	resister**anno**	**avrà** resistito	**avranno** resistito
condizionale presente		condizionale passato	
resist**erei**	resist**eremmo**	**avrei** resistito	**avremmo** resistito
resist**eresti**	resist**ereste**	**avresti** resistito	**avreste** resistito
resist**erebbe**	resist**erebbero**	**avrebbe** resistito	**avrebbero** resistito
congiuntivo presente		congiuntivo passato	
resist**a**	resist**iamo**	**abbia** resistito	**abbiamo** resistito
resist**a**	resist**iate**	**abbia** resistito	**abbiate** resistito
resist**a**	resist**ano**	**abbia** resistito	**abbiano** resistito
congiuntivo imperfetto		congiuntivo trapassato	
resist**essi**	resist**essimo**	**avessi** resistito	**avessimo** resistito
resist**essi**	resist**este**	**avessi** resistito	**aveste** resistito
resist**esse**	resist**essero**	**avesse** resistito	**avessero** resistito
imperativo			
	resistiamo		
resisti; non resistere	resistete		
resista	resistano		

gerundio **respirando** participio passato **respirato**

SINGULAR	PLURAL	SINGULAR	PLURAL
indicativo presente		passato prossimo	
respir**o**	respir**iamo**	**ho** respirato	**abbiamo** respirato
respir**i**	respir**ate**	**hai** respirato	**avete** respirato
respir**a**	respir**ano**	**ha** respirato	**hanno** respirato
imperfetto		trapassato prossimo	
respira**vo**	respira**vamo**	**avevo** respirato	**avevamo** respirato
respira**vi**	respira**vate**	**avevi** respirato	**avevate** respirato
respira**va**	respira**vano**	**aveva** respirato	**avevano** respirato
passato remoto		trapassato remoto	
respir**ai**	respir**ammo**	**ebbi** respirato	**avemmo** respirato
respir**asti**	respir**aste**	**avesti** respirato	**aveste** respirato
respir**ò**	respir**arono**	**ebbe** respirato	**ebbero** respirato
futuro semplice		futuro anteriore	
respirer**ò**	respirer**emo**	**avrò** respirato	**avremo** respirato
respirer**ai**	respirer**ete**	**avrai** respirato	**avrete** respirato
respirer**à**	respirer**anno**	**avrà** respirato	**avranno** respirato
condizionale presente		condizionale passato	
respir**erei**	respir**eremmo**	**avrei** respirato	**avremmo** respirato
respir**eresti**	respir**ereste**	**avresti** respirato	**avreste** respirato
respir**erebbe**	respir**erebbero**	**avrebbe** respirato	**avrebbero** respirato
congiuntivo presente		congiuntivo passato	
respir**i**	respir**iamo**	**abbia** respirato	**abbiamo** respirato
respir**i**	respir**iate**	**abbia** respirato	**abbiate** respirato
respir**i**	respir**ino**	**abbia** respirato	**abbiano** respirato
congiuntivo imperfetto		congiuntivo trapassato	
respir**assi**	respir**assimo**	**avessi** respirato	**avessimo** respirato
respir**assi**	respir**aste**	**avessi** respirato	**aveste** respirato
respir**asse**	respir**assero**	**avesse** respirato	**avessero** respirato
imperativo			
	respiriamo		
respira; non respirare	respirate		
respiri	respirino		

restare — to stay

gerundio **restando** — participio passato **restato**

SINGULAR	PLURAL	SINGULAR	PLURAL
indicativo presente		*passato prossimo*	
rest**o**	rest**iamo**	**sono** restato(a)	**siamo** restati(e)
rest**i**	rest**ate**	**sei** restato(a)	**siete** restati(e)
rest**a**	rest**ano**	**è** restato(a)	**sono** restati(e)
imperfetto		*trapassato prossimo*	
resta**vo**	resta**vamo**	**ero** restato(a)	**eravamo** restati(e)
resta**vi**	resta**vate**	**eri** restato(a)	**eravate** restati(e)
resta**va**	resta**vano**	**era** restato(a)	**erano** restati(e)
passato remoto		*trapassato remoto*	
resta**i**	rest**ammo**	**fui** restato(a)	**fummo** restati(e)
rest**asti**	rest**aste**	**fosti** restato(a)	**foste** restati(e)
rest**ò**	rest**arono**	**fu** restato(a)	**furono** restati(e)
futuro semplice		*futuro anteriore*	
rester**ò**	rester**emo**	**sarò** restato(a)	**saremo** restati(e)
rester**ai**	rester**ete**	**sarai** restato(a)	**sarete** restati(e)
rester**à**	rester**anno**	**sarà** restato(a)	**saranno** restati(e)
condizionale presente		*condizionale passato*	
rest**erei**	rest**eremmo**	**sarei** restato(a)	**saremmo** restati(e)
rest**eresti**	rest**ereste**	**saresti** restato(a)	**sareste** restati(e)
rest**erebbe**	rest**erebbero**	**sarebbe** restato(a)	**sarebbero** restati(e)
congiuntivo presente		*congiuntivo passato*	
rest**i**	rest**iamo**	**sia** restato(a)	**siamo** restati(e)
rest**i**	rest**iate**	**sia** restato(a)	**siate** restati(e)
rest**i**	rest**ino**	**sia** restato(a)	**siano** restati(e)
congiuntivo imperfetto		*congiuntivo trapassato*	
rest**assi**	rest**assimo**	**fossi** restato(a)	**fossimo** restati(e)
rest**assi**	rest**aste**	**fossi** restato(a)	**foste** restati(e)
rest**asse**	rest**assero**	**fosse** restato(a)	**fossero** restati(e)

imperativo

	restiamo
resta; non restare	restate
resti	restino

to return, to give back **restituire**

gerundio **restituendo** participio passato **restituito**

SINGULAR	PLURAL
indicativo presente	
restituisc**o**	restitu**iamo**
restituisc**i**	restitu**ite**
restituisc**e**	restituisc**ono**
imperfetto	
restitui**vo**	restitui**vamo**
restitui**vi**	restitui**vate**
restitui**va**	restitui**vano**
passato remoto	
restitu**ii**	restitu**immo**
restitu**isti**	restitu**iste**
restituì	restitu**irono**
futuro semplice	
restituir**ò**	restituir**emo**
restituir**ai**	restituir**ete**
restituir**à**	restituir**anno**
condizionale presente	
restitu**irei**	restitu**iremmo**
restitu**iresti**	restitu**ireste**
restitu**irebbe**	restitu**irebbero**
congiuntivo presente	
restitu**isca**	restitu**iamo**
restitu**isca**	restitu**iate**
restitu**isca**	restituisc**ano**
congiuntivo imperfetto	
restitu**issi**	restitu**issimo**
restitu**issi**	restitu**iste**
restitu**isse**	restitu**issero**
imperativo	
	restituiamo
restituisci; non restituire	restituite
restituisca	restituiscano

SINGULAR	PLURAL
passato prossimo	
ho restituito	**abbiamo** restituito
hai restituito	**avete** restituito
ha restituito	**hanno** restituito
trapassato prossimo	
avevo restituito	**avevamo** restituito
avevi restituito	**avevate** restituito
aveva restituito	**avevano** restituito
trapassato remoto	
ebbi restituito	**avemmo** restituito
avesti restituito	**aveste** restituito
ebbe restituito	**ebbero** restituito
futuro anteriore	
avrò restituito	**avremo** restituito
avrai restituito	**avrete** restituito
avrà restituito	**avranno** restituito
condizionale passato	
avrei restituito	**avremmo** restituito
avresti restituito	**avreste** restituito
avrebbe restituito	**avrebbero** restituito
congiuntivo passato	
abbia restituito	**abbiamo** restituito
abbia restituito	**abbiate** restituito
abbia restituito	**abbiano** restituito
congiuntivo trapassato	
avessi restituito	**avessimo** restituito
avessi restituito	**aveste** restituito
avesse restituito	**avessero** restituito

riassumere — to re-employ, to summarize

gerundio **riassumendo** — participio passato **riassunto**

SINGULAR	PLURAL
indicativo presente	
riassum**o**	riassum**iamo**
riassum**i**	riassum**ete**
riassum**e**	riassum**ono**
imperfetto	
riassume**vo**	riassume**vamo**
riassume**vi**	riassume**vate**
riassume**va**	riassume**vano**
passato remoto	
riassuns**i**	riassum**emmo**
riassum**esti**	riassum**este**
riassuns**e**	riassuns**ero**
futuro semplice	
riassumer**ò**	riassumer**emo**
riassumer**ai**	riassumer**ete**
riassumer**à**	riassumer**anno**
condizionale presente	
riassum**erei**	riassum**eremmo**
riassum**eresti**	riassum**ereste**
riassum**erebbe**	riassum**erebbero**
congiuntivo presente	
riassum**a**	riassum**iamo**
riassum**a**	riassum**iate**
riassum**a**	riassum**ano**
congiuntivo imperfetto	
riassum**essi**	riassum**essimo**
riassum**essi**	riassum**este**
riassum**esse**	riassum**essero**
imperativo	
	riassumiamo
riassumi; non riassumere	riassumete
riassuma	riassumano

SINGULAR	PLURAL
passato prossimo	
ho riassunto	**abbiamo** riassunto
hai riassunto	**avete** riassunto
ha riassunto	**hanno** riassunto
trapassato prossimo	
avevo riassunto	**avevamo** riassunto
avevi riassunto	**avevate** riassunto
aveva riassunto	**avevano** riassunto
trapassato remoto	
ebbi riassunto	**avemmo** riassunto
avesti riassunto	**aveste** riassunto
ebbe riassunto	**ebbero** riassunto
futuro anteriore	
avrò riassunto	**avremo** riassunto
avrai riassunto	**avrete** riassunto
avrà riassunto	**avranno** riassunto
condizionale passato	
avrei riassunto	**avremmo** riassunto
avresti riassunto	**avreste** riassunto
avrebbe riassunto	**avrebbero** riassunto
congiuntivo passato	
abbia riassunto	**abbiamo** riassunto
abbia riassunto	**abbiate** riassunto
abbia riassunto	**abbiano** riassunto
congiuntivo trapassato	
avessi riassunto	**avessimo** riassunto
avessi riassunto	**aveste** riassunto
avesse riassunto	**avessero** riassunto

to receive **ricevere**

gerundio **ricevendo** participio passato **ricevuto**

SINGULAR	PLURAL
indicativo presente	
ricev**o**	ricev**iamo**
ricev**i**	ricev**ete**
ricev**e**	ricev**ono**
imperfetto	
riceve**vo**	riceve**vamo**
riceve**vi**	riceve**vate**
riceve**va**	riceve**vano**
passato remoto	
ricev**ei** (ricevetti)	ricev**emmo**
ricev**esti**	ricev**este**
ricev**é** (ricevette)	ricev**erono** (ricevettero)
futuro semplice	
ricever**ò**	ricever**emo**
ricever**ai**	ricever**ete**
ricever**à**	ricever**anno**
condizionale presente	
ricev**erei**	ricev**eremmo**
ricev**eresti**	ricev**ereste**
ricev**erebbe**	ricev**erebbero**
congiuntivo presente	
ricev**a**	ricev**iamo**
ricev**a**	ricev**iate**
ricev**a**	ricev**ano**
congiuntivo imperfetto	
ricev**essi**	ricev**essimo**
ricev**essi**	ricev**este**
ricev**esse**	ricev**essero**
imperativo	
	riceviamo
ricevi; non ricevere	ricevete
riceva	ricevano

SINGULAR	PLURAL
passato prossimo	
ho ricevuto	**abbiamo** ricevuto
hai ricevuto	**avete** ricevuto
ha ricevuto	**hanno** ricevuto
trapassato prossimo	
avevo ricevuto	**avevamo** ricevuto
avevi ricevuto	**avevate** ricevuto
aveva ricevuto	**avevano** ricevuto
trapassato remoto	
ebbi ricevuto	**avemmo** ricevuto
avesti ricevuto	**aveste** ricevuto
ebbe ricevuto	**ebbero** ricevuto
futuro anteriore	
avrò ricevuto	**avremo** ricevuto
avrai ricevuto	**avrete** ricevuto
avrà ricevuto	**avranno** ricevuto
condizionale passato	
avrei ricevuto	**avremmo** ricevuto
avresti ricevuto	**avreste** ricevuto
avrebbe ricevuto	**avrebbero** ricevuto
congiuntivo passato	
abbia ricevuto	**abbiamo** ricevuto
abbia ricevuto	**abbiate** ricevuto
abbia ricevuto	**abbiano** ricevuto
congiuntivo trapassato	
avessi ricevuto	**avessimo** ricevuto
avessi ricevuto	**aveste** ricevuto
avesse ricevuto	**avessero** ricevuto

ricominciare — to begin again

gerundio **ricominciando** participio passato **ricominciato**

SINGULAR	PLURAL
indicativo presente	
ricominci**o**	ricominci**amo**
ricominc**i**	ricominci**ate**
ricominci**a**	ricominci**ano**
imperfetto	
ricomincia**vo**	ricomincia**vamo**
ricomincia**vi**	ricomincia**vate**
ricomincia**va**	ricomincia**vano**
passato remoto	
ricomincia**i**	ricominci**ammo**
ricominci**asti**	ricominci**aste**
ricominci**ò**	ricominci**arono**
futuro semplice	
ricomincer**ò**	ricomincer**emo**
ricomincer**ai**	ricomincer**ete**
ricomincer**à**	ricomincer**anno**
condizionale presente	
ricominc**erei**	ricominc**eremmo**
ricominc**eresti**	ricominc**ereste**
ricominc**erebbe**	ricominc**erebbero**
congiuntivo presente	
ricominc**i**	ricominci**amo**
ricominc**i**	ricominci**ate**
ricominc**i**	ricominc**ino**
congiuntivo imperfetto	
ricominci**assi**	ricominci**assimo**
ricominci**assi**	ricominci**aste**
ricominci**asse**	ricominci**assero**
imperativo	
	ricominciamo
ricomincia; non ricominciare	ricominciate
ricominci	ricomincino

SINGULAR	PLURAL
passato prossimo	
ho ricominciato	**abbiamo** ricominciato
hai ricominciato	**avete** ricominciato
ha ricominciato	**hanno** ricominciato
trapassato prossimo	
avevo ricominciato	**avevamo** ricominciato
avevi ricominciato	**avevate** ricominciato
aveva ricominciato	**avevano** ricominciato
trapassato remoto	
ebbi ricominciato	**avemmo** ricominciato
avesti ricominciato	**aveste** ricominciato
ebbe ricominciato	**ebbero** ricominciato
futuro anteriore	
avrò ricominciato	**avremo** ricominciato
avrai ricominciato	**avrete** ricominciato
avrà ricominciato	**avranno** ricominciato
condizionale passato	
avrei ricominciato	**avremmo** ricominciato
avresti ricominciato	**avreste** ricominciato
avrebbe ricominciato	**avrebbero** ricominciato
congiuntivo passato	
abbia ricominciato	**abbiamo** ricominciato
abbia ricominciato	**abbiate** ricominciato
abbia ricominciato	**abbiano** ricominciato
congiuntivo trapassato	
avessi ricominciato	**avessimo** ricominciato
avessi ricominciato	**aveste** ricominciato
avesse ricominciato	**avessero** ricominciato

gerundio **ricompensando** participio passato **ricompensato**

SINGULAR	PLURAL
indicativo presente	
ricompens**o**	ricompens**iamo**
ricompens**i**	ricompens**ate**
ricompens**a**	ricompens**ano**
imperfetto	
ricompensa**vo**	ricompensa**vamo**
ricompensa**vi**	ricompensa**vate**
ricompensa**va**	ricompensa**vano**
passato remoto	
ricompensa**i**	ricompens**ammo**
ricompens**asti**	ricompens**aste**
ricompens**ò**	ricompens**arono**
futuro semplice	
ricompenser**ò**	ricompenser**emo**
ricompenser**ai**	ricompenser**ete**
ricompenser**à**	ricompenser**anno**
condizionale presente	
ricompens**erei**	ricompens**eremmo**
ricompens**eresti**	ricompens**ereste**
ricompens**erebbe**	ricompens**erebbero**
congiuntivo presente	
ricompens**i**	ricompens**iamo**
ricompens**i**	ricompens**iate**
ricompens**i**	ricompens**ino**
congiuntivo imperfetto	
ricompens**assi**	ricompens**assimo**
ricompens**assi**	ricompens**aste**
ricompens**asse**	ricompens**assero**
imperativo	
	ricompensiamo
ricompensa; non ricompensare	ricompensate
ricompensi	ricompensino

SINGULAR	PLURAL
passato prossimo	
ho ricompensato	**abbiamo** ricompensato
hai ricompensato	**avete** ricompensato
ha ricompensato	**hanno** ricompensato
trapassato prossimo	
avevo ricompensato	**avevamo** ricompensato
avevi ricompensato	**avevate** ricompensato
aveva ricompensato	**avevano** ricompensato
trapassato remoto	
ebbi ricompensato	**avemmo** ricompensato
avesti ricompensato	**aveste** ricompensato
ebbe ricompensato	**ebbero** ricompensato
futuro anteriore	
avrò ricompensato	**avremo** ricompensato
avrai ricompensato	**avrete** ricompensato
avrà ricompensato	**avranno** ricompensato
condizionale passato	
avrei ricompensato	**avremmo** ricompensato
avresti ricompensato	**avreste** ricompensato
avrebbe ricompensato	**avrebbero** ricompensato
congiuntivo passato	
abbia ricompensato	**abbiamo** ricompensato
abbia ricompensato	**abbiate** ricompensato
abbia ricompensato	**abbiano** ricompensato
congiuntivo trapassato	
avessi ricompensato	**avessimo** ricompensato
avessi ricompensato	**aveste** ricompensato
avesse ricompensato	**avessero** ricompensato

riconoscere — to recognize

gerundio **riconoscendo** participio passato **riconosciuto**

SINGULAR	PLURAL
indicativo presente	
riconosc**o**	riconosc**iamo**
riconosc**i**	riconosc**ete**
riconosc**e**	riconosc**ono**
imperfetto	
riconosce**vo**	riconosce**vamo**
riconosce**vi**	riconosce**vate**
riconosce**va**	riconosce**vano**
passato remoto	
riconobb**i**	riconosc**emmo**
riconosc**esti**	riconosc**este**
riconobb**e**	riconobb**ero**
futuro semplice	
riconoscer**ò**	riconoscer**emo**
riconoscer**ai**	riconoscer**ete**
riconoscer**à**	riconoscer**anno**
condizionale presente	
riconosc**erei**	riconosc**eremmo**
riconosc**eresti**	riconosc**ereste**
riconosc**erebbe**	riconosc**erebbero**
congiuntivo presente	
riconosc**a**	riconosc**iamo**
riconosc**a**	riconosc**iate**
riconosc**a**	riconosc**ano**
congiuntivo imperfetto	
riconosc**essi**	riconosc**essimo**
riconosc**essi**	riconosc**este**
riconosc**esse**	riconosc**essero**
imperativo	
	riconosciamo
riconosci; non riconoscere	riconoscete
riconosca	riconoscano

SINGULAR	PLURAL
passato prossimo	
ho riconosciuto	**abbiamo** riconosciuto
hai riconosciuto	**avete** riconosciuto
ha riconosciuto	**hanno** riconosciuto
trapassato prossimo	
avevo riconosciuto	**avevamo** riconosciuto
avevi riconosciuto	**avevate** riconosciuto
aveva riconosciuto	**avevano** riconosciuto
trapassato remoto	
ebbi riconosciuto	**avemmo** riconosciuto
avesti riconosciuto	**aveste** riconosciuto
ebbe riconosciuto	**ebbero** riconosciuto
futuro anteriore	
avrò riconosciuto	**avremo** riconosciuto
avrai riconosciuto	**avrete** riconosciuto
avrà riconosciuto	**avranno** riconosciuto
condizionale passato	
avrei riconosciuto	**avremmo** riconosciuto
avresti riconosciuto	**avreste** riconosciuto
avrebbe riconosciuto	**avrebbero** riconosciuto
congiuntivo passato	
abbia riconosciuto	**abbiamo** riconosciuto
abbia riconosciuto	**abbiate** riconosciuto
abbia riconosciuto	**abbiano** riconosciuto
congiuntivo trapassato	
avessi riconosciuto	**avessimo** riconosciuto
avessi riconosciuto	**aveste** riconosciuto
avesse riconosciuto	**avessero** riconosciuto

to remember, to remind **ricordare**

gerundio **ricordando** participio passato **ricordato**

SINGULAR	PLURAL	SINGULAR	PLURAL
indicativo presente		*passato prossimo*	
ricord**o**	ricord**iamo**	**ho** ricordato	**abbiamo** ricordato
ricord**i**	ricord**ate**	**hai** ricordato	**avete** ricordato
ricord**a**	ricord**ano**	**ha** ricordato	**hanno** ricordato
imperfetto		*trapassato prossimo*	
ricorda**vo**	ricorda**vamo**	**avevo** ricordato	**avevamo** ricordato
ricorda**vi**	ricorda**vate**	**avevi** ricordato	**avevate** ricordato
ricorda**va**	ricorda**vano**	**aveva** ricordato	**avevano** ricordato
passato remoto		*trapassato remoto*	
ricorda**i**	ricord**ammo**	**ebbi** ricordato	**avemmo** ricordato
ricord**asti**	ricord**aste**	**avesti** ricordato	**aveste** ricordato
ricord**ò**	ricord**arono**	**ebbe** ricordato	**ebbero** ricordato
futuro semplice		*futuro anteriore*	
ricorder**ò**	ricorder**emo**	**avrò** ricordato	**avremo** ricordato
ricorder**ai**	ricorder**ete**	**avrai** ricordato	**avrete** ricordato
ricorder**à**	ricorder**anno**	**avrà** ricordato	**avranno** ricordato
condizionale presente		*condizionale passato*	
ricord**erei**	ricord**eremmo**	**avrei** ricordato	**avremmo** ricordato
ricord**eresti**	ricord**ereste**	**avresti** ricordato	**avreste** ricordato
ricord**erebbe**	ricord**erebbero**	**avrebbe** ricordato	**avrebbero** ricordato
congiuntivo presente		*congiuntivo passato*	
ricord**i**	ricord**iamo**	**abbia** ricordato	**abbiamo** ricordato
ricord**i**	ricord**iate**	**abbia** ricordato	**abbiate** ricordato
ricord**i**	ricord**ino**	**abbia** ricordato	**abbiano** ricordato
congiuntivo imperfetto		*congiuntivo trapassato*	
ricord**assi**	ricord**assimo**	**avessi** ricordato	**avessimo** ricordato
ricord**assi**	ricord**aste**	**avessi** ricordato	**aveste** ricordato
ricord**asse**	ricord**assero**	**avesse** ricordato	**avessero** ricordato
imperativo			
	ricordiamo		
ricorda; non ricordare	ricordate		
ricordi	ricordino		

ricordarsi — to remember

gerundio **ricordandosi** participio passato **ricordatosi**

SINGULAR	PLURAL
indicativo presente	
mi ricord**o**	**ci** ricord**iamo**
ti ricord**i**	**vi** ricord**ate**
si ricord**a**	**si** ricord**ano**
imperfetto	
mi ricorda**vo**	**ci** ricorda**vamo**
ti ricorda**vi**	**vi** ricorda**vate**
si ricorda**va**	**si** ricorda**vano**
passato remoto	
mi ricord**ai**	**ci** ricord**ammo**
ti ricord**asti**	**vi** ricord**aste**
si ricord**ò**	**si** ricord**arono**
futuro semplice	
mi ricorder**ò**	**ci** ricorder**emo**
ti ricorder**ai**	**vi** ricorder**ete**
si ricorder**à**	**si** ricorder**anno**
condizionale presente	
mi ricord**erei**	**ci** ricord**eremmo**
ti ricord**eresti**	**vi** ricord**ereste**
si ricord**erebbe**	**si** ricord**erebbero**
congiuntivo presente	
mi ricord**i**	**ci** ricord**iamo**
ti ricord**i**	**vi** ricord**iate**
si ricord**i**	**si** ricord**ino**
congiuntivo imperfetto	
mi ricord**assi**	**ci** ricord**assimo**
ti ricord**assi**	**vi** ricord**aste**
si ricord**asse**	**si** ricord**assero**
imperativo	
	ricordiamoci
ricordati; non ti ricordare	ricordatevi
si ricordi	si ricordino

SINGULAR	PLURAL
passato prossimo	
mi sono ricordato(a)	**ci siamo** ricordati(e)
ti sei ricordato(a)	**vi siete** ricordati(e)
si è ricordato(a)	**si sono** ricordati(e)
trapassato prossimo	
mi ero ricordato(a)	**ci eravamo** ricordati(e)
ti eri ricordato(a)	**vi eravate** ricordati(e)
si era ricordato(a)	**si erano** ricordati(e)
trapassato remoto	
mi fui ricordato(a)	**ci fummo** ricordati(e)
ti fosti ricordato(a)	**vi foste** ricordati(e)
si fu ricordato(a)	**si furono** ricordati(e)
futuro anteriore	
mi sarò ricordato(a)	**ci saremo** ricordati(e)
ti sarai ricordato(a)	**vi sarete** ricordati(e)
si sarà ricordato(a)	**si saranno** ricordati(e)
condizionale passato	
mi sarei ricordato(a)	**ci saremmo** ricordati(e)
ti saresti ricordato(a)	**vi sareste** ricordati(e)
si sarebbe ricordato(a)	**si sarebbero** ricordati(e)
congiuntivo passato	
mi sia ricordato(a)	**ci siamo** ricordati(e)
ti sia ricordato(a)	**vi siate** ricordati(e)
si sia ricordato(a)	**si siano** ricordati(e)
congiuntivo trapassato	
mi fossi ricordato(a)	**ci fossimo** ricordati(e)
ti fossi ricordato(a)	**vi foste** ricordati(e)
si fosse ricordato(a)	**si fossero** ricordati(e)

to laugh — ridere

gerundio **ridendo** participio passato **riso**

SINGULAR	PLURAL	SINGULAR	PLURAL
indicativo presente		passato prossimo	
rid**o**	rid**iamo**	**ho** riso	**abbiamo** riso
rid**i**	rid**ete**	**hai** riso	**avete** riso
rid**e**	rid**ono**	**ha** riso	**hanno** riso
imperfetto		trapassato prossimo	
ride**vo**	ride**vamo**	**avevo** riso	**avevamo** riso
ride**vi**	ride**vate**	**avevi** riso	**avevate** riso
ride**va**	ride**vano**	**aveva** riso	**avevano** riso
passato remoto		trapassato remoto	
ris**i**	rid**emmo**	**ebbi** riso	**avemmo** riso
rid**esti**	rid**este**	**avesti** riso	**aveste** riso
ris**e**	ris**ero**	**ebbe** riso	**ebbero** riso
futuro semplice		futuro anteriore	
rider**ò**	rider**emo**	**avrò** riso	**avremo** riso
rider**ai**	rider**ete**	**avrai** riso	**avrete** riso
rider**à**	rider**anno**	**avrà** riso	**avranno** riso
condizionale presente		condizionale passato	
rid**erei**	rid**eremmo**	**avrei** riso	**avremmo** riso
rid**eresti**	rid**ereste**	**avresti** riso	**avreste** riso
rid**erebbe**	rid**erebbero**	**avrebbe** riso	**avrebbero** riso
congiuntivo presente		congiuntivo passato	
rid**a**	rid**iamo**	**abbia** riso	**abbiamo** riso
rid**a**	rid**iate**	**abbia** riso	**abbiate** riso
rid**a**	rid**ano**	**abbia** riso	**abbiano** riso
congiuntivo imperfetto		congiuntivo trapassato	
rid**essi**	rid**essimo**	**avessi** riso	**avessimo** riso
rid**essi**	rid**este**	**avessi** riso	**aveste** riso
rid**esse**	rid**essero**	**avesse** riso	**avessero** riso

imperativo

	ridiamo
ridi; non ridere	ridete
rida	ridano

R

ridire — to repeat

gerundio **ridicendo** participio passato **ridetto**

SINGULAR	PLURAL
indicativo presente	
ridic**o**	ridic**iamo**
ridic**i**	rid**ite**
ridic**e**	ridic**ono**
imperfetto	
ridice**vo**	ridice**vamo**
ridice**vi**	ridice**vate**
ridice**va**	ridice**vano**
passato remoto	
ridiss**i**	ridic**emmo**
ridic**esti**	ridic**este**
ridiss**e**	ridiss**ero**
futuro semplice	
ridir**ò**	ridir**emo**
ridir**ai**	ridir**ete**
ridir**à**	ridir**anno**
condizionale presente	
rid**irei**	rid**iremmo**
rid**iresti**	rid**ireste**
rid**irebbe**	rid**irebbero**
congiuntivo presente	
ridic**a**	ridic**iamo**
ridic**a**	ridic**iate**
ridic**a**	ridic**ano**
congiuntivo imperfetto	
ridic**essi**	ridic**emmo**
ridic**essi**	ridic**este**
ridic**esse**	ridic**essero**
imperativo	
	ridiciamo
ridi'; non ridire	ridite
ridica	ridicano

SINGULAR	PLURAL
passato prossimo	
ho ridetto	**abbiamo** ridetto
hai ridetto	**avete** ridetto
ha ridetto	**hanno** ridetto
trapassato prossimo	
avevo ridetto	**avevamo** ridetto
avevi ridetto	**avevate** ridetto
aveva ridetto	**avevano** ridetto
trapassato remoto	
ebbi ridetto	**avemmo** ridetto
avesti ridetto	**aveste** ridetto
ebbe ridetto	**ebbero** ridetto
futuro anteriore	
avrò ridetto	**avremo** ridetto
avrai ridetto	**avrete** ridetto
avrà ridetto	**avranno** ridetto
condizionale passato	
avrei ridetto	**avremmo** ridetto
avresti ridetto	**avreste** ridetto
avrebbe ridetto	**avrebbero** ridetto
congiuntivo passato	
abbia ridetto	**abbiamo** ridetto
abbia ridetto	**abbiate** ridetto
abbia ridetto	**abbiano** ridetto
congiuntivo trapassato	
avessi ridetto	**avessimo** ridetto
avessi ridetto	**aveste** ridetto
avesse ridetto	**avessero** ridetto

gerundio **riducendo** participio passato **ridotto**

SINGULAR	PLURAL	SINGULAR	PLURAL
indicativo presente		passato prossimo	
ridu**co**	riduc**iamo**	**ho** ridotto	**abbiamo** ridotto
riduc**i**	riduc**ete**	**hai** ridotto	**avete** ridotto
riduc**e**	riduc**ono**	**ha** ridotto	**hanno** ridotto
imperfetto		trapassato prossimo	
riduce**vo**	riduce**vamo**	**avevo** ridotto	**avevamo** ridotto
riduce**vi**	riduce**vate**	**avevi** ridotto	**avevate** ridotto
riduce**va**	riduce**vano**	**aveva** ridotto	**avevano** ridotto
passato remoto		trapassato remoto	
ridu**ssi**	riduc**emmo**	**ebbi** ridotto	**avemmo** ridotto
riduc**esti**	riduc**este**	**avesti** ridotto	**aveste** ridotto
ridu**sse**	ridu**ssero**	**ebbe** ridotto	**ebbero** ridotto
futuro semplice		futuro anteriore	
ridurr**ò**	ridurr**emo**	**avrò** ridotto	**avremo** ridotto
ridurr**ai**	ridurr**ete**	**avrai** ridotto	**avrete** ridotto
ridurr**à**	ridurr**anno**	**avrà** ridotto	**avranno** ridotto
condizionale presente		condizionale passato	
ridurr**ei**	ridurr**emmo**	**avrei** ridotto	**avremmo** ridotto
ridurr**esti**	ridurr**este**	**avresti** ridotto	**avreste** ridotto
ridurr**ebbe**	ridurr**ebbero**	**avrebbe** ridotto	**avrebbero** ridotto
congiuntivo presente		congiuntivo passato	
riduc**a**	riduc**iamo**	**abbia** ridotto	**abbiamo** ridotto
riduc**a**	riduc**iate**	**abbia** ridotto	**abbiate** ridotto
riduc**a**	riduc**ano**	**abbia** ridotto	**abbiano** ridotto
congiuntivo imperfetto		congiuntivo trapassato	
riduc**essi**	riduc**essimo**	**avessi** ridotto	**avessimo** ridotto
riduc**essi**	riduc**este**	**avessi** ridotto	**aveste** ridotto
riduc**esse**	riduc**essero**	**avesse** ridotto	**avessero** ridotto
imperativo			
	riduciamo		
riduci; non ridurre	riducete		
riduca	riducano		

riempire — to fill

gerundio **riempiendo** participio passato **riempito**

SINGULAR	PLURAL	SINGULAR	PLURAL
indicativo presente		passato prossimo	
riempi**o**	riempi**amo**	**ho** riempito	**abbiamo** riempito
riemp**i**	riemp**ite**	**hai** riempito	**avete** riempito
riempi**e**	riempi**ono**	**ha** riempito	**hanno** riempito
imperfetto		trapassato prossimo	
riempi**vo**	riempi**vamo**	**avevo** riempito	**avevamo** riempito
riempi**vi**	riempi**vate**	**avevi** riempito	**avevate** riempito
riempi**va**	riempi**vano**	**aveva** riempito	**avevano** riempito
passato remoto		trapassato remoto	
riempi**i**	riemp**immo**	**ebbi** riempito	**avemmo** riempito
riemp**isti**	riemp**iste**	**avesti** riempito	**aveste** riempito
riemp**ì**	riemp**irono**	**ebbe** riempito	**ebbero** riempito
futuro semplice		futuro anteriore	
riempir**ò**	riempir**emo**	**avrò** riempito	**avremo** riempito
riempir**ai**	riempir**ete**	**avrai** riempito	**avrete** riempito
riempir**à**	riempir**anno**	**avrà** riempito	**avranno** riempito
condizionale presente		condizionale passato	
riemp**irei**	riemp**iremmo**	**avrei** riempito	**avremmo** riempito
riemp**iresti**	riemp**ireste**	**avresti** riempito	**avreste** riempito
riemp**irebbe**	riemp**irebbero**	**avrebbe** riempito	**avrebbero** riempito
congiuntivo presente		congiuntivo passato	
riempi**a**	riempi**amo**	**abbia** riempito	**abbiamo** riempito
riempi**a**	riempi**ate**	**abbia** riempito	**abbiate** riempito
riempi**a**	riempi**ano**	**abbia** riempito	**abbiano** riempito
congiuntivo imperfetto		congiuntivo trapassato	
riemp**issi**	riemp**issimo**	**avessi** riempito	**avessimo** riempito
riemp**issi**	riemp**iste**	**avessi** riempito	**aveste** riempito
riemp**isse**	riemp**issero**	**avesse** riempito	**avessero** riempito

R

imperativo

	riempiamo
riempi; non riempire	riempite
riempia	riempiano

to do again **rifare**

gerundio **rifacendo** participio passato **rifatto**

SINGULAR	PLURAL
indicativo presente	
rifacci**o**	rifacc**iamo**
rifa**i**	rif**ate**
rif**à**	rif**anno**
imperfetto	
riface**vo**	riface**vamo**
riface**vi**	riface**vate**
riface**va**	riface**vano**
passato remoto	
rifec**i**	rifac**emmo**
rifac**esti**	rifac**este**
rifec**e**	rifec**ero**
futuro semplice	
rifar**ò**	rifar**emo**
rifar**ai**	rifar**ete**
rifar**à**	rifar**anno**
condizionale presente	
rif**arei**	rif**aremmo**
rif**aresti**	rif**areste**
rif**arebbe**	rif**arebbero**
congiuntivo presente	
rifacci**a**	rifacc**iamo**
rifacci**a**	rifacc**iate**
rifacci**a**	rifacc**iano**
congiuntivo imperfetto	
rifac**essi**	rifac**essimo**
rifac**essi**	rifac**este**
rifac**esse**	rifac**essero**
imperativo	
	rifacciamo
rifai; non rifare	rifate
rifaccia	rifacciano

SINGULAR	PLURAL
passato prossimo	
ho rifatto	**abbiamo** rifatto
hai rifatto	**avete** rifatto
ha rifatto	**hanno** rifatto
trapassato prossimo	
avevo rifatto	**avevamo** rifatto
avevi rifatto	**avevate** rifatto
aveva rifatto	**avevano** rifatto
trapassato remoto	
ebbi rifatto	**avemmo** rifatto
avesti rifatto	**aveste** rifatto
ebbe rifatto	**ebbero** rifatto
futuro anteriore	
avrò rifatto	**avremo** rifatto
avrai rifatto	**avrete** rifatto
avrà rifatto	**avranno** rifatto
condizionale passato	
avrei rifatto	**avremmo** rifatto
avresti rifatto	**avreste** rifatto
avrebbe rifatto	**avrebbero** rifatto
congiuntivo passato	
abbia rifatto	**abbiamo** rifatto
abbia rifatto	**abbiate** rifatto
abbia rifatto	**abbiano** rifatto
congiuntivo trapassato	
avessi rifatto	**avessimo** rifatto
avessi rifatto	**aveste** rifatto
avesse rifatto	**avessero** rifatto

rifiutare — to reject, to refuse

gerundio **rifiutando** — participio passato **rifiutato**

SINGULAR	PLURAL
indicativo presente	
rifiut**o**	rifiut**iamo**
rifiut**i**	rifiut**ate**
rifiut**a**	rifiut**ano**
imperfetto	
rifiuta**vo**	rifiuta**vamo**
rifiuta**vi**	rifiuta**vate**
rifiuta**va**	rifiuta**vano**
passato remoto	
rifiut**ai**	rifiut**ammo**
rifiut**asti**	rifiut**aste**
rifiut**ò**	rifiut**arono**
futuro semplice	
rifiuter**ò**	rifiuter**emo**
rifiuter**ai**	rifiuter**ete**
rifiuter**à**	rifiuter**anno**
condizionale presente	
rifiut**erei**	rifiut**eremmo**
rifiut**eresti**	rifiut**ereste**
rifiut**erebbe**	rifiut**erebbero**
congiuntivo presente	
rifiut**i**	rifiut**iamo**
rifiut**i**	rifiut**iate**
rifiut**i**	rifiut**ino**
congiuntivo imperfetto	
rifiut**assi**	rifiut**assimo**
rifiut**assi**	rifiut**aste**
rifiut**asse**	rifiut**assero**
imperativo	
	rifiutiamo
rifiuta; non rifiutare	rifiutate
rifiuti	rifiutino

SINGULAR	PLURAL
passato prossimo	
ho rifiutato	**abbiamo** rifiutato
hai rifiutato	**avete** rifiutato
ha rifiutato	**hanno** rifiutato
trapassato prossimo	
avevo rifiutato	**avevamo** rifiutato
avevi rifiutato	**avevate** rifiutato
aveva rifiutato	**avevano** rifiutato
trapassato remoto	
ebbi rifiutato	**avemmo** rifiutato
avesti rifiutato	**aveste** rifiutato
ebbe rifiutato	**ebbero** rifiutato
futuro anteriore	
avrò rifiutato	**avremo** rifiutato
avrai rifiutato	**avrete** rifiutato
avrà rifiutato	**avranno** rifiutato
condizionale passato	
avrei rifiutato	**avremmo** rifiutato
avresti rifiutato	**avreste** rifiutato
avrebbe rifiutato	**avrebbero** rifiutato
congiuntivo passato	
abbia rifiutato	**abbiamo** rifiutato
abbia rifiutato	**abbiate** rifiutato
abbia rifiutato	**abbiano** rifiutato
congiuntivo trapassato	
avessi rifiutato	**avessimo** rifiutato
avessi rifiutato	**aveste** rifiutato
avesse rifiutato	**avessero** rifiutato

to think, to reflect — riflettere

gerundio **riflettendo** participio passato **riflettuto**

SINGULAR	PLURAL
indicativo presente	
riflett**o**	riflett**iamo**
riflett**i**	riflett**ete**
riflett**e**	riflett**ono**
imperfetto	
riflette**vo**	riffletteva**mo**
riflette**vi**	riflette**vate**
riflette**va**	riflette**vano**
passato remoto	
riflett**ei** (rifless**i**)	riflett**emmo**
riflett**esti**	riflett**este**
riflett**é** (rifless**e**)	riflett**erono** (refl**essero**)
futuro semplice	
rifletter**ò**	rifletter**emo**
rifletter**ai**	rifletter**ete**
rifletter**à**	rifletter**anno**
condizionale presente	
riflett**erei**	riflett**eremmo**
riflett**eresti**	riflett**ereste**
riflett**erebbe**	riflett**erebbero**
congiuntivo presente	
riflett**a**	riflett**iamo**
riflett**a**	riflett**iate**
riflett**a**	riflett**ano**
congiuntivo imperfetto	
riflett**essi**	riflett**essimo**
riflett**essi**	riflett**este**
riflett**esse**	riflett**essero**
imperativo	
	riflettiamo
rifletti; non riflettere	riflettete
rifletta	riflettano

SINGULAR	PLURAL
passato prossimo	
ho riflettuto	**abbiamo** riflettuto
hai riflettuto	**avete** riflettuto
ha riflettuto	**hanno** riflettuto
trapassato prossimo	
avevo riflettuto	**avevamo** riflettuto
avevi riflettuto	**avevate** riflettuto
aveva riflettuto	**avevano** riflettuto
trapassato remoto	
ebbi riflettuto	**avemmo** riflettuto
avesti riflettuto	**aveste** riflettuto
ebbe riflettuto	**ebbero** riflettuto
futuro anteriore	
avrò riflettuto	**avremo** riflettuto
avrai riflettuto	**avrete** riflettuto
avrà riflettuto	**avranno** riflettuto
condizionale passato	
avrei riflettuto	**avremmo** riflettuto
avresti riflettuto	**avreste** riflettuto
avrebbe riflettuto	**avrebbero** riflettuto
congiuntivo passato	
abbia riflettuto	**abbiamo** riflettuto
abbia riflettuto	**abbiate** riflettuto
abbia riflettuto	**abbiano** riflettuto
congiuntivo trapassato	
avessi riflettuto	**avessimo** riflettuto
avessi riflettuto	**aveste** riflettuto
avesse riflettuto	**avessero** riflettuto

rilassarsi — to relax

gerundio **rilassandosi** participio passato **rilassatosi**

SINGULAR	PLURAL	SINGULAR	PLURAL
indicativo presente		passato prossimo	
mi rilass**o**	**ci** rilass**iamo**	**mi sono** rilassato(a)	**ci siamo** rilassati(e)
ti rilass**i**	**vi** rilass**ate**	**ti sei** rilassato(a)	**vi siete** rilassati(e)
si rilass**a**	**si** rilass**ano**	**si è** rilassato(a)	**si sono** rilassati(e)
imperfetto		trapassato prossimo	
mi rilassa**vo**	**ci** rilassa**vamo**	**mi ero** rilassato(a)	**ci eravamo** rilassati(e)
ti rilassa**vi**	**vi** rilassa**vate**	**ti eri** rilassato(a)	**vi eravate** rilassati(e)
si rilassa**va**	**si** rilassa**vano**	**si era** rilassato(a)	**si erano** rilassati(e)
passato remoto		trapassato remoto	
mi rilass**ai**	**ci** rilass**ammo**	**mi fui** rilassato(a)	**ci fummo** rilassati(e)
ti rilass**asti**	**vi** rilass**aste**	**ti fosti** rilassato(a)	**vi foste** rilassati(e)
si rilass**ò**	**si** rilass**arono**	**si fu** rilassato(a)	**si furono** rilassati(e)
futuro semplice		futuro anteriore	
mi rilasser**ò**	**ci** rilasser**emo**	**mi sarò** rilassato(a)	**ci saremo** rilassati(e)
ti rilasser**ai**	**vi** rilasser**ete**	**ti sarai** rilassato(a)	**vi sarete** rilassati(e)
si rilasser**à**	**si** rilasser**anno**	**si sarà** rilassato(a)	**si saranno** rilassati(e)
condizionale presente		condizionale passato	
mi rilass**erei**	**ci** rilass**eremmo**	**mi sarei** rilassato(a)	**ci saremmo** rilassati(e)
ti rilass**eresti**	**vi** rilass**ereste**	**ti saresti** rilassato(a)	**vi sareste** rilassati(e)
si rilass**erebbe**	**si** rilass**erebbero**	**si sarebbe** rilassato(a)	**si sarebbero** rilassati(e)
congiuntivo presente		congiuntivo passato	
mi rilass**i**	**ci** rilass**iamo**	**mi sia** rilassato(a)	**ci siamo** rilassati(e)
ti rilass**i**	**vi** rilass**iate**	**ti sia** rilassato(a)	**vi siate** rilassati(e)
si rilass**i**	**si** rilass**ino**	**si sia** rilassato(a)	**si siano** rilassati(e)
congiuntivo imperfetto		congiuntivo trapassato	
mi rilass**assi**	**ci** rilass**assimo**	**mi fossi** rilassato(a)	**ci fossimo** rilassati(e)
ti rilass**assi**	**vi** rilass**aste**	**ti fossi** rilassato(a)	**vi foste** rilassati(e)
si rilass**asse**	**si** rilass**assero**	**si fosse** rilassato(a)	**si fossero** rilassati(e)

imperativo

	rilassiamoci
rilassati; non rilassarti/ non ti rilassare	rilassatevi
si rilassi	si rilassino

to remain, to stay **rimanere**

gerundio **rimanendo** participio passato **rimasto**

SINGULAR	PLURAL	SINGULAR	PLURAL
indicativo presente		passato prossimo	
rimang**o**	rimani**amo**	**sono** rimasto(a)	**siamo** rimasti(e)
riman**i**	riman**ete**	**sei** rimasto(a)	**siete** rimasti(e)
riman**e**	rimang**ono**	**è** rimasto(a)	**sono** rimasti(e)
imperfetto		trapassato prossimo	
rimane**vo**	rimane**vamo**	**ero** rimasto(a)	**eravamo** rimasti(e)
rimane**vi**	rimane**vate**	**eri** rimasto(a)	**eravate** rimasti(e)
rimane**va**	rimane**vano**	**era** rimasto(a)	**erano** rimasti(e)
passato remoto		trapassato remoto	
rimas**i**	rimane**mmo**	**fui** rimasto(a)	**fummo** rimasti(e)
rimane**sti**	rimane**ste**	**fosti** rimasto(a)	**foste** rimasti(e)
rimas**e**	rimane**sero**	**fu** rimasto(a)	**furono** rimasti(e)
futuro semplice		futuro anteriore	
rimarr**ò**	rimarr**emo**	**sarò** rimasto(a)	**saremo** rimasti(e)
rimarr**ai**	rimarr**ete**	**sarai** rimasto(a)	**sarete** rimasti(e)
rimarr**à**	rimarr**anno**	**sarà** rimasto(a)	**saranno** rimasti(e)
condizionale presente		condizionale passato	
rimar**rei**	rimar**remmo**	**sarei** rimasto(a)	**saremmo** rimasti(e)
rimar**resti**	rimar**reste**	**saresti** rimasto(a)	**sareste** rimasti(e)
rimar**rebbe**	rimar**rebbero**	**sarebbe** rimasto(a)	**sarebbero** rimasti(e)
congiuntivo presente		congiuntivo passato	
rimang**a**	rimani**amo**	**sia** rimasto(a)	**siamo** rimasti(e)
rimang**a**	rimani**ate**	**sia** rimasto(a)	**siate** rimasti(e)
rimang**a**	rimang**ano**	**sia** rimasto(a)	**siano** rimasti(e)
congiuntivo imperfetto		congiuntivo trapassato	
rimane**ssi**	rimane**ssimo**	**fossi** rimasto(a)	**fossimo** rimasti(e)
rimane**ssi**	rimane**ste**	**fossi** rimasto(a)	**foste** rimasti(e)
rimane**sse**	rimane**ssero**	**fosse** rimasto(a)	**fossero** rimasti(e)
imperativo			
	rimaniamo		
rimani; non rimanere	rimanete		
rimanga	rimangano		

R

rimproverare — to scold

gerundio **rimproverando** — participio passato **rimproverato**

SINGULAR	PLURAL	SINGULAR	PLURAL
indicativo presente		passato prossimo	
rimprover**o**	rimprover**iamo**	**ho** rimproverato	**abbiamo** rimproverato
rimprover**i**	rimprover**ate**	**hai** rimproverato	**avete** rimproverato
rimprover**a**	rimprover**ano**	**ha** rimproverato	**hanno** rimproverato
imperfetto		trapassato prossimo	
rimprovera**vo**	rimprovera**vamo**	**avevo** rimproverato	**avevamo** rimproverato
rimprovera**vi**	rimprovera**vate**	**avevi** rimproverato	**avevate** rimproverato
rimprovera**va**	rimprovera**vano**	**aveva** rimproverato	**avevano** rimproverato
passato remoto		trapassato remoto	
rimprover**ai**	rimprover**ammo**	**ebbi** rimproverato	**avemmo** rimproverato
rimprover**asti**	rimprover**aste**	**avesti** rimproverato	**aveste** rimproverato
rimprover**ò**	rimprover**arono**	**ebbe** rimproverato	**ebbero** rimproverato
futuro semplice		futuro anteriore	
rimproverer**ò**	rimproverer**emo**	**avrò** rimproverato	**avremo** rimproverato
rimproverer**ai**	rimproverer**ete**	**avrai** rimproverato	**avrete** rimproverato
rimproverer**à**	rimproverer**anno**	**avrà** rimproverato	**avranno** rimproverato
condizionale presente		condizionale passato	
rimprover**erei**	rimprover**eremmo**	**avrei** rimproverato	**avremmo** rimproverato
rimprover**eresti**	rimprover**ereste**	**avresti** rimproverato	**avreste** rimproverato
rimprover**erebbe**	rimprover**erebbero**	**avrebbe** rimproverato	**avrebbero** rimproverato
congiuntivo presente		congiuntivo passato	
rimprover**i**	rimprover**iamo**	**abbia** rimproverato	**abbiamo** rimproverato
rimprover**i**	rimprover**iate**	**abbia** rimproverato	**abbiate** rimproverato
rimprover**i**	rimprover**ino**	**abbia** rimproverato	**abbiano** rimproverato
congiuntivo imperfetto		congiuntivo trapassato	
rimprover**assi**	rimprover**assimo**	**avessi** rimproverato	**avessimo** rimproverato
rimprover**assi**	rimprover**aste**	**avessi** rimproverato	**aveste** rimproverato
rimprover**asse**	rimprover**assero**	**avesse** rimproverato	**avessero** rimproverato

R

imperativo

	rimproveriamo
rimprovera; non rimproverare	rimproverate
rimproveri	rimproverino

to regret **rincrescere**

gerundio **rincrescendo** participio passato **rincresciuto**

SINGULAR	PLURAL	SINGULAR	PLURAL
indicativo presente		passato prossimo	
rincresc**o**	rincresc**iamo**	**sono** rincresciuto(a)	**siamo** rincresciuti(e)
rincresc**i**	rincresc**ete**	**sei** rincresciuto(a)	**siete** rincresciuti(e)
rincresc**e**	rincresc**ono**	**è** rincresciuto(a)	**sono** rincresciuti(e)
imperfetto		trapassato prossimo	
rincresce**vo**	rincresce**vamo**	**ero** rincresciuto(a)	**eravamo** rincresciuti(e)
rincresce**vi**	rincresce**vate**	**eri** rincresciuto(a)	**eravate** rincresciuti(e)
rincresce**va**	rincresce**vano**	**era** rincresciuto(a)	**erano** rincresciuti(e)
passato remoto		trapassato remoto	
rincrebb**i**	rincresc**emmo**	**fui** rincresciuto(a)	**fummo** rincresciuti(e)
rincresc**esti**	rincresc**este**	**fosti** rincresciuto(a)	**foste** rincresciuti(e)
rincrebb**e**	rincrebb**ero**	**fu** rincresciuto(a)	**furono** rincresciuti(e)
futuro semplice		futuro anteriore	
rincrescer**ò**	rincrescer**emo**	**sarò** rincresciuto(a)	**saremo** rincresciuti(e)
rincrescer**ai**	rincrescer**ete**	**sarai** rincresciuto(a)	**sarete** rincresciuti(e)
rincrescer**à**	rincrescer**anno**	**sarà** rincresciuto(a)	**saranno** rincresciuti(e)
condizionale presente		condizionale passato	
rincresc**erei**	rincresc**eremmo**	**sarei** rincresciuto(a)	**saremmo** rincresciuti(e)
rincresc**eresti**	rincresc**ereste**	**saresti** rincresciuto(a)	**sareste** rincresciuti(e)
rincresc**erebbe**	rincresc**erebbero**	**sarebbe** rincresciuto(a)	**sarebbero** rincresciuti(e)
congiuntivo presente		congiuntivo passato	
rincresc**a**	rincresc**iamo**	**sia** rincresciuto(a)	**siamo** rincresciuti(e)
rincresc**a**	rincresc**iate**	**sia** rincresciuto(a)	**siate** rincresciuti(e)
rincresc**a**	rincresc**ano**	**sia** rincresciuto(a)	**siano** rincresciuti(e)
congiuntivo imperfetto		congiuntivo trapassato	
rincresc**essi**	rincresc**essimo**	**fossi** rincresciuto(a)	**fossimo** rincresciuti(e)
rincresc**essi**	rincresc**este**	**fossi** rincresciuto(a)	**foste** rincresciuti(e)
rincresc**esse**	rincresc**essero**	**fosse** rincresciuto(a)	**fossero** rincresciuti(e)

imperativo

	rincresciamo
rincresci; non rincrescere	rincrescete
rincresca	rincrescano

ringraziare — to thank

gerundio **ringraziando** participio passato **ringraziato**

SINGULAR	PLURAL	SINGULAR	PLURAL
indicativo presente		passato prossimo	
ringrazi**o**	ringrazi**amo**	**ho** ringraziato	**abbiamo** ringraziato
ringraz**i**	ringrazi**ate**	**hai** ringraziato	**avete** ringraziato
ringrazi**a**	ringrazi**ano**	**ha** ringraziato	**hanno** ringraziato
imperfetto		trapassato prossimo	
ringrazia**vo**	ringrazia**vamo**	**avevo** ringraziato	**avevamo** ringraziato
ringrazia**vi**	ringrazia**vate**	**avevi** ringraziato	**avevate** ringraziato
ringrazia**va**	ringrazia**vano**	**aveva** ringraziato	**avevano** ringraziato
passato remoto		trapassato remoto	
ringrazi**ai**	ringrazi**ammo**	**ebbi** ringraziato	**avemmo** ringraziato
ringrazi**asti**	ringrazi**aste**	**avesti** ringraziato	**aveste** ringraziato
ringrazi**ò**	ringrazi**arono**	**ebbe** ringraziato	**ebbero** ringraziato
futuro semplice		futuro anteriore	
ringrazier**ò**	ringrazier**emo**	**avrò** ringraziato	**avremo** ringraziato
ringrazier**ai**	ringrazer**ete**	**avrai** ringraziato	**avrete** ringraziato
ringrazier**à**	ringrazier**anno**	**avrà** ringraziato	**avranno** ringraziato
condizionale presente		condizionale passato	
ringrazi**erei**	ringrazi**eremmo**	**avrei** ringraziato	**avremmo** ringraziato
ringrazi**eresti**	ringrazi**ereste**	**avresti** ringraziato	**avreste** ringraziato
ringrazi**erebbe**	ringrazi**erebbero**	**avrebbe** ringraziato	**avrebbero** ringraziato
congiuntivo presente		congiuntivo passato	
ringraz**i**	ringrazi**amo**	**abbia** ringraziato	**abbiamo** ringraziato
ringraz**i**	ringrazi**ate**	**abbia** ringraziato	**abbiate** ringraziato
ringraz**i**	ringraz**ino**	**abbia** ringraziato	**abbiano** ringraziato
congiuntivo imperfetto		congiuntivo trapassato	
ringrazi**assi**	ringrazi**assimo**	**avessi** ringraziato	**avessimo** ringraziato
ringrazi**assi**	ringrazi**aste**	**avessi** ringraziato	**aveste** ringraziato
ringrazi**asse**	ringrazi**assero**	**avesse** ringraziato	**avessero** ringraziato

R

imperativo

SINGULAR	PLURAL
	ringraziamo
ringrazia; non ringraziare	ringraziate
ringrazi	ringrazino

to renew **rinnovare**

gerundio **rinnovando** participio passato **rinnovato**

indicativo presente

SINGULAR	PLURAL
rinnov**o**	rinnov**iamo**
rinnov**i**	rinnov**ate**
rinnov**a**	rinnov**ano**

imperfetto

SINGULAR	PLURAL
rinnova**vo**	rinnova**vamo**
rinnova**vi**	rinnova**vate**
rinnova**va**	rinnova**vano**

passato remoto

SINGULAR	PLURAL
rinnov**ai**	rinnov**ammo**
rinnov**asti**	rinnov**aste**
rinnov**ò**	rinnov**arono**

futuro semplice

SINGULAR	PLURAL
rinnover**ò**	rinnover**emo**
rinnover**ai**	rinnover**ete**
innover**à**	rinnover**anno**

condizionale presente

SINGULAR	PLURAL
rinnov**erei**	rinnov**eremmo**
rinnov**eresti**	rinnov**ereste**
rinnov**erebbe**	rinnov**erebbero**

congiuntivo presente

SINGULAR	PLURAL
rinnov**i**	rinnov**iamo**
rinnov**i**	rinnov**iate**
rinnov**i**	rinnov**ino**

congiuntivo imperfetto

SINGULAR	PLURAL
rinnov**assi**	rinnov**assimo**
rinnov**assi**	rinnov**aste**
rinnov**asse**	rinnov**assero**

imperativo

SINGULAR	PLURAL
	rinnoviamo
rinnova; non rinnovare	rinnovate
rinnovi	rinnovino

passato prossimo

SINGULAR	PLURAL
ho rinnovato	**abbiamo** rinnovato
hai rinnovato	**avete** rinnovato
ha rinnovato	**hanno** rinnovato

trapassato prossimo

SINGULAR	PLURAL
avevo rinnovato	**avevamo** rinnovato
avevi rinnovato	**avevate** rinnovato
aveva rinnovato	**avevano** rinnovato

trapassato remoto

SINGULAR	PLURAL
ebbi rinnovato	**avemmo** rinnovato
avesti rinnovato	**aveste** rinnovato
ebbe rinnovato	**ebbero** rinnovato

futuro anteriore

SINGULAR	PLURAL
avrò rinnovato	**avremo** rinnovato
avrai rinnovato	**avrete** rinnovato
avrà rinnovato	**avranno** rinnovato

condizionale passato

SINGULAR	PLURAL
avrei rinnovato	**avremmo** rinnovato
avresti rinnovato	**avreste** rinnovato
avrebbe rinnovato	**avrebbero** rinnovato

congiuntivo passato

SINGULAR	PLURAL
abbia rinnovato	**abbiamo** rinnovato
abbia rinnovato	**abbiate** rinnovato
abbia rinnovato	**abbiano** rinnovato

congiuntivo trapassato

SINGULAR	PLURAL
avessi rinnovato	**avessimo** rinnovato
avessi rinnovato	**aveste** rinnovato
avesse rinnovato	**avessero** rinnovato

riparare — to fix, to repair

gerundio **riparando** — participio passato **riparato**

SINGULAR	PLURAL	SINGULAR	PLURAL
indicativo presente		*passato prossimo*	
ripar**o**	ripar**iamo**	**ho** riparato	**abbiamo** riparato
ripar**i**	ripar**ate**	**hai** riparato	**avete** riparato
ripar**a**	ripar**ano**	**ha** riparato	**hanno** riparato
imperfetto		*trapassato prossimo*	
ripara**vo**	ripara**vamo**	**avevo** riparato	**avevamo** riparato
ripara**vi**	ripara**vate**	**avevi** riparato	**avevate** riparato
ripara**va**	ripara**vano**	**aveva** riparato	**avevano** riparato
passato remoto		*trapassato remoto*	
ripar**ai**	ripar**ammo**	**ebbi** riparato	**avemmo** riparato
ripar**asti**	ripar**aste**	**avesti** riparato	**aveste** riparato
ripar**ò**	ripar**arono**	**ebbe** riparato	**ebbero** riparato
futuro semplice		*futuro anteriore*	
riparer**ò**	riparer**emo**	**avrò** riparato	**avremo** riparato
riparer**ai**	riparer**ete**	**avrai** riparato	**avrete** riparato
riparer**à**	riparer**anno**	**avrà** riparato	**avranno** riparato
condizionale presente		*condizionale passato*	
ripar**erei**	ripar**eremmo**	**avrei** riparato	**avremmo** riparato
ripar**eresti**	ripar**ereste**	**avresti** riparato	**avreste** riparato
ripar**erebbe**	ripar**erebbero**	**avrebbe** riparato	**avrebbero** riparato
congiuntivo presente		*congiuntivo passato*	
ripar**i**	ripar**iamo**	**abbia** riparato	**abbiamo** riparato
ripar**i**	ripar**iate**	**abbia** riparato	**abbiate** riparato
ripar**i**	ripar**ino**	**abbia** riparato	**abbiano** riparato
congiuntivo imperfetto		*congiuntivo trapassato*	
ripar**assi**	ripar**assimo**	**avessi** riparato	**avessimo** riparato
ripar**assi**	ripar**aste**	**avessi** riparato	**aveste** riparato
ripar**asse**	ripar**assero**	**avesse** riparato	**avessero** riparato
imperativo			
	ripariamo		
ripara; non riparare	riparate		
ripari	riparino		

gerundio **ripetendo** participio passato **ripetuto**

SINGULAR	PLURAL	SINGULAR	PLURAL
indicativo presente		passato prossimo	
ripet**o**	ripet**iamo**	**ho** ripetuto	**abbiamo** ripetuto
ripet**i**	ripet**ete**	**hai** ripetuto	**avete** ripetuto
ripet**e**	ripet**ono**	**ha** ripetuto	**hanno** ripetuto
imperfetto		trapassato prossimo	
ripete**vo**	ripete**vamo**	**avevo** ripetuto	**avevamo** ripetuto
ripete**vi**	ripete**vate**	**avevi** ripetuto	**avevate** ripetuto
ripete**va**	ripete**vano**	**aveva** ripetuto	**avevano** ripetuto
passato remoto		trapassato remoto	
ripet**ei**	ripet**emmo**	**ebbi** ripetuto	**avemmo** ripetuto
ripet**esti**	ripet**este**	**avesti** ripetuto	**aveste** ripetuto
ripet**é**	ripet**erono**	**ebbe** ripetuto	**ebbero** ripetuto
futuro semplice		futuro anteriore	
ripeter**ò**	ripeter**emo**	**avrò** ripetuto	**avremo** ripetuto
ripeter**ai**	ripeter**ete**	**avrai** ripetuto	**avrete** ripetuto
ripeter**à**	ripeter**anno**	**avrà** ripetuto	**avranno** ripetuto
condizionale presente		condizionale passato	
ripet**erei**	ripet**eremmo**	**avrei** ripetuto	**avremmo** ripetuto
ripet**eresti**	ripet**ereste**	**avresti** ripetuto	**avreste** ripetuto
ripet**erebbe**	ripet**erebbero**	**avrebbe** ripetuto	**avrebbero** ripetuto
congiuntivo presente		congiuntivo passato	
ripet**a**	ripet**iamo**	**abbia** ripetuto	**abbiamo** ripetuto
ripet**a**	ripet**iate**	**abbia** ripetuto	**abbiate** ripetuto
ripet**a**	ripet**ano**	**abbia** ripetuto	**abbiano** ripetuto
congiuntivo imperfetto		congiuntivo trapassato	
ripet**essi**	ripet**essimo**	**avessi** ripetuto	**avessimo** ripetuto
ripet**essi**	ripet**este**	**avessi** ripetuto	**aveste** ripetuto
ripet**esse**	ripet**essero**	**avesse** ripetuto	**avessero** ripetuto
imperativo			
	ripetiamo		
ripeti; non ripetere	ripetete		
ripeta	ripetano		

riposarsi — to rest

gerundio **riposandosi** participio passato **riposatosi**

SINGULAR	PLURAL	SINGULAR	PLURAL
indicativo presente		passato prossimo	
mi ripos**o**	**ci** ripos**iamo**	**mi sono** riposato(a)	**ci siamo** riposati(e)
ti ripos**i**	**vi** ripos**ate**	**ti sei** riposato(a)	**vi siete** riposati(e)
si ripos**a**	**si** ripos**ano**	**si è** riposato(a)	**si sono** riposati(e)
imperfetto		trapassato prossimo	
mi riposa**vo**	**ci** riposa**vamo**	**mi ero** riposato(a)	**ci eravamo** riposati(e)
ti riposa**vi**	**vi** riposa**vate**	**ti eri** riposato(a)	**vi eravate** riposati(e)
si riposa**va**	**si** riposa**vano**	**si era** riposato(a)	**si erano** riposati(e)
passato remoto		trapassato remoto	
mi ripos**ai**	**ci** riposa**mmo**	**mi fui** riposato(a)	**ci fummo** riposati(e)
ti riposa**sti**	**vi** riposa**ste**	**ti fosti** riposato(a)	**vi foste** riposati(e)
si ripos**ò**	**si** ripos**arono**	**si fu** riposato(a)	**si furono** riposati(e)
futuro semplice		futuro anteriore	
mi riposer**ò**	**ci** riposer**emo**	**mi sarò** riposato(a)	**ci saremo** riposati(e)
ti riposer**ai**	**vi** riposer**ete**	**ti sarai** riposato(a)	**vi sarete** riposati(e)
si riposer**à**	**si** riposer**anno**	**si sarà** riposato(a)	**si saranno** riposati(e)
condizionale presente		condizionale passato	
mi ripos**erei**	**ci** ripos**eremmo**	**mi sarei** riposato(a)	**ci saremmo** riposati(e)
ti ripos**eresti**	**vi** ripos**ereste**	**ti saresti** riposato(a)	**vi sareste** riposati(e)
si ripos**erebbe**	**si** ripos**erebbero**	**si sarebbe** riposato(a)	**si sarebbero** riposati(e)
congiuntivo presente		congiuntivo passato	
mi riposi	**ci** ripos**iamo**	**mi sia** riposato(a)	**ci siamo** riposati(e)
ti riposi	**vi** ripos**iate**	**ti sia** riposato(a)	**vi siate** riposati(e)
si riposi	**si** ripos**ino**	**si sia** riposato(a)	**si siano** riposati(e)
congiuntivo imperfetto		congiuntivo trapassato	
mi riposa**ssi**	**ci** riposa**ssimo**	**mi fossi** riposato(a)	**ci fossimo** riposati(e)
ti riposa**ssi**	**vi** riposa**ste**	**ti fossi** riposato(a)	**vi foste** riposati(e)
si riposa**sse**	**si** riposa**ssero**	**si fosse** riposato(a)	**si fossero** riposati(e)

R

imperativo

	riposiamoci
riposati; non riposarti/ non ti riposare	riposatevi
si riposi	si riposino

to heat, to warm up — riscaldare

gerundio **riscaldando** participio passato **riscaldato**

SINGULAR	PLURAL
indicativo presente	
riscaldo	riscaldiamo
riscaldi	riscaldate
riscalda	riscaldano
imperfetto	
riscaldavo	riscaldavamo
riscaldavi	riscaldavate
riscaldava	riscaldavano
passato remoto	
riscaldai	riscaldammo
riscaldasti	riscaldaste
riscaldò	riscaldarono
futuro semplice	
riscalderò	riscalderemo
riscalderai	riscalderete
riscalderà	riscalderanno
condizionale presente	
riscalderei	riscalderemmo
riscalderesti	riscaldereste
riscalderebbe	riscalderebbero
congiuntivo presente	
riscaldi	riscaldiamo
riscaldi	riscaldiate
riscaldi	riscaldino
congiuntivo imperfetto	
riscaldassi	riscaldassimo
riscaldassi	riscaldaste
riscaldasse	riscaldassero
imperativo	
	riscaldiamo
riscalda; non riscaldare	riscaldate
riscaldi	riscaldino

SINGULAR	PLURAL
passato prossimo	
ho riscaldato	abbiamo riscaldato
hai riscaldato	avete riscaldato
ha riscaldato	hanno riscaldato
trapassato prossimo	
avevo riscaldato	avevamo riscaldato
avevi riscaldato	avevate riscaldato
aveva riscaldato	avevano riscaldato
trapassato remoto	
ebbi riscaldato	avemmo riscaldato
avesti riscaldato	aveste riscaldato
ebbe riscaldato	ebbero riscaldato
futuro anteriore	
avrò riscaldato	avremo riscaldato
avrai riscaldato	avrete riscaldato
avrà riscaldato	avranno riscaldato
condizionale passato	
avrei riscaldato	avremmo riscaldato
avresti riscaldato	avreste riscaldato
avrebbe riscaldato	avrebbero riscaldato
congiuntivo passato	
abbia riscaldato	abbiamo riscaldato
abbia riscaldato	abbiate riscaldato
abbia riscaldato	abbiano riscaldato
congiuntivo trapassato	
avessi riscaldato	avessimo riscaldato
avessi riscaldato	aveste riscaldato
avesse riscaldato	avessero riscaldato

risolvere — to resolve, to solve

gerundio **risolvendo** participio passato **risolto**

SINGULAR	PLURAL	SINGULAR	PLURAL
indicativo presente		passato prossimo	
risolv**o**	risolv**iamo**	**ho** risolto	**abbiamo** risolto
risolv**i**	risolv**ete**	**hai** risolto	**avete** risolto
risolv**e**	risolv**ono**	**ha** risolto	**hanno** risolto
imperfetto		trapassato prossimo	
risolve**vo**	risolve**vamo**	**avevo** risolto	**avevamo** risolto
risolve**vi**	risolve**vate**	**avevi** risolto	**avevate** risolto
risolve**va**	risolve**vano**	**aveva** risolto	**avevano** risolto
passato remoto		trapassato remoto	
risols**i**	risolv**emmo**	**ebbi** risolto	**avemmo** risolto
risolv**esti**	risolv**este**	**avesti** risolto	**aveste** risolto
risols**e**	risols**ero**	**ebbe** risolto	**ebbero** risolto
futuro semplice		futuro anteriore	
risolver**ò**	risolver**emo**	**avrò** risolto	**avremo** risolto
risolver**ai**	risolver**ete**	**avrai** risolto	**avrete** risolto
risolver**à**	risolver**anno**	**avrà** risolto	**avranno** risolto
condizionale presente		condizionale passato	
risolv**erei**	risolv**eremmo**	**avrei** risolto	**avremmo** risolto
risolv**eresti**	risolv**ereste**	**avresti** risolto	**avreste** risolto
risolv**erebbe**	risolv**erebbero**	**avrebbe** risolto	**avrebbero** risolto
congiuntivo presente		congiuntivo passato	
risolv**a**	risolv**iamo**	**abbia** risolto	**abbiamo** risolto
risolv**a**	risolv**iate**	**abbia** risolto	**abbiate** risolto
risolv**a**	risolv**ano**	**abbia** risolto	**abbiano** risolto
congiuntivo imperfetto		congiuntivo trapassato	
risolv**essi**	risolv**essimo**	**avessi** risolto	**avessimo** risolto
risolv**essi**	risolv**este**	**avessi** risolto	**aveste** risolto
risolv**esse**	risolv**essero**	**avesse** risolto	**avessero** risolto

R

imperativo

SINGULAR	PLURAL
	risolviamo
risolvi; non risolvere	risolvete
risolva	risolvano

gerundio **rispettando** participio passato **rispettato**

SINGULAR	PLURAL
indicativo presente	
rispett**o**	rispett**iamo**
rispett**i**	rispett**ate**
rispett**a**	rispett**ano**
imperfetto	
rispetta**vo**	rispetta**vamo**
rispetta**vi**	rispetta**vate**
rispetta**va**	rispetta**vano**
passato remoto	
rispett**ai**	rispett**ammo**
rispett**asti**	rispett**aste**
rispett**ò**	rispett**arono**
futuro semplice	
rispetter**ò**	rispetter**emo**
rispetter**ai**	rispetter**ete**
rispetter**à**	rispetter**anno**
condizionale presente	
rispett**erei**	rispett**eremmo**
rispett**eresti**	rispett**ereste**
rispett**erebbe**	rispett**erebbero**
congiuntivo presente	
rispett**i**	rispett**iamo**
rispett**i**	rispett**iate**
rispett**i**	rispett**ino**
congiuntivo imperfetto	
rispett**assi**	rispett**assimo**
rispett**assi**	rispett**aste**
rispett**asse**	rispett**assero**
imperativo	
	rispettiamo
rispetta; non rispettare	rispettate
rispetti	rispettino

SINGULAR	PLURAL
passato prossimo	
ho rispettato	**abbiamo** rispettato
hai rispettato	**avete** rispettato
ha rispettato	**hanno** rispettato
trapassato prossimo	
avevo rispettato	**avevamo** rispettato
avevi rispettato	**avevate** rispettato
aveva rispettato	**avevano** rispettato
trapassato remoto	
ebbi rispettato	**avemmo** rispettato
avesti rispettato	**aveste** rispettato
ebbe rispettato	**ebbero** rispettato
futuro anteriore	
avrò rispettato	**avremo** rispettato
avrai rispettato	**avrete** rispettato
avrà rispettato	**avranno** rispettato
condizionale passato	
avrei rispettato	**avremmo** rispettato
avresti rispettato	**avreste** rispettato
avrebbe rispettato	**avrebbero** rispettato
congiuntivo passato	
abbia rispettato	**abbiamo** rispettato
abbia rispettato	**abbiate** rispettato
abbia rispettato	**abbiano** rispettato
congiuntivo trapassato	
avessi rispettato	**avessimo** rispettato
avessi rispettato	**aveste** rispettato
avesse rispettato	**avessero** rispettato

rispondere — to answer

gerundio **rispondendo** participio passato **risposto**

SINGULAR	PLURAL	SINGULAR	PLURAL
indicativo presente		passato prossimo	
rispond**o**	rispond**iamo**	**ho** risposto	**abbiamo** risposto
rispond**i**	rispond**ete**	**hai** risposto	**avete** risposto
rispond**e**	rispond**ono**	**ha** risposto	**hanno** risposto
imperfetto		trapassato prossimo	
risponde**vo**	risponde**vamo**	**avevo** risposto	**avevamo** risposto
risponde**vi**	risponde**vate**	**avevi** risposto	**avevate** risposto
risponde**va**	risponde**vano**	**aveva** risposto	**avevano** risposto
passato remoto		trapassato remoto	
rispos**i**	rispond**emmo**	**ebbi** risposto	**avemmo** risposto
rispond**esti**	rispond**este**	**avesti** risposto	**aveste** risposto
rispos**e**	rispos**ero**	**ebbe** risposto	**ebbero** risposto
futuro semplice		futuro anteriore	
risponder**ò**	risponder**emo**	**avrò** risposto	**avremo** risposto
risponder**ai**	risponder**ete**	**avrai** risposto	**avrete** risposto
risponder**à**	risponder**anno**	**avrà** risposto	**avranno** risposto
condizionale presente		condizionale passato	
rispond**erei**	rispond**eremmo**	**avrei** risposto	**avremmo** risposto
rispond**eresti**	rispond**ereste**	**avresti** risposto	**avreste** risposto
rispond**erebbe**	rispond**erebbero**	**avrebbe** risposto	**avrebbero** risposto
congiuntivo presente		congiuntivo passato	
rispond**a**	rispond**iamo**	**abbia** risposto	**abbiamo** risposto
rispond**a**	rispond**iate**	**abbia** risposto	**abbiate** risposto
rispond**a**	rispond**ano**	**abbia** risposto	**abbiano** risposto
congiuntivo imperfetto		congiuntivo trapassato	
rispond**essi**	rispond**essimo**	**avessi** risposto	**avessimo** risposto
rispond**essi**	rispond**este**	**avessi** risposto	**aveste** risposto
rispond**esse**	rispond**essero**	**avesse** risposto	**avessero** risposto

imperativo

	rispondiamo
rispondi; non rispondere	rispondete
risponda	rispondano

to hold, to stop, to believe **ritenere**

gerundio **ritenendo** participio passato **ritenuto**

SINGULAR	PLURAL
indicativo presente	
riteng**o**	riten**iamo**
ritien**i**	riten**ete**
ritien**e**	riteng**ono**
imperfetto	
ritene**vo**	ritene**vamo**
ritene**vi**	ritene**vate**
ritene**va**	ritene**vano**
passato remoto	
ritenn**i**	riten**emmo**
riten**esti**	riten**este**
ritenn**e**	ritenn**ero**
futuro semplice	
riterr**ò**	riterr**emo**
riterr**ai**	riterr**ete**
riterr**à**	riterr**anno**
condizionale presente	
rit**errei**	rit**erremmo**
rit**erresti**	rit**erreste**
rit**errebbe**	rit**errebbero**
congiuntivo presente	
riteng**a**	riten**iamo**
riteng**a**	riten**iate**
riteng**a**	riteng**ano**
congiuntivo imperfetto	
riten**essi**	riten**essimo**
riten**essi**	riten**este**
riten**esse**	riten**essero**
imperativo	
	riteniamo
ritieni; non ritenere	ritenete
ritenga	ritengano

SINGULAR	PLURAL
passato prossimo	
ho ritenuto	**abbiamo** ritenuto
hai ritenuto	**avete** ritenuto
ha ritenuto	**hanno** ritenuto
trapassato prossimo	
avevo ritenuto	**avevamo** ritenuto
avevi ritenuto	**avevate** ritenuto
aveva ritenuto	**avevano** ritenuto
trapassato remoto	
ebbi ritenuto	**avemmo** ritenuto
avesti ritenuto	**aveste** ritenuto
ebbe ritenuto	**ebbero** ritenuto
futuro anteriore	
avrò ritenuto	**avremo** ritenuto
avrai ritenuto	**avrete** ritenuto
avrà ritenuto	**avranno** ritenuto
condizionale passato	
avrei ritenuto	**avremmo** ritenuto
avresti ritenuto	**avreste** ritenuto
avrebbe ritenuto	**avrebbero** ritenuto
congiuntivo passato	
abbia ritenuto	**abbiamo** ritenuto
abbia ritenuto	**abbiate** ritenuto
abbia ritenuto	**abbiano** ritenuto
congiuntivo trapassato	
avessi ritenuto	**avessimo** ritenuto
avessi ritenuto	**aveste** ritenuto
avesse ritenuto	**avessero** ritenuto

ritornare

to return, to go back

gerundio **ritornando** participio passato **ritornato**

SINGULAR	PLURAL
indicativo presente	
ritorn**o**	ritorn**iamo**
ritorn**i**	ritorn**ate**
ritorn**a**	ritorn**ano**
imperfetto	
ritorna**vo**	ritorna**vamo**
ritorna**vi**	ritorna**vate**
ritorna**va**	ritorna**vano**
passato remoto	
ritorn**ai**	ritorn**ammo**
ritorn**asti**	ritorn**aste**
ritorn**ò**	ritorn**arono**
futuro semplice	
ritorner**ò**	ritorner**emo**
ritorner**ai**	ritorner**ete**
ritorner**à**	ritorner**anno**
condizionale presente	
ritorn**erei**	ritorn**eremmo**
ritorn**eresti**	ritorn**ereste**
ritorn**erebbe**	ritorn**erebbero**
congiuntivo presente	
ritorn**i**	ritorn**iamo**
ritorn**i**	ritorn**iate**
ritorn**i**	ritorn**ino**
congiuntivo imperfetto	
ritorn**assi**	ritorn**assimo**
ritorn**assi**	ritorn**aste**
ritorn**asse**	ritorn**assero**
imperativo	
	ritorniamo
ritorna; non ritornare	ritornate
ritorni	ritornino

SINGULAR	PLURAL
passato prossimo	
sono ritornato(a)	**siamo** ritornati(e)
sei ritornato(a)	**siete** ritornati(e)
è ritornato(a)	**sono** ritornati(e)
trapassato prossimo	
ero ritornato(a)	**eravamo** ritornati(e)
eri ritornato(a)	**eravate** ritornati(e)
era ritornato(a)	**erano** ritornati(e)
trapassato remoto	
fui ritornato(a)	**fummo** ritornati(e)
fosti ritornato(a)	**foste** ritornati(e)
fu ritornato(a)	**furono** ritornati(e)
futuro anteriore	
sarò ritornato(a)	**saremo** ritornati(e)
sarai ritornato(a)	**sarete** ritornati(e)
sarà ritornato(a)	**saranno** ritornati(e)
condizionale passato	
sarei ritornato(a)	**saremmo** ritornati(e)
saresti ritornato(a)	**sareste** ritornati(e)
sarebbe ritornato(a)	**sarebbero** ritornati(e)
congiuntivo passato	
sia ritornato(a)	**siamo** ritornati(e)
sia ritornato(a)	**siate** ritornati(e)
sia ritornato(a)	**siano** ritornati(e)
congiuntivo trapassato	
fossi ritornato(a)	**fossimo** ritornati(e)
fossi ritornato(a)	**foste** ritornati(e)
fosse ritornato(a)	**fossero** ritornati(e)

to withdraw, to portray **ritrarre**

gerundio **ritraendo** participio passato **ritratto**

SINGULAR	PLURAL	SINGULAR	PLURAL
indicativo presente		passato prossimo	
ritragg**o**	ritra**iamo**	**ho** ritratto	**abbiamo** ritratto
ritra**i**	ritra**ete**	**hai** ritratto	**avete** ritratto
ritra**e**	ritragg**ono**	**ha** ritratto	**hanno** ritratto
imperfetto		trapassato prossimo	
ritrae**vo**	ritrae**vamo**	**avevo** ritratto	**avevamo** ritratto
ritrae**vi**	ritrae**vate**	**avevi** ritratto	**avevate** ritratto
ritrae**va**	ritrae**vano**	**aveva** ritratto	**avevano** ritratto
passato remoto		trapassato remoto	
ritrass**i**	ritra**emmo**	**ebbi** ritratto	**avemmo** ritratto
ritra**esti**	ritra**este**	**avesti** ritratto	**aveste** ritratto
ritrass**e**	ritrass**ero**	**ebbe** ritratto	**ebbero** ritratto
futuro semplice		futuro anteriore	
ritrarr**ò**	ritrarr**emo**	**avrò** ritratto	**avremo** ritratto
ritrarr**ai**	ritrarr**ete**	**avrai** ritratto	**avrete** ritratto
ritrarr**à**	ritrarr**anno**	**avrà** ritratto	**avranno** ritratto
condizionale presente		condizionale passato	
ritrarr**ei**	ritrarr**emmo**	**avrei** ritratto	**avremmo** ritratto
ritrarr**esti**	ritrarr**este**	**avresti** ritratto	**avreste** ritratto
ritrarr**ebbe**	ritrarr**ebbero**	**avrebbe** ritratto	**avrebbero** ritratto
congiuntivo presente		congiuntivo passato	
ritragg**a**	ritra**iamo**	**abbia** ritratto	**abbiamo** ritratto
ritragg**a**	ritra**iate**	**abbia** ritratto	**abbiate** ritratto
ritragg**a**	ritragg**ano**	**abbia** ritratto	**abbiano** ritratto
congiuntivo imperfetto		congiuntivo trapassato	
ritra**essi**	ritra**essimo**	**avessi** ritratto	**avessimo** ritratto
ritra**essi**	ritra**este**	**avessi** ritratto	**aveste** ritratto
ritra**esse**	ritra**essero**	**avesse** ritratto	**avessero** ritratto
imperativo			
	ritraiamo		
ritrai; non ritrarre	ritraete		
ritragga	ritraggano		

R

riunire — to reunite

gerundio **riunendo** — participio passato **riunito**

SINGULAR	PLURAL	SINGULAR	PLURAL
indicativo presente		passato prossimo	
riun**isco**	riun**iamo**	**ho** riunito	**abbiamo** riunito
riun**isci**	riun**ite**	**hai** riunito	**avete** riunito
riun**isce**	riun**iscono**	**ha** riunito	**hanno** riunito
imperfetto		trapassato prossimo	
riuni**vo**	riuni**vamo**	**avevo** riunito	**avevamo** riunito
riuni**vi**	riuni**vate**	**avevi** riunito	**avevate** riunito
riuni**va**	riuni**vano**	**aveva** riunito	**avevano** riunito
passato remoto		trapassato remoto	
riun**ii**	riun**immo**	**ebbi** riunito	**avemmo** riunito
riun**isti**	riun**iste**	**avesti** riunito	**aveste** riunito
riun**ì**	riun**irono**	**ebbe** riunito	**ebbero** riunito
futuro semplice		futuro anteriore	
riunir**ò**	riunir**emo**	**avrò** riunito	**avremo** riunito
riunir**ai**	riunir**ete**	**avrai** riunito	**avrete** riunito
riunir**à**	riunir**anno**	**avrà** riunito	**avranno** riunito
condizionale presente		condizionale passato	
riun**irei**	riun**iremmo**	**avrei** riunito	**avremmo** riunito
riun**iresti**	riun**ireste**	**avresti** riunito	**avreste** riunito
riun**irebbe**	riun**irebbero**	**avrebbe** riunito	**avrebbero** riunito
congiuntivo presente		congiuntivo passato	
riun**isca**	riun**iamo**	**abbia** riunito	**abbiamo** riunito
riun**isca**	riun**iate**	**abbia** riunito	**abbiate** riunito
riun**isca**	riun**iscano**	**abbia** riunito	**abbiano** riunito
congiuntivo imperfetto		congiuntivo trapassato	
riun**issi**	riun**issimo**	**avessi** riunito	**avessimo** riunito
riun**issi**	riun**iste**	**avessi** riunito	**aveste** riunito
riun**isse**	riun**issero**	**avesse** riunito	**avessero** riunito

R

imperativo

	riuniamo
riunisci; non riunire	riunite
riunisca	riuniscano

gerundio **riuscendo** participio passato **riuscito**

SINGULAR	PLURAL
indicativo presente	
riesc**o**	riusc**iamo**
riesc**i**	riusc**ite**
riesc**e**	riesc**ono**
imperfetto	
riusci**vo**	riusci**vamo**
riusci**vi**	riusci**vate**
riusci**va**	riusci**vano**
passato remoto	
riusc**ii**	riusc**immo**
riusc**isti**	riusc**iste**
riusc**ì**	riusc**irono**
futuro semplice	
riuscir**ò**	riuscir**emo**
riuscir**ai**	riuscir**ete**
riuscir**à**	riuscir**anno**
condizionale presente	
riusc**irei**	riusc**iremmo**
riusc**iresti**	riusc**ireste**
riusc**irebbe**	riusc**irebbero**
congiuntivo presente	
riesc**a**	riusc**iamo**
riesc**a**	riusc**iate**
riesc**a**	riesc**ano**
congiuntivo imperfetto	
riusc**issi**	riusc**issimo**
riusc**issi**	riusc**iste**
riusc**isse**	riusc**issero**
imperativo	
	riusciamo
riesci; non riuscire	riuscite
riesca	riescano

SINGULAR	PLURAL
passato prossimo	
sono riuscito(a)	**siamo** riusciti(e)
sei riuscito(a)	**siete** riusciti(e)
è riuscito(a)	**sono** riusciti(e)
trapassato prossimo	
ero riuscito(a)	**eravamo** riusciti(e)
eri riuscito(a)	**eravate** riusciti(e)
era riuscito(a)	**erano** riusciti(e)
trapassato remoto	
fui riuscito(a)	**fummo** riusciti(e)
fosti riuscito(a)	**foste** riusciti(e)
fu riuscito(a)	**furono** riusciti(e)
futuro anteriore	
sarò riuscito(a)	**saremo** riusciti(e)
sarai riuscito(a)	**sarete** riusciti(e)
sarà riuscito(a)	**saranno** riusciti(e)
condizionale passato	
sarei riuscito(a)	**saremmo** riusciti(e)
saresti riuscito(a)	**sareste** riusciti(e)
sarebbe riuscito(a)	**sarebbero** riusciti(e)
congiuntivo passato	
sia riuscito(a)	**siamo** riusciti(e)
sia riuscito(a)	**siate** riusciti(e)
sia riuscito(a)	**siano** riusciti(e)
congiuntivo trapassato	
fossi riuscito(a)	**fossimo** riusciti(e)
fossi riuscito(a)	**foste** riusciti(e)
fosse riuscito(a)	**fossero** riusciti(e)

rivolgersi — to turn to, to turn around

gerundio **rivolgendosi** participio passato **rivoltosi**

SINGULAR	PLURAL
indicativo presente	
mi rivolg**o**	**ci** rivolg**iamo**
ti rivolg**i**	**vi** rivolg**ete**
si rivolg**e**	**si** rivolg**ono**
imperfetto	
mi rivolge**vo**	**ci** rivolge**vamo**
ti rivolge**vi**	**vi** rivolge**vate**
si rivolge**va**	**si** rivolge**vano**
passato remoto	
mi rivols**i**	**ci** rivolg**emmo**
ti rivolg**esti**	**vi** rivolg**este**
si rivols**e**	**si** rivols**ero**
futuro semplice	
mi rivolger**ò**	**ci** rivolger**emo**
ti rivolger**ai**	**vi** rivolger**ete**
si rivolger**à**	**si** rivolger**anno**
condizionale presente	
mi rivolg**erei**	**ci** rivolg**eremmo**
ti rivolg**eresti**	**vi** rivolg**ereste**
si rivolg**erebbe**	**si** rivolg**erebbero**
congiuntivo presente	
mi rivolg**a**	**ci** rivolg**iamo**
ti rivolg**a**	**vi** rivolg**iate**
si rivolg**a**	**si** rivolg**ano**
congiuntivo imperfetto	
mi rivolg**essi**	**ci** rivolg**essimo**
ti rivolg**essi**	**vi** rivolg**este**
si rivolg**esse**	**si** rivolg**essero**
imperativo	
	rivolgiamoci
rivolgiti; non rivolgerti/ non ti rivolgere	rivolgetevi
si rivolga	si rivolgano

SINGULAR	PLURAL
passato prossimo	
mi sono rivolto(a)	**ci siamo** rivolti(e)
ti sei rivolto(a)	**vi siete** rivolti(e)
si è rivolto(a)	**si sono** rivolti(e)
trapassato prossimo	
mi ero rivolto(a)	**ci eravamo** rivolti(e)
ti eri rivolto(a)	**vi eravate** rivolti(e)
si era rivolto(a)	**si erano** rivolti(e)
trapassato remoto	
mi fui rivolto(a)	**ci fummo** rivolti(e)
ti fosti rivolto(a)	**vi foste** rivolti(e)
si fu rivolto(a)	**si furono** rivolti(e)
futuro anteriore	
mi sarò rivolto(a)	**ci saremo** rivolti(e)
ti sarai rivolto(a)	**vi sarete** rivolti(e)
si sarà rivolto(a)	**si saranno** rivolti(e)
condizionale passato	
mi sarei rivolto(a)	**ci saremmo** rivolti(e)
ti saresti rivolto(a)	**vi sareste** rivolti(e)
si sarebbe rivolto(a)	**si sarebbero** rivolti(e)
congiuntivo passato	
mi sia rivolto(a)	**ci siamo** rivolti(e)
ti sia rivolto(a)	**vi siate** rivolti(e)
si sia rivolto(a)	**si siano** rivolti(e)
congiuntivo trapassato	
mi fossi rivolto(a)	**ci fossimo** rivolti(e)
ti fossi rivolto(a)	**vi foste** rivolti(e)
si fosse rivolto(a)	**si fossero** rivolti(e)

to turn inside out, to upset **rivoltare**

gerundio **rivoltando** participio passato **rivoltato**

SINGULAR	PLURAL	SINGULAR	PLURAL
indicativo presente		passato prossimo	
rivolt**o**	rivolt**iamo**	**ho** rivoltato	**abbiamo** rivoltato
rivolt**i**	rivolt**ate**	**hai** rivoltato	**avete** rivoltato
rivolt**a**	rivolt**ano**	**ha** rivoltato	**hanno** rivoltato
imperfetto		trapassato prossimo	
rivolta**vo**	rivolta**vamo**	**avevo** rivoltato	**avevamo** rivoltato
rivolta**vi**	rivolta**vate**	**avevi** rivoltato	**avevate** rivoltato
rivolta**va**	rivolta**vano**	**aveva** rivoltato	**avevano** rivoltato
passato remoto		trapassato remoto	
rivolt**ai**	rivolt**ammo**	**ebbi** rivoltato	**avemmo** rivoltato
rivolt**asti**	rivolt**aste**	**avesti** rivoltato	**aveste** rivoltato
rivolt**ò**	rivolt**arono**	**ebbe** rivoltato	**ebbero** rivoltato
futuro semplice		futuro anteriore	
rivolter**ò**	rivolter**emo**	**avrò** rivoltato	**avremo** rivoltato
rivolter**ai**	rivolter**ete**	**avrai** rivoltato	**avrete** rivoltato
rivolter**à**	rivolter**anno**	**avrà** rivoltato	**avranno** rivoltato
condizionale presente		condizionale passato	
rivolt**erei**	rivolt**eremmo**	**avrei** rivoltato	**avremmo** rivoltato
rivolt**eresti**	rivolt**ereste**	**avresti** rivoltato	**avreste** rivoltato
rivolt**erebbe**	rivolt**erebbero**	**avrebbe** rivoltato	**avrebbero** rivoltato
congiuntivo presente		congiuntivo passato	
rivolt**i**	rivolt**iamo**	**abbia** rivoltato	**abbiamo** rivoltato
rivolt**i**	rivolt**iate**	**abbia** rivoltato	**abbiate** rivoltato
rivolt**i**	rivolt**ino**	**abbia** rivoltato	**abbiano** rivoltato
congiuntivo imperfetto		congiuntivo trapassato	
rivolt**assi**	rivolt**assimo**	**avessi** rivoltato	**avessimo** rivoltato
rivolt**assi**	rivolt**aste**	**avessi** rivoltato	**aveste** rivoltato
rivolt**asse**	rivolt**assero**	**avesse** rivoltato	**avessero** rivoltato
imperativo			
	rivoltiamo		
rivolta; non rivoltare	rivoltate		
rivolti	rivoltino		

rodere — to gnaw

gerundio **rodendo**   participio passato **roso**

SINGULAR	PLURAL
indicativo presente	
rod**o**	rod**iamo**
rod**i**	rod**ete**
rod**e**	rod**ono**
imperfetto	
rode**vo**	rode**vamo**
rode**vi**	rode**vate**
rode**va**	rode**vano**
passato remoto	
ros**i**	rod**emmo**
rod**esti**	rod**este**
ros**e**	ros**ero**
futuro semplice	
roder**ò**	roder**emo**
roder**ai**	roder**ete**
roder**à**	roder**anno**
condizionale presente	
rod**erei**	rod**eremmo**
rod**eresti**	rod**ereste**
rod**erebbe**	rod**erebbero**
congiuntivo presente	
rod**a**	rod**iamo**
rod**a**	rod**iate**
rod**a**	rod**ano**
congiuntivo imperfetto	
rod**essi**	rod**essimo**
rod**essi**	rod**este**
rod**esse**	rod**essero**
imperativo	
	rodiamo
rodi; non rodere	rodete
roda	rodano

SINGULAR	PLURAL
passato prossimo	
ho roso	**abbiamo** roso
hai roso	**avete** roso
ha roso	**hanno** roso
trapassato prossimo	
avevo roso	**avevamo** roso
averi roso	**avevate** roso
aveva roso	**avevano** roso
trapassato remoto	
ebbi roso	**avemmo** roso
avesti roso	**aveste** roso
ebbe roso	**ebbero** roso
futuro anteriore	
avrò roso	**avremo** roso
avrai roso	**avrete** roso
avrà roso	**avranno** roso
condizionale passato	
avrei roso	**avremmo** roso
avresti roso	**avreste** roso
avrebbe roso	**avrebbero** roso
congiuntivo passato	
abbia roso	**abbiamo** roso
abbia roso	**abbiate** roso
abbia roso	**abbiano** roso
congiuntivo trapassato	
avessi roso	**avessimo** roso
avessi roso	**aveste** roso
avesse roso	**avessero** roso

to break — rompere

gerundio **rompendo** participio passato **rotto**

SINGULAR	PLURAL	SINGULAR	PLURAL
indicativo presente		passato prossimo	
romp**o**	romp**iamo**	**ho** rotto	**abbiamo** rotto
romp**i**	romp**ete**	**hai** rotto	**avete** rotto
romp**e**	romp**ono**	**ha** rotto	**hanno** rotto
imperfetto		trapassato prossimo	
rompe**vo**	rompe**vamo**	**avevo** rotto	**avevamo** rotto
rompe**vi**	rompe**vate**	**avevi** rotto	**avevate** rotto
rompe**va**	rompe**vano**	**aveva** rotto	**avevano** rotto
passato remoto		trapassato remoto	
rupp**i**	romp**emmo**	**ebbi** rotto	**avemmo** rotto
romp**esti**	romp**este**	**avesti** rotto	**aveste** rotto
rupp**e**	rupp**ero**	**ebbe** rotto	**ebbero** rotto
futuro semplice		futuro anteriore	
romper**ò**	romper**emo**	**avrò** rotto	**avremo** rotto
romper**ai**	romper**ete**	**avrai** rotto	**avrete** rotto
romper**à**	romper**anno**	**avrà** rotto	**avranno** rotto
condizionale presente		condizionale passato	
romp**erei**	romp**eremmo**	**avrei** rotto	**avremmo** rotto
romp**eresti**	romp**ereste**	**avresti** rotto	**avreste** rotto
romp**erebbe**	romp**erebbero**	**avrebbe** rotto	**avrebbero** rotto
congiuntivo presente		congiuntivo passato	
romp**a**	romp**iamo**	**abbia** rotto	**abbiamo** rotto
romp**a**	romp**iate**	**abbia** rotto	**abbiate** rotto
romp**a**	romp**ano**	**abbia** rotto	**abbiano** rotto
congiuntivo imperfetto		congiuntivo trapassato	
romp**essi**	romp**essimo**	**avessi** rotto	**avessimo** rotto
romp**essi**	romp**este**	**avessi** rotto	**aveste** rotto
romp**esse**	romp**essero**	**avesse** rotto	**avessero** rotto
imperativo			
	rompiamo		
rompi; non rompere	rompete		
rompa	rompano		

rubare — to steal

gerundio **rubando** participio passato **rubato**

SINGULAR	PLURAL	SINGULAR	PLURAL
indicativo presente		passato prossimo	
rub**o**	rub**iamo**	**ho** rubato	**abbiamo** rubato
rub**i**	rub**ate**	**hai** rubato	**avete** rubato
rub**a**	rub**ano**	**ha** rubato	**hanno** rubato
imperfetto		trapassato prossimo	
ruba**vo**	ruba**vamo**	**avevo** rubato	**avevamo** rubato
ruba**vi**	ruba**vate**	**avevi** rubato	**avevate** rubato
ruba**va**	ruba**vano**	**aveva** rubato	**avevano** rubato
passato remoto		trapassato remoto	
rub**ai**	rub**ammo**	**ebbi** rubato	**avemmo** rubato
rub**asti**	rub**aste**	**avesti** rubato	**aveste** rubato
rub**ò**	rub**arono**	**ebbe** rubato	**ebbero** rubato
futuro semplice		futuro anteriore	
ruber**ò**	ruber**emo**	**avrò** rubato	**avremo** rubato
ruber**ai**	ruber**ete**	**avrai** rubato	**avrete** rubato
ruber**à**	ruber**anno**	**avrà** rubato	**avranno** rubato
condizionale presente		condizionale passato	
rub**erei**	rub**eremmo**	**avrei** rubato	**avremmo** rubato
rub**eresti**	rub**ereste**	**avresti** rubato	**avreste** rubato
rub**erebbe**	rub**erebbero**	**avrebbe** rubato	**avrebbero** rubato
congiuntivo presente		congiuntivo passato	
rub**i**	rub**iamo**	**abbia** rubato	**abbiamo** rubato
rub**i**	rub**iate**	**abbia** rubato	**abbiate** rubato
rub**i**	rub**ino**	**abbia** rubato	**abbiano** rubato
congiuntivo imperfetto		congiuntivo trapassato	
rub**assi**	rub**assimo**	**avessi** rubato	**avessimo** rubato
rub**assi**	rub**aste**	**avessi** rubato	**aveste** rubato
rub**asse**	rub**assero**	**avesse** rubato	**avessero** rubato

imperativo

	rubiamo
ruba; non rubare	rubate
rubi	rubino

gerundio **salendo** participio passato **salito**

SINGULAR	PLURAL	SINGULAR	PLURAL
indicativo presente		passato prossimo	
salg**o**	sal**iamo**	**sono** salito(a)	**siamo** saliti(e)
sal**i**	sal**ite**	**sei** salito(a)	**siete** saliti(e)
sal**e**	salg**ono**	**è** salito(a)	**sono** saliti(e)
imperfetto		trapassato prossimo	
sali**vo**	sali**vamo**	**ero** salito(a)	**eravamo** saliti(e)
sali**vi**	sali**vate**	**eri** salito(a)	**eravate** saliti(e)
sali**va**	sali**vano**	**era** salito(a)	**erano** saliti(e)
passato remoto		trapassato remoto	
sal**ii**	sal**immo**	**fui** salito(a)	**fummo** saliti(e)
sal**isti**	sal**iste**	**fosti** salito(a)	**foste** saliti(e)
sal**ì**	sal**irono**	**fu** salito(a)	**furono** saliti(e)
futuro semplice		futuro anteriore	
salir**ò**	salir**emo**	**sarò** salito(a)	**saremo** saliti(e)
salir**ai**	salir**ete**	**sarai** salito(a)	**sarete** saliti(e)
salir**à**	salir**anno**	**sarà** salito(a)	**saranno** saliti(e)
condizionale presente		condizionale passato	
sal**irei**	sal**iremmo**	**sarei** salito(a)	**saremmo** saliti(e)
sal**iresti**	sal**ireste**	**saresti** salito(a)	**sareste** saliti(e)
sal**irebbe**	sal**irebbero**	**sarebbe** salito(a)	**sarebbero** saliti(e)
congiuntivo presente		congiuntivo passato	
salg**a**	sal**iamo**	**sia** salito(a)	**siamo** saliti(e)
salg**a**	sal**iate**	**sia** salito(a)	**siate** saliti(e)
salg**a**	salg**ano**	**sia** salito(a)	**siano** saliti(e)
congiuntivo imperfetto		congiuntivo trapassato	
sal**issi**	sal**issimo**	**fossi** salito(a)	**fossimo** saliti(e)
sal**issi**	sal**iste**	**fossi** salito(a)	**foste** saliti(e)
sal**isse**	sal**issero**	**fosse** salito(a)	**fossero** saliti(e)
imperativo			
	saliamo		
sali; non salire	salite		
salga	salgano		

saltare — to jump

gerundio **saltando** participio passato **saltato**

SINGULAR	PLURAL	SINGULAR	PLURAL
indicativo presente		passato prossimo	
salt**o**	salt**iamo**	**ho** saltato	**abbiamo** saltato
salt**i**	salt**ate**	**hai** saltato	**avete** saltato
salt**a**	salt**ano**	**ha** saltato	**hanno** saltato
imperfetto		trapassato prossimo	
salta**vo**	salta**vamo**	**avevo** saltato	**avevamo** saltato
salta**vi**	salta**vate**	**avevi** saltato	**avevate** saltato
salta**va**	salta**vano**	**aveva** saltato	**avevano** saltato
passato remoto		trapassato remoto	
salt**ai**	salt**ammo**	**ebbi** saltato	**avemmo** saltato
salt**asti**	salt**aste**	**avesti** saltato	**aveste** saltato
salt**ò**	salt**arono**	**ebbe** saltato	**ebbero** saltato
futuro semplice		futuro anteriore	
salter**ò**	salter**emo**	**avrò** saltato	**avremo** saltato
salter**ai**	salter**ete**	**avrai** saltato	**avrete** saltato
salter**à**	salter**anno**	**avrà** saltato	**avranno** saltato
condizionale presente		condizionale passato	
salt**erei**	salt**eremmo**	**avrei** saltato	**avremmo** saltato
salt**eresti**	salt**ereste**	**avresti** saltato	**avreste** saltato
salt**erebbe**	salt**erebbero**	**avrebbe** saltato	**avrebbero** saltato
congiuntivo presente		congiuntivo passato	
salt**i**	salt**iamo**	**abbia** saltato	**abbiamo** saltato
salt**i**	salt**iate**	**abbia** saltato	**abbiate** saltato
salt**i**	salt**ino**	**abbia** saltato	**abbiano** saltato
congiuntivo imperfetto		congiuntivo trapassato	
salt**assi**	salt**assimo**	**avessi** saltato	**avessimo** saltato
salt**assi**	salt**aste**	**avessi** saltato	**aveste** saltato
salt**asse**	salt**assero**	**avesse** saltato	**avessero** saltato
imperativo			
	saltiamo		
salta; non saltare	saltate		
salti	saltino		

to greet **salutare**

gerundio **salutando** participio passato **salutato**

indicativo presente

SINGULAR	PLURAL
salut**o**	salut**iamo**
salut**i**	salut**ate**
salut**a**	salut**ano**

imperfetto

SINGULAR	PLURAL
saluta**vo**	saluta**vamo**
saluta**vi**	saluta**vate**
saluta**va**	saluta**vano**

passato remoto

SINGULAR	PLURAL
salut**ai**	salut**ammo**
salut**asti**	salut**aste**
salut**ò**	salut**arono**

futuro semplice

SINGULAR	PLURAL
saluter**ò**	saluter**emo**
saluter**ai**	saluter**ete**
saluter**à**	saluter**anno**

condizionale presente

SINGULAR	PLURAL
salut**erei**	salut**eremmo**
salut**eresti**	salut**ereste**
salut**erebbe**	salut**erebbero**

congiuntivo presente

SINGULAR	PLURAL
salut**i**	salut**iamo**
salut**i**	salut**iate**
salut**i**	salut**ino**

congiuntivo imperfetto

SINGULAR	PLURAL
salut**assi**	salut**assimo**
salut**assi**	salut**aste**
salut**asse**	salut**assero**

imperativo

SINGULAR	PLURAL
	salutiamo
saluta; non salutare	salutate
saluti	salutino

passato prossimo

SINGULAR	PLURAL
ho salutato	**abbiamo** salutato
hai salutato	**avete** salutato
ha salutato	**hanno** salutato

trapassato prossimo

SINGULAR	PLURAL
avevo salutato	**avevamo** salutato
avevi salutato	**avevate** salutato
aveva salutato	**avevano** salutato

trapassato remoto

SINGULAR	PLURAL
ebbi salutato	**avemmo** salutato
avesti salutato	**aveste** salutato
ebbe salutato	**ebbero** salutato

futuro anteriore

SINGULAR	PLURAL
avrò salutato	**avremo** salutato
avrai salutato	**avrete** salutato
avrà salutato	**avranno** salutato

condizionale passato

SINGULAR	PLURAL
avrei salutato	**avremmo** salutato
avresti salutato	**avreste** salutato
avrebbe salutato	**avrebbero** salutato

congiuntivo passato

SINGULAR	PLURAL
abbia salutato	**abbiamo** salutato
abbia salutato	**abbiate** salutato
abbia salut	**abbiano** salutato

congiuntivo trapassato

SINGULAR	PLURAL
avessi salutato	**avessimo** salutato
avessi salutato	**aveste** salutato
avesse salutato	**avessero** salutato

MUST KNOW VERB

salvare — to save

gerundio **salvando** participio passato **salvato**

SINGULAR	PLURAL	SINGULAR	PLURAL
indicativo presente		passato prossimo	
salv**o**	salv**iamo**	**ho** salvato	**abbiamo** salvato
salv**i**	salv**ate**	**hai** salvato	**avete** salvato
salv**a**	salv**ano**	**ha** salvato	**hanno** salvato
imperfetto		trapassato prossimo	
salva**vo**	salva**vamo**	**avevo** salvato	**avevamo** salvato
salva**vi**	salva**vate**	**avevi** salvato	**avevate** salvato
salva**va**	salva**vano**	**aveva** salvato	**avevano** salvato
passato remoto		trapassato remoto	
salv**ai**	salv**ammo**	**ebbi** salvato	**avemmo** salvato
salv**asti**	salv**aste**	**avesti** salvato	**aveste** salvato
salv**ò**	salv**arono**	**ebbe** salvato	**ebbero** salvato
futuro semplice		futuro anteriore	
salver**ò**	salver**emo**	**avrò** salvato	**avremo** salvato
salver**ai**	salver**ete**	**avrai** salvato	**avrete** salvato
salver**à**	salver**anno**	**avrà** salvato	**avranno** salvato
condizionale presente		condizionale passato	
salv**erei**	salv**eremmo**	**avrei** salvato	**avremmo** salvato
salv**eresti**	salv**ereste**	**avresti** salvato	**avreste** salvato
salv**erebbe**	salv**erebbero**	**avrebbe** salvato	**avrebbero** salvato
congiuntivo presente		congiuntivo passato	
salv**i**	salv**iamo**	**abbia** salvato	**abbiamo** salvato
salv**i**	salv**iate**	**abbia** salvato	**abbiate** salvato
salv**i**	salv**ino**	**abbia** salvato	**abbiano** salvato
congiuntivo imperfetto		congiuntivo trapassato	
salv**assi**	salv**assimo**	**avessi** salvato	**avessimo** salvato
salv**assi**	salv**aste**	**avessi** salvato	**aveste** salvato
salv**asse**	salv**assero**	**avesse** salvato	**avessero** salvato

imperativo

	salviamo
salva; non salvare	salvate
salvi	salvino

to know, to learn, to be able to **sapere**

gerundio **sapendo** participio passato **saputo**

SINGULAR	PLURAL	SINGULAR	PLURAL
indicativo presente		passato prossimo	
so	sap**piamo**	**ho** saputo	**abbiamo** saputo
sai	sap**ete**	**hai** saputo	**avete** saputo
sa	san**no**	**ha** saputo	**hanno** saputo
imperfetto		trapassato prossimo	
sape**vo**	sape**vamo**	**avevo** saputo	**avevamo** saputo
sape**vi**	sape**vate**	**avevi** saputo	**avevate** saputo
sape**va**	sape**vano**	**aveva** saputo	**avevano** saputo
passato remoto		trapassato remoto	
seppi	sap**emmo**	**ebbi** saputo	**avemmo** saputo
sap**esti**	sap**este**	**avesti** saputo	**aveste** saputo
seppe	sep**pero**	**ebbe** saputo	**ebbero** saputo
futuro semplice		futuro anteriore	
sap**rò**	sap**remo**	**avrò** saputo	**avremo** saputo
sap**rai**	sap**rete**	**avrai** saputo	**avrete** saputo
sap**rà**	sap**ranno**	**avrà** saputo	**avranno** saputo
condizionale presente		condizionale passato	
sap**rei**	sap**remmo**	**avrei** saputo	**avremmo** saputo
sap**resti**	sap**reste**	**avresti** saputo	**avreste** saputo
sap**rebbe**	sap**rebbero**	**avrebbe** saputo	**avrebbero** saputo
congiuntivo presente		congiuntivo passato	
sap**pia**	sap**piamo**	**abbia** saputo	**abbiamo** saputo
sap**pia**	sap**piate**	**abbia** saputo	**abbiate** saputo
sap**pia**	sap**piano**	**abbia** saputo	**abbiano** saputo
congiuntivo imperfetto		congiuntivo trapassato	
sap**essi**	sap**essimo**	**avessi** saputo	**avessimo** saputo
sap**essi**	sap**este**	**avessi** saputo	**aveste** saputo
sap**esse**	sap**essero**	**avesse** saputo	**avessero** saputo
imperativo			
	sappiamo		
sappi; non sapere	sappiate		
sappia	sappiano		

sbagliare — to make a mistake, to be wrong

gerundio **sbagliando** participio passato **sbagliato**

SINGULAR	PLURAL	SINGULAR	PLURAL
indicativo presente		passato prossimo	
sbagli**o**	sbagli**amo**	**ho** sbagliato	**abbiamo** sbagliato
sbagli	sbagli**ate**	**hai** sbagliato	**avete** sbagliato
sbagli**a**	sbagli**ano**	**ha** sbagliato	**hanno** sbagliato
imperfetto		trapassato prossimo	
sbaglia**vo**	sbaglia**vamo**	**avevo** sbagliato	**avevamo** sbagliato
sbaglia**vi**	sbaglia**vate**	**avevi** sbagliato	**avevate** sbagliato
sbaglia**va**	sbaglia**vano**	**aveva** sbagliato	**avevano** sbagliato
passato remoto		trapassato remoto	
sbagli**ai**	sbagli**ammo**	**ebbi** sbagliato	**avemmo** sbagliato
sbagli**asti**	sbagli**aste**	**avesti** sbagliato	**aveste** sbagliato
sbagli**ò**	sbagli**arono**	**ebbe** sbagliato	**ebbero** sbagliato
futuro semplice		futuro anteriore	
sbaglier**ò**	sbaglier**emo**	**avrò** sbagliato	**avremo** sbagliato
sbaglier**ai**	sbaglier**ete**	**avrai** sbagliato	**avrete** sbagliato
sbaglier**à**	sbaglier**anno**	**avrà** sbagliato	**avranno** sbagliato
condizionale presente		condizionale passato	
sbagli**erei**	sbagli**eremmo**	**avrei** sbagliato	**avremmo** sbagliato
sbagli**eresti**	sbagli**ereste**	**avresti** sbagliato	**avreste** sbagliato
sbagli**erebbe**	sbagli**erebbero**	**avrebbe** sbagliato	**avrebbero** sbagliato
congiuntivo presente		congiuntivo passato	
sbagl**i**	sbagli**amo**	**abbia** sbagliato	**abbiamo** sbagliato
sbagl**i**	sbagli**ate**	**abbia** sbagliato	**abbiate** sbagliato
sbagl**i**	sbagl**ino**	**abbia** sbagliato	**abbiano** sbagliato
congiuntivo imperfetto		congiuntivo trapassato	
sbagli**assi**	sbagli**assimo**	**avessi** sbagliato	**avessimo** sbagliato
sbagli**assi**	sbagli**aste**	**avessi** sbagliato	**aveste** sbagliato
sbagli**asse**	sbagli**assero**	**avesse** sbagliato	**avessero** sbagliato

imperativo

	sbagliamo
sbaglia; non sbagliare	sbagliate
sbagli	sbaglino

to make a mistake, to be wrong **sbagliarsi**

gerundio **sbagliandosi** participio passato **sbagliatosi**

SINGULAR	PLURAL	SINGULAR	PLURAL
indicativo presente		passato prossimo	
mi sbagli**o**	**ci** sbagli**amo**	**mi sono** sbagliato(a)	**ci siamo** sbagliati(e)
ti sbagli	**vi** sbagli**ate**	**ti sei** sbagliato(a)	**vi siete** sbagliati(e)
si sbagli**a**	**si** sbagli**ano**	**si è** sbagliato(a)	**si sono** sbagliati(e)
imperfetto		trapassato prossimo	
mi sbaglia**vo**	**ci** sbaglia**vamo**	**mi ero** sbagliato(a)	**ci eravamo** sbagliati(e)
ti sbaglia**vi**	**vi** sbaglia**vate**	**ti eri** sbagliato(a)	**vi eravate** sbagliati(e)
si sbaglia**va**	**si** sbaglia**vano**	**si era** sbagliato(a)	**si erano** sbagliati(e)
passato remoto		trapassato remoto	
mi sbagli**ai**	**ci** sbagli**ammo**	**mi fui** sbagliato(a)	**ci fummo** sbagliati(e)
ti sbagli**asti**	**vi** sbagli**aste**	**ti fosti** sbagliato(a)	**vi foste** sbagliati(e)
si sbagli**ò**	**si** sbagli**arono**	**si fu** sbagliato(a)	**si furono** sbagliati(e)
futuro semplice		futuro anteriore	
mi sbaglier**ò**	**ci** sbaglier**emo**	**mi sarò** sbagliato(a)	**ci saremo** sbagliati(e)
ti sbaglier**ai**	**vi** sbaglier**ete**	**ti sarai** sbagliato(a)	**vi sarete** sbagliati(e)
si sbaglier**à**	**si** sbaglier**anno**	**si sarà** sbagliato(a)	**si saranno** sbagliati(e)
condizionale presente		condizionale passato	
mi sbagli**erei**	**ci** sbagli**eremmo**	**mi sarei** sbagliato(a)	**ci saremmo** sbagliati(e)
ti sbagli**eresti**	**vi** sbagli**ereste**	**ti saresti** sbagliato(a)	**vi sareste** sbagliati(e)
si sbagli**erebbe**	**si** sbagli**erebbero**	**si sarebbe** sbagliato(a)	**si sarebbero** sbagliati(e)
congiuntivo presente		congiuntivo passato	
mi sbagli	**ci** sbagli**amo**	**mi sia** sbagliato(a)	**ci siamo** sbagliati(e)
ti sbagli	**vi** sbagli**ate**	**ti sia** sbagliato(a)	**vi siate** sbagliati(e)
si sbagli	**si** sbagli**no**	**si sia** sbagliato(a)	**si siano** sbagliati(e)
congiuntivo imperfetto		congiuntivo trapassato	
mi sbagli**assi**	**ci** sbagli**assimo**	**mi fossi** sbagliato(a)	**ci fossimo** sbagliati(e)
ti sbagli**assi**	**vi** sbagli**aste**	**ti fossi** sbagliato(a)	**vi foste** sbagliati(e)
si sbagli**asse**	**si** sbagli**assero**	**si fosse** sbagliato(a)	**si fossero** sbagliati(e)

imperativo

	sbagliamoci
sbagliati; non sbagliarti/non ti sbagliare	sbagliatevi
si sbagli	si sbaglino

sbarcare — to land, to disembark

gerundio **sbarcando** participio passato **sbarcato**

SINGULAR	PLURAL	SINGULAR	PLURAL
indicativo presente		passato prossimo	
sbarc**o**	sbarch**iamo**	**sono** sbarcato(a)	**siamo** sbarcati(e)
sbarch**i**	sbarc**ate**	**sei** sbarcato(a)	**siete** sbarcati(e)
sbarc**a**	sbarc**ano**	**è** sbarcato(a)	**sono** sbarcati(e)
imperfetto		trapassato prossimo	
sbarca**vo**	sbarca**vamo**	**ero** sbarcato(a)	**eravamo** sbarcati(e)
sbarca**vi**	sbarca**vate**	**eri** sbarcato(a)	**eravate** sbarcati(e)
sbarca**va**	sbarca**vano**	**era** sbarcato(a)	**erano** sbarcati(e)
passato remoto		trapassato remoto	
sbarc**ai**	sbarc**ammo**	**fui** sbarcato(a)	**fummo** sbarcati(e)
sbarc**asti**	sbarc**aste**	**fosti** sbarcato(a)	**foste** sbarcati(e)
sbarc**ò**	sbarc**arono**	**fu** sbarcato(a)	**furono** sbarcati(e)
futuro semplice		futuro anteriore	
sbarcher**ò**	sbarcher**emo**	**sarò** sbarcato(a)	**saremo** sbarcati(e)
sbarcher**ai**	sbarcher**ete**	**sarai** sbarcato(a)	**sarete** sbarcati(e)
sbarcher**à**	sbarcher**anno**	**sarà** sbarcato(a)	**saranno** sbarcati(e)
condizionale presente		condizionale passato	
sbarch**erei**	sbarch**eremmo**	**sarei** sbarcato(a)	**saremmo** sbarcati(e)
sbarch**eresti**	sbarch**ereste**	**saresti** sbarcato(a)	**sareste** sbarcati(e)
sbarch**erebbe**	sbarch**erebbero**	**sarebbe** sbarcato(a)	**sarebbero** sbarcati(e)
congiuntivo presente		congiuntivo passato	
sbarch**i**	sbarch**iamo**	**sia** sbarcato(a)	**siamo** sbarcati(e)
sbarch**i**	sbarch**iate**	**sia** sbarcato(a)	**siate** sbarcati(e)
sbarch**i**	sbarch**ino**	**sia** sbarcato(a)	**siano** sbarcati(e)
congiuntivo imperfetto		congiuntivo trapassato	
sbarc**assi**	sbarc**assimo**	**fossi** sbarcato(a)	**fossimo** sbarcati(e)
sbarc**assi**	sbarc**aste**	**fossi** sbarcato(a)	**foste** sbarcati(e)
sbarc**asse**	sbarc**assero**	**fosse** sbarcato(a)	**fossero** sbarcati(e)
imperativo			
	sbarchiamo		
sbarca; non sbarcare	sbarcate		
sbarchi	sbarchino		

gerundio **scaldando** participio passato **scaldato**

SINGULAR	PLURAL	SINGULAR	PLURAL
indicativo presente		passato prossimo	
scald**o**	scald**iamo**	**ho** scaldato	**abbiamo** scaldato
scald**i**	scald**ate**	**hai** scaldato	**avete** scaldato
scald**a**	scald**ano**	**ha** scaldato	**hanno** scaldato
imperfetto		trapassato prossimo	
scalda**vo**	scalda**vamo**	**avevo** scaldato	**avevamo** scaldato
scalda**vi**	scalda**vate**	**avevi** scaldato	**avevate** scaldato
scalda**va**	scalda**vano**	**aveva** scaldato	**avevano** scaldato
passato remoto		trapassato remoto	
scald**ai**	scald**ammo**	**ebbi** scaldato	**avemmo** scaldato
scald**asti**	scald**aste**	**avesti** scaldato	**aveste** scaldato
scald**ò**	scald**arono**	**ebbe** scaldato	**ebbero** scaldato
futuro semplice		futuro anteriore	
scalder**ò**	scalder**emo**	**avrò** scaldato	**avremo** scaldato
scalder**ai**	scalder**ete**	**avrai** scaldato	**avrete** scaldato
scalder**à**	scalder**anno**	**avrà** scaldato	**avranno** scaldato
condizionale presente		condizionale passato	
scald**erei**	scald**eremmo**	**avrei** scaldato	**avremmo** scaldato
scald**eresti**	scald**ereste**	**avresti** scaldato	**avreste** scaldato
scald**erebbe**	scald**erebbero**	**avrebbe** scaldato	**avrebbero** scaldato
congiuntivo presente		congiuntivo passato	
scald**i**	scald**iamo**	**abbia** scaldato	**abbiamo** scaldato
scald**i**	scald**iate**	**abbia** scaldato	**abbiate** scaldato
scald**i**	scald**ino**	**abbia** scaldato	**abbiano** scaldato
congiuntivo imperfetto		congiuntivo trapassato	
scald**assi**	scald**assimo**	**avessi** scaldato	**avessimo** scaldato
scald**asi**	scald**aste**	**avessi** scaldato	**aveste** scaldato
scald**asse**	scald**asero**	**avesse** scaldato	**avessero** scaldato

imperativo

SINGULAR	PLURAL
	scaldiamo
scalda; non scaldare	scaldate
scaldi	scaldino

scambiare — to exchange

gerundio **scambiando** participio passato **scambiato**

SINGULAR	PLURAL
indicativo presente	
scamb**io**	scamb**iamo**
scamb**i**	scamb**iate**
scamb**ia**	scamb**iano**
imperfetto	
scambia**vo**	scambia**vamo**
scambia**vi**	scambia**vate**
scambia**va**	scambia**vano**
passato remoto	
scamb**iai**	scamb**iammo**
scamb**iasti**	scamb**iaste**
scamb**iò**	scamb**iarono**
futuro semplice	
scambier**ò**	scambier**emo**
scambier**ai**	scambier**ete**
scambier**à**	scambier**anno**
condizionale presente	
scambi**erei**	scambi**eremmo**
scambi**eresti**	scambi**ereste**
scambi**erebbe**	scambi**erebbero**
congiuntivo presente	
scamb**i**	scamb**iamo**
scamb**i**	scamb**iate**
scamb**i**	scamb**ino**
congiuntivo imperfetto	
scambi**assi**	scambi**assimo**
scambi**assi**	scambi**aste**
scambi**asse**	scambi**assero**
imperativo	
	scambiamo
scambia; non scambiare	scambiate
scambi	scambino

SINGULAR	PLURAL
passato prossimo	
ho scambiato	**abbiamo** scambiato
hai scambiato	**avete** scambiato
ha scambiato	**hanno** scambiato
trapassato prossimo	
avevo scambiato	**avevamo** scambiato
avevi scambiato	**avevate** scambiato
aveva scambiato	**avevano** scambiato
trapassato remoto	
ebbi scambiato	**avemmo** scambiato
avesti scambiato	**aveste** scambiato
ebbe scambiato	**ebbero** scambiato
futuro anteriore	
avrò scambiato	**avremo** scambiato
avrai scambiato	**avrete** scambiato
avrà scambiato	**avranno** scambiato
condizionale passato	
avrei scambiato	**avremmo** scambiato
avresti scambiato	**avreste** scambiato
avrebbe scambiato	**avrebbero** scambiato
congiuntivo passato	
abbia scambiato	**abbiamo** scambiato
abbia scambiato	**abbiate** scambiato
abbia scambiato	**abbiano** scambiato
congiuntivo trapassato	
avessi scambiato	**avessimo** scambiato
avessi scambiato	**aveste** scambiato
avesse scambiato	**avessero** scambiato

to choose, to select **sceglière**

gerundio **scegliendo**

participio passato **scelto**

indicativo presente

SINGULAR	PLURAL
scelg**o**	scegli**amo**
scegl**i**	scegli**ete**
scegli**e**	scelg**ono**

imperfetto

SINGULAR	PLURAL
sceglie**vo**	sceglie**vamo**
sceglie**vi**	sceglie**vate**
sceglie**va**	sceglie**vano**

passato remoto

SINGULAR	PLURAL
scel**si**	scegli**emmo**
scegli**esti**	scegli**este**
scel**se**	scel**sero**

futuro semplice

SINGULAR	PLURAL
sceglier**ò**	sceglier**emo**
sceglier**ai**	sceglier**ete**
sceglier**à**	sceglier**anno**

condizionale presente

SINGULAR	PLURAL
scegli**erei**	scegli**eremmo**
scegli**eresti**	scegli**ereste**
scegli**erebbe**	scegli**erebbero**

congiuntivo presente

SINGULAR	PLURAL
scelg**a**	scegli**amo**
scelg**a**	scegli**ate**
scelg**a**	scelg**ano**

congiuntivo imperfetto

SINGULAR	PLURAL
scegli**essi**	scegli**essimo**
scegli**essi**	scegli**este**
scegli**esse**	scegli**essero**

imperativo

SINGULAR	PLURAL
	scegliamo
scegli; non scegliere	scegliete
scelga	scelgano

passato prossimo

SINGULAR	PLURAL
ho scelto	**abbiamo** scelto
hai scelto	**avete** scelto
ha scelto	**hanno** scelto

trapassato prossimo

SINGULAR	PLURAL
avevo scelto	**avevamo** scelto
avevi scelto	**avevate** scelto
aveva scelto	**avevano** scelto

trapassato remoto

SINGULAR	PLURAL
ebbi scelto	**avemmo** scelto
avesti scelto	**aveste** scelto
ebbe scelto	**ebbero** scelto

futuro anteriore

SINGULAR	PLURAL
avrò scelto	**avremo** scelto
avrai scelto	**avrete** scelto
avrà scelto	**avranno** scelto

condizionale passato

SINGULAR	PLURAL
avrei scelto	**avremmo** scelto
avresti scelto	**avreste** scelto
avrebbe scelto	**avrebbero** scelto

congiuntivo passato

SINGULAR	PLURAL
abbia scelto	**abbiamo** scelto
abbia scelto	**abbiate** scelto
abbia scelto	**abbiano** scelto

congiuntivo trapassato

SINGULAR	PLURAL
avessi scelto	**avessimo** scelto
avessi scelto	**aveste** scelto
avesse scelto	**avessero** scelto

scendere — to descend, to go/come down

gerundio **scendendo** — participio passato **sceso**

SINGULAR	PLURAL	SINGULAR	PLURAL
indicativo presente		passato prossimo	
scend**o**	scend**iamo**	**sono** sceso(a)	**siamo** scesi(e)
scend**i**	scend**ete**	**sei** sceso(a)	**siete** scesi(e)
scend**e**	scend**ono**	**è** sceso(a)	**sono** scesi(e)
imperfetto		trapassato prossimo	
scende**vo**	scende**vamo**	**ero** sceso(a)	**eravamo** scesi(e)
scende**vi**	scende**vate**	**eri** sceso(a)	**eravate** scesi(e)
scende**va**	scende**vano**	**era** sceso(a)	**erano** scesi(e)
passato remoto		trapassato remoto	
sces**i**	scend**emmo**	**fui** sceso(a)	**fummo** scesi(e)
scend**esti**	scend**este**	**fosti** sceso(a)	**foste** scesi(e)
sces**e**	sces**ero**	**fu** sceso(a)	**furono** scesi(e)
futuro semplice		futuro anteriore	
scender**ò**	scender**emo**	**sarò** sceso(a)	**saremo** scesi(e)
scender**ai**	scender**ete**	**sarai** sceso(a)	**sarete** scesi(e)
scender**à**	scender**anno**	**sarà** sceso(a)	**saranno** scesi(e)
condizionale presente		condizionale passato	
scend**erei**	scend**eremmo**	**sarei** sceso(a)	**saremmo** scesi(e)
scend**eresti**	scend**ereste**	**saresti** sceso(a)	**sareste** scesi(e)
scend**erebbe**	scend**erebbero**	**sarebbe** sceso(a)	**sarebbero** scesi(e)
congiuntivo presente		congiuntivo passato	
scend**a**	scend**iamo**	**sia** sceso(a)	**siamo** scesi(e)
scend**a**	scend**iate**	**sia** sceso(a)	**siate** scesi(e)
scend**a**	scend**ano**	**sia** sceso(a)	**siano** scesi(e)
congiuntivo imperfetto		congiuntivo trapassato	
scend**essi**	scend**essimo**	**fossi** sceso(a)	**fossimo** scesi(e)
scend**essi**	scend**este**	**fossi** sceso(a)	**foste** scesi(e)
scend**esse**	scend**essero**	**fosse** sceso(a)	**fossero** scesi(e)

imperativo

	scendiamo
scendi; non scendere	scendete
scenda	scendano

SINGULAR	PLURAL	SINGULAR	PLURAL
indicativo presente		passato prossimo	
scherz**o**	scherz**iamo**	**ho** scherzato	**abbiamo** scherzato
scherz**i**	scherz**ate**	**hai** scherzato	**avete** scherzato
scherz**a**	scherz**ano**	**ha** scherzato	**hanno** scherzato
imperfetto		trapassato prossimo	
scherza**vo**	scherza**vamo**	**avevo** scherzato	**avevamo** scherzato
scherza**vi**	scherza**vate**	**avevi** scherzato	**avevate** scherzato
scherza**va**	scherza**vano**	**aveva** scherzato	**avevano** scherzato
passato remoto		trapassato remoto	
scherz**ai**	scherz**ammo**	**ebbi** scherzato	**avemmo** scherzato
scherz**asti**	scherz**aste**	**avesti** scherzato	**aveste** scherzato
scherz**ò**	scherz**arono**	**ebbe** scherzato	**ebbero** scherzato
futuro semplice		futuro anteriore	
scherzer**ò**	scherzer**emo**	**avrò** scherzato	**avremo** scherzato
scherzer**ai**	scherzer**ete**	**avrai** scherzato	**avrete** scherzato
scherzer**à**	scherzer**anno**	**avrà** scherzato	**avranno** scherzato
condizionale presente		condizionale passato	
scherz**erei**	scherz**eremmo**	**avrei** scherzato	**avremmo** scherzato
scherz**eresti**	scherz**ereste**	**avresti** scherzato	**avreste** scherzato
scherz**erebbe**	scherz**erebbero**	**avrebbe** scherzato	**avrebbero** scherzato
congiuntivo presente		congiuntivo passato	
scherz**i**	scherz**iamo**	**abbia** scherzato	**abbiamo** scherzato
scherz**i**	scherz**iate**	**abbia** scherzato	**abbiate** scherzato
scherz**i**	scherz**ino**	**abbia** scherzato	**abbiano** scherzato
congiuntivo imperfetto		congiuntivo trapassato	
scherz**assi**	scherz**assimo**	**avessi** scherzato	**avessimo** scherzato
scherz**assi**	scherz**aste**	**avessi** scherzato	**aveste** scherzato
scherz**asse**	scherz**assero**	**avesse** scherzato	**avessero** scherzato
imperativo			
	scherziamo		
scherza; non scherzare	scherzate		
scherzi	scherzino		

S

sciare — to ski

gerundio **sciando** participio passato **sciato**

SINGULAR	PLURAL
indicativo presente	
scio	sciamo
scii	sciate
scia	sciano
imperfetto	
sciavo	sciavamo
sciavi	sciavate
sciava	sciavano
passato remoto	
sciai	sciammo
sciasti	sciaste
sciò	sciarono
futuro semplice	
scierò	scieremo
scierai	scierete
scierà	scieranno
condizionale presente	
scierei	scieremmo
scieresti	sciereste
scierebbe	scierebbero
congiuntivo presente	
scii	sciamo
scii	sciate
scii	sciino
congiuntivo imperfetto	
sciassi	sciassimo
sciassi	sciaste
sciasse	sciassero
imperativo	
	sciamo
scia; non sciare	sciate
scii	sciino

SINGULAR	PLURAL
passato prossimo	
ho sciato	abbiamo sciato
hai sciato	avete sciato
ha sciato	hanno sciato
trapassato prossimo	
avevo sciato	avevamo sciato
avevi sciato	avevate sciato
aveva sciato	avevano sciato
trapassato remoto	
ebbi sciato	avemmo sciato
avesti sciato	aveste sciato
ebbe sciato	ebbero sciato
futuro anteriore	
avrò sciato	avremo sciato
avrai sciato	avrete sciato
avrà sciato	avranno sciato
condizionale passato	
avrei sciato	avremmo sciato
avresti sciato	avreste sciato
avrebbe sciato	avrebbero sciato
congiuntivo passato	
abbia sciato	abbiamo sciato
abbia sciato	abbiate sciato
abbia sciato	abbiano sciato
congiuntivo trapassato	
avessi sciato	avessimo sciato
avessi sciato	aveste sciato
avesse sciato	avessero sciato

to disappear — scomparire

gerundio **scomparendo** participio passato **scomparso**

SINGULAR	PLURAL
indicativo presente	
scompai**o**	scompar**iamo**
scompar**i**	scompar**ite**
scompar**e**	scompai**ono**
imperfetto	
scompari**vo**	scompari**vamo**
scompari**vi**	scompari**vate**
scompari**va**	scompari**vano**
passato remoto	
scompar**vi**	scompar**immo**
scompar**isti**	scompar**iste**
scompar**ve**	scompar**vero**
futuro semplice	
scomparir**ò**	scomparir**emo**
scomparir**ai**	scomparir**ete**
scomparir**à**	scomparir**anno**
condizionale presente	
scompar**irei**	scompar**iremmo**
scompar**iresti**	scompar**ireste**
scompar**irebbe**	scompar**irebbero**
congiuntivo presente	
scompai**a**	scompar**iamo**
scompai**a**	scompar**iate**
scompai**a**	scompai**ano**
congiuntivo imperfetto	
scompar**issi**	scompar**issimo**
scompar**issi**	scompar**iste**
scompar**isse**	scompar**issero**
imperativo	
	scompariamo
scompari; non scomparire	scomparite
scompaia	scompaiano

SINGULAR	PLURAL
passato prossimo	
sono scomparso(a)	**siamo** scomparsi(e)
sei scomparso(a)	**siete** scomparsi(e)
è scomparso(a)	**sono** scomparsi(e)
trapassato prossimo	
ero scomparso(a)	**eravamo** scomparsi(e)
eri scomparso(a)	**eravate** scomparsi(e)
era scomparso(a)	**erano** scomparsi(e)
trapassato remoto	
fui scomparso(a)	**fummo** scomparsi(e)
fosti scomparso(a)	**foste** scomparsi(e)
fu scomparso(a)	**furono** scomparsi(e)
futuro anteriore	
sarò scomparso(a)	**saremo** scomparsi(e)
sarai scomparso(a)	**sarete** scomparsi(e)
sarà scomparso(a)	**saranno** scomparsi(e)
condizionale passato	
sarei scomparso(a)	**saremmo** scomparsi(e)
saresti scomparso(a)	**sareste** scomparsi(e)
sarebbe scomparso(a)	**sarebbero** scomparsi(e)
congiuntivo passato	
sia scomparso(a)	**siamo** scomparsi(e)
sia scomparso(a)	**siate** scomparsi(e)
sia scomparso(a)	**siano** scomparsi(e)
congiuntivo trapassato	
fossi scomparso(a)	**fossimo** scomparsi(e)
fossi scomparso(a)	**foste** scomparsi(e)
fosse scomparso(a)	**fossero** scomparsi(e)

sconfiggere — to defeat

gerundio **sconfiggendo** participio passato **sconfitto**

SINGULAR	PLURAL
indicativo presente	
sconfigg**o**	sconfigg**iamo**
sconfigg**i**	sconfigg**ete**
sconfigg**e**	sconfigg**ono**
imperfetto	
sconfigge**vo**	sconfigge**vamo**
sconfigge**vi**	sconfigge**vate**
sconfigge**va**	sconfigge**vano**
passato remoto	
sconfiss**i**	sconfigg**emmo**
sconfigg**esti**	sconfigg**este**
sconfiss**e**	sconfiss**ero**
futuro semplice	
sconfigger**ò**	sconfigger**emo**
sconfigger**ai**	sconfigger**ete**
sconfigger**à**	sconfigger**anno**
condizionale presente	
sconfigg**erei**	sconfigg**eremmo**
sconfigg**eresti**	sconfigg**ereste**
sconfigg**erebbe**	sconfigg**erebbero**
congiuntivo presente	
sconfigg**a**	sconfigg**iamo**
sconfigg**a**	sconfigg**iate**
sconfigg**a**	sconfigg**ano**
congiuntivo imperfetto	
sconfigg**essi**	sconfigg**essimo**
sconfigg**essi**	sconfigg**este**
sconfigg**esse**	sconfigg**essero**
imperativo	
	sconfiggiamo
sconfiggi; non sconfiggere	sconfiggete
sconfigga	sconfiggano

SINGULAR	PLURAL
passato prossimo	
ho sconfitto	**abbiamo** sconfitto
hai sconfitto	**avete** sconfitto
ha sconfitto	**hanno** sconfitto
trapassato prossimo	
avevo sconfitto	**avevamo** sconfitto
avevi sconfitto	**avevate** sconfitto
aveva sconfitto	**avevano** sconfitto
trapassato remoto	
ebbi sconfitto	**avemmo** sconfitto
avesti sconfitto	**aveste** sconfitto
ebbe sconfitto	**ebbero** sconfitto
futuro anteriore	
avrò sconfitto	**avremo** sconfitto
avrai sconfitto	**avrete** sconfitto
avrà sconfitto	**avranno** sconfitto
condizionale passato	
avrei sconfitto	**avremmo** sconfitto
avresti sconfitto	**avreste** sconfitto
avrebbe sconfitto	**avrebbero** sconfitto
congiuntivo passato	
abbia sconfitto	**abbiamo** sconfitto
abbia sconfitto	**abbiate** sconfitto
abbia sconfitto	**abbiano** sconfitto
congiuntivo trapassato	
avessi sconfitto	**avessimo** sconfitto
avessi sconfitto	**aveste** sconfitto
avesse sconfitto	**avessero** sconfitto

gerundio **scoprendo** participio passato **scoperto**

SINGULAR	PLURAL	SINGULAR	PLURAL
indicativo presente		passato prossimo	
scopr**o**	scopr**iamo**	**ho** scoperto	**abbiamo** scoperto
scopr**i**	scopr**ite**	**hai** scoperto	**avete** scoperto
scopr**e**	scopr**ono**	**ha** scoperto	**hanno** scoperto
imperfetto		trapassato prossimo	
scopri**vo**	scopri**vamo**	**avevo** scoperto	**avevamo** scoperto
scopri**vi**	scopri**vate**	**avevi** scoperto	**avevate** scoperto
scopri**va**	scopri**vano**	**aveva** scoperto	**avevano** scoperto
passato remoto		trapassato remoto	
scopr**ii**, scopers**i**	scopr**immo**	**ebbi** scoperto	**avemmo** scoperto
scopr**isti**	scopr**iste**	**avesti** scoperto	**aveste** scoperto
scopr**ì**, scop**erse**	scopr**irono**, scop**ersero**	**ebbe** scoperto	**ebbero** scoperto
futuro semplice		futuro anteriore	
scoprir**ò**	scoprir**emo**	**avrò** scoperto	**avremo** scoperto
scoprir**ai**	scoprir**ete**	**avrai** scoperto	**avrete** scoperto
scoprir**à**	scoprir**anno**	**avrà** scoperto	**avranno** scoperto
condizionale presente		condizionale passato	
scopr**irei**	scopr**iremmo**	**avrei** scoperto	**avremmo** scoperto
scopr**iresti**	scopr**ireste**	**avresti** scoperto	**avreste** scoperto
scopr**irebbe**	scopr**irebbero**	**avrebbe** scoperto	**avrebbero** scoperto
congiuntivo presente		congiuntivo passato	
scopr**a**	scopr**iamo**	**abbia** scoperto	**abbiamo** scoperto
scopr**a**	scopr**iate**	**abbia** scoperto	**abbiate** scoperto
scopr**a**	scopr**ano**	**abbia** scoperto	**abbiano** scoperto
congiuntivo imperfetto		congiuntivo trapassato	
scopr**issi**	scopr**issimo**	**avessi** scoperto	**avessimo** scoperto
scopr**issi**	scopr**iste**	**avessi** scoperto	**aveste** scoperto
scopr**isse**	scopr**issero**	**avesse** scoperto	**avessero** scoperto
imperativo			
	scopriamo		
scopri; non scoprire	scoprite		
scopra	scoprano		

scrivere — to write

gerundio **scrivendo** participio passato **scritto**

SINGULAR	PLURAL	SINGULAR	PLURAL
indicativo presente		passato prossimo	
scriv**o**	scriv**iamo**	**ho** scritto	**abbiamo** scritto
scriv**i**	scriv**ete**	**hai** scritto	**avete** scritto
scriv**e**	scriv**ono**	**ha** scritto	**hanno** scritto
imperfetto		trapassato prossimo	
scrive**vo**	scrive**vamo**	**avevo** scritto	**avevamo** scritto
scrive**vi**	scrive**vate**	**avevi** scritto	**avevate** scritto
scrive**va**	scrive**vano**	**aveva** scritto	**avevano** scritto
passato remoto		trapassato remoto	
scriss**i**	scriv**emmo**	**ebbi** scritto	**avemmo** scritto
scriv**esti**	scriv**este**	**avesti** scritto	**aveste** scritto
scriss**e**	scriss**ero**	**ebbe** scritto	**ebbero** scritto
futuro semplice		futuro anteriore	
scriver**ò**	scriver**emo**	**avrò** scritto	**avremo** scritto
scriver**ai**	scriver**ete**	**avrai** scritto	**avrete** scritto
scriver**à**	scriver**anno**	**avrà** scritto	**avranno** scritto
condizionale presente		condizionale passato	
scriv**erei**	scriv**eremmo**	**avrei** scritto	**avremmo** scritto
scriv**eresti**	scriv**ereste**	**avresti** scritto	**avreste** scritto
scriv**erebbe**	scriv**erebbero**	**avrebbe** scritto	**avrebbero** scritto
congiuntivo presente		congiuntivo passato	
scriv**a**	scriv**iamo**	**abbia** scritto	**abbiamo** scritto
scriv**a**	scriv**iate**	**abbia** scritto	**abbiate** scritto
scriv**a**	scriv**ano**	**abbia** scritto	**abbiano** scritto
congiuntivo imperfetto		congiuntivo trapassato	
scriv**essi**	scriv**essimo**	**avessi** scritto	**avessimo** scritto
scriv**essi**	scriv**este**	**avessi** scritto	**aveste** scritto
scriv**esse**	scriv**essero**	**avesse** scritto	**avessero** scritto

imperativo

	scriviamo
scrivi; non scrivere	scrivete
scriva	scrivano

gerundio **scuotendo** participio passato **scosso**

SINGULAR	PLURAL	SINGULAR	PLURAL
indicativo presente		passato prossimo	
scuot**o**	scuot**iamo**	**ho** scosso	**abbiamo** scosso
scuot**i**	scuot**ete**	**hai** scosso	**avete** scosso
scuot**e**	scuot**ono**	**ha** scosso	**hanno** scosso
imperfetto		trapassato prossimo	
scuote**vo**	scuote**vamo**	**avevo** scosso	**avevamo** scosso
scuote**vi**	scuote**vate**	**avevi** scosso	**avevate** scosso
scuote**va**	scuote**vano**	**aveva** scosso	**avevano** scosso
passato remoto		trapassato remoto	
scoss**i**	scuot**emmo**	**ebbi** scosso	**avemmo** scosso
scuot**esti**	scuot**este**	**avesti** scosso	**aveste** scosso
scoss**e**	scoss**ero**	**ebbe** scosso	**ebbero** scosso
futuro semplice		futuro anteriore	
scuoter**ò**	scuoter**emo**	**avrò** scosso	**avremo** scosso
scuoter**ai**	scuoter**ete**	**avrai** scosso	**avrete** scosso
scuoter**à**	scuoter**anno**	**avrà** scosso	**avranno** scosso
condizionale presente		condizionale passato	
scuot**erei**	scuot**eremmo**	**avrei** scosso	**avremmo** scosso
scuot**eresti**	scuot**ereste**	**avresti** scosso	**avreste** scosso
scuot**erebbe**	scuot**erebbero**	**avrebbe** scosso	**avrebbero** scosso
congiuntivo presente		congiuntivo passato	
scuot**a**	scuot**iamo**	**abbia** scosso	**abbiamo** scosso
scuot**a**	scuot**iate**	**abbia** scosso	**abbiate** scosso
scuot**a**	scuot**ano**	**abbia** scosso	**abbiano** scosso
congiuntivo imperfetto		congiuntivo trapassato	
scuot**essi**	scuot**essimo**	**avessi** scosso	**avessimo** scosso
scuot**essi**	scuot**este**	**avessi** scosso	**aveste** scosso
scuot**esse**	scuot**essero**	**avesse** scosso	**avessero** scosso
imperativo			
	scuotiamo		
scuoti; non scuotere	scuotete		
scuota	scuotano		

scusare — to excuse

gerundio **scusando** participio passato **scusato**

SINGULAR	PLURAL	SINGULAR	PLURAL
indicativo presente		passato prossimo	
scus**o**	scus**iamo**	**ho** scusato	**abbiamo** scusato
scus**i**	scus**ate**	**hai** scusato	**avete** scusato
scus**a**	scus**ano**	**ha** scusato	**hanno** scusato
imperfetto		trapassato prossimo	
scusa**vo**	scusa**vamo**	**avevo** scusato	**avevamo** scusato
scusa**vi**	scusa**vate**	**avevi** scusato	**avevate** scusato
scusa**va**	scusa**vano**	**aveva** scusato	**avevano** scusato
passato remoto		trapassato remoto	
scus**ai**	scus**ammo**	**ebbi** scusato	**avemmo** scusato
scus**asti**	scus**aste**	**avesti** scusato	**aveste** scusato
scus**ò**	scus**arono**	**ebbe** scusato	**ebbero** scusato
futuro semplice		futuro anteriore	
scuser**ò**	scuser**emo**	**avrò** scusato	**avremo** scusato
scuser**ai**	scuser**ete**	**avrai** scusato	**avrete** scusato
scuser**à**	scuser**anno**	**avrà** scusato	**avranno** scusato
condizionale presente		condizionale passato	
scus**erei**	scus**eremmo**	**avrei** scusato	**avremmo** scusato
scus**eresti**	scus**ereste**	**avresti** scusato	**avreste** scusato
scus**erebbe**	scus**erebbero**	**avrebbe** scusato	**avrebbero** scusato
congiuntivo presente		congiuntivo passato	
scus**i**	scus**iamo**	**abbia** scusato	**abbiamo** scusato
scus**i**	scus**iate**	**abbia** scusato	**abbiate** scusato
scus**i**	scus**ino**	**abbia** scusato	**abbiano** scusato
congiuntivo imperfetto		congiuntivo trapassato	
scus**assi**	scus**assimo**	**avessi** scusato	**avessimo** scusato
scus**assi**	scus**aste**	**avessi** scusato	**aveste** scusato
scus**asse**	scus**assero**	**avesse** scusato	**avessero** scusato
imperativo			
	scusiamo		
scusa; non scusare	scusate		
scusi	scusino		

to apologize, to excuse oneself **scusarsi**

gerundio **scusandosi** participio passato **scusatosi**

SINGULAR	PLURAL	SINGULAR	PLURAL
indicativo presente		passato prossimo	
mi scus**o**	**ci** scus**iamo**	**mi sono** scusato(a)	**ci siamo** scusati(e)
ti scus**i**	**vi** scus**ate**	**ti sei** scusato(a)	**vi siete** scusati(e)
si scus**a**	**si** scus**ano**	**si è** scusato(a)	**si sono** scusati(e)
imperfetto		trapassato prossimo	
mi scusa**vo**	**ci** scusa**vamo**	**mi ero** scusato(a)	**ci eravamo** scusati(e)
ti scusa**vi**	**vi** scusa**vate**	**ti eri** scusato(a)	**vi eravate** scusati(e)
si scusa**va**	**si** scusa**vano**	**si era** scusato(a)	**si erano** scusati(e)
passato remoto		trapassato remoto	
mi scus**ai**	**ci** scus**ammo**	**mi fui** scusato(a)	**ci fummo** scusati(e)
ti scus**asti**	**vi** scus**aste**	**ti fosti** scusato(a)	**vi foste** scusati(e)
si scus**ò**	**si** scus**arono**	**si fu** scusato(a)	**si furono** scusati(e)
futuro semplice		futuro anteriore	
mi scuser**ò**	**ci** scuser**emo**	**mi sarò** scusato(a)	**ci saremo** scusati(e)
ti scuser**ai**	**vi** scuser**ete**	**ti sarai** scusato(a)	**vi sarete** scusati(e)
si scuser**à**	**si** scuser**anno**	**si sarà** scusato(a)	**si saranno** scusati(e)
condizionale presente		condizionale passato	
mi scus**erei**	**ci** scus**eremmo**	**mi sarei** scusato(a)	**ci saremmo** scusati(e)
ti scus**eresti**	**vi** scus**ereste**	**ti saresti** scusato(a)	**vi sareste** scusati(e)
si scus**erebbe**	**si** scus**erebbero**	**si sarebbe** scusato(a)	**si sarebbero** scusati(e)
congiuntivo presente		congiuntivo passato	
mi scus**i**	**ci** scus**iamo**	**mi sia** scusato(a)	**ci siamo** scusati(e)
ti scus**i**	**vi** scus**iate**	**ti sia** scusato(a)	**vi siate** scusati(e)
si scus**i**	**si** scus**ino**	**si sia** scusato(a)	**si siano** scusati(e)
congiuntivo imperfetto		congiuntivo trapassato	
mi scus**assi**	**ci** scus**assimo**	**mi fossi** scusato(a)	**ci fossimo** scusati(e)
ti scus**assi**	**vi** scus**aste**	**ti fossi** scusato(a)	**vi foste** scusati(e)
si scus**asse**	**si** scus**assero**	**si fosse** scusato(a)	**si fossero** scusati(e)

imperativo

	scusiamoci
scusati; non scusarti/ non ti scusare	scusatevi
si scusi	si scusino

sedere — to sit

gerundio **sedendo** participio passato **seduto**

SINGULAR	PLURAL	SINGULAR	PLURAL
indicativo presente		passato prossimo	
sied**o**	sed**iamo**	**ho** seduto	**abbiamo** seduto
sied**i**	sed**ete**	**hai** seduto	**avete** seduto
sied**e**	sied**ono**	**ha** seduto	**hanno** seduto
imperfetto		trapassato prossimo	
sed**evo**	sed**evamo**	**avevo** seduto	**avevamo** seduto
sed**evi**	sed**evate**	**avevi** seduto	**avevate** seduto
sed**eva**	sed**evano**	**aveva** seduto	**avevano** seduto
passato remoto		trapassato remoto	
sed**ei**, sed**etti**	sed**emmo**	**ebbi** seduto	**avemmo** seduto
sed**esti**	sed**este**	**avesti** seduto	**aveste** seduto
sed**é**, sed**ette**	sed**erono**, sed**ettero**	**ebbe** seduto	**ebbero** seduto
futuro semplice		futuro anteriore	
seder**ò**	seder**emo**	**avrò** seduto	**avremo** seduto
seder**ai**	seder**ete**	**avrai** seduto	**avrete** seduto
seder**à**	seder**anno**	**avrà** seduto	**avranno** seduto
condizionale presente		condizionale passato	
sed**erei**	sed**eremmo**	**avrei** seduto	**avremmo** seduto
sed**eresti**	sed**ereste**	**avresti** seduto	**avreste** seduto
sed**erebbe**	sed**erebbero**	**avrebbe** seduto	**avrebbero** seduto
congiuntivo presente		congiuntivo passato	
sied**a**	sed**iamo**	**abbia** seduto	**abbiamo** seduto
sied**a**	sed**iate**	**abbia** seduto	**abbiate** seduto
sied**a**	sied**ano**	**abbia** seduto	**abbiano** seduto
congiuntivo imperfetto		congiuntivo trapassato	
sed**essi**	sed**essimo**	**avessi** seduto	**avessimo** seduto
sed**essi**	sed**este**	**avessi** seduto	**aveste** seduto
sed**esse**	sed**essero**	**avesse** seduto	**avessero** seduto

imperativo

SINGULAR	PLURAL
	sediamo
siedi; non sedere	sedete
sieda	siedano

to sit down **sedersi**

gerundio **sedendosi** participio passato **sedutosi**

SINGULAR	PLURAL
indicativo presente	
mi sied**o**	**ci** sed**iamo**
ti sied**i**	**vi** sed**ete**
si sied**e**	**si** sied**ono**
imperfetto	
mi sede**vo**	**ci** sede**vamo**
ti sede**vi**	**vi** sede**vate**
si sede**va**	**si** sede**vano**
passato remoto	
mi sed**ei**, **mi** sed**etti**	**ci** sed**emmo**
ti sed**esti**	**vi** sed**este**
si sed**é**, **si** sed**ette**	**si** sed**erono**, **si** sed**ettero**
futuro semplice	
mi seder**ò**	**ci** seder**emo**
ti seder**ai**	**vi** seder**ete**
si seder**à**	**si** seder**anno**
condizionale presente	
mi sed**erei**	**ci** sed**eremmo**
ti sed**eresti**	**vi** sed**ereste**
si sed**erebbe**	**si** sed**erebbero**
congiuntivo presente	
mi sied**a**	**ci** sed**iamo**
ti sed**a**	**vi** sed**iate**
si sed**a**	**si** sied**ano**
congiuntivo imperfetto	
mi sed**essi**	**ci** sed**essimo**
ti sed**essi**	**vi** sed**este**
si sed**esse**	**si** sed**essero**
imperativo	
	sediamoci
siediti; non sederti/ non ti sedere	sedetevi
si sieda	si siedano

SINGULAR	PLURAL
passato prossimo	
mi sono seduto(a)	**ci siamo** seduti(e)
ti sei seduto(a)	**vi siete** seduti(e)
si è seduto(a)	**si sono** seduti(e)
trapassato prossimo	
mi ero seduto(a)	**ci eravamo** seduti(e)
ti eri seduto(a)	**vi eravate** seduti(e)
si era seduto(a)	**si erano** seduti(e)
trapassato remoto	
mi fui seduto(a)	**ci fummo** seduti(e)
ti fosti seduto(a)	**vi foste** seduti(e)
si fu seduto(a)	**si furono** seduti(e)
futuro anteriore	
mi sarò seduto(a)	**ci saremo** seduti(e)
ti sarai seduto(a)	**vi sarete** seduti(e)
si sarà seduto(a)	**si saranno** seduti(e)
condizionale passato	
mi sarei seduto(a)	**ci saremmo** seduti(e)
ti saresti seduto(a)	**vi sareste** seduti(e)
si sarebbe seduto(a)	**si sarebbero** seduti(e)
congiuntivo passato	
mi sia seduto(a)	**ci siamo** seduti(e)
ti sia seduto(a)	**vi siate** seduti(e)
si sia seduto(a)	**si siano** seduti(e)
congiuntivo trapassato	
mi fossi seduto(a)	**ci fossimo** seduti(e)
ti fossi seduto(a)	**vi foste** seduti(e)
si fosse seduto(a)	**si fossero** seduti(e)

seguire — to follow

gerundio **seguendo** participio passato **seguito**

SINGULAR	PLURAL
indicativo presente	
segu**o**	segu**iamo**
segu**i**	segu**ite**
segu**e**	segu**ono**
imperfetto	
segui**vo**	segui**vamo**
segui**vi**	segui**vate**
segui**va**	segui**vano**
passato remoto	
segu**ii**	segu**immo**
segu**isti**	segu**iste**
segu**ì**	segu**irono**
futuro semplice	
seguir**ò**	seguir**emo**
seguir**ai**	seguir**ete**
seguir**à**	seguir**anno**
condizionale presente	
segu**irei**	segu**iremmo**
segu**iresti**	segu**ireste**
segu**irebbe**	segu**irebbero**
congiuntivo presente	
segu**a**	segu**iamo**
segu**a**	segu**iate**
segu**a**	segu**ano**
congiuntivo imperfetto	
segu**issi**	segu**issimo**
segu**issi**	segu**iste**
segu**isse**	segu**issero**
imperativo	
	seguiamo
segui; non seguire	seguite
segua	seguano

SINGULAR	PLURAL
passato prossimo	
ho seguito	**abbiamo** seguito
hai seguito	**avete** seguito
ha seguito	**hanno** seguito
trapassato prossimo	
avevo seguito	**avevamo** seguito
avevi seguito	**avevate** seguito
aveva seguito	**avevano** seguito
trapassato remoto	
ebbi seguito	**avemmo** seguito
avesti seguito	**aveste** seguito
ebbe seguito	**ebbero** seguito
futuro anteriore	
avrò seguito	**avremo** seguito
avrai seguito	**avrete** seguito
avrà seguito	**avranno** seguito
condizionale passato	
avrei seguito	**avremmo** seguito
avresti seguito	**avreste** seguito
avrebbe seguito	**avrebbero** seguito
congiuntivo passato	
abbia seguito	**abbiamo** seguito
abbia seguito	**abbiate** seguito
abbia seguito	**abbiano** seguito
congiuntivo trapassato	
avessi seguito	**avessimo** seguito
avessi seguito	**aveste** seguito
avesse seguito	**avessero** seguito

to seem, to appear **sembrare**

gerundio **sembrando** participio passato **sembrato**

SINGULAR	PLURAL	SINGULAR	PLURAL
indicativo presente		passato prossimo	
sembr**o**	sembr**iamo**	**sono** sembrato(a)	**siamo** sembrati(e)
sembr**i**	sembr**ate**	**sei** sembrato(a)	**siete** sembrati(e)
sembr**a**	sembr**ano**	**è** sembrato(a)	**sono** sembrati(e)
imperfetto		trapassato prossimo	
sembra**vo**	sembra**vamo**	**ero** sembrato(a)	**eravamo** sembrati(e)
sembra**vi**	sembra**vate**	**eri** sembrato(a)	**eravate** sembrati(e)
sembra**va**	sembra**vano**	**era** sembrato(a)	**erano** sembrati(e)
passato remoto		trapassato remoto	
sembr**ai**	sembr**ammo**	**fui** sembrato(a)	**fummo** sembrati(e)
sembr**asti**	sembr**aste**	**fosti** sembrato(a)	**foste** sembrati(e)
sembr**ò**	sembr**arono**	**fu** sembrato(a)	**furono** sembrati(e)
futuro semplice		futuro anteriore	
sembrer**ò**	sembrer**emo**	**sarò** sembrato(a)	**saremo** sembrati(e)
sembrer**ai**	sembrer**ete**	**sarai** sembrato(a)	**sarete** sembrati(e)
sembrer**à**	sembrer**anno**	**sarà** sembrato(a)	**saranno** sembrati(e)
condizionale presente		condizionale passato	
sembr**erei**	sembr**eremmo**	**sarei** sembrato(a)	**saremmo** sembrati(e)
sembr**eresti**	sembr**ereste**	**saresti** sembrato(a)	**sareste** sembrati(e)
sembr**erebbe**	sembr**erebbero**	**sarebbe** sembrato(a)	**sarebbero** sembrati(e)
congiuntivo presente		congiuntivo passato	
sembr**i**	sembr**iamo**	**sia** sembrato(a)	**siamo** sembrati(e)
sembr**i**	sembr**iate**	**sia** sembrato(a)	**siate** sembrati(e)
sembr**i**	sembr**ino**	**sia** sembrato(a)	**siano** sembrati(e)
congiuntivo imperfetto		congiuntivo trapassato	
sembr**assi**	sembr**assimo**	**fossi** sembrato(a)	**fossimo** sembrati(e)
sembr**assi**	sembr**aste**	**fossi** sembrato(a)	**foste** sembrati(e)
sembr**asse**	sembr**assero**	**fosse** sembrato(a)	**fossero** sembrati(e)

sentire — to feel, to hear

gerundio **sentendo** participio passato **sentito**

SINGULAR	PLURAL	SINGULAR	PLURAL
indicativo presente		passato prossimo	
sent**o**	sent**iamo**	**ho** sentito	**abbiamo** sentito
sent**i**	sent**ite**	**hai** sentito	**avete** sentito
sent**e**	sent**ono**	**ha** sentito	**hanno** sentito
imperfetto		trapassato prossimo	
senti**vo**	senti**vamo**	**avevo** sentito	**avevamo** sentito
senti**vi**	senti**vate**	**avevi** sentito	**avevate** sentito
senti**va**	senti**vano**	**aveva** sentito	**avevano** sentito
passato remoto		trapassato remoto	
sent**ii**	sent**immo**	**ebbi** sentito	**avemmo** sentito
sent**isti**	sent**iste**	**avesti** sentito	**aveste** sentito
sent**ì**	sent**irono**	**ebbe** sentito	**ebbero** sentito
futuro semplice		futuro anteriore	
sentir**ò**	sentir**emo**	**avrò** sentito	**avremo** sentito
sentir**ai**	sentir**ete**	**avrai** sentito	**avrete** sentito
sentir**à**	sentir**anno**	**avrà** sentito	**avranno** sentito
condizionale presente		condizionale passato	
sent**irei**	sent**iremmo**	**avrei** sentito	**avremmo** sentito
sent**iresti**	sent**ireste**	**avresti** sentito	**avreste** sentito
sent**irebbe**	sent**irebbero**	**avrebbe** sentito	**avrebbero** sentito
congiuntivo presente		congiuntivo passato	
sent**a**	sent**iamo**	**abbia** sentito	**abbiamo** sentito
sent**a**	sent**iate**	**abbia** sentito	**abbiate** sentito
sent**a**	sent**ano**	**abbia** sentito	**abbiano** sentito
congiuntivo imperfetto		congiuntivo trapassato	
sent**issi**	sent**issimo**	**avessi** sentito	**avessimo** sentito
sent**issi**	sent**iste**	**avessi** sentito	**aveste** sentito
sent**isse**	sent**issero**	**avesse** sentito	**avessero** sentito

imperativo

	sentiamo
senti; non sentire	sentite
senta	sentano

to separate, to divide — **separare**

gerundio **separando** participio passato **separato**

SINGULAR	PLURAL	SINGULAR	PLURAL
indicativo presente		passato prossimo	
separ**o**	separ**iamo**	**ho** separato	**abbiamo** separato
separ**i**	separ**ate**	**hai** separato	**avete** separato
separ**a**	separ**ano**	**ha** separato	**hanno** separato
imperfetto		trapassato prossimo	
separa**vo**	separa**vamo**	**avevo** separato	**avevamo** separato
separa**vi**	separa**vate**	**avevi** separato	**avevate** separato
separa**va**	separa**vano**	**aveva** separato	**avevano** separato
passato remoto		trapassato remoto	
separ**ai**	separ**ammo**	**ebbi** separato	**avemmo** separato
separ**asti**	separ**aste**	**avesti** separato	**aveste** separato
separ**ò**	separ**arono**	**ebbe** separato	**ebbero** separato
futuro semplice		futuro anteriore	
separer**ò**	separer**emo**	**avrò** separato	**avremo** separato
separer**ai**	separer**ete**	**avrai** separato	**avrete** separato
separer**à**	separer**anno**	**avrà** separato	**avanno** separato
condizionale presente		condizionale passato	
separ**erei**	separ**eremmo**	**avrei** separato	**avremmo** separato
separ**eresti**	separ**ereste**	**avresti** separato	**avreste** separato
separ**erebbe**	separ**erebbero**	**avrebbe** separato	**avrebbero** separato
congiuntivo presente		congiuntivo passato	
separ**i**	separ**iamo**	**abbia** separato	**abbiamo** separato
separ**i**	separ**iate**	**abbia** separato	**abbiate** separato
separ**i**	separ**ino**	**abbia** separato	**abbiano** separato
congiuntivo imperfetto		congiuntivo trapassato	
separ**assi**	separ**assimo**	**avessi** separato	**avessimo** separato
separ**assi**	separ**aste**	**avessi** separato	**aveste** separato
separ**asse**	separ**assero**	**avesse** separato	**avessero** separato

imperativo

	separiamo
separa; non separare	separate
separi	separino

S

serrare — to shut, to close

gerundio **serrando** — participio passato **serrato**

indicativo presente

SINGULAR	PLURAL
serr**o**	serr**iamo**
serr**i**	serr**ate**
serr**a**	serr**ano**

imperfetto

SINGULAR	PLURAL
serra**vo**	serra**vamo**
serra**vi**	serra**vate**
serra**va**	serra**vano**

passato remoto

SINGULAR	PLURAL
serr**ai**	serr**ammo**
serr**asti**	serr**aste**
serr**ò**	serr**arono**

futuro semplice

SINGULAR	PLURAL
serrer**ò**	serrer**emo**
serrer**ai**	serrer**ete**
serrer**à**	serrer**anno**

condizionale presente

SINGULAR	PLURAL
serr**erei**	serr**eremmo**
serr**eresti**	serr**ereste**
serr**erebbe**	serr**erebbero**

congiuntivo presente

SINGULAR	PLURAL
serr**i**	serr**iamo**
serr**i**	serr**iate**
serr**i**	serr**ino**

congiuntivo imperfetto

SINGULAR	PLURAL
serr**assi**	serr**assimo**
serr**assi**	serr**aste**
serr**asse**	serr**assero**

imperativo

SINGULAR	PLURAL
	serriamo
serra; non serrare	serrate
serri	serrino

passato prossimo

SINGULAR	PLURAL
ho serrato	**abbiamo** serrato
hai serrato	**avete** serrato
ha serrato	**hanno** serrato

trapassato prossimo

SINGULAR	PLURAL
avevo serrato	**avevamo** serrato
avevi serrato	**avevate** serrato
aveva serrato	**avevano** serrato

trapassato remoto

SINGULAR	PLURAL
ebbi serrato	**avemmo** serrato
avesti serrato	**aveste** serrato
ebbe serrato	**ebbero** serrato

futuro anteriore

SINGULAR	PLURAL
avrò serrato	**avremo** serrato
avrai serrato	**avrete** serrato
avrà serrato	**avranno** serrato

condizionale passato

SINGULAR	PLURAL
avrei serrato	**avremmo** serrato
avresti serrato	**avreste** serrato
avrebbe serrato	**avrebbero** serrato

congiuntivo passato

SINGULAR	PLURAL
abbia serrato	**abbiamo** serrato
abbia serrato	**abbiate** serrato
abbia serrato	**abbiano** serrato

congiuntivo trapassato

SINGULAR	PLURAL
avessi serrato	**avessimo** serrato
avessi serrato	**aveste** serrato
avesse serrato	**avessero** serrato

gerundio **servendo** participio passato **servito**

SINGULAR	PLURAL	SINGULAR	PLURAL
indicativo presente		passato prossimo	
serv**o**	serv**iamo**	**ho** servito	**abbiamo** servito
serv**i**	serv**ite**	**hai** servito	**avete** servito
serv**e**	serv**ono**	**ha** servito	**hanno** servito
imperfetto		trapassato prossimo	
servi**vo**	servi**vamo**	**avevo** servito	**avevamo** servito
servi**vi**	servi**vate**	**avevi** servito	**avevate** servito
servi**va**	servi**vano**	**aveva** servito	**avevano** servito
passato remoto		trapassato remoto	
serv**ii**	serv**immo**	**ebbi** servito	**avemmo** servito
serv**isti**	serv**iste**	**avesti** servito	**aveste** servito
serv**ì**	serv**irono**	**ebbe** servito	**ebbero** servito
futuro semplice		futuro anteriore	
servir**ò**	servir**emo**	**avrò** servito	**avremo** servito
servir**ai**	servir**ete**	**avrai** servito	**avrete** servito
servir**à**	servir**anno**	**avrà** servito	**avranno** servito
condizionale presente		condizionale passato	
serv**irei**	serv**iremmo**	**avrei** servito	**avremmo** servito
serv**iresti**	serv**ireste**	**avresti** servito	**avreste** servito
serv**irebbe**	serv**irebbero**	**avrebbe** servito	**avrebbero** servito
congiuntivo presente		congiuntivo passato	
serv**a**	serv**iamo**	**abbia** servito	**abbiamo** servito
serv**a**	serv**iate**	**abbia** servito	**abbiate** servito
serv**a**	serv**ano**	**abbia** servito	**abbiano** servito
congiuntivo imperfetto		congiuntivo trapassato	
serv**issi**	serv**issimo**	**avessi** servito	**avessimo** servito
serv**issi**	serv**iste**	**avessi** servito	**aveste** servito
serv**isse**	serv**issero**	**avesse** servito	**avessero** servito
imperativo			
	serviamo		
servi; non servire	servite		
serva	servano		

S

gerundio **sgridando** participio passato **sgridato**

SINGULAR	PLURAL	SINGULAR	PLURAL
indicativo presente		passato prossimo	
sgrid**o**	sgrid**iamo**	**ho** sgridato	**abbiamo** sgridato
sgrid**i**	sgrid**ate**	**hai** sgridato	**avete** sgridato
sgrid**a**	sgrid**ano**	**ha** sgridato	**hanno** sgridato
imperfetto		trapassato prossimo	
sgrida**vo**	sgrida**vamo**	**avevo** sgridato	**avevamo** sgridato
sgrida**vi**	sgrida**vate**	**avevi** sgridato	**avevate** sgridato
sgrida**va**	sgrida**vano**	**aveva** sgridato	**avevano** sgridato
passato remoto		trapassato remoto	
sgrid**ai**	sgrid**ammo**	**ebbi** sgridato	**avemmo** sgridato
sgrid**asti**	sgrid**aste**	**avesti** sgridato	**aveste** sgridato
sgrid**ò**	sgrid**arono**	**ebbe** sgridato	**ebbero** sgridato
futuro semplice		futuro anteriore	
sgrider**ò**	sgrider**emo**	**avrò** sgridato	**avremo** sgridato
sgrider**ai**	sgrider**ete**	**avrai** sgridato	**avrete** sgridato
sgrider**à**	sgrider**anno**	**avrà** sgridato	**avranno** sgridato
condizionale presente		condizionale passato	
sgrid**erei**	sgrid**eremmo**	**avrei** sgridato	**avremmo** sgridato
sgrid**eresti**	sgrid**ereste**	**avresti** sgridato	**avreste** sgridato
sgrid**erebbe**	sgrid**erebbero**	**avrebbe** sgridato	**avrebbero** sgridato
congiuntivo presente		congiuntivo passato	
sgrid**i**	sgrid**iamo**	**abbia** sgridato	**abbiamo** sgridato
sgrid**i**	sgrid**iate**	**abbia** sgridato	**abbiate** sgridato
sgrid**i**	sgrid**ino**	**abbia** sgridato	**abbiano** sgridato
congiuntivo imperfetto		congiuntivo trapassato	
sgrid**assi**	sgrid**assimo**	**avessi** sgridato	**avessimo** sgridato
sgrid**assi**	sgrid**aste**	**avessi** sgridato	**aveste** sgridato
sgrid**asse**	sgrid**assero**	**avesse** sgridato	**avessero** sgridato
imperativo			
	sgridiamo		
sgrida; non sgridare	sgridate		
sgridi	sgridino		

to mean, to signify **significare**

gerundio **significando** participio passato **significato**

SINGULAR	PLURAL	SINGULAR	PLURAL
indicativo presente		passato prossimo	
signific**o**	significh**iamo**	**ho** significato	**abbiamo** significato
significh**i**	signific**ate**	**hai** significato	**avete** significato
signific**a**	signific**ano**	**ha** significato	**hanno** significato
imperfetto		trapassato prossimo	
significa**vo**	significa**vamo**	**avevo** significato	**avevamo** significato
significa**vi**	significa**vate**	**avevi** significato	**avevate** significato
significa**va**	significa**vano**	**aveva** significato	**avevano** significato
passato remoto		trapassato remoto	
signific**ai**	signific**ammo**	**ebbi** significato	**avemmo** significato
signific**asti**	signific**aste**	**avesti** significato	**aveste** significato
signific**ò**	signific**arono**	**ebbe** significato	**ebbero** significato
futuro semplice		futuro anteriore	
significher**ò**	significher**emo**	**avrò** significato	**avremo** significato
significher**ai**	significher**este**	**avrai** significato	**avrete** significato
significher**à**	significher**anno**	**avrà** significato	**avranno** significato
condizionale presente		condizionale passato	
significh**erei**	significh**eremmo**	**avrei** significato	**avremmo** significato
significh**eresti**	significh**ereste**	**avresti** significato	**avreste** significato
significh**erebbe**	significh**erebbero**	**avrebbe** significato	**avrebbero** significato
congiuntivo presente		congiuntivo passato	
significh**i**	significh**iamo**	**abbia** significato	**abbiamo** significato
significh**i**	significh**iate**	**abbia** significato	**abbiate** significato
significh**i**	significh**ino**	**abbia** significato	**abbiano** significato
congiuntivo imperfetto		congiuntivo trapassato	
signific**assi**	signific**assimo**	**avessi** significato	**avessimo** significato
signific**assi**	signific**aste**	**avessi** significato	**aveste** significato
signific**asse**	signific**assero**	**avesse** significato	**avessero** significato

soddisfare — to fulfill, to satisfy

gerundio **soddisfacendo** participio passato **soddisfatto**

SINGULAR	PLURAL	SINGULAR	PLURAL
indicativo presente		passato prossimo	
soddisf**o**	soddisf**iamo**	**ho** soddisfatto	**abbiamo** soddisfatto
soddisf**i**	soddisf**ate**	**hai** soddisfatto	**avete** soddisfatto
soddisf**a**	soddisf**anno**	**ha** soddisfatto	**hanno** soddisfatto
imperfetto		trapassato prossimo	
soddisface**vo**	soddisface**vamo**	**avevo** soddisfatto	**avevamo** soddisfatto
soddisface**vi**	soddisface**vate**	**avevi** soddisfatto	**avevate** soddisfatto
soddisface**va**	soddisface**vano**	**aveva** soddisfatto	**avevano** soddisfatto
passato remoto		trapassato remoto	
soddisf**eci**	soddisf**acemmo**	**ebbi** soddisfatto	**avemmo** soddisfatto
soddisf**acesti**	soddisf**aceste**	**avesti** soddisfatto	**aveste** soddisfatto
soddisf**ece**	soddisf**ecero**	**ebbe** soddisfatto	**ebbero** soddisfatto
futuro semplice		futuro anteriore	
soddisfar**ò**	soddisfar**emo**	**avrò** soddisfatto	**avremo** soddisfatto
soddisfar**ai**	soddisfar**ete**	**avrai** soddisfatto	**avrete** soddisfatto
soddisfar**à**	soddisfar**anno**	**avrà** soddisfatto	**avranno** soddisfatto
condizionale presente		condizionale passato	
soddisf**arei**	soddisf**aremmo**	**avrei** soddisfatto	**avremmo** soddisfatto
soddisf**aresti**	soddisf**areste**	**avresti** soddisfatto	**avreste** soddisfatto
soddisf**arebbe**	soddisf**arebbero**	**avrebbe** soddisfatto	**avrebbero** soddisfatto
congiuntivo presente		congiuntivo passato	
soddisf**i**	soddisf**iamo**	**abbia** soddisfatto	**abbiamo** soddisfatto
soddisf**i**	soddisf**iate**	**abbia** soddisfatto	**abbiate** soddisfatto
soddisf**i**	soddisf**ino**	**abbia** soddisfatto	**abbiano** soddisfatto
congiuntivo imperfetto		congiuntivo trapassato	
soddisf**acessi**	soddisf**acessimo**	**avessi** soddisfatto	**avessimo** soddisfatto
soddisf**acessi**	soddisf**aceste**	**avessi** soddisfatto	**aveste** soddisfatto
soddisf**acesse**	soddisf**acessero**	**avesse** soddisfatto	**avessero** soddisfatto

imperativo

	soddisfiamo
soddisfa; non soddisfare	soddisfate
soddisfi	soddisfino

to suffer — soffrire

gerundio **soffrendo** participio passato **sofferto**

SINGULAR	PLURAL
indicativo presente	
soffr**o**	soffr**iamo**
soffr**i**	soffr**ite**
soffr**e**	soffr**ono**
imperfetto	
soffri**vo**	soffri**vamo**
soffri**vi**	soffri**vate**
soffri**va**	soffri**vano**
passato remoto	
soffr**ii**	soffr**immo**
soffr**isti**	soffr**iste**
soffr**ì**	soffr**irono**
futuro semplice	
soffrir**ò**	soffrir**emo**
soffrir**ai**	soffrir**ete**
soffrir**à**	soffrir**anno**
condizionale presente	
soffr**irei**	soffr**iremmo**
soffr**iresti**	soffr**ireste**
soffr**irebbe**	soffr**irebbero**
congiuntivo presente	
soffr**a**	soffr**iamo**
soffr**a**	soffr**iate**
soffr**a**	soffr**ano**
congiuntivo imperfetto	
soffr**issi**	soffr**issimo**
soffr**issi**	soffr**iste**
soffr**isse**	soffr**issero**
imperativo	
	soffriamo
soffri; non soffrire	soffrite
soffra	soffrano

SINGULAR	PLURAL
passato prossimo	
ho sofferto	**abbiamo** sofferto
hai sofferto	**avete** sofferto
ha sofferto	**hanno** sofferto
trapassato prossimo	
avevo sofferto	**avevamo** sofferto
avevi sofferto	**avevate** sofferto
aveva sofferto	**avevano** sofferto
trapassato remoto	
ebbi sofferto	**avemmo** sofferto
avesti sofferto	**aveste** sofferto
ebbe sofferto	**ebbero** sofferto
futuro anteriore	
avrò sofferto	**avremo** sofferto
avrai sofferto	**avrete** sofferto
avrà sofferto	**avranno** sofferto
condizionale passato	
avrei sofferto	**avremmo** sofferto
avresti sofferto	**avreste** sofferto
avrebbe sofferto	**avrebbero** sofferto
congiuntivo passato	
abbia sofferto	**abbiamo** sofferto
abbia sofferto	**abbiate** sofferto
abbia sofferto	**abbiano** sofferto
congiuntivo trapassato	
avessi sofferto	**avessimo** sofferto
avessi sofferto	**aveste** sofferto
avesse sofferto	**avessero** sofferto

sognare — to dream

gerundio **sognando** participio passato **sognato**

SINGULAR	PLURAL
indicativo presente	
sogn**o**	sogn**iamo**
sogn**i**	sogn**ate**
sogn**a**	sogn**ano**
imperfetto	
sogna**vo**	sogna**vamo**
sogna**vi**	sogna**vate**
sogna**va**	sogna**vano**
passato remoto	
sogn**ai**	sogn**ammo**
sogn**asti**	sogn**aste**
sogn**ò**	sogn**arono**
futuro semplice	
sogner**ò**	sogner**emo**
sogner**ai**	sogner**ete**
sogner**à**	sogner**anno**
condizionale presente	
sogn**erei**	sogn**eremmo**
sogn**eresti**	sogn**ereste**
sogn**erebbe**	sogn**erebbero**
congiuntivo presente	
sogn**i**	sogn**iamo**
sogn**i**	sogn**iate**
sogn**i**	sogn**ino**
congiuntivo imperfetto	
sogn**assi**	sogn**assimo**
sogn**assi**	sogn**aste**
sogn**asse**	sogn**assero**
imperativo	
	sogniamo
sogna; non sognare	sognate
sogni	sognino

SINGULAR	PLURAL
passato prossimo	
ho sognato	**abbiamo** sognato
hai sognato	**avete** sognato
ha sognato	**hanno** sognato
trapassato prossimo	
avevo sognato	**avevamo** sognato
avevi sognato	**avevate** sognato
aveva sognato	**avevano** sognato
trapassato remoto	
ebbi sognato	**avemmo** sognato
avesti sognato	**aveste** sognato
ebbe sognato	**ebbero** sognato
futuro anteriore	
avrò sognato	**avremo** sognato
avrai sognato	**avrete** sognato
avrà sognato	**avranno** sognato
condizionale passato	
avrei sognato	**avremmo** sognato
avresti sognato	**avreste** sognato
avrebbe sognato	**avrebbero** sognato
congiuntivo passato	
abbia sognato	**abbiamo** sognato
abbia sognato	**abbiate** sognato
abbia sognato	**abbiano** sognato
congiuntivo trapassato	
avessi sognato	**avessimo** sognato
avessi sognato	**aveste** sognato
avesse sognato	**avessero** sognato

to rise — sorgere

gerundio **sorgendo** participio passato **sorto**

SINGULAR	PLURAL	SINGULAR	PLURAL
indicativo presente		passato prossimo	
sorg**o**	sorg**iamo**	**sono** sorto(a)	**siamo** sorti(e)
sorg**i**	sorg**ete**	**sei** sorto(a)	**siete** sorti(e)
sorg**e**	sorg**ono**	**è** sorto(a)	**sono** sorti(e)
imperfetto		trapassato prossimo	
sorge**vo**	sorge**vamo**	**ero** sorto(a)	**eravamo** sorti(e)
sorge**vi**	sorge**vate**	**eri** sorto(a)	**eravate** sorti(e)
sorge**va**	sorge**vano**	**era** sorto(a)	**erano** sorti(e)
passato remoto		trapassato remoto	
sors**i**	sorg**emmo**	**fui** sorto(a)	**fummo** sorti(e)
sorg**esti**	sorg**este**	**fosti** sorto(a)	**foste** sorti(e)
sors**e**	sors**ero**	**fu** sorto(a)	**furono** sorti(e)
futuro semplice		futuro anteriore	
sorger**ò**	sorger**emo**	**sarò** sorto(a)	**saremo** sorti(e)
sorger**ai**	sorger**ete**	**sarai** sorto(a)	**sarete** sorti(e)
sorger**à**	sorger**anno**	**sarà** sorto(a)	**saranno** sorti(e)
condizionale presente		condizionale passato	
sorg**erei**	sorg**eremmo**	**sarei** sorto(a)	**saremmo** sorti(e)
sorg**eresti**	sorg**ereste**	**saresti** sorto(a)	**sareste** sorti(e)
sorg**erebbe**	sorg**erebbero**	**sarebbe** sorto(a)	**sarebbero** sorti(e)
congiuntivo presente		congiuntivo passato	
sorg**a**	sorg**iamo**	**sia** sorto(a)	**siamo** sorti(e)
sorg**a**	sorg**iate**	**sia** sorto(a)	**siate** sorti(e)
sorg**a**	sorg**ano**	**sia** sorto(a)	**siano** sorti(e)
congiuntivo imperfetto		congiuntivo trapassato	
sorg**essi**	sorg**essimo**	**fossi** sorto(a)	**fossimo** sorti(e)
sorg**essi**	sorg**este**	**fossi** sorto(a)	**foste** sorti(e)
sorg**esse**	sorg**essero**	**fosse** sorto(a)	**fossero** sorti(e)
imperativo			
	sorgiamo		
sorgi; non sorgere	sorgete		
sorga	sorgano		

sorprendere — to surprise

gerundio **sorprendendo** participio passato **sorpreso**

SINGULAR	PLURAL	SINGULAR	PLURAL
indicativo presente		passato prossimo	
sorprend**o**	sorprend**iamo**	**ho** sorpreso	**abbiamo** sorpreso
sorprend**i**	sorprend**ete**	**hai** sorpreso	**avete** sorpreso
sorprend**e**	sorprend**ono**	**ha** sorpreso	**hanno** sorpreso
imperfetto		trapassato prossimo	
sorprende**vo**	sorprende**vamo**	**avevo** sorpreso	**avevamo** sorpreso
sorprende**vi**	sorprende**vate**	**avevi** sorpreso	**avevate** sorpreso
sorprende**va**	sorprende**vano**	**aveva** sorpreso	**avevano** sorpreso
passato remoto		trapassato remoto	
sorpres**i**	sorprend**emmo**	**ebbi** sorpreso	**avemmo** sorpreso
sorprend**esti**	sorprend**este**	**avesti** sorpreso	**aveste** sorpreso
sorpres**e**	sorpres**ero**	**ebbe** sorpreso	**ebbero** sorpreso
futuro semplice		futuro anteriore	
sorprender**ò**	sorprender**emo**	**avrò** sorpreso	**avremo** sorpreso
sorprender**ai**	sorprend**erete**	**avrai** sorpreso	**avrete** sorpreso
sorprender**à**	sorprender**anno**	**avrà** sorpreso	**avranno** sorpreso
condizionale presente		condizionale passato	
sorprend**erei**	sorprend**eremmo**	**avrei** sorpreso	**avremmo** sorpreso
sorprend**eresti**	sorprend**ereste**	**avresti** sorpreso	**avreste** sorpreso
sorprend**erebbe**	sorprend**erebbero**	**avrebbe** sorpreso	**avrebbero** sorpreso
congiuntivo presente		congiuntivo passato	
sorprend**a**	sorprend**iamo**	**abbia** sorpreso	**abbiamo** sorpreso
sorprend**a**	sorprend**iate**	**abbia** sorpreso	**abbiate** sorpreso
sorprend**a**	sorprend**ano**	**abbia** sorpreso	**abbiano** sorpreso
congiuntivo imperfetto		congiuntivo trapassato	
sorprend**essi**	sorprend**essimo**	**avessi** sorpreso	**avessimo** sorpreso
sorprend**essi**	sorprend**este**	**avessi** sorpreso	**aveste** sorpreso
sorprend**esse**	sorprend**essero**	**avesse** sorpreso	**avessero** sorpreso

imperativo

	sorprendiamo
sorprendi; non sorprendere	sorprendete
sorprenda	sorprendano

S

gerundio **sorridendo** participio passato **sorriso**

SINGULAR	PLURAL	SINGULAR	PLURAL
indicativo presente		passato prossimo	
sorrid**o**	sorrid**iamo**	**ho** sorriso	**abbiamo** sorriso
sorrid**i**	sorrid**ete**	**hai** sorriso	**avete** sorriso
sorrid**e**	sorrid**ono**	**ha** sorriso	**hanno** sorriso
imperfetto		trapassato prossimo	
sorride**vo**	sorride**vamo**	**avevo** sorriso	**avevamo** sorriso
sorride**vi**	sorride**vate**	**avevi** sorriso	**avevate** sorriso
sorride**va**	sorride**vano**	**aveva** sorriso	**avevano** sorriso
passato remoto		trapassato remoto	
sorris**i**	sorrid**emmo**	**ebbi** sorriso	**avemmo** sorriso
sorrid**esti**	sorrid**este**	**avesti** sorriso	**aveste** sorriso
sorris**e**	sorris**ero**	**ebbe** sorriso	**ebbero** sorriso
futuro semplice		futuro anteriore	
sorrider**ò**	sorrider**emo**	**avrò** sorriso	**avremo** sorriso
sorrider**ai**	sorrider**ete**	**avrai** sorriso	**avrete** sorriso
sorrider**à**	sorrider**anno**	**avrà** sorriso	**avranno** sorriso
condizionale presente		condizionale passato	
sorrid**erei**	sorrid**eremmo**	**avrei** sorriso	**avremmo** sorriso
sorrid**eresti**	sorrid**ereste**	**avresti** sorriso	**avreste** sorriso
sorrid**erebbe**	sorrid**erebbero**	**avrebbe** sorriso	**avrebbero** sorriso
congiuntivo presente		congiuntivo passato	
sorrid**a**	sorrid**iamo**	**abbia** sorriso	**abbiamo** sorriso
sorrid**a**	sorrid**iate**	**abbia** sorriso	**abbiate** sorriso
sorrid**a**	sorrid**ano**	**abbia** sorriso	**abbiano** sorriso
congiuntivo imperfetto		congiuntivo trapassato	
sorrid**essi**	sorrid**essimo**	**avessi** sorriso	**avessimo** sorriso
sorrid**essi**	sorrid**este**	**avessi** sorriso	**aveste** sorriso
sorrid**esse**	sorrid**essero**	**avesse** sorriso	**avessero** sorriso
imperativo			
	sorridiamo		
sorridi; non sorridere	sorridete		
sorrida	sorridano		

sospendere — to hang up, to suspend

gerundio **sospendendo** — participio passato **sospeso**

SINGULAR	PLURAL	SINGULAR	PLURAL
indicativo presente		passato prossimo	
sospend**o**	sospend**iamo**	**ho** sospeso	**abbiamo** sospeso
sospend**i**	sospend**ete**	**hai** sospeso	**avete** sospeso
sospend**e**	sospend**ono**	**ha** sospeso	**hanno** sospeso
imperfetto		trapassato prossimo	
sospende**vo**	sospende**vamo**	**avevo** sospeso	**avevamo** sospeso
sospende**vi**	sospende**vate**	**avevi** sospeso	**avevate** sospeso
sospende**va**	sospende**vano**	**aveva** sospeso	**avevano** sospeso
passato remoto		trapassato remoto	
sospes**i**	sospend**emmo**	**ebbi** sospeso	**avemmo** sospeso
sospend**esti**	sospend**este**	**avesti** sospeso	**aveste** sospeso
sospes**e**	sospes**ero**	**ebbe** sospeso	**ebbero** sospeso
futuro semplice		futuro anteriore	
sospender**ò**	sospender**emo**	**avrò** sospeso	**avremo** sospeso
sospender**ai**	sospender**ete**	**avrai** sospeso	**avrete** sospeso
sospender**à**	sospender**anno**	**avrà** sospeso	**avranno** sospeso
condizionale presente		condizionale passato	
sospend**erei**	sospend**eremmo**	**avrei** sospeso	**avremmo** sospeso
sospend**eresti**	sospend**ereste**	**avresti** sospeso	**avreste** sospeso
sospend**erebbe**	sospend**erebbero**	**avrebbe** sospeso	**avrebbero** sospeso
congiuntivo presente		congiuntivo passato	
sospend**a**	sospend**iamo**	**abbia** sospeso	**abbiamo** sospeso
sospend**a**	sospend**iate**	**abbia** sospeso	**abbiate** sospeso
sospend**a**	sospend**ano**	**abbia** sospeso	**abbiano** sospeso
congiuntivo imperfetto		congiuntivo trapassato	
sospend**essi**	sospend**essimo**	**avessi** sospeso	**avessimo** sospeso
sospend**essi**	sospend**este**	**avessi** sospeso	**aveste** sospeso
sospend**esse**	sospend**essero**	**avesse** sospeso	**avessero** sospeso

imperativo

	sospendiamo
sospendi; non sospendere	sospendete
sospenda	sospendano

to sustain, to support — sostenere

gerundio **sostenendo** participio passato **sostenuto**

SINGULAR	PLURAL
indicativo presente	
sosteng**o**	sosten**iamo**
sostien**i**	sosten**ete**
sostien**e**	sosteng**ono**
imperfetto	
sostene**vo**	sostene**vamo**
sostene**vi**	sostene**vate**
sostene**va**	sostene**vano**
passato remoto	
sosten**ni**	sosten**emmo**
sosten**esti**	sosten**este**
sosten**ne**	sosten**nero**
futuro semplice	
sosterr**ò**	sosterr**emo**
sosterr**ai**	sosterr**ete**
sosterr**à**	sosterr**anno**
condizionale presente	
sost**errei**	sost**erremmo**
sost**erresti**	sost**erreste**
sost**errebbe**	sost**errebbero**
congiuntivo presente	
sosteng**a**	sosten**iamo**
sosteng**a**	sosten**iate**
sosteng**a**	sosteng**ano**
congiuntivo imperfetto	
sost**enessi**	soten**essimo**
sost**enessi**	soten**este**
sost**enesse**	soten**essero**
imperativo	
	sosteniamo
sostieni; non sostenere	sostenete
sostenga	sostengano

SINGULAR	PLURAL
passato prossimo	
ho sostenuto	**abbiamo** sostenuto
hai sostenuto	**avete** sostenuto
ha sostenuto	**hanno** sostenuto
trapassato prossimo	
avevo sostenuto	**avevamo** sostenuto
avevi sostenuto	**avevate** sostenuto
aveva sostenuto	**avevano** sostenuto
trapassato remoto	
ebbi sostenuto	**avemmo** sostenuto
avesti sostenuto	**aveste** sostenuto
ebbe sostenuto	**ebbero** sostenuto
futuro anteriore	
avrò sostenuto	**avremo** sostenuto
avrai sostenuto	**avrete** sostenuto
avrà sostenuto	**avranno** sostenuto
condizionale passato	
avrei sostenuto	**avremmo** sostenuto
avresti sostenuto	**avreste** sostenuto
avrebbe sostenuto	**avrebbero** sostenuto
congiuntivo passato	
abbia sostenuto	**abbiamo** sostenuto
abbia sostenuto	**abbiate** sostenuto
abbia sostenuto	**abbiano** sostenuto
congiuntivo trapassato	
avessi sostenuto	**avessimo** sostenuto
avessi sostenuto	**aveste** sostenuto
avesse sostenuto	**avessero** sostenuto

sottomettere — to submit, to subject

gerundio **sottomettendo** — participio passato **sottomesso**

SINGULAR	PLURAL
indicativo presente	
sottomett**o**	sottomett**iamo**
sottomett**i**	sottomett**ete**
sottomett**e**	sottomett**ono**
imperfetto	
sottomette**vo**	sottomette**vamo**
sottomette**vi**	sottomette**vato**
sottomette**va**	sottomette**vano**
passato remoto	
sottomis**i**	sottomett**emmo**
sottomett**esti**	sottomett**este**
sottomis**e**	sottomis**ero**
futuro semplice	
sottometter**ò**	sottometter**emo**
sottometter**ai**	sottometter**ete**
sottometter**à**	sottometter**anno**
condizionale presente	
sottomett**erei**	sottomett**eremmo**
sottomett**eresti**	sottomett**ereste**
sottomett**erebbe**	sottomett**erebbero**
congiuntivo presente	
sottomett**a**	sottomett**iamo**
sottomett**a**	sottomett**iate**
sottomett**a**	sottomett**ano**
congiuntivo imperfetto	
sottomett**essi**	sottomett**essimo**
sottomett**essi**	sottomett**este**
sottomett**esse**	sottomett**essero**
imperativo	
	sottomettiamo
sottometti; non sottomettere	sottomettete
sottometa	sottomettano

SINGULAR	PLURAL
passato prossimo	
ho sottomesso	**abbiamo** sottomesso
hai sottomesso	**avete** sottomesso
ha sottomesso	**hanno** sottomesso
trapassato prossimo	
avevo sottomesso	**avevamo** sottomesso
avevi sottomesso	**avevate** sottomesso
aveva sottomesso	**avevano** sottomesso
trapassato remoto	
ebbi sottomesso	**avemmo** sottomesso
avesti sottomesso	**aveste** sottomesso
ebbe sottomesso	**ebbero** sottomesso
futuro anteriore	
avrò sottomesso	**avremo** sottomesso
avrai sottomesso	**avrete** sottomesso
avrà sottomesso	**avranno** sottomesso
condizionale passato	
avrei sottomesso	**avremmo** sottomesso
avresti sottomesso	**avreste** sottomesso
avrebbe sottomesso	**avrebbero** sottomesso
congiuntivo passato	
abbia sottomesso	**abbiamo** sottomesso
abbia sottomesso	**abbiate** sottomesso
abbia sottomesso	**abbiano** sottomesso
congiuntivo trapassato	
avessi sottomesso	**avessimo** sottomesso
avessi sottomesso	**aveste** sottomesso
avesse sottomesso	**avessero** sottomesso

gerundio **sottraendo** participio passato **sottratto**

SINGULAR	PLURAL	SINGULAR	PLURAL
indicativo presente		passato prossimo	
sottra**ggo**	sottra**iamo**	**ho** sottratto	**abbiamo** sottratto
sottra**i**	sottra**ete**	**hai** sottratto	**avete** sottratto
sottra**e**	sottra**ggono**	**ha** sottratto	**hanno** sottratto
imperfetto		trapassato prossimo	
sottrae**vo**	sottrae**vamo**	**avevo** sottratto	**avevamo** sottratto
sottrae**vi**	sottrae**vate**	**avevi** sottratto	**avevate** sottratto
sottrae**va**	sottrae**vano**	**aveva** sottratto	**avevano** sottratto
passato remoto		trapassato remoto	
sottra**ssi**	sottra**emmo**	**ebbi** sottratto	**avemmo** sottratto
sottra**esti**	sottra**este**	**avesti** sottratto	**aveste** sottratto
sottra**sse**	sottra**ssero**	**ebbe** sottratto	**ebbero** sottratto
futuro semplice		futuro anteriore	
sottrarr**ò**	sottrarr**emo**	**avrò** sottratto	**avremo** sottratto
sottrarr**ai**	sottrarr**ete**	**avrai** sottratto	**avrete** sottratto
sottrarr**à**	sottrarr**anno**	**avrà** sottratto	**avranno** sottratto
condizionale presente		condizionale passato	
sottra**rrei**	sottra**rremmo**	**avrei** sottratto	**avremmo** sottratto
sottra**rresti**	sottra**rreste**	**avresti** sottratto	**avreste** sottratto
sottra**rrebbe**	sottra**rrebbero**	**avrebbe** sottratto	**avrebbero** sottratto
congiuntivo presente		congiuntivo passato	
sottra**gga**	sottra**iamo**	**abbia** sottratto	**abbiamo** sottratto
sottra**gga**	sottra**iate**	**abbia** sottratto	**abbiate** sottratto
sottra**gga**	sottra**ggano**	**abbia** sottratto	**abbiano** sottratto
congiuntivo imperfetto		congiuntivo trapassato	
sottra**essi**	sottra**essimo**	**avessi** sottratto	**avessimo** sottratto
sottra**essi**	sottra**este**	**avessi** sottratto	**aveste** sottratto
sottra**esse**	sottra**essero**	**avesse** sottratto	**avessero** sottratto
imperativo			
	sottraiamo		
sottrai; non sottrarre	sottraete		
sottragga	sottraggano		

S

spandere — to spread

gerundio **spandendo** participio passato **spanto**

SINGULAR	PLURAL
indicativo presente	
spand**o**	spand**iamo**
spand**i**	spand**ete**
spand**e**	spand**ono**
imperfetto	
spande**vo**	spande**vamo**
spande**vi**	spande**vate**
spande**va**	spande**vano**
passato remoto	
spand**ei**	spand**emmo**
spand**esti**	spand**este**
spand**é**	spand**erono**
futuro semplice	
spander**ò**	spander**emo**
spander**ai**	spander**ete**
spander**à**	spander**anno**
condizionale presente	
spand**erei**	spand**eremmo**
spand**eresti**	spand**ereste**
spand**erebbe**	spand**erebbero**
congiuntivo presente	
spand**a**	spand**iamo**
spand**a**	spand**iate**
spand**a**	spand**ano**
congiuntivo imperfetto	
spand**essi**	spand**essimo**
spand**essi**	spand**este**
spand**esse**	spand**essero**
imperativo	
	spandiamo
spandi; non spandere	spandete
spanda	spandano

SINGULAR	PLURAL
passato prossimo	
ho spanso, spanto	**abbiamo** spanso, spanto
hai spanso, spanto	**avete** spanso, spanto
ha spanso, spanto	**hanno** spanso, spanto
trapassato prossimo	
avevo spanso, spanto	**avevamo** spanso, spanto
avevi spanso, spanto	**avevate** spanso, spanto
aveva spanso, spanto	**avevano** spanso, spanto
trapassato remoto	
ebbi spanso, spanto	**avemmo** spanso, spanto
avesti spanso, spanto	**aveste** spanso, spanto
ebbe spanso, spanto	**ebbero** spanso, spanto
futuro anteriore	
avrò spanso, spanto	**avremo** spanso, spanto
avrai spanso, spanto	**avrete** spanso, spanto
avrà spanso, spanto	**avranno** spanso, spanto
condizionale passato	
avrei spanso, spanto	**avremmo** spanso, spanto
avresti spanso, spanto	**avreste** spanso, spanto
avrebbe spanso, spanto	**avrebbero** spanso, spanto
congiuntivo passato	
abbia spanso, spanto	**abbiamo** spanso, spanto
abbia spanso, spanto	**abbiate** spanso, spanto
abbia spanso, spanto	**abbiano** spanso, spanto
congiuntivo trapassato	
avessi spanso, spanto	**avessimo** spanso, spanto
avessi spanso, spanto	**aveste** spanso, spanto
avesse spanso, spanto	**avessero** spanso, spanto

gerundio **spargendo** participio passato **sparso**

SINGULAR	PLURAL
indicativo presente	
spargo	spargiamo
spargi	spargete
sparge	spargono
imperfetto	
spargevo	spargevamo
spargevi	spargevate
spargeva	spargevano
passato remoto	
sparsi	spargemmo
spargesti	spargeste
sparse	sparsero
futuro semplice	
spargerò	spargeremo
spargerai	spargerete
spargerà	spargeranno
condizionale presente	
spargerei	spargeremmo
spargeresti	spargereste
spargerebbe	spargerebbero
congiuntivo presente	
sparga	spargiamo
sparga	spargiate
sparga	spargano
congiuntivo imperfetto	
spargessi	spargessimo
spargessi	spargeste
spargesse	spargessero
imperativo	
	spargiamo
spargi; non spargere	spargete
sparga	spargano

SINGULAR	PLURAL
passato prossimo	
ho sparso	abbiamo sparso
hai sparso	avete sparso
ha sparso	hanno sparso
trapassato prossimo	
avevo sparso	avevamo sparso
avevi sparso	avevate sparso
aveva sparso	avevano sparso
trapassato remoto	
ebbi sparso	avemmo sparso
avesti sparso	aveste sparso
ebbe sparso	ebbero sparso
futuro anteriore	
avrò sparso	avremo sparso
avrai sparso	avrete sparso
avrà sparso	avranno sparso
condizionale passato	
avrei sparso	avremmo sparso
avresti sparso	avreste sparso
avrebbe sparso	avrebbero sparso
congiuntivo passato	
abbia sparso	abbiamo sparso
abbia sparso	abbiate sparso
abbia sparso	abbiano sparso
congiuntivo trapassato	
avessi sparso	avessimo sparso
avessi sparso	aveste sparso
avesse sparso	avessero sparso

spaventarsi — to be frightened, to be scared

gerundio **spaventandosi** participio passato **spaventatosi**

SINGULAR	PLURAL
indicativo presente	
mi spavent**o**	**ci** spavent**iamo**
ti spavent**i**	**vi** spavent**ate**
si spavent**a**	**si** spavent**ano**
imperfetto	
mi spaventa**vo**	**ci** spaventa**vamo**
ti spaventa**vi**	**vi** spaventa**vate**
si spaventa**va**	**si** spaventa**vano**
passato remoto	
mi spavent**ai**	**ci** spavent**ammo**
ti spavent**asti**	**vi** spavent**aste**
si spavent**ò**	**si** spavent**arono**
futuro semplice	
mi spavente**rò**	**ci** spavente**remo**
ti spavente**rai**	**vi** spavente**rete**
si spavente**rà**	**si** spavente**ranno**
condizionale presente	
mi spavent**erei**	**ci** spavent**eremmo**
ti spavent**eresti**	**vi** spavent**ereste**
si spavent**erebbe**	**si** spavent**erebbero**
congiuntivo presente	
mi spavent**i**	**ci** spavent**iamo**
ti spavent**i**	**vi** spavent**iate**
si spavent**i**	**si** spavent**ino**
congiuntivo imperfetto	
mi spavent**assi**	**ci** spavent**assimo**
ti spavent**assi**	**vi** spavent**aste**
si spavent**asse**	**si** spavent**assero**
imperativo	
	spaventiamoci
spaventati; non spaventarti/ non ti spaventare	spaventatevi
si spaventi	si spaventino

SINGULAR	PLURAL
passato prossimo	
mi sono spaventato(a)	**ci siamo** spaventati(e)
ti sei spaventato(a)	**vi siete** spaventati(e)
si è spaventato(a)	**si sono** spaventati(e)
trapassato prossimo	
mi ero spaventato(a)	**ci eravamo** spaventati(e)
ti eri spaventato(a)	**vi eravate** spaventati(e)
si era spaventato(a)	**si erano** spaventati(e)
trapassato remoto	
mi fui spaventato(a)	**ci fummo** spaventati(e)
ti fosti spaventato(a)	**vi foste** spaventati(e)
si fu spaventato(a)	**si furono** spaventati(e)
futuro anteriore	
mi sarò spaventato(a)	**ci saremo** spaventati(e)
ti sarai spaventato(a)	**vi sarete** spaventati(e)
si sarà spaventato(a)	**si saranno** spaventati(e)
condizionale passato	
mi sarei spaventato(a)	**ci saremmo** spaventati(e)
ti saresti spaventato(a)	**vi sareste** spaventati(e)
si sarebbe spaventato(a)	**si sarebbero** spaventati(e)
congiuntivo passato	
mi sia spaventato(a)	**ci siamo** spaventati(e)
ti sia spaventato(a)	**vi siate** spaventati(e)
si sia spaventato(a)	**si siano** spaventati(e)
congiuntivo trapassato	
mi fossi spaventato(a)	**ci fossimo** spaventati(e)
ti fossi spaventato(a)	**vi foste** spaventati(e)
si fosse spaventato(a)	**si fossero** spaventati(e)

to send, to mail **spedire**

gerundio **spedendo**

participio passato **spedito**

SINGULAR	PLURAL
indicativo presente	
spedisc**o**	sped**iamo**
spedisc**i**	sped**ite**
spedisc**e**	spedisc**ono**
imperfetto	
spedi**vo**	spedi**vamo**
spedi**vi**	spedi**vate**
spedi**va**	spedi**vano**
passato remoto	
sped**ii**	sped**immo**
sped**isti**	sped**iste**
sped**ì**	sped**irono**
futuro semplice	
spedir**ò**	spedir**emo**
spedir**ai**	spedir**ete**
spedir**à**	spedir**anno**
condizionale presente	
sped**irei**	sped**iremmo**
sped**iresti**	sped**ireste**
sped**irebbe**	sped**irebbero**
congiuntivo presente	
spedisc**a**	sped**iamo**
spedisc**a**	sped**iate**
spedisc**a**	spedisc**ano**
congiuntivo imperfetto	
sped**issi**	sped**issimo**
sped**issi**	sped**iste**
sped**isse**	sped**issero**
imperativo	
	spediamo
spedisci; non spedire	spedite
spedisca	spediscano

SINGULAR	PLURAL
passato prossimo	
ho spedito	**abbiamo** spedito
hai spedito	**avete** spedito
ha spedito	**hanno** spedito
trapassato prossimo	
avevo spedito	**avevamo** spedito
avevi spedito	**avevate** spedito
aveva spedito	**avevano** spedito
trapassato remoto	
ebbi spedito	**avemmo** spedito
avesti spedito	**aveste** spedito
ebbe spedito	**ebbero** spedito
futuro anteriore	
avrò spedito	**avremo** spedito
avrai spedito	**avrete** spedito
avrà spedito	**avranno** spedito
condizionale passato	
avrei spedito	**avremmo** spedito
avresti spedito	**avreste** spedito
avrebbe spedito	**avrebbero** spedito
congiuntivo passato	
abbia spedito	**abbiamo** spedito
abbia spedito	**abbiate** spedito
abbia spedito	**abbiano** spedito
congiuntivo trapassato	
avessi spedito	**avessimo** spedito
avessi spedito	**aveste** spedito
avesse spedito	**avessero** spedito

spegnere — to turn off, to extinguish

gerundio **spegnendo** participio passato **spento**

SINGULAR	PLURAL	SINGULAR	PLURAL
indicativo presente		passato prossimo	
speng**o**	spegn**iamo**	**ho** spento	**abbiamo** spento
spegn**i**	spegn**ete**	**hai** spento	**avete** spento
spegn**e**	speng**ono**	**ha** spento	**hanno** spento
imperfetto		trapassato prossimo	
spegne**vo**	spegne**vamo**	**avevo** spento	**avevamo** spento
spegne**vi**	spegne**vate**	**avevi** spento	**avevate** spento
spegne**va**	spegne**vano**	**aveva** spento	**avevano** spento
passato remoto		trapassato remoto	
spens**i**	spegn**emmo**	**ebbi** spento	**avemmo** spento
spegn**esti**	spegn**este**	**avesti** spento	**aveste** spento
spen**se**	spens**erono**	**ebbe** spento	**ebbero** spento
futuro semplice		futuro anteriore	
spegner**ò**	spegner**emo**	**avrò** spento	**avremo** spento
spegner**ai**	spegner**ete**	**avrai** spento	**avrete** spento
spegner**à**	spegner**anno**	**avrà** spento	**avranno** spento
condizionale presente		condizionale passato	
spegn**erei**	spegn**eremmo**	**avrei** spento	**avremmo** spento
spegn**eresti**	spegn**ereste**	**avresti** spento	**avreste** spento
spegn**erebbe**	spegn**erebbero**	**avrebbe** spento	**avrebbero** spento
congiuntivo presente		congiuntivo passato	
speng**a**	spegn**iamo**	**abbia** spento	**abbiamo** spento
speng**a**	spegn**iate**	**abbia** spento	**abbiate** spento
speng**a**	speng**ano**	**abbia** spento	**abbiano** spento
congiuntivo imperfetto		congiuntivo trapassato	
spegn**essi**	spegn**essimo**	**avessi** spento	**avessimo** spento
spegn**essi**	spegn**este**	**avessi** spento	**aveste** spento
spegn**esse**	spegn**essero**	**avesse** spento	**avessero** spento

imperativo

	spegniamo
spegni; non spegnere	spegnete
spenga	spengano

to spend, to expend — spendere

gerundio **spendendo** participio passato **speso**

SINGULAR	PLURAL

indicativo presente

spend**o**	spend**iamo**
spend**i**	spend**ete**
spend**e**	spend**ono**

imperfetto

spende**vo**	spende**vamo**
spende**vi**	spende**vate**
spende**va**	spende**vano**

passato remoto

spes**i**	spend**emmo**
spend**esti**	spend**este**
spes**e**	spes**erono**

futuro semplice

spender**ò**	spender**emo**
spender**ai**	spender**ete**
spender**à**	spender**anno**

condizionale presente

spend**erei**	spend**eremmo**
spend**eresti**	spend**ereste**
spend**erebbe**	spend**erebbero**

congiuntivo presente

spend**a**	spend**iamo**
spend**a**	spend**iate**
spend**a**	spend**ano**

congiuntivo imperfetto

spend**essi**	spend**essimo**
spend**essi**	spend**este**
spend**esse**	spend**essero**

imperativo

	spendiamo
spendi; non spendere	spendete
spenda	spendano

SINGULAR	PLURAL

passato prossimo

ho speso	**abbiamo** speso
hai speso	**avete** speso
ha speso	**hanno** speso

trapassato prossimo

avevo speso	**avevamo** speso
avevi speso	**avevate** speso
aveva speso	**avevano** speso

trapassato remoto

ebbi speso	**avemmo** speso
avesti speso	**aveste** speso
ebbe speso	**ebbero** speso

futuro anterioro

avrò speso	**avremo** speso
avrai speso	**avrete** speso
avrà speso	**avranno** speso

condizionale passato

avrei speso	**avremmo** speso
avresti speso	**avreste** speso
avrebbe speso	**avrebbero** speso

congiuntivo passato

abbia speso	**abbiamo** speso
abbia speso	**abbiate** speso
abbia speso	**abbiano** speso

congiuntivo trapassato

avessi speso	**avessimo** speso
avessi speso	**aveste** speso
avesse speso	**avessero** speso

spiegare — to explain

gerundio **spiegando** participio passato **spiegato**

SINGULAR	PLURAL	SINGULAR	PLURAL
indicativo presente		passato prossimo	
spieg**o**	spiegh**iamo**	**ho** spiegato	**abbiamo** spiegato
spiegh**i**	spieg**ate**	**hai** spiegato	**avete** spiegato
spieg**a**	spieg**ano**	**ha** spiegato	**hanno** spiegato
imperfetto		trapassato prossimo	
spiega**vo**	spiega**vamo**	**avevo** spiegato	**avevamo** spiegato
spiega**vi**	spiega**vate**	**avevi** spiegato	**avevate** spiegato
spiega**va**	spiega**vano**	**aveva** spiegato	**avevano** spiegato
passato remoto		trapassato remoto	
spieg**ai**	spieg**ammo**	**ebbi** spiegato	**avemmo** spiegato
spieg**asti**	spieg**aste**	**avesti** spiegato	**aveste** spiegato
spieg**ò**	spieg**arono**	**ebbe** spiegato	**ebbero** spiegato
futuro semplice		futuro anteriore	
spiegher**ò**	spiegher**emo**	**avrò** spiegato	**avremo** spiegato
spiegher**ai**	spiegher**ete**	**avrai** spiegato	**avrete** spiegato
spiegher**à**	spiegher**anno**	**avrà** spiegato	**avranno** spiegato
condizionale presente		condizionale passato	
spiegh**erei**	spiegh**eremmo**	**avrei** spiegato	**avremmo** spiegato
spiegh**eresti**	spiegh**ereste**	**avresti** spiegato	**avreste** spiegato
spiegh**erebbe**	spiegh**erebbero**	**avrebbe** spiegato	**avrebbero** spiegato
congiuntivo presente		congiuntivo passato	
spiegh**i**	spiegh**iamo**	**abbia** spiegato	**abbiamo** spiegato
spiegh**i**	spiegh**iate**	**abbia** spiegato	**abbiate** spiegato
spiegh**i**	spiegh**ino**	**abbia** spiegato	**abbiano** spiegato
congiuntivo imperfetto		congiuntivo trapassato	
spieg**assi**	spieg**assimo**	**avessi** spiegato	**avessimo** spiegato
spieg**assi**	spieg**aste**	**avessi** spiegato	**aveste** spiegato
spieg**asse**	spieg**assero**	**avesse** spiegato	**avessero** spiegato

imperativo

	spieghiamo
spiega; non spiegare	spiegate
spieghi	spieghino

gerundio **spingendo** participio passato **spinto**

SINGULAR	PLURAL
indicativo presente	
sping**o**	sping**iamo**
sping**i**	sping**ete**
sping**e**	sping**ono**
imperfetto	
spinge**vo**	spinge**vamo**
spinge**vi**	spinge**vate**
spinge**va**	spinge**vano**
passato remoto	
spins**i**	sping**emmo**
sping**esti**	sping**este**
spins**e**	spins**erono**
futuro semplice	
spinger**ò**	spinger**emo**
spinger**ai**	spinger**ete**
spinger**à**	spinger**anno**
condizionale presente	
sping**erei**	sping**eremmo**
sping**eresti**	sping**ereste**
sping**erebbe**	sping**erebbero**
congiuntivo presente	
sping**a**	sping**iamo**
sping**a**	sping**iate**
sping**a**	sping**ano**
congiuntivo imperfetto	
sping**essi**	sping**essimo**
sping**essi**	sping**este**
sping**esse**	sping**essero**
imperativo	
	spingiamo
spingi; non spingere	spingete
spinga	spingano

SINGULAR	PLURAL
passato prossimo	
ho spinto	**abbiamo** spinto
hai spinto	**avete** spinto
ha spinto	**hanno** spinto
trapassato prossimo	
avevo spinto	**avevamo** spinto
avevi spinto	**avevate** spinto
aveva spinto	**avevano** spinto
trapassato remoto	
ebbi spinto	**avemmo** spinto
avesti spinto	**aveste** spinto
ebbe spinto	**ebbero** spinto
futuro anteriore	
avrò spinto	**avremo** spinto
avrai spinto	**avrete** spinto
avrà spinto	**avranno** spinto
condizionale passato	
avrei spinto	**avremmo** spinto
avresti spinto	**avreste** spinto
avrebbe spinto	**avrebbero** spinto
congiuntivo passato	
abbia spinto	**abbiamo** spinto
abbia spinto	**abbiate** spinto
abbia spinto	**abbiano** spinto
congiuntivo trapassato	
avessi spinto	**avessimo** spinto
avessi spinto	**aveste** spinto
avesse spinto	**avessero** spinto

sporcare — to dirty

gerundio **sporcando** participio passato **sporcato**

indicativo presente

SINGULAR	PLURAL
sporc**o**	sporch**iamo**
sporch**i**	sporc**ate**
sporc**a**	sporc**ano**

imperfetto

SINGULAR	PLURAL
sporca**vo**	sporca**vamo**
sporca**vi**	sporca**vate**
sporca**va**	sporca**vano**

passato remoto

SINGULAR	PLURAL
sporc**ai**	sporc**ammo**
sporc**asti**	sporc**aste**
sporc**ò**	sporc**arono**

futuro semplice

SINGULAR	PLURAL
sporcher**ò**	sporcher**emo**
sporcher**ai**	sporcher**ete**
sporcher**à**	sporcher**anno**

condizionale presente

SINGULAR	PLURAL
sporch**erei**	sporch**eremmo**
sporch**eresti**	sporch**ereste**
sporch**erebbe**	sporch**erebbero**

congiuntivo presente

SINGULAR	PLURAL
sporch**i**	sporch**iamo**
sporch**i**	sporch**iate**
sporch**i**	sporch**ino**

congiuntivo imperfetto

SINGULAR	PLURAL
sporc**assi**	sporc**assimo**
sporc**assi**	sporc**aste**
sporc**asse**	sporc**assero**

imperativo

SINGULAR	PLURAL
	sporchiamo
sporca; non sporcare	sporcate
sporchi	sporchino

passato prossimo

SINGULAR	PLURAL
ho sporcato	**abbiamo** sporcato
hai sporcato	**avete** sporcato
ha sporcato	**hanno** sporcato

trapassato prossimo

SINGULAR	PLURAL
avevo sporcato	**avevamo** sporcato
avevi sporcato	**avevate** sporcato
aveva sporcato	**avevano** sporcato

trapassato remoto

SINGULAR	PLURAL
ebbi sporcato	**avemmo** sporcato
avesti sporcato	**aveste** sporcato
ebbe sporcato	**ebbero** sporcato

futuro anteriore

SINGULAR	PLURAL
avrò sporcato	**avremo** sporcato
avrai sporcato	**avrete** sporcato
avrà sporcato	**avranno** sporcato

condizionale passato

SINGULAR	PLURAL
avrei sporcato	**avremmo** sporcato
avresti sporcato	**avreste** sporcato
avrebbe sporcato	**avrebbero** sporcato

congiuntivo passato

SINGULAR	PLURAL
abbia sporcato	**abbiamo** sporcato
abbia sporcato	**abbiate** sporcato
abbia sporcato	**abbiano** sporcato

congiuntivo trapassato

SINGULAR	PLURAL
avessi sporcato	**avessimo** sporcato
avessi sporcato	**aveste** sporcato
avesse sporcato	**avessero** sporcato

gerundio **sposando** participio passato **sposato**

SINGULAR	PLURAL
indicativo presente	
spos**o**	spos**iamo**
spos**i**	spos**ate**
spos**a**	spos**ano**
imperfetto	
sposa**vo**	sposa**vamo**
sposa**vi**	sposa**vate**
sposa**va**	sposa**vano**
passato remoto	
spos**ai**	spos**ammo**
spos**asti**	spos**aste**
spos**ò**	spos**arono**
futuro semplice	
sposer**ò**	sposer**emo**
sposer**ai**	sposer**ete**
sposer**à**	sposer**anno**
condizionale presente	
spos**erei**	spos**eremmo**
spos**eresti**	spos**ereste**
spos**erebbe**	spos**erebbero**
congiuntivo presente	
spos**i**	spos**iamo**
spos**i**	spos**iate**
spos**i**	spos**ino**
congiuntivo imperfetto	
spos**assi**	spos**assimo**
spos**assi**	spos**aste**
spos**asse**	spos**assero**
imperativo	
	sposiamo
sposa; non sposare	sposate
sposi	sposino

SINGULAR	PLURAL
passato prossimo	
ho sposato	**abbiamo** sposato
hai sposato	**avete** sposato
ha sposato	**hanno** sposato
trapassato prossimo	
avevo sposato	**avevamo** sposato
avevi sposato	**avevate** sposato
aveva sposato	**avevano** sposato
trapassato remoto	
ebbi sposato	**avemmo** sposato
avesti sposato	**aveste** sposato
ebbe sposato	**ebbero** sposato
futuro anteriore	
avrò sposato	**avremo** sposato
avrai sposato	**avrete** sposato
avrà sposato	**avranno** sposato
condizionale passato	
avrei sposato	**avremmo** sposato
avresti sposato	**avreste** sposato
avrebbe sposato	**avrebbero** sposato
congiuntivo passato	
abbia sposato	**abbiamo** sposato
abbia sposato	**abbiate** sposato
abbia sposato	**abbiano** sposato
congiuntivo trapassato	
avessi sposato	**avessimo** sposato
avessi sposato	**aveste** sposato
avesse sposato	**avessero** sposato

sposarsi — to get married

gerundio **sposandosi** — participio passato **sposatosi**

SINGULAR	PLURAL
indicativo presente	
mi spos**o**	**ci** spos**iamo**
ti spos**i**	**vi** spos**ate**
si spos**a**	**si** spos**ano**
imperfetto	
mi sposa**vo**	**ci** sposa**vamo**
ti sposa**vi**	**vi** sposa**vate**
si sposa**va**	**si** sposa**vano**
passato remoto	
mi spos**ai**	**ci** spos**ammo**
ti spos**asti**	**vi** spos**aste**
si spos**ò**	**si** spos**arono**
futuro semplice	
mi sposer**ò**	**ci** sposer**emo**
ti sposer**ai**	**vi** sposer**ete**
si sposer**à**	**si** sposer**anno**
condizionale presente	
mi spos**erei**	**ci** spos**eremmo**
ti spos**eresti**	**vi** spos**ereste**
si spos**erebbe**	**si** spos**erebbero**
congiuntivo presente	
mi sposi	**ci** spos**iamo**
ti sposi	**vi** spos**iate**
si sposi	**si** spos**ino**
congiuntivo imperfetto	
mi sposa**ssi**	**ci** sposa**ssimo**
ti sposa**ssi**	**vi** sposa**ste**
si sposa**sse**	**si** sposa**ssero**
imperativo	
	sposiamoci
sposati; non sposarti/ non ti sposare	sposatevi
si sposi	si sposino

SINGULAR	PLURAL
passato prossimo	
mi sono sposato(a)	**ci siamo** sposati(e)
ti sei sposato(a)	**vi siete** sposati(e)
si è sposato(a)	**si sono** sposati(e)
trapassato prossimo	
mi ero sposato(a)	**ci eravamo** sposati(e)
ti eri sposato(a)	**vi eravate** sposati(e)
si era sposato(a)	**si erano** sposati(e)
trapassato remoto	
mi fui sposato(a)	**ci fummo** sposati(e)
ti fosti sposato(a)	**vi foste** sposati(e)
si fu sposato(a)	**si furono** sposati(e)
futuro anteriore	
mi sarò sposato(a)	**ci saremo** sposati(e)
ti sarai sposato(a)	**vi sarete** sposati(e)
si sarà sposato(a)	**si saranno** sposati(e)
condizionale passato	
mi sarei sposato(a)	**ci saremmo** sposati(e)
ti saresti sposato(a)	**vi sareste** sposati(e)
si sarebbe sposato(a)	**si sarebbero** sposati(e)
congiuntivo passato	
mi sia sposato(a)	**ci siamo** sposati(e)
ti sia sposato(a)	**vi siate** sposati(e)
si sia sposato(a)	**si siano** sposati(e)
congiuntivo trapassato	
mi fossi sposato(a)	**ci fossimo** sposati(e)
ti fossi sposato(a)	**vi foste** sposati(e)
si fosse sposato(a)	**si fossero** sposati(e)

gerundio **spostando** participio passato **spostato**

SINGULAR	PLURAL
indicativo presente	
sposto	spostiamo
sposti	spostate
sposta	spostano
imperfetto	
spostavo	spostavamo
spostavi	spostavate
spostava	spostavano
passato remoto	
spostai	spostammo
spostasti	spostaste
spostò	spostarono
futuro semplice	
sposterò	sposteremo
sposterai	sposterete
sposterà	sposteranno
condizionale presente	
sposterei	sposteremmo
sposteresti	spostereste
sposterebbe	sposterebbero
congiuntivo presente	
sposti	spostiamo
sposti	spostiate
sposti	spostino
congiuntivo imperfetto	
spostassi	spostassimo
spostassi	spostaste
spostasse	spostassero
imperativo	
	spostiamo
sposta; non spostare	spostate
sposti	spostino

SINGULAR	PLURAL
passato prossimo	
ho spostato	abbiamo spostato
hai spostato	avete spostato
ha spostato	hanno spostato
trapassato prossimo	
avevo spostato	avevamo spostato
avevi spostato	avevate spostato
aveva spostato	avevano spostato
trapassato remoto	
ebbi spostato	avemmo spostato
avesti spostato	aveste spostato
ebbe spostato	ebbero spostato
futuro anteriore	
avrò spostato	avremo spostato
avrai spostato	avrete spostato
avrà spostato	avranno spostato
condizionale passato	
avrei spostato	avremmo spostato
avresti spostato	avreste spostato
avrebbe spostato	avrebbero spostato
congiuntivo passato	
abbia spostato	abbiamo spostato
abbia spostato	abbiate spostato
abbia spostato	abbiano spostato
congiuntivo trapassato	
avessi spostato	avessimo spostato
avessi spostato	aveste spostato
avesse spostato	avessero spostato

stabilire — to establish, to set

gerundio **stabilendo** participio passato **stabilito**

SINGULAR	PLURAL
indicativo presente	
stabilisc**o**	stabili**amo**
stabilisc**i**	stabili**te**
stabilisc**e**	stabilisc**ono**
imperfetto	
stabili**vo**	stabili**vamo**
stabili**vi**	stabili**vate**
stabili**va**	stabili**vano**
passato remoto	
stabil**ii**	stabil**immo**
stabil**isti**	stabil**iste**
stabil**ì**	stabil**irono**
futuro semplice	
stabilir**ò**	stabilir**emo**
stabilir**ai**	stabilir**ete**
stabilir**à**	stabilir**anno**
condizionale presente	
stabil**irei**	stabil**iremmo**
stabil**iresti**	stabil**ireste**
stabil**irebbe**	stabil**irebbero**
congiuntivo presente	
stabilisc**a**	stabili**amo**
stabilisc**a**	stabil**iate**
stabilisc**a**	stabilisc**ano**
congiuntivo imperfetto	
stabil**issi**	stabil**issimo**
stabil**issi**	stabil**iste**
stabil**isse**	stabil**issero**
imperativo	
	stabiliamo
stabilisci; non stabilire	stabilite
stabilisca	stabiliscano

SINGULAR	PLURAL
passato prossimo	
ho stabilito	**abbiamo** stabilito
hai stabilito	**avete** stabilito
ha stabilito	**hanno** stabilito
trapassato prossimo	
avevo stabilito	**avevamo** stabilito
avevi stabilito	**avevate** stabilito
aveva stabilito	**avevano** stabilito
trapassato remoto	
ebbi stabilito	**avemmo** stabilito
avesti stabilito	**aveste** stabilito
ebbe stabilito	**ebbero** stabilito
futuro anteriore	
avrò stabilito	**avremo** stabilito
avrai stabilito	**avrete** stabilito
avrà stabilito	**avranno** stabilito
condizionale passato	
avrei stabilito	**avremmo** stabilito
avresti stabilito	**avreste** stabilito
avrebbe stabilito	**avrebbero** stabilito
congiuntivo passato	
abbia stabilito	**abbiamo** stabilito
abbia stabilito	**abbiate** stabilito
abbia stabilito	**abbiano** stabilito
congiuntivo trapassato	
avessi stabilito	**avessimo** stabilito
avessi stabilito	**aveste** stabilito
avesse stabilito	**avessero** stabilito

gerundio **stando** participio passato **stato**

SINGULAR	PLURAL	SINGULAR	PLURAL
indicativo presente		passato prossimo	
st**o**	st**iamo**	**sono** stato(a)	**siamo** stati(e)
st**ai**	st**ate**	**sei** stato(a)	**siete** stati(e)
st**a**	st**anno**	**è** stato(a)	**sono** stati(e)
imperfetto		trapassato prossimo	
sta**vo**	sta**vamo**	**ero** stato(a)	**eravamo** stati(e)
sta**vi**	sta**vate**	**eri** stato(a)	**eravate** stati(e)
sta**va**	sta**vano**	**era** stato(a)	**erano** stati(e)
passato remoto		trapassato remoto	
st**etti**	st**emmo**	**fui** stato(a)	**fummo** stati(e)
st**esti**	st**este**	**fossti** stato(a)	**fosste** stati(e)
st**ette**	st**ettero**	**fu** stato(a)	**furono** stati(e)
futuro semplice		futuro anteriore	
star**ò**	star**emo**	**sarò** stato(a)	**saremo** stati(e)
star**ai**	star**ete**	**sarai** stato(a)	**sarete** stati(e)
star**à**	star**anno**	**sarà** stato(a)	**saranno** stati(e)
condizionale presente		condizionale passato	
st**arei**	st**aremmo**	**sarei** stato(a)	**saremmo** stati(e)
st**aresti**	st**areste**	**saresti** stato(a)	**sareste** stati(e)
st**arebbe**	st**arebbero**	**sarebbe** stato(a)	**sarebbero** stati(e)
congiuntivo presente		congiuntivo passato	
st**ia**	st**iamo**	**sia** stato(a)	**siamo** stati(e)
st**ia**	st**iate**	**sia** stato(a)	**siate** stati(e)
st**ia**	st**iano**	**sia** stato(a)	**siano** stati(e)
congiuntivo imperfetto		congiuntivo trapassato	
st**essi**	st**essimo**	**fossi** stato(a)	**fossimo** stati(e)
st**essi**	st**este**	**fossi** stato(a)	**foste** stati(e)
st**esse**	st**essero**	**fosse** stato(a)	**fossero** stati(e)
imperativo			
	stiamo		
sta'/stai; non stare	state		
stia	stiano		

S

stendere — to spread, to extend

gerundio **stendendo** — participio passato **steso**

SINGULAR	PLURAL
indicativo presente	
stend**o**	stend**iamo**
stend**i**	stend**ete**
stend**e**	stend**ono**
imperfetto	
stende**vo**	stende**vamo**
stende**vi**	stende**vate**
stende**va**	stende**vano**
passato remoto	
stes**i**	stend**emmo**
stend**esti**	stend**este**
stes**e**	stes**ero**
futuro semplice	
stender**ò**	stender**emo**
stender**ai**	stender**ete**
stender**à**	stender**anno**
condizionale presente	
stend**erei**	stend**eremmo**
stend**eresti**	stend**ereste**
stend**erebbe**	stend**erebbero**
congiuntivo presente	
stend**a**	stend**iamo**
stend**a**	stend**iate**
stend**a**	stend**ano**
congiuntivo imperfetto	
stend**essi**	stend**essimo**
stend**essi**	stend**este**
stend**esse**	stend**essero**
imperativo	
	stendiamo
stendi; non stendere	stendete
stenda	stendano

SINGULAR	PLURAL
passato prossimo	
ho steso	**abbiamo** steso
hai steso	**avete** steso
ha steso	**hanno** steso
trapassato prossimo	
avevo steso	**avevamo** steso
avevi steso	**avevate** steso
aveva steso	**avevano** steso
trapassato remoto	
ebbi steso	**avemmo** steso
avesti steso	**aveste** steso
ebbe steso	**ebbero** steso
futuro anteriore	
avrò steso	**avremo** steso
avrai steso	**avrete** steso
avrà steso	**avranno** steso
condizionale passato	
avrei steso	**avremmo** steso
avresti steso	**avreste** steso
avrebbe steso	**avrebbero** steso
congiuntivo passato	
abbia steso	**abbiamo** steso
abbia steso	**abbiate** steso
abbia steso	**abbiano** steso
congiuntivo trapassato	
avessi steso	**avessimo** steso
avessi steso	**aveste** steso
avesse steso	**avessero** steso

to press, to squeeze **stringere**

gerundio **stringendo** participio passato **stretto**

SINGULAR	PLURAL	SINGULAR	PLURAL
indicativo presente		passato prossimo	
string**o**	string**iamo**	**ho** stretto	**abbiamo** stretto
string**i**	string**ete**	**hai** stretto	**avete** stretto
string**e**	string**ono**	**ha** stretto	**hanno** stretto
imperfetto		trapassato prossimo	
stringe**vo**	stringe**vamo**	**avevo** stretto	**avevamo** stretto
stringe**vi**	stringe**vate**	**avevi** stretto	**avevate** stretto
stringe**va**	stringe**vano**	**aveva** stretto	**avevano** stretto
passato remoto		trapassato remoto	
strins**i**	string**emmo**	**ebbi** stretto	**avemmo** stretto
string**esti**	string**este**	**avesti** stretto	**aveste** stretto
strins**e**	strins**ero**	**ebbe** stretto	**ebbero** stretto
futuro semplice		futuro anteriore	
stringer**ò**	stringer**emo**	**avrò** stretto	**avremo** stretto
stringer**ai**	stringer**ete**	**avrai** stretto	**avrete** stretto
stringer**à**	stringer**anno**	**avrà** stretto	**avranno** stretto
condizionale presente		condizionale passato	
string**erei**	string**eremmo**	**avrei** stretto	**avremmo** stretto
string**eresti**	string**ereste**	**avresti** stretto	**avreste** stretto
string**erebbe**	string**erebbero**	**avrebbe** stretto	**avrebbero** stretto
congiuntivo presente		congiuntivo passato	
string**a**	string**iamo**	**abbia** stretto	**abbiamo** stretto
string**a**	string**iate**	**abbia** stretto	**abbiate** stretto
string**a**	string**ano**	**abbia** stretto	**abbiano** stretto
congiuntivo imperfetto		congiuntivo trapassato	
string**essi**	string**essimo**	**avessi** stretto	**avessimo** stretto
string**essi**	string**este**	**avessi** stretto	**aveste** stretto
string**esse**	string**essero**	**avesse** stretto	**avessero** stretto
imperativo			
	stringiamo		
stringi; non stringere	stringete		
stringa	stringano		

S

studiare — to study

gerundio **studiando** — participio passato **studiato**

SINGULAR	PLURAL	SINGULAR	PLURAL
indicativo presente		passato prossimo	
stud**io**	stud**iamo**	**ho** studiato	**abbiamo** studiato
stud**i**	stud**iate**	**hai** studiato	**avete** studiato
stud**ia**	stud**iano**	**ha** studiato	**hanno** studiato
imperfetto		trapassato prossimo	
studia**vo**	studia**vamo**	**avevo** studiato	**avevamo** studiato
studia**vi**	studia**vate**	**avevi** studiato	**avevate** studiato
studia**va**	studia**vano**	**aveva** studiato	**avevano** studiato
passato remoto		trapassato remoto	
studi**ai**	studi**ammo**	**ebbi** studiato	**avemmo** studiato
studi**asti**	studi**aste**	**avesti** studiato	**aveste** studiato
studi**ò**	studi**arono**	**ebbe** studiato	**ebbero** studiato
futuro semplice		futuro anteriore	
studier**ò**	studier**emo**	**avrò** studiato	**avremo** studiato
studier**ai**	studier**ete**	**avrai** studiato	**avrete** studiato
studier**à**	studier**anno**	**avrà** studiato	**avranno** studiato
condizionale presente		condizionale passato	
studi**erei**	studi**eremmo**	**avrei** studiato	**avremmo** studiato
studi**eresti**	studi**ereste**	**avresti** studiato	**avreste** studiato
studi**erebbe**	studi**erebbero**	**avrebbe** studiato	**avrebbero** studiato
congiuntivo presente		congiuntivo passato	
stud**i**	stud**iamo**	**abbia** studiato	**abbiamo** studiato
stud**i**	stud**iate**	**abbia** studiato	**abbiate** studiato
stud**i**	stud**ino**	**abbia** studiato	**abbiano** studiato
congiuntivo imperfetto		congiuntivo trapassato	
studi**assi**	studi**assimo**	**avessi** studiato	**avessimo** studiato
studi**assi**	studi**aste**	**avessi** studiato	**aveste** studiato
studi**asse**	studi**assero**	**avesse** studiato	**avessero** studiato
imperativo			
	studiamo		
studia; non studiare	studiate		
studi	studino		

to happen, to occur **succedere**

gerundio **succedendo** participio passato **successo**

SINGULAR	PLURAL	SINGULAR	PLURAL
indicativo presente		passato prossimo	
succed**e**	succed**ono**	**è** successo(a)	**sono** successi(e)
imperfetto		trapassato prossimo	
succed**eva**	succed**evano**	**era** successo(a)	**erano** successi(e)
passato remoto		trapassato remoto	
success**e**	success**ero**	**fu** successo(a)	**furono** successi(e)
futuro semplice		futuro anteriore	
succeder**à**	succeder**anno**	**sarà** successo(a)	**saranno** successi(e)
condizionale presente		condizionale passato	
succed**erebbe**	succed**erebbero**	**sarebbe** successo(a)	**sarebbero** successi(e)
congiuntivo presente		congiuntivo passato	
succed**a**	succed**ano**	**sia** successo(a)	**siano** successi(e)
congiuntivo imperfetto		congiuntivo trapassato	
succed**esse**	succed**essero**	**fosse** successo(a)	**fossero** successi(e)

MEMORY TIP

Success was destined to **occur**.

suggerire — to suggest, to advise

gerundio **suggerendo** participio passato **suggerito**

SINGULAR	PLURAL	SINGULAR	PLURAL
indicativo presente		passato prossimo	
suggerisc**o**	sugger**iamo**	**ho** suggerito	**abbiamo** suggerito
suggerisc**i**	sugger**ite**	**hai** suggerito	**avete** suggerito
suggerisc**e**	suggerisc**ono**	**ha** suggerito	**hanno** suggerito
imperfetto		trapassato prossimo	
sugger**ivo**	sugger**ivamo**	**avevo** suggerito	**avevamo** suggerito
sugger**ivi**	sugger**ivate**	**avevi** suggerito	**avevate** suggerito
sugger**iva**	sugger**ivano**	**aveva** suggerito	**avevano** suggerito
passato remoto		trapassato remoto	
sugger**ii**	sugger**immo**	**ebbi** suggerito	**avemmo** suggerito
sugger**isti**	sugger**iste**	**avesti** suggerito	**aveste** suggerito
sugger**ì**	sugger**irono**	**ebbe** suggerito	**ebbero** suggerito
futuro semplice		futuro anteriore	
suggerir**ò**	suggerir**emo**	**avrò** suggerito	**avremo** suggerito
suggerir**ai**	suggerir**ete**	**avrai** suggerito	**avrete** suggerito
suggerir**à**	suggerir**anno**	**avrà** suggerito	**avranno** suggerito
condizionale presente		condizionale passato	
sugger**irei**	sugger**iremmo**	**avrei** suggerito	**avremmo** suggerito
sugger**iresti**	sugger**ireste**	**avresti** suggerito	**avreste** suggerito
sugger**irebbe**	sugger**irebbero**	**avrebbe** suggerito	**avrebbero** suggerito
congiuntivo presente		congiuntivo passato	
suggerisc**a**	sugger**iamo**	**abbia** suggerito	**abbiamo** suggerito
suggerisc**a**	sugger**iate**	**abbia** suggerito	**abbiate** suggerito
suggerisc**a**	suggerisc**ano**	**abbia** suggerito	**abbiano** suggerito
congiuntivo imperfetto		congiuntivo trapassato	
sugger**issi**	sugger**issimo**	**avessi** suggerito	**avessimo** suggerito
sugger**issi**	sugger**iste**	**avessi** suggerito	**aveste** suggerito
sugger**isse**	sugger**issero**	**avesse** suggerito	**avessero** suggerito
imperativo			
	suggeriamo		
suggerisci; non suggerire	suggerite		
suggerisca	suggeriscano		

to ring, to play (an instrument) **suonare**

gerundio **suonando** participio passato **suonato**

SINGULAR	PLURAL	SINGULAR	PLURAL
indicativo presente		passato prossimo	
suon**o**	suon**iamo**	**ho** suonato	**abbiamo** suonato
suon**i**	suon**ate**	**hai** suonato	**avete** suonato
suon**a**	suon**ano**	**ha** suonato	**hanno** suonato
imperfetto		trapassato prossimo	
suona**vo**	suona**vamo**	**avevo** suonato	**avevamo** suonato
suona**vi**	suona**vate**	**avevi** suonato	**avevate** suonato
suona**va**	suona**vano**	**aveva** suonato	**avevano** suonato
passato remoto		trapassato remoto	
suon**ai**	suon**ammo**	**ebbi** suonato	**avemmo** suonato
suon**asti**	suon**aste**	**avesti** suonato	**aveste** suonato
suon**ò**	suon**arono**	**ebbe** suonato	**ebbero** suonato
futuro semplice		futuro anteriore	
suoner**ò**	suoner**emo**	**avrò** suonato	**avremo** suonato
suoner**ai**	suoner**ete**	**avrai** suonato	**avrete** suonato
suoner**à**	suoner**anno**	**avrà** suonato	**avranno** suonato
condizionale presente		condizionale passato	
suon**erei**	suon**eremmo**	**avrei** suonato	**avremmo** suonato
suon**eresti**	suon**ereste**	**avresti** suonato	**avreste** suonato
suon**erebbe**	suon**erebbero**	**avrebbe** suonato	**avrebbero** suonato
congiuntivo presente		congiuntivo passato	
suon**i**	suon**iamo**	**abbia** suonato	**abbiamo** suonato
suon**i**	suon**iate**	**abbia** suonato	**abbiate** suonato
suon**i**	suon**ino**	**abbia** suonato	**abbiano** suonato
congiuntivo imperfetto		congiuntivo trapassato	
suon**assi**	suon**assimo**	**avessi** suonato	**avessimo** suonato
suon**assi**	suon**aste**	**avessi** suonato	**aveste** suonato
suon**asse**	suon**assero**	**avesse** suonato	**avessero** suonato
imperativo			
	suoniamo		
suona; non suonare	suonate		
suoni	suonino		

supporre — to suppose, to assume

gerundio **supponendo** — participio passato **supposto**

SINGULAR	PLURAL
indicativo presente	
suppon**go**	suppon**iamo**
suppon**i**	suppon**ete**
suppon**e**	suppong**ono**
imperfetto	
suppone**vo**	suppone**vamo**
suppone**vi**	suppone**vate**
suppone**va**	suppone**vano**
passato remoto	
suppo**si**	suppon**emmo**
suppon**esti**	suppon**este**
suppo**se**	suppo**sero**
futuro semplice	
supporr**ò**	supporr**emo**
supporr**ai**	supporr**ete**
supporr**à**	supporr**anno**
condizionale presente	
supp**orrei**	supp**orremmo**
supp**orresti**	supp**orreste**
supp**orrebbe**	supp**orrebbero**
congiuntivo presente	
suppong**a**	suppon**iamo**
suppong**a**	suppon**iate**
suppong**a**	suppong**ano**
congiuntivo imperfetto	
suppon**essi**	suppon**essimo**
suppon**essi**	suppon**este**
suppon**esse**	suppon**essero**
imperativo	
	supponiamo
supponi;	supponete
non supporre	
supponga	supponigano

SINGULAR	PLURAL
passato prossimo	
ho supposto	**abbiamo** supposto
hai supposto	**avete** supposto
ha supposto	**hanno** supposto
trapassato prossimo	
avevo supposto	**avevamo** supposto
avevi supposto	**avevate** supposto
aveva supposto	**avevano** supposto
trapassato remoto	
ebbi supposto	**avemmo** supposto
avesti supposto	**aveste** supposto
ebbe supposto	**ebbero** supposto
futuro anteriore	
avrò supposto	**avremo** supposto
avrai supposto	**avrete** supposto
avrà supposto	**avranno** supposto
condizionale passato	
avrei supposto	**avremmo** supposto
avresti supposto	**avreste** supposto
avrebbe supposto	**avrebbero** supposto
congiuntivo passato	
abbia supposto	**abbiamo** supposto
abbia supposto	**abbiate** supposto
abbia supposto	**abbiano** supposto
congiuntivo trapassato	
avessi supposto	**avessimo** supposto
avessi supposto	**aveste** supposto
avesse supposto	**avessero** supposto

gerundio **svanendo** participio passato **svanito**

SINGULAR	PLURAL	SINGULAR	PLURAL
indicativo presente		passato prossimo	
svanisc**o**	svan**iamo**	**sono** svanito(a)	**siamo** svaniti(e)
svanisc**i**	svan**ite**	**sei** svanito(a)	**siete** svaniti(e)
svanisc**e**	svanisc**ono**	**è** svanito(a)	**sono** svaniti(e)
imperfetto		trapassato prossimo	
svani**vo**	svani**vamo**	**ero** svanito(a)	**eravamo** svaniti(e)
svani**vi**	svani**vate**	**eri** svanito(a)	**eravate** svaniti(e)
svani**va**	svani**vano**	**era** svanito(a)	**erano** svaniti(e)
passato remoto		trapassato remoto	
svan**ii**	svan**immo**	**fui** svanito(a)	**fummo** svaniti(e)
svan**isti**	svan**iste**	**fosti** svanito(a)	**foste** svaniti(e)
svan**ì**	svan**irono**	**fu** svanito(a)	**furono** svaniti(e)
futuro semplice		futuro anteriore	
svanir**ò**	svanir**emo**	**sarò** svanito(a)	**saremo** svaniti(e)
svanir**ai**	svanir**ete**	**sarai** svanito(a)	**sarete** svaniti(e)
svanir**à**	svanir**anno**	**sarà** svanito(a)	**saranno** svaniti(e)
condizionale presente		condizionale passato	
svan**irei**	svan**iremmo**	**sarei** svanito(a)	**saremmo** svaniti(e)
svan**iresti**	svan**ireste**	**saresti** svanito(a)	**sareste** svaniti(e)
svan**irebbe**	svan**irebbero**	**sarebbe** svanito(a)	**sarebbero** svaniti(e)
congiuntivo presente		congiuntivo passato	
svanisc**a**	svan**iamo**	**sia** svanito(a)	**siamo** svaniti(e)
svanisc**a**	svan**iate**	**sia** svanito(a)	**siate** svaniti(e)
svanisc**a**	svan**iscano**	**sia** svanito(a)	**siano** svaniti(e)
congiuntivo imperfetto		congiuntivo trapassato	
svan**issi**	svan**issimo**	**fossi** svanito(a)	**fossimo** svaniti(e)
svan**issi**	svan**iste**	**fossi** svanito(a)	**foste** svaniti(e)
svan**isse**	svan**issero**	**fosse** svanito(a)	**fossero** svaniti(e)
imperativo			
	svaniamo		
svanisci; non svanire	svanite		
svanisca	svaniscano		

svegliare — to wake up

gerundio **svegliando** participio passato **svegliato**

SINGULAR	PLURAL
indicativo presente	
svegli**o**	svegli**amo**
svegli	svegli**ate**
svegli**a**	svegli**ano**
imperfetto	
sveglia**vo**	sveglia**vamo**
sveglia**vi**	sveglia**vate**
sveglia**va**	sveglia**vano**
passato remoto	
svegli**ai**	svegli**ammo**
svegli**asti**	svegli**aste**
svegli**ò**	svegli**arono**
futuro semplice	
sveglier**ò**	sveglier**emo**
sveglier**ai**	sveglier**ete**
sveglier**à**	svegler**anno**
condizionale presente	
svegli**erei**	svegli**eremmo**
svegli**eresti**	svegli**ereste**
svegli**erebbe**	svegli**erebbero**
congiuntivo presente	
svegl**i**	svegli**amo**
svegl**i**	svegli**ate**
svegl**i**	svegl**ino**
congiuntivo imperfetto	
svegli**assi**	svegli**assimo**
svegli**assi**	svegli**aste**
svegli**asse**	svegli**assero**
imperativo	
	svegliamo
sveglia; non svegliare	svegliate
svegli	sveglino

SINGULAR	PLURAL
passato prossimo	
ho svegliato	**abbiamo** svegliato
hai svegliato	**avete** svegliato
ha svegliato	**hanno** svegliato
trapassato prossimo	
avevo svegliato	**avevamo** svegliato
avevi svegliato	**avevate** svegliato
aveva svegliato	**avevano** svegliato
trapassato remoto	
ebbi svegliato	**avemmo** svegliato
avesti svegliato	**aveste** svegliato
ebbe svegliato	**ebbero** svegliato
futuro anteriore	
avrò svegliato	**avremo** svegliato
avrai svegliato	**avrete** svegliato
avrà svegliato	**avranno** svegliato
condizionale passato	
avrei svegliato	**avremmo** svegliato
avresti svegliato	**avreste** svegliato
avrebbe svegliato	**avrebbero** svegliato
congiuntivo passato	
abbia svegliato	**abbiamo** svegliato
abbia svegliato	**abbiate** svegliato
abbia svegliato	**abbiano** svegliato
congiuntivo trapassato	
avessi svegliato	**avessimo** svegliato
avessi svegliato	**aveste** svegliato
avesse svegliato	**avessero** svegliato

gerundio **svegliandosi** participio passato **svegliatosi**

SINGULAR	PLURAL
indicativo presente	
mi svegli**o**	**ci** svegli**amo**
ti svegli	**vi** svegli**ate**
si svegli**a**	**si** svegli**ano**
imperfetto	
mi sveglia**vo**	**ci** sveglia**vamo**
ti sveglia**vi**	**vi** sveglia**vate**
si sveglia**va**	**si** sveglia**vano**
passato remoto	
mi svegli**ai**	**ci** svegli**ammo**
ti svegli**asti**	**vi** svegli**aste**
si svegli**ò**	**si** svegli**arono**
futuro semplice	
mi sveglier**ò**	**ci** sveglier**emo**
ti sveglier**ai**	**vi** sveglier**ete**
si sveglier**à**	**si** sveglier**anno**
condizionale presente	
mi sveglier**ei**	**ci** sveglier**emmo**
ti svegli**eresti**	**vi** svegli**ereste**
si svegli**erebbe**	**si** svegli**erebbero**
congiuntivo presente	
mi svegli	**ci** svegli**amo**
ti svegli	**vi** svegli**ate**
si svegli	**si** svegl**ino**
congiuntivo imperfetto	
mi svegli**assi**	**ci** svegli**assimo**
ti svegli**assi**	**vi** svegli**aste**
si svegli**asse**	**si** svegli**assero**
imperativo	
	svegliamoci
svegliati; non svegliarti/ non ti svegliare	svegliatevi
si svegli	si sveglino

SINGULAR	PLURAL
passato prossimo	
mi sono svegliato(a)	**ci siamo** svegliati(e)
ti sei svegliato(a)	**vi siete** svegliati(e)
si è svegliato(a)	**si sono** svegliati(e)
trapassato prossimo	
mi ero svegliato(a)	**ci eravamo** svegliati(e)
ti eri svegliato(a)	**vi eravate** svegliati(e)
si era svegliato(a)	**si erano** svegliati(e)
trapassato remoto	
mi fui svegliato(a)	**ci fummo** svegliati(e)
ti fosti svegliato(a)	**vi foste** svegliati(e)
si fu svegliato(a)	**si furono** svegliati(e)
futuro anteriore	
mi sarò svegliato(a)	**ci saremo** svegliati(e)
ti sarai svegliato(a)	**vi sarete** svegliati(e)
si sarà svegliato(a)	**si saranno** svegliati(e)
condizionale passato	
mi sarei svegliato(a)	**ci saremmo** svegliati(e)
ti saresti svegliato(a)	**vi sareste** svegliati(e)
si sarebbe svegliato(a)	**si sarebbero** svegliati(e)
congiuntivo passato	
mi sia svegliato(a)	**ci siamo** svegliati(e)
ti sia svegliato(a)	**vi siate** svegliati(e)
si sia svegliato(a)	**si siano** svegliati(e)
congiuntivo trapassato	
mi fossi svegliato(a)	**ci fossimo** svegliati(e)
ti fossi svegliato(a)	**vi foste** svegliati(e)
si fosse svegliato(a)	**si fossero** svegliati(e)

svenire — to faint

gerundio **svenendo** participio passato **svenuto**

SINGULAR	PLURAL
indicativo presente	
sveng**o**	sven**iamo**
svien**i**	sven**ite**
svien**e**	sveng**ono**
imperfetto	
sveni**vo**	sveni**vamo**
sveni**vi**	sveni**vate**
sveni**va**	sveni**vano**
passato remoto	
sven**ni**	sven**immo**
sven**isti**	sven**iste**
sven**ne**	sven**nero**
futuro semplice	
sverr**ò**	sverr**emo**
sverr**ai**	sverr**ete**
sverr**à**	sverr**anno**
condizionale presente	
sver**rei**	sver**remmo**
sver**resti**	sver**reste**
sver**rebbe**	sver**rebbero**
congiuntivo presente	
sveng**a**	sven**iamo**
sveng**a**	sven**iate**
sveng**a**	sveng**ano**
congiuntivo imperfetto	
sven**issi**	sven**issimo**
sven**issi**	sven**iste**
sven**isse**	sven**issero**
imperativo	
	sveniamo
svieni; non svenire	svenite
svenga	svengano

SINGULAR	PLURAL
passato prossimo	
sono svenuto(a)	**siamo** svenuti(e)
sei svenuto(a)	**siete** svenuti(e)
è svenuto(a)	**sono** svenuti(e)
trapassato prossimo	
ero svenuto(a)	**eravamo** svenuti(e)
eri svenuto(a)	**eravate** svenuti(e)
era svenuto(a)	**erano** svenuti(e)
trapassato remoto	
fui svenuto(a)	**fummo** svenuti(e)
fosti svenuto(a)	**foste** svenuti(e)
fu svenuto(a)	**furono** svenuti(e)
futuro anteriore	
sarò svenuto(a)	**saremo** svenuti(e)
sarai svenuto(a)	**sarete** svenuti(e)
sarà svenuto(a)	**saranno** svenuti(e)
condizionale passato	
sarei svenuto(a)	**saremmo** svenuti(e)
saresti svenuto(a)	**sareste** svenuti(e)
sarebbe svenuto(a)	**sarebbero** svenuti(e)
congiuntivo passato	
sia svenuto(a)	**siamo** svenuti(e)
sia svenuto(a)	**siate** svenuti(e)
sia svenuto(a)	**siano** svenuti(e)
congiuntivo trapassato	
fossi svenuto(a)	**fossimo** svenuti(e)
fossi svenuto(a)	**foste** svenuti(e)
fosse svenuto(a)	**fossero** svenuti(e)

gerundio **sviluppando** participio passato **sviluppato**

SINGULAR	PLURAL	SINGULAR	PLURAL
indicativo presente		passato prossimo	
svilupp**o**	svilupp**iamo**	**ho** sviluppato	**abbiamo** sviluppato
svilupp**i**	svilupp**ate**	**hai** sviluppato	**avete** sviluppato
svilupp**a**	svilupp**ano**	**ha** sviluppato	**hanno** sviluppato
imperfetto		trapassato prossimo	
sviluppa**vo**	sviluppa**vamo**	**avevo** sviluppato	**avevamo** sviluppato
sviluppa**vi**	sviluppa**vate**	**avevi** sviluppato	**avevate** sviluppato
sviluppa**va**	sviluppa**vano**	**aveva** sviluppato	**avevano** sviluppato
passato remoto		trapassato remoto	
svilupp**ai**	svilupp**ammo**	**ebbi** sviluppato	**avemmo** sviluppato
svilupp**asti**	svilupp**aste**	**avesti** sviluppato	**aveste** sviluppato
svilupp**ò**	svilupp**arono**	**ebbe** sviluppato	**ebbero** sviluppato
futuro semplice		futuro anteriore	
svilupper**ò**	svilupper**emo**	**avrò** sviluppato	**avremo** sviluppato
svilupper**ai**	svilupper**ete**	**avrai** sviluppato	**avrete** sviluppato
svilupper**à**	svilupper**anno**	**avrà** sviluppato	**avranno** sviluppato
condizionale presente		condizionale passato	
svilupp**erei**	svilupp**eremmo**	**avrei** sviluppato	**avremmo** sviluppato
svilupp**eresti**	svilupp**ereste**	**avresti** sviluppato	**avreste** sviluppato
svilupp**erebbe**	svilupp**erebbero**	**avrebbe** sviluppato	**avrebbero** sviluppato
congiuntivo presente		congiuntivo passato	
svilupp**i**	svilupp**iamo**	**abbia** sviluppato	**abbiamo** sviluppato
svilupp**i**	svilupp**iate**	**abbia** sviluppato	**abbiate** sviluppato
svilupp**i**	svilupp**ino**	**abbia** sviluppato	**abbiano** sviluppato
congiuntivo imperfetto		congiuntivo trapassato	
svilupp**assi**	svilupp**assimo**	**avessi** sviluppato	**avessimo** sviluppato
svilupp**assi**	svilupp**aste**	**avessi** sviluppato	**aveste** sviluppato
svilupp**asse**	svilupp**assero**	**avesse** sviluppato	**avessero** sviluppato
imperativo			
	sviluppiamo		
sviluppa; non sviluppare	sviluppate		
sviluppi	sviluppino		

svolgere — to develop, to take place

gerundio **svolgendo** — participio passato **svolto**

SINGULAR	PLURAL
indicativo presente	
svolg**o**	svolg**iamo**
svolg**i**	svolg**ete**
svolg**e**	svolg**ono**
imperfetto	
svolge**vo**	svolge**vamo**
svolge**vi**	svolge**vate**
svolge**va**	svolge**vano**
passato remoto	
svols**i**	svolg**emmo**
svolg**esti**	svolg**este**
svols**e**	svols**ero**
futuro semplice	
svolger**ò**	svolger**emo**
svolger**ai**	svolger**ete**
svolger**à**	svolger**anno**
condizionale presente	
svolg**erei**	svolg**eremmo**
svolg**eresti**	svolg**ereste**
svolg**erebbe**	svolg**erebbero**
congiuntivo presente	
svolg**a**	svolg**iamo**
svolg**a**	svolg**iate**
svolg**a**	svolg**ano**
congiuntivo imperfetto	
svolg**essi**	svolg**essimo**
svolg**essi**	svolg**este**
svolg**esse**	svolg**essero**
imperativo	
	svolgiamo
svolgi; non svolgere	svolgete
svolga	svolgano

SINGULAR	PLURAL
passato prossimo	
ho svolto	**abbiamo** svolto
hai svolto	**avete** svolto
ha svolto	**hanno** svolto
trapassato prossimo	
avevo svolto	**avevamo** svolto
avevi svolto	**avevate** svolto
aveva svolto	**avevano** svolto
trapassato remoto	
ebbi svolto	**avemmo** svolto
avesti svolto	**aveste** svolto
ebbe svolto	**ebbero** svolto
futuro anteriore	
avrò svolto	**avremo** svolto
avrai svolto	**avrete** svolto
avrà svolto	**avranno** svolto
condizionale passato	
avrei svolto	**avremmo** svolto
avresti svolto	**avreste** svolto
avrebbe svolto	**avrebbero** svolto
congiuntivo passato	
abbia svolto	**abbiamo** svolto
abbia svolto	**abbiate** svolto
abbia svolto	**abbiano** svolto
congiuntivo trapassato	
avessi svolto	**avessimo** svolto
avessi svolto	**aveste** svolto
avesse svolto	**avessero** svolto

to be silent **tacere**

gerundio **tacendo**   participio passato **taciuto**

indicativo presente

SINGULAR	PLURAL
tacci**o**	tac**iamo**
tac**i**	tac**ete**
tac**e**	tacci**ono**

imperfetto

SINGULAR	PLURAL
tace**vo**	tace**vamo**
tace**vi**	tace**vate**
tace**va**	tace**vano**

passato remoto

SINGULAR	PLURAL
tacqu**i**	tac**emmo**
tac**esti**	tac**este**
tacqu**e**	tacqu**ero**

futuro semplice

SINGULAR	PLURAL
tacer**ò**	tacer**emo**
tacer**ai**	tacer**ete**
tacer**à**	tacer**anno**

condizionale presente

SINGULAR	PLURAL
tac**erei**	tac**eremmo**
tac**eresti**	tac**ereste**
tac**erebbe**	tac**erebbero**

congiuntivo presente

SINGULAR	PLURAL
tacci**a**	tac(c)**iamo**
tacci**a**	tac(c)**iate**
tacci**a**	tacc**iano**

congiuntivo imperfetto

SINGULAR	PLURAL
tac**essi**	tac**essimo**
tac**essi**	tac**este**
tac**esse**	tac**essero**

imperativo

SINGULAR	PLURAL
	tacciamo
taci; non tacere	tacete
taccia	tacciano

passato prossimo

SINGULAR	PLURAL
ho taciuto	**abbiamo** taciuto
hai taciuto	**avete** taciuto
ha taciuto	**hanno** taciuto

trapassato prossimo

SINGULAR	PLURAL
avevo taciuto	**avevamo** taciuto
avevi taciuto	**avevate** taciuto
aveva taciuto	**avevano** taciuto

trapassato remoto

SINGULAR	PLURAL
ebbi taciuto	**avemmo** taciuto
avesti taciuto	**aveste** taciuto
ebbe taciuto	**ebbero** taciuto

futuro anteriore

SINGULAR	PLURAL
avrò taciuto	**avremo** taciuto
avrai taciuto	**avrete** taciuto
avrà taciuto	**avranno** taciuto

condizionale passato

SINGULAR	PLURAL
avrei taciuto	**avremmo** taciuto
avresti taciuto	**avreste** taciuto
avrebbe taciuto	**avrebbero** taciuto

congiuntivo passato

SINGULAR	PLURAL
abbia taciuto	**abbiamo** taciuto
abbia taciuto	**abbiate** taciuto
abbia taciuto	**abbiano** taciuto

congiuntivo trapassato

SINGULAR	PLURAL
avessi taciuto	**avessimo** taciuto
avessi taciuto	**aveste** taciuto
avesse taciuto	**avessero** taciuto

tagliare	**to cut, to slice, to cut up**
gerundio **tagliando**	participio passato **tagliato**

SINGULAR	PLURAL	SINGULAR	PLURAL
indicativo presente		passato prossimo	
tagli**o**	tagli**amo**	**ho** tagliato	**abbiamo** tagliato
tagl**i**	tagli**ate**	**hai** tagliato	**avete** tagliato
tagli**a**	tagli**ano**	**ha** tagliato	**hanno** tagliato
imperfetto		trapassato prossimo	
taglia**vo**	taglia**vamo**	**avevo** tagliato	**avevamo** tagliato
taglia**vi**	taglia**vate**	**avevi** tagliato	**avevate** tagliato
taglia**va**	taglia**vano**	**aveva** tagliato	**avevano** tagliato
passato remoto		trapassato remoto	
taglia**i**	tagli**ammo**	**ebbi** tagliato	**avemmo** tagliato
tagli**asti**	tagli**aste**	**avesti** tagliato	**aveste** tagliato
tagli**ò**	tagliar**ono**	**ebbe** tagliato	**ebbero** tagliato
futuro semplice		futuro anteriore	
taglier**ò**	taglier**emo**	**avrò** tagliato	**avremo** tagliato
taglier**ai**	taglier**ete**	**avrai** tagliato	**avrete** tagliato
taglier**à**	taglier**anno**	**avrà** tagliato	**avranno** tagliato
condizionale presente		condizionale passato	
tagli**erei**	tagli**eremmo**	**avrei** tagliato	**avremmo** tagliato
tagli**eresti**	tagli**ereste**	**avresti** tagliato	**avreste** tagliato
tagli**erebbe**	tagli**erebbero**	**avrebbe** tagliato	**avrebbero** tagliato
congiuntivo presente		congiuntivo passato	
tagl**i**	tagl**iamo**	**abbia** tagliato	**abbiamo** tagliato
tagl**i**	tagl**iate**	**abbia** tagliato	**abbiate** tagliato
tagl**i**	tagl**ino**	**abbia** tagliato	**abbiano** tagliato
congiuntivo imperfetto		congiuntivo trapassato	
tagli**assi**	tagli**assimo**	**avessi** tagliato	**avessimo** tagliato
tagli**assi**	tagli**aste**	**avessi** tagliato	**aveste** tagliato
tagli**asse**	tagli**assero**	**avesse** tagliato	**avessero** tagliato
imperativo			
	tagliamo		
taglia; non tagliare	tagliate		
tagli	taglino		

T

to telephone, to call — telefonare

gerundio **telefonando** participio passato **telefonato**

SINGULAR	PLURAL	SINGULAR	PLURAL
indicativo presente		passato prossimo	
telefon**o**	telefon**iamo**	**ho** telefonato	**abbiamo** telefonato
telefon**i**	telefon**ate**	**hai** telefonato	**avete** telefonato
telefon**a**	telefon**ano**	**ha** telefonato	**hanno** telefonato
imperfetto		trapassato prossimo	
telefona**vo**	telefona**vamo**	**avevo** telefonato	**avevamo** telefonato
telefona**vi**	telefona**vate**	**avevi** telefonato	**avevate** telefonato
telefona**va**	telefona**vano**	**aveva** telefonato	**avevano** telefonato
passato remoto		trapassato remoto	
telefona**i**	telefon**ammo**	**ebbi** telefonato	**avemmo** telefonato
telefon**asti**	telefon**aste**	**avesti** telefonato	**aveste** telefonato
telefon**ò**	telefonar**ono**	**ebbe** telefonato	**ebbero** telefonato
futuro semplice		futuro anteriore	
telefoner**ò**	telefoner**emo**	**avrò** telefonato	**avremo** telefonato
telefoner**ai**	telefoner**ete**	**avrai** telefonato	**avrete** telefonato
telefoner**à**	telefoner**anno**	**avrà** telefonato	**avranno** telefonato
condizionale presente		condizionale passato	
telefon**erei**	telefon**eremmo**	**avrei** telefonato	**avremmo** telefonato
telefon**eresti**	telefon**ereste**	**avresti** telefonato	**avreste** telefonato
telefon**erebbe**	telefon**erebbero**	**avrebbe** telefonato	**avrebbero** telefonato
congiuntivo presente		congiuntivo passato	
telefon**i**	telefon**iamo**	**abbia** telefonato	**abbiamo** telefonato
telefon**i**	telefon**iate**	**abbia** telefonato	**abbiate** telefonato
telefon**i**	telefon**ino**	**abbia** telefonato	**abbiano** telefonato
congiuntivo imperfetto		congiuntivo trapassato	
telefon**assi**	telefon**assimo**	**avessi** telefonato	**avessimo** telefonato
telefon**assi**	telefon**aste**	**avessi** telefonato	**aveste** telefonato
telefon**asse**	telefon**assero**	**avesse** telefonato	**avessero** telefonato
imperativo			
	telefoniamo		
telefona; non telefonare	telefonate		
telefoni	telefonino		

temere — to be afraid of

gerundio **temendo** participio passato **temuto**

SINGULAR	PLURAL	SINGULAR	PLURAL
indicativo presente		passato prossimo	
tem**o**	tem**iamo**	**ho** temuto	**abbiamo** temuto
tem**i**	tem**ete**	**hai** temuto	**avete** temuto
tem**e**	tem**ono**	**ha** temuto	**hanno** temuto
imperfetto		trapassato prossimo	
teme**vo**	teme**vamo**	**avevo** temuto	**avevamo** temuto
teme**vi**	teme**vate**	**avevi** temuto	**avevate** temuto
teme**va**	teme**vano**	**aveva** temuto	**avevano** temuto
passato remoto		trapassato remoto	
teme**i**, tem**etti**	tem**emmo**	**ebbi** temuto	**avemmo** temuto
tem**esti**	tem**este**	**avesti** temuto	**aveste** temuto
tem**é**, tem**ette**	temer**ono**, tem**ettero**	**ebbe** temuto	**ebbero** temuto
futuro semplice		futuro anteriore	
temer**ò**	temer**emo**	**avrò** temuto	**avremo** temuto
temer**ai**	temer**ete**	**avrai** temuto	**avrete** temuto
temer**à**	temer**anno**	**avrà** temuto	**avranno** temuto
condizionale presente		condizionale passato	
tem**erei**	tem**eremmo**	**avrei** temuto	**avremmo** temuto
tem**eresti**	tem**ereste**	**avresti** temuto	**avreste** temuto
tem**erebbe**	tem**erebbero**	**avrebbe** temuto	**avrebbero** temuto
congiuntivo presente		congiuntivo passato	
tem**a**	tem**iamo**	**abbia** temuto	**abbiamo** temuto
tem**a**	tem**iate**	**abbia** temuto	**abbiate** temuto
tem**a**	tem**ano**	**abbia** temuto	**abbiano** temuto
congiuntivo imperfetto		congiuntivo trapassato	
tem**essi**	tem**essimo**	**avessi** temuto	**avessimo** temuto
tem**essi**	tem**este**	**avessi** temuto	**aveste** temuto
tem**esse**	tem**essero**	**avesse** temuto	**avessero** temuto
imperativo			
	temiamo		
temi; non temere	temete		
tema	temano		

T

gerundio **tendendo** participio passato **teso**

SINGULAR	PLURAL	SINGULAR	PLURAL
indicativo presente		passato prossimo	
tend**o**	tend**iamo**	**ho** teso	**abbiamo** teso
tend**i**	tend**ete**	**hai** teso	**avete** teso
tend**e**	tend**ono**	**ha** teso	**hanno** teso
imperfetto		trapassato prossimo	
tende**vo**	tende**vamo**	**avevo** teso	**avevamo** teso
tende**vi**	tende**vate**	**avevi** teso	**avevate** teso
tende**va**	tende**vano**	**aveva** teso	**avevano** teso
passato remoto		trapassato remoto	
tes**i**	tend**emmo**	**ebbi** teso	**avemmo** teso
tend**esti**	tend**este**	**avesti** teso	**aveste** teso
tes**e**	tes**ero**	**ebbe** teso	**ebbero** teso
futuro semplice		futuro anteriore	
tender**ò**	tender**emo**	**avrò** teso	**avremo** teso
tender**ai**	tender**ete**	**avrai** teso	**avrete** teso
tender**à**	tender**anno**	**avrà** teso	**avranno** teso
condizionale presente		condizionale passato	
tend**erei**	tend**eremmo**	**avrei** teso	**avremmo** teso
tend**eresti**	tend**ereste**	**avresti** teso	**avreste** teso
tend**erebbe**	tend**erebbero**	**avrebbe** teso	**avrebbero** teso
congiuntivo presente		congiuntivo passato	
tend**a**	tend**iamo**	**abbia** teso	**abbiamo** teso
tend**a**	tend**iate**	**abbia** teso	**abbiate** teso
tend**a**	tend**ano**	**abbia** teso	**abbiano** teso
congiuntivo imperfetto		congiuntivo trapassato	
tend**essi**	tend**essimo**	**avessi** teso	**avessimo** teso
tend**essi**	tend**este**	**avessi** teso	**aveste** teso
tend**esse**	tend**essero**	**avesse** teso	**avessero** teso
imperativo			
	tendiamo		
tendi; non tendere	tendete		
tenda	tendano		

T

tenere — to keep, to hold

gerundio **tenendo** participio passato **tenuto**

SINGULAR	PLURAL	SINGULAR	PLURAL
indicativo presente		passato prossimo	
teng**o**	ten**iamo**	**ho** tenuto	**abbiamo** tenuto
tien**i**	ten**ete**	**hai** tenuto	**avete** tenuto
tien**e**	teng**ono**	**ha** tenuto	**hanno** tenuto
imperfetto		trapassato prossimo	
tene**vo**	tene**vamo**	**avevo** tenuto	**avevamo** tenuto
tene**vi**	tene**vate**	**avevi** tenuto	**avevate** tenuto
tene**va**	tene**vano**	**aveva** tenuto	**avevano** tenuto
passato remoto		trapassato remoto	
tenn**i**	ten**emmo**	**ebbi** tenuto	**avemmo** tenuto
ten**esti**	ten**este**	**avesti** tenuto	**aveste** tenuto
tenn**e**	tenn**ero**	**ebbe** tenuto	**ebbero** tenuto
futuro semplice		futuro anteriore	
terr**ò**	terr**emo**	**avrò** tenuto	**avremo** tenuto
terr**ai**	terr**ete**	**avrai** tenuto	**avrete** tenuto
terr**à**	terr**anno**	**avrà** tenuto	**avranno** tenuto
condizionale presente		condizionale passato	
terrei	**terremmo**	**avrei** tenuto	**avremmo** tenuto
terresti	**terreste**	**avresti** tenuto	**avreste** tenuto
terrebbe	**terrebbero**	**avrebbe** tenuto	**avrebbero** tenuto
congiuntivo presente		congiuntivo passato	
teng**a**	ten**iamo**	**abbia** tenuto	**abbiamo** tenuto
teng**a**	ten**iate**	**abbia** tenuto	**abbiate** tenuto
teng**a**	teng**ano**	**abbia** tenuto	**abbiano** tenuto
congiuntivo imperfetto		congiuntivo trapassato	
ten**essi**	ten**essimo**	**avessi** tenuto	**avessimo** tenuto
ten**essi**	ten**este**	**avessi** tenuto	**aveste** tenuto
ten**esse**	ten**essero**	**avesse** tenuto	**avessero** tenuto

imperativo

	teniamo
tieni; non tenere	tenete
tenga	tengano

T

gerundio **tentando** participio passato **tentato**

SINGULAR	PLURAL	SINGULAR	PLURAL
indicativo presente		passato prossimo	
tent**o**	tent**iamo**	**ho** tentato	**abbiamo** tentato
tent**i**	tent**ate**	**hai** tentato	**avete** tentato
tent**a**	tent**ano**	**ha** tentato	**hanno** tentato
imperfetto		trapassato prossimo	
tenta**vo**	tenta**vamo**	**avevo** tentato	**avevamo** tentato
tenta**vi**	tenta**vate**	**avevi** tentato	**avevate** tentato
tenta**va**	tenta**vano**	**aveva** tentato	**avevano** tentato
passato remoto		trapassato remoto	
tent**ai**	tent**ammo**	**ebbi** tentato	**avemmo** tentato
tent**asti**	tent**aste**	**avesti** tentato	**aveste** tentato
tent**ò**	tentar**ono**	**ebbe** tentato	**ebbero** tentato
futuro semplice		futuro anteriore	
tenter**ò**	tenter**emo**	**avrò** tentato	**avremo** tentato
tenter**ai**	tenter**ete**	**avrai** tentato	**avrete** tentato
tenter**à**	tenter**anno**	**avrà** tentato	**avranno** tentato
condizionale presente		condizionale passato	
tent**erei**	tent**eremmo**	**avrei** tentato	**avremmo** tentato
tent**eresti**	tent**ereste**	**avresti** tentato	**avreste** tentato
tent**erebbe**	tent**erebbero**	**avrebbe** tentato	**avrebbero** tentato
congiuntivo presente		congiuntivo passato	
tent**i**	tent**iamo**	**abbia** tentato	**abbiamo** tentato
tent**i**	tent**iate**	**abbia** tentato	**abbiate** tentato
tent**i**	tent**ino**	**abbia** tentato	**abbiano** tentato
congiuntivo imperfetto		congiuntivo trapassato	
tent**assi**	tent**assimo**	**avessi** tentato	**avessimo** tentato
tent**assi**	tent**aste**	**avessi** tentato	**aveste** tentato
tent**asse**	tent**assero**	**avesse** tentato	**avessero** tentato
imperativo			
	tentiamo		
tenta; non tentare	tentate		
tenti	tentino		

T

tingere — to dye

gerundio **tingendo** — participio passato **tinto**

SINGULAR	PLURAL
indicativo presente	
ting**o**	ting**iamo**
ting**i**	ting**ete**
ting**e**	ting**ono**
imperfetto	
tinge**vo**	tinge**vamo**
tinge**vi**	tinge**vate**
tinge**va**	tinge**vano**
passato remoto	
tins**i**	ting**emmo**
ting**esti**	ting**este**
tins**e**	tins**ero**
futuro semplice	
tinger**ò**	tinger**emo**
tinger**ai**	tinger**ete**
tinger**à**	tinger**anno**
condizionale presente	
ting**erei**	ting**eremmo**
ting**eresti**	ting**ereste**
ting**erebbe**	ting**erebbero**
congiuntivo presente	
ting**a**	ting**iamo**
ting**a**	ting**iate**
ting**a**	ting**ano**
congiuntivo imperfetto	
ting**essi**	ting**essimo**
ting**essi**	ting**este**
ting**esse**	ting**essero**
imperativo	
	tingiamo
tingi; non tingere	tingete
tinga	tingano

SINGULAR	PLURAL
passato prossimo	
ho tinto	**abbiamo** tinto
hai tinto	**avete** tinto
ha tinto	**hanno** tinto
trapassato prossimo	
avevo tinto	**avevamo** tinto
avevi tinto	**avevate** tinto
aveva tinto	**avevano** tinto
trapassato remoto	
ebbi tinto	**avemmo** tinto
avesti tinto	**aveste** tinto
ebbe tinto	**ebbero** tinto
futuro anteriore	
avrò tinto	**avremo** tinto
avrai tinto	**avrete** tinto
avrà tinto	**avranno** tinto
condizionale passato	
avrei tinto	**avremmo** tinto
avresti tinto	**avreste** tinto
avrebbe tinto	**avrebbero** tinto
congiuntivo passato	
abbia tinto	**abbiamo** tinto
abbia tinto	**abbiate** tinto
abbia tinto	**abbiano** tinto
congiuntivo trapassato	
avessi tinto	**avessimo** tinto
avessi tinto	**aveste** tinto
avesse tinto	**avessero** tinto

gerundio **tirando** participio passato **tirato**

SINGULAR	PLURAL	SINGULAR	PLURAL
indicativo presente		passato prossimo	
tir**o**	tir**iamo**	**ho** tirato	**abbiamo** tirato
tir**i**	tir**ate**	**hai** tirato	**avete** tirato
tir**a**	tir**ano**	**ha** tirato	**hanno** tirato
imperfetto		trapassato prossimo	
tira**vo**	tira**vamo**	**avevo** tirato	**avevamo** tirato
tira**vi**	tira**vate**	**avevi** tirato	**avevate** tirato
tira**va**	tira**vano**	**aveva** tirato	**avevano** tirato
passato remoto		trapassato remoto	
tira**i**	tir**ammo**	**ebbi** tirato	**avemmo** tirato
tir**asti**	tir**aste**	**avesti** tirato	**aveste** tirato
tir**ò**	tirar**ono**	**ebbe** tirato	**ebbero** tirato
futuro semplice		futuro anteriore	
tirer**ò**	tirer**emo**	**avrò** tirato	**avremo** tirato
tirer**ai**	tirer**ete**	**avrai** tirato	**avrete** tirato
tirer**à**	tirer**anno**	**avrà** tirato	**avranno** tirato
condizionale presente		condizionale passato	
tir**erei**	tir**eremmo**	**avrei** tirato	**avremmo** tirato
tir**eresti**	tir**ereste**	**avresti** tirato	**avreste** tirato
tir**erebbe**	tir**erebbero**	**avrebbe** tirato	**avrebbero** tirato
congiuntivo presente		congiuntivo passato	
tir**i**	tir**iamo**	**abbia** tirato	**abbiamo** tirato
tir**i**	tir**iate**	**abbia** tirato	**abbiate** tirato
tir**i**	tir**ino**	**abbia** tirato	**abbiano** tirato
congiuntivo imperfetto		congiuntivo trapassato	
tir**assi**	tir**assimo**	**avessi** tirato	**avessimo** tirato
tir**assi**	tir**aste**	**avessi** tirato	**aveste** tirato
tir**asse**	tir**assero**	**avesse** tirato	**avessero** tirato
imperativo			
	tiriamo		
tira; non tirare	tirate		
tiri	tirino		

toccare — to touch, to handle

gerundio **toccando** — participio passato **toccato**

SINGULAR	PLURAL
indicativo presente	
tocc**o**	tocch**iamo**
tocch**i**	tocc**ate**
tocc**a**	tocc**ano**
imperfetto	
tocca**vo**	tocca**vamo**
tocca**vi**	tocca**vate**
tocca**va**	tocca**vano**
passato remoto	
tocca**i**	tocc**ammo**
tocc**asti**	tocc**aste**
tocc**ò**	toccar**ono**
futuro semplice	
toccher**ò**	toccher**emo**
toccher**ai**	toccher**ete**
toccher**à**	toccher**anno**
condizionale presente	
tocch**erei**	tocch**eremmo**
tocch**eresti**	tocch**ereste**
tocch**erebbe**	tocch**erebbero**
congiuntivo presente	
tocch**i**	tocch**iamo**
tocch**i**	tocch**iate**
tocch**i**	tocch**ino**
congiuntivo imperfetto	
tocc**assi**	tocc**assimo**
tocc**assi**	tocc**aste**
tocc**asse**	tocc**assero**
imperativo	
	tocchiamo
tocca; non toccare	toccate
tocchi	tocchino

SINGULAR	PLURAL
passato prossimo	
ho toccato	**abbiamo** toccato
hai toccato	**avete** toccato
ha toccato	**hanno** toccato
trapassato prossimo	
avevo toccato	**avevamo** toccato
avevi toccato	**avevate** toccato
aveva toccato	**avevano** toccato
trapassato remoto	
ebbi toccato	**avemmo** toccato
avesti toccato	**aveste** toccato
ebbe toccato	**ebbero** toccato
futuro anteriore	
avrò toccato	**avremo** toccato
avrai toccato	**avrete** toccato
avrà toccato	**avranno** toccato
condizionale passato	
avrei toccato	**avremmo** toccato
avresti toccato	**avreste** toccato
avrebbe toccato	**avrebbero** toccato
congiuntivo passato	
abbia toccato	**abbiamo** toccato
abbia toccato	**abbiate** toccato
abbia toccato	**abbiano** toccato
congiuntivo trapassato	
avessi toccato	**avessimo** toccato
avessi toccato	**aveste** toccato
avesse toccato	**avessero** toccato

to remove **togliere**

gerundio **togliendo** participio passato **tolto**

SINGULAR	PLURAL	SINGULAR	PLURAL
indicativo presente		passato prossimo	
tolg**o**	togl**iamo**	**ho** tolto	**abbiamo** tolto
togl**i**	togli**ete**	**hai** tolto	**avete** tolto
togli**e**	tolg**ono**	**ha** tolto	**hanno** tolto
imperfetto		trapassato prossimo	
toglie**vo**	toglie**vamo**	**avevo** tolto	**avevamo** tolto
toglie**vi**	toglie**vate**	**avevi** tolto	**avevate** tolto
toglie**va**	toglie**vano**	**aveva** tolto	**avevano** tolto
passato remoto		trapassato remoto	
tols**i**	togli**emmo**	**ebbi** tolto	**avemmo** tolto
togli**esti**	togli**este**	**avesti** tolto	**aveste** tolto
tols**e**	tols**ero**	**ebbe** tolto	**ebbero** tolto
futuro semplice		futuro anteriore	
toglier**ò**	toglier**emo**	**avrò** tolto	**avremo** tolto
toglier**ai**	toglier**ete**	**avrai** tolto	**avrete** tolto
toglier**à**	toglier**anno**	**avrà** tolto	**avranno** tolto
condizionale presente		condizionale passato	
togli**erei**	togli**eremmo**	**avrei** tolto	**avremmo** tolto
togli**eresti**	togli**ereste**	**avresti** tolto	**avreste** tolto
togli**erebbe**	togli**erebbero**	**avrebbe** tolto	**avrebbero** tolto
congiuntivo presente		congiuntivo passato	
tolg**a**	togl**iamo**	**abbia** tolto	**abbiamo** tolto
tolg**a**	togl**iate**	**abbia** tolto	**abbiate** tolto
tolg**a**	tolg**ano**	**abbia** tolto	**abbiano** tolto
congiuntivo imperfetto		congiuntivo trapassato	
togli**essi**	togli**essimo**	**avessi** tolto	**avessimo** tolto
togli**essi**	togli**este**	**avessi** tolto	**aveste** tolto
togli**esse**	togli**essero**	**avesse** tolto	**avessero** tolto
imperativo			
	togliamo		
togli; non togliere	togliete		
tolga	tolgano		

T

torcere — to twist

gerundio **torcendo** — participio passato **torto**

SINGULAR	PLURAL
indicativo presente	
torc**o**	torc**iamo**
torc**i**	torc**ete**
torc**e**	torc**ono**
imperfetto	
torce**vo**	torce**vamo**
torce**vi**	torce**vate**
torce**va**	torce**vano**
passato remoto	
tors**i**	torc**emmo**
torc**esti**	torc**este**
tors**e**	tors**ero**
futuro semplice	
torcer**ò**	torcer**emo**
torcer**ai**	torcer**ete**
torcer**à**	torcer**anno**
condizionale presente	
torc**erei**	torc**eremmo**
torc**eresti**	torc**ereste**
torc**erebbe**	torc**erebbero**
congiuntivo presente	
torc**a**	torc**iamo**
torc**a**	torc**iate**
torc**a**	torc**ano**
congiuntivo imperfetto	
torc**essi**	torc**essimo**
torc**essi**	torc**este**
torc**esse**	torc**essero**
imperativo	
	torciamo
torci; non torcere	torcete
torca	torcano

SINGULAR	PLURAL
passato prossimo	
ho torto	**abbiamo** torto
hai torto	**avete** torto
ha torto	**hanno** torto
trapassato prossimo	
avevo torto	**avevamo** torto
avevi torto	**avevate** torto
aveva torto	**avevano** torto
trapassato remoto	
ebbi torto	**avemmo** torto
avesti torto	**aveste** torto
ebbe torto	**ebbero** torto
futuro anteriore	
avrò torto	**avremo** torto
avrai torto	**avrete** torto
avrà torto	**avranno** torto
condizionale passato	
avrei torto	**avremmo** torto
avresti torto	**avreste** torto
avrebbe torto	**avrebbero** torto
congiuntivo passato	
abbia torto	**abbiamo** torto
abbia torto	**abbiate** torto
abbia torto	**abbiano** torto
congiuntivo trapassato	
avessi torto	**avessimo** torto
avessi torto	**aveste** torto
avesse torto	**avessero** torto

to return, to go back **tornare**

gerundio **tornando** participio passato **tornato**

SINGULAR	PLURAL	SINGULAR	PLURAL
indicativo presente		passato prossimo	
torn**o**	torn**iamo**	**sono** tornato(a)	**siamo** tornati(e)
torn**i**	torn**ate**	**sei** tornato(a)	**siete** tornati(e)
torn**a**	torn**ano**	**è** tornato(a)	**sono** tornati(e)
imperfetto		trapassato prossimo	
torna**vo**	torna**vamo**	**ero** tornato(a)	**eravamo** tornati(e)
torna**vi**	torna**vate**	**eri** tornato(a)	**eravate** tornati(e)
torna**va**	torna**vano**	**era** tornato(a)	**erano** tornati(e)
passato remoto		trapassato remoto	
torna**i**	torn**ammo**	**fui** tornato(a)	**fummo** tornati(e)
torn**asti**	torn**aste**	**fosti** tornato(a)	**foste** tornati(e)
torn**ò**	tornar**ono**	**fu** tornato(a)	**furono** tornati(e)
futuro semplice		futuro anteriore	
torner**ò**	torner**emo**	**sarò** tornato(a)	**saremo** tornati(e)
torner**ai**	torner**ete**	**sarai** tornato(a)	**sarete** tornati(e)
torner**à**	torner**anno**	**sarà** tornato(a)	**saranno** tornati(e)
condizionale presente		condizionale passato	
torn**erei**	torn**eremmo**	**sarei** tornato(a)	**saremmo** tornati(e)
torn**eresti**	torn**ereste**	**saresti** tornato(a)	**sareste** tornati(e)
torn**erebbe**	torn**erebbero**	**sarebbe** tornato(a)	**sarebbero** tornati(e)
congiuntivo presente		congiuntivo passato	
torn**i**	torni**amo**	**sia** tornato(a)	**siamo** tornati(e)
torn**i**	torni**ate**	**sia** tornato(a)	**siate** tornati(e)
torn**i**	torn**ino**	**sia** tornato(a)	**siano** tornati(e)
congiuntivo imperfetto		congiuntivo trapassato	
torn**assi**	torn**assimo**	**fossi** tornato(a)	**fossimo** tornati(e)
torn**assi**	torn**aste**	**fossi** tornato(a)	**foste** tornati(e)
torn**asse**	torn**assero**	**fosse** tornato(a)	**fossero** tornati(e)
imperativo			
	torniamo		
torna; non tornare	tornate		
torni	tornino		

T

MUST KNOW VERB

tradire — to betray, to deceive

gerundio **tradendo** — participio passato **tradito**

SINGULAR	PLURAL
indicativo presente	
tradisc**o**	trad**iamo**
tradisc**i**	trad**ite**
tradisc**e**	tradisc**ono**
imperfetto	
tradi**vo**	tradi**vamo**
tradi**vi**	tradi**vate**
tradi**va**	tradi**vano**
passato remoto	
tradi**i**	trad**immo**
trad**isti**	trad**iste**
trad**ì**	tradir**ono**
futuro semplice	
tradir**ò**	tradir**emo**
tradir**ai**	tradir**ete**
tradir**à**	tradir**anno**
condizionale presente	
trad**irei**	trad**iremmo**
trad**iresti**	trad**ireste**
trad**irebbe**	trad**irebbero**
congiuntivo presente	
tradisc**a**	trad**iamo**
tradisc**a**	trad**iate**
tradisc**a**	tradisc**ano**
congiuntivo imperfetto	
trad**issi**	trad**issimo**
trad**issi**	trad**iste**
trad**isse**	trad**issero**
imperativo	
	tradiamo
tradisci; non tradire	tradite
tradisca	tradiscano

SINGULAR	PLURAL
passato prossimo	
ho tradito	**abbiamo** tradito
hai tradito	**avete** tradito
ha tradito	**hanno** tradito
trapassato prossimo	
avevo tradito	**avevamo** tradito
avevi tradito	**avevate** tradito
aveva tradito	**avevano** tradito
trapassato remoto	
ebbi tradito	**avemmo** tradito
avesti tradito	**aveste** tradito
ebbe tradito	**ebbero** tradito
futuro anteriore	
avrò tradito	**avremo** tradito
avrai tradito	**avrete** tradito
avrà tradito	**avranno** tradito
condizionale passato	
avrei tradito	**avremmo** tradito
avresti tradito	**avreste** tradito
avrebbe tradito	**avrebbero** tradito
congiuntivo passato	
abbia tradito	**abbiamo** tradito
abbia tradito	**abbiate** tradito
abbia tradito	**abbiano** tradito
congiuntivo trapassato	
avessi tradito	**avessimo** tradito
avessi tradito	**aveste** tradito
avesse tradito	**avessero** tradito

gerundio **traducendo** participio passato **tradotto**

SINGULAR	PLURAL	SINGULAR	PLURAL
indicativo presente		passato prossimo	
traduc**o**	traduc**iamo**	**ho** tradotto	**abbiamo** tradotto
traduc**i**	traduc**ete**	**hai** tradotto	**avete** tradotto
traduc**e**	traduc**ono**	**ha** tradotto	**hanno** tradotto
imperfetto		trapassato prossimo	
traduce**vo**	traduce**vamo**	**avevo** tradotto	**avevamo** tradotto
traduce**vi**	traduce**vate**	**avevi** tradotto	**avevate** tradotto
traduce**va**	traduce**vano**	**aveva** tradotto	**avevano** tradotto
passato remoto		trapassato remoto	
traduss**i**	traduc**emmo**	**ebbi** tradotto	**avemmo** tradotto
traduc**esti**	traduc**este**	**avesti** tradotto	**aveste** tradotto
traduss**e**	traduss**ero**	**ebbe** tradotto	**ebbero** tradotto
futuro semplice		futuro anteriore	
tradurr**ò**	tradurr**emo**	**avrò** tradotto	**avremo** tradotto
tradurr**ai**	tradurr**ete**	**avrai** tradotto	**avrete** tradotto
tradurr**à**	tradurr**anno**	**avrà** tradotto	**avranno** tradotto
condizionale presente		condizionale passato	
tradurr**ei**	tradurr**emmo**	**avrei** tradotto	**avremmo** tradotto
tradurr**esti**	tradurr**este**	**avresti** tradotto	**avreste** tradotto
tradurr**ebbe**	tradurr**ebbero**	**avrebbe** tradotto	**avrebbero** tradotto
congiuntivo presente		congiuntivo passato	
traduc**a**	traduc**iamo**	**abbia** tradotto	**abbiamo** tradotto
traduc**a**	traduc**iate**	**abbia** tradotto	**abbiate** tradotto
traduc**a**	traduc**ano**	**abbia** tradotto	**abbiano** tradotto
congiuntivo imperfetto		congiuntivo trapassato	
traduc**essi**	traduc**essimo**	**avessi** tradotto	**avessimo** tradotto
traduc**essi**	traduc**este**	**avessi** tradotto	**aveste** tradotto
traduc**esse**	traduc**essero**	**avesse** tradotto	**avessero** tradotto
imperativo			
	traduciamo		
traduci; non tradurre	traducete		
traduca	traducano		

trarre — to draw, to pull

gerundio **traendo** — participio passato **tratto**

SINGULAR	PLURAL	SINGULAR	PLURAL
indicativo presente		passato prossimo	
tragg**o**	tra**iamo**	**ho** tratto	**abbiamo** tratto
tra**i**	tra**ete**	**hai** tratto	**avete** tratto
tra**e**	tragg**ono**	**ha** tratto	**hanno** tratto
imperfetto		trapassato prossimo	
trae**vo**	trae**vamo**	**avevo** tratto	**avevamo** tratto
trae**vi**	trae**vate**	**avevi** tratto	**avevate** tratto
trae**va**	trae**vano**	**aveva** tratto	**avevano** tratto
passato remoto		trapassato remoto	
trass**i**	tra**emmo**	**ebbi** tratto	**avemmo** tratto
tra**esti**	tra**este**	**avesti** tratto	**aveste** tratto
trass**e**	trass**ero**	**ebbe** tratto	**ebbero** tratto
futuro semplice		futuro anteriore	
trarr**ò**	trarr**emo**	**avrò** tratto	**avremo** tratto
trarr**ai**	trarr**ete**	**avrai** tratto	**avrete** tratto
trarr**à**	trarr**anno**	**avrà** tratto	**avranno** tratto
condizionale presente		condizionale passato	
trarr**ei**	trarr**emmo**	**avrei** tratto	**avremmo** tratto
trarr**esti**	trarr**este**	**avresti** tratto	**avreste** tratto
trarr**ebbe**	trarr**ebbero**	**avrebbe** tratto	**avrebbero** tratto
congiuntivo presente		congiuntivo passato	
tragg**a**	tra**iamo**	**abbia** tratto	**abbiamo** tratto
tragg**a**	tra**iate**	**abbia** tratto	**abbiate** tratto
tragg**a**	tragg**ano**	**abbia** tratto	**abbiano** tratto
congiuntivo imperfetto		congiuntivo trapassato	
tra**essi**	tra**essimo**	**avessi** tratto	**avessimo** tratto
tra**essi**	tra**este**	**avessi** tratto	**aveste** tratto
tra**esse**	tra**essero**	**avesse** tratto	**avessero** tratto

imperativo

	traiamo
trai; non trarre	traete
tragga	traggano

T

to drag **trascinare**

gerundio **trascinando** participio passato **trascinato**

SINGULAR	PLURAL
indicativo presente	
trascin**o**	trascin**iamo**
trascin**i**	trascin**ate**
trascin**a**	trascin**ano**
imperfetto	
trascina**vo**	trascina**vamo**
trascina**vi**	trascina**vate**
trascina**va**	trascina**vano**
passato remoto	
trascina**i**	trascin**ammo**
trascin**asti**	trascin**aste**
trascin**ò**	trascinar**ono**
futuro semplice	
trasciner**ò**	trasciner**emo**
trasciner**ai**	trasciner**ete**
trasciner**à**	trasciner**anno**
condizionale presente	
trascin**erei**	trascin**eremmo**
trascin**eresti**	trascin**ereste**
trascin**erebbe**	trascin**erebbero**
congiuntivo presente	
trascin**i**	trascin**iamo**
trascin**i**	trascin**iate**
trascin**i**	trascin**ino**
congiuntivo imperfetto	
trascin**assi**	trascin**assimo**
trascin**assi**	trascin**aste**
trascin**asse**	trascin**assero**
imperativo	
	trasciniamo
trascina; non trascinare	trascinate
trascini	trascinino

SINGULAR	PLURAL
passato prossimo	
ho trascinato	**abbiamo** trascinato
hai trascinato	**avete** trascinato
ha trascinato	**hanno** trascinato
trapassato prossimo	
avevo trascinato	**avevamo** trascinato
avevi trascinato	**avevate** trascinato
aveva trascinato	**avevano** trascinato
trapassato remoto	
ebbi trascinato	**avemmo** trascinato
avesti trascinato	**aveste** trascinato
ebbe trascinato	**ebbero** trascinato
futuro anteriore	
avrò trascinato	**avremo** trascinato
avrai trascinato	**avrete** trascinato
avrà trascinato	**avranno** trascinato
condizionale passato	
avrei trascinato	**avremmo** trascinato
avresti trascinato	**avreste** trascinato
avrebbe trascinato	**avrebbero** trascinato
congiuntivo passato	
abbia trascinato	**abbiamo** trascinato
abbia trascinato	**abbiate** trascinato
abbia trascinato	**abbiano** trascinato
congiuntivo trapassato	
avessi trascinato	**avessimo** trascinato
avessi trascinato	**aveste** trascinato
avesse trascinato	**avessero** trascinato

trascorrere — to spend, to pass

gerundio **trascorrendo** participio passato **trascorso**

SINGULAR	PLURAL
indicativo presente	
trascorr**o**	trascorr**iamo**
trascorr**i**	trascorr**ete**
trascorr**e**	trascorr**ono**
imperfetto	
trascorre**vo**	trascorre**vamo**
trascorre**vi**	trascorre**vate**
trascorre**va**	trascorre**vano**
passato remoto	
trascors**i**	trascorr**emmo**
trascorr**esti**	trascorr**este**
trascors**e**	trascors**ero**
futuro semplice	
trascorrer**ò**	trascorrer**emo**
trascorrer**ai**	trascorrer**ete**
trascorrer**à**	trascorrer**anno**
condizionale presente	
trascorr**erei**	trascorr**eremmo**
trascorr**eresti**	trascorr**ereste**
trascorr**erebbe**	trascorr**erebbero**
congiuntivo presente	
trascorr**a**	trascorr**iamo**
trascorr**a**	trascorr**iate**
trascorr**a**	trascorr**ano**
congiuntivo imperfetto	
trascorr**essi**	trascorr**essimo**
trascorr**essi**	trascorr**este**
trascorr**esse**	trascorr**essero**
imperativo	
	trascorriamo
trascorri; non trascorrere	trascorrete
trascorra	trascorrano

SINGULAR	PLURAL
passato prossimo	
ho trascorso	**abbiamo** trascorso
hai trascorso	**avete** trascorso
ha trascorso	**hanno** trascorso
trapassato prossimo	
avevo trascorso	**avevamo** trascorso
avevi trascorso	**avevate** trascorso
aveva trascorso	**avevano** trascorso
trapassato remoto	
ebbi trascorso	**avemmo** trascorso
avesti trascorso	**aveste** trascorso
ebbe trascorso	**ebbero** trascorso
futuro anteriore	
avrò trascorso	**avremo** trascorso
avrai trascorso	**avrete** trascorso
avrà trascorso	**avranno** trascorso
condizionale passato	
avrei trascorso	**avremmo** trascorso
avresti trascorso	**avreste** trascorso
avrebbe trascorso	**avrebbero** trascorso
congiuntivo passato	
abbia trascorso	**abbiamo** trascorso
abbia trascorso	**abbiate** trascorso
abbia trascorso	**abbiano** trascorso
congiuntivo trapassato	
avessi trascorso	**avessimo** trascorso
avessi trascorso	**aveste** trascorso
avesse trascorso	**avessero** trascorso

to transfer, to move (somewhere) **trasferire**

gerundio **trasferendo** participio passato **trasferito**

SINGULAR	PLURAL
indicativo presente	
trasferisc**o**	trasfer**iamo**
trasferisc**i**	trasfer**ite**
trasferisc**e**	trasferisc**ono**
imperfetto	
trasferi**vo**	trasferi**vamo**
trasferi**vi**	trasferi**vate**
trasferi**va**	trasferi**vano**
passato remoto	
trasferi**i**	trasfer**immo**
trasfer**isti**	trasfer**iste**
trasfer**ì**	trasferir**ono**
futuro semplice	
trasferir**ò**	trasferir**emo**
trasferir**ai**	trasferir**ete**
trasferir**à**	trasferir**anno**
condizionale presente	
trasfer**irei**	trasfer**iremmo**
trasfer**iresti**	trasfer**ireste**
trasfer**irebbe**	trasfer**irebbero**
congiuntivo presente	
trasferisc**a**	trasfer**iamo**
trasferisc**a**	trasfer**iate**
trasferisc**a**	trasferisc**ano**
congiuntivo imperfetto	
trasfer**issi**	trasfer**issimo**
trasfer**issi**	trasfer**iste**
trasfer**isse**	trasfer**issero**
imperativo	
	trasferiamo
trasferisci; non trasferire	trasferite
trasferisca	trasferiscano

SINGULAR	PLURAL
passato prossimo	
ho trasferito	**abbiamo** trasferito
hai trasferito	**avete** trasferito
ha trasferito	**hanno** trasferito
trapassato prossimo	
avevo trasferito	**avevamo** trasferito
avevi trasferito	**avevate** trasferito
aveva trasferito	**avevano** trasferito
trapassato remoto	
ebbi trasferito	**avemmo** trasferito
avesti trasferito	**aveste** trasferito
ebbe trasferito	**ebbero** trasferito
futuro anteriore	
avrò trasferito	**avremo** trasferito
avrai trasferito	**avrete** trasferito
avrà trasferito	**avranno** trasferito
condizionale passato	
avrei trasferito	**avremmo** trasferito
avresti trasferito	**avreste** trasferito
avrebbe trasferito	**avrebbero** trasferito
congiuntivo passato	
abbia trasferito	**abbiamo** trasferito
abbia trasferito	**abbiate** trasferito
abbia trasferito	**abbiano** trasferito
congiuntivo trapassato	
avessi trasferito	**avessimo** trasferito
avessi trasferito	**aveste** trasferito
avesse trasferito	**avessero** trasferito

trasmettere — to transmit, to convey

gerundio **trasmettendo** — participio passato **trasmesso**

SINGULAR	PLURAL	SINGULAR	PLURAL
indicativo presente		passato prossimo	
trasmett**o**	trasmett**iamo**	**ho** trasmesso	**abbiamo** trasmesso
trasmett**i**	trasmett**ete**	**hai** trasmesso	**avete** trasmesso
trasmett**e**	trasmett**ono**	**ha** trasmesso	**hanno** trasmesso
imperfetto		trapassato prossimo	
trasmette**vo**	trasmette**vamo**	**avevo** trasmesso	**avevamo** trasmesso
trasmette**vi**	trasmette**vate**	**avevi** trasmesso	**avevate** trasmesso
trasmette**va**	trasmette**vano**	**aveva** trasmesso	**avevano** trasmesso
passato remoto		trapassato remoto	
trasmis**i**	trasmett**emmo**	**ebbi** trasmesso	**avemmo** trasmesso
trasmett**esti**	trasmett**este**	**avesti** trasmesso	**aveste** trasmesso
trasmis**e**	trasmis**ero**	**ebbe** trasmesso	**ebbero** trasmesso
futuro semplice		futuro anteriore	
trasmetter**ò**	trasmetter**emo**	**avrò** trasmesso	**avremo** trasmesso
trasmetter**ai**	trasmetter**ete**	**avrai** trasmesso	**avrete** trasmesso
trasmetter**à**	trasmetter**anno**	**avrà** trasmesso	**avranno** trasmesso
condizionale presente		condizionale passato	
trasmett**erei**	trasmett**eremmo**	**avrei** trasmesso	**avremmo** trasmesso
trasmett**eresti**	trasmett**ereste**	**avresti** trasmesso	**avreste** trasmesso
trasmett**erebbe**	trasmett**erebbero**	**avrebbe** trasmesso	**avrebbero** trasmesso
congiuntivo presente		congiuntivo passato	
trasmett**a**	trasmett**iamo**	**abbia** trasmesso	**abbiamo** trasmesso
trasmett**a**	trasmett**iate**	**abbia** trasmesso	**abbiate** trasmesso
trasmett**a**	trasmett**ano**	**abbia** trasmesso	**abbiano** trasmesso
congiuntivo imperfetto		congiuntivo trapassato	
trasmett**essi**	trasmett**essimo**	**avessi** trasmesso	**avessimo** trasmesso
trasmett**essi**	trasmett**este**	**avessi** trasmesso	**aveste** trasmesso
trasmett**esse**	trasmett**essero**	**avesse** trasmesso	**avessero** trasmesso
imperativo			
	trasmettiamo		
trasmetti; non trasmettere	trasmettete		
trasmetta	trasmettano		

gerundio **trattando** participio passato **trattato**

SINGULAR	PLURAL	SINGULAR	PLURAL
indicativo presente		passato prossimo	
tratt**o**	tratt**iamo**	**ho** trattato	**abbiamo** trattato
tratt**i**	tratt**ate**	**hai** trattato	**avete** trattato
tratt**a**	tratt**ano**	**ha** trattato	**hanno** trattato
imperfetto		trapassato prossimo	
tratta**vo**	tratta**vamo**	**avevo** trattato	**avevamo** trattato
tratta**vi**	tratta**vate**	**avevi** trattato	**avevate** trattato
tratta**va**	tratta**vano**	**aveva** trattato	**avevano** trattato
passato remoto		trapassato remoto	
tratta**i**	tratt**ammo**	**ebbi** trattato	**avemmo** trattato
tratt**asti**	tratt**aste**	**avesti** trattato	**aveste** trattato
tratt**ò**	trattar**ono**	**ebbe** trattato	**ebbero** trattato
futuro semplice		futuro anteriore	
tratter**ò**	tratter**emo**	**avrò** trattato	**avremo** trattato
tratter**ai**	tratter**ete**	**avrai** trattato	**avrete** trattato
tratter**à**	tratter**anno**	**avrà** trattato	**avranno** trattato
condizionale presente		condizionale passato	
tratt**erei**	tratt**eremmo**	**avrei** trattato	**avremmo** trattato
tratt**eresti**	tratt**ereste**	**avresti** trattato	**avreste** trattato
tratt**erebbe**	tratt**erebbero**	**avrebbe** trattato	**avrebbero** trattato
congiuntivo presente		congiuntivo passato	
tratt**i**	tratt**iamo**	**abbia** trattato	**abbiamo** trattato
tratt**i**	tratt**iate**	**abbia** trattato	**abbiate** trattato
tratt**i**	tratt**ino**	**abbia** trattato	**abbiano** trattato
congiuntivo imperfetto		congiuntivo trapassato	
tratt**assi**	tratt**assimo**	**avessi** trattato	**avessimo** trattato
tratt**assi**	tratt**aste**	**avessi** trattato	**aveste** trattato
tratt**asse**	tratt**assero**	**avesse** trattato	**avessero** trattato

imperativo

	trattiamo
tratta; non trattare	trattate
tratti	trattino

trattenere — to keep back, to restrain

gerundio **trattenendo** participio passato **trattenuto**

SINGULAR	PLURAL
indicativo presente	
tratteng**o**	tratten**iamo**
trattien**i**	tratten**ete**
trattien**e**	tratteng**ono**
imperfetto	
trattene**vo**	trattene**vamo**
trattene**vi**	trattene**vate**
trattene**va**	trattene**vano**
passato remoto	
trattenn**i**	tratten**emmo**
tratten**esti**	tratten**este**
trattenn**e**	trattenn**ero**
futuro semplice	
tratterr**ò**	tratterr**emo**
tratterr**ai**	tratterr**ete**
tratterr**à**	tratterr**anno**
condizionale presente	
tratt**errei**	tratt**erremmo**
tratt**erresti**	tratt**erreste**
tratt**errebbe**	tratt**errebbero**
congiuntivo presente	
tratteng**a**	tratten**iamo**
tratteng**a**	tratten**iate**
tratteng**a**	tratteng**ano**
congiuntivo imperfetto	
tratten**essi**	tratten**essimo**
tratten**essi**	tratten**este**
tratten**esse**	tratten**essero**
imperativo	
	tratteniamo
trattieni; non trattenere	trattenete
trattenga	trattengano

SINGULAR	PLURAL
passato prossimo	
ho trattenuto	**abbiamo** trattenuto
hai trattenuto	**avete** trattenuto
ha trattenuto	**hanno** trattenuto
trapassato prossimo	
avevo trattenuto	**avevamo** trattenuto
avevi trattenuto	**avevate** trattenuto
aveva trattenuto	**avevano** trattenuto
trapassato remoto	
ebbi trattenuto	**avemmo** trattenuto
avesti trattenuto	**aveste** trattenuto
ebbe trattenuto	**ebbero** trattenuto
futuro anteriore	
avrò trattenuto	**avremo** trattenuto
avrai trattenuto	**avrete** trattenuto
avrà trattenuto	**avranno** trattenuto
condizionale passato	
avrei trattenuto	**avremmo** trattenuto
avresti trattenuto	**avreste** trattenuto
avrebbe trattenuto	**avrebbero** trattenuto
congiuntivo passato	
abbia trattenuto	**abbiamo** trattenuto
abbia trattenuto	**abbiate** trattenuto
abbia trattenuto	**abbiano** trattenuto
congiuntivo trapassato	
avessi trattenuto	**avessimo** trattenuto
avessi trattenuto	**aveste** trattenuto
avesse trattenuto	**avessero** trattenuto

gerundio **tremando** participio passato **tremato**

SINGULAR	PLURAL	SINGULAR	PLURAL
indicativo presente		passato prossimo	
trem**o**	trem**iamo**	**ho** tremato	**abbiamo** tremato
trem**i**	trem**ate**	**hai** tremato	**avete** tremato
trem**a**	trem**ano**	**ha** tremato	**hanno** tremato
imperfetto		trapassato prossimo	
trema**vo**	trema**vamo**	**avevo** tremato	**avevamo** tremato
trema**vi**	trema**vate**	**avevi** tremato	**avevate** tremato
trema**va**	trema**vano**	**aveva** tremato	**avevano** tremato
passato remoto		trapassato remoto	
trema**i**	trem**ammo**	**ebbi** tremato	**avemmo** tremato
trem**asti**	trem**aste**	**avesti** tremato	**aveste** tremato
trem**ò**	tremar**ono**	**ebbe** tremato	**ebbero** tremato
futuro semplice		futuro anteriore	
tremer**ò**	tremer**emo**	**avrò** tremato	**avremo** tremato
tremer**ai**	tremer**ete**	**avrai** tremato	**avrete** tremato
tremer**à**	tremer**anno**	**avrà** tremato	**avranno** tremato
condizionale presente		condizionale passato	
trem**erei**	trem**eremmo**	**avrei** tremato	**avremmo** tremato
trem**eresti**	trem**ereste**	**avresti** tremato	**avreste** tremato
trem**erebbe**	trem**erebbero**	**avrebbe** tremato	**avrebbero** tremato
congiuntivo presente		congiuntivo passato	
trem**i**	tremi**amo**	**abbia** tremato	**abbiamo** tremato
trem**i**	tremi**ate**	**abbia** tremato	**abbiate** tremato
trem**i**	trem**ino**	**abbia** tremato	**abbiano** tremato
congiuntivo imperfetto		congiuntivo trapassato	
trem**assi**	trem**assimo**	**avessi** tremato	**avessimo** tremato
trem**assi**	trem**aste**	**avessi** tremato	**aveste** tremato
trem**asse**	trem**assero**	**avesse** tremato	**avessero** tremato
imperativo			
	tremiamo		
trema; non tremare	tremate		
tremi	tremino		

T

trovare — to find

gerundio **trovando** participio passato **trovato**

SINGULAR	PLURAL	SINGULAR	PLURAL
indicativo presente		passato prossimo	
trov**o**	trov**iamo**	**ho** trovato	**abbiamo** trovato
trov**i**	trov**ate**	**hai** trovato	**avete** trovato
trov**a**	trov**ano**	**ha** trovato	**hanno** trovato
imperfetto		trapassato prossimo	
trova**vo**	trova**vamo**	**avevo** trovato	**avevamo** trovato
trova**vi**	trova**vate**	**avevi** trovato	**avevate** trovato
trova**va**	trova**vano**	**aveva** trovato	**avevano** trovato
passato remoto		trapassato remoto	
trova**i**	trov**ammo**	**ebbi** trovato	**avemmo** trovato
trov**asti**	trov**aste**	**avesti** trovato	**aveste** trovato
trov**ò**	trovar**ono**	**ebbe** trovato	**ebbero** trovato
futuro semplice		futuro anteriore	
trover**ò**	trover**emo**	**avrò** trovato	**avremo** trovato
trover**ai**	trover**ete**	**avrai** trovato	**avrete** trovato
trover**à**	trover**anno**	**avrà** trovato	**avranno** trovato
condizionale presente		condizionale passato	
trov**erei**	trov**eremmo**	**avrei** trovato	**avremmo** trovato
trov**eresti**	trov**ereste**	**avresti** trovato	**avreste** trovato
trov**erebbe**	trov**erebbero**	**avrebbe** trovato	**avrebbero** trovato
congiuntivo presente		congiuntivo passato	
trov**i**	trov**iamo**	**abbia** trovato	**abbiamo** trovato
trov**i**	trov**iate**	**abbia** trovato	**abbiate** trovato
trov**i**	trov**ino**	**abbia** trovato	**abbiano** trovato
congiuntivo imperfetto		congiuntivo trapassato	
trov**assi**	trov**assimo**	**avessi** trovato	**avessimo** trovato
trov**assi**	trov**aste**	**avessi** trovato	**aveste** trovato
trov**asse**	trov**assero**	**avesse** trovato	**avessero** trovato

imperativo

	troviamo
trova; non trovare	trovate
trovi	trovino

gerundio **turbandosi** participio passato **turbatosi**

SINGULAR	PLURAL
indicativo presente	
mi turb**o**	**ci** turb**iamo**
ti turb**i**	**vi** turb**ate**
si turb**a**	**si** turb**ano**
imperfetto	
mi turba**vo**	**ci** turba**vamo**
ti turba**vi**	**vi** turba**vate**
si turba**va**	**si** turba**vano**
passato remoto	
mi turb**ai**	**ci** turb**ammo**
ti turb**asti**	**vi** turb**aste**
si turb**ò**	**si** turbar**ono**
futuro semplice	
mi turber**ò**	**ci** turber**emo**
ti turber**ai**	**vi** turber**ete**
si turber**à**	**si** turber**anno**
condizionale presente	
mi turb**erei**	**ci** turb**eremmo**
ti turb**eresti**	**vi** turb**ereste**
si turb**erebbe**	**si** turb**erebbero**
congiuntivo presente	
mi turb**i**	**ci** turb**iamo**
ti turb**i**	**vi** turb**iate**
si turb**i**	**si** turb**ino**
congiuntivo imperfetto	
mi turb**assi**	**ci** turb**assimo**
ti turb**assi**	**vi** turb**aste**
si turb**asse**	**si** turb**assero**
imperativo	
	turbiamoci
turbati; non turbarti/ non ti turbare	turbatevi
si turbi	si turbino

SINGULAR	PLURAL
passato prossimo	
mi sono turbato(a)	**ci siamo** turbati(e)
ti sei turbato(a)	**vi siete** turbati(e)
si è turbato(a)	**si sono** turbati(e)
trapassato prossimo	
mi ero turbato(a)	**ci eravamo** turbati(e)
ti eri turbato(a)	**vi eravate** turbati(e)
si era turbato(a)	**si erano** turbati(e)
trapassato remoto	
mi fui turbato(a)	**ci fummo** turbati(e)
ti fosti turbato(a)	**vi foste** turbati(e)
si fu turbato(a)	**si furono** turbati(e)
futuro anteriore	
mi sarò turbato(a)	**ci saremo** turbati(e)
ti sarai turbato(a)	**vi sarete** turbati(e)
si sarà turbato(a)	**si saranno** turbati(e)
condizionale passato	
mi sarei turbato(a)	**ci saremmo** turbati(e)
ti saresti turbato(a)	**vi sareste** turbati(e)
si sarebbe turbato(a)	**si sarebbero** turbati(e)
congiuntivo passato	
mi sia turbato(a)	**ci siamo** turbati(e)
ti sia turbato(a)	**vi siate** turbati(e)
si sia turbato(a)	**si siano** turbati(e)
congiuntivo trapassato	
mi fossi turbato(a)	**ci fossimo** turbati(e)
ti fossi turbato(a)	**vi foste** turbati(e)
si fosse turbato(a)	**si fossero** turbati(e)

ubbidire — to obey

gerundio **ubbidendo** participio passato **ubbidito**

	SINGULAR	PLURAL
indicativo presente		
	ubbidisc**o**	ubbid**iamo**
	ubbidisc**i**	ubbid**ite**
	ubbidisc**e**	ubbidisc**ono**
imperfetto		
	ubbidi**vo**	ubbidi**vamo**
	ubbidi**vi**	ubbidi**vate**
	ubbidi**va**	ubbidi**vano**
passato remoto		
	ubbid**ii**	ubbid**immo**
	ubbid**isti**	ubbid**iste**
	ubbidì	ubbid**irono**
futuro semplice		
	ubbidir**ò**	ubbidir**emo**
	ubbidir**ai**	ubbider**ete**
	ubbidir**à**	ubbidir**anno**
condizionale presente		
	ubbid**irei**	ubbid**iremmo**
	ubbid**iresti**	ubbid**ireste**
	ubbid**irebbe**	ubbid**irebbero**
congiuntivo presente		
	ubbidisc**a**	ubbid**iamo**
	ubbidisc**a**	ubbid**iate**
	ubbidisc**a**	ubbid**iscano**
congiuntivo imperfetto		
	ubbid**issi**	ubbid**issimo**
	ubbid**issi**	ubbid**iste**
	ubbid**isse**	ubbid**issero**
imperativo		
		ubbidiamo
	ubbidisci; non ubbidire	ubbidite
	ubbidisca	ubbidiscano

	SINGULAR	PLURAL
passato prossimo		
	ho ubbidito	**abbiamo** ubbidito
	hai ubbidito	**avete** ubbidito
	ha ubbidito	**hanno** ubbidito
trapassato prossimo		
	avevo ubbidito	**avevamo** ubbidito
	avevi ubbidito	**avevate** ubbidito
	aveva ubbidito	**avevano** ubbidito
trapassato remoto		
	ebbi ubbidito	**avemmo** ubbidito
	avesti ubbidito	**aveste** ubbidito
	ebbe ubbidito	**ebbero** ubbidito
futuro anteriore		
	avrò ubbidito	**avremo** ubbidito
	avrai ubbidito	**avrete** ubbidito
	avrà ubbidito	**avranno** ubbidito
condizionale passato		
	avrei ubbidito	**avremmo** ubbidito
	avresti ubbidito	**avreste** ubbidito
	avrebbe ubbidito	**avrebbero** ubbidito
congiuntivo passato		
	abbia ubbidito	**abbiamo** ubbidito
	abbia ubbidito	**abbiate** ubbidito
	abbia ubbidito	**abbiano** ubbidito
congiuntivo trapassato		
	avessi ubbidito	**avessimo** ubbidito
	avessi ubbidito	**aveste** ubbidito
	avesse ubbidito	**avessero** ubbidito

to get drunk, to become intoxicated **ubriacarsi**

gerundio **ubriacandosi** participio passato **ubriacatosi**

SINGULAR	PLURAL
indicativo presente	
mi ubriac**o**	**ci** ubriach**iamo**
ti ubriach**i**	**vi** ubriac**ate**
si ubriac**a**	**si** ubriac**ano**
imperfetto	
mi ubriac**avo**	**ci** ubriac**avamo**
ti ubriac**avi**	**vi** ubriac**avate**
si ubriac**ava**	**si** ubriac**avano**
passato remoto	
mi ubriac**ai**	**ci** ubriac**ammo**
ti ubriac**asti**	**vi** ubriac**aste**
si ubriac**ò**	**si** ubriac**arono**
futuro semplice	
mi ubriacher**ò**	**ci** ubriacher**emo**
ti ubriacher**ai**	**vi** ubriacher**ete**
si ubriacher**à**	**si** ubriacher**anno**
condizionale presente	
mi ubriach**erei**	**ci** ubriach**eremmo**
ti ubriach**eresti**	**vi** ubriach**ereste**
si ubriach**erebbe**	**si** ubriach**erebbero**
congiuntivo presente	
mi ubriach**i**	**ci** ubriach**iamo**
ti ubriach**i**	**vi** ubriach**iate**
si ubriach**i**	**si** ubriach**ino**
congiuntivo imperfetto	
mi ubriac**assi**	**ci** ubriac**assimo**
ti ubriac**assi**	**vi** ubriac**aste**
si ubriac**asse**	**si** ubriac**assero**
imperativo	
	ubriachiamoci
ubriacati; non ubriacarti/ non ti ubriacare	ubriacatevi
si ubriachi	si ubriachino

SINGULAR	PLURAL
passato prossimo	
mi sono ubriacato(a)	**ci siamo** ubriacati(e)
ti sei ubriacato(a)	**vi siete** ubriacati(e)
si è ubriacato(a)	**si sono** ubriacati(e)
trapassato prossimo	
mi ero ubriacato(a)	**ci eravamo** ubriacati(e)
ti eri ubriacato(a)	**vi eravate** ubriacati(e)
si era ubriacato(a)	**si erano** ubriacati(e)
trapassato remoto	
mi fui ubriacato(a)	**ci fummo** ubriacati(e)
ti fosti ubriacato(a)	**vi foste** ubriacati(e)
si fu ubriacato(a)	**si furono** ubriacati(e)
futuro anteriore	
mi sarò ubriacato(a)	**ci saremo** ubriacati(e)
ti sarai ubriacato(a)	**vi sarete** ubriacati(e)
si sarà ubriacato(a)	**si saranno** ubriacati(e)
condizionale passato	
mi sarei ubriacato(a)	**ci saremmo** ubriacati(e)
ti saresti ubriacato(a)	**vi sareste** ubriacati(e)
si sarebbe ubriacato(a)	**si sarebbero** ubriacati(e)
congiuntivo passato	
mi sia ubriacato(a)	**ci siamo** ubriacati(e)
ti sia ubriacato(a)	**vi siate** ubriacati(e)
si sia ubriacato(a)	**si siano** ubriacati(e)
congiuntivo trapassato	
mi fossi ubriacato(a)	**ci fossimo** ubriacati(e)
ti fossi ubriacato(a)	**vi foste** ubriacati(e)
si fosse ubriacato(a)	**si fossero** ubriacati(e)

uccidere — to kill

gerundio **uccidendo** — participio passato **ucciso**

SINGULAR	PLURAL
indicativo presente	
uccid**o**	uccid**iamo**
uccid**i**	uccid**ete**
uccid**e**	uccid**ono**
imperfetto	
uccid**evo**	uccid**evamo**
uccid**evi**	uccid**evate**
uccid**eva**	uccid**evano**
passato remoto	
uccis**i**	uccid**emmo**
uccid**esti**	uccid**este**
uccis**e**	uccis**ero**
futuro semplice	
ucciderò	uccider**emo**
uccider**ai**	uccider**ete**
ucciderà	uccider**anno**
condizionale presente	
uccid**erei**	uccid**eremmo**
uccid**eresti**	uccid**ereste**
uccid**erebbe**	uccid**erebbero**
congiuntivo presente	
uccid**a**	uccid**iamo**
uccid**a**	uccid**iate**
uccid**a**	uccid**ano**
congiuntivo imperfetto	
uccid**essi**	uccid**essimo**
uccid**essi**	uccid**este**
uccid**esse**	uccid**essero**
imperativo	
	uccidiamo
uccidi; non uccidere	uccidete
uccida	uccidano

SINGULAR	PLURAL
passato prossimo	
ho ucciso	**abbiamo** ucciso
hai ucciso	**avete** ucciso
ha ucciso	**hanno** ucciso
trapassato prossimo	
avevo ucciso	**avevamo** ucciso
avevi ucciso	**avevate** ucciso
aveva ucciso	**avevano** ucciso
trapassato remoto	
ebbi ucciso	**avemmo** ucciso
avesti ucciso	**aveste** ucciso
ebbe ucciso	**ebbero** ucciso
futuro anteriore	
avrò ucciso	**avremo** ucciso
avrai ucciso	**avrete** ucciso
avrà ucciso	**avranno** ucciso
condizionale passato	
avrei ucciso	**avremmo** ucciso
avresti ucciso	**avreste** ucciso
avrebbe ucciso	**avrebbero** ucciso
congiuntivo passato	
abbia ucciso	**abbiamo** ucciso
abbia ucciso	**abbiate** ucciso
abbia ucciso	**abbiano** ucciso
congiuntivo trapassato	
avessi ucciso	**avessimo** ucciso
avessi ucciso	**aveste** ucciso
avesse ucciso	**avessero** ucciso

gerundio **udendo** participio passato **udito**

SINGULAR	PLURAL	SINGULAR	PLURAL
indicativo presente		passato prossimo	
od**o**	ud**iamo**	**ho** udito	**abbiamo** udito
od**i**	ud**ite**	**hai** udito	**avete** udito
od**e**	od**ono**	**ha** udito	**hanno** udito
imperfetto		trapassato prossimo	
ud**ivo**	ud**ivamo**	**avevo** udito	**avevamo** udito
ud**ivi**	ud**ivate**	**avevi** udito	**avevate** udito
ud**iva**	ud**ivano**	**aveva** udito	**avevano** udito
passato remoto		trapassato remoto	
ud**ii**	ud**immo**	**ebbi** udito	**avemmo** udito
ud**isti**	ud**iste**	**avesti** udito	**aveste** udito
ud**ì**	ud**irono**	**ebbe** udito	**ebbero** udito
futuro semplice		futuro anteriore	
ud(i)r**ò**	ud(i)r**emo**	**avrò** udito	**avremo** udito
ud(i)r**ai**	ud(i)r**ete**	**avrai** udito	**avrete** udito
ud(i)r**à**	ud(i)r**anno**	**avrà** udito	**avranno** udito
condizionale presente		condizionale passato	
ud**(i)rei**	ud**iremmo**	**avrei** udito	**avremmo** udito
ud**(i)resti**	ud**(i)reste**	**avresti** udito	**avreste** udito
ud**(i)rebbe**	ud**(i)rebbero**	**avrebbe** udito	**avrebbero** udito
congiuntivo presente		congiuntivo passato	
od**a**	ud**iamo**	**abbia** udito	**abbiamo** udito
od**a**	ud**iate**	**abbia** udito	**abbiate** udito
od**a**	od**ano**	**abbia** udito	**abbiano** udito
congiuntivo imperfetto		congiuntivo trapassato	
ud**issi**	ud**issimo**	**avessi** udito	**avessimo** udito
ud**issi**	ud**iste**	**avessi** udito	**aveste** udito
ud**isse**	ud**issero**	**avesse** udito	**avessero** udito
imperativo			
	udiamo		
odi; non udire	udite		
oda	odano		

umiliare — to humiliate

gerundio **umiliando** participio passato **umiliato**

indicativo presente

SINGULAR	PLURAL
umil**io**	umil**iamo**
umil**i**	umil**iate**
umil**ia**	umil**iano**

imperfetto

SINGULAR	PLURAL
umili**avo**	umili**avamo**
umili**avi**	umili**avate**
umili**ava**	umili**avano**

passato remoto

SINGULAR	PLURAL
umili**ai**	umili**ammo**
umili**asti**	umili**aste**
umili**ò**	umili**arono**

futuro semplice

SINGULAR	PLURAL
umilier**ò**	umilier**emo**
umilier**ai**	umilier**ete**
umilier**à**	umilier**anno**

condizionale presente

SINGULAR	PLURAL
umili**erei**	umili**eremmo**
umili**eresti**	umili**ereste**
umili**erebbe**	umil**erebbero**

congiuntivo presente

SINGULAR	PLURAL
umil**i**	umil**iamo**
umil**i**	umil**iate**
umil**i**	umil**ino**

congiuntivo imperfetto

SINGULAR	PLURAL
umili**assi**	umili**assimo**
umili**assi**	umili**aste**
umili**asse**	umili**assero**

imperativo

SINGULAR	PLURAL
	umiliamo
umilia; non umiliare	umiliate
umili	umilino

passato prossimo

SINGULAR	PLURAL
ho umiliato	**abbiamo** umiliato
hai umiliato	**avete** umiliato
ha umiliato	**hanno** umiliato

trapassato prossimo

SINGULAR	PLURAL
avevo umiliato	**avevamo** umiliato
avevi umiliato	**avevate** umiliato
aveva umiliato	**avevano** umiliato

trapassato remoto

SINGULAR	PLURAL
ebbi umiliato	**avemmo** umiliato
avesti umiliato	**aveste** umiliato
ebbe umiliato	**ebbero** umiliato

futuro anteriore

SINGULAR	PLURAL
avrò umiliato	**avremo** umiliato
avrai umiliato	**avrete** umiliato
avrà umiliato	**avranno** umiliato

condizionale passato

SINGULAR	PLURAL
avrei umiliato	**avremmo** umiliato
avresti umiliato	**avreste** umiliato
avrebbe umiliato	**avrebbero** umiliato

congiuntivo passato

SINGULAR	PLURAL
abbia umiliato	**abbiamo** umiliato
abbia umiliato	**abbiate** umiliato
abbia umiliato	**abbiano** umiliato

congiuntivo trapassato

SINGULAR	PLURAL
avessi umiliato	**avessimo** umiliato
avessi umiliato	**aveste** umiliato
avesse umiliato	**avessero** umiliato

gerundio **ungendo** participio passato **unto**

SINGULAR	PLURAL	SINGULAR	PLURAL
indicativo presente		passato prossimo	
ung**o**	ung**iamo**	**ho** unto	**abbiamo** unto
ung**i**	ung**ete**	**hai** unto	**avete** unto
ung**e**	ung**ono**	**ha** unto	**hanno** unto
imperfetto		trapassato prossimo	
ung**evo**	ung**evamo**	**avevo** unto	**avevamo** unto
ung**evi**	ung**evate**	**avevi** unto	**avevate** unto
ung**eva**	ung**evano**	**aveva** unto	**avevano** unto
passato remoto		trapassato remoto	
uns**i**	ung**emmo**	**ebbi** unto	**avemmo** unto
ung**esti**	ung**este**	**avesti** unto	**aveste** unto
uns**e**	uns**ero**	**ebbe** unto	**ebbero** unto
futuro semplice		futuro anteriore	
unger**ò**	unger**emo**	**avrò** unto	**avremo** unto
unger**ai**	unger**ete**	**avrai** unto	**avrete** unto
unger**à**	unger**anno**	**avrà** unto	**avranno** unto
condizionale presente		condizionale passato	
ung**erei**	ung**eremmo**	**avrei** unto	**avremmo** unto
ung**eresti**	ung**ereste**	**avresti** unto	**avreste** unto
ung**erebbe**	ung**erebbero**	**avrebbe** unto	**avrebbero** unto
congiuntivo presente		congiuntivo passato	
ung**a**	ung**iamo**	**abbia** unto	**abbiamo** unto
ung**a**	ung**iate**	**abbia** unto	**abbiate** unto
ung**a**	ung**ano**	**abbia** unto	**abbiano** unto
congiuntivo imperfetto		congiuntivo trapassato	
ung**essi**	ung**essimo**	**avessi** unto	**avessimo** unto
ung**essi**	ung**este**	**avessi** unto	**aveste** unto
ung**esse**	ung**essero**	**avesse** unto	**avessero** unto
imperativo			
	ungiamo		
ungi; non ungere	ungete		
unga	ungano		

unire — to unite, to join together

gerundio **unendo** participio passato **unito**

SINGULAR	PLURAL
indicativo presente	
unisc**o**	un**iamo**
unisc**i**	un**ite**
unisc**e**	unisc**ono**
imperfetto	
un**ivo**	un**ivamo**
un**ivi**	un**ivate**
un**iva**	un**ivano**
passato remoto	
un**ii**	un**immo**
un**isti**	un**iste**
un**ì**	un**irono**
futuro semplice	
unir**ò**	unir**emo**
unir**ai**	unir**ete**
unir**à**	unir**anno**
condizionale presente	
un**irei**	un**iremmo**
un**iresti**	un**ireste**
un**irebbe**	un**irebbero**
congiuntivo presente	
unisc**a**	un**iamo**
unisc**a**	un**iate**
unisc**a**	unisc**ano**
congiuntivo imperfetto	
un**issi**	un**issimo**
un**issi**	un**iste**
un**isse**	un**issero**
imperativo	
	uniamo
unisci; non unire	unite
unisca	uniscano

SINGULAR	PLURAL
passato prossimo	
ho unito	**abbiamo** unito
hai unito	**avete** unito
ha unito	**hanno** unito
trapassato prossimo	
avevo unito	**avevamo** unito
avevi unito	**avevate** unito
aveva unito	**avevano** unito
trapassato remoto	
ebbi unito	**avemmo** unito
avesti unito	**aveste** unito
ebbe unito	**ebbero** unito
futuro anteriore	
avrò unito	**avremo** unito
avrai unito	**avrete** unito
avrà unito	**avranno** unito
condizionale passato	
avrei unito	**avremmo** unito
avresti unito	**avreste** unito
avrebbe unito	**avrebbero** unito
congiuntivo passato	
abbia unito	**abbiamo** unito
abbia unito	**abbiate** unito
abbia unito	**abbiano** unito
congiuntivo trapassato	
avessi unito	**avessimo** unito
avessi unito	**aveste** unito
avesse unito	**avessero** unito

gerundio **urlando** participio passato **urlato**

SINGULAR	PLURAL	SINGULAR	PLURAL
indicativo presente		passato prossimo	
urlo	urliamo	**ho** urlato	**abbiamo** urlato
urli	urlate	**hai** urlato	**avete** urlato
urla	urlano	**ha** urlato	**hanno** urlato
imperfetto		trapassato prossimo	
urlavo	urlavamo	**avevo** urlato	**avevamo** urlato
urlavi	urlavate	**avevi** urlato	**avevate** urlato
urlava	urlavano	**aveva** urlato	**avevano** urlato
passato remoto		trapassato remoto	
urlai	urlammo	**ebbi** urlato	**avemmo** urlato
urlasti	urlaste	**avesti** urlato	**aveste** urlato
urlò	urlarono	**ebbe** urlato	**ebbero** urlato
futuro semplice		futuro anteriore	
urlerò	urleremo	**avrò** urlato	**avremo** urlato
urlerai	urlerete	**avrai** urlato	**avrete** urlato
urlerà	urleranno	**avrà** urlato	**avranno** urlato
condizionale presente		condizionale passato	
urlerei	urleremmo	**avrei** urlato	**avremmo** urlato
urleresti	urlereste	**avresti** urlato	**avreste** urlato
urlerebbe	urlerebbero	**avrebbe** urlato	**avrebbero** urlato
congiuntivo presente		congiuntivo passato	
urli	urliamo	**abbia** urlato	**abbiamo** urlato
urli	urliate	**abbia** urlato	**abbiate** urlato
urli	urlino	**abbia** urlato	**abbiano** urlato
congiuntivo imperfetto		congiuntivo trapassato	
urlassi	urlassimo	**avessi** urlato	**avessimo** urlato
urlassi	urlaste	**avessi** urlato	**aveste** urlato
urlasse	urlassero	**avesse** urlato	**avessero** urlato
imperativo			
	urliamo		
urla; non urlare	urlate		
urli	urlino		

usare — to use

gerundio **usando** participio passato **usato**

SINGULAR	PLURAL	SINGULAR	PLURAL
indicativo presente		passato prossimo	
us**o**	us**iamo**	**ho** usato	**abbiamo** usato
us**i**	us**ate**	**hai** usato	**avete** usato
us**a**	us**ano**	**ha** usato	**hanno** usato
imperfetto		trapassato prossimo	
us**avo**	us**avamo**	**avevo** usato	**avevamo** usato
us**avi**	us**avate**	**avevi** usato	**avevate** usato
us**ava**	us**avano**	**aveva** usato	**avevano** usato
passato remoto		trapassato remoto	
us**ai**	us**ammo**	**ebbi** usato	**avemmo** usato
us**asti**	us**aste**	**avesti** usato	**aveste** usato
us**ò**	us**arono**	**ebbe** usato	**ebbero** usato
futuro semplice		futuro anteriore	
user**ò**	user**emo**	**avrò** usato	**avremo** usato
user**ai**	user**ete**	**avrai** usato	**avrete** usato
user**à**	user**anno**	**avrà** usato	**avranno** usato
condizionale presente		condizionale passato	
us**erei**	us**eremmo**	**avrei** usato	**avremmo** usato
us**eresti**	us**ereste**	**avresti** usato	**avreste** usato
us**erebbe**	us**erebbero**	**avrebbe** usato	**avrebbero** usato
congiuntivo presente		congiuntivo passato	
usi	us**iamo**	**abbia** usato	**abbiamo** usato
usi	us**iate**	**abbia** usato	**abbiate** usato
usi	us**ino**	**abbia** usato	**abbiano** usato
congiuntivo imperfetto		congiuntivo trapassato	
us**assi**	us**assimo**	**avessi** usato	**avessimo** usato
us**assi**	us**aste**	**avessi** usato	**aveste** usato
us**asse**	us**assero**	**avesse** usato	**avessero** usato

imperativo

	usiamo
usa; non usare	usate
usi	usino

U

to go out, to come out — uscire

gerundio **uscendo** participio passato **uscito**

SINGULAR	PLURAL	SINGULAR	PLURAL
indicativo presente		passato prossimo	
esc**o**	usc**iamo**	**sono** uscito(a)	**siamo** usciti(e)
esc**i**	usc**ite**	**sei** uscito(a)	**siete** usciti(e)
esc**e**	esc**ono**	**è** uscito(a)	**sono** usciti(e)
imperfetto		trapassato prossimo	
usc**ivo**	usc**ivamo**	**ero** uscito(a)	**eravamo** usciti(e)
usc**ivi**	usc**ivate**	**eri** uscito(a)	**eravate** usciti(e)
usc**iva**	usc**ivano**	**era** uscito(a)	**erano** usciti(e)
passato remoto		trapassato remoto	
usc**ii**	usc**immo**	**fui** uscito(a)	**fummo** usciti(e)
usc**isti**	usc**iste**	**fosti** uscito(a)	**foste** usciti(e)
usc**ì**	usc**irono**	**fu** uscito(a)	**furono** usciti(e)
futuro semplice		futuro anteriore	
usci**rò**	usci**remo**	**sarò** uscito(a)	**saremo** usciti(e)
usci**rai**	usci**rete**	**sarai** uscito(a)	**sarete** usciti(e)
usci**rà**	usci**ranno**	**sarà** uscito(a)	**saranno** usciti(e)
condizionale presente		condizionale passato	
usc**irei**	usc**iremmo**	**sarei** uscito(a)	**saremmo** usciti(e)
usc**iresti**	usc**ireste**	**saresti** uscito(a)	**sareste** usciti(e)
usc**irebbe**	usc**irebbero**	**sarebbe** uscito(a)	**sarebbero** usciti(e)
congiuntivo presente		congiuntivo passato	
esc**a**	usc**iamo**	**sia** uscito(a)	**siamo** usciti(e)
esc**a**	usc**iate**	**sia** uscito(a)	**siate** usciti(e)
esc**a**	esc**ano**	**sia** uscito(a)	**siano** usciti(e)
congiuntivo imperfetto		congiuntivo trapassato	
usc**issi**	usc**issimo**	**fossi** uscito(a)	**fossimo** usciti(e)
usc**issi**	usc**iste**	**fossi** uscito(a)	**foste** usciti(e)
usc**isse**	usc**issero**	**fosse** uscito(a)	**fossero** usciti(e)

imperativo

	usciamo
esci; non uscire	uscite
esca	escano

MUST KNOW VERB

U

valere to be of value, to be of worth

gerundio **valendo** participio passato **valso**

SINGULAR	PLURAL	SINGULAR	PLURAL
indicativo presente		*passato prossimo*	
valg**o**	val**iamo**	**sono** valso(a)	**siamo** valsi(e)
val**i**	val**ete**	**sei** valso(a)	**siete** valsi(e)
val**e**	valg**ono**	**è** valso(a)	**sono** valsi(e)
imperfetto		*trapassato prossimo*	
vale**vo**	vale**vamo**	**ero** valso(a)	**eravamo** valsi(e)
vale**vi**	vale**vate**	**eri** valso(a)	**eravate** valsi(e)
vale**va**	vale**vano**	**era** valso(a)	**erano** valsi(e)
passato remoto		*trapassato remoto*	
vals**i**	val**emmo**	**fui** valso(a)	**fummo** valsi(e)
val**esti**	val**este**	**fosti** valso(a)	**foste** valsi(e)
vals**e**	vals**ero**	**fu** valso(a)	**furono** valsi(e)
futuro semplice		*futuro anteriore*	
varr**ò**	varr**emo**	**sarò** valso(a)	**saremo** valsi(e)
varr**ai**	varr**ete**	**sarai** valso(a)	**sarete** valsi(e)
varr**à**	varr**anno**	**sarà** valso(a)	**saranno** valsi(e)
condizionale presente		*condizionale passato*	
varr**ei**	varr**emmo**	**sarei** valso(a)	**saremmo** valsi(e)
varr**esti**	varr**este**	**saresti** valso(a)	**sareste** valsi(e)
varr**ebbe**	varr**ebbero**	**sarebbe** valso(a)	**sarebbero** valsi(e)
congiuntivo presente		*congiuntivo passato*	
valg**a**	val**iamo**	**sia** valso(a)	**siamo** valsi(e)
valg**a**	val**iate**	**sia** valso(a)	**siate** valsi(e)
valg**a**	valg**ano**	**sia** valso(a)	**siano** valsi(e)
congiuntivo imperfetto		*congiuntivo trapassato*	
val**essi**	val**essimo**	**fossi** valso(a)	**fossimo** valsi(e)
val**essi**	val**este**	**fossi** valso(a)	**foste** valsi(e)
val**esse**	val**essero**	**fosse** valso(a)	**fossero** valsi(e)

to brag, to be proud — vantarsi

gerundio **vantandosi** participio passato **vantatosi**

SINGULAR	PLURAL
indicativo presente	
mi vant**o**	**ci** vant**iamo**
ti vant**i**	**vi** vant**ate**
si vant**a**	**si** vant**ano**
imperfetto	
mi vanta**vo**	**ci** vanta**vamo**
ti vanta**vi**	**vi** vanta**vate**
si vanta**va**	**si** vanta**vano**
passato remoto	
mi vant**ai**	**ci** vant**ammo**
ti vant**asti**	**vi** vant**aste**
si vant**ò**	**si** vant**arono**
futuro semplice	
mi vanter**ò**	**ci** vanter**emo**
ti vanter**ai**	**vi** vanter**ete**
si vanter**à**	**si** vanter**anno**
condizionale presente	
mi vant**erei**	**ci** vant**eremmo**
ti vant**eresti**	**vi** vant**ereste**
si vant**erebbe**	**si** vant**erebbero**
congiuntivo presente	
mi vanti	**ci** vant**iamo**
ti vanti	**vi** vant**iate**
si vanti	**si** vant**ino**
congiuntivo imperfetto	
mi vant**assi**	**ci** vant**assimo**
ti vant**assi**	**vi** vant**aste**
si vant**asse**	**si** vant**assero**
imperativo	
	vantiamoci
vantati; non vantarti/ non ti vantare	vantatevi
si vanti	si vantino

SINGULAR	PLURAL
passato prossimo	
mi sono vantato(a)	**ci siamo** vantati(e)
ti sei vantato(a)	**vi siete** vantati(e)
si è vantato(a)	**si sono** vantati(e)
trapassato prossimo	
mi ero vantato(a)	**ci eravamo** vantati(e)
ti eri vantato(a)	**vi eravate** vantati(e)
si era vantato(a)	**si erano** vantati(e)
trapassato remoto	
mi fui vantato(a)	**ci fummo** vantati(e)
ti fosti vantato(a)	**vi foste** vantati(e)
si fu vantato(a)	**si furono** vantati(e)
futuro anteriore	
mi sarò vantato(a)	**ci saremo** vantati(e)
ti sarai vantato(a)	**vi sarete** vantati(e)
si sarà vantato(a)	**si saranno** vantati(e)
condizionale passato	
mi sarei vantato(a)	**ci saremmo** vantati(e)
ti saresti vantato(a)	**vi sareste** vantati(e)
si sarebbe vantato(a)	**si sarebbero** vantati(e)
congiuntivo passato	
mi sia vantato(a)	**ci siamo** vantati(e)
ti sia vantato(a)	**vi siate** vantati(e)
si sia vantato(a)	**si siano** vantati(e)
congiuntivo trapassato	
mi fossi vantato(a)	**ci fossimo** vantati(e)
ti fossi vantato(a)	**vi foste** vantati(e)
si fosse vantato(a)	**si fossero** vantati(e)

variare — to vary, to change

gerundio **variando** — participio passato **variato**

SINGULAR	PLURAL	SINGULAR	PLURAL
indicativo presente		*passato prossimo*	
var**io**	var**iamo**	**ho** variato	**abbiamo** variato
var**i**	var**iate**	**hai** variato	**avete** variato
var**ia**	var**iano**	**ha** variato	**hanno** variato
imperfetto		*trapassato prossimo*	
varia**vo**	varia**vamo**	**avevo** variato	**avevamo** variato
varia**vi**	varia**vate**	**avevi** variato	**avevate** variato
varia**va**	varia**vano**	**aveva** variato	**avevano** variato
passato remoto		*trapassato remoto*	
var**iai**	var**iammo**	**ebbi** variato	**avemmo** variato
var**iasti**	var**iaste**	**avesti** variato	**aveste** variato
var**iò**	var**iarono**	**ebbe** variato	**ebbero** variato
futuro semplice		*futuro anteriore*	
varier**ò**	varier**emo**	**avrò** variato	**avremo** variato
varier**ai**	varier**ete**	**avrai** variato	**avrete** variato
varier**à**	varier**anno**	**avrà** variato	**avranno** variato
condizionale presente		*condizionale passato*	
var**ierei**	varier**emmo**	**avrei** variato	**avremmo** variato
var**ieresti**	varier**este**	**avresti** variato	**avreste** variato
var**ierebbe**	varier**ebbero**	**avrebbe** variato	**avrebbero** variato
congiuntivo presente		*congiuntivo passato*	
var**i**	var**iamo**	**abbia** variato	**abbiamo** variato
var**i**	var**iate**	**abbia** variato	**abbiate** variato
var**i**	var**ino**	**abbia** variato	**abbiano** variato
congiuntivo imperfetto		*congiuntivo trapassato*	
var**iassi**	var**iassimo**	**avessi** variato	**avessimo** variato
var**iassi**	var**iaste**	**avessi** variato	**aveste** variato
var**iasse**	var**iassero**	**avesse** variato	**avessero** variato
imperativo			
	variamo		
varia; non variare	variate		
vari	varino		

to see **vedere**

gerundio **vedendo** participio passato **visto**

SINGULAR	PLURAL	SINGULAR	PLURAL
indicativo presente		passato prossimo	
ved**o**	ved**iamo**	**ho** visto	**abbiamo** visto
ved**i**	ved**ete**	**hai** visto	**avete** visto
ved**e**	ved**ono**	**ha** visto	**hanno** visto
imperfetto		trapassato prossimo	
vede**vo**	vede**vamo**	**avevo** visto	**avevamo** visto
vede**vi**	vede**vate**	**avevi** visto	**avevate** visto
vede**va**	vede**vano**	**aveva** visto	**avevano** visto
passato remoto		trapassato remoto	
vid**i**	ved**emmo**	**ebbi** visto	**avemmo** visto
ved**esti**	ved**este**	**avesti** visto	**aveste** visto
vid**e**	vid**ero**	**ebbe** visto	**ebbero** visto
futuro semplice		futuro anteriore	
vedr**ò**	vedr**emo**	**avrò** visto	**avremo** visto
vedr**ai**	vedr**ete**	**avrai** visto	**avrete** visto
vedr**à**	vedr**anno**	**avrà** visto	**avranno** visto
condizionale presente		condizionale passato	
vedr**ei**	vedr**emmo**	**avrei** visto	**avremmo** visto
vedr**esti**	vedr**este**	**avresti** visto	**avreste** visto
vedr**ebbe**	vedr**ebbero**	**avrebbe** visto	**avrebbero** visto
congiuntivo presente		congiuntivo passato	
ved**a**	ved**iamo**	**abbia** visto	**abbiamo** visto
ved**a**	ved**iate**	**abbia** visto	**abbiate** visto
ved**a**	ved**ano**	**abbia** visto	**abbiano** visto
congiuntivo imperfetto		congiuntivo trapassato	
ved**essi**	ved**essimo**	**avessi** visto	**avessimo** visto
ved**essi**	ved**este**	**avessi** visto	**aveste** visto
ved**esse**	ved**essero**	**avesse** visto	**avessero** visto
imperativo			
	vediamo		
vedi; non vedere	vedete		
veda	vedano		

vendere — to sell

gerundio **vendendo** participio passato **venduto**

	SINGULAR	PLURAL
indicativo presente	vend**o**	vend**iamo**
	vend**i**	vend**ete**
	vend**e**	vend**ono**
imperfetto	vende**vo**	vende**vamo**
	vende**vi**	vende**vate**
	vende**va**	vende**vano**
passato remoto	vend**ei**, vend**etti**	vend**emmo**
	vend**esti**	vend**este**
	vend**é**, vend**ette**	vend**erono**, vend**ettero**
futuro semplice	vender**ò**	vender**emo**
	vender**ai**	vender**ete**
	vender**à**	vender**anno**
condizionale presente	vend**erei**	vend**eremmo**
	vend**eresti**	vend**ereste**
	vend**erebbe**	vend**erebbero**
congiuntivo presente	vend**a**	vend**iamo**
	vend**a**	vend**iate**
	vend**a**	vend**ano**
congiuntivo imperfetto	vend**essi**	vend**essimo**
	vend**essi**	vend**este**
	vend**esse**	vend**essero**
imperativo		vendiamo
	vendi;	vendete
	non vendere	
	venda	vendano

	SINGULAR	PLURAL
passato prossimo	**ho** venduto	**abbiamo** venduto
	hai venduto	**avete** venduto
	ha venduto	**hanno** venduto
trapassato prossimo	**avevo** venduto	**avevamo** venduto
	avevi venduto	**avevate** venduto
	aveva venduto	**avevano** venduto
trapassato remoto	**ebbi** venduto	**avemmo** venduto
	avesti venduto	**aveste** venduto
	ebbe venduto	**ebbero** venduto
futuro anteriore	**avrò** venduto	**avremo** venduto
	avrai venduto	**avrete** venduto
	avrà venduto	**avranno** venduto
condizionale passato	**avrei** venduto	**avremmo** venduto
	avresti venduto	**avreste** venduto
	avrebbe venduto	**avrebbero** venduto
congiuntivo passato	**abbia** venduto	**abbiamo** venduto
	abbia venduto	**abbiate** venduto
	abbia venduto	**abbiano** venduto
congiuntivo trapassato	**avessi** venduto	**avessimo** venduto
	avessi venduto	**aveste** venduto
	avesse venduto	**avessero** venduto

MUST KNOW VERB

gerundio **venendo** participio passato **venuto**

SINGULAR	PLURAL	SINGULAR	PLURAL
indicativo presente		passato prossimo	
veng**o**	ven**iamo**	**sono** venuto(a)	**siamo** venuti(e)
vien**i**	ven**ite**	**sei** venuto(a)	**siete** venuti(e)
vien**e**	veng**ono**	**è** venuto(a)	**sono** venuti(e)
imperfetto		trapassato prossimo	
veni**vo**	veni**vamo**	**ero** venuto(a)	**eravamo** venuti(e)
veni**vi**	veni**vate**	**eri** venuto(a)	**eravate** venuti(e)
veni**va**	veni**vano**	**era** venuto(a)	**erano** venuti(e)
passato remoto		trapassato remoto	
ven**ni**	ven**immo**	**fui** venuto(a)	**fummo** venuti(e)
ven**isti**	ven**iste**	**fosti** venuto(a)	**foste** venuti(e)
ven**ne**	venn**ero**	**fu** venuto(a)	**furono** venuti(e)
futuro semplice		futuro anteriore	
verr**ò**	verr**emo**	**sarò** venuto(a)	**saremo** venuti(e)
verr**ai**	verr**ete**	**sarai** venuto(a)	**sarete** venuti(e)
verr**à**	verr**anno**	**sarà** venuto(a)	**saranno** venuti(e)
condizionale presente		condizionale passato	
verr**ei**	verr**emmo**	**sarei** venuto(a)	**saremmo** venuti(e)
verr**esti**	verr**este**	**saresti** venuto(a)	**sareste** venuti(e)
verr**ebbe**	verr**ebbero**	**sarebbe** venuto(a)	**sarebbero** venuti(e)
congiuntivo presente		congiuntivo passato	
veng**a**	ven**iamo**	**sia** venuto(a)	**siamo** venuti(e)
veng**a**	ven**iate**	**sia** venuto(a)	**siate** venuti(e)
veng**a**	veng**ano**	**sia** venuto(a)	**siano** venuti(e)
congiuntivo imperfetto		congiuntivo trapassato	
ven**issi**	ven**issimo**	**fossi** venuto(a)	**fossimo** venuti(e)
ven**issi**	ven**iste**	**fossi** venuto(a)	**foste** venuti(e)
ven**isse**	ven**issero**	**fosse** venuto(a)	**fossero** venuti(e)
imperativo			
	veniamo		
vieni; non venire	venite		
venga	vengano		

MUST KNOW VERB

vergognarsi — to feel ashamed, to be shy

gerundio **vergognandosi** participio passato **vergognatosi**

SINGULAR	PLURAL
indicativo presente	
mi vergogn**o**	**ci** vergogn**iamo**
ti vergogn**i**	**vi** vergogn**ate**
si vergogn**a**	**si** vergogn**ano**
imperfetto	
mi vergogna**vo**	**ci** vergogna**vamo**
ti vergogna**vi**	**vi** vergogna**vate**
si vergogna**va**	**si** vergogna**vano**
passato remoto	
mi vergogn**ai**	**ci** vergogn**ammo**
ti vergogn**asti**	**vi** vergogn**aste**
si vergogn**ò**	**si** vergogn**arono**
futuro semplice	
mi vergogner**ò**	**ci** vergogner**emo**
ti vergogner**ai**	**vi** vergogner**ete**
si vergogner**à**	**si** vergogner**anno**
condizionale presente	
mi vergogn**erei**	**ci** vergogn**eremmo**
ti vergogn**eresti**	**vi** vergogn**ereste**
si vergogn**erebbe**	**si** vergogn**erebbero**
congiuntivo presente	
mi vergogn**i**	**ci** vergogn**iamo**
ti vergogn**i**	**vi** vergogn**iate**
si vergogn**i**	**si** vergogn**ino**
congiuntivo imperfetto	
mi vergogn**assi**	**ci** vergogn**assimo**
ti vergogn**assi**	**vi** vergogn**aste**
si vergogn**asse**	**si** vergogn**assero**
imperativo	
	vergogniamoci
vergognati; non vergognarti/ non ti vergognare	vergognatevi
si vergogni	si vergognino

SINGULAR	PLURAL
passato prossimo	
mi sono vergognato(a)	**ci siamo** vergognati(e)
ti sei vergognato(a)	**vi siete** vergognati(e)
si è vergognato(a)	**si sono** vergognati(e)
trapassato prossimo	
mi ero vergognato(a)	**ci eravamo** vergognati(e)
ti eri vergognato(a)	**vi eravate** vergognati(e)
si era vergognato(a)	**si erano** vergognati(e)
trapassato remoto	
mi fui vergognato(a)	**ci fummo** vergognati(e)
ti fosti vergognato(a)	**vi foste** vergognati(e)
si fu vergognato(a)	**si furono** vergognati(e)
futuro anteriore	
mi sarò vergognato(a)	**ci saremo** vergognati(e)
ti sarai vergognato(a)	**vi sarete** vergognati(e)
si sarà vergognato(a)	**si saranno** vergognati(e)
condizionale passato	
mi sarei vergognato(a)	**ci saremmo** vergognati(e)
ti saresti vergognato(a)	**vi sareste** vergognati(e)
si sarebbe vergognato(a)	**si sarebbero** vergognati(e)
congiuntivo passato	
mi sia vergognato(a)	**ci siamo** vergognati(e)
ti sia vergognato(a)	**vi siate** vergognati(e)
si sia vergognato(a)	**si siano** vergognati(e)
congiuntivo trapassato	
mi fossi vergognato(a)	**ci fossimo** vergognati(e)
ti fossi vergognato(a)	**vi foste** vergognati(e)
si fosse vergognato(a)	**si fossero** vergognati(e)

gerundio **verificando** participio passato **verificato**

SINGULAR	PLURAL
indicativo presente	
verifi**co**	verific**hiamo**
verific**hi**	verifi**cate**
verifi**ca**	verifi**cano**
imperfetto	
verifica**vo**	verifica**vamo**
verifica**vi**	verifica**vate**
verifica**va**	verifica**vano**
passato remoto	
verifi**cai**	verifi**cammo**
verifi**casti**	verifi**caste**
verifi**cò**	verifi**carono**
futuro semplice	
verifichер**ò**	verificher**emo**
verificher**ai**	verificher**ete**
verificher**à**	verificher**anno**
condizionale presente	
verific**herei**	verific**heremmo**
verific**heresti**	verific**hereste**
verific**herebbe**	verific**herebbero**
congiuntivo presente	
verific**hi**	verific**hiamo**
verific**hi**	verific**hiate**
verific**hi**	verific**hino**
congiuntivo imperfetto	
verifi**cassi**	verifi**cassimo**
verifi**cassi**	verifi**caste**
verifi**casse**	verifi**cassero**
imperativo	
	verifichiamo
verifica; non verificare	verificate
verifichi	verifichino

SINGULAR	PLURAL
passato prossimo	
ho verificato	**abbiamo** verificato
hai verificato	**avete** verificato
ha verificato	**hanno** verificato
trapassato prossimo	
avevo verificato	**avevamo** verificato
avevi verificato	**avevate** verificato
aveva verificato	**avevano** verificato
trapassato remoto	
ebbi verificato	**avemmo** verificato
avesti verificato	**aveste** verificato
ebbe verificato	**ebbero** verificato
futuro anteriore	
avrò verificato	**avremo** verificato
avrai verificato	**avrete** verificato
avrà verificato	**avranno** verificato
condizionale passato	
avrei verificato	**avremmo** verificato
avresti verificato	**avreste** verificato
avrebbe verificato	**avrebbero** verificato
congiuntivo passato	
abbia verificato	**abbiamo** verificato
abbia verificato	**abbiate** verificato
abbia verificato	**abbiano** verificato
congiuntivo trapassato	
avessi verificato	**avessimo** verificato
avessi verificato	**aveste** verificato
avesse verificato	**avessero** verificato

versare — to pour, to deposit (money)

gerundio **versando** — participio passato **versato**

SINGULAR	PLURAL	SINGULAR	PLURAL
indicativo presente		*passato prossimo*	
vers**o**	vers**iamo**	**ho** versato	**abbiamo** versato
vers**i**	vers**ate**	**hai** versato	**avete** versato
vers**a**	vers**ano**	**ha** versato	**hanno** versato
imperfetto		*trapassato prossimo*	
versa**vo**	versa**vamo**	**avevo** versato	**avevamo** versato
versa**vi**	versa**vate**	**avevi** versato	**avevate** versato
versa**va**	versa**vano**	**aveva** versato	**avevano** versato
passato remoto		*trapassato remoto*	
vers**ai**	vers**ammo**	**ebbi** versato	**avemmo** versato
vers**asti**	vers**aste**	**avesti** versato	**aveste** versato
vers**ò**	vers**arono**	**ebbe** versato	**ebbero** versato
futuro semplice		*futuro anteriore*	
verser**ò**	verser**emo**	**avrò** versato	**avremo** versato
verser**ai**	verser**ete**	**avrai** versato	**avrete** versato
verser**à**	verser**anno**	**avrà** versato	**avranno** versato
condizionale presente		*condizionale passato*	
verser**ei**	verser**emmo**	**avrei** versato	**avremmo** versato
verser**esti**	verser**este**	**avresti** versato	**avreste** versato
verser**ebbe**	verser**ebbero**	**avrebbe** versato	**avrebbero** versato
congiuntivo presente		*congiuntivo passato*	
vers**i**	vers**iamo**	**abbia** versato	**abbiamo** versato
vers**i**	vers**iate**	**abbia** versato	**abbiate** versato
vers**i**	vers**ino**	**abbia** versato	**abbiano** versato
congiuntivo imperfetto		*congiuntivo trapassato*	
vers**assi**	vers**assimo**	**avessi** versato	**avessimo** versato
vers**assi**	vers**aste**	**avessi** versato	**aveste** versato
vers**asse**	vers**assero**	**avesse** versato	**avessero** versato
imperativo			
	versiamo		
versa; non versare	versate		
versi	versino		

to dress oneself **vestirsi**

gerundio **vestendosi**

participio passato **vestitosi**

indicativo presente

SINGULAR	PLURAL
mi vest**o**	**ci** vest**iamo**
ti vest**i**	**vi** vest**ite**
si vest**e**	**si** vest**ono**

imperfetto

SINGULAR	PLURAL
mi vesti**vo**	**ci** vesti**vamo**
ti vesti**vi**	**vi** vesti**vate**
si vesti**va**	**si** vesti**vano**

passato remoto

SINGULAR	PLURAL
mi vest**ii**	**ci** vest**immo**
ti vest**isti**	**vi** vest**iste**
si vest**ì**	**si** vest**irono**

futuro semplice

SINGULAR	PLURAL
mi vestir**ò**	**ci** vestir**emo**
ti vestir**ai**	**vi** vestir**ete**
si vestir**à**	**si** vestir**anno**

condizionale presente

SINGULAR	PLURAL
mi vest**irei**	**ci** vest**iremmo**
ti vest**iresti**	**vi** vest**ireste**
si vest**irebbe**	**si** vest**irebbero**

congiuntivo presente

SINGULAR	PLURAL
mi vest**a**	**ci** vest**iamo**
ti vest**a**	**vi** vest**iate**
si vest**a**	**si** vest**ano**

congiuntivo imperfetto

SINGULAR	PLURAL
mi vest**issi**	**ci** vest**issimo**
ti vest**issi**	**vi** vest**iste**
si vest**isse**	**si** vest**issero**

imperativo

SINGULAR	PLURAL
	vestiamoci
vestiti; non vestirti/ non ti vestire	vestitevi
si vesta	si vestano

passato prossimo

SINGULAR	PLURAL
mi sono vestito(a)	**ci siamo** vestiti(e)
ti sei vestito(a)	**vi siete** vestiti(e)
si è vestito(a)	**si sono** vestiti(e)

trapassato prossimo

SINGULAR	PLURAL
mi ero vestito(a)	**ci eravamo** vestiti(e)
ti eri vestito(a)	**vi eravate** vestiti(e)
si era vestito(a)	**si erano** vestiti(e)

trapassato remoto

SINGULAR	PLURAL
mi fui vestito(a)	**ci fummo** vestiti(e)
ti fosti vestito(a)	**vi foste** vestiti(e)
si fu vestito(a)	**si furono** vestiti(e)

futuro anteriore

SINGULAR	PLURAL
mi sarò vestito(a)	**ci saremo** vestiti(e)
ti sarai vestito(a)	**vi sarete** vestiti(e)
si sarà vestito(a)	**si saranno** vestiti(e)

condizionale passato

SINGULAR	PLURAL
mi sarei vestito(a)	**ci saremmo** vestiti(e)
ti saresti vestito(a)	**vi sareste** vestiti(e)
si sarebbe vestito(a)	**si sarebbero** vestiti(e)

congiuntivo passato

SINGULAR	PLURAL
mi sia vestito(a)	**ci siamo** vestiti(e)
ti sia vestito(a)	**vi siate** vestiti(e)
si sia vestito(a)	**si siano** vestiti(e)

congiuntivo trapassato

SINGULAR	PLURAL
mi fossi vestito(a)	**ci fossimo** vestiti(e)
ti fossi vestito(a)	**vi foste** vestiti(e)
si fosse vestito(a)	**si fossero** vestiti(e)

viaggiare — to travel

gerundio **viaggiando** participio passato **viaggiato**

SINGULAR	PLURAL	SINGULAR	PLURAL
indicativo presente		passato prossimo	
viaggi**o**	viaggi**amo**	**ho** viaggiato	**abbiamo** viaggiato
viagg**i**	viaggi**ate**	**hai** viaggiato	**avete** viaggiato
viaggi**a**	viaggi**ano**	**ha** viaggiato	**hanno** viaggiato
imperfetto		trapassato prossimo	
viaggia**vo**	viaggia**vamo**	**avevo** viaggiato	**avevamo** viaggiato
viaggia**vi**	viaggia**vate**	**avevi** viaggiato	**avevate** viaggiato
viaggia**va**	viaggia**vano**	**aveva** viaggiato	**avevano** viaggiato
passato remoto		trapassato remoto	
viaggi**ai**	viaggi**ammo**	**ebbi** viaggiato	**avemmo** viaggiato
viaggi**asti**	viaggi**aste**	**avesti** viaggiato	**aveste** viaggiato
viaggi**ò**	viaggi**arono**	**ebbe** viaggiato	**ebbero** viaggiato
futuro semplice		futuro anteriore	
viagger**ò**	viagger**emo**	**avrò** viaggiato	**avremo** viaggiato
viagger**ai**	viagger**ete**	**avrai** viaggiato	**avrete** viaggiato
viagger**à**	viagger**anno**	**avrà** viaggiato	**avranno** viaggiato
condizionale presente		condizionale passato	
viagger**ei**	viagger**emmo**	**avrei** viaggiato	**avremmo** viaggiato
viagger**esti**	viagger**este**	**avresti** viaggiato	**avreste** viaggiato
viagger**ebbe**	viagger**ebbero**	**avrebbe** viaggiato	**avrebbero** viaggiato
congiuntivo presente		congiuntivo passato	
viagg**i**	viaggi**amo**	**abbia** viaggiato	**abbiamo** viaggiato
viagg**i**	viaggi**ate**	**abbia** viaggiato	**abbiate** viaggiato
viagg**i**	viagg**ino**	**abbia** viaggiato	**abbiano** viaggiato
congiuntivo imperfetto		congiuntivo trapassato	
viaggi**assi**	viaggi**assimo**	**avessi** viaggiato	**avessimo** viaggiato
viaggi**assi**	viaggi**aste**	**avessi** viaggiato	**aveste** viaggiato
viaggi**asse**	viaggi**assero**	**avesse** viaggiato	**avessero** viaggiato
imperativo			
	viaggiamo		
viaggia; non viaggiare	viaggiate		
viaggi	viaggino		

to prohibit, to forbid **vietare**

gerundio **vietando** participio passato **vietato**

SINGULAR	PLURAL
indicativo presente	
viet**o**	viet**iamo**
viet**i**	viet**ate**
viet**a**	viet**ano**
imperfetto	
vieta**vo**	vieta**vamo**
vieta**vi**	vieta**vate**
vieta**va**	vieta**vano**
passato remoto	
viet**ai**	viet**ammo**
viet**asti**	viet**aste**
viet**ò**	viet**arono**
futuro semplice	
vieter**ò**	vieter**emo**
vieter**ai**	vieter**ete**
vieter**à**	vieter**anno**
condizionale presente	
viet**erei**	viet**eremmo**
viet**eresti**	viet**ereste**
viet**erebbe**	viet**erebbero**
congiuntivo presente	
viet**i**	viet**iamo**
viet**i**	viet**iate**
viet**i**	viet**ino**
congiuntivo imperfetto	
viet**assi**	viet**assimo**
viet**assi**	viet**aste**
viet**asse**	viet**assero**
imperativo	
	vietiamo
vieta; non vietare	vietate
vieti	vietino

SINGULAR	PLURAL
passato prossimo	
ho vietato	**abbiamo** vietato
hai vietato	**avete** vietato
ha vietato	**hanno** vietato
trapassato prossimo	
avevo vietato	**avevamo** vietato
avevi vietato	**avevate** vietato
aveva vietato	**avevano** vietato
trapassato remoto	
ebbi vietato	**avemmo** vietato
avesti vietato	**aveste** vietato
ebbe vietato	**ebbero** vietato
futuro anteriore	
avrò vietato	**avremo** vietato
avrai vietato	**avrete** vietato
avrà vietato	**avranno** vietato
condizionale passato	
avrei vietato	**avremmo** vietato
avresti vietato	**avreste** vietato
avrebbe vietato	**avrebbero** vietato
congiuntivo passato	
abbia vietato	**abbiamo** vietato
abbia vietato	**abbiate** vietato
abbia vietato	**abbiano** vietato
congiuntivo trapassato	
avessi vietato	**avessimo** vietato
avessi vietato	**aveste** vietato
avesse vietato	**avessero** vietato

vincere — to conquer, to win

gerundio **vincendo** participio passato **vinto**

SINGULAR	PLURAL	SINGULAR	PLURAL
indicativo presente		passato prossimo	
vinc**o**	vinc**iamo**	**ho** vinto	**abbiamo** vinto
vinc**i**	vinc**ete**	**hai** vinto	**avete** vinto
vinc**e**	vinc**ono**	**ha** vinto	**hanno** vinto
imperfetto		trapassato prossimo	
vince**vo**	vince**vamo**	**avevo** vinto	**avevamo** vinto
vince**vi**	vince**vate**	**avevi** vinto	**avevate** vinto
vince**va**	vince**vano**	**aveva** vinto	**avevano** vinto
passato remoto		trapassato remoto	
vins**i**	vinc**emmo**	**ebbi** vinto	**avemmo** vinto
vinc**esti**	vinc**este**	**avesti** vinto	**aveste** vinto
vins**e**	vins**ero**	**ebbe** vinto	**ebbero** vinto
futuro semplice		futuro anteriore	
vincer**ò**	vincer**emo**	**avrò** vinto	**avremo** vinto
vincer**ai**	vincer**ete**	**avrai** vinto	**avrete** vinto
vincer**à**	vincer**anno**	**avrà** vinto	**avranno** vinto
condizionale presente		condizionale passato	
vinc**erei**	vinc**eremmo**	**avrei** vinto	**avremmo** vinto
vinc**eresti**	vinc**ereste**	**avresti** vinto	**avreste** vinto
vinc**erebbe**	vinc**erebbero**	**avrebbe** vinto	**avrebbero** vinto
congiuntivo presente		congiuntivo passato	
vinc**a**	vinc**iamo**	**abbia** vinto	**abbiamo** vinto
vinc**a**	vinc**iate**	**abbia** vinto	**abbiate** vinto
vinc**a**	vinc**ano**	**abbia** vinto	**abbiano** vinto
congiuntivo imperfetto		congiuntivo trapassato	
vinc**essi**	vinc**essimo**	**avessi** vinto	**avessimo** vinto
vinc**essi**	vinc**este**	**avessi** vinto	**aveste** vinto
vinc**esse**	vinc**essero**	**avesse** vinto	**avessero** vinto

imperativo

	vinciamo
vinci; non vincere	vincete
vinca	vincano

V

to visit, to examine (medically) visitare

gerundio **visitando** participio passato **visitato**

SINGULAR	PLURAL	SINGULAR	PLURAL
indicativo presente		passato prossimo	
visit**o**	visit**iamo**	**ho** visitato	**abbiamo** visitato
visit**i**	visit**ate**	**hai** visitato	**avete** visitato
visit**a**	visit**ano**	**ha** visitato	**hanno** visitato
imperfetto		trapassato prossimo	
visita**vo**	visita**vamo**	**avevo** visitato	**avevamo** visitato
visita**vi**	visita**vate**	**avevi** visitato	**avevate** visitato
visita**va**	visita**vano**	**aveva** visitato	**avevano** visitato
passato remoto		trapassato remoto	
visit**ai**	visit**ammo**	**ebbi** visitato	**avemmo** visitato
visit**asti**	visit**aste**	**avesti** visitato	**aveste** visitato
visit**ò**	visit**arono**	**ebbe** visitato	**ebbero** visitato
futuro semplice		futuro anteriore	
visiter**ò**	visiter**emo**	**avrò** visitato	**avremo** visitato
visiter**ai**	visiter**ete**	**avrai** visitato	**avrete** visitato
visiter**à**	visiter**anno**	**avrà** visitato	**avranno** visitato
condizionale presente		condizionale passato	
visit**erei**	visit**eremmo**	**avrei** visitato	**avremmo** visitato
visit**eresti**	visit**ereste**	**avresti** visitato	**avreste** visitato
visit**erebbe**	visit**erebbero**	**avrebbe** visitato	**avrebbero** visitato
congiuntivo presente		congiuntivo passato	
visit**i**	visit**iamo**	**abbia** visitato	**abbiamo** visitato
visit**i**	visit**iate**	**abbia** visitato	**abbiate** visitato
visit**i**	visit**ino**	**abbia** visitato	**abbiano** visitato
congiuntivo imperfetto		congiuntivo trapassato	
visit**assi**	visit**assimo**	**avessi** visitato	**avessimo** visitato
visit**assi**	visit**aste**	**avessi** visitato	**aveste** visitato
visit**asse**	visit**assero**	**avesse** visitato	**avessero** visitato

imperativo

	visitiamo
visita; non visitare	visitate
visiti	visitino

vivere — to live

gerundio **vivendo** participio passato **vissuto**

SINGULAR	PLURAL	SINGULAR	PLURAL
indicativo presente		passato prossimo	
viv**o**	viv**iamo**	**ho** vissuto	**abbiamo** vissuto
viv**i**	viv**ete**	**hai** vissuto	**avete** vissuto
viv**e**	viv**ono**	**ha** vissuto	**hanno** vissuto
imperfetto		trapassato prossimo	
vive**vo**	vive**vamo**	**avevo** vissuto	**avevamo** vissuto
vive**vi**	vive**vate**	**avevi** vissuto	**avevate** vissuto
vive**va**	vive**vano**	**aveva** vissuto	**avevano** vissuto
passato remoto		trapassato remoto	
viss**i**	viv**emmo**	**ebbi** vissuto	**avemmo** vissuto
viv**esti**	viv**este**	**avesti** vissuto	**aveste** vissuto
viss**e**	viss**ero**	**ebbe** vissuto	**ebbero** vissuto
futuro semplice		futuro anteriore	
vivr**ò**	vivr**emo**	**avrò** vissuto	**avremo** vissuto
vivr**ai**	vivr**ete**	**avrai** vissuto	**avrete** vissuto
vivr**à**	vivr**anno**	**avrà** vissuto	**avranno** vissuto
condizionale presente		condizionale passato	
vivr**ei**	vivr**emmo**	**avrei** vissuto	**avremmo** vissuto
vivr**esti**	vivr**este**	**avresti** vissuto	**avreste** vissuto
vivr**ebbe**	vivr**ebbero**	**avrebbe** vissuto	**avrebbero** vissuto
congiuntivo presente		congiuntivo passato	
viv**a**	viv**iamo**	**abbia** vissuto	**abbiamo** vissuto
viv**a**	viv**iate**	**abbia** vissuto	**abbiate** vissuto
viv**a**	viv**ano**	**abbia** vissuto	**abbiano** vissuto
congiuntivo imperfetto		congiuntivo trapassato	
viv**essi**	viv**essimo**	**avessi** vissuto	**avessimo** vissuto
viv**essi**	viv**este**	**avessi** vissuto	**aveste** vissuto
viv**esse**	viv**essero**	**avesse** vissuto	**avessero** vissuto
imperativo			
	viviamo		
vivi; non vivere	vivete		
viva	vivano		

V

to fly — volare

gerundio **volando** participio passato **volato**

SINGULAR	PLURAL	SINGULAR	PLURAL
indicativo presente		passato prossimo	
vol**o**	vol**iamo**	**ho** volato	**abbiamo** volato
vol**i**	vol**ate**	**hai** volato	**avete** volato
vol**a**	vol**ano**	**ha** volato	**hanno** volato
imperfetto		trapassato prossimo	
vola**vo**	vola**vamo**	**avevo** volato	**avevamo** volato
vola**vi**	vola**vate**	**avevi** volato	**avevate** volato
vola**va**	vola**vano**	**aveva** volato	**avevano** volato
passato remoto		trapassato remoto	
vol**ai**	vol**ammo**	**ebbi** volato	**avemmo** volato
vol**asti**	vol**aste**	**avesti** volato	**aveste** volato
vol**ò**	vol**arono**	**ebbe** volato	**ebbero** volato
futuro semplice		futuro anteriore	
voler**ò**	voler**emo**	**avrò** volato	**avremo** volato
voler**ai**	voler**ete**	**avrai** volato	**avrete** volato
voler**à**	voler**anno**	**avrà** volato	**avranno** volato
condizionale presente		condizionale passato	
vol**erei**	vol**eremmo**	**avrei** volato	**avremmo** volato
vol**eresti**	vol**ereste**	**avresti** volato	**avreste** volato
vol**erebbe**	vol**erebbero**	**avrebbe** volato	**avrebbero** volato
congiuntivo presente		congiuntivo passato	
vol**i**	vol**iamo**	**abbia** volato	**abbiamo** volato
vol**i**	vol**iate**	**abbia** volato	**abbiate** volato
vol**i**	vol**ino**	**abbia** volato	**abbiano** volato
congiuntivo imperfetto		congiuntivo trapassato	
vol**assi**	vol**assimo**	**avessi** volato	**avessimo** volato
vol**assi**	vol**aste**	**avessi** volato	**aveste** volato
vol**asse**	vol**assero**	**avesse** volato	**avessero** volato
imperativo			
	voliamo		
vola; non volare	volate		
voli	volino		

V

volere — to want

gerundio **volendo** participio passato **voluto**

SINGULAR	PLURAL	SINGULAR	PLURAL
indicativo presente		passato prossimo	
vogl**io**	vogl**iamo**	**ho** voluto	**abbiamo** voluto
vuo**i**	vol**ete**	**hai** voluto	**avete** voluto
vuol**e**	vogl**iono**	**ha** voluto	**hanno** voluto
imperfetto		trapassato prossimo	
vole**vo**	vole**vamo**	**avevo** voluto	**avevamo** voluto
vole**vi**	vole**vate**	**avevi** voluto	**avevate** voluto
vole**va**	vole**vano**	**aveva** voluto	**avevano** voluto
passato remoto		trapassato remoto	
vol**li**	vol**emmo**	**ebbi** voluto	**avemmo** voluto
vol**esti**	vol**este**	**avesti** voluto	**aveste** voluto
vol**le**	vol**lero**	**ebbe** voluto	**ebbero** voluto
futuro semplice		futuro anteriore	
vorr**ò**	vorr**emo**	**avrò** voluto	**avremo** voluto
vorr**ai**	vorr**ete**	**avrai** voluto	**avrete** voluto
vorr**à**	vorr**anno**	**avrà** voluto	**avranno** voluto
condizionale presente		condizionale passato	
vorr**ei**	vorr**emmo**	**avrei** voluto	**avremmo** voluto
vorre**sti**	vorr**este**	**avresti** voluto	**avreste** voluto
vorre**bbe**	vorr**ebbero**	**avrebbe** voluto	**avrebbero** voluto
congiuntivo presente		congiuntivo passato	
vogl**ia**	vogl**iamo**	**abbia** voluto	**abbiamo** voluto
vogl**ia**	vogl**iate**	**abbia** voluto	**abbiate** voluto
vogl**ia**	vogl**iano**	**abbia** voluto	**abbiano** voluto
congiuntivo imperfetto		congiuntivo trapassato	
vol**essi**	vol**essimo**	**avessi** voluto	**avessimo** voluto
vol**essi**	vol**este**	**avessi** voluto	**aveste** voluto
vol**esse**	vol**esserro**	**avesse** voluto	**avessero** voluto

gerundio **volgendo** participio passato **volto**

SINGULAR	PLURAL	SINGULAR	PLURAL
indicativo presente		passato prossimo	
volg**o**	volg**iamo**	**ho** volto	**abbiamo** volto
volg**i**	volg**ete**	**hai** volto	**avete** volto
volg**e**	volg**ono**	**ha** volto	**hanno** volto
imperfetto		trapassato prossimo	
volge**vo**	volge**vamo**	**avevo** volto	**avevamo** volto
volge**vi**	volge**vate**	**avevi** volto	**avevate** volto
volge**va**	volge**vano**	**aveva** volto	**avevano** volto
passato remoto		trapassato remoto	
vols**i**	volg**emmo**	**ebbi** volto	**avemmo** volto
volg**esti**	volg**este**	**avesti** volto	**aveste** volto
vols**e**	vols**ero**	**ebbe** volto	**ebbero** volto
futuro semplice		futuro anteriore	
volger**ò**	volger**emo**	**avrò** volto	**avremo** volto
volger**ai**	volger**ete**	**avrai** volto	**avrete** volto
volger**à**	volger**anno**	**avrà** volto	**avranno** volto
condizionale presente		condizionale passato	
volg**erei**	volg**eremmo**	**avrei** volto	**avremmo** volto
volg**eresti**	volg**ereste**	**avresti** volto	**avreste** volto
volg**erebbe**	volg**erebbero**	**avrebbe** volto	**avrebbero** volto
congiuntivo presente		congiuntivo passato	
volg**a**	volg**iamo**	**abbia** volto	**abbiamo** volto
volg**a**	volg**iate**	**abbia** volto	**abbiate** volto
volg**a**	volg**ano**	**abbia** volto	**abbiano** volto
congiuntivo imperfetto		congiuntivo trapassato	
volg**essi**	volg**essimo**	**avessi** volto	**avessimo** volto
volg**essi**	volg**este**	**avessi** volto	**aveste** volto
volg**esse**	volg**essero**	**avesse** volto	**avessero** volto
imperativo			
	volgiamo		
volgi; non volgere	volgete		
volga	volgano		

V

votare — to vote

gerundio **votando** — participio passato **votato**

SINGULAR	PLURAL	SINGULAR	PLURAL
indicativo presente		passato prossimo	
vot**o**	vot**iamo**	**ho** votato	**abbiamo** votato
vot**i**	vot**ate**	**hai** votato	**avete** votato
vot**a**	vot**ano**	**ha** votato	**hanno** votato
imperfetto		trapassato prossimo	
vota**vo**	vota**vamo**	**avevo** votato	**avevamo** votato
vota**vi**	vota**vate**	**avevi** votato	**avevate** votato
vota**va**	vota**vano**	**aveva** votato	**avevano** votato
passato remoto		trapassato remoto	
vot**ai**	vot**ammo**	**ebbi** votato	**avemmo** votato
vot**asti**	vot**aste**	**avesti** votato	**aveste** votato
vot**ò**	vot**arono**	**ebbe** votato	**ebbero** votato
futuro semplice		futuro anteriore	
voter**ò**	voter**emo**	**avrò** votato	**avremo** votato
voter**ai**	voter**ete**	**avrai** votato	**avrete** votato
voter**à**	voter**anno**	**avrà** votato	**avranno** votato
condizionale presente		condizionale passato	
vot**erei**	vot**eremmo**	**avrei** votato	**avremmo** votato
vot**eresti**	vot**ereste**	**avresti** votato	**avreste** votato
vot**erebbe**	vot**erebbero**	**avrebbe** votato	**avrebbero** votato
congiuntivo presente		congiuntivo passato	
vot**i**	vot**iamo**	**abbia** votato	**abbiamo** votato
vot**i**	vot**iate**	**abbia** votato	**abbiate** votato
vot**i**	vot**ino**	**abbia** votato	**abbiano** votato
congiuntivo imperfetto		congiuntivo trapassato	
vot**assi**	vot**assimo**	**avessi** votato	**avessimo** votato
vot**assi**	vot**aste**	**avessi** votato	**aveste** votato
vot**asse**	vot**assero**	**avesse** votato	**avessero** votato
imperativo			
	votiamo		
vota; non votare	votate		
voti	votino		

V

gerundio **zoppicando** participio passato **zoppicato**

SINGULAR	PLURAL	SINGULAR	PLURAL
indicativo presente		passato prossimo	
zoppic**o**	zoppic**hiamo**	**ho** zoppicato	**abbiamo** zoppicato
zoppic**hi**	zoppic**ate**	**hai** zoppicato	**avete** zoppicato
zoppic**a**	zoppic**ano**	**ha** zoppicato	**hanno** zoppicato
imperfetto		trapassato prossimo	
zoppica**vo**	zoppica**vamo**	**avevo** zoppicato	**avevamo** zoppicato
zoppica**vi**	zoppica**vate**	**avevi** zoppicato	**avevate** zoppicato
zoppica**va**	zoppica**vano**	**aveva** zoppicato	**avevano** zoppicato
passato remoto		trapassato remoto	
zoppic**ai**	zoppic**ammo**	**ebbi** zoppicato	**avemmo** zoppicato
zoppic**asti**	zoppic**aste**	**avesti** zoppicato	**aveste** zoppicato
zoppic**ò**	zoppic**arono**	**ebbe** zoppicato	**ebbero** zoppicato
futuro semplice		futuro anteriore	
zoppicher**ò**	zoppicher**emo**	**avrò** zoppicato	**avremo** zoppicato
zoppicher**ai**	zoppicher**ete**	**avrai** zoppicato	**avrete** zoppicato
zoppicher**à**	zoppicher**anno**	**avrà** zoppicato	**avranno** zoppicato
condizionale presente		condizionale passato	
zoppich**erei**	zoppich**eremmo**	**avrei** zoppicato	**avremmo** zoppicato
zoppich**eresti**	zoppich**ereste**	**avresti** zoppicato	**avreste** zoppicato
zoppich**erebbe**	zoppich**erebbero**	**avrebbe** zoppicato	**avrebbero** zoppicato
congiuntivo presente		congiuntivo passato	
zoppich**i**	zoppich**iamo**	**abbia** zoppicato	**abbiamo** zoppicato
zoppich**i**	zoppich**iate**	**abbia** zoppicato	**abbiate** zoppicato
zoppich**i**	zoppich**ino**	**abbia** zoppicato	**abbiano** zoppicato
congiuntivo imperfetto		congiuntivo trapassato	
zoppic**assi**	zoppic**assimo**	**avessi** zoppicato	**avessimo** zoppicato
zoppic**assi**	zoppic**aste**	**avessi** zoppicato	**aveste** zoppicato
zoppic**asse**	zoppic**assero**	**avesse** zoppicato	**avessero** zoppicato
imperativo			
	zoppichiamo		
zoppica; non zoppicare	zoppicate		
zoppichi	zoppichino		

Exercise 1

Rewrite these sentences. Give the appropriate verbs to reflect the change in subject.

1. *Vado* a dormire alle nove e mezzo perché la mattina *mi sveglio* alle sei. [tu; noi; Lucia; i miei nonni]
2. Roberto *si è iscritto* a un corso di storia e *ha conosciuto* tanti ragazzi interessanti. [noi; voi; i tuoi cugini; tu]
3. Spero che stasera alla festa *si divertano*. [Marta; io e Mario; tu; voi]
4. *Affrettiamoci* perché il pullman arriverà fra poco. [tu; voi; Paola e Chiara; il dott. Randazzo]
5. Adesso *ti accorgi* di che cosa succede quando *ti comporti* male con i clienti. [voi; io; io e Giulia; l'avvocato]
6. Per favore avvocato, *rispetti* i diritti degli altri. [tu; noi; voi; loro]
7. Ho *lodato* lo studente perché aveva fatto un bel lavoro. [tu; Filomena; noi; tu ed Elena]
8. I miei amici *parteciperanno* alla conferenza. [tu; voi; Lianna; io]
9. Quando *informate* i clienti della nuova gestione? [Giuseppe; noi; le ragazze; tu]
10. Michela *ha trascorso* l'estate in montagna. [io; Franco e Paolo; noi; tu]

Exercise 2

Choose the synonym of these verbs.

1. spalancare, dischiudere
2. ostentare, sfoggiare
3. prendere in giro, beffare, ridicolizzare
4. prendersela, incavolarsi, irritarsi
5. ascoltare, eseguire
6. proibire, negare, rifiutare
7. riconsegnare, sdebitarsi
8. brontolare, borbottare, protestare
9. dire bugie, ingannare, fingere
10. detestare, disprezzare

Exercise 3

Contrari: Choose the antonym of these verbs.

1. svanire, sparire, scomparire
2. benedire, lodare, ringraziare
3. disordinare, scompigliare
4. accendere, avviare, infiammare
5. tranquillizzarsi, rassicurarsi

Exercise 4

Complete the sentences by conjugating the verbs in brackets in the subjunctive mood. In some cases two answers are possible.

1. Non credo che ______________________ [lui, riuscire] ad arrivare in tempo alla stazione.
2. È improbabile che ieri ______________________ [voi, studiare] per l'esame di storia.
3. Se ________________ [loro, chiamare], potremmo convincerli.
4. Penso che tu non __________________ [essere] capace di risolvere il problema.
5. Avresti continuato a dormire se io non ______________________ [io, suonare] il campanello.

Exercise 5

Translate these sentences.

1. I will go to the museum tomorrow morning.
2. You (pl.) have to book the hotel for the vacation.
3. Yesterday, Elena and Lucia received three letters.
4. As a kid, Luca used to sing in the choir.
5. If you see Laura, invite her!

Exercise 6

Choose whether the following statements require the *passato prossimo* or the imperfect.

1. [Raccontavo/Ho raccontato] la barzelletta a Paola tre volte
2. [Volevi/Hai voluto] studiare a Parigi ma non avevi i soldi
3. Da giovane mia moglie [ha dipinto/dipingeva] ogni giorno.
4. Da bambina Matilde [leggeva/ha letto] molti libri.
5. Ogni fine settimana mia madre [spostava/ha spostato] i mobili del soggiorno
6. [Abbiamo pulito/Pulivamo] il bagno per un'ora
7. La settimana scorsa [ho partecipato/partecipavo] a una gara di scacchi
8. Quando è arrivato in ospedale, il bambino [ha respirato/respirava] a fatica
9. Marco [ha giurato/giurava] ai genitori di studiare di più
10. Da piccoli Mimmo e Giacomo [hanno suonato/suonavano] il clarinetto

Exercise 7

Complete the sentences by conjugating the verbs in the present subjunctive, indicative or infinitive.

1. Pensi sempre di ______________ [sbagliare] strada.
2. Ho paura che loro ______________ [scegliere] sempre gli amici sbagliati.
3. Ci aspettiamo che voi ______________ [comportarsi] correttamente.
4. Io ______________ [mostare] sempre tanto affetto ai miei parenti.
5. La famiglia Alberti pensa di ______________ [trasferirsi] all'estero nei prossimi mesi.

Exercise 8

Complete the sentences by conjugating the verbs in brackets.

1. Che cosa ______________ [accadere] nella prossima puntata?
2. Stamani in riunione i clienti ______________ [nominare] un altro avvocato.
3. Prima di partire per Roma io avevo prenotato l'albergo e Luca ______________ (noleggiare) una macchina.
4. Ieri sera alla festa tu ______________ [versare] un bicchiere di aranciata sul vestito di un invitato.
5. La settimana prossima io e Claudio ______________ [sposarsi] a Las Vegas.
6. Erano stanchi perché ______________ [nuotare] tutta la mattina.

7. Non riesco a ______________ [rifiutare] un'offerta del genere.

8. A Milano, quando ero bambina, ______________ [piovere] sempre.

9. Quando siamo arrivati in pizzeria i ragazzi __________ appena ______________ [ordinare] la pizza.

10. Quando non abbiamo niente da fare ______________ [annoiarsi].

Exercise 9

Complete the passage by conjugating the verbs in brackets.

Vorrei che tu ____________________ [1. discutere] della data del matrimonio con Laura. Domani lei __________________ [2. organizzare] un piccolo ricevimento per festeggiare il vostro fidanzamento. Penso che tu ____________ [3. dovere] parlare con lei perché Paola __________ già ____________ [4. stabilire] la data del matrimonio ma ____________________ [5. valere] la pena discutere insieme gli ultimi dettagli.

Exercise 10

Complete the following crossword puzzle using the clues below.

Orizzontale	Verticale
5. Io (pranzare) imperfetto 8. Io e Luca (formare) futuro 9. Tu e Paola (offrire) presente indicativo 10. Voi (lottare) passato prossimo	1. I presidenti (governare) condizionale presente 2. Loro (spendere) futuro semplice 3. Noi (trascinare) presente indicativo 4. I signori Paoli (ospitare) passato prossimo 6. Noi (ferire) passato prossimo 7. Tu (limitare) condizionale presente

Exercise 11

Complete the sentences by conjugating the verbs in brackets in the past perfect subjunctive mood.

1. Avrei preferito che loro ______________ [partire] alle tre.
2. Luigi ha pensato che voi ______________ [finire] i compiti.
3. Avresti preferito che Elena ______________ [portare] il computer.
4. Pensavi che noi non ______________ [andare] alla riunione.
5. Temevo che Paolo ______________ [avere] un incidente.
6. Era felice che tu ______________ [fare] un viaggio in Europa.
7. Credevo che voi ______________ [dire] la verità.
8. Avrebbe preferito che Eleonora ______________ [uscire] prima dal cinema.

Exercise 12

Complete the passage by conjugating the verbs provided below in the present, future or imperfect indicative.

Cucinare, giocare, diventare, commuoversi, chiedere, vivere, piacere, spiegare

1. Quando abitava a Roma Laura ____________________ dei primi piatti squisiti.
2. La settimana prossima noi ____________________ un aumento di stipendio.
3. Durante lo scorso semestre agli studenti del professor Carli ____________________ parlare dei giovani italiani.
4. Domani io ____________________ a calcio nel nuovo stadio.
5. La bambina di Monica ____________________ ogni giorno più bella.
6. Mentre la professoressa di storia ____________________ la lezione è entrato in classe il nuovo preside.
7. Tu ____________________ sempre quando guardi i film d'amore.
8. Da bambini Luca e Susanna ____________________ nello stesso quartiere.

Exercise 13

Create a sentence using elements from each column and conjugating the verbs accordingly.

A	B
1. L'anno scorso io [giocare]	sempre la verità
2. Da bambina Laura [cantare]	per le vacanze
3. Domani i signori Renzi [partire]	mangiare cibi più sani
4. Penso che voi [dovere]	un corso di spagnolo
5. Vorrei che tu [dire]	il sassofono
6. La settimana prossima noi [suonare]	una lettera a un'amica
7. Ieri Paola [spedire]	a tennis
8. Quest'estate voi [seguire]	molto bene

Exercise 14

Presente/passato progressivo: Complete the following sentences with the present or past progressive.

1. Stamattina in classe Laura ______________ [leggere] un brano del Manzoni.
2. Ieri sera noi ______________ [cenare] in una pizzeria italiana.
3. La maestra ______________ [spiegare] una lezione interessante quando è finita l'ora.
4. Claudia e Luca ______________ [passeggiare] quando hanno incontrato Sofia Loren.
5. Posso venire a prenderti o (tu) ______________ [mangiare]?
6. Alla stazione avete incontrato i nonni che ______________ [partire] per Parigi
7. (io) ______________ [fare] un bellissimo sogno quando è suonata la sveglia.
8. (noi) ______________ ancora ______________ [cenare], ti chiamo più tardi.

Exercise 15

Parole intrecciate: Conjugate the verbs indicated below and then find them in the grid.

Y O L I U N E D V K A G V P O
P X N G B S V C O S F O E S L
W G W N C Q T O C V N J N A V
P K R O A E E O E A R B I F P
H P N V G R L H V G F E V H C
L O G T E T E A D O R M I V A
B E U Q E A D G J E U O V J C
S M G R A N I Q G G G R M W L
D P E N A O G A P E A E B B L
L M J N E E Q V J I L B C R J
O E T S E R E C N I V B Z P E
D F M V K Z X V A R H E I R L
E J Q I E R D Z G W M R H G A
X V Q F I S P Q P Q D A R U H
S L Y S C L V P D O E D T F D

1. Loro (andare) imperfetto
2. Noi (ascoltare) futuro semplice
3. Loro (dare) condizionale presente
4. Lei (dormire) imperfetto
5. Io (dovere) condizionale presente
6. Loro (uscire) presente indicativo
7. Loro (leggere) futuro semplice
8. Io (pagare) presente indicativo
9. Tu (venire) imperfetto
10. Voi (vincere) condizionale presente

Exercise 16

Passato remoto/passato prossimo: Change the following verbs from the past absolute into the past tense.

1. fui
2. conobbi
3. scelsero
4. spiegasti
5. visse
6. venni
7. metteste
8. rimanemmo
9. nacquero
10. avesti

Exercise 17

L'intruso: For each group of verbs select the one that does not belong.

1. ballare, danzare, andare in discoteca, esibirsi, digerire
2. pregare, meditare, pensare, ubriacarsi, filosofare
3. cucinare, cuocere, dipingere, arrostire, friggere
4. viaggiare, girare, visitare, camminare, scavare
5. saltare, disegnare, dipingere, colorare, tinteggiare

Must Know Verbs

Here is a list of Must Know Verbs. Each is followed by the page number on which you will find its conjugation in this book.

Test Prep Verb List

Here is a list of useful test prep verbs. Each is followed by a number, which refers either to the page with the conjugation of the model verb or to the page where the verb is conjugated, i.e.: *aumentare* (90), *avere* (122). For *aumentare*, 90 refers to the page with the conjugation of the model verb *amare*; the verb *aumentare* is conjugated like the model verb *amare*. For *avere*, 122 refers to the page where the verb *avere* is conjugated.

1. aiutare (85)
2. alzarsi (89)
3. amare (90)
4. andare (93)
5. arrivare (108)
6. ascoltare (110)
7. aumentare (90)
8. avere (122)
9. bere (132)
10. cenare (155)
11. cercare (156)
12. chiedere (159)
13. comprare (170)
14. conoscere (178)
15. costruire (199)
16. creare (90)
17. crescere (201)
18. dare (206)
19. dimenticare (221)
20. dimostrare (223)
21. dire (226)
22. domandare (246)
23. dormire (247)
24. dovere (248)
25. esistere (263)
26. essere (265)
27. fare (271)
28. fare colazione (271)
29. farsi male (271)
30. giocare (295)
31. guardare (306)
32. incontrare (325)
33. iniziare (330)
34. insegnare (333)
35. introdurre (339)
36. lavorare (352)
37. leggere (354)
38. mandare (365)
39. mangiare (366)
40. mantenere (367)
41. meritare (373)
42. morire (382)
43. nascere (386)
44. offrire (405)
45. partire (424)
46. passare (425)
47. pensare (430)
48. piovere (442)
49. portare (447)
50. possedere (448)
51. potere (449)
52. pranzare (450)
53. prendere (455)
54. prestare (460)
55. pulire (477)
56. ricordare (507)
57. ridere (509)
58. sapere (543)
59. scegliere (549)
60. scrivere (556)
61. seguire (562)
62. sentire (564)
63. soffrire (571)
64. spiegare (586)
65. stare (593)
66. studiare (596)
67. suonare (599)
68. togliere (617)
69. tornare (619)
70. uscire (641)
71. vedere (645)
72. venire (647)
73. viaggiare (652)
74. vincere (654)
75. volere (658)

Tech **VERB** list

Useful tech verbs in *italiano*:

apply	**applicare**
back up	**fare una copia di sicurezza**
boldface	**mettere in grassetto**
cancel	**annullare**
choose	**selezionare**
clear	**cancellare, eliminare**
click	**cliccare**
close	**chiudere**
copy	**copiare**
create shortcut	**creare collegamento**
delete	**eliminare**

Tech **VERB** list

Useful tech verbs in *italiano*:

double click	**fare doppio clic**
download (music)	**scaricare (musica)**
drag	**trascinare**
drag-and-drop	**trascinare e lasciare**
edit	**modificare**
exit	**uscire**
explore	**esplorare**
find	**cercare, trovare**
find next	**trova successivo**
finish	**terminare**
print	**stampare**
scan	**scansionare/ scannerizzare**

italian **TEXT** messaging

Text your friends in *italiano.*

-	meno	*less*
:(	triste	*sad*
:), =)	felice, allegro	*happy*
:D	ghigno	*grin*
:p	linguaccia	*tongue sticking out*
;)	occhiolino	*wink*
+	più	*more*
+o-	più o meno	*more or less*
=	uguale	*the same*
6	sei, sei?	*you are/are you?*
a dp	a dopo, ci vediamo dopo	*see you later*
am	amore	*love*
anke	anche	*also*
bb	bebè	*baby*
br	bere	*to drink*
c 6	ci sei?	*are you there?*
c sent	ci sentiamo	*speak to you later*
cad	cadauno	*each*
cam	camera, stanza	*room*
ce	c'è	*is there?, there is...*
ce ness1	c'è nessuno?	*is anybody there?*
ciao	ciao	*hello, goodbye*
cm	come	*as, how, like*
cm va	come va?	*what's up?*
cmq	comunque	*anyway*
cn	con	*with*
cs dc?	cosa mi dici?	*what's up?*
d	da, di	*from, of*
diff	difficile	*difficult*
dim	dimmi	*tell me*
dl	del, dello, della, degli, delle	*of the*

Text your friends in *italiano.*

dm	domani	*tomorrow*
dp skuola	dopo le lezioni, dopo scuola	*after class*
dp	dopo	*after*
dr	dire	*say*
dtt	detto	*said*
dv	dove?	*where?*
dv 6	dove sei?	*where are you?*
dx	destra	*right*
fiko	fico!	*cool!*
frs	forse	*maybe*
fsta	festa	*party*
ft	fatto, finito	*done*
grrr	arrabbiato	*angry*
ke	che, che?	*what, what?*
ke fai	che fai?	*what are you doing?*
ke noia	che noia!	*what a drag!*
ke vuoi	che vuoi?	*what do you want?*
ki	chi, chi?	*who, who?*
ko	sono sfinito	*I'm exhausted*
ksa	casa	*house, home*
lol	che ridere	*what a laugh!*
m1m+t	mandami un messaggio più tardi	*send me a message later*
mah	non so	*I don't know*
-male	meno male	*thank goodness*
mim	missione impossibile	*mission impossible*
mlt	molto	*a lot*
mmt+	mi manchi tantissimo	*I miss you a lot*
msg	messaggio	*message*
n	in, no	*in, no*

italian **TEXT** messaging

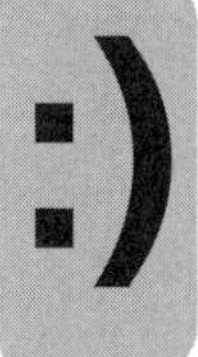

Text your friends in *italiano.*

nm	numero	*number*
nn	non	*not*
nn succ nnt	non succede niente	*nothing is happening*
nnt	niente	*nothing*
npp	non posso parlare	*I can't talk now*
ntt	notte	*night*
ok	bene	*good, OK*
pco	poco	*a little*
pf, pls	per favore	*please*
prox	prossimo	*next*
qlc	qualche	*some*
qlc1	qualcuno	*someone*
qlcs	qualcosa	*something*
qnd	quando	*when*
qndi	quindi	*therefore*
qnt	quanto, quanti	*how much, how many*
qst	questo, questa	*this*
rsp	risposta	*answer*
rst	resto	*I'm staying*
s	sì, si	*yes, if*
sh	zitto!	*shut up*
sl	solo	*only, alone*
smpr	sempre	*always*
sms	sms	*text*
sn	sono	*I am, they are*
sx	sinistra	*left*
sxo	spero	*I hope*
t	ti, tu	*you*
t tel + trd	ti telefono + tardi	*I'll ring you later*
tat	ti amo tanto	*I love you a lot (for bf/gf)*

italian **TEXT** messaging

Text your friends in *italiano.*

tel m	telefonami	*call me*
tnt	tanto	*very, much*
trnki	tranquillo	*don't worry*
trp	troppo	*too, too much*
tt	tutto, tutti	*all, everyone*
tt bn	tutto bene?	*are you OK?*
tvb	ti voglio bene	*I love you (for friends/relatives)*
tvtb	ti voglio tanto bene	*I love you a lot (for friends/relatives)*
tx, thx, grz	grazie	*thanks*
uni	università	*university, college*
vd	vado, devo andare	*I'm going, I have to go*
vlv	volevo	*I wanted*
vn?	vieni?	*are you coming?*
we	fine settimana	*weekend*
x	per	*for, to*
xciò	perciò	*therefore*
xdono	perdono	*sorry*
xh	per ora	*for now*
xké	perché, perché?	*because, why?*
xò	però	*but*
xsona	persona	*person*
xxx	baci	*kisses*
zzz	dormire	*to sleep*

Test Prep Guide

Taking an Italian test or quiz soon? Preparing for a test is not only about studying content such as Italian verbs, reading, vocabulary, useful expressions or culture, it is also about practicing and using your learning skills.

The Berlitz authors, review and editorial team would like to share with you some test-taking strategies that have worked for them. Many of these strategies may be familiar to you, but it's always helpful to review them again. Remember that enhancing your learning skills will help you with all of your classes!

In bocca al lupo!

General Test-Taking Tips: Before the Test

- Review test-taking strategies to help you get a head start on the test.
- Prepping for an exam really begins on your first day of class.
  Reading, reviewing and keeping up with your classwork is the first step to test prep.
- Take good notes in class, especially when your teacher suggests that you write something down.
- Review your notes on a regular basis (at least twice a week).
- Review additional classroom assignments, such as worksheets, in class activities, assignments or readings.
- Review previous quizzes, tests and any test preparation materials related to your class.
- Study with a partner or with a small group of classmates.
- If your teacher has a review session be sure that you attend the review session.
- During the review session, be sure to ask questions, ask for clarification and for additional practice activities.
- Prepare a brief tip sheet for yourself in which you summarize important information, conjugation endings, vocabulary definitions and ideas so that you can review at a glance.
- Spend additional time on material that is more challenging for you and remember there is material that you do know and probably know quite well!
- Get a good night of sleep. Remember that "all nighters" deprive you of the sleep you need to perform well.
- Be sure to eat well before your test.

Test-Taking Tips: During the Test

- Be sure to bring extra pencils, pens, paper, erasers or any other materials and resources that your teacher has allowed you to use for the test.
- Arrive early so that you are not stressed.
- Bring a watch to class so that you can manage your time.
- Scan the entire test before you begin so that you know what you will need to do to manage your time.
- Read instruction lines carefully. Be sure that you answer what you are being asked.
- Do the sections that you know well first so that you can move to the sections that are more challenging.
- Balance the amount of time that you spend on each question. If you find that you are spending too much time on one question, skip the question and come back to it later.
- Be sure that you save about 10 minutes at the end of the test to review. You may be able to catch your own mistakes.

Test-Taking Tips: After the Test

- Review your test and see if you can identify your own mistakes. If you can't identify your mistakes, ask your teacher.
- Correct your test mistakes in your notebook for future reference.
- Review the test to see what sections you did well on and what sections you need to review again. Make a list so that you can begin to prepare for your next quiz or test.
- Keep your test for future reference and for review and practice.

Verb Activities Answer Key

Exercise 1

1. vai, ti svegli; andiamo, ci svegliamo; va, si sveglia; vanno, si svegliano.
2. ci siamo iscritti, abbiamo conosciuto; vi siete iscritti, avete conosciuto; si sono iscritti, hanno conosciuto; ti sei iscritto, hai conosciuto
3. si diverta; ci divertiamo; ti diverta; vi divertiate
4. affrettati; affrettatevi; si affrettino; si affretti
5. vi accorgete, vi comportate; mi accorgo, mi comporto; ci accorgiamo, ci comportiamo; si accorge, si comporta
6. rispetta; rispettiamo; rispettate, rispettino
7. hai lodato; ha lodato; abbiamo lodato; avete lodato
8. parteciperai; parteciperete; parteciperà; parteciperò
9. informa; informiamo; informano; informi
10. ho trascorso; hanno trascorso; abbiamo trascorso; hai trascorso

Exercise 2

1. aprire
2. esibire
3. burlarsi
4. arrabbiarsi
5. ubbidire
6. vietare
7. restituire
8. lagnarsi
9. mentire
10. odiare

Verb Activities Answer Key

Exercise 3

1. comparire
2. maledire
3. ordinare
4. spegnere
5. preoccuparsi

Exercise 4

1. riesca/sia riuscito
2. abbiate studiato
3. chiamassero
4. sia/sia stato
5. avessi suonato

Exercise 5

1. Andrò al museo domani mattina
2. Dovete prenotare l'albergo per le vacanze
3. Ieri Elena e Lucia hanno ricevuto tre lettere
4. Da bambino Luca cantava nel coro
5. Se vedi Laura, invitala!

Exercise 6

1. Ho raccontato
2. Volevi
3. dipingeva
4. leggeva
5. spostava

6. abbiamo pulito
7. ho partecipato
8. respirava
9. ha giurato
10. suonavano

Exercise 7

1. sbagliare
2. scelgano
3. vi comportiate
4. mostro
5. trasferirsi

Exercise 8

1. accadrà
2. hanno nominato
3. aveva noleggiato
4. hai versato
5. ci sposeremo
6. avevano nuotato
7. rifiutare
8. pioveva
9. avevano ordinato
10. ci annoiamo

Exercise 9

1. discutessi
2. organizzerà
3. debba
4. ha stabilito
5. varrebbe

Exercise 10

Orizzontale

5. pranzavo; 8. formeremo; 9. offrite; 10. avete lottato

Verticale

1. governerebbero; 2. spenderanno; 3. trasciniamo; 4. hanno ospitato; 6. abbiamo ferito; 7. limiteresti

Exercise 11

1. fossero partiti
2. aveste finito
3. avesse portato
4. fossimo andati
5. avesse avuto
6. avessi fatto
7. aveste detto
8. fosse uscita

Exercise 12

1. cucinava
2. chiederemo
3. piaceva

4. giocherò
5. diventa
6. spiegava
7. ti commuovi
8. vivevano

Exercise 13

1. L'anno scorso io ho giocato a tennis
2. Da bambina Laura cantava molto bene
3. Domani i signori Renzi partiranno per le vacanze
4. Penso che voi dobbiate mangiare cibi più sani
5. Vorrei che tu dicessi sempre la verità
6. La settimana prossima noi suoneremo il sassofono
7. Ieri Paola ha spedito una lettera a un'amica
8. Quest'estate voi seguirete un corso di spagnolo

Exercise 14

1. stava leggendo
2. stavamo cenando
3. stava spiegando
4. stavano passeggiando
5. stai mangiando
6. stavano partendo
7. stavo facendo
8. Stiamo cenando

Verb Activities Answer Key

Exercise 15

1. andavano
2. ascolteremo
3. darebbero
4. dormiva
5. dovrei
6. escono
7. leggeranno
8. pago
9. venivi
10. vincereste

Exercise 16

1. sono stato/a
2. ho conosciuto
3. hanno scelto
4. hai spiegato
5. ha vissuto
6. sono venuto/a
7. avete messo
8. siamo rimasti/e
9. sono nati/e
10. hai avuto

Exercise 17

1. digerire
2. ubriacarsi
3. dipingere
4. scavare
5. saltare

Index of over 1900 Italian Verbs

Model Verbs

Below, you will find a list of model verbs. We have included these verbs since most other Italian verbs are conjugated like one of these model forms. We suggest that you study these model verbs; once you know these conjugations you will be able to conjugate almost any verb!

On the following pages, you will find an index of an additional 1900 verbs. Each verb is followed by an English translation. The English translation is followed by a number, for example: **remare** to row (90). The number 90 refers to the page number where you will find the conjugation of the verb *amare*. The verb *remare* is conjugated like the model verb *amare*.

Index of over 1900 Italian Verbs

F

Q

riguardare to look at again, to concern (90)
rigurgitare to regurgitate (90)
rilasciare to release (163)
rilassare to relax, to calm down (516)
rilegare to tie up again (419)
rilevare to point out (90)
rimandare to delay (90)
rimarginare to heal (90)
rimbalzare to rebound (90)
rimbambire to become inane (280)
rimediare to remedy (146)
rimettere to put back (374)
rinfrescare to refresh (295)
rimpatriare to return to one's homeland (146)
rimpicciolirsi to diminish, to become smaller (280)
rimuovere to remove (384)
rinascere to be reborn (386)
rinfacciare to reproach (163)
rinforzare to reinforce (90)
rinfrescare to refresh (295)
ringiovanire to become youthful again (280)
rinnegare to deny (419)
rintracciare to track down (163)
rinunciare to reject (163)
rinviare to postpone (146)
ripensare to think over (90)
riposare to relax (90)
riporre to put back (445)
ripulire to clean up (280)
risalire to go up again (539)
risaltare to project out, to jump again (90)
risanare to heal (90)
risapere to find out (543)
risarcire to compensate, to indemnify (280)
riscattare to ransom (90)
rischiare to risk (146)
rischiarire to become clear (280)
riscrivere to rewrite (556)
risentire to hear again, to feel (564)
risorgere to rise again (573)
risparmiare to save, to spare (146)
rispecchiarsi to be reflected (146)
ristringere to clasp again (595)
risuscitare to resurrect (90)
risvegliare to reawaken (544)
ritardare to delay, to be late (90)
ritirare to withdraw (90)
rotolare to roll (90)
rovesciare to overturn (163)

For iPod:

Introduction

Berlitz® Italian Essential Words and Phrases for iPod® is a unique digital e-phrase book that contains 300 travel-related words and phrases—all for use on your iPod.

Simply download the software from our web site at www.berlitzpublishing.com/601verbs to your computer, run the automatic installer and instantly your iPod Classic or Nano will be loaded with words, phrases, pictures and audio for your trip — no need to carry a phrase book, CD or separate audio device! The program is easily organized into thematic menus, so you can quickly scroll to find the phrase you're looking for. This easy-to-navigate technology ensures that you can communicate in a variety of situations immediately: at the airport, train station, hotel, restaurant, shopping area, Internet café, and more.

System Requirements

Windows 2000, XP, Vista or Windows 7, Internet Explorer
Mac OS 10.4 or later, Safari
25MB of available hard disk space.

iTunes Requirements:
Windows or Mac Version 8.0 or later

iPod Requirements:
iPod Classic 5th generation or later; iPod Nano 3rd generation or later.

Installation Instructions

> For error-free installation, make sure your iPod is connected and iTunes is open. Wait until your iPod appears in the iTunes Source Menu.
> In iTunes, make sure your iPod has the Options boxes checked as illustrated here:

For PC iPods

> On Windows PCs, the installer screen will automatically extract the zipped content and prompt you to start the installation process. Follow the installer menus to properly install the text into the Notes folder of your iPod and the audio into your iTunes Library. Your iTunes will then sync to your iPod to transfer the audio into your iPod's music folder. Note: if you have "Manually manage music and videos" checked under your iTunes Options, you will have to drag the audio files from the iTunes Library to your iPod after installation.

For Mac iPods

> On your Mac, open the folder called Berlitz_IT_LT_unzipped.
> Double click the MacBook Installer icon. Follow the installation menus as they lead you through the process.
> Eject your iPod and go to the iPod Extras; then go to the Notes folder. You'll find Berlitz® Italian there.

Technical Support

For technical support issues for this product, please refer to our help page at www.ipreppress.com/iphrase.htm. You can also contact us by phone at 1-866-439-5032 (toll free U.S. only) or 1-215-321-0447 Monday through Friday, 9 a.m. to 6 p.m. EST, or email us at help@ipreppress.com.